Lecture Notes in Computer Sci

T0238119

Commenced Publication in 1973
Founding and Former Series Editors:
Gerhard Goos, Juris Hartmanis, and Jan van Leeuwen

Rudolf Eigenmann   Zhiyuan Li
Samuel P. Midkiff (Eds.)

Languages and Compilers for High Performance Computing

17th International Workshop, LCPC 2004
West Lafayette, IN, USA, September 22-24, 2004
Revised Selected Papers

 Springer

Volume Editors

Rudolf Eigenmann
Samuel P. Midkiff
Purdue University, School of Electrical and Computer Engineering
West Lafayette,, IN 47906, USA
E-mail: {eigenman, smidkiff}@ecn.purdue.edu

Zhiyuan Li
Purdue University, Department of Computer Sciences
West Lafayette, IN 47906, USA
E-mail: li@cs.purdue.edu

Library of Congress Control Number: 2005929713

CR Subject Classification (1998): D.3, D.1.3, F.1.2, B.2.1, C.2.4, C.2, E.1, D.4

ISSN   0302-9743
ISBN-10   3-540-28009-X Springer Berlin Heidelberg New York
ISBN-13   978-3-540-28009-5 Springer Berlin Heidelberg New York

Springer is a part of Springer Science+Business Media

springeronline.com

© Springer-Verlag Berlin Heidelberg 2005
Printed in Germany

Typesetting: Camera-ready by author, data conversion by Scientific Publishing Services, Chennai, India
Printed on acid-free paper   SPIN: 11532378   06/3142   5 4 3 2 1 0

Preface

The 17th International Workshop on Languages and Compilers for High Performance Computing was hosted by Purdue University in September 2004 on Purdue campus in West Lafayette, Indiana, USA. The workshop is an annual international forum for leading research groups to present their current research activities and the latest results, covering languages, compiler techniques, run-time environments, and compiler-related performance evaluation for parallel and high-performance computing. Eighty-six researchers from Canada, France, Japan, Korea, P. R. China, Spain, Taiwan and the United States attended the workshop.

A new feature of LCPC 2004 was its mini-workshop on Research-Compiler Infrastructures. Representatives from four projects, namely Cetus, LLVM, ORC and Trimaran, gave a 90-minute long presentation each. In addition, 29 research papers were presented at the workshop. These papers were reviewed by the program committee. External reviewers were used as needed. The authors received additional comments during the workshop. The revisions after the workshop are now assembled into these final proceedings.

A panel session was organized by Samuel Midkiff on the question of "What is Good Compiler Research – Theory, Practice or Complexity?" The workshop also had the honor and pleasure to have two keynote speakers, Peter Kogge of the University of Notre Dame and David Kuck of Intel Inc., both pioneers in high performance computing. Peter Kogge gave a presentation titled "Architectures and Execution Models: How New Technologies May Affect How Languages Play on Future HPC Systems". David Kuck presented Intel's vision and roadmap for parallel and distributed solutions.

The workshop was sponsored by the National Science Foundation and by International Business Machines Corporation. Their generous contribution is greatly appreciated. We wish to acknowledge Purdue's Office for Continuing Education and Conferences, Thomas L. Robertson in particular, for their assistance in organizing the workshop. Eighteen graduate students affiliated with Purdue's Advanced Computer Systems Laboratory (ACSL) volunteered their time to assist in the workshop's operations. Our special thanks go to the LCPC 2004 program committee and the nameless external reviewers for their efforts in reviewing the submissions. Advice and suggestions from both the steering committee and the program committee have helped the smooth preparation of the workshop. Finally, we wish to thank all the authors and participants for their contribution and lively discussions which made the workshop a success.

May 2005   Rudolf Eigenmann, Zhiyuan Li, Samuel P. Midkiff

Organization

Committees

Program Co-chairs:	Rudolf Eigenmann (Purdue University, USA)
	Zhiyuan Li (Purdue University, USA)
	Samuel P. Midkiff (Purdue University, USA)
Program Committee:	Nancy Amato (Texas A&M University, USA)
	Rudolf Eigenmann (Purdue University, USA)
	Zhiyuan Li (Purdue University, USA)
	Sam Midkiff (Purdue University USA)
	Bill Pugh (University of Maryland, USA)
	J. Ramanujam (Louisiana State University, USA)
	Lawrence Rauchwerger (Texas A&M University, USA)
	P. Sadayappan (Ohio State University, USA)
	Bjarne Stroustrup (Texas A&M University, USA)
	Chau-Wen Tseng (University of Maryland, USA)
Conference Co-chairs:	Rudolf Eigenmann (Purdue University, USA)
	Zhiyuan Li (Purdue University, USA)
	Samuel P. Midkiff (Purdue University, USA)
Steering Committee:	Utpal Banerjee (Intel Corporation, USA)
	Alex Nicolau (University of California, Irvine, USA)
	David Gelernter (Yale University, USA)
	David Padua (University of Illinois at Urbana-Champaign, USA)

Sponsors

National Science Foundation, USA
International Business Machines Corporation

Table of Contents

Experiences in Using Cetus
for Source-to-Source Transformations*

Troy A. Johnson, Sang-Ik Lee, Long Fei, Ayon Basumallik,
Gautam Upadhyaya, Rudolf Eigenmann, and Samuel P. Midkiff

School of Electrical & Computer Engineering,
Purdue University, West Lafayette IN 47906, USA
{troyj, sangik, lfei, basumall, gupadhya, eigenman,
smidkiff}@ecn.purdue.edu
http://www.ece.purdue.edu/ParaMount

Abstract. Cetus is a compiler infrastructure for the source-to-source transformation of programs. Since its creation nearly three years ago, it has grown to over 12,000 lines of Java code, been made available publically on the web, and become a basis for several research projects. We discuss our experience using Cetus for a selection of these research projects. The focus of this paper is not the projects themselves, but rather how Cetus made these projects possible, how the needs of these projects influenced the development of Cetus, and the solutions we applied to problems we encountered with the infrastructure. We believe the research community can benefit from such a discussion, as shown by the strong interest in the mini-workshop on compiler research infrastructures where some of this information was first presented.

1 Introduction

Parallelizing compiler technology is most mature for the Fortran 77 language [1,3,12,13,16]. The simplicity of the language without pointers or user-defined types makes it easy to analyze and to develop many advanced compiler passes. By contrast, parallelization technology for modern languages, such as Java, C++, or even C, is still in its infancy. When trying to engage in such research, we were faced with a serious challenge. We were unable to find a parallelizing compiler infrastructure that supported interprocedural analysis, exhibited state-of-the-art software engineering techniques to help shorten development time, and allowed us to compile large, realistic applications. We feel these properties are of paramount importance because they enable a compiler writer to develop "production strength" passes. Production strength passes, in turn, can work in the context of the most up-to-date compiler technology and lead to compiler research that can be evaluated with full suites of realistic applications. The lack of such thorough evaluations in many current research papers has been

---

* This material is based upon work supported in part by the National Science Foundation under Grant No. 9703180, 9975275, 9986020, and 9974976.

R. Eigenmann et al. (Eds.): LCPC 2004, LNCS 3602, pp. 1–14, 2005.

observed and criticized by many. The availability of an easy-to-use compiler infrastructure would help improve this situation significantly. Hence, continuous research and development in this area are among the most important tasks of the compiler community.

Cetus was created with those needs in mind. It supports analyses and transformations at the source level; other infrastructures are more appropriate for instruction-level compiler research. Cetus is composed of over 10,000 lines of Java code that implements the Cetus intermediate representation (IR), over 1,500 lines of code that implements source transformations, a C parser using Antlr, and standalone C and C++ Bison parsers that have yet to be integrated completely into Cetus. The Cetus IR is the product of three graduate students working part-time over two years. Several others have contributed analysis and transformation passes, as well as used Cetus for their own research projects. We discuss these projects in this paper from the perspective of how Cetus made these projects possible, how the needs of these projects influenced the development of Cetus, and the solutions we applied to problems we encountered with the infrastructure. We believe the research community can benefit from such a discussion, as shown by the strong interest in the mini-workshop on compiler research infrastructures where some of this information was first presented.

Section 2 briefly covers the Cetus IR. In Section 3, we cover basic analysis, transformation, and instrumentation passes. Section 4 contains five case studies of more complex passes. Section 5 discusses the effects of user-feedback on the project. Finally, Section 6 concludes.

2   Cetus Intermediate Representation

For the design of the IR we chose an abstract representation, implemented in the form of a class hierarchy and accessed through the class member functions. We consider a strong separation between the implementation and the interface to be very important. In this way, a change to the implementation may be done while maintaining the API for its users. It also permits passes to be written before the IR implementation is ready. These concepts had already proved their value in the implementation of the Polaris infrastructure [2], which served as an important example for the Cetus design. Polaris was rewritten three to four times over its lifetime while keeping the interface, and hence all compilation passes, nearly unmodified [5]. Cetus has a similar design, shown in Figure 1, where the high-level interface insulates the pass writer from changes in the base.

Our design goal was a simple IR class hierarchy easily understood by users. It should also be easy to maintain, while being rich enough to enable future extension without major modification. The basic building blocks of a program are the *translation units*, which represent the content of a source file, and *procedures*, which represent individual functions. Procedures include a list of simple or compound statements, representing the program control flow in a hierarchical way. That is, compound statements, such as *IF*-constructs and *FOR*-loops include inner (simple or compound) statements, representing *then* and *else* blocks

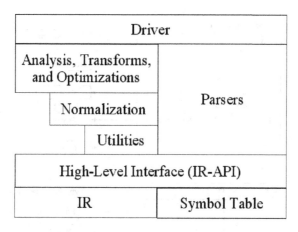

Fig. 1. Cetus components and interfaces: Components of Cetus only call methods of the components beneath them. The driver interprets command-line arguments and initiates the appropriate parser for the input language, which in turn uses the high-level interface to build the IR. The driver then initiates analysis and transformation passes. Normalization passes and utilities are provided to perform complex operations that are useful to multiple passes. The interface functions are kept lean and generally provide only a single way of performing IR manipulations

or loop bodies, respectively. *Expressions* represent the operations being done on variables, including the assignments to variables.

Cetus' IR contrasts with the Polaris Fortran translator's IR in that it uses a hierarchical statement structure. The Cetus IR directly reflects the block structure of a program. Polaris lists the statements of each procedure in a flat way, with a reference to the outer statement being the only way for determining the block structure. There are also important differences in the representation of expressions, which further reflects the differences between C and Fortran. The Polaris IR includes assignment statements, whereas Cetus represents assignments in the form of expressions. This corresponds to the C language's feature to include assignment side effects in any expression.

The IR is structured such that the original source program can be reproduced, but this is where source-to-source translators face an intrinsic dilemma. Keeping the IR and output similar to the input will make it easy for the user to recognize the transformations applied by the compiler. On the other hand, keeping the IR language-independent leads to a simpler compiler architecture, but may make it impossible to reproduce the original source code as output. In Cetus, the concept of statements and expressions are closely related to the syntax of the C language, facilitating easy source-to-source translation. The correspondence between syntax and IR is shown in Figure 2. However, the drawback is increased complexity for pass writers (since they must think in terms of C syntax) and limited extensibility of Cetus to additional languages. That problem is mitigated by the provision of several interfaces that represent generic control constructs. Generic

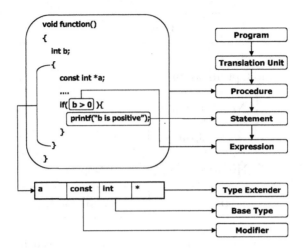

Fig. 2. A program fragment and its IR in Cetus. IR relationships are similar to the program structure and a symbol table is associated with each block scope

passes can be written using the abstract interface, while more language-specific passes can use the derived classes. For example, the classes that represent for-loops and while-loops both implement a loop interface. A pass that manipulates loops may be written using the generic loop interface if the exact type of loop is not important.

The high-level interface, or IR-API, is the interface presented to compiler writers. In general the IR-API is kept minimal and free of redundant functionality, so as to make it easy to learn about its basic operation and easy to debug. IR-API calls expect the IR to be in a consistent state upon entry and ensure the state is consistent upon their return. Cetus also provides a utility package, that offers convenience to pass writers. The utility package provides additional functions, where needed by more than a single compiler pass. Obviously, this criterion will depend on the passes that will be written in the future. Hence, the utilities will evolve, while we expect the base to remain stable. The utility functions operate using only the IR-API.

2.1   Navigating the IR

Traversing the IR is a fundamental operation that will be used by every compiler pass. Therefore, it is important that traversals be easy to perform and require little code. Cetus provides an abstract IRIterator class that implements the standard Java Iterator interface. The classes BreadthFirstIterator, Depth-FirstIterator, and FlatIterator are all derived from IRIterator. The constructor for each of these classes accepts as its only parameter a Traversable object which defines the root of the traversal. Traversable is an interface that ensures any implementing class can act as a node of a tree by providing methods to access its parent and children. A design alternative here was to have every class provide a getIterator method instead of passing the root object to an iterator constructor, but that required adding an implementation of getIterator to every class, and was rejected.[1] The DepthFirstIterator visits statements and expressions sequentially in program order without regard to block scope. The BreadthFirstIterator visits all children of an object before visiting the children's children; i.e., block scope is respected with outer objects visited first. The FlatIterator does not visit the root of the traversal and instead visits the root's children sequentially without visiting the children's children.

In addition to providing a `next` method, as all Iterators must, an IRIterator provides `next(Class)`, `next(Set)`, and `nextExcept(Set)` to allow the caller to specify that only objects of a certain class, or that belong or do not belong to a particular set of classes, are of interest. When these methods were first introduced, we were able to rewrite older Cetus passes using considerably fewer lines of code. Figure 3 shows the usefulness of these methods.

```
/* Look for loops in a procedure. Assumes proc is a Procedure object. */

BreadthFirstIterator iter = new BreadthFirstIterator(proc);
try {
  while (true)
  {
    Loop loop = (Loop)iter.next(Loop.class);
    // Do something with the loop
  }
} catch (NoSuchElementException e) {
}
```

Fig. 3. Using iterators to find loops within a procedure. Outer loops are discovered first

2.2   Type System and Symbol Table

Modern programming languages provide rich type systems. In order to keep the Cetus type system flexible, we divided the elements of a type into three concepts: base types, extenders, and modifiers. A complete type is described by a combination of these three elements. Base types include built-in primitive types, which have a predefined meaning in programming languages, and user-defined types. User-defined types are new types introduced into the program by providing the layout of the structure and the semantics. These include typedef, struct, union, and enum types in C. Base types are often combined with type extenders. Examples of type extenders are arrays, pointers, and functions. The last concept is modifiers which express an attribute of a type, such as const and volatile in C. They can decorate any part of the type definition. Types

---

[1] The decision was primarily due to Java's lack of multiple inheritance, since in most cases inheritance had already been used.

are understood by decoding the description one element at a time, which is a sequential job in nature. We use a list structure to hold type information so that types can be understood easily by looking at the elements in the list one at a time.

Another important concept is a symbol, which represents the declaration of a variable in the program. Symbols are not part of the IR tree and reside in symbol tables. Our concept of a symbol table is a mapping from a variable name to its point of declaration, which is located in a certain scope and has all of the type information. As a result, scope always must be considered when dealing with symbols. In C, a block structure defines a scope. Therefore, structs in C are also scopes and their members are represented as local symbols within that scope. A compiler may use one large symbol table with hashing to locate symbols [4]. In Cetus, since source transformations can move, add, or remove scopes, we use distributed symbol tables where each scope has a separate physical symbol table. The logical symbol table for a scope includes its physical symbol table and the physical symbol tables of the enclosing scopes, with inner declarations hiding outer declarations. There are certain drawbacks to this approach, namely the need to search through the full hierarchy of symbol tables to reach a global symbol [6], but we find it to be convenient. For example, all the declarations in a scope can be manipulated as a group simply by manipulating that scope's symbol table. It is especially convenient in allowing Cetus to support object-oriented languages, where classes and namespaces may introduce numerous scopes whose relationships can be expressed through the symbol table hierarchy.

3   Capabilities for Writing Passes

Cetus has a number of features that are useful to pass writers. Classes that support program analysis, normalization, and modification are discussed below.

3.1   Analysis

Call Graph. Cetus provides a CallGraph class that creates a call graph from a Program object. The call graph maps callers to callees as well as callees to callers. A pass can query the call graph to determine if a procedure is a leaf of the call graph or if a procedure is recursive.

Control-Flow Graph. Cetus provides a ControlFlowGraph class, which creates a control-flow graph from a Program object. The graph represents the structure of each procedure in terms of its basic blocks connected by control-flow edges.

3.2   Normalization

Single Return. Compiler passes often become simpler if they can assume that each procedure has a single exit point. A procedure with multiple return statements complicates such actions as inserting code that should execute just prior to a procedure returning to its caller. To eliminate this problem, the single-return pass creates a new variable to hold the return value, identifies all return statements, and replaces the return statements with an assignment to the variable followed immediately by a goto to the end of the procedure. Then, the procedure is appended with a single return statement that returns the value of the variable.

Single Call. Instrumentation passes sometimes need to place code before and after procedure calls, but most languages allow multiple calls per statement. Thus, the pass writer has two choices: find a way within the language to insert their code into an already complex statement, or separate all the calls so there is one per statement. The first option often is not possible, and when it is, such as by using the comma operator in C, it results in obfuscated code. Therefore, Cetus provides a single-call pass to separate statements with multiple calls, including "unwrapping" nested calls. New variables are introduced to hold return values and the calls are placed in the appropriate order. It is worth noting that the C language standard leaves undefined the order of execution of multiple calls in a statement at the same nesting level. Arbitrarily ordering such calls left to right did not appear to affect any programs that we tested.

Single Declarator. Languages allow multiple symbols to be introduced by a single declaration. An example is int x, y, z; in C. If a pass needs to copy, move, or remove the declaration of a single variable, then it must be careful not to change the rest of the declaration. Cetus provides a single-declarator pass that would separate the example above into three declarations, allowing passes to work on individual declarations.

3.3   Modifying the Program

Annotation System. The Cetus IR provides an Annotation class that is derived from the general Declaration class. Annotations can appear wherever declarations can appear, allowing them to appear both inside and outside of procedures. They can be used to insert comments, pragmas, raw text, or a hash map to act as a database that facilitates the exchange of information between passes.

Inserting New Code. All of the statement and expression classes in the Cetus IR have constructors that can be used to create new IR. These constructors are used by the parser to create the IR for the program. Therefore, pass writers are able to insert new IR in exactly the same way as the parser creates the IR for the original code. The constructors and other methods of the IR classes check their arguments to ensure that the IR remains consistent at all times. For example, an exception is thrown if a duplicate symbol is about to be created, or if an attempt is made to place the same IR object in two parts of the IR tree.

4   Case Studies

Here we present five case studies in which Cetus was used to accomplish more complex analyses and transformations. Each case study was written by the person who used Cetus for that purpose, so this section represents the experiences and opinions of five different people.

4.1   Extraction of Loops into Subroutines

A number of loop transformations are more easily applied if the loop is available as a separate subroutine. The micro-tasking implementation described below in Section 4.2 is one such example. Separating a loop from a procedure and moving it to its own procedure faces several issues. There will be values used by the loop that are defined above the loop and must be passed by value into the new procedure. There will be values used below the loop that are defined within the loop and must be passed by reference (or by pointer) into the new procedure. Cetus has basic use-def analysis to support both of these.

A Cetus utility method to search and replace variables by name is very useful to this pass. For example, if a variable p is passed to the new procedure via a pointer (i.e., it was not a pointer in the original code) then all occurrences of p, must be replaced with *p in the new procedure. The search and replace method must know to skip replacing names that are structure members, because, for example, x.*p is not legal C code.

4.2   Translation of OpenMP Applications

One of the early experiences in using Cetus was the creation of an OpenMP translator pass. OpenMP is currently one of the most popular paradigms for programming shared-memory parallel applications [7]. Unlike programming with MPI (message-passing interface), where one inserts communication library calls, OpenMP programmers use directives that have semantics understood by the compiler.

Compiler functionality for translating OpenMP falls into two broad categories. The first category deals with the translation of the OpenMP work-sharing constructs into a micro-tasking form, requiring the extraction of the work-sharing code (such as the bodies of parallel loops) into separate micro-tasking subroutines. It also requires inserting corresponding function calls and synchronization. Cetus provides functionality that is sufficient for these transformations. The second category deals with the translation of the OpenMP data clauses, which requires support for accessing and modifying symbol table entries. Cetus provides several ways in which the pass writer can access the symbol table to add and delete symbols or change their scope. There are currently two different OpenMP translators which have been implemented using Cetus. Both of them use the same OpenMP front end. One translator generates code for shared-memory systems using the POSIX threads API. The other translator targets software distributed shared memory systems and was developed as part of a project to extend OpenMP to cluster systems [11]. Although the entire OpenMP 2.0 specification is not supported yet, the translators are powerful enough to handle benchmarks such as art and equake , two of the larger applications from the SPEC OMPM2001 suite.

Cetus is also being used in an ongoing project to translate OpenMP applications directly to MPI. The project is also a source-to-source translation, but it makes use of a wider range of compiler techniques and Cetus functionality. One major component of this transformation is the interprocedural analysis of array accesses. A regular array section analysis pass was implemented in Cetus to summarize array accesses within loops using Regular Section Descriptors [8]. The flow graph described in Section 3, along with the regular section analysis pass, was used to implement an array dataflow pass. The array dataflow pass is then used to resolve producer-consumer relationships for shared data, and to insert MPI calls to satisfy these relationships. Three aspects of Cetus greatly facilitated the development of these passes. First, Cetus provides a rich set of iterators for program traversal. Second, Cetus provides functions for conveniently accessing the symbol tables visible within specific scopes, as well as their parent scopes. Finally, Cetus provides a convenient interface for the insertion of function calls at the source level in a program. These aspects of Cetus allowed us to conveniently create the requisite dataflow passes and insert the MPI calls.

4.3 Pointer Alias Analysis

Pointer analysis generally has two different variations. Points-to analysis is a program analysis pass that determines the set of memory objects that a pointer could point to at a given place in the program. Similarly, alias analysis is a program analysis pass that determines if two pointers can point to the same memory object at a given place in the program. These two analyses are related in the sense that alias analysis could be done by doing a points-to analysis first and then applying set intersection operations.

The goal was to write a context-sensitive and flow-sensitive points-to analysis. The pass was written using an earlier version of Cetus [10] and updated to use newer features. To implement a points-to analysis pass, the underlying compiler has to support several basic features. First, pointer variables should be easy to identify. This requires adequate symbol table operations. Second, our points-to analysis is an iterative analysis that traverses the entire program, finding pointer related expressions and evaluating them until reaching a fixed-point. While the earlier Cetus version provided limited flexibility for traversing the program IR, the new functionality mentioned in Section 2 greatly simplified this task.

Writing a flow-sensitive analysis pass requires a control-flow graph, as described in Section 3.1. Additionally, program normalization functionality, as per Section 3.2, helped reduce the complexity of the pass substantially. It resulted in more regular expressions that needed less special-case handling. Similarly, normalizing each statement to have a single function call simplified the interprocedural analysis pass. We also normalized each statement to have a single assignment. Flow sensitive analysis requires keeping track of changes to points-to sets at every program point. Saving the entire points-to set per statement requires excessive memory, so an incremental way of recording the points-to set change is needed. We implemented a method that records the change to the points-to set at each program location only. When the pass needs to look at the entire points-to set, all reaching definitions are looked up. We implemented this functionality by representing the program in SSA form. The availability of a control-flow graph was useful for creating the SSA representation.

4.4 Software Debugging

Cetus is a useful tool for source-level instrumentation. The high-level IR keeps all of the information available from source code. The hierarchical-structured IR and iterators make it easy to traverse the IR tree. Each object in the IR tree has its direct corresponding element in the source code. Each **Statement** object keeps the line number in the source file of the statement it represents. With all this information, the user can write an instrumentation pass that does the transformation analogous to the transformation the user would directly apply on the source code. That is, the gap between the abstract instrumentation pass in Cetus and the concrete instrumentation that user expects to apply to the source code is small. The small gap makes it easy for the user to design an instrumentation pass with Cetus.

However, there are still limitations. First, creating an IR object (e.g. **Symbol**, **Expression**, **Statement**) is not easy. For instance, if the user wishes to add a **Statement** object into the IR tree, he/she has to create the whole subtree (with the **Statement** object as its root). Because the user typically thinks in C, there is a big gap between the concept of inserting instrumentation into the source code and creating an IR subtree in the existing IR. It is impractical for the instrumentation pass writer to build the IR subtree corresponding to the instrumentation he/she wishes to insert if the instrumentation is complex or if the pass writer has insufficient knowledge about Cetus parsing and IR implementation. It would be useful to have an on-demand utility that can properly parse the instrumentation the user wishes to add (expressed in C) and return a legal IR subtree that fits into the context. For instance, if the user wishes to add a **printf** statement which displays the value of a local variable, the utility should translate (**printf("value = %d", local_symbol);**) into an IR subtree and return it to the user. The utility should also make proper changes to the symbol table and make proper reference to the local symbol used in the instrumentation. Such a utility has not been implemented in Cetus because it requires maintaining multiple parsers (e.g., one for the entire C language, one only for statements, and one only for expressions), or a parser generator that supports multiple starting productions.

Second, the requirement to keep the IR tree consistent, as per Section 2, makes it less flexible to instrument the IR tree. It is a design specification that every operation on the IR tree should result in a legal IR tree, i.e. in a series of operations, the IR tree should be consistent after every operation. This requirement trades the flexibility in manipulating the IR tree for correctness and robustness of the IR. However, it is commonplace that instrumentation is done out of order. For example, if the instrumentation uses temporary data structures, and an analysis pass is performed after the instrumentation pass to determine how many of the data structures can be reused to avoid excessive waste of memory, it is not determined what temporary data structures really needed to be declared until we finish the analysis pass. In this scenario, it is desirable to add the uses of the temporary data structures in the instrumentation pass before we add the declarations of those temporary data structures that are really needed after the analysis pass. It is sometimes infeasible or not desirable for modularization reasons to interleave the redundancy analysis with the instrumentation pass.

In order to avoid the two limitations discussed above, we develop a two-phased instrumentation utility. The first phase is a Cetus instrumentation pass that traverses the IR tree, performs analysis, and logs the instrumentation operations needed to be performed (in any order) in an instrumentation profile. The second phase is an instrumentation program, which reads in the instrumentation profile generated by the instrumentation pass, rearranges the instrumentation operations into a proper ordering, and performs the instrumentation operations on the source files. Different instrumentation tasks need to have different Cetus instrumentation passes, while the second phase is shared. This instrumentation utility is used in our past research on the AccMon project [17], where instrumentation is added to turn on runtime monitoring on memory locations that need to be monitored.

4.5   A Java Byte-Code Translator

We used Cetus to construct a bytecode-to-bytecode translator with the purpose of experimenting with optimization passes for the Java programming language. With this infrastructure, we plan on performing quasi-static [14] optimizations at the bytecode level – these are ahead-of-time optimizations in which assumptions about other classes are checked at runtime (by an intelligent classloader [9]) to verify the correctness of the off-line optimizations. We will initially target numerical programs, but longer term will explore more general purpose optimizations. Our input was a bytecode (Java class) file. We broke up the translation process as follows. First we read in the bytecode and stored it in standard Java data structures. Then we constructed an intermediate representation (IR) based on the data we had gathered. This IR was then used to drive the back-end which translated the IR into bytecode. Optimization passes will be added to the tool by acting at the IR, rather than the bytecode, level. Cetus was used as the IR of choice for our project. We converted our bytecode to Cetus by

1. reading in bytecode into an internal ClassFile data structure, as specified by Sun in the JVM documentation [15]
2. parsing the ClassFile data structure and extracting information about individual statements/declarations/ definitions and
3. constructing Cetus IR by performing a mapping between the parsed data and (Cetus) IR classes.

Our experiences with Cetus have been extremely favorable to date. The object-orientedness of the tool combined with the abundance of good documentation allowed us to construct our IR in a very short time-span. The only problem encountered was with the fact that Cetus was designed with C++ and not Java in mind and while the similarities in the approaches are self-evident, we did need to modify the code occasionally to facilitate our target language, i.e. Java. However, the fact that Cetus was written almost entirely in Java proved to be extremely beneficial since changes made were minimal and rapidly implemented.

5   Users' Influence on Cetus Development

Beginning with its first usable version and continuing throughout its development, Cetus has been used for both research projects and course projects. Feedback from the people involved in those projects provided direction for further development.

One of the first suggestions was to improve the iterators. A tree-structured IR requires that there be code to traverse the tree. Completely exposing the traversal code to pass writers places an unnecessary burden on them; hence, iterators were provided. However, the iterators were not initially provided as they have been described in this paper – only the standard form of the `next` method was provided. Pass writers noted that much of their code was spent type-checking the object returned by `next` to decide whether or not it was an object of interest to them. The solution was to allow the type of the desired object to be passed to the `next` method, allowing the method internally to skip over objects that did not match the specified type, thus hiding the type-checking code. The savings to the pass writer is only a few lines of code, but those lines are saved each time an iterator is used. Consensus was that the improved iterators allowed for shorter, more readable code.

Another example of user-driven improvement was the AssignmentExpression class. Originally, there was only a BinaryExpression class that was used to represent all types of binary expressions. The users found this to be very inconvenient because they often wished to find definitions of a variable. Finding definitions required them first to search for instances of BinaryExpression and then to test if each instance was any of the many forms of assignment that the C language provides. Not only was this process inconvenient, but inefficient, since typical programs contain a large number of binary expressions. The solution was to split the duties of the BinaryExpression class by deriving from it an AssignmentExpression class. If an object was an instance of AssignmentExpression, then users knew automatically that it was a binary expression that modified its lefthand side. Combined with the improved iterators, users could skip the other binary expressions by requesting that `next` only return AssignmentExpressions.

6   Conclusion

We briefly discussed the Cetus IR and presented five case studies that used Cetus to perform non-trivial operations. Cetus was shown to have an API sufficient for a variety of applications. The API has been improved based on users' feedback. We observe that most of the difficulties that users encountered were in using

Cetus to find the part of the program they wished to transform or optimize (i.e., to find statements or expressions satisfying a certain property); few complaints dealt with using Cetus to perform the actual transformation. It is interesting to consider if developers of other compiler infrastructures have noticed a similar phenomenon.

Overall, Cetus' users have found it to be a useful tool, and with the program and source code now available for download, we expect that more people will make use of Cetus. Future development focuses on adding support for C++ and finding additional ways to shorten the code necessary for writing passes.

References

1. P. Banerjee, J. A. Chandy, M. Gupta, et al. The PARADIGM Compiler for Distributed-Memory Multicomputers. *IEEE Computer*, 28(10):37–47, October 1995.
2. W. Blume, R. Doallo, R. Eigenmann, et al. Advanced Program Restructuring for High-Performance Computers with Polaris. *IEEE Computer*, pages 78–82, December 1996.
3. W. Blume, R. Eigenmann, et al. Restructuring Programs for High-Speed Computers with Polaris. In *ICPP Workshop*, pages 149–161, 1996.
4. R. P. Cook and T. J. LeBlanc. A Symbol Table Abstraction to Implement Languages with Explicit Scope Control. *IEEE Transactions on Software Engineering*, 9(1):8–12, January 1983.
5. K. A. Faigin, S. A. Weatherford, J. P. Hoeflinger, D. A. Padua, and P. M. Petersen. The Polaris Internal Representation. *International Journal of Parallel Programming*, 22(5):553–586, 1994.
6. C. N. Fischer and R. J. LeBlanc Jr. *Crafting a Compiler*. Benjamin/Cummings, 1988.
7. O. Forum. OpenMP: A Proposed Industry Standard API for Shared Memory Programming. Technical report, Oct. 1997.
8. P. Havlak and K. Kennedy. An implementation of interprocedural bounded regular section analysis. *IEEE Transactions on Parallel and Distributed Systems*, 2(3):350–360, 1991.
9. G. C. Lee and S. P. Midkiff. Ninja 2: Towards fast, portable, numerical Java. In *Workshop on Compilers for Parallel Computing*, July 2004.
10. S.-I. Lee, T. A. Johnson, and R. Eigenmann. Cetus - An Extensible Compiler Infrastructure for Source-to-Source Transformation. In *16th International Workshop on Languages and Compilers for Parallel Computing (LCPC)*, pages 539–553, October 2003.
11. S.-J. Min, A. Basumallik, and R. Eigenmann. Optimizing OpenMP programs on Software Distributed Shared Memory Systems. *International Journal of Parallel Programming*, 31(3):225–249, June 2003.
12. T. N. Nguyen, J. Gu, and Z. Li. An Interprocedural Parallelizing Compiler and Its Support for Memory Hierarchy Research. In *Proceedings of the International Workshop on Languages and Compilers for Parallel Computing (LCPC)*, pages 96–110, 1995.
13. C. Polychronopoulos, M. B. Girkar, et al. The Structure of Parafrase-2: An Advanced Parallelizing Compiler for C and Fortran. In *Languages and Compilers for Parallel Computing*. MIT Press, 1990.

14. M. J. Serrano, R. Bordawekar, S. P. Midkiff, and M. Gupta. Quicksilver: a Quasi-Static Compiler for Java. In *Conference on Object-Oriented Programming, Systems, Languages, and Applications (OOPSLA)*, pages 66–82, 2000.

15. Sun Microsystems. *The Java Virtual Machine Specification*.

16. R. P. Wilson, R. S. French, et al. SUIF: An Infrastructure for Research on Parallelizing and Optimizing Compilers. *SIGPLAN Notices*, 29(12):31–37, 1994.

17. P. Zhou, W. Liu, L. Fei, S. Lu, F. Qin, Y. Zhou, S. Midkiff, and J. Torrellas. AccMon: Automatically detecting memory-related bugs via program counter-based invariants. In *Proceedings of the 37th Annual IEEE/ACM International Symposium on Micro-architecture (MICRO'04)*, 2004.

The LLVM Compiler Framework and Infrastructure Tutorial

Chris Lattner and Vikram Adve

University of Illinois at Urbana-Champaign
{lattner, vadve}@cs.uiuc.edu

Abstract. The LLVM Compiler Infrastructure (http://llvm.cs.uiuc.edu) is a robust system that is well suited for a wide variety of research and development work. This brief paper introduces the LLVM system and provides pointers to more extensive documentation, complementing the tutorial presented at LCPC.

1 Brief Overview and Goals

The LLVM Compiler Infrastructure [2] is a language and target-independent compiler system, designed for both static and dynamic compilation. LLVM (Low Level Virtual Machine) can be used to build both traditional optimizing compilers for high performance programming languages as well as compiler-based tools such as Just-In-Time (JIT) translators, profilers, binary translators, memory sandboxing tools, static analysis tools, and others.

A major goal of the LLVM development community is to provide a fast, robust, and well-documented core framework to support high-quality compilers and tools. A second major goal is to develop a broad community of contributors to ensure that the software continues to grow and be relevant, and to maintain its robustness and quality. A third goal is to provide a flexible infrastructure for new compiler development and research.

2 Key LLVM Design Features

The LLVM system has three main components: the LLVM Virtual Instruction Set, a collection of reusable libraries for analysis, transformation and code generation; and tools built from these libraries. The LLVM framework is characterized by a clean, simple, and modular design, which allows new users to understand the representation, write new analyses, transformations, and tools easily.

The LLVM Virtual Instruction Set is the common intermediate representation shared by all of the LLVM subsystems. It is a simple, mid-level, three-address code representation that is designed to be both language-independent and target-independent [1]. The instruction set provides explicit control-flow graphs, explicit dataflow information (in SSA form), and a mid-level, language

R. Eigenmann et al. (Eds.): LCPC 2004, LNCS 3602, pp. 15–16, 2005.

independent type system. The type system is rich enough to support sophisticated, language-independent compiler techniques, including pointer analysis, dependence analysis, and interprocedural dataflow analyses, and transformations based on them. Exactly the same instruction set is used both as a persistent, external representation for compiled code and as the internal representation for all mid-level compiler passes. Making this representation persistent enables all LLVM passes to be used at compile-time, link-time, load-time, run-time, and "idle-time" (between program runs). The key design features and the innovative aspects of the code representation are are described in a paper [2], and the complete instruction set is described in an online reference manual [1].

The LLVM source base mostly consists of modular and reusable libraries. These components include analyses and optimizations, native code generators, JIT compiler support, profile-guided feedback, etc. These compiler components reduce the cost and difficulty of building compilers for new platforms, new source languages, and for building new kinds of tools (debuggers, profilers, etc).

The LLVM system also includes several complete tools built from these components, including an ANSI-conforming C/C++ compiler (which uses the GNU Compiler Collection (GCC) parsers). The C/C++ compiler applies a large number of module-level (compile-time) and cross-module (link-time) optimizations. Other LLVM tools include programs to manipulate the IR (e.g. convert between ASCII and binary formats, extract functions from a program, etc), a modular optimizer (which can run any LLVM optimization on an program, driven from the command line), automated compiler debugging tools, and others.

3   Status

LLVM 1.0 was released on October 2003, and has had three releases (1.1 - 1.3) since then. Each release adds new features and improves performance, stability, and compliance. As of LLVM 1.3, LLVM can compile C, C++, and Stacker (a Forth-like language) to native X86, Sparc V9 and PowerPC machine code, and includes JIT compilers for X86 and Sparc V9. Other language front-ends and code generators are under development.

LLVM includes extensive documentation [4] and an active developer community, making it easy to dig in and come up to speed quickly. A broad range of information about LLVM is accessible through its web page [3], including mailing lists, publications, and the slides that correspond to this presentation.

References

1. C. Lattner and V. Adve. LLVM Language Reference Manual. http://llvm.cs.uiuc.edu/docs/LangRef.html.
2. C. Lattner and V. Adve. LLVM: A Compilation Framework for Lifelong Program Analysis and Transformation. In *Proc. 2004 Int'l Symposium on Code Generation and Optimization*, San Jose, USA, Mar 2004.
3. LLVM Development Group. LLVM Home Page. http://llvm.cs.uiuc.edu/.
4. LLVM Development Group. LLVM Online Docs. http://llvm.cs.uiuc.edu/docs/.

An Overview of the Open Research Compiler

Chengyong Wu[1], Ruiqi Lian[1], Junchao Zhang[1], Roy Ju[2],
Sun Chan[2], Lixia Liu[2], Xiaobing Feng[1], and Zhaoqing Zhang[1]

[1] Institute of Computing Technology, Chinese Academy of Sciences,
Beijing 100080, P. R. China
{cwu, lrq, jczhang, fxb, zqzhang}@ict.ac.cn
[2] Microprocessor Technology Labs, Intel Corporation,
Santa Clara, CA 95052
{roy.ju, sun.c.chan, lixia.liu}@intel.com

Abstract. The Open Research Compiler (ORC), jointly developed by Intel Microprocessor Technology Labs and the Institute of Computing Technology at Chinese Academy of Sciences, has become the leading open source compiler on the Itanium[TM] Processor Family (IPF, previously known as IA-64). Since its first release in 2002, it has been widely used in academia and industry worldwide as a compiler and architecture research infrastructure and as code base for further development. In this paper, we present an overview of the design of the major components in ORC, especially those new features in the code generator. We discuss the development methodology that is important to achieving the objectives of ORC. Performance comparisons with other IPF compilers and a brief summary of the research work based on ORC are also presented.

1 Introduction

The Explicitly Parallel Instruction Computing (EPIC) architecture exemplified by the Itanium[TM] Processor Family (IPF, previously known as IA-64) [18] provides wide execution resources and rich hardware supports to compiler optimization. It is also an ideal platform for research on instruction-level parallelism compilation and architecture technology. However, the lack of a robust, flexible, and high performance compiler infrastructure impeded the adoption of the IPF platform in the research community. The Microprocessor Technology Labs (MTL) at Intel initiated the Open Research Compiler (ORC) project [21], and collaborated with the Institute of Computing Technology (ICT) at Chinese Academy of Sciences (CAS). The objective of the project is to provide a leading open source IPF compiler infrastructure to the research community, to encourage and facilitate compiler and architecture research.

The design of ORC stresses on the following aspects: compatibility to other open source tools, robustness of the entire infrastructure, flexibility and modularity for quick prototyping of novel ideas, and leading performance among IPF open source compilers. Researchers are invited to explore all aspects of compiler and architecture research on ORC, e.g. performance-driven optimizations, thread-level parallelism, co-design of software and hardware features, power management, design and implemen-

R. Eigenmann et al. (Eds.): LCPC 2004, LNCS 3602, pp. 17–31, 2005.

tation of type-safe languages, co-design of static and dynamic compilation, optimizations for memory hierarchies, etc.

To best leverage existing resources and make timely deliverables, ORC is based on the Pro64 compiler[1] from SGI [13]. Pro64 includes a comprehensive set of components: front-ends for C/C++ and Fortran 90, inter-procedural analyzer and optimizer, loop-nest optimizer, scalar global optimizer, and code generator for IPF. It incorporates many state-of-the-art technologies. In the first set of deliverables, ORC had focused its efforts on largely redesign of the code generator mainly from two aspects: new optimizations to better utilize IPF architectural features and infrastructure functionality to facilitate future research. The new IPF optimizations include instruction scheduling integrated with finite-state-automaton-based resource management, control and data speculation with recovery code generation, if-conversion and predicate analysis. The research infrastructure features include region-based compilation, profiling support, and parameterized machine model. In the subsequent releases of ORC, the entire compiler was significantly enhanced and additional features were added to take full advantage of the architectural features of IPF. As a result, ORC has become a widely used open source compiler infrastructure with leading IPF performance.

The rest of the paper is organized as follows. Section 2 provides an overview of the design of the major components in ORC, with a particular focus on those new features of the code generator. Section 3 discusses the development methodology that is important to accomplishing the objectives of ORC. Section 4 presents performance comparisons with other IPF compilers. Section 5 lists selective research projects based on ORC. Section 6 concludes the paper.

2   Overview of ORC

2.1   Framework and Major Components

ORC inherited several major components, e.g. the front-ends, inter-procedural optimizer (IPA), loop-nest optimizer (LNO), and global scalar optimizer (WOPT), from Pro64. The framework and the major components of ORC are shown in Fig. 1. The front-ends include C and C++ front-ends from GNU, and a Fortran 90 front-end developed by SGI/Cray. The different front-ends translate the different languages into a common intermediate representation (IR) called WHIRL [32], which is organized in a strict tree form and serves as the common interface among most of the backend components except code generation (CG). To meet the different requirements of various optimizations and allow efficient implementation, WHIRL has multiple levels of representations. The very-high level is output by the front-ends and well corresponds to the source program, while the lowest level exposes the most machine details. Each optimization phase is supposed to work on a specific level. The compilation process can be viewed as a process of continuous lowering of the semantic level of the IR. The low-level WHIRL is translated to CG's internal IR, which corresponds to machine instructions.

---

[1] A continuation of Pro64, also called Open64 in the user community, has been maintained by Prof. G. Gao and CAPSL. At present, ORC is a major contributor to Open64. More information can be found at http://open64.sourceforge.net/.

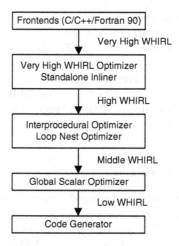

Fig. 1. Framework and major components of ORC

The interprocedural optimizer (IPA)[2] has a two-stage implementation: IPL and IPA main stage. The IPL stage collects summary information local to a procedure, e.g. call-site specific formals and actuals, mod/ref counts of variables, Fortran common shape, array section and shape, and call site frequencies. The IPA main stage also consists of two phases: analysis and optimization. The analysis phase performs a set of interprocedural analyses, e.g. alias analysis, mod/ref analysis, and array section analysis, etc. The implementation can handle relocatable object files and archives, as well as dynamic shared objects (a.k.a dynamic linked libraries), so as to support whole program analysis (WPA). It also considers symbol preemption attributes so that WPA effect is achieved without the need to access full source code. Some of the optimization decisions are also made in this phase, e.g. inlining and array padding/splitting. Based on these information, the optimization phase performs a set of optimizations, e.g. data promotion, constant propagation, function cloning, and dead function/variable elimination.

The loop nest optimizer (LNO) [35] contains a rather complete set of loop transformations to improve register reuse, locality of memory hierarchy, and loop-level parallelism[3]. LNO includes fission, fusion, unroll and jam, loop interchange, peeling, tiling, and vector data prefetching, etc. The locality optimizations assume a traditional memory hierarchy consists of several levels of caches and a flat, uniformly addressed memory space. It has its own cache model, which chooses the best tiling and block size. It supports both perfect and imperfect loop nests. It also supports OpenMP[4].

The global scalar optimizer (WOPT) performs classical machine independent optimizations. It works on its internal IR called HSSA, which is a static single assignment (SSA) form with extensions to incorporate aliases and indirect memory references [8]. HSSA introduces two pseudo operators to represent the effects of aliasing

---

[2] The IPA phase was not fully functional until ORC 1.1.

[3] Several loop transformations improving instruction-level parallelism are performed in CG.

[4] The OpenMP support in ORC has been enhanced by Tsinghua Univ [33].

and virtual variables to characterize the aliasing behavior of indirect memory references. The scalar variables and virtual variables are represented uniformly in HSSA via hashing-based global value numbering. WOPT takes the WHIRL representation of a program unit as input, and converts it to HSSA in a series of steps. It then performs such optimizations as induction variable recognition and elimination, copy propagation, unreachable code and dead store elimination, control flow transformations, SSA-based partial redundancy elimination [7, 25], and register variable identification [28], etc. After all work done, the internal IR is translated back to WHIRL before being fed to CG.

2.2 New Features of Code Generator

The framework and the major phases of the code generator (CG) are shown in Fig. 2, where the grayed phases are those existing phases in Pro64. The new features can be classified into two categories: IPF specific optimizations and research infrastructure. The IPF specific optimizations include instruction scheduling integrated with finite-state-automaton-based resource management, control and data speculation with recovery code generation, if-conversion and predicate analysis. The research infrastructure features include region-based compilation, profiling support, and parameterized machine model.

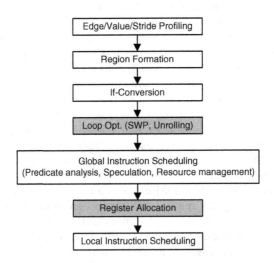

Fig. 2. Framework and major phases of the code generator

In CG, first we do profiling to collect the needed runtime information. Then a region hierarchy is formed for the compilation unit. Most of the newly added phases work in the scope of a region. If-conversion converts control flows into straightline, predicated code to eliminate branches and enlarge the scope for other ILP optimizations. Loop optimizations, including software pipelining and loop unrolling, are existing phases in Pro64, but have been adapted to coexist with the region hierarchy. After that, global instruction scheduling is invoked for each region, from innermost outside. It drives a number of machine dependent analyses and optimizations, e.g. predicate analysis, control and data speculation, and integrates a finite-state-automaton based resource management to handle instruction templates and dispersal rules. The global and local register allocation are performed for the whole compilation unit. Finally, a post pass of local instruction scheduling, which shares the same implementation with the global one, is invoked for those basic blocks with spill code inserted.

2.2.1 Region-Based Compilation

Compared to the traditional, function-based backend compilation framework, a region-based framework provides a way to better control the compilation time and space overhead, especially for those expensive algorithms that could often be found in modern optimizing compilers. Furthermore, for regions of some specific shapes or with some expected properties, more effective or efficient algorithms can be devised. Several kinds of regions with specific shapes have been proposed, e.g. trace [12], superblock [17], hyperblock [30], treegion [15], etc. and a more general notion of region has also been proposed to cover a wide range of optimizations [14]. Hank also proposed a region-based compilation framework [14], but the region structure there is a flat one, i.e. nested regions are not allowed.

In ORC, we proposed and implemented a more flexible and general region-based compilation framework. Informally, a region is simply a connected sub-component of the control flow graph (CFG). Depending on the shape and other characteristics of the internal CFG and the numbers of entries and exits, regions can be further classified as loop region, single-entry-multiple-exit (SEME) region, multiple-entry-multiple-exit (MEME) region, and improper region[5]. A set of optimization-guiding attributes are attached to each region to indicate the limitations on subsequent phases, e.g. whether the region is allowed to be further optimized, whether optimizations across the region boundary can be performed, etc. Regions can also be nested to form a hierarchy or region tree, with the root node being the outmost region corresponding to the whole function. An inner region is collapsed into a single node in the outer region's CFG. The region hierarchy can be constructed and destructed at different points, to meet the requirements of different optimization phases. Most of the newly added phases in CG have been made region-based. Several original phases have been adapted to maintain the region structure or observe the specified region attributes.

The region hierarchy is formed in two steps. In the first step, after a preprocessing of the CFG, we form the root region and identify the intervals. We then form loop regions or improper regions for the intervals. In the second step, large regions are decomposed into smaller SEME or MEME regions based on a predetermined size limit. An enhanced version of the MEME region formation algorithm proposed in [14] is used to form MEME regions. Then an algorithm considering code duplication ratio and main exit probability is used to form SEME regions. Tail duplication is judiciously applied in this process to avoid excessive code expansion and adverse I-cache effect. Details of the region formation algorithms can be found in [27].

---

[5] We defined an improper region to be a region with irreducible control flow.

2.2.2 Profiling Support

Profiling is important to compilers for EPIC architecture since many optimization decisions need to base on the feedback information. Various profiling techniques collecting different runtime information have been proposed, such as edge profiling [1], path profiling [2], value profiling [5], and stride profiling [36], etc. As a research infrastructure feature, the emphasis here is to provide some common supports so that researchers can build the instrumentation and feedback loop of the specific profiling they need more easily.

There is already an edge profiling in Pro64[6] which is performed on the WHIRL IR before CG. However, propagating the edge frequencies across all the optimizations that may change control flow significantly to the phases in CG could in general be difficult. Hence, we decided to provide a flexible profiling framework in CG. This includes some common supports to various kinds of profiling, such as generation and use interface of the feedback information, common (or parameterized with the profiling type) instrumentation library, etc. The implementation allows various instrumentation points in CG and verifies that feedback information is properly maintained. To demonstrate the capability of the framework and to improve the performance of the compiler, we also implemented several kinds of profiling, including edge profiling, value profiling, and stride profiling. They have been shown to be important to the performance of the compiler.

2.2.3 Machine Model

The purpose of a centralized machine model is to encapsulate architectural and microarchitectural details in a well-interfaced module, and to ease the porting of the compiler to future generations of IPF or even other architectures. A flexible machine model also facilitates the study of hardware/compiler co-design. In ORC, machine model consists of two parts: a parameterized machine description system and a microscheduler.

The machine description system, shown in the right part of Fig. 3, reads the architectural and micro-architectural parameters from a knobsfile published by Intel [20], and automatically generates the machine description tables internally used by the compiler. It also provides a set of query functions on various machine parameters, such as the machine width, number of functional units in each type, number of registers in each class, etc.

The EPIC architecture introduces a new notion of instruction templates and a set of complicated dispersal rules as critical resource constraints in addition to the traditional pipeline resource hazards [19]. This has presented challenges to instruction scheduler in its ability to manage resource constraints effectively and efficiently, which has already been one of the most complex phases in an optimizing compiler. To shield the complicated resource management of the EPIC architecture from instruction scheduler, we propose to use a micro-level scheduler to handle the placement of instructions and resource management within a cycle. At the core is a functional-unit-based finite state automaton (or FU-FSA in short) that models the resource usage of a schedule cycle. Each state in the FU-FSA represents the set of functional units that are in use in a schedule cycle. Instructions scheduled into a cycle are treated

---

[6] The original profiling implementation is incomplete and fully functional only after ORC 1.1.

as a sequence of FU-FSA state transitions. Instruction templates and dispersal rules are modeled in each state by a list of legal template assignments of the state. A template assignment is legal for a state if its FU usage set is a superset of the FU usage set of the state. Only those states with at least one legal template assignment are included in the FU-FSA.

The proposed approach has been fully implemented in ORC and experimental results showed that it provides not only good performance improvements but also compilation time efficiency [6]. We have ported ORC to Itanium2™ rather straightforwardly. This demonstrates the effectiveness of the proposed machine model.

2.2.4 Instruction Scheduling
Instruction scheduling has been intensively studied in literature [11]. In ORC, we proposed and implemented an approach of integrated instruction scheduling, as illustrated in Fig. 3, where the high-level scheduler considers dependences and latencies to determine the issue cycle of each instruction, and the micro-level scheduler takes care of the placement of each instruction and resource management within a cycle. Both the high-level and micro-level scheduler retrieve machine information from the machine descriptions generated offline by a machine model builder (MM builder).

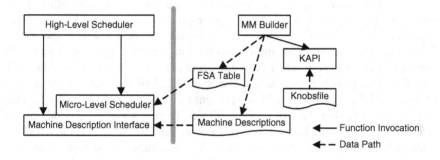

Fig. 3. High-level structure of the ORC integrated instruction scheduler

The high-level and micro-level scheduler cooperate in the following way. The high-level instruction scheduler repeatedly picks the best candidate from a list of instructions that are ready for scheduling. It then consults the micro-level scheduler to check whether there is any available FU and legal template assignment that satisfies instruction dependence constraints, if exist. The micro-level scheduler simply picks an available FU for the candidate instruction and then consults the FU-FSA for a legal state transition. When there is no intra-cycle instruction dependence, the legal FU-FSA transition check is simply verifying the new FU usage set is indeed a state in the FU-FSA. The construction of FU-FSA guarantees that at least one legal template assignment exists for each state. When intra-cycle dependences exist, the legal FU-FSA transition check needs to scan through the list of legal template assignments of the new FU-FSA state to ensure the existence of at least one template assignment that can lay out instructions in the required dependence order.

Two passes of instruction scheduling are performed to solve the phase ordering problem of instruction scheduling and register allocation. The prepass, global instruction scheduling uses a forward, cycle scheduling framework [4] but works on the scope of SEME regions with internal control flow transfers. The enhanced cost function is based on the path lengths in the global dependence DAG built for the region and weighted by execution frequencies. The global instruction scheduling also drives a number of machine-dependent optimizations to fully utilize the architectural features. These include control and data speculation to move load instructions across branches and potential aliasing stores. The scheduler also performs partially ready code motion to exploit the potential parallelism. In case there are spills from register allocation, a postpass, local instruction scheduling is invoked for the affected basic blocks.

2.2.5 Control and Data Speculation

Control and data speculation are effective ways to improve instruction level parallelism [29]. ORC implemented an unified control and data speculation framework based on [24], and it consists of two de-coupled phases: speculative code motion and recovery code generation.

The speculative code motion is driven by global instruction scheduling. First, speculative edges are marked in dependence graph, meaning that the corresponding dependence is not a "hard" one and can be violated via speculation. A speculative edge is also annotated with its type of speculation, e.g. an edge from a store (cf. branch) to a load may be marked as "data-speculative" (cf. "control-speculative"), means that it is possible to schedule the load ahead of the store speculatively. Such unresolved dependences will not prevent the load being added into the candidate list. But whether the speculation will finally be committed depends on the scheduling priority of the load, compared to other candidates. If a load is scheduled speculatively, it is converted to a speculative load according to the type of speculation, and a *check* instruction is inserted at the home location. The dependence graph is then updated based on the inserted *check* instruction. Updating dependence graph includes building incoming and outgoing edges for the *check* instruction. The incoming edges are to prevent the *check* instruction from being scheduled across the speculative load and its unsatisfied speculative predecessors. The outgoing edges are to prevent those "unrecoverable" instructions from being scheduled across the *check*.

The decoupled phase of recovery code generation locates between instruction scheduling and register allocation so that the virtual registers in recovery blocks can be colored. Two kinds of instructions must be put into the recovery block: instructions that are flow-dependent on the speculative load and instructions output-dependent on those already in the recovery block. The recovery code generation goes through each execution path from the speculative load to the corresponding *check* to collect such instructions into the recovery block.

The implementation can handle more complicated cases, such as cascaded speculation (e.g. a speculative load directly or indirectly feeds another speculative load scheduled before the *check* of the first load.), speculation with predication, etc.

2.2.6 If-Conversion and Predicate Analysis

Predicated execution can effectively eliminate branches to expose more instruction level parallelism [30]. While IPF provides the necessary architectural support, compiler needs to convert conditionals to straightline, predicated code through if-conversion. ORC contains a region-based implementation of if-conversion. The framework is simple and effective. The first step is to iteratively traverse the input CFG in a topological order to find out the candidate sub-regions by matching the patterns shown in Fig 4, i.e. the *sequential, if-then* and *if-then-else* patterns.

Each sub-region needs to go through a legality and profitability check to become a candidate of if-conversion. In subsequent iterations, a marked candidate will be treated as a single CFG node and can be merged with other candidates. Finally, all candidates are converted to predicated code and the branches within them are removed.

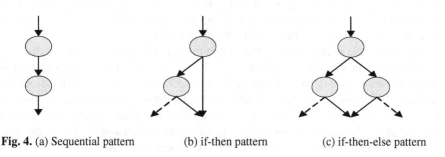

Fig. 4. (a) Sequential pattern   (b) if-then pattern   (c) if-then-else pattern

The cost model considers critical path length, resource usage, approximate branch mis-prediction rate and penalty, and instruction counts, etc. The framework can be extended to consider more factors.

If-conversion generates predicated code, which make the traditional data-flow analysis too conservative. To support predicate-aware analysis [10], ORC contains a predicate analysis [22] phase, which constructs a predicate relation database (PRDB) and provides query interfaces on various relations like disjoint, subset, superset, complementary, etc. A partition graph is used as the core of the PRDB to track the relations between predicates. Both control flow and materialized predicates are considered. The information can be incrementally updated or recomputed at different phases in CG.

2.3 Other Performance Enhancements

In addition to the features presented above, there are a number of performance enhancements that have been added into ORC. They include, but not limited to: C++ optimizations, inter-procedural RSE model to balance RSE traffic and explicit spills, stride prefetching, structure splitting/field reordering framework, type-based memory disambiguation, multi-way branch synthesis, Cache optimizations to reduce cache line/bank conflicts on Itanium2, loop-invariant code motion in CG, and switch optimization. More details can be found in [23].

3 Development Methodology

From the very beginning, ORC was intended to be a research infrastructure, not a production compiler. The potential users are researchers in academia and industry, as well as developers in open source community. The requirements to ORC are prioritized as the following: robustness, flexibility, performance, and compilation time and space. The robustness and stability of the compiler is the top priority. To meet these requirements, several guidelines were set and reinforced in the process of design and implementation. For example, software/code reuse has been encouraged in the project as a way both to improve the robustness of the compiler and to minimize the development efforts needed. Whenever possible, we reuse the components and utility routines in Pro64. We have leveraged many existing phases in CG except for those discussed in the previous section. Unless there is a strong need, we avoid changing IR since such a change usually has a widespread impact. The C++ standard template library (STL) [33] has been heavily used in ORC. These different levels of reuse of matured code contribute to the stability of the compiler.

We have made many efforts in the design to keep a clean infrastructure which will allow easy extensions. We developed clear and well-defined interfaces to each of our focused phases. Within each phase, assertion checkings of the states of various data structures were placed as many as reasonable. To improve modularity, the information communicated between phases is minimized if it can be reconstructed at a reasonable cost. The result of these efforts is a flexible infrastructure. Within the stated and checked constraints, it is possible to reorder these optimization phases or invoke them multiple times. It also allows an easy replacement of an existing implementation of a phase with a new one while conducting research.

We also understood that good coding style not only improves readability and maintainability, but also helps correctness and efficiency. We adopted a revised version of the Pro64 coding convention and tried our best to keep the style of the code to be consistent with the old one. We applied design reviews and code inspections in the project. These practices helped to expose a significant number of potential bugs. At the same time, built-in testability and debugability are always important considerations in the design and implementation.

Another lesson we learned from the development of ORC is that the time and efforts spent on tools pay off well. Various tools have been developed along with the compiler, to cover almost all aspects of the project life cycle, especially testing, debugging, and performance analysis.

Testing is one of the major parts of every developer's daily work. A well-designed testing environment integrating various compilers and test suites with tools written in portable script languages can greatly reduce tedious manual work and improve productivity. The testing environment in ORC can handle all complexities due to OS and library versions, allow users to customize the testing through specifying the compilers and test suites, the optimization levels and specific compilation/linkage flags, and the different testing requirements, e.g. correctness testing, performance testing, checkin testing and regression testing, etc. The environment is user-friendly. Performing any testing need no more manual operation than typing in a simple command line. And the whole process can be made automatic via crontab settings.

Debugging a compiler of hundreds of thousands of lines of code is another difficult task, especially when the failing benchmark consists of tens of files and thousands of functions and the only symptom is the wrong results. To ease the work, we developed a triage tool to narrow down the search scope in a top-down manner. We first identify an erroneous object file and a compilation unit (function) through binary search. This requires the compiler to generate correct code at a lower optimization level. We can then pinpoint a specific erroneous compiler phase through turning off the phases bottom-up, one by one. For some phases, we can further reduce the scope to region, basic block, or even a single instruction. Although a final manual work is still needed to identify the root cause of the failure, a number of mechanical steps have been automated.

Performance analysis may be the hardest work to be automated. But we still developed a set of tools to make it easier. One is a cycle-counting tool, which can count the cycles caused by stop bits and latencies, but cycles due to runtime events are not counted[7]. A set of preselected hot functions are counted to quickly find out potential performance regressions or identify possible opportunities. Performance analysis always requires much manual inspection of assembly code of large functions, which is tedious. According to the 90:10 rule, focusing only on hot paths is much more efficient. Hence, we developed a hot path enumeration tool to find out the hot paths in a function. The hot paths are sorted according to their execution frequencies, and one can visualize the hot paths in the CFG.

4 Evaluation

While we don't have a full repertoire of test suites, we have done as much testing as our resources available for each release of ORC. We also permuted compiler options to improve the testing coverage. Various combinations of OS and libraries have been experienced.

We have also measured the performance of ORC 2.1 on both Itanium and Itanium2 systems, against the GNU GCC compiler, and the best performing Linux-based production compiler, Intel's ECC compiler. The evaluation was done at the time of ORC 2.1 release in July 2003. Fig. 5 and Fig. 6 show the testing configurations and the performance comparisons with ECC 7.0 and GCC 3.1, on Itanium and Itanium2, respectively, using SPEC CINT2000 benchmarks. All benchmarks are compiled with SPEC base options for Ecc 7.0, -O3 for GCC 3.1, and "-peak" option for ORC[8], and linked with standard libraries on Redhat Linux. All data are normalized to that of ECC. From the figures we can see that on Itanium the performance of ORC 2.1 is on par with ECC 7.0, and on Itanium2, the difference is about 5%. While on both systems, ORC 2.1 is 30% ahead of GCC 3.1.

---

[7] Runtime events on IPF can be counted using tools like pfmon or VTune.

[8] The "-peak" option of ORC will invoke three passes of compilations, with the first two passes for WHIRL profiling and CG edge profiling. More information can be found at [21].

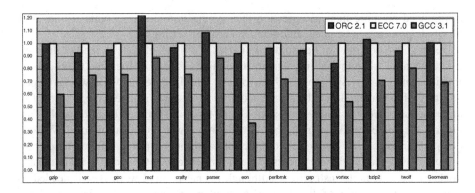

Fig. 5. Performance comparison with ECC 7.0 and GCC 3.1 on Itanium. Testing environment: HP i2000 workstation with 733MHz Itanium, 2MB L3 Cache, 1GB Memory, Redhat 7.2

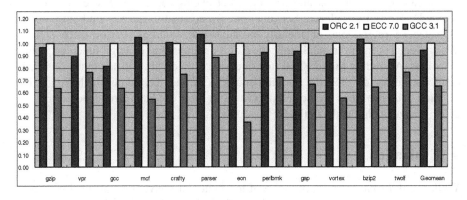

Fig. 6. Performance comparison with ECC 7.0 and GCC 3.1 on Itanium2. Testing environment: 4-way 900MHz Itanium2, 16KB L1 DCache,16KB L1 ICache, 256KB L2 Cache, 3MB L3 Cache, 1GB Memory, Redhat AS2.1

5   Proliferation of Open64 and ORC

As an open research compiler, Open64/ORC has been widely used by both academia and industry for its robustness, flexibility, and performance. Many universities and companies worldwide have adopted ORC/Open64 as the infrastructure for their research and development. At the time of writing, there have been about 15,000 downloads since the first release of ORC. In this section, we briefly describe a number of selective research projects based on ORC/Open64 in academia and industry, while the overall uses of the compiler infrastructure have grown steadily.

Many projects utilize the optimizations and WHIRL2C/WHIRL2F tools in ORC/Open64 to do source to source translation. U.C. Berkeley and Lawrence Berkeley National Lab have a joint project on Berkeley Unified Parallel C (UPC) [3]. UPC is an extension of the C programming language designed for high performance computing on large-scale parallel machines. The Berkeley UPC compiler has an Open64-based UPC-to-C translator. Through the UPC front end processing and backend lowering, UPC code is converted into the high level WHIRL, which is later translated back into ANSI-compliant C code by a WHIRL2C tool. Similarly, the Open64 project at Rice University makes use of WHIRL2F in the source to source transformation of Fortran 90 programs with extensions [31].

Using ORC/Open64 as a vehicle, novel ideas and research topics are implemented and verified. Prof. K. Palem at Georgia Institute of Technology uses ORC in design space exploration and memory optimizations like data remapping, cache sensitive scheduling, static Markovian-based data prefetching, etc. Prof. P. Yew and Prof. W. Hsu at University of Minnesota use ORC to study a general speculative analysis and optimization framework and as an instrumentation and profiling tool to study alias and data dependence profiling on optimizations for sequential and parallel code [26]. Ghent University of Belgium reuses the distance-based cache hint selection in ORC. Tsinghua University of China uses ORC as a platform to study software pipelining, including heuristics of software pipelining and cache latency aware modulo-scheduling.

Prof. G. Gao at University of Delaware uses Open64/ORC to do low power research on loop transformation and SWP. University of Houston uses Open64 as an infrastructure for OpenMP research [16]. By exploiting existing analyses inside Open64, they have developed a tool for browsing OpenMP programs and displaying analysis results. Tsinghua University also has a project to make ORC compliant to OpenMP standard [34]. Our ICT compiler group has engrafted ORC with an automatic parallelizing compiler for distributed memory machines.

Several universities have used ORC/Open64 in their courses. For instance, Prof. J. N. Amaral at University of Alberta has used ORC/Open64 as class projects on machine SSA, pointer-based prefetching, and hardware support for SWP. Prof. W. Hsu at University of Minnesota has used ORC as an instructional tool for a compiler optimization course.

ORC/Open64 has also been used in the industry. Intel initiated several projects based on ORC. Intel's speculative multithreading projects took advantage of ORC's region-based optimizations to support multithreading [9]. Intel's StarJIT project leveraged the micro-scheduler of ORC. Intel's ongoing Shangri-La project, which aims to create a high level programming environment for network processors, is also based on ORC. A number of companies also leverage Open64 in their development targeting different platforms.

6 Conclusion and Future Work

We have presented an overview of the Open Research Compiler (ORC), including the design of the framework and the major components, focusing on the new features in the code generator. The new features can be classified into two categories: IPF specific optimizations and research infrastructure. These features, along with a number of performance enhancements and a complete set of development-aiding tools, make ORC an ideal infrastructure for compiler and architecture research. We introduced the development methodology of ORC. We also showed performance comparisons with other IPF compilers. We demonstrated how robustness, high performance and a clean, flexible infrastructure can be achieved simultaneously. Finally, we summarized the proliferation of Open64/ORC in wide and diverse research areas.

Both Intel and CAS will keep working on ORC, to improve it's robustness and performance, and to conduct compiler and architecture research. We welcome contributions and suggestions from the user community and would like to see the community keeps growing.

Acknowledgements

We would like to thank the entire ORC team at Chinese Academy of Sciences and Intel China Research Center, for the design and implementation of the ORC compiler. We also would like to thank the colleagues in the Programming Systems Lab at Intel Microprocessor Technology Labs for their valuable inputs to this project.

References

1. T. Ball and J. Larus, Optimally profiling and tracing programs, ACM Transactions on Programming Languages and Systems, 16(3): 1319-1360, Jul. 1994.
2. T. Ball and J. Larus, Efficient path profiling. In Proc. 29th Annual Intl. Symp. on Microarchitecture, Dec. 1996.
3. Berkeley Unified Parallel C (UPC) Project: http://upc.lbl.gov.
4. D. Berstein, M. Rodeh, Global Instruction Scheduling for Superscalar Machines, Proc. of SIGPLAN '91 Conference on Programming Language Design and Implementation, 1991.
5. B. Calder, P. Feller, and A. Eustance, Value Profiling, In Proc. 30th Annual Intl. Symp. on Microarchitecture, Dec. 1997.
6. D. Chen, L. Liu, C.Fu, S. Yang, C. Wu, and R. Ju, Efficient Resource Management during Instruction Scheduling for the EPIC Architecture, Proc. of the 12th International Conference on Parallel Architectures and Compilation Techniques, New Orleans, Sep. 2003.
7. F. Chow, S. Chan, R. Kennedy, S. Liu, R. Lo, and P. Tu, A New Algorithm for Partial Redundancy Elimination Based on SSA Form, Proc. of SIGPLAN '97 Conf. on Programming Language Design and Implementation, May 1997.
8. F. Chow, R. Lo, S. Liu, S. Chan, and M. Streich, Effective Representation of Aliases and Indirect Memory Operations in SSA Form, Proc. of 6th Int'l Conf. on Compiler Construction, Apr. 1996.
9. Z. Du, C. Lim, X. Li, C. Yang, Q. Zhao, T. Ngai, A Cost-Driven Compilation Framework for Speculative Parallelization of Sequential Programs. In Proc. of the ACM SIGPLAN'04 Conference on Programming Language Design and Implementation, 2004.
10. A. Eichenberger and E. Davidson, Register allocation for predicated code, in Proc. of the 28th Annual International Symposium on Microarchitecture, Dec. 1995.
11. P. Faraboschi, J. Fisher and C Young, Instruction Scheduling for Instruction Level Parallel Processors, Proceedings of the IEEE, vol. 89, No. 11, Nov. 2001.
12. J. Fisher, Trace scheduling: A Technique for Global Microcode Compaction, IEEE Trans. on Computers, Vol. No. 7, 1981.
13. G. Gao, J. Amaral, J. Dehnert, and R. Towle, The SGI Pro64 Compiler Infrastructure, 2000 International Conference on Parallel Architectures and Compilation Techniques, Tutorial, Oct. 2000.

14. R. Hank, Region Based Compilation, Doctoral thesis, University of Illinois at Urbana Champaign, 1996.
15. W. Havanki, Treegion Scheduling for VLIW Processors, MS Thesis, Dept.of Electrical and Computer Engineering, North Carolina State University, Raleigh, NC, 1997.
16. University of Houston, Dragon Analysis Tool: http://www2.cs.uh.edu/~dragon.
17. W. Hwu, S. Mahlke, W. Chen, P. Chang, N. Warter, R. Bringmann, R. Ouellette, R. Hank, T. Kiyohara, G. Haab, J. Holm, and D. Lavery, The Superblock: An Effective Technique for VLIW and Superscalar Compilation. Journal of Supercomputing, 7(1,2):229--248, March 1993.
18. Intel, Intel Itanium Architecture Software Developer's Manual, Vol. 1, Oct. 2002.
19. Intel, Itanium Processor Microarchitecture Reference, Mar. 2000.
20. Intel, Itanium Microarchitecture Knobs API Programmer's Guide, 2001.
21. Intel, ICT, The Open Research Compiler Project: http://ipf-orc.sourceforge.net.
22. R. Johnson and M. Schlansker, Analysis technique for predicated code, in Proceedings of the 29th International Symposium on Microarchitecture, Dec. 1996.
23. R. Ju, S. Chan, T. Ngai, C. Wu, Y. Lu, J. Zhang, Open Research Compiler (ORC) 2.0 and Tuning Performance on Itanium, Micro-35 Tutorial, Istanbul, Turkey, November 19, 2002.
24. R. Ju, K. Nomura, U. Mahadevan, and L. Wu, A Unified Compiler Framework for Control and Data Speculation, 2000 International Conference on Parallel Architectures and Compilation Techniques, Oct. 2000.
25. R. Kennedy, S. Chan, S. Liu, R. Lo, P. Tu, and F. Chow, Partial Redundancy Elimination in SSA Form, TOPLAS 21(3), May 1999.
26. J. Lin, T. Chen, W. Hsu, P. Yew, R. Ju, T. Ngai, and S. Chan, A Compiler Framework for Speculative Analysis and Optimizations. In Proc. of the ACM SIGPLAN'03 Conference on Programming Language Design and Implementation, 2003.
27. Y. Liu, Z. Zhang, R. Qiao, and R. Ju, A Region-Based Compilation Infrastructure, Proc. of the 7th Workshop on Interaction between Compilers and Computer Architectures, 2003.
28. R. Lo, F. Chow, R. Kennedy, S. Liu, and P. Tu, Register Promotion by Sparse Partial Redundancy Elimination of Loads and Stores, Proc. of SIGPLAN '98 Conf. on Programming Language Design and Implementation, Jun. 1998.
29. S. Mahlke, W. Chen, W. Hwu, B. Rau, and M. Schlansker, Sentinel Scheduling for Superscalar and VLIW Processors, in Proc. of the 5th Int'l Conference on Ar-chitectural Support for Programming Languages and Operating Systems, Oct. 1992.
30. S. Mahlke, D. Lin, W. Chen, R. Hank, and R. Bringmann, Effective Compiler Support for Predicted Execution Using the Hyperblock, Proceedings of 25th international symposium of Microarchitecture, 1992.
31. Rice University, Open64 Project: http://www.hipersoft.rice.edu/open64.
32. SGI, WHIRL Intermediate Language Specification, http://open64.sourceforge.net.
33. SGI, Standard Template Library Programmer's Guide, http://www.sgi.com/tech/stl.
34. Tsinghua University, ORC-OpenMP Project: http://sourceforge.net/projects/orc-openmp.
35. M. Wolf, D. Maydan, and D. Chen, Combining Loop Transformations Considering Caches and Scheduling, MICRO-29, Dec. 1996.
36. Y. Wu, Efficient Discovery of Regular Stride Patterns In Irregular Programs and Its Use in Compiler Prefetching, PLDI 2002, Berlin, Germany, Jun. 2002.

Trimaran: An Infrastructure for Research in Instruction-Level Parallelism

Lakshmi N. Chakrapani[1], John Gyllenhaal[2], Wen-mei W. Hwu[3],
Scott A. Mahlke[4], Krishna V. Palem[1], and Rodric M. Rabbah[5]

[1] Georgia Institute of Technology
{nsimhan, palem}@cc.gatech.edu
[2] Lawrence Livermore National Laboratory
gyllen@llnl.gov
[3] University of Illinois, Urbana-Champaign
w-hwu@uiuc.edu
[4] University of Michigan
mahlke@umich.edu
[5] Massachusetts Institute of Technology
rabbah@mit.edu

Abstract. Trimaran is an integrated compilation and performance monitoring infrastructure. The architecture space that Trimaran covers is characterized by HPL-PD, a parameterized processor architecture supporting novel features such as predication, control and data speculation and compiler controlled management of the memory hierarchy. Trimaran also consists of a full suite of analysis and optimization modules, as well as a graph-based intermediate language. Optimizations and analysis modules can be easily added, deleted or bypassed, thus facilitating compiler optimization research. Similarly, computer architecture research can be conducted by varying the HPL-PD machine via the machine description language HMDES. Trimaran also provides a detailed simulation environment and a flexible performance monitoring environment that automatically tracks the machine as it is varied.

1 Introduction

Trimaran is a compiler infrastructure for supporting state of the art research in compiling for Instruction Level Parallel (ILP) architectures. The system is currently oriented toward Explicitly Parallel Instruction Computing (EPIC) [24], and supports a variety of compiler research, including instruction scheduling, register allocation, and software pipelining. The Trimaran compiler infrastructure is comprised of the following components:

- A parameterized ILP architecture called HPL-PD.
- A machine description facility for describing HPL-PD architectures.
- An optimizing compiler with a large suite of optimizations. The compiler is designed such that it may be easily modified and extended by a compiler researcher. The compiler employs an extensible IR (intermediate program

R. Eigenmann et al. (Eds.): LCPC 2004, LNCS 3602, pp. 32–41, 2005.

representation) which has both an internal and textual representation, with conversion routines between the two. The IR supports modern compiler techniques by representing control flow, data and control dependence, and many other attributes.
- A detailed HPL-PD architecture simulator which is parameterized via a machine description and provides run-time information on execution time, branch frequencies, and resource utilization. This information can be used for profile-driven optimizations as well as to provide validation of new optimizations.
- A Graphical User Interface (GUI) for configuring and running the Trimaran system.
- Various tools for the graphical visualization of the program intermediate representation and of the performance results.

The infrastructure is used for designing, implementing, and testing new compilation optimizations, as well as the evaluation of various architectural innovations.

Although there are several compiler infrastructures available to the research community, Trimaran is unique in that it is especially geared toward ILP and EPIC research. It provides a rich compilation framework. The parameterized ILP architecture (HPL-PD) space allows the user to experiment with machines that vary considerably in the number and kinds of functional units and register files, as well as their instruction latencies. The modular nature of the compiler and the hierarchical intermediate program representation used throughout the compiler makes the construction and insertion of new compilation modules into the compiler especially easy. The framework is already populated with a large number of existing compilation modules, providing leverage for new compiler research and supporting meaningful experimentation. The Trimaran Graphical Interface makes the configuration and use of the system surprisingly easy. There is a commitment on our part to releasing a robust, tested, and documented software system. Our website (http://www.trimaran.org) provides the latest information on Trimaran, and includes extensive documentation, and facilities to download the infrastructure and other useful material.

The next section briefly describes the Trimaran user community and provides examples of how the infrastructure has been used to further research. In addition, Section 2 also discusses the quality of the code produced by the Trimaran compiler. Section 3 describes the parametric HPL-PD architecture space, and Section 4 presents an overview of the machine description facility for describing HPL-PD architectures. This is followed by an overview of Trimaran compilation technology (Section 5). Section 6 describes the Trimaran simulation environment, and Section 7 concludes the paper.

2   User Community and Field Tests

The Trimaran user community has steadily grown since the first public release of the infrastructure. Today, the user community spans many universities worldwide, and papers which used Trimaran as their evaluation and experimentation vehicle have appeared in numerous conferences on programming languages, compilers, and computer architecture. Trimaran is also used in several classroom settings where it facilitates student projects in compilation technology and VLIW architecture research.

Trimaran has proved to be a versatile infrastructure, and examples of its many uses include research in predicated static single assignment [4] and predicate-aware scheduling [27], software pipelining that is sensitive to register pressure [2], implementation strategies that improve the performance of object oriented codes [3], and optimizations for improving the performance of the memory system [18,19]. Other published works have leveraged Trimaran as a vehicle for architectural design space exploration and processor customization [5,17].

Furthermore, researchers have extended Trimaran so that it can target real architectures such as the Itanium [10], ARM [6], and WIMS (wireless integrated micro systems) [32]. A Trimaran extension which generates ARM assembly is distributed on our website [30]. The Itanium-specific Trimaran is a collaborative effort between the National University of Singapore and the George Washington University [31].

The compiler, in addition to being versatile, is robust and competitive with widely used compilers (e.g., gcc). Trimaran can successfully compile several benchmark suites including SPEC [28], Mediabench [13], and Olden [16] to name a few. Furthermore, an extensive set of results was presented at the 2004 International Symposium on Computer Architecture (ISCA) to demonstrate that Trimaran is on-par with state of the art compilation technology for EPIC architectures [26]. The code quality produced by Trimaran is largely controlled by the compiler front-end which applies a series of transformations as the code is lowered from the input source language. The compilation process begins with application profiling, followed by procedure inlining to reduce function call overhead, alias analysis, classical optimization, and a slew of structural transformation for enhancing ILP (as discussed in the later portions of this paper).

3   Architecture Space

The architecture space targeted by Trimaran is the HPL-PD parametric processor [11]. HPL-PD was designed to promote research in instruction-level parallelism and serves as a vehicle to investigate ILP architectures and the compiler technology needed to effectively exploit such architectures.

HPL-PD is a parametric architecture in that it admits machines of different composition and scale, especially with respect to the amount of parallelism offered. The HPL-PD parameter space includes the number and types of functional units, the composition of the register files, operation latencies and descriptors that specify when operands may be read and written, instruction formats, and resource usage behavior of each operation.

The architecture's instruction set is akin to a RISC load-store architecture, with standard arithmetic and memory operations. It also supports speculative and predicated execution, compiler exposed memory systems, a decoupled branch mechanism, and software pipelining. The following briefly describe the advanced features of HPL-PD which are geared toward enhancing and exploiting ILP. The interested reader can review the HPL-PD architecture specification [11] for a more thorough description of the architecture.

3.1 Speculative Execution

HPL-PD supports control and data speculation. The former represents code motion across conditional branches. When an instructions is *control speculated*, it is moved above a branch and unconditionally executed, whereas previously it was executed conditionally. This transformation is generally safe but may lead to exceptions. For example, if instructions are speculated from the "taken" path following a branch, but the branch resolves to the "not taken" path, then any exceptions that may have been encountered during speculative execution must be ignored. If on the other hand the branch is taken, then the exception must be exposed. HPL-PD provides the necessary support to enable speculative execution [14]. Briefly, if an exception occurs during a speculative operation, the exception is not raised. Instead, a bit is set in the result register to indicate that such a condition occurred. If a non-speculative operation has an operand with its speculative bit set, the exception is immediately raised.

Another form of speculation known as *data speculation* is geared toward increasing the range of code motion for memory instructions [7,23]. For example, a long latency read operation may not be hoisted above an intervening memory write because the load and the store instructions may access (alias) the same location. It is often difficult for the compiler to determine when such a conflict occurs. In order to safely move the data fetch above a store—to better mask an access latency for example—some form of alias detection and recovery support is necessary. The HPL-PD ISA provides the necessary support to enable data speculation.

3.2 Predicated Execution

In HPL-PD, operations can be predicated, or in other words, their execution is guarded by a predicate. For example (p) LOAD rd = [rs] is a predicate memory read: the operation is nullified (i.e., the state of the machine does not change) when the predicate is not set (p = 0). If on the other hand the predicate is affirmed (p = 1) the operation fetches the data stored at address rs and writes it to register rd (in other words the instruction is issued and allowed to update the state of the machine).

In HPL-PD, a predicate instruction requires an additional operand. The extra operand is a one-bit predicate register whose value guards the execution of the instruction. The value of a predicate register is usually defined using compare-to-predicate instructions (CMPP) that are a part of the ISA. The ISA provides a rich set of these operations. The CMPP instructions are unique in that they define two predicate registers simultaneously, subject to a specified *action*. For example, a CMPP may write the value of a comparison to one predicate, and the complementary value to the other predicate. There is a sufficient number of actions defined in the ISA to cover most of the requirements imposed by the various uses of predicates. Furthermore, the architecture permits multiple operations to write into a register simultaneously, provided all producers generate the same value. These write semantics are particularly valuable for the efficient evaluation of boolean reductions as carried out by the CMPP instructions.

Predication is most notably used to eliminate hard-to-predict branches. Predicate execution is also used in software pipelining as noted in a subsequent section.

3.3   Exposed Memory Hierarchy

The HPL-PD memory hierarchy is unusual in that it is visible to the compiler. The ISA includes instructions for managing data across the hierarchy, for saving and restoring registers, and for performing run-time data disambiguation.

The instructions that manage the memory hierarchy do so by way of latency specifications and cache directives. For example, a store instructions can specify the highest level in the hierarchy where the stored data should be left for use by subsequent memory operations. A load instructions can also specify a cache directive to indicate its view of the highest level in the memory hierarchy where the fetched data should be left. In addition, a load may specify its expectation as to where its source operand (i.e., data address) is cached. Concomitantly, this hint also specifies the operation latency that is assumed for scheduling.

In order to support run-time disambiguation, HPL-PD provides instructions that can speculatively load data from memory and then verify that the address read was not updated by an intervening store; if it was, then the appropriate register is updated. The ISA also permits a branch to compensation code when the verification fails.

3.4   Branch Architecture

In HPL-PD, there is a rich repertoire of branches, and it includes operations to support software pipelining, and as noted earlier, run-time memory disambiguation. HPL-PD replaces conventional branch operations with two operations. A prepare-to-branch instruction loads the target address into a branch target register and initiates a prefetch of the branch target to minimize delays. The instruction may also hint that a branch is taken or not. A branch instruction updates the program counter according to its source branch target operand and perform the actual transfer of control.

3.5   Software Pipelining

Software pipelining [12,20] is a technique for exploiting parallelism across iterations of a loop. In software pipelining, the loop iterations are overlapped such that new iterations begin execution before previous iterations are complete. The set of instructions that are in flight at steady state constitute a *kernel*. To reach steady state, a subset of the instruction in the kernel are executed during a *prologue* stage; similarly, another subset is executed during an *epilogue* stage to complete the loop. During the prologue and epilogue stages, predication is used to nullify the appropriate subsets of the kernel.

HPL-PD supports both static and rotating registers. The latter provide automatic register renaming across iterations such that a register `r[i]` in one iteration is referenced as `r[i+1]` in the next.

4   Machine Model

HPL-PD adopts an EPIC philosophy whereby the compiler is responsible for statically orchestrating the execution of a program. Thus, a compiler must have exact information pertaining to the particulars of the architecture definition within the HPL-PD space. In Trimaran, a machine-description (MDES) database specifies those particulars which include the register file structure, the operation repertoire, the set of resources in the architectures (e.g., functional units and memory hierarchy), the resource utilization patterns for each instruction, and the latency descriptors that define when an operand may be read or written after an instruction is issued.

The architecture is defined using a human-readable, high-level machine description (HMDES) language [8]. The description is translated to a low-level language that specifies the same information but in a format that is suitable for a compiler. A MDES Query System (mQS) relays the information to a compiler through a procedural interface. The MDES methodology allows for a retargetable compiler infrastructure and enables experimentation with numerous performance-oriented compiler algorithms (e.g., register allocation, scheduling) as well as architecture-exploration algorithms [29,25] that attempt to discover a machine description best suited for one or more applications of interest.

5   Optimizing Compiler

The Trimaran optimizing compiler is a profile/feedback driven compiler: applications are instrumented and executed using representative workloads to generate information that describes the salient tendencies of the program. For example, profiling information quantifies the likelihood of executing different regions of the program, the predominant control flow paths in the program, and the extent of load-store address aliasing.

The Trimaran compiler generates a control flow graph (CFG) for an input program, where nodes in the graph represent a *basic block* or an atomic unit of execution, and edges connecting nodes represent control flow. The compiler's front-end is charged with applying classic optimizations as well as advanced region formation for boosting ILP. In particular, the compiler leverages profiling information to form traces or long sequences of basic blocks that traverse a frequently occurring control flow path in the CFG. The traces are known as *super blocks* [9] and *hyper blocks* [15]; the later uses predication to merge paths that forge out of a conditional branch. The trace formation algorithms enable many scheduling optimizations and afford more opportunities for control and data speculation.

In addition to these transformations, the compiler's back-end can apply many novel optimizations, many of which are machine specific (e.g., register allocation and scheduling). The back-end is especially rich in scheduling technology and complements the ILP optimizations applied in the front-end.

The Trimaran compiler is highly modularized and is designed to operate in a plug-and-play manner. Thus, the optimizations represent modules that are invoked by a top level driver as dictated by an elaborate set of compiler parameters.

The driver has at its disposal several acyclic scheduling algorithms, including inter-region scheduling [1] where scheduling decisions made in one block affect those made in subsequent blocks. In addition, the compiler can perform modulo scheduling [21], a widely used technique for software pipelining. There are also compiler modules that perform rotating register allocation for software pipelined loops [22], and register allocation for acyclic regions.

The compiler also includes (*i*) techniques to eliminate redundant array loads and stores within loop iterations, and redundant register-to-register moves; (*ii*) if-conversion to form predicated code to enable software pipelining, or to reduce critical path length through a computation; (*iii*) a sophisticated region-based register allocator with predicate code analysis to reduce register saves and restores; and (*iv*) scheduling strategies to tolerate branch and memory latencies.

The intermediate representation (IR) used in the Trimaran compiler is a graph-based IR that is easy to use and extend. The IR is also hierarchical with a *program* node at the root. A program consists of a set of *procedures* which in turn are composed of *blocks*. A block is made up of operations which consist of source and destination operands. The compiler provides many built-in utilities for traversing, transforming, and visualizing the IR. There is also a textual, human-readable equivalent for the internal representation. In Trimaran, all optimizations are IR to IR transformations. This greatly simplifies the design of the compiler and makes the tool chain easy to use and extend.

6   Instruction Set Simulator

The Trimaran infrastructure also includes an instruction set simulator (ISS). The ISS consumes the output of the Trimaran compiler to generate an executable binary which can simulate the original program. The simulator was specifically engineered to allow for an intermixing of HPL-PD and native code. This allows subsets of a large application to be compiled using Trimaran and linked against the remaining portions of the program that are compiled using a native compiler (e.g., gcc). The advantage of such a design is faster simulation.

The main simulation loop processes a table of operations and for each operation it invokes a function that implements the semantics of the opcode. These functions are automatically generated from the machine description file which defines the ISA. Thus, the main simulation core is small and extensible.

The ISS also includes a device stack model to support various components of the architecture such as a branch predictor, an instruction buffer, and any reasonable memory hierarchy configuration. The simulator also tracks many different events and generates a plethora of data and statistics with varying levels of granularity. For example, the ISS can track the execution frequency of a single instruction, as well as its memory system behavior (e.g., how often fetching the instruction resulted in an instruction cache miss). The statistics are also aggregated at the block, procedure, and program levels.

The ISS supports all of the HPL-PD features, including speculation, predication, software pipelining and rotating registers, as well as various register write semantics. It can simulate unscheduled code (i.e., serial execution), unregister allocated code, and allows for intermixing of the different modes. It is also amenable to integration with other tools such as Wattch[1] which would enable power-based experimentation and evaluation.

7   Concluding Remarks

We have described Trimaran, a compilation and simulation infrastructure that was designed to support research in instruction level parallelism. Trimaran is founded upon HPL-PD, a parametric architecture that scales in the amount of parallelism it affords. The architecture and compiler support a variety of ILP-enhancing techniques, including speculation, predication, and software pipelining. Trimaran also provides a detailed instruction set simulator to facilitate experimentation and evaluation of architecture features and compiler optimizations.

We invite researchers who have interests in ILP and EPIC computing to adopt Trimaran and join the user community which currently spans numerous universities worldwide. We encourage users to contribute to the infrastructure to provide a greater repertoire of ideas in a unified environment. This will aid in the comparison of results and the evaluation of ideas. Trimaran is currently evolving to address important research questions that are facing architects and compiler engineers as we forge ahead into a new era of computer system design and organization. We will try to ensure that the evolution takes place in a controlled, coordinated, and timely manner.

Acknowledgments

Trimaran is the result of many man-years of research and development. It began as a collaborative effort between the Compiler and Architecture Research (CAR) Group at Hewlett Packard Laboratories, the IMPACT Group at the University

---

[1] Wattch is available for download from http://www.eecs.harvard.edu/~dbrooks/wattch-form.html.

of Illinois, and the Center for Research on Embedded Systems and Technology (CREST) at the Georgia Institute of Technology. CREST was the ReaCT-ILP Laboratory at New York University. Many thanks to the former members of the CAR group—especially Santosh Abraham, Sadun Anik, Shail Aditya Gupta, Richard Johnson, Vinod Kathail, Mike Schlansker, Robert Schreiber, Greg Snider, and of course, the late Bob Rau—for their many years of support and contributions, without which, Trimaran would not be possible.

References

1. S. Abraham, V. Kathail, and B. Deitrich. Meld scheduling: A technique for relaxing scheduling constraints. Technical Report HPL-1997-39, Hewlett Packard Laboratories, Feb. 1997.
2. G. Altemose and C. Norris. Register pressure responsive software pipelining. In *Proceedings of the 2001 ACM symposium on Applied computing*, 2001.
3. M. Arnold, M. Hsiao, U. Kremer, and B. G. Ryder. Instruction scheduling in the presence of java's runtime exceptions. In *Proceedings of the 12th International Workshop on Languages and Compilers for Parallel Computing*, 2000.
4. L. Carter, B. Simon, B. Calder, L. Carter, and J. Ferrante. Predicated static single assignment. In *Proceedings of the International Conference on Parallel Architectures and Compilation Techniques*, 1999.
5. N. Clark, W. Tang, and S. Mahlke. Automatically generating custom instruction set extensions. In *Proceedings of the 1st Annual Workshop on Application-Specific Processors*, Nov. 2002.
6. S. Furber. ARM *System Architecture*. Addison Wesley, 1996.
7. D. Gallagher, W. Chen, S. Mahlke, J. Gyllenhaal, and W. Hwu. Dynamic memory disambiguation using the memory conflict buffer. In *Proceedings of the 6th International Conference on Architectural Support for Programming Languages and Operating Systems*, pages 183–195, 1994.
8. J. Gyllenhaal, W. Hwu, and B. R. Rau. Hmdes version 2.0 specification. Technical Report IMPACT-96-3, University of Illinois, Urbana, 1996.
9. W. Hwu, S. Mahlke, W. Chen, P. Chang, N. Warter, R. Bringmann, R. Ouellette, R. Hank, T. Kiyohara, G. Haab, J. Holm, and D. Lavery. The superblock: An effective technique for VLIW and superscalar compilation. *Journal of Supercomputing*, Jan. 1993.
10. Intel Itanium Processors. `http://www.intel.com/itanium/`.
11. V. Kathail, M. Schlansker, and B. R. Rau. HPL-PD architecture specification: Version 1.1. Technical Report HPL-9380 (R.1), Hewlett Packard Laboratories, Feb. 2000.
12. M. Lam. Software Pipelining: An Effective Scheduling Technique for VLIW Machines. In *Proceedings of the ACM SIGPLAN Conference on Programming Language Design and Implementation*, pages 318–328, Atlanta, GA, June 1988.
13. C. Lee, M. Potkonjak, and W. H. Mangione-Smith. MediaBench: A Tool for Evaluating and Synthesizing Multimedia and Communications Systems. In *Proceedings of the 30th Annual International Symposium on Microarchitecture (MICRO-30)*, Research Triangle Park, NC, December 1997. IEEE Computer Society.
14. S. Mahlke, W. Chen, R. Bringmann, R.Hank, W. Hwu, B. R. Rau, and M. Schlansker. Sentinel scheduling: a model for compiler-controlled speculative execution. *ACM Transactions on Computer Systems*, 11(4), Nov. 1993.

15. S. Mahlke, D. Lin, W. Chen, R. Hank, and R. Bringmann. Effective compiler support for predicated execution using the hyperblock. In *Proceedings of the 25th Annual International Symposium on Microarchitecture*, pages 45–54, Dec. 1992.
16. OLDEN benchmark suite. http://www.cs.princeton.edu/~mcc/olden.html.
17. K. Palem, L. Chakrapani, and S. Yalamanchili. A framework for compiler driven design space exploration for embedded system customization. In *Proceedings of the 9th Asian Computing Science Conference*, Dec. 2004.
18. R. Rabbah and K. Palem. Data remapping for design space optimization of embedded memory systems. *To appear in a Special Issue of the ACM Transactions in Embedded Computing Systems*, 2003.
19. R. Rabbah, H. Sandanagobalane, M. Ekpanyapong, and W.-F. Wong. Compiler orchestrated prefetching via speculation and predication. In *Proceedings of the 11th International Conference on Architectural Support for Programming Languages and Operating Systems*, Oct. 2004.
20. B. R. Rau. Iterative Modulo Scheduling. Technical Report HPL-94-115, Hewlett Packard Company, November 1995.
21. B. R. Rau. Iterative modulo scheduling. Technical Report Technical Report HPL-94-115, Hewlett-Packard Laboratories, Nov. 1995.
22. B. R. Rau, M. Lee, P. Tirumalai, and M. Schlansker. Register allocation for modulo scheduled loops: Strategies, algorithms and heuristics. Technical Report HPL-1992-48, Hewlett Packard Laboratories, May 1992.
23. A. Rogers and K. Li. Software support for speculative loads. In *Proceedings of the 5th International Conference on Architectural Support for Programming Languages and Operating Systems*, pages 38–50, 1992.
24. M. Schlansker and B. Rau. EPIC: Explicitly Parallel Instruction Computing. *IEEE Computer*, 33(2):37–45, 2000.
25. R. Schreiber, S. Aditya, S. Mahlke, V. Kathail, B. R. Rau, D. Cronquist, and M. Sivaraman. PICO-NPA: High-level synthesis of nonprogrammable hardware accelerators. *Journal of VLSI Signal Processing*, 31(2), June 2002.
26. J. W. Sias, S. zee Ueng, G. A. Kent, I. M. Steiner, E. M. Nystrom, and W. mei W. Hwu. Field-testing impact epic research results in itanium 2. In *Proceedings of the 31st annual international symposium on Computer architecture*, June 2004.
27. M. Smelyanskiy, S. Mahlke, E. Davidson, , and H.-H. Lee. Predicate-aware scheduling: A technique for reducing resource constraints. In *Proceedings of the 1st International Symposium on Code Generation and Optimization*, Mar. 2003.
28. STANDARD PERFORMANCE EVALUATION CORPORATION benchmark suite. http://www.spec.org.
29. S. Talla. *Adaptive explicitly parallel instruction computing*. PhD thesis, New York University, 2000.
30. TRICEPS: A TRIMARAN-based ARM code generator. http://www.trimaran.org/triceps.shtml.
31. TRITANIUM: A TRIMARAN-based Itanium code generator. http://hydrogen.cs.gwu.edu/tritanium.
32. Wireless integrated microsystems. http://www.wimserc.org.

Phase-Based Miss Rate Prediction Across Program Inputs

Xipeng Shen, Yutao Zhong, and Chen Ding

Computer Science Department, University of Rochester
{xshen, ytzhong, cding}@cs.rochester.edu

Abstract. Previous work shows the possibility of predicting the cache miss rate (CMR) for all inputs of a program. However, most optimization techniques need to know more than the miss rate of the whole program. Many of them benefit from knowing miss rate of each execution phase of a program for all inputs.

In this paper, we describe a method that divides a program into phases that have a regular locality pattern. Using a regression model, it predicts the reuse signature and then the cache miss rate of each phase for all inputs. We compare the prediction with the actual measurement. The average prediction is over 98% accurate for a set of floating-point programs. The predicted CMR-traces matches the simulated ones in spite of dramatic fluctuations of the miss rate over time. This technique can be used for improving dynamic optimization, benchmarking, and compiler design.

1 Introduction

Memory hierarchy provides a way to ameliorate the problem of the widening speed gap between memory and CPU. The cache miss rate (CMR) measures the effect of the program reference patterns on a cache configuration. It determines the effectiveness of the memory hierarchy. Program reference patterns depend on program inputs. Therefore, to fully understand the behavior of a program, it is important to know the cache performance across all input data sets. In [32], Zhong *et. al.* present a method for predicting the average CMR of a whole program across different inputs. However, an average CMR is just a summary. A program's execution may include billions of instructions. Different parts have different computations and sometimes dramatically different behavior. The overall miss rate summarizes the behavior of billions of instructions into one number. The information loss is substantial. The loss becomes important as on-line dynamic techniques are more widely used. It is desirable to accurately predict the behavior of each execution phase of a program across all inputs. This paper reports our preliminary results toward this goal.

We build a locality-trace prediction system based on the locality phase analysis [29] and the miss-rate prediction [11,28]. In our system, we first cut a program into phases that have regular locality patterns. They are called locality phases. We then build a regression model to predict the reuse signature of each phase on any given input, from which we predict the cache miss rate of each phase. We use a simple but effective method to predict the new phase sequence. The new CMR trace for the execution is

R. Eigenmann et al. (Eds.): LCPC 2004, LNCS 3602, pp. 42–55, 2005.

generated by aligning the predicted miss rates along the phase sequence. Our preliminary experiments show that the average prediction accuracy is over 98% for the cache hit rate of each phase [1]. The predicted cache behavior matches with the measured behavior, despite the dramatically different cache behavior in different phases.

One use of this technique is for dynamic hardware and software optimization. In recent years, for their high flexibility of on-line adaptation to program executions, dynamic techniques are widely studied in both the hardware design and software optimization. These techniques tune the hardware (e.g. cache size) or optimization parameters (e.g. unrolling level) during a program's execution. To find the best configuration, most techniques explore various configurations during the execution. The run-time exploration brings much overhead given many options to explore. Furthermore, because they use recent history to predict future behavior, the prediction tends to miss the best configuration when program behavior changes dramatically. Our technique helps to solve those two problems. It accurately predicts the locality and CMR of each section of an execution, which improves the efficiency of run-time exploration and helps to find the best system configuration.

Also, locality trace prediction helps benchmarking and the compiler design. It helps the selection of benchmarks and inputs, thus enables the comprehensive evaluation of dynamic techniques. It also helps to test and design compiler techniques since locality traces reveal the effects of the techniques on different phases of a program.

Our system adds a new dimension—the time—to program locality prediction. Most previous work varies the cache characteristics and measures the average CMR of a given program. Mattson et al. [25] measured CMR for a wide range of cache configurations in one pass; Hill [18] extended it to cache with limited associativity. Ding et. al. [11,32,28] enabled the prediction of changes across different inputs, but only for the overall cache miss rate. Our work moves one step further and predicts the temporal changes in program locality.

In the rest of this paper, we first review the locality measurement, i.e. reuse signature, and its prediction in Section 2. Then we describe locality phase analysis in Section 3 and phase sequence prediction in Section 6. Section 4 shows our phase trace prediction system, followed by evaluations in Section 5. Finally, this paper concludes with related work and conclusions.

2   Locality Measurement and Prediction

In 1970, Mattson et al. defined the *LRU-stack distance* as the number of distinct data elements accessed between two consecutive references to the same element [25]. They summarized the locality of an execution by the distance histogram, which determines the miss rate of fully-associative LRU cache of all sizes. Building on decades of development by others, Ding and Zhong analyzed large traces by reducing the analysis cost to near linear time. They found that reuse-distance histograms change in predictable patterns in many programs [11]. For brevity we call the LRU stack distance the *reuse distance* as Ding and Zhong did.

---

[1] The relative error on the miss rate can be large when the miss rate is small.

We measure the program locality by the histogram of the reuse distance. Figure 1 shows an example, where each bin shows the percentage of memory references whose reuse distance falls within a range. Reuse distance histogram is also called the *reuse signature*. It provides the basis for CMR estimation. Given a cache size S, for fully-associative cache, all references with a reuse distance less than S are cache hits and the others are misses. Zhong *et al.* first estimated CMR according to this observation [32].

In [11], Ding and Zhong showed that reuse distance of many programs has a consistent pattern across different inputs. The pattern is a formula with the data size [2] as the parameter. For a given program input, it predicts the reuse signature of the corresponding execution. The pattern analysis method in [11] has two limitations. First, it uses only two training runs and is likely misled by their noises. Second, the accuracy is limited by the precision of data collection. Accurate prediction requires using large size program inputs and fine-grained reuse distance histograms. The space and time cost of the analysis is consequently high.

In [28], Shen *et al.* presented a set of techniques that overcome these limitations in two ways. First, they use regression to extract signature pattern from more than two training runs. Second, they employ multiple models. They provide a set of prediction methods with higher accuracy and lower overhead. The basic idea is as follows.

To predict the reuse signature of the run on a new input, the key step is to build a model reflecting the reuse pattern with the data size as the parameter. Multiple profiling-runs on inputs of different sizes generate multiple reuse signatures. An arbitrary one is picked as the standard reuse signature and its input as the standard input. It is assumed that the standard reuse signature is composed of multiple models, e.g. constant, linear, sub-linear models. Each model is a function mapping from the data size to the reuse distance. For example, linear model means the reuse distance lengthens linearly with the increase of the program input size. Those models split the standard reuse signature into many chunks. Other training reuse signatures can be formulated as combinations of those chunks. These formulas compose a large group of equations. The least-square linear regression gives the solution, i.e. the size of each chunk in the standard reuse signature. This concludes the building of reuse models. Since any reuse signature can be formulated as a combination of those chunks, the reuse signature of new inputs can be easily computed from the reuse model once the data size is known.

We use the same estimation method as Shen *et al.*, except that our task is to estimate the CMR of each phase instead of the whole execution.

3   Locality Phase Analysis

We use the locality phase analysis to cut a program into phases [29]. It was proposed recently by Shen *et al.*, using program locality for program phase analysis and combines both the data and control information. Figure 2 shows the reuse-distance trace of Tomcatv, a vectorized mesh generation program from SPEC95. X-axis shows the logical time, i.e. the number of memory accesses from the beginning of the execution, and

---

[2] The data size is measured by distance-based sampling [11]. For most programs, it is proportional to the number of different data elements or cache blocks accessed during an execution.

Y-axis shows the reuse distance of each data access. A point (x, y) shows that the memory access at the logical time x has the reuse distance y. The disruptive changes in the reuse patterns divide the trace into clearly separated phases. The same phases repeat in a fixed sequence. Shen *et al.* use wavelet filtering and optimal phase partitioning to find these phase-changing points. They then insert static markers into the program binary to enable on-line phase prediction. Their results show high consistency of CMRs for each phase—most with a standard deviation less than 0.00001.

Many phase-analysis methods exist: some start from the measurement of program behavior using a shifting window [3,4,9,10,12,30] and some start from program structures, e.g. loops and subroutines [19,22,23]. There are three reasons for us to choose the locality phase analysis. First, locality phases have highly consistent behavior. Second, the analysis does not depend on the code structure being the same as the phase structure. Two iterations of a loop may have dramatically different behavior because of different data. Finally, the cache miss rate is closely related with the program locality.

4 Phase-Based CMR Prediction System

In this section, we describe our whole prediction system as shown in Figure 4. The rectangles with thick boundaries show the four main steps of the system. We use gray parallel rectangles for input and output of the system, white parallel rectangles for intermediate results, and squares for operations.

The upper dotted box shows the training process, which constructs two models— the reuse signature model for each phase and the sequence model of all phases. Given a binary program, the first step is to the locality phase analysis. It takes a training input to profile and apply wavelet filtering, optimal phase partitioning, and static marker insertions to generate a binary program with static phase markers. The second step is to execute the marked binary on each training input to collect the reuse-distance signature of each phase on each input and also the phase sequence of each execution. Regression analysis on those reuse signatures yields a reuse-signature model for each phase. A phase sequence model is built from the analysis of phase sequences.

After the construction of the two models, program locality-trace prediction is straightforward. The lower dotted box in Figure 4 shows the prediction process. Given a new input, the two models generated in the training process will give the corresponding reuse signatures and phase sequence according to the new data size. The CMR of each phase for any cache size can be estimated from its reuse signature. The CMR temporal trace can be obtained by aligning the CMRs along the new phase sequence.

5 Evaluation

We test five benchmarks, shown in table 1. FFT is an implementation from a textbook, Swim and Tomcatv are from SPEC95 suit. All have four training inputs and one test input. We pick these programs because they are readily available from our previous studies.

We use ATOM to instrument the programs for data collection and phase marker insertion. All programs are compiled by the Alpha compiler using "-O3" flag.

Table 1. The input size and phase numbers of benchmarks with descriptions

	Applu	Compress	FFT	Swim	Tomcatv
Train-1	12^3	10^2	32x4	160^2	100^2
Train-2	20^3	10^3	64x4	200^2	200^2
Train-3	32^3	10^4	128x4	300^2	300^2
Train-4	40^3	10^6	256x4	400^2	400^2
Test	60^3	1.4×10^8	512x4	512^2	513^2
Number of static phases	195	4	7	17	9
Number of dynamic phases	645	52	37	92	15
Source	Spec95	Spec95	Textbook	Spec95	Spec95
Description	solution of five coupled nonlinear PDE's	an in-memory version of the common UNIX compression utility	fast Fourier transform	finite difference approximations for shallow water equation	vectorized mesh generation

Our phase analysis cuts a program into phases. In table 1, the static phase numbers show the number of distinct phases. Dynamic phase number is the number of occurrences of static phases during an whole execution. At this step, we control the input so that all runs of a benchmark have the same phase sequence. The reason is to focus on phase-based CMR prediction, instead of being distracted by changing phase sequences.

5.1   Experiment Results

Table 2 shows the average accuracy of the predicted phase reuse signatures and cache hit rates. The first row shows the accuracy when we measure the reuse of data elements. The second row shows the accuracy when we consider cache block reuse (of 32-byte blocks). While the prediction accuracy for the element pattern is less than 90% for some programs, the accuracy for the cache-block pattern is never below 93%.

Figure 4 shows the real and the predicted reuse signature of one phase of FFT, Swim and Tomcatv. We use black bars for real data, labeled by the benchmark names, and use gray bars for estimated data, labeled by the benchmark names with suffix "-p". Most data references have large reuse distances for Swim; while as to Tomcatv, about 79% references have reuse distance shorter than 32. All graphs show accurate prediction.

Table 2. Average accuracy of phase reuse signature prediction and cache-hit-rate prediction

Benchmark	Applu	Compress	FFT	Swim	Tomcatv	Average
Element reuse	0.867	0.841	0.963	0.832	0.921	0.885
Block reuse (32 bytes)	0.942	0.933	0.968	0.938	0.963	0.949
Cache-hit-rate (32 bytes)	0.982	0.980	0.983	0.982	0.979	0.981

Figure 5 shows the real and the predicted CMR-traces for FFT, Swim, and Tomcatv. (The Swim graph is enlarged for readability.) These three benchmarks have very different CMR curves. FFT has only 15 dynamic phases, whose hit rates are all larger than 0.7. The measured curve of *Swim* fluctuates dramatically. Some phases almost have no short-distance data reuse so that the cache hit rates are close to zero. The hit rates of other phases are greater than 0.79. For this dramatically changing curve, our method also yields accurate prediction. Tomcatv is a benchmark with less varying hit rates. It has twice as many phases as FFT has. All predicted curves are very close to the measured ones.

The last row of table 2 shows the average accuracy of the hit-rate prediction on an instance of fully associative cache of 32KB with 32-byte blocks. Our prediction method yields 98.1% average accuracy. The experiment on set-associative caches remains our future work. We expect a similar accuracy based on the previous results [32].

The prediction accuracy is similar to that of whole program hit rate prediction in [32]. The purpose of this work is not to improve the accuracy but to explore the possibility of predicting more—the prediction with time as a new dimension. The results show that the locality-phase based approach can work well for tests in the experiments.

6   Phase Sequence Prediction

The phase sequence of a program may be different for different inputs. We represent phase sequence as regular expressions. Expression 1 shows an example of the regular expression of a phase trace, where p_x represents a phase ID. Brackets separate the phases into segments. The exponents show the repetitions of a segment. For many programs, the regular expressions from different runs have the same structure but different exponent values. To predict the phase sequence for these programs, we need to determine the value of the exponents for any given input. We now describe our prediction method.

$$p_1 p_2 \ldots p_{15} \left(p_{16} p_{17} \left(p_{18} \ldots p_{25} \left(p_{26} p_{27} \right)^2 p_{28} p_{29} p_{30} \right)^5 p_{31} p_{32} \right)^{50} \tag{1}$$

We first manually find the input parameters, i.e. the numbers that change from an input to another input. The parameters can be the number of iterations, the data size, or the data content. We need to identify the parameters that control the phase sequence.

Through several training runs on different inputs, we collect multiple phase sequences and convert them into regular expressions. We use the following steps to find the correlation between the exponent values in the phase sequences and the parameters from the inputs.

- If an exponent value does not change in the training runs, its value is constant and independent of the input.
- If an exponent changes its value, we find the input parameter that has the same value.
- The remaining exponents are more complex functions of the input parameters. They may depend on multiple input parameters (e.g. the number of rows and columns of

an input matrix). In the worst case, no automatic method can find the formula since it is not computable. Still we can often determine or approximate the formula by studying the contribution of each parameter separately. Suppose in training runs we can change the value of just one parameter at a time. If we assume simple polynomials (linear, root, square, or constant patterns), then a fixed number of training runs are enough to determine the coefficients through the following regression technique: first to determine the coefficient for each polynomial to fit the exponents of training runs; then to find the polynomial that generates the regular expressions closest to the phase sequences.

We studied five benchmarks shown in table 1. They come from different sources. Applu, FFT, Tomcatv, and Swim have parameters in their input files affecting the phase sequence. For Compress, its phase sequence can be changed by changing constants in its source code. Their inputs are either the matrix size or iteration numbers. Those benchmarks have simple phase sequence patterns—the exponents take either a constant or the same value as some input parameter. The first two steps in the previous list are enough to obtain perfect phase-sequence prediction.

7 Related Work

Cache behavior measurement. Much work has been done in trace-driven simulation. Mattson *et al.* measured cache misses for all cache sizes in one simulation using a stack algorithm [25]. Hill extended the algorithm to cache systems with limited associativity [18]. Zhong *et al.* predicted cache misses across different program inputs by utilizing data reuse signature patterns [32]. They predicted the average cache miss rate of the whole program's execution. Shen *et al.* extended their method using regression techniques and achieved more accurate locality prediction with less overhead [28]. Marin and Mellor-Crummey reported similar reuse-distance prediction used inside a comprehensive performance tool [24]. Fang *et al.* examined the reuse pattern of each program instruction of 11 SPEC2K CFP benchmark programs and predicted the miss rate of 90% of instructions with a 97% accuracy [13]. Our work, for the first time, predicts cache temporal behavior through the execution of a program across different inputs.

Phase analysis. In this work, we use locality-based phase analysis [29], which yields program phases with different data access patterns. Those patterns can be used for accurate locality prediction. There are many other studies in program phase analysis. Allen and Cocke pioneered interval analysis to convert a program control flow into a hierarchy of regions [1]. Hsu and Kremer used program regions to control processor voltages to save energy [20]. Balasubramonian *et al.* [3], Huang *et al.* [22], and Magklis *et al.* [23] selected large enough procedures and loops as phases. Balasubramonian *et al.* and later researchers divide an execution into fixed-size windows, classify past intervals using machine or code-based metrics, and predict future intervals using last value, Markov, or table-driven predictors [3,4,9,10,12,30]. The advantage of locality-based phase analysis is that each phase has its own data access pattern and the pattern is stable across multiple phase occurrences.

Locality analysis and prediction. Dependence analysis analyzes data accesses and is used extensively in program locality measurement and improvement. In [2], Allen and Kennedy gave a comprehensive description on this subject. Gannon *et al.* estimated the amount of memory needed by a loop [15]. Other researchers used various types of array sections to measure data access in loops and procedures. Such analysis includes linearization for high-dimensional arrays by Burke and Cytron [5], linear inequalities for convex sections by Triolet *et al.* [31], regular sections by Callahan and Kennedy [6], and reference list by Li *et al.* [21]. Havlak and Kennedy studied the effect of array section analysis on a wide range of programs [17]. Cascaval and Padua extended the dependence analysis to estimate the distance of data reuses [7]. One limitation of dependence analysis is that it does not model cache interference caused by the data layout. Ferrente *et al.* gave an efficient approximation of cache interference in a loop nest [14]. Recent studies used more expensive (worst-case super-exponential) tools to find the exact number of cache misses. Ghosh *et al.* modeled cache misses of a perfect loop nest as solutions to a set of linear Diophantine equations [16]. Chatterjee *et al.* studied solutions of general integer equations and used Presburger solvers like Omega [8]. The precise methods are effective for a single loop nest. For full applications, researchers have combined compiler analysis with cache simulation. McKinley and Temam carefully measured various types of reference locality within and between loop nests [26]. Mellor-Crummey *et al.* measured fine-grained reuse and program balance through a tool called HPCView [27].

8   Conclusions

In this paper, we described an approach to predict the temporal CMR-trace for all inputs to a program. Through locality phase analysis, we cut a program into segments with regular locality patterns. By building a regression model, we accurately predict the reuse signature of each phase for a new input. CMR estimation yields the new CMR of each phase. We have developed a method for determining the phase sequence from input parameters. The CMR-trace for the new input is then calculated from the phase sequence and the per-phase locality prediction. Our experiment shows over 98% average accuracy of the phase CMR prediction. The CMR-traces predicted by our method coincides with the real CMR-trace very well for even dramatically changing curves. This approach is important to reduce explorations in dynamic systems and improve the accuracy of the prediction. It can also be used in benchmark and compiler design.

Our technique enables a new dimension of program locality prediction—the time. We expect that a similar technique can help to predict the temporal pattern of other performance metrics and yield better understanding of computer programs.

References

1. F. Allen and J. Cocke. A proram data flow analysis procedure. *Communications of the ACM*, 19:137–147, 1976.
2. R. Allen and K. Kennedy. *Optimizing Compilers for Modern Architectures: A Dependence-based Approach.* Morgan Kaufmann Publishers, October 2001.

3. R. Balasubramonian, D. Albonesi, A. Buyuktosunoglu, and S. Dwarkadas. Memory hierarchy reconfiguration for energy and performance in general-purpose processor architectures. In *Proceedings of the 33rd International Symposium on Microarchitecture*, Monterey, California, December 2000.

4. R. Balasubramonian, S. Dwarkadas, and D. H. Albonesi. Dynamically managing the communication-parallelism trade-off in future clustered processors. In *Proceedings of International Symposium on Computer Architecture*, San Diego, CA, June 2003.

5. M. Burke and R. Cytron. Interprocedural dependence analysis and parallelization. In *Proceedings of the SIGPLAN '86 Symposium on Compiler Construction*, Palo Alto, CA, June 1986.

6. D. Callahan, J. Cocke, and K. Kennedy. Analysis of interprocedural side effects in a parallel programming environment. *Journal of Parallel and Distributed Computing*, 5(5):517–550, October 1988.

7. C. Cascaval and D. A. Padua. Estimating cache misses and locality using stack distances. In *Proceedings of International Conference on Supercomputing*, San Francisco, CA, June 2003.

8. S. Chatterjee, E. Parker, P. J. Hanlon, and A. R. Lebeck. Exact analysis of the cache behavior of nested loops. In *Proceedings of ACM SIGPLAN Conference on Programming Language Design and Implementation*, Snowbird, UT, 2001.

9. A. S. Dhodapkar and J. E. Smith. Managing multi-configuration hardware via dynamic working-set analysis. In *Proceedings of International Symposium on Computer Architecture*, Anchorage, Alaska, June 2002.

10. A. S. Dhodapkar and J. E. Smith. Comparing program phase detection techniques. In *Proceedings of International Symposium on Microarchitecture*, December 2003.

11. C. Ding and Y. Zhong. Predicting whole-program locality with reuse distance analysis. In *Proceedings of ACM SIGPLAN Conference on Programming Language Design and Implementation*, San Diego, CA, June 2003.

12. E. Duesterwald, C. Cascaval, and S. Dwarkadas. Characterizing and predicting program behavior and its variability. In *Proceedings of International Conference on Parallel Architectures and Compilation Techniques*, New Orleans, Louisiana, September 2003.

13. C. Fang, S. Carr, S. Onder, and Z. Wang. Reuse-distance-based miss-rate prediction on a per instruction basis. In *Proceedings of the first ACM SIGPLAN Workshop on Memory System Performance*, Washington DC, June 2004.

14. J. Ferrante, V. Sarkar, and W. Thrash. On estimating and enhancing cache effectiveness. In U. Banerjee, D. Gelernter, A. Nicolau, and D. Padua, editors, *Languages and Compilers for Parallel Computing, Fourth International Workshop*, Santa Clara, CA, August 1991. Springer-Verlag.

15. K. Gallivan, W. Jalby, and D. Gannon. On the problem of optimizing data transfers for complex memory systems. In *Proceedings of the Second International Conference on Supercomputing*, St. Malo, France, July 1988.

16. S. Ghosh, M. Martonosi, and S. Malik. Cache miss equations: A compiler framework for analyzing and tuning memory behavior. *ACM Transactions on Programming Languages and Systems*, 21(4), 1999.

17. P. Havlak and K. Kennedy. An implementation of interprocedural bounded regular section analysis. *IEEE Transactions on Parallel and Distributed Systems*, 2(3):350–360, July 1991.

18. M. D. Hill. *Aspects of cache memory and instruction buffer performance*. PhD thesis, University of California, Berkeley, November 1987.

19. C.-H. Hsu and U. Kermer. The design, implementation and evaluation of a compiler algorithm for CPU energy reduction. In *Proceedings of ACM SIGPLAN Conference on Programming Language Design and Implementation*, San Diego, CA, June 2003.

20. C.-H. Hsu, U. Kremer, and M. Hsiao. Compiler-directed dynamic frequency and voltage scaling. In *Workshop on Power-Aware Computer Systems*, Cambridge, MA, November 2000.

21. Z. Li, P. Yew, and C. Zhu. An efficient data dependence analysis for parallelizing compilers. *IEEE Transactions on Parallel and Distributed Systems*, 1(1):26–34, January 1990.
22. M. Huang and J. Renau and J. Torrellas. Positional adaptation of processors: application to energy reduction. In *Proceedings of the International Symposium on Computer Architecture*, San Diego, CA, June 2003.
23. G. Magklis, M. L. Scott, G. Semeraro, D. H. Albonesi, and S. Dropsho. Profile-based dynamic voltage and frequency scaling for a multiple clock domain microprocessor. In *Proceedings of the International Symposium on Computer Architecture*, San Diego, CA, June 2003.
24. G. Marin and J. Mellor-Crummey. Cross architecture performance predictions for scientific applications using parameterized models. In *Proceedings of Joint International Conference on Measurement and Modeling of Computer Systems*, New York City, NY, June 2004.
25. R. L. Mattson, J. Gecsei, D. Slutz, and I. L. Traiger. Evaluation techniques for storage hierarchies. *IBM System Journal*, 9(2):78–117, 1970.
26. K. S. McKinley and O. Temam. Quantifying loop nest locality using SPEC'95 and the perfect benchmarks. *ACM Transactions on Computer Systems*, 17(4):288–336, 1999.
27. J. Mellor-Crummey, R. Fowler, and D. B. Whalley. Tools for application-oriented performance tuning. In *Proceedings of the 15th ACM International Conference on Supercomputing*, Sorrento, Italy, June 2001.
28. X. Shen, Y. Zhong, and C. Ding. Regression-based multi-model prediction of data reuse signature. In *Proceedings of the 4th Annual Symposium of the Las Alamos Computer Science Institute*, Sante Fe, New Mexico, November 2003.
29. X. Shen, Y. Zhong, and C. Ding. Locality phase prediction. In *Proceedings of the Eleventh International Conference on Architect ural Support for Programming Languages and Operating Systems (ASPLOS XI)*, Boston, MA, 2004. (To appear).
30. T. Sherwood, S. Sair, and B. Calder. Phase tracking and prediction. In *Proceedings of International Symposium on Computer Architecture*, San Diego, CA, June 2003.
31. R. Triolet, F. Irigoin, and P. Feautrier. Direct parallelization of CALL statements. In *Proceedings of the SIGPLAN '86 Symposium on Compiler Construction*, Palo Alto, CA, June 1986.
32. Y. Zhong, S. G. Dropsho, and C. Ding. Miss rate prediction across all program inputs. In *Proceedings of the 12th International Conference on Parallel Architectures and Compilation Techniques*, New Orleans, Louisiana, September 2003.

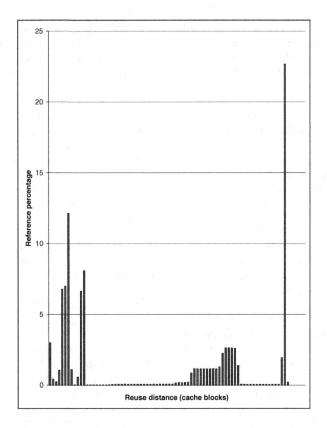

Fig. 1. The reuse distance histogram example

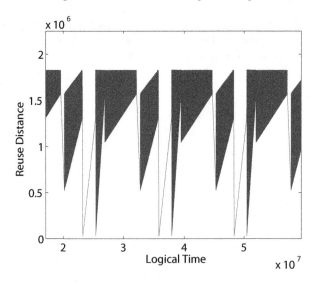

Fig. 2. The reuse-distance trace of Tomcatv

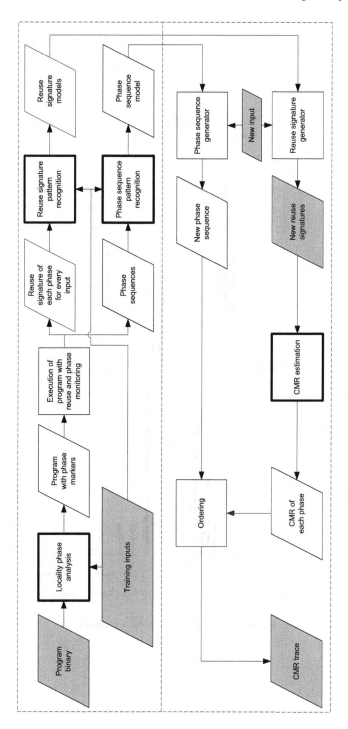

Fig. 3. Locality-trace prediction system

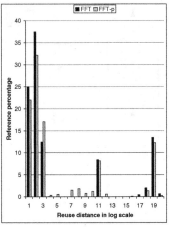

(a) A phase of FFT

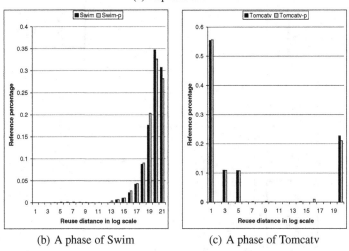

(b) A phase of Swim   (c) A phase of Tomcatv

Fig. 4. Real and predicted reuse signatures

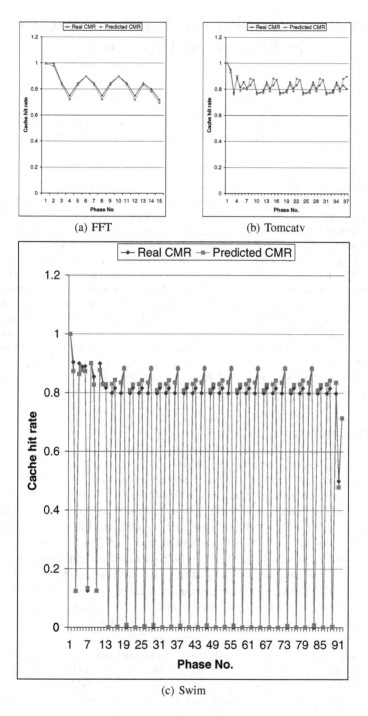

(a) FFT   (b) Tomcatv

(c) Swim

Fig. 5. Cache hit rate prediction

Speculative Subword Register Allocation in Embedded Processors[*]

Bengu Li[1], Youtao Zhang[2], and Rajiv Gupta[1]

[1] The Univ. of Arizona, Dept. of Computer Science, Tucson, Arizona
[2] The Univ. of Texas at Dallas, Dept. of Computer Science, Richardson, Texas

Abstract. Multimedia and network processing applications make extensive use of subword data. Since registers are capable of holding a full data word, when a subword variable is assigned a register only part of the register is used. We propose an instruction set extension to the ARM embedded processor which allows two data items to reside in a register as long as each of them can be stored in 16 bits. The instructions are used by the register allocator to speculatively move the value of an otherwise spilled variable into a register which has already been assigned to another variable. The move is speculative because it only succeeds if the two values (value already present in the register and the value being moved into the register) can be simultaneously held in the register using 16 bits each. When this value is reloaded for further use, an attempt is first made to retrieve the value from its speculatively assigned register. If this attempt succeeds, load from memory is avoided. On an average our technique avoids 47% of dynamic reloads caused by spills.

1 Introduction

Recent research has shown that embedded applications, including network and media processing applications, contain significant amounts of narrow width data [4,13]. Network processing applications usually pack the data before transmission and unpack it before processing. The unpacked data is composed of subword data. Media applications typically process byte streams. Since subword data requires fewer bits to store than the machine word size, its presence can be exploited by many optimizations that can help satisfy the tight area, performance and power constraints of embedded systems. Recent work has focused on exploiting narrow width data to carry out memory related optimizations [5,14,15,16]. In this paper we show how narrow width data can be exploited to make effective use of small number of registers provided by embedded processors. We address this problem in context of the ARM processor [10].

The main objective of this work is to develop the architectural and compiler support through which the registers can be used more effectively in presence of subword data. In particular, our goal is to allow two variables to be simultaneously assigned to the same register such that if their values can be represented

---

[*] Supported by Microsoft, Intel, and NSF grants CCR-0324969, CCR-0220334, CCR-0208756, CCR-0105355, and EIA-0080123 to the Univ. of Arizona.

R. Eigenmann et al. (Eds.): LCPC 2004, LNCS 3602, pp. 56–71, 2005.

using 16 bits, they can be simultaneously held in a register. To demonstrate that this objective is worth pursuing we collected some data by executing a set of embedded applications. We found that the average bitwidth across all variables over entire program execution ranges from 15.87 to 20.74 bits across the benchmarks. We also found that the percentage of variables whose average width for the entire execution does not exceed 16 bits ranges from 33% to 61% across the benchmarks. Thus, it is quite clear that many variables can be stored using 16 bits for significant periods of time during execution.

Table 1. Dynamically observed narrow width data

Benchmark	Dynamic Bitwidth	Variables $\leq$ 16 Bits
g721.decode	17.43	49%
g721.encode	18.99	44%
epic	16.35	61%
unepic	19.52	45%
mpeg2.decode	17.59	45%
mpeg2.encode	15.87	59%
adpcm.dec	17.07	50%
adpcm.enc	16.87	54%
drr	18.81	35%
frag	20.52	33%
reed	20.74	38%
rtr	19.03	38%

Generally the observed subword data can be divided into two categories: (static) a variable is declared as a word but in reality the values assigned to the variable can never exceed 16 bits; and (dynamic) a variable is declared as a word but in practice the values assigned to it do not exceed 16 bits most of the time during a program run. In our prior work on bitwidth aware register allocation, the compiler is responsible for identifying the upperbound on the bitwidth of variables and then multiple subword variables are packed into individual registers during register allocation [11,6]. This approach exploits only the opportunities due to static subword data.

In this paper, we propose a *speculative subword register allocation* (SSRA) scheme. A *speculative* allocation pass is introduced after the *normal* register allocation pass. In the speculative pass, an additional variable may be allocated to a register which was assigned to another variable in the normal pass. A decision to assign another variable to an already allocated register is made only if the value profile data indicates that *most of the time* the two variables can fit into a single register. While the value of variable assigned to the register in the normal pass is guaranteed to be present in the register, the value of the variable assigned to the same register in the speculative pass may or may not be present in the register depending upon whether the two values can fit into a single register or not. Code is generated in a way that while loads are generated to reload the value of the variable assigned a register during the speculative pass, these loads are only executed if the value cannot be saved in the register. While the benefit of this approach is the reduction in the number of dynamically executed loads, in case the value cannot be kept in the register we pay an extra cost. This extra cost is due to additional instructions introduced to save and retrieve speculatively stored values in registers. The main advantage of this approach is that both categories of subword data (static and dynamic) can be exploited. Moreover, static bitwidth analysis [9,11,3] that is otherwise used to compute bitwidths of variables in no longer needed. Instead, speculative register allocation is driven by value profiles. It should be noted that our work is orthogonal to speculative register promotion technique of [7]. While speculative register promotion allows allocation of registers to variables in presence of aliasing, our work assigns already allocated registers to additional variables when no free registers are available.

The rest of the paper is organized as follows. In section 2 we discuss bitwidth aware register allocation and identify the challenges in developing a speculative register allocation scheme. The architectural support is introduced in section 3. Section 4 discusses the speculative register allocation algorithm. The implementation and experimental results are presented in section 5. Related work and conclusions are given in sections 6 and 7.

2   Bitwidth Aware Register Allocation: Static Versus Dynamic Narrow Width Data

The discussion of register allocation in this paper targets embedded processors where small modifications can be made to effectively manipulate subword data. Each register R can contain up to two entities that are of same size, i.e. it can hold a whole word $R_{1..32}$ or two half-words $R_{1..16}$ and $R_{17..32}$.

Let us consider the existing approach to bitwidth aware register allocation [11]. Figure 1(a) contains a code fragment in which variables b and c are assigned to registers $R1$ and $R2$ respectively. Moreover there is no free register for variable a. Thus, spill code is generated to store new value of a back to memory after computation and a load is introduced to bring the value from memory before a is used (Figure 1(b)). The approach in [11] determines the bitwidths of the variables using data flow analysis. Let us assume that the resulting bitwidths indicate that all three variables can be stored in 16 bits. Thus, the variables can each be assigned to use half of a register as shown in Figure 1(c). In the transformed code, instead of being spilled to memory, variable a is assigned to use half of a register $R1_{17..32}$ while the other half of the same register is used to hold the value of variable b.

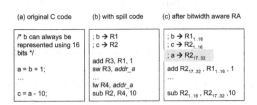

(a) original C code	(b) with spill code	(c) after bitwidth aware RA

/* b can always be represented using 16 bits */
 	
a = b + 1;
...
c = a - 10;
	; b → R1
	; c → R2
	
	add R3, R1, 1
	sw R3, addr_a
	...
	lw R4, addr_a
	sub R2, R4, 10
		; b → R1$_{1..16}$
		; c → R2$_{1..16}$
		; a → R2$_{17..32}$
		add R2$_{17..32}$, R1$_{1..16}$, 1
		...
		sub R2$_{1..16}$, R2$_{17..32}$,10

Fig. 1. Bitwidth aware register allocation

While the above approach is effective, there are situations under which opportunities for subword register allocation cannot be detected and/or exploited. It is possible that the compiler is unable to establish that variables a, b and c occupy only half a word or that they occupy half a word most of the time and only rarely take up more space. In particular, the three situations under which the above approach fails are as follows: (a) The program does not contain enough information to enable discovery of true bitwidths. For example, an input variable may be declared as a full word variable although the valid inputs do not exceed 16 bits. The compiler will fail to realize that the input variable represents subword data; in addition, bitwidths of variables that depend upon this input will also be likely overestimated; (b) Even if the program contains information to infer the true bitwidths of variables, the imprecision in static analysis may lead us to conclude that the bitwidths exceed 16 bits; and (c) We miss the opportunity to optimize variables that represent subword data most of the time but only sometimes exceed 16 bits. For example, for the code in Figure 3(a) the value profiles may show that for most executions or for most of the time during a single execution variables a, b, and c take values that can be represented in 16 bits. However, existing register allocation techniques cannot exploit this information and will introduce spill code as in Figure 1(b).

In summary we can say that while the existing method for bitwidth aware register allocation can take advantage of statically known subword data, it cannot take advantage of dynamically observed subword data. In this paper we address this issue by proposing a speculative mechanism for packing two variables into a single register. Profiling information is used to identify variables which when packed together are highly likely to always have their values fit into a single register. If the values do fit into the same register, loads associated with reloading of values are avoided; otherwise they are executed. While the basic idea of our approach is clear, there are architectural and compiler challenges to achieving such a solution which are as follows:

Architectural Support. The key challenge here is to design instruction set extensions through which the mechanism for speculative packing of two variables into one register can be exposed to the compiler. Compiler should be able to control which variable is *guaranteed* to be found in a register and which variable is *expected* to be present. Instruction for speculatively storing a value into a register and *checking* whether it is present are needed. Finally once two values are present in a register we need to be able to *address* them.

Compiler Support. We need to develop an algorithm for global register allocation such that it leads to performance improvements when speculative register assignments are made. This requires that we carefully choose the pair of variables that are assigned to the same register. The compiler must choose the variable whose value is guaranteed to be found in the register and one whose value is expected to be found in the register. Since there is extra cost due to checking whether a speculatively stored value is present in a register, the compiler must use profile data to pair variables such that it is highly likely that the values of both variables will be able to reside simultaneously in the same register. Finally speculative register assignment should be carefully integrated into conventional global register allocation algorithm.

3   Architectural Support

In this section, we discuss the necessary architectural support to enable speculative subword register allocation. To support subword accesses, we attach one bit with each register, allocate a global bit in status word register and add four new instructions. These extensions are described in greater detail next.

3.1   Register File Enhancement

The register file in ARM processors includes 16 user visible 32-bit registers. We add one extra bit B to each register which is used to indicate whether the register currently holds subword data. As shown in Figure 2, when the bit is cleared, the register stores one 32-bit value. When the bit B is set, the two halves of the register store two 16-bit values. The upper half of the register is used to store the speculatively saved value and it can be separately accessed by the four new instructions we add (discussed later). When accessing the value that is definitely present, i.e. when register is accessed by normal instructions, the lower half is accessed.

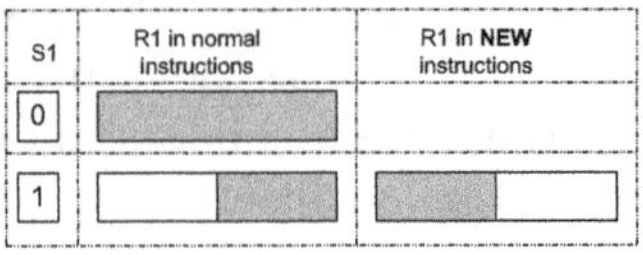

Fig. 2. Accessing registers

3.2   Instruction Set Support

To speculatively store a value in the upper half of the register and to access it later on, we propose four new instructions. We also add an additional G bit to the status word register which is set and examined by these new instructions. These instructions are described in detail below. The first two instructions are used together to speculatively assign a value to an already occupied register while the last two are used to access a speculatively saved value.

Speculative Store: Ssw Rs, addr. This instruction stores the value of Rs into the memory address addr. In addition, it checks the value for compressibility. In particular, it sets the G bit in the status register if the higher order 16 bits are the same as its 16th bit, i.e. they are sign extensions.

Store Move: Smv Rd, Rs. This instruction checks the global condition bit G and the non-speculative value residing in Rd for compressibility. If G is set, and the higher order 16 bits of Rd are the same as its 16th bit, the lower order 16 bits of Rs are moved into upper half of Rd. The B bit of Rd is set to indicate that it now contains two values.

Extract Move: Emv Rd, Rs. This instruction checks the B bit of Rs. If the bit is set, the higher order 16 bits of Rs are sign extended and then moved to Rd. In addition, the global condition G is set to indicate that the instruction was successful in finding the speculatively stored value in Rs. If the B bit of Rs is not set, G is cleared to indicate that the value was not found.

Speculative Load: Sld Rd, addr. This instruction checks the G bit in the status word. If it is clear, the value stored in memory address `addr` is loaded into Rd; otherwise, the instruction acts as a null instruction. In the latter case the load is not issued to memory because the preceding instruction must have located the speculatively saved value in the specified register.

Let us reconsider the example in Figure 3(a) where value of a is being spilled because no register is free. Let us assume that we would like to speculatively save the spilled value of a in register which holds the value of c (say register $R2$). The code in Figure 3(b) shows how instructions Ssw and Smv are used to speculatively save the value in $R2$ and then later instructions Emv and Sld are used to reload the value of a from $R2$ into $R4$. If the speculative save of a is successful, the Sld instruction turns into a null operation; otherwise the value of a is reloaded from memory.

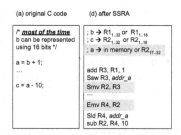

Fig. 3. Example illustrating the use of new instructions

From the above discussion it is clear that we pay a cost for speculatively saving and reloading a compressed value. While traditional code would have included a store and a load, in our case we also introduce two extra move instructions (Smov and Emov). However, the benefits of eliminating loads are much greater as not only loads have longer latency, they can also cause cache misses which leads to even greater delays. Moreover our compiler will only perform speculative register assignment when it is highly likely that it would lead to elimination of loads.

3.3   Hardware Implementation

Other modifications must be made to the processor pipeline when the above mentioned instructions are introduced. Normal instructions must always check the B bit of a register that it reads or writes to. This is needed so that it knows how to interpret and update the contents of the register. Changes are needed when results are being written or operands are being read. For modern embedded processors such as ARM SA-110 (see Figure 4(a)) changes affect the second and fourth stage of the pipeline.

ALU instructions compute the result in *execute* stage while the register is updated at *write back* stage. A small component can thus be added in the intervening *buffer* stage to ensure that the higher order bits are sign extensions. If not, the entire register is used to hold the result and the corresponding B bit of the register is cleared. For memory access instructions that use a register as the destination, i.e. load instructions, register is ready at the end of *buffer* stage and thus we do not have time to perform validation. We simply clear its B bit and use all the bits in this case.

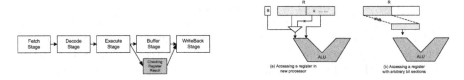

Fig. 4. (a) ARM processor pipeline; and (b) Accessing registers with subword support

Since the flag bit B of a register determines whether a 16-bit or a 32-bit value is involved in a computation, we need a multiplexer for the higher order 16 bits. Therefore in comparison to a machine without subword support, we introduce extra delay due to the multiplexer shown in Figure 4(b). However, this delay is smaller than the delays in processors that support accesses to arbitrary bit sections such as the Infineon processor [8].

4   Speculative Subword Register Allocation

Given the hardware support designed in the preceding section, we now discuss compiler support needed to carry out speculative subword register allocation (SSRA). Since we have designed our algorithms so that they can be integrated into the gcc compiler, we first briefly introduce the implementation of register allocation in gcc compiler. Next we describe the details of the three passes that implement SSRA. The *profiling pass* collects information about how likely it is that the two variables can fit into one register and how long is the lifetime during which they coexist. Based on this information, the new *speculative allocation pass* determines a subset of physical registers and speculatively assigns other variables to each of them. The variables picked up in this pass are those that otherwise are spilled into memory. The decision is made to achieve speculatively best performance in terms of reduction in the number of reload operations that are executed. In the *enhanced reload pass*, the compiler generates transformed code utilizing the newly designed instructions.

4.1   Register Allocation in the gcc Compiler

The `gcc` compiler [2] performs register allocation in three passes: local register allocation pass, global register allocation pass, and reload pass. These passes operate on the intermediate representation – register transfer language (RTL). Operands are mapped to virtual registers before register allocation. The local and global register allocation passes do not actually modify the RTL representation. Instead, the results of these passes is an assignment of physical registers to virtual registers. It is the responsibility of reload pass to modify the RTL and insert spill code if necessary.

The local register allocation pass allocates physical registers to virtual registers that are both generated and killed within one basic block, i.e. live ranges that are completely local to a basic block are handled in this pass. The allocation is driven by live range priorities. Register coalescing is also performed in this pass. Since local register allocation works on linear code, it is inexpensive. Local allocation reduces the amount of work that must be performed by the more expensive global allocation pass.

The global register allocation pass allocates physical registers to the remaining virtual registers. This pass may change some of the allocation decisions made during the local register allocation pass. This pass performs allocation by coloring the global interference graph [1]. Virtual registers are considered for coloring in an order determined by weighted counts. If a physical register cannot be found for a virtual register, none is assigned and the virtual register is handled by generation of spill code in the reload pass.

The reload pass replaces the virtual registers references by physical register names in the RTL according to the allocations determined by the previous two passes. Stack slots are assigned to those virtual registers that were not allocated a physical register in the preceding passes. Reload pass also generates spill code for them. Unlike Chaitin-style [1] graph-coloring allocation, which spills a symbolic register, a physical register is spilled. For each point where a virtual register must be in a physical register, it is temporarily copied into a "reload register" which is a temporarily freed physical register. Reload registers are allocated locally for every instruction that needs reloads.

4.2   The SSRA Algorithm

In this section we first discuss how SSRA is integrated into the `gcc` register allocator described above. The details of SSRA are also discussed later. The modified design of `gcc` register allocator after integration of SSRA into it is shown in Figure 5. In integrating SSRA with the `gcc` allocator we keep the following in mind. There are three types of accesses allowed in our architecture: register

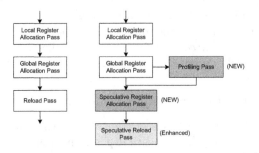

Fig. 5. Framework for speculative register allocation

accesses for values definitely present in registers – these accesses are the fastest; memory accesses that are the slowest; and register accesses for speculatively assigned values which have an intermediate access cost as an additional Sld instruction is required.

In light of the above observation, we first carry out local register allocation and global register allocation passes in exactly the same way. This is because the variables that are referenced more frequently are assigned physical registers in these passes. At run time, the variables that are assigned physical registers in these phases occupy either the whole physical register or possibly just the lower half. Following the above passes SSRA is used to speculatively assign physical registers to virtual registers that are not colored by the first two passes. Finally, the virtual registers that are still not colored are handled by generating memory references by the reload pass. The reload pass is enhanced to generate the newly designed instructions.

During the speculative allocation pass, the upper halves of the physical registers are made speculatively available for the variables that are not colored by the preceding passes. However, it is important that the savings expected by finding the speculatively assigned values in registers exceeds the additional cost of executing Emv instructions when the values are not found in the registers and must be loaded from memory. The savings depend on how frequently the variables are able to be coalesced and how often the references to memory can be avoided. We add a profiling pass which instruments the code and records the information needed to estimate the savings. Since we can only coalesce one variable which already has a register with one variable which does not have a register, we only need to collect profile information for relevant pairs of values. The SSRA pass makes its decisions to achieve speculatively best performance by avoiding maximum number of reload operations. After the decisions are made, a speculative reload pass generates the code according to the decisions made in all of the previous passes. It inserts spill code and the code for speculatively allocated virtual registers. When there are no spilled variables, the behavior of our modified allocator is identical to the behavior of the original gcc allocator.

Next we describe the details of the SSRA algorithm. Three main parts of our algorithm are discussed: priority based allocation algorithm; profiling pass details; and the speculative reload pass.

Priority Based Speculative Allocation. The decision to speculatively allocate an occupied register to another variable is made based upon profile information consisting of the following: *coexisting lifetime* of variables $v1$ and $v2$ refers to the period of time during which $v1$ and $v2$ are both live during program execution; and *coalescing probability* of variables $v1$ and $v2$ refers to the percentage of the coexisting lifetime during which $v1$ and $v2$ can be coalesced. The coalesce probability is undefined if two variables never coexist. Note that during program execution one variable may be coalesced with different variables at different program points.

The speculative allocation pass makes use of two interference graphs. One is called the *Annotated Interference Graph* (AIG) which contains the information needed to make coloring decisions while the coloring itself is performed on another interference graph called the *Residual Interference Graph* (RIG). A more detailed description of these graphs follows.

The *Annotated Interference Graph* (AIG) graph is built from the interference graph after global allocation pass in which some nodes are not colored. For each non-colored node, we annotate the edges between this node and its colored neighbors with a 2-tuple (coalescing probability, coexisting lifetime). Figure 6(a) shows a simple example with nine virtual registers and two physical registers. After global register allocation pass, nodes 1-6 are colored with two colors and nodes 7-9 are not colored. The edge labels are interpreted as follows. Label (0.9, 800) on edge (7,1) indicates that during 90% of 800 units of the time that variables 1 and 7 coexist, both of them are expected to require no more than 16 bits to represent and thus they can simultaneously reside in one register.

The *Residual Interference Graph* (RIG) is a subgraph of AIG that consists of non-colored nodes and edges between them. RIG is not annotated. The RIG for the above example is shown in Figure 6(b). Note that two variables in RIG may be speculatively allocated to the same register if they do not interfere with each other.

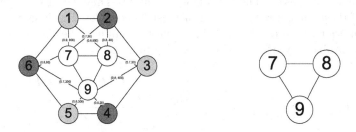

Fig. 6. (a) Annotated interference graph; and (b) Residual interference graph

The speculative allocation pass colors the nodes in RIG using the annotation information in AIG. After coloring a node in RIG, it shares the same color as at least one of its colored neighbors in AIG. While all colored nodes in AIG are colored in the local or global allocation passes, the colored nodes in RIG are colored in the speculative pass.

Next let us discuss in greater detail how nodes are chosen for coloring from RIG and how colors are selected for them. This process is also priority driven because there are limited physical register resources to which additional variables can be speculatively assigned. Our priority function is based net savings that are expected to result by speculatively assigning a virtual register to a physical register. The savings result from avoiding cost of reloads from memory; however, a cost of one cycle is incurred for each reference due to an extra instruction required when values are speculatively accessed from registers. The savings are also a function of coalescing probabilities. Priority of node n, which is the estimated net savings by speculatively assigning a register to n, is given by:

$$Priority(n) = READ(n) \times READCOST \times MCP(n) - REF(n)$$

where $READ(n)$ is the total number of reads of node n, $REF(n)$ is the total number of references (reads and writes) to node n, $READCOST$ is the number of cycles needed to finish a normal read from memory (i.e., it is the memory latency), and $MCP(n)$ is the maximum coalescing probability of n. Note that the above $Priority$ value can be negative for some nodes in which case they are not considered for speculative register assignment. Nodes with higher priority are considered before those with lower priority.

The maximum coalescing probability of n, i.e. $MCP(n)$, is determined by considering all available colors for n and finding which color is expected to result in most savings. The best choice for a color depends upon the following factors. The higher the coalescing probability of a pair of variables, the more beneficial it is to allocate them to the same register. The longer two variables co-exist, the more beneficial it is to allocate them to the same register. Based upon these two factors we compute the maximum coalescing probability. Moreover we should also note that the physical register being speculatively assigned to a node n in RIG may have been allocated to several non-interfering virtual registers in earlier passes. The coalescing probabilities and lengths of coexistence of each of these virtual registers with n must be considered as long as a virtual register interferes with n. The following equation computes the current maximum coalescing probability $MCP(n)$ for a node n in RIG:

$$MCP(n) = \max_{c \in C(n, RIG)} \frac{\sum_{n' \in Nb(n, AIG) \wedge Cl(n')=c} CLt(n, n') \times CPb(n, n')}{\sum_{n' \in Nb(n, AIG) \wedge Cl(n')=c} CLt(n, n')}$$

Where $C(n, RIG)$ is the set of currently available colors for node n in RIG (i.e., these colors have not been assigned to neighbors of n in RIG), $Nb(n, AIG)$ is the set of neighboring nodes of n in AIG (i.e., these nodes were colored during local or global allocation passes), $CLt(n, n')$ is the length of coexisting lifetime of nodes n and n', $CPb(n, n')$ is coalescing probability of nodes n and n' and $Cl(n')$ is the color assigned to node n'. The max function finds the maximum coalescing probability across all potential colors in $C(n, RIG)$.

Profiling Pass. The speculative allocation pass depends on the coalescing probability and coexisting lifetime profiling information. We implement the profiling by instrumenting the intermediate representation of the code. Profiling is performed after the global allocation pass when the objects of our optimization, those variables which do not get a register, have been identified. At this time the liveness information of the variables at each program points is available since data flow analysis is done before register allocation. The intermediate representation used still contains virtual registers instead of physical register since register reloading pass has not been done.

We are only interested in the relation between colored and non-colored nodes. Whether two variables can be coalesced or not depends on the status of the variables (i.e., whether they fit in 16 bits or not). A variable read will not change the status of the variables and thus consecutive variable reads will share the same coalescing probability. Variable definitions can change the status of variables and thus change the coalescing probability between two variables. Therefore variable definitions play an important role in the coexisting lifetime of two variables. In the priority function described earlier, the number of references has already been considered. Here, we use the length of the status history of two variables to approximate the coexisting lifetime.

Two arrays, $lifetime[i][j][k]$ and $count[i][j][k]$, are used during profiling. Here index i identifies the function, index j identifies the colored variable, and index k identifies the non-colored variable. The lifetime array records the length of overlap of live ranges of two variables while the count array records the duration over which the two variables are likely coalescable. The coalescing probability is computed by dividing latter by the former.

Speculative Reload Pass. Our speculative reload pass is an enhanced version of the gcc reload pass. According to the decisions made in the previous passes, we generate code to access physical registers, access upper halves of physical registers and access memory. In summary, we have three categories of variables to handle in this pass.

First, for variables that are assigned to physical registers in local and global register allocation, the compiler replaces the virtual register names with physical register names in the intermediate representation.

Second, for variables that remain in virtual registers after speculative allocation pass, the compiler allocates slots on the stack and generates spill code. For each definition or use point, we identify a reload register and generate spill code by placing the store after the definition and load before the use.

Finally, for variables that are assigned in the speculative pass, we still need to allocate slots on the stack and generate spill code for them. Instead of using ordinary load and store instructions, we generate speculative load and store instructions. At a definition point, the compiler identifies a reload register and temporarily stores the computed value into this register. A speculative store instruction Ssw is generated to speculative store the value back to the stack slot. It is followed by a speculative Smv instruction which speculatively moves the value from the temporary register into the upper half of the assigned register.

At each use point, we identify a reload register and try to speculatively extract the value from the assigned upper half of the register using a speculative Emv instructions. It is followed by a speculative load instruction Sld which actually loads the value from the stack slot if at runtime the required value is not in the register.

5　Experimental Results

We have implemented and evaluated the proposed technique. The speculative subword register allocation algorithms have been incorporated in the gcc Compiler for the ARM processor. All the phases have been implemented including the profiling pass, speculative allocation pass, and enhanced register reloading pass to generate spill code. While new instructions are generated, to avoid the effort of modifying the assembler and the linker, we insert nop instructions in their place in the code and generate an additional file in which the new instructions and the absolute addresses in the binary where these instructions must replace the nop instructions are provided. The code generated by the compiler is executed on the ARM version of the Simplescalar simulator. The simulator was modified to implement the proposed architectural enhancements including the newly incorporated instructions, registers with B bits, the G bit in the status word, and the logic needed to access lower or upper half of the register.

We carried out experiments using some embedded benchmarks from the Mediabench and Commbench suites. We also took a couple of SPEC2000 benchmarks to see if the technique we have developed can be useful for general purpose applications. We ran the programs with different memory latencies such that when speculative reloads from registers are successful, the number of *cycles saved* in comparison to reloading from memory is 1, 2, 3 and 4 cycles. Our evaluation is aimed at determining the percentage of dynamic reloads from memory that are successfully transformed into speculative dynamic reloads from registers. We also considered the overall reduction in execution time of the program as a result of avoiding these reloads.

In Table 2 we present the benchmark characteristics. The first six programs are taken from embedded suite while the last two from SPEC2000. The table presents the number of residual virtual registers present in the intermediate code generated by the gcc compiler following the global register allocation pass, the number of static reloads generated by the gcc reload pass, and the number of dynamic reloads that can be attributed to these static reloads during the execution of the benchmarks.

Table 2. Benchmark characteristics   **Table 3.** Improvement in cycles

Benchmarks	Res. Vir. Regs	Static Reloads	Dynamic Reloads
Embedded			
mpeg2.decode	114	483	952060
mpeg2.encode	278	1234	29738119
epic	109	527	6307287
unepic	48	225	107759
g721.encode	9	33	3543596
g721.decode	9	33	4046653
rtr	12	28	3855503
General Purpose			
176.gcc	1755	10200	99248047
164.gzip	77	365	53069259

Saving = 1 Cycle	Saving = 2 Cycles	Saving = 3 Cycles	Saving = 4 Cycles
Embedded			
0.38%	0.65%	0.97%	1.27%
2.53%	4.09%	5.70%	7.33%
0.38%	1.31%	3.06%	5.17%
0.10%	0.21%	0.32%	0.45%
0.95%	1.53%	2.11%	2.71%
1.13%	1.82%	2.53%	3.26%
0.79%	1.20%	1.61%	2.02%
General Purpose			
5.06%	8.97%	13.04%	17.20%
1.08%	1.77%	2.59%	3.42%

The results of studying the effectiveness of our technique in avoiding dynamic reloads are given in Figure 7. We present two numbers for each program: *Speculation percentage* is the percentage of dynamic memory reloads that were changed into speculative dynamic register reloads by our technique; and *Avoidance percentage* is the percentage of dynamic memory reloads for which the speculative register reloads were successful, i.e. the value was found in the register. The above values vary with the savings (1, 2, 3, or 4 cycles) that can be expected from using speculative register reloads. This is because the savings effect the priorities of nodes in *RIG* and therefore the code generated by by the SSRA algorithm. For greater values of savings SSRA will perform speculative register allocation more aggressively.

The results show that on average, the *Speculation percentage* is 57% when the saving is one cycle and 82% when saving is four cycles. Furthermore, when the saving is one cycle, SSRA achieved an average *Avoidance percentage* of 41% (with upper bound of 91% and lower bound of 5%). When the saving is four cycles, *Avoidance percentage* increases to 47% (with upper bound of 93% and lower bound of 16%). From these results we notice that the minimal savings of one cycle is enough to get most of the reduction in memory reloads.

Table 3 shows the performance improvement in cycles. On average, our method achieved performance improvement of 4.76% when the saving is four cycles and 1.38% when the saving is one cycle. While we had originally designed this technique for embedded applications, we notice that for a general purpose application like 176.gcc the savings are much higher (5.05% to 17.20%). This is because, due to extensive use of pointers, this benchmark contains a much larger number of dynamic reloads. Moreover narrow width values appear in sufficient abundance in this application for SSRA to be successful.

6   Conclusions

In this paper we presented a technique that exploits presence of narrow width data in programs to more effectively make use of limited register resources in embedded processors. Values otherwise spilled by a coloring allocator are spec-

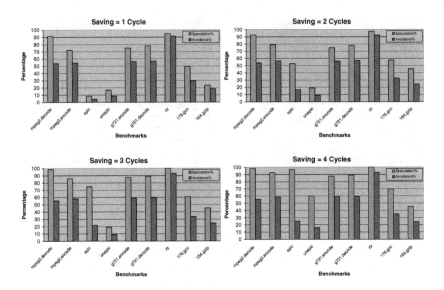

Fig. 7. Effectiveness in avoiding memory reloads

ulatively saved in registers occupied by other variables. Speculative assignment is made such that it is expected that the definitely assigned and speculatively assigned values will be able to simultaneously reside in the same register. We designed a small set of four new instructions through which the feature of speculative register assignment can be implemented without requiring significant amounts of instruction encoding space. The coloring based register allocator was extended by developing a new pass for speculative register allocation. The results of our experiments show that SSRA avoided an average of 47% of dynamic reloads leading to a significant savings in execution time. While our technique was designed for embedded applications, it is also of value for general purpose applications.

References

1. G.J. Chaitin, M.A. Auslander, A.K. Chandra, J. Cocke, M.E. Hopkins, P.W. Markstein, "Register Allocation Via Coloring," *Computer Languages*, 6(1):47-57, 1981.
2. C.E. Foster and H.C. Grossman, "An Empirical Investigation of the Haifa Register Allocation in the GNU C Compiler," *IEEE Southeast Conference*, pages 776-779, vol.2 , April 1992.
3. R. Gupta, E. Mehofer, and Y. Zhang, "A Representation for Bit Section based Analysis and Optimization," *International Conference on Compiler Construction* (CC), pages 62-77, Grenoble, France, Apr 2002.
4. C. Lee, M. Potkonjak, and W.H. Mangione-Smith, "Mediabench: A Tool for Evaluating and Synthesizing Multimedia and Communication Systems," *IEEE/ACM International Symposium on Microarchitecture* (MICRO), December 1997.

5. B. Li and R. Gupta, "Simple Offset Assignment in Presence of Subword Data," *International Conference on Compilers, Architecture, and Synthesis of Embedded Systems* (CASES), San Jose, CA, October 2003.
6. B. Li and R. Gupta, "Bit Section Instruction Set Extension of ARM for Embedded Applications," *International Conference on Compilers, Architecture, and Synthesis of Embedded Systems* (CASES), pages 69-78, Grenoble, France, October 2002.
7. J. Lin, T. Chen, W.C. Hsu, and P.C. Yew, "Speculative Register Promotion Using Advanced Load Address Table (ALAT)," *International Symposium on Code Generation and Optimization* (CGO), 2003.
8. X. Nie, L. Gazsi, F. Engel, and G. Fettweis, "A New Network Processor Architecture for High Speed Communications," *IEEE Workshop on Signal Processing Systems* (SiPS), pages 548-557, 1999.
9. M. Stephenson, J. Babb, and S. Amarasinghe, "Bitwidth Analysis with Application to Silicon Compilation," *ACM SIGPLAN Conference on Programming Language Design and Implementation* (PLDI), pages 108-120, 2000.
10. D. Seal, Editor, "ARM Architectural Reference Manual," Second Edition, Addison-Wesley.
11. S. Tallam and R. Gupta, "Bitwidth Aware Global Register Allocation," *30th Annual ACM SIGPLAN-SIGACT Symposium on Principles of Programming Languages* (POPL), pages 85-96, New Orleans, LA, January 2003.
12. J. Wagner and R. Leupers, "C Compiler Design for an Industrial Network Processor," *ACM SIGPLAN Workshop on Languages, Compilers, and Tools for Embedded Systems* (LCTES), pages 155-164, June 2001.
13. T. Wolf and M. Franklin, "Commbench - A Telecommunications Benchmark for Network Processor," *IEEE International Symposium on Performance Analysis of Systems and Software* (ISPASS), April 2000.
14. J. Yang and R. Gupta, "Energy Efficient Frequent Value Data Cache Design," *IEEE/ACM 35th International Symposium on Microarchitecture* (MICRO), pages 197-207, Istanbul, Turkey, November 2002.
15. Y. Zhang and R. Gupta, "Data Compression Transformations for Dynamically Allocated Data Structures," *International Conference on Compiler Construction* (CC), pages 14-28, Grenoble, France, Apr 2002.
16. Y. Zhang and R. Gupta, "Enabling Partial Cache Line Prefetching Through Data Compression," *International Conference on Parallel Processing* (ICPP), Kaohsiung, Taiwan, October 2003.

Empirical Performance-Model Driven Data Layout Optimization*

Qingda Lu[1], Xiaoyang Gao[1], Sriram Krishnamoorthy[1], Gerald Baumgartner[2],
J. Ramanujam[3], and P. Sadayappan[1]

[1] Department of Computer Science and Engineering,
The Ohio State University, Columbus, OH 43210, USA
{luq, gaox, krishnsr, saday}@cse.ohio-state.edu
[2] Department of Computer Science,
Louisiana State University, Baton Rouge, LA 70803, USA
gb@csc.lsu.edu
[3] Department of Electrical and Computer Engineering,
Louisiana State University, Baton Rouge, LA 70803, USA
jxr@ece.lsu.edu

Abstract. Empirical optimizers like ATLAS have been very effective in optimizing computational kernels in libraries. The best choice of parameters such as tile size and degree of loop unrolling is determined by executing different versions of the computation. In contrast, optimizing compilers use a model-driven approach to program transformation. While the model-driven approach of optimizing compilers is generally orders of magnitude faster than ATLAS-like library generators, its effectiveness can be limited by the accuracy of the performance models used. In this paper, we describe an approach where a class of computations is modeled in terms of constituent operations that are empirically measured, thereby allowing modeling of the overall execution time. The performance model with empirically determined cost components is used to perform data layout optimization in the context of the Tensor Contraction Engine, a compiler for a high-level domain-specific language for expressing computational models in quantum chemistry. The effectiveness of the approach is demonstrated through experimental measurements on some representative computations from quantum chemistry.

1 Introduction

Optimizing compilers use high-level program transformations to generate efficient code. The computation is modeled in some form and its cost is derived in terms of metrics such as reuse distance. Program transformations are then applied to the computational model to minimize its cost. The large number of parameters and the variety of programs to be handled limits optimizing compilers to model-driven optimization with relatively simple cost models. Approaches to empirically optimize a computation, such as ATLAS [22], generate solutions for different structures of the optimized code and determine the

---

* Supported in part by the National Science Foundation through the Information Technology Research program (CHE-0121676 and CHE-0121706), by NSF grant CCF-0073800 and by a grant from the Environmental Protection Agency.

R. Eigenmann et al. (Eds.): LCPC 2004, LNCS 3602, pp. 72–86, 2005.

parameters that optimize the execution time by running different versions of the code and choosing the optimal one. But empirical optimization of large complex applications can be prohibitively expensive. In this paper, we decompose a class of computations into its constituent operations and model the execution time of the computation in terms of empirical characterization of its constituent operations. The empirical measurements allow modeling of the overall execution time of the computation while decomposition enables offline determination of the cost model and efficient global optimization across multiple constituent operations.

Our domain of interest is the calculation of electronic structure properties using ab initio quantum chemistry models such as the coupled cluster models [17]. We are developing an automatic synthesis system called the Tensor Contraction Engine (TCE), to generate efficient parallel programs from high-level expressions, for a class of computations expressible as tensor contractions [3,7,6]. These calculations employ multidimensional tensors in contractions, which are essentially generalized matrix multiplications. The computation is represented by an operator tree, in which each node represents the contraction of two tensors to produce a result tensor. The order of indices of the intermediate tensors (multidimensional arrays) is not constrained.

Computational kernels such as Basic Linear Algebra Subroutines (BLAS) [8] have been tuned to achieve very high performance. These hand-tuned or empirically optimized kernels generally achieve better performance than conventional general-purpose compilers [23]. If General Matrix Multiplication (GEMM) routines available in BLAS libraries are used to perform tensor contractions, the multi-dimensional intermediate arrays that arise in tensor contractions must be transformed to group the indices to allow a two-dimensional view of the arrays, as required by GEMM. We observe that the performance of the GEMM routines is significantly influenced by the choice of parameters used in their invocation. We determine the layouts of the intermediate arrays and the choice of parameters to the GEMM invocations that minimize the overall execution time. The overall execution time is estimated from the GEMM and index permutation times. Empirically-derived costs for these constituent operations are used to determine the GEMM parameters and array layouts.

The approach presented in this paper may be viewed as an instance of the telescoping languages approach described in [15]. The telescoping languages approach aims at facilitating a high-level *scripting* interface for a domain-specific computation to the user, while achieving high performance that is portable across machine architectures, and compilation time that only grows linearly with the size of the user script. In this paper, we evaluate the performance of the relevant libraries empirically. Parallel code is generated using the Global Arrays (GA) library [20]. Parallel matrix multiplication is performed using the Cannon matrix multiplication algorithm [4], extended to handle non-square distribution of matrices amongst the processors. The matrix multiplication within each node is performed using GEMM. The parallel matrix multiplication and parallel index transformation costs are estimated from the local GEMM and transformation costs and the communication cost. We then use the empirical results to construct a performance model that enables the code generator to determine the appropriate choice of array layouts and distributions and usage modalities for library calls.

The paper is organized as follows. In Section 2, we elaborate on the computational context, demonstrate potential optimization opportunities and then define our problem. Section 3 discusses the constituent operations in the computation and the parameters to be determined to generate optimal parallel code. Section 4 describes the determination of the constituent operation costs. Section 5 discusses the determination of the parameters of the generated code from the constituent operation costs. Results are presented in Section 6. Section 7 discusses related work. Section 8 concludes the paper.

2   The Computational Context

The Tensor Contraction Engine (TCE) [3,7,6] is a domain-specific compiler for developing accurate ab initio models in quantum chemistry. The TCE takes as input a high-level specification of a computation expressed as a set of tensor contraction expressions and transforms it into efficient parallel code. In the class of computations considered, the final result to be computed can be expressed as multi-dimensional summations of the product of several input arrays.

Consider the following tensor contraction expression.

$$E[i, j, k] = \text{Sum}\{a, b, c\} A[a, b, c] B[a, i] C[b, j] D[c, k]$$

where all indices range over N. a, b, c are the summation indices. The direct way to compute this would require $O(N^6)$ arithmetic operations. Instead, by computing the following intermediate partial results, the number of operations can be reduced to $O(N^4)$.

$$T1[a, b, k] = \text{Sum}\{c\} A[a, b, c] D[c, k]$$
$$T2[a, j, k] = \text{Sum}\{b\} T1[a, b, k] C[b, j]$$
$$E[i, j, k] = \text{Sum}\{a\} T2[a, j, k] B[a, i]$$

This form of the computation is represented as an operator tree. For example, Fig. 1(a) shows the operator tree for a sub-expression from the CCSD (Coupled Cluster Singles and Doubles) model [17]. The curly braces around the indices indicate the fact that there is no implied ordering between the indices. The computation represented by such an operator tree could be implemented as a collection of nested loops, one per node of the operator tree. However, optimizing the resulting collection of a large number of nested loops to minimize execution time is a difficult challenge. But each contraction is essentially a generalized matrix multiplication, for which efficient tuned library Generalized Matrix Multiplication (GEMM) routines exist. Hence it is attractive to translate the computation for each tensor contraction node into a call to GEMM. For the above 3-contraction example, the first contraction can be implemented directly as a call to GEMM with A viewed as an $N^2 \times N$ rectangular matrix and D as an $N \times N$ matrix. The second contraction, however, cannot be directly implemented as a GEMM call because the summation index b is the middle index of $T1$. GEMM requires the summation indices and non-summation indices in the contraction to be collected into two separate contiguous groups. In order to use GEMM, $T1$ needs to be "reshaped", e.g. $T1[a, b, k] \rightarrow T1r[a, k, b]$. Then GEMM can be invoked with the first operand $T1r$ viewed as an $N^2 \times N$ array and the second input operand C as an $N \times N$ array. The result, which has the index order $[a, k, j]$, would have to be reshaped to give $T2[a, j, k]$.

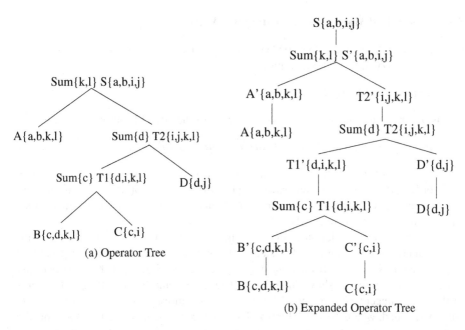

Fig. 1. Operator tree for a sub-expression in the CCSD equation. (a) Original operator tree (b) The expanded operator tree used for optimal code generation

Since $T2$ is only a temporary intermediate array, the order of its dimensions could be chosen to be $[a, k, j]$ instead of $[a, j, k]$, which avoids the need to reshape the output array produced by GEMM. Considering the last contraction, it might seem that some reshaping would be necessary in order to use GEMM. However, GEMM allows one or both of its input operands to be transposed. Thus, the contraction can be achieved by invoking GEMM with B as the first operand in transposed form, and $T2[a, j, k]$ as the second operand, with shape $N \times N^2$. But, as will be shown later, the performance of GEMM for transposed and non-transposed input operands could differ significantly.

In general, a sequence of multi-dimensional tensor contractions can be implemented using a sequence of GEMM calls, possibly with some additional array reordering operations interspersed. We represent this computation as an expanded operator tree. For example, Fig. 1(b) shows the expanded operator tree derived from the operator tree in Fig. 1(a). Each node in the operator tree is replicated to represent a possible array reordering. The problem addressed in this paper is: given a sequence of tensor contractions (expressed as an expanded operator tree), determine the layout (i.e., dimension order) and distribution (among multiple processors) of the tensors, and the modes of invocation of GEMM so that the specified computation is executed in minimal time.

3   Constituent Operations

In this section we discuss the various operations within the computation and their influence on the execution time. The parameters that influence these costs, and hence the overall execution time, are detailed.

3.1   Generalized Matrix Multiplication (GEMM)

General Matrix Multiplication (GEMM) is a set of matrix multiplication subroutines in the BLAS library. It is used to compute

C := alpha*op(A)*op(B) + beta*C.

In this paper, we use the double precision version of the GEMM routine of the form

$$dgemm(transa, transb, m, n, k, alpha, A, lda, B, ldb, beta, C, ldc),$$

where $transa$ ($transb$) specifies whether A (B) is in the transposed form. When $transa$ is $'n'$ or $'N'$, $op(A) = A$; when $transa$ equals to $'t'$ or $'T'$, $op(A) = A^T$; $alpha$ and $beta$ are scalars; C is an $M \times N$ matrix; $op(A)$ and $op(B)$ are matrices of dimensions $M \times K$ and $K \times N$, respectively.

We measured the variation in the performance of GEMM with variation in its input parameters on the Itanium 2 Cluster at the Ohio Supercomputer Center (Dual 900 MHz processors with 4 GB memory, interconnected by Myrinet 2000 network). The cluster's configuration is shown in Table 1. The latency and bandwidth measurements of the interconnect were obtained from [1]. Matrix multiplications of the form $A * B$ were performed, where B was a 4000×4000 matrix and A was an $M \times 4000$ matrix, with M varied from 1 to 300. Matrix multiplications involving such oblong matrices is quite typical in quantum chemistry computations. Two BLAS libraries available in the Itanium 2 Cluster, ATLAS [22] and the Intel Math Kernel Library (MKL) [10] were evaluated. The $transb$ argument was specified as $'t'$ for the results shown in Fig. 3(a) and Fig. 4(a). Fig. 3(b) and Fig. 4(b) show the results for $transb$ being $'n'$. The x-axis shows the value of M and the y-axis represents the performance of matrix multiplication in GFLOPS. We observe that the performance of the GEMM operation for the transposed and untransposed versions cannot be interpreted as the cost of transposition at the beginning of the computation for the experiments with transposed B. For example, in some of the experiments with the ATLAS library, the transposed version performs better. Thus the parameters of the DGEMM invocations need to be determined so as to optimize the overall execution time.

Cannon's Matrix Multiplication Algorithm. Several approaches have been proposed for implementing parallel matrix multiplication [9,8]. In this paper, we consider an extension to Cannon's algorithm [4], which removes the restriction of using a square grid of processors for array distribution.

The extended Cannon algorithm for a 4×2 processors grid is illustrated for the matrix multiplication $C(M, N)$ += $A(M, K) * B(K, N)$ in Fig. 2. The processors form

Table 1. Configuration of the Itanium 2 cluster at OSC

Node	Memory	OS	Compilers	TLB	Network Latency	Interconnect	Commn. library
Dual 900MHz Itanium 2	4GB	Linux 2.4.21smp	g77, ifc	128 entry	17.8 μ s	Myrinet 2000	ARMCI

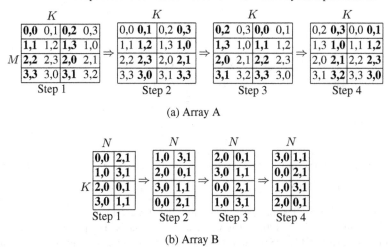

(a) Array A

(b) Array B

Fig. 2. The processing steps in the extended Cannon Algorithm. Initially processor P_{ij} holds blocks labeled B_{ij} and $A_{i(j:j+1)}$. The portion of data accessed in each step is shown in bold

a logical rectangular grid. All the arrays are distributed amongst the processors in the gird in an identical fashion. Each processor holds a block of arrays A, B and C. The algorithm divides the common dimension (K in this illustration) to have the same number of sub-blocks. Each step operates on a sub-block and not on the entire data local to each processor. In each step, if the sub-block required is local to the processor, no communication is required. Fig. 2 shows in bold the sub-blocks of arrays A and B accessed in each step. It shows that the entire B array is accessed in each step.

Given a processor grid, the number of steps is given by the number of sub-blocks along the common dimension (K). The number of blocks of A that are needed by one processor corresponds to the number of processors along the common dimension, and that of B correspond to the other dimension. The number of steps and the number of remote blocks required per processor depend on the distribution of the arrays amongst the processors. The block size for communication is independent of the dimensions. It can be seen that different distributions have different costs for each of the components.

The relative sizes of the arrays A and B determine the optimal distribution. When one array is much larger than the other, the cost can be reduced by skewing the distribution to reduce the number of remote blocks accessed for that array. The shape of the array that is local to each processor affects the local DGEMM cost. Thus, the array distribution influences the communication and computation costs and is an important parameter to be determined.

3.2 Index Permutation

DGEMM requires a two-dimensional view of the input matrices. This means that the summation and non-summation indices of a tensor contraction must be grouped into two contiguous sets of indices. Thus the layout of a multi-dimensional array might have to be transformed to be used as input to DGEMM. Further, additional index permutation

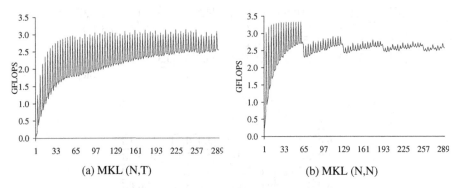

Fig. 3. The matrix multiplication times using the MKL library for $C(M, N)$ += $A(M, K)$ * $B(K, N)$ where $K = N = 4000$. M is varied along the x-axis. The performance obtained in shown on the y-axis in GFLOPS. (a) transb='t' (b) transb='n' in input argument to dgemm

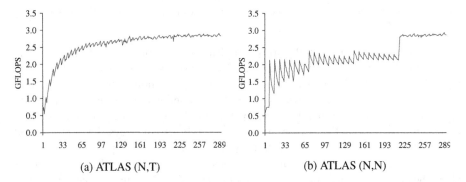

Fig. 4. The matrix multiplication times using the ATLAS library for $C(M, N)$ += $A(M, K)$ * $B(K, N)$ where $K = N = 4000$. M is varied along the x-axis. The performance obtained in shown on the y-axis in GFLOPS. (a) transb='t' (b) transb='n' in input argument to dgemm

cost might be worth paying if it can reduce the DGEMM cost through the use of a transposed (or non-transposed) argument form.

We implemented a collection of index permutation routines, one each for a different number of dimensions. The routines were tiled in the fastest varying indices in the source and target arrays. We observed that performing the computation such that the target arrays are traversed in the order of their storage resulted in better performance than biasing the access to the source array. The execution times for different tile sizes was determined and the best tile size was chosen. The performance of the routines was evaluated on a number of permutations to determine the tile sizes.

We measured the execution times of these routines for some index permutations on four-dimensional arrays of size $N \times N \times N \times N$, with N varying from 15 to 85. The results are shown in Fig. 5. Different permutations are observed to incur different costs. We also notice that the use of different compilers leads to different performances.

The layout of the arrays influences the index permutation costs and is the parameter to be determined to evaluate the index permutation cost. Parallel index permutation can

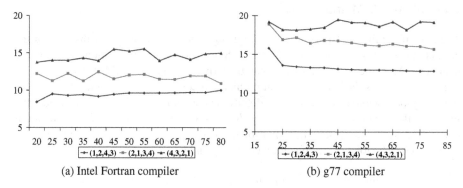

Fig. 5. Index permutation times for three different permutations for an $N \times N \times N \times N$ matrix using (a) Intel Fortran compiler (b) g77 compiler. N is varied along the x-axis. The y-axis shows the execution time per double word in clock cycles

be viewed as a combination of local index permutation and array redistribution. The extended Cannon's algorithm requires that the summation and non-summation index groups be distributed along the slowest varying index in that group. The number of processors along the dimension in the processor grid corresponding to a group can also be varied to determine the shape/size of arrays used in the local DGEMM calls. Thus, in addition to the layout of the arrays, their distribution needs to be determined as well.

Note that the layout of input and output arrays for a DGEMM invocation uniquely determines its parameters. Thus the problem of determination of the DGEMM parameters can be reduced to the layout optimization problem. The variation in the cost of DGEMM with its parameters has the effect of increasing the search space to be explored.

4   Empirical Measurement of Constituent Operations

GEMM Cost

The DGEMM cost can be determined by executing the DGEMM routine with the specified parameters on the target machine. Alternatively, the cost of DGEMM routines in a library on a particular system can be modeled by sampling it offline. The DGEMM cost for the relevant parameters can then be estimated from the sampled data set. Executing the DGEMM at runtime increases the code generation time, while estimating it leads to potential inaccuracies in the cost model.

In this paper, we determine the cost of DGEMM by executing it with the specified parameters. In the operator tree model considered, in which each non-leaf node requires exactly one invocation of the DGEMM, this could result in compilation times that are as long as the execution times. But in real quantum chemistry computations, which require out-of-core treatment [16], tiles of multi-dimensional arrays are brought into memory and operated upon. These loops are in turn enclosed in an outermost loop in iterative chemical methods. Thus each node in the operator tree requires multiple invocations of DGEMM. Thus the compilation time is much less than the execution time.

Cannon's Matrix Multiplication

The cost of parallel matrix multiplication using Cannon's algorithm is the sum of the computation and the communication costs. Since the local computation is performed using DGEMM, the computation cost can be derived from the DGEMM cost. The communication cost is the sum of the communication costs at the beginning of each step. A latency-bandwidth model is used to determine the communication cost. Consider the matrix multiplication $C(M, N) \mathrel{+}= A(M, K) * B(K, N)$. Let P_M, P_K, P_N be the number of processors into which the array is distributed along the M, N and K dimensions, respectively. The total communication cost is given by

$$CommnCost = CommnCost_A + CommnCost_B$$
$$CommnCost_A = (T_s + \frac{M * K}{BW * P_M * P_K}) * (P_K - P_K/P_M)$$
$$CommnCost_B = (T_s + \frac{K * N}{BW * P_K * P_N}) * (P_K - P_K/P_N)$$

where T_s is the latency of the interconnect shown in Table 1. BW, the bandwidth is estimated from a table constructed from the bandwidth curve in [1].

Index Permutation

Fig. 5 shows the performance of our index permutation routines for some permutations. The performance of the implementation appears to be relatively independent of the array dimensions, but is influenced by the permutation being performed.

An analysis of the implementation revealed that the variation in the per-element permutation cost was primarily influenced by the variation in the TLB misses for different permutations and the capability of compilers to perform efficient register tiling.

We estimated the index permutation cost to consist of two components. The first component is the basic copy cost, the minimum cost required to copy a multi-dimensional array, together with the index calculation. We determined two types of basic copy costs. The first, referred to as c_0, is the one in which both the source and target arrays are traversed to have sufficient locality. The other basic copy cost, referred to as c_1, is one in which only the target array is traversed to have locality. Depending on the permutation and the size of the arrays, one of these basic copy costs is chosen. Note that with multi-level tiling of the routines there would be only one basic copy cost. The basic costs c_0 and c_1 were found to be compiler dependent. They were determined to be 9.5 and 11.3 cycles, respectively, per double word with the Intel Fortran Compiler and 12.9 and 15.9 cycles, respectively, per double word with g77. The second component is the TLB miss cost. Each processor on the Itanium-2 cluster had an 128 entry fully-associative TLB with a miss penalty of 25 cycles. Different permutations can lead to different blocks of data being contiguously accessed and at different strides. The permutation to be performed and the array size are used to determine the TLB cost.

In the parallel version of the algorithm, index permutation is coupled with array redistribution. Transformation from one layout and distribution configuration to another is accomplished in two steps, a local index permutation followed by array redistribution.

A combination of index permutation and redistribution can result in each processor communicating its data to more than one processor. The communication cost is estimated differently for different cases. When the target patch written to is local to a processor no communication is required. When the layout transformation is such that each processor needs to communicate its data to exactly one other processor, the cost is uniform across all the processors and is estimated as the cost of communicating that block. In all other cases, we estimate the communication cost to be the cost incurred by the processor whose data is scattered among the most number of processors.

5   Composite Performance Model

In this section, we discuss how the empirical measurements of the constituent operations are used to determine the parameters that optimize the overall execution time.

Constraints and Array Layouts and Distributions

The input and output arrays are constrained to have one layout each. The feasible layouts for the other nodes is given by the following equation.

$$
\mathcal{S}(n) = \begin{cases} \bigcup(\forall l \in \mathcal{P}(NSI(n')))(\forall r \in \mathcal{P}(NSI(n'')))\{(l,r) \cup (r,l)\} \\ \qquad\qquad \text{if } n \text{ is contraction node} \\ \bigcup(\forall l \in \mathcal{P}(SI(n)))(\forall r \in \mathcal{P}(NSI(n)))\{(l,r) \cup (r,l)\} \\ \qquad\qquad \text{if } n \text{ is an index permutation node} \end{cases}
$$

where $\mathcal{S}(n)$ is the set of possible layouts, $SI(n)$ the set of summation indices and $NSI(n)$ the set of non-summation indices in node n. $\mathcal{P}$ is the set of all permutations of its argument. n' and n'' are the left and right child of node n, respectively. (l,r) denotes the concatenation of the sequences l and r.

A tree node C corresponding to a DGEMM computation of the form $C(M,N) \mathrel{+}= A(M,K) * B(K,N)$ can have layouts corresponding to the cross-product of the permutations of the non-summation indices of its children. The remaining nodes are index permutation nodes and are constrained by the layouts acceptable by their parent (i.e., the contraction node to which they act as input). They have layouts corresponding to the cross-product of the permutations of their summation and non-summation indices.

For example, if A and B contain 3 non-summation and 2 summation indices (as determined by the C array) each, A and B have $3! * 2! * 2 = 24$ possible layouts each and C has $3! * 3! * 2 = 72$ possible layouts.

The extended Cannon algorithm requires all distributions to be rectangular in nature. In addition, the children of each contraction node in the operator tree are required to have the same distribution as that node. Thus, for each distribution of a contraction node, there is a corresponding distribution for its children. There is no restriction on the distribution of the contraction nodes themselves.

Determination of Optimal Parameters

For the specified layout and distribution of the root and leaves of the operator tree, we determine the layouts and distributions of the intermediate arrays. For each layout of an array produced by DGEMM, the arrays corresponding to its children nodes are required to have a compatible layout, i.e. the order in which the summation and non-summation indices are grouped is required to be identical in the produced and consumed arrays. This is because the DGEMM does not perform any index permutation within a group. This restriction is used to prune candidate layouts.

The configuration of an array is represented by a layout-distribution pair. Dynamic programming is used to determine the optimal configuration for the intermediate arrays. The cost of a node is determined as the least cost to compute its children and subsequently compute it from its children. It is as follows.

$$
\mathcal{C}_t(n, d, l) = \begin{cases} \min_{\forall d' \in \mathcal{D}, \forall l' \in \mathcal{L}} \mathcal{C}_t(n', d', l') + \mathcal{C}_{ip}((n', d', l') \to (n, d, l)) \\ \qquad \text{if } n \text{ is a index permute node} \\ \min_{\forall l', l'' \in \mathcal{L}} \mathcal{C}_t(n', d, l') + \mathcal{C}_t(n'', d, l'') + \\ \quad \mathcal{C}_{dg}((n', d, l') \times (n'', d, l'') \to (n, d, l)) \\ \qquad \text{if } n \text{ is a contraction node} \end{cases}
$$

where

$$\mathcal{C}_t \equiv \text{Total cost of computing a node with relevant } (d, l)$$

$$\mathcal{C}_{ip} \equiv \text{Cost of the required index permutation}$$

$$\mathcal{C}_{dg} \equiv \text{Cost of the required DGEMM invocation}$$

$$\mathcal{D}(\mathcal{L}) \equiv \text{All feasible distributions (layouts) of relevant node}$$

$$n'(n') \equiv \text{Left(Right) child of } n$$

The expanded operator tree for the example in Fig. 1(a) is shown in Fig. 1(b). The replicated nodes correspond to the index permutations. The original nodes correspond to the contractions. Thus, in the expanded operator tree, each non-leaf node is computed from its children by either index permutation or contraction. Therefore, the total cost of computation of each non-leaf, for different configurations, can be determined from the cost of computing its children from the leaf nodes and the cost of the basic operation, index permutation or GEMM, to compute the node from its children. The algorithm first determines the feasible layouts for each of the nodes in the expanded operator tree. The optimal cost of the root node is subsequently computed using the dynamic programming formulation described above.

6   Experimental Results

We evaluated our approach on the OSC Itanium-2 cluster whose configuration is shown in Table 1. All the experiment programs were compiled with the Intel Itanium Fortran Compiler for Linux. We considered two computations in our domain.

1. CCSD: We used a typical sub-expression from the CCSD theory used to determine electronic structures.

$$
\begin{aligned}
S(j, i, b, a) = \text{Sum}\{l, k\} \, (A\{l, k, b, a\} \\
\times (\text{Sum}\{d\} \, (\text{Sum}\{c\}(B\{d, c, l, k\} \times C\{i, c\}) \times D\{j, d\})))
\end{aligned}
$$

All the array dimensions were 64 for the sequential experiments and 96 for the parallel experiments.

Table 2. Layouts and distributions for the CCSD computation for the unoptimized and optimized versions of the code

Array	Unoptimized				Optimized			
	Distribution	Dist. Index	Layout	GEMM. Parameters	Distribution	Dist. Index	Layout	GEMM. Parameters
A	(2,2)	(k,a)	(l,k,b,a)	–	(1,4)	(k,a)	(l,k,b,a)	–
A'	(2,2)	(a,k)	(b,a,l,k)	–	–	–	–	–
B	(2,2)	(c,k)	(d,c,l,k)	–	(1,4)	(c,k)	(d,c,l,k)	–
B'	(2,2)	(k,c)	(d,l,k,c)	–	(1,4)	(c,k)	(c,d,l,k)	–
C	(2,2)	(i,c)	(i,c)	–	(1,4)	(i,c)	(i,c)	–
C'	(2,2)	(c,i)	(c,i)	–	–	–	–	–
D	(2,2)	(j,d)	(j,d)	–	(1,4)	(j,d)	(j,d)	–
D'	(2,2)	(d,j)	(d,j)	–	–	–	–	–
T1	(2,2)	(k,i)	(d,l,k,i)	B',C',('n','n')	(1,4)	(i,k)	(i,d,l,k)	C,B',('n','n')
T1'	(2,2)	(i,d)	(l,k,i,d)	–	(1,4)	(d,k)	(d,i,l,k)	–
T2	(2,2)	(i,j)	(l,k,i,j)	T1',D',('n','n')	(1,4)	(j,k)	(j,i,l,k)	D,T1',('n','n')
T2'	(2,2)	(k,j)	(l,k,i,j)	–	–	–	–	–
S'	(2,2)	(a,j)	(b,a,i,j)	A',T2,('n','n')	(4,1)	(a,i)	(b,a,j,i)	A,T2, ('t','t')
S	(2,2)	(i,a)	(j,i,b,a)	–	(1,4)	(i,a)	(j,i,b,a)	–

2. AO-to-MO transform: This expression, henceforth referred to as the 4-index transform, is commonly used to transform two-electron integrals from atomic orbital (AO) basis to molecular orbital (MO) basis.

$$B(a,b,c,d) = \text{Sum}\{s\}\,(C1\{s,d\} \times \text{Sum}\{r\}\,(C2\{r,c\}\times$$
$$\text{Sum}\{q\}\,(C3\{q,b\} \times \text{Sum}\{p\}\,(C4\{p,a\} \times A\{p,q,r,s\}))))$$

The array dimensions were 80 and 96 for the sequential and parallel experiments.

We compared our approach with the baseline implementation in which an initial layout for the arrays is provided. A fixed $\sqrt{P} \times \sqrt{P}$ array distribution is required throughout the computation. This approach was, in fact, used in our early implementations. The optimized version is allowed flexibility in the distribution of the input and output arrays.

Table 2 shows the configurations chosen for each array in the parallel experiment for the unoptimized and optimized cases. A first look reveals that the number of intermediate arrays is reduced by effective choice of layouts and distributions. The GEMM parameters for all three GEMM invocations is different, either in the order chosen for the input arrays or in the transposition of the input parameters. The distribution chosen for all the arrays is different from those for the unoptimized version of the computation.

Table 3 and Table 4 show the sequential and parallel results respectively. In the parallel experiments, the GEMM and index permutation times reported subsume the communication costs. The optimized version has close to 20% improvement over the unoptimized version in almost all cases. The parallel 4-index transform has an improvement of more than 75% over the unoptimized version. The effective choice of GEMM parameters results in a noticeable improvement in the GEMM cost for most cases. The

Table 3. Sequential performance results for ccsd and 4index-transform

	Unoptimized (secs)				Optimized(secs)			
	GEMM	Index Permutation	Exec. Time	GFLOPS	GEMM	Index Permutation	Exec. Time	GFLOPS
ccsd	55.28	1.41	56.69	2.50	45.58	0.78	46.36	3.06
4index	10.06	2.58	12.64	2.07	10.58	0.0	10.58	2.48

Table 4. Parallel performance results on 4 processors for ccsd and 4index-transform

	Unoptimized(secs)				Optimized(secs)			
	GEMM	Index Permutation	Exec. Time	GFLOPS	GEMM	Index Permutation	Exec. Time	GFLOPS
ccsd	157.93	7.21	165.14	9.68	136.41	2.86	139.27	11.71
4index	12.23	7.74	19.97	3.27	7.57	3.64	11.21	5.83

index permutation cost is either improved or totally eliminated. The trade-off between the GEMM and the index permutation costs can be observed in the sequential 4-index transform experiment. In this experiment, the optimization process chooses an inferior configuration for the GEMM computation, so as to eliminate the index permutation cost completely, and hence reduce the overall execution time.

7   Related Work

There has been prior work that has attempted to use data layout optimizations to improve spatial locality in programs, either in addition to or instead of loop transformations. Leung and Zahorjan [18] were the first to demonstrate cases where loop transformations fail (for a variety of reasons) for which data transformations are useful. The data transformations they consider correspond to non-singular linear transformations of the data space. O'Boyle and Knijnenburg [21] present techniques for generating efficient code for several layout optimizations such as linear transformations memory layouts, alignment of arrays to page boundaries, and page replication. Several authors [2,11] discuss the use of data transformations to improve locality on shared memory machines. Kandemir et al. [14] present a hyperplane representation of memory layouts of multi-dimensional arrays and show how to use this representation to derive very general data transformations for a single perfectly-nested loop. In the absence of dynamic data layouts, the layout of an array has an impact on the spatial locality characteristic of all the loop nests in the program which access the array. As a result, Kandemir et al. [12,13,14] and Leung and Zahorjan [18] present a global approach to this problem; of these, [12] considers dynamic layouts.

Some authors have addressed unifying loop and data transformations into a single framework. These works [5,13] use loop permutations and array dimension permutations in an exhaustive search to determine the appropriate loop and data transformations for a single nest and then extend it to handle multiple nests.

FFTW [19] and ATLAS [22] produce high performance libraries for specific computation kernels, by executing different versions of the computation and choosing the parameters that optimize the overall execution time. Our approach is similar to these in that we perform empirical evaluation of the constituent operations for various possible parameters. But our work focuses on a more general class of computations than a single kernel. This forbids an exhaustive search strategy.

8 Conclusions

We have described an approach to the synthesis of efficient parallel code that minimizes the overall execution time. The approach was developed for a program synthesis system targeted at the quantum chemistry domain. The code was generated as a sequence of DGEMM calls interspersed with index permutation and redistribution to enable to use of the BLAS libraries and to improve overall performance. The costs of the constituent operations in the computation were empirically measured and were used to model the cost of the computation. This computational model was used to determine layouts and distributions that minimize the overall execution time. Experimental results were provided that showed the effectiveness of our approach.

In future, we intend to further explore the trade-offs between empirical measurement and estimation of the cost of constituent operations, so that it can be tuned by the user to achieve the level of accuracy desired. We also plan to evaluate our approach with other parallel matrix multiplication algorithms.

References

1. Aggregate Remote Memory Copy Interface. http://www.emsl.pnl.gov/docs/parsoft/armci/.
2. J. M. Anderson, S. P. Amarasinghe, and M. S. Lam. Data and Computation Transformations for Multiprocessors. In *Proc. of the Fifth ACM SIGPLAN Symposium on Principles and Practice of Parallel Processing*, July 1995.
3. G. Baumgartner, D.E. Bernholdt, D. Cociorva, R. Harrison, S. Hirata, C. Lam, M. Nooijen, R. Pitzer, J. Ramanujam, and P. Sadayappan. A High-Level Approach to Synthesis of High-Performance Codes for Quantum Chemistry. In *Proc. of SC 2002*, November 2002.
4. L. Cannon. *A Cellular Computer to Implement the Kalman Filter Algorithm*. PhD thesis, Montana State University, 1969.
5. M. Cierniak and W. Li. Unifying data and control transformations for distributed shared memory machines. In *ACM SIGPLAN IPDPS*, pages 205–217, 1995.
6. D. Cociorva, G. Baumgartner, C. Lam, J. Ramanujam P. Sadayappan, M. Nooijen, D. Bernholdt, and R. Harrison. Space-Time Trade-Off Optimization for a Class of Electronic Structure Calculations. In *Proc. of ACM SIGPLAN PLDI 2002*, pages 177–186, 2002.
7. D. Cociorva, X. Gao, S. Krishnan, G. Baumgartner, C. Lam, P. Sadayappan, and J. Ramanujam. Global Communication Optimization for Tensor Contraction Expressions under Memory Constraints. In *Proc. of IPDPS*, 2003.
8. J. J. Dongarra, J. D. Croz, I. S. Duff, and S. Hammarling. A set of level-3 basic linear algebra subprograms. *ACM Transactions on Mathematical Software*, 16(1):1–17, 1990.
9. R. A. Van De Geijn and J. Watts. SUMMA: scalable universal matrix multiplication algorithm. *Concurrency: Practice and Experience*, 9(4):255–274, 1997.

10. Intel Math Kernel Library. http://www.intel.com/software/products/mkl/features.htm.

11. Y. Ju and H. Dietz. Reduction of cache coherence overhead by compiler data layout and loop transformation. In *Proc. of LCPC*, pages 344–358. Springer-Verlag, 1992.

12. M. Kandemir, P. Banerjee, A. Choudhary, J. Ramanujam, and E. Ayguade. Static and dynamic locality optimizations using integer linear programming. *IEEE Transactions on Parallel and Distributed Systems*, 12(9):922–941, 2001.

13. M. Kandemir, A. Choudhary, J. Ramanujam, and P. Banerjee. Improving locality using loop and data transformations in an integrated framework. In *International Symposium on Microarchitecture*, pages 285–297, 1998.

14. M. Kandemir, A. Choudhary, N. Shenoy, P. Banerjee, and J. Ramanujam. A linear algebra framework for automatic determination of optimal data layouts. *IEEE Transactions on Parallel and Distributed Systems*, 10(2):115–135, 1999.

15. K. Kennedy, B. Broom, K. Cooper, J. Dongarra, R. Fowler, D. Gannon, L. Johnsson, J. M. Crummey, and L. Torczon. Telescoping languages: A strategy for automatic generation of scientific problem-solving systems from annotated libraries. *JPDC*, 61(12):1803–1826, December 2001.

16. S. Krishnan, S. Krishnamoorthy, G. Baumgartner, D. Cociorva, C. Lam, P. Sadayappan, J. Ramanujam, D. E. Bernholdt, and V. Choppella. Data Locality Optimization for Synthesis of Efficient Out-of-Core Algorithms. In *Proc. of HiPC*. Springer Verlag, 2003.

17. T. J. Lee and G. E. Scuseria. Achieving chemical accuracy with coupled cluster theory. In S. R. Langhoff, editor, *Quantum Mechanical Electronic Structure Calculations with Chemical Accuracy*, pages 47–109. Kluwer Academic, 1997.

18. S. Leung and J. Zahorjan. Optimizing data locality by array restructuring. Technical Report TR-95-09-01, Dept. Computer Science, University of Washington, Seattle, WA, 1995.

19. M. Frigo and S. Johnson. FFTW: An adaptive software architecture for the FFT. In *Proc. of ICASSP 98*, volume 3, pages 1381–1384, 1998.

20. J. Nieplocha, R. J. Harrison, and R. J. Littlefield. Global arrays: a portable programming model for distributed memory computers. In *Supercomputing*, pages 340–349, 1994.

21. M. F. P. O'Boyle and P. M. W. Knijnenburg. Non-singular data transformations: definition, validity, applications. In *Proc. of CPC'96*, pages 287–297, 1996.

22. R. Whaley and J. Dongarra. Automatically Tuned Linear Algebra Software (ATLAS). In *Proc. of Supercomputing '98*, 1998.

23. K. Yotov, X. Li, G. Ren, M. Cibulskis, G. DeJong, M. Garzaran, D. Padua, D. Pingali, P. Stodghill, and P. Wu. A comparison of empirical and model-driven optimization. *SIGPLAN Not.*, 38(5):63–76, 2003.

Implementation of Parallel Numerical Algorithms Using Hierarchically Tiled Arrays*

Ganesh Bikshandi[1], Basilio B. Fraguela[2], Jia Guo[1], María J. Garzarán[1],
Gheorghe Almási[3], José Moreira[3], and David Padua[1]

[1] Dept. of Computer Science, University of Illinois at Urbana-Champaign, USA
{bikshand, jiaguo, garzaran, padua}@cs.uiuc.edu
[2] Dept. de Electrónica e Sistemas, Universidade da Coruña, Spain
basilio@udc.es
[3] IBM Thomas J. Watson Research Center. Yorktown Heights, NY, USA
{gheorghe, jmoreira}@us.ibm.com

Abstract. In this paper, we describe our experience in writing parallel numerical algorithms using Hierarchically Tiled Arrays (HTAs). HTAs are classes of objects that encapsulate parallelism. HTAs allow the construction of single-threaded parallel programs where a master process distributes tasks to be executed by a collection of servers holding the components (tiles) of the HTAs.

The tiled and recursive nature of HTAs facilitates the development of algorithms with a high degree of parallelism as well as locality. We have implemented HTAs as a MATLAB™ toolbox, overloading conventional operators and array functions such that HTA operations appear to the programmer as extensions of MATLAB™. We have successfully used it to write some widely used parallel numerical programs. The resulting programs are easier to understand and maintain than their MPI counterparts.

1 Introduction

Parallel programs are difficult to develop and maintain. This is particularly true in the case of distributed memory machines, where every piece of data that needs to be accessed by two or more processors must be communicated by means of messages in the program, and where the user must make sure that every machine is working with the latest version of the data. Parallel execution also makes debugging a difficult task. Moreover, more factors influence the performance of parallel programs than that of sequential programs. For example, systems may be

* This work was supported in part by the National Science Foundation under grants CCR 01-21401 ITR and 03-25687 ITR/NGS; by DARPA under contract NBCH30390004; and by gifts from INTEL and IBM. It has also been supported in part by the Ministry of Science and Technology of Spain under contract TIC2001-3694-C02-02, and by the Xunta de Galicia under contract PGIDIT03-TIC10502PR. This work is not necessarily representative of the positions or policies of the Army or Government.

R. Eigenmann et al. (Eds.): LCPC 2004, LNCS 3602, pp. 87–101, 2005.

heterogeneous; the architecture to consider involves a communication network, and different operating system layers and user libraries may be involved in the passing of a message. As a result, performance tuning is also much harder. The language and compiler community has come up with several approaches to help programmers deal with these issues.

The first approach to ease the burden on the programmer when developing distributed memory programs was based on standard message passing libraries like MPI [8] or PVM [7] which improve the portability of the parallel applications. Data distribution and synchronization must be completely managed by the programmer. The SPMD programming model typically used in conjunction with these libraries leads to unstructured codes in which communication may take place between widely separated sections of code and in which a given communication statement could interact with several different statements during the execution of the program. Some programming languages like Co-Array FORTRAN [11] and UPC [5] improve the readability of the programs by replacing library calls with array assignments, but they still have all the drawbacks of the SPMD approach.

Another strategy to facilitate the programming of distributed memory systems consists of writing the programs as a single thread and letting the compiler take care of the problems of distributing the data and assigning the parallel tasks. This is for example the approach of the High Performance Fortran[9,10]. Unfortunately, compiler technology is not always capable of generating code that matches the performance of hand-written code.

In this paper we explore the possibility of extending a single-threaded object-oriented programming language with a *new class, called Hierarchically Tiled Array or HTA [3], that encapsulates the parallelism in the code.* HTA operators overload the standard operators of the language. HTA data can be distributed across a collection of servers, and its operations can be scheduled on the appropriate processors. The HTA class provides a flexible indexing scheme for its tiles that allows communication between servers to be expressed by means of simple array assignments. As a result, HTA based programs are single-threaded, which improves readability and ease development and maintenance. Furthermore, the compiler support required by our parallel programming approach is minimal since the implementation of the class itself takes care of the parallelization. In MATLAB^{TM} we have found an ideal platform for the implementation and testing of HTAs. MATLAB^{TM} provides a high-level programming language with object-oriented features that is easy to extend using the *toolbox approach.*

The rest of this paper is structured as follows. HTA syntax and semantics are described in the next Section. Section 3 provides several code examples that use HTA. Section 4 describes the implementation of the HTA language extension as a MATLAB^{TM} toolbox. Section 5 presents our implementation of NAS benchmark kernels using HTA. In Section 6 we analyze two aspects of our approach - performance and programmability. In Section 7 an analytical comparison of HTA with other related languages is given. Finally we conclude in Section 8 with several future directions.

2   Hierarchically Tiled Arrays: Syntax and Semantics

We define a *tiled array* as an array partitioned into tiles in such a way that adjacent tiles have the same size along the dimension of adjacency. A *hierarchically tiled array* (HTA) is a tiled array where each tile is either an unpartitioned array or an HTA. Note that our definition does not require all tiles to have the same size: both HTAs in Fig. 1 are legal.

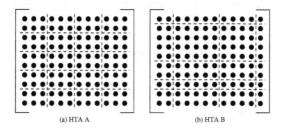

Fig. 1. Two tiled arrays A (a) and B (b)

2.1   Dereferencing the Contents of an HTA

Given an arbitrary HTA, there are two basic ways to address its contents: *hierarchical* or *flat*. Hierarchical addressing identifies a subset of the HTA at the top level of the hierarchy, then identifies subsets of those elements at lower levels of the hierarchy, and so on down to possibly the lowest level.

Flat addressing disregards the hierarchical nature of the HTA and addresses elements by their absolute indices, as in a normal array. Flattening can be applied to any level of the hierarchy. Thus, a series of intermediate possibilities lie between hierarchical and flat addressing.

As an example, consider HTA A shown in Fig. 1(a). The element in its fifth row and sixth column can be referenced using flat addressing as A(5,6). The same element can be referenced using hierarchical addressing as A{3,2}(1,3), where curly brackets are used to index tiles and parentheses are used to index the elements in the bottommost tile. Indexing using triple notation init:step:limit is also provided for both hierarchical and flattened addressing.

2.2   HTA Arithmetic Operations

The semantics of HTA arithmetic operations depend on the operands. The following are the types of operations and the resulting semantics.

- HTA $\oplus$ Scalar: In this case, the scalar is operated with the scalars of each tile of the HTA.
- HTA $\oplus$ Matrix: In this case, the matrix is promoted to an HTA with a single tile and operated with each of the tiles of the HTA. Matrix promotion requires a legality check. The condition for legality of operations depend on

the operator - an addition or a subtraction requires the matrix to match the shape of each tile of the HTA, while multiplication requires the number of columns of the matrix to be same as that of rows of each tile of the HTA.

− HTA ⊕ HTA: Two cases are distinguished here. The first one involves two HTAs with the *same topology* - with the same number of tiles in every dimension at the top level and the corresponding tiles being legally operable. The resulting HTA has the same topology as the input ones, with each of its tiles associated to the computation of the corresponding input tiles. The other case involves HTAs in which one of them as a whole has the same topology as each one of the tiles of the other one at a given level of subdivision. In this situation, the semantics is similar to that of HTA ⊕ Matrix.

2.3 HTA Assignments

The semantics for assignments to HTAs are similar to those for binary operators. When a scalar is assigned to a range of positions within an HTA, the scalar gets replicated in all of them. When an array is assigned to a range of tiles of an HTA, the array is replicated in all of the tiles if the HTA resulting from the assignment is legal. Finally, an HTA can be assigned to another HTA (or a range of tiles of it) if the copy of the correspondingly selected tiles from the right-hand side (RHS) HTA to those selected in the left-hand side (LHS) one is legal. When the right HTA has a single tile, it is replicated in each one of the tiles selected in the left HTA.

2.4 Construction of HTAs

The simplest way to build an HTA is by providing a source array and a series of delimiters in each dimension where the array should be cut into tiles. For example, the HTAs A and B from Fig. 1 could be created as follows, using a source matrix MX:

```
A = hta(MX, {1:2:10,1:3:12});
B = hta(MX, {[1,2,6,8,9], [1,3,8,12]});
```

The HTAs built above are local. In order to request the distribution of the top-level tiles of the HTA on a mesh of processors, the last argument of the constructor must be a vector specifying the shape of the mesh. The distribution is currently fixed to be block-cyclic.

HTAs can also be built as structures whose tiles are empty. In this case the constructor is called just with the number of tiles desired in each dimension. The empty tiles can be filled in later by means of assignments. As an, example, the following statement generates an empty 4×4 HTA whose tiles are distributed on a 2×2 processor mesh:

```
A = hta(4, 4, [2, 2]);
```

3   Parallel Programming Using HTAs

Codes using HTAs have a single thread of execution that runs in a client (master). The client is connected to a distributed memory machine with an array of processors, called servers. HTAs can be created on the client side and their tiles can be distributed to the severs. An operator involving HTA requires the client to broadcast the operation to the servers where they are executed in parallel. Some operators, once initiated by the client, involve communication among severs without the further involvement of the client. Some other operators involve accessing arbitrary tiles across different severs, mediated by the client. We will see some of these common examples in this section.

The first example we consider is the Cannon's matrix multiplication algorithm shown in Fig. 2. Cannon's matrix multiplication algorithm [4] is an example of code that requires communication between the servers. In our implementation of the algorithm, the operands, denoted a and b respectively, are HTAs tiled in two dimensions. The HTAs are mapped onto a mesh of $n \times n$ processors. In each iteration of the algorithm's main loop, each server executes a matrix multiplication of the tiles of a and b that currently reside on that server. The result of the multiplication is accumulated in a (local) tile of the result HTA, c. After the local matrix multiplication, the tiles of b and a are circularly shifted in the first and second dimensions respectively. The effect of this operation is that the tiles of a are sent to the left processor in the mesh and the tiles of b are sent to the lower processor in the mesh. The left-most processor transfers its tile of a to the right-most processor in its row and the bottom-most processor transfers its tile of b to the top-most processor in its column. The statement $c=a*b$, in Fig. 2, initiates the above mentioned parallel computation with circular shift after each iteration. The circular shift is done by `circshift`, an HTA-overloaded version of the native `circshift` in MATLAB^{TM} . In this code the function involves communication because the HTAs are distributed.

The next example shows how to reference arbitrary elements of HTAs. The blocked Jacobi relaxation code in Fig. 3 requires a given element to compute its new value as a function of the values of its four neighbors. Each block is represented by a tile of the HTA v. In addition the tiles also contain extra rows and columns for use as border regions exchanging information with the neighbors. Border exchange is executed in the first four statements of the main loop. The actual computation step (last statement in the loop) uses only local data.

```
for i = 1:n
    c = c + a * b;
    a = circshift(a, [0, -1] );
    b = circshift(b, [-1, 0] );
end
```

Fig. 2. Main loop in Cannon's algorithm

```
while ~converged
  v{2:n,:}(1,:) = v{1:n-1,:}(d+1,:);
  v{1:n-1,:}(d+2,:) = v{2:n,:}(2,:);
  v{:,2:n}(:,1) = v{:,1:n-1}(:,d+1);
  v{:,1:n-1}(:,d+2) = v{:,2:n}(:,2);

  u{:,:}(2:d+1,2:d+1) = K * (v{:,:}(2:d+1,1:d) + v{:,:}(1:d,2:d+1)...
                        + v{:,:}(2:d+1,3:d+2) + v{:,:}(3:d+2,2:d+1));
end
```

Fig. 3. Parallel Jacobi relaxation

```
input = hta(px, py, [px py]);
input{:, :} = zeros(px, py);
output = parHTAFunc(@randx, input);
```

Fig. 4. Filling an HTA with uniform random numbers

Easy programming of embarrassingly parallel and MIMD style codes is also possible using HTAs thanks to the parHTAFunc function. It allows the execution of a function in parallel on different tiles of the same HTA. A call to this function has the form parHTAFunc(@func, arg1, arg2, ...), where @func is a pointer to the function to execute in parallel, and arg1, arg2,... are its arguments. At least one of these arguments must be a distributed HTA. The function func will be executed over each of the tiles, on their owning servers. If the server keeps several tiles, the function will be executed for each of these. Several arguments to parHTAFunc can be distributed HTAs. In this case they all must have the same number of tiles in every dimension and the same mapping.

Fig. 4 illustrates the usage of parHTAFunc to fill an array represented as HTA with uniform random numbers in the range [0,1]. A distributed HTA input with one tile per processor is built and is sent as the argument to randx via the parHTAFunc. The function randx is similar to rand in MATLAB^{TM} but generates a different sequence on each processor. Specific details of this function is ignored for brevity. The result of the parallel execution of the function is a distributed HTA output that has the same mapping as input and keeps a single tile per processor with the random numbers filled in.

4 Execution Model and Implementation

HTAs can be added to almost any object-based or object-oriented language. We chose the MATLAB^{TM} environment as the host for our implementation, for 3 main reasons: wide user base, support of polymorphism and extensibility as a toolbox. HTAs are implemented as a new type of object, accessible through the constructors described in Section 2.

The HTA class methods have been written either in MATLAB^{TM} or in C that interfaces with MATLAB^{TM} (version R13 or above) through MEX. In general,

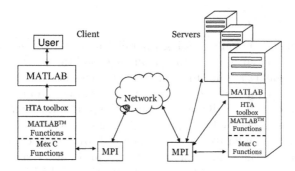

Fig. 5. HTA implementation in MATLAB^{TM}

methods that do not involve communications, such as those that test the legality of operations, were written in MATLAB^{TM} to simplify their development. Small methods used very frequently were written in C for performance reasons. Communications between the client and the servers are implemented using the MPI [8] library, thus methods that involve communication were written in C in order to use the message-passing library.

The architecture of our MATLAB^{TM} implementation is shown in Fig. 5. MATLAB^{TM} is used both in the client, where the code is executed following a single thread, and in the servers, where it is used as a computational engine for the distributed operations on the HTAs. The lower layers of the HTA toolbox deal with communication, while the higher layers implement the syntax.

Our implementation supports both dense and sparse matrices with double precision data, which can be real or complex. Any number of levels of tiling is allowed in the HTAs, although every tile must have the same number of levels of decomposition.

When an HTA is distributed, the client keeps an image of its complete structure, so that legality checks can always be made locally. As the number of servers grows, the centralized legality check and the required broadcast of commands from the client will become a bottleneck. Thus HTA implementations for highly-parallel systems should be based on compilers in order to scale as required.

5   NAS Benchmark Suite

In this section we present our experience with writing highly parallel numerical programs using HTA. Specifically, we deal with the kernels of the NAS benchmarks [1]. We have successfully implemented four kernels so far - *cg*, *ep*, *mg* and *ft*. We are also in the process of implementing the other kernels. We first created serial versions of the programs in MATLAB^{TM} and incrementally parallelized them with minimal efforts using the HTA representation. In the following subsections we present a detailed description of *ep*, *mg* and *ft*.

5.1 NAS *Kernel ep*

The NAS kernel *ep* is an embarrassingly parallel application that generates pairs of uniformly distributed pseudo-random numbers and tabulates those pairs that lie in successive square annuli. In the parallel implementation of the algorithm, each processor generates its section of random numbers and does the above mentioned computation locally and exchange the results through a reduction at the end. This is implemented using the `parHTAFunc` described in Section 3. The resulting code looks similar to that shown in Fig. 4, with additional computations that involves finding the number of pairs that lie in the successive square annuli. All these steps are encoded inside the `randx` function of the Fig. 4 that is called via the `parHTAFunc`. Function `myHTARank` is used to identify the rank of the servers in execution, inside `randx`.

5.2 NAS *Kernel mg*

The NAS kernel *mg* solves the Poisson's equation, $\nabla^2 u = v$, in 3D using a multigrid V-cycle. An outline of the algorithm, as presented in [1] is shown in Fig. 6. P, Q, A and S are arrays of coefficients. Each iteration of the algorithm consists of two steps, 1 and 2, listed in Fig. 6. The step 2 is recursive and is also explained in the same figure. The step 1 consists of finding the residual $r = v - Au$. The step 2 consists of solving the residual equation $Ae = r$ and updating the current solution u, $u = u + e$. Solving the residual equation is done using the V-cycle approach, described as M^k, in the figure. The first step of the V-cycle is restricting (`restrict`) larger grids to smaller ones (step 3) successively (step 4), until we reach the smallest grid that could be solved trivially (step 8). Then the reverse process of interpolation (`interpolate`) takes place where a smaller grid is expanded to a larger grid (step 5). The above sequence is repeated for several iterations until the solution converges.

The grids v and u are 3-dimensional and are represented as 3-dimensional arrays. $r_i, 0 < i < k$, is an array of grids with the kth grid being the largest. Each grid is 3-dimensional and is represented in the same way as u. P, Q, A and S are banded diagonal matrices with the same 4 values in each row. Hence they are represented using a vector with 4 values. Given the above representations, it is straight forward to implement the above algorithm in MATLAB^{TM}. In order to parallelize this algorithm, the grids must be divided into several chunks along each dimension and each such chunk must be allocated to a processor, using a processor map. After each operation, communication of the boundary values in each dimension should be performed. Shadow regions are allocated in each chunk to hold the boundary values.

In a typical MPI program, the programmer is responsible for doing all the above mentioned steps. The algorithm is implemented in parallel using the HTA representation in an easy manner as follows. The grids v and u are represented as a 3-D HTAs of size $dx \times dy \times dz$. r_i is represented as an array of HTAs, with each HTA representing a grid of size i. Fig. 7 presents an outline of this step. Also shown in the figure is the allocation of extra space for shadow regions in each

$$(1) \quad r = v - A\,u$$
$$(2) \quad u = u + M^k\,r$$

where M^k is defined as follows:
$z_k = M^k\,r_k :$

$\qquad$ if $k > 1$

(3) [restrict] $\qquad\qquad r_{k-1} = P r_k$

(4) [recursive solve] $\qquad z_{k-1} = M^{k-1}\,r_{k-1}$

(5) [interpolate] $\qquad\quad z_k = Q z_{k-1}$

(6) [evaluate residue] $\quad r_k = r_k - A\,z_k$

(7) [smoothen] $\qquad\quad\ z_k = z_k + S\,r_k$

$\qquad$ else

(8) $\qquad\qquad\qquad\qquad z_1 = S\,r_1$

$\qquad$ end

Fig. 6. *mg* - Outline of the algorithm

```
%px, py, pz are processors along X, Y and Z axes
for i = 1 : k
%add shadow regions for the boundaries
      sx = nx(i) + 2 * px;
      sy = ny(i) + 2 * py;
      sz = nz(i) + 2 * pz;
      r{i} = hta(zeros(sx, sy, sz), {1 : sx/px : sx, 1 : sy/py : sy, 1 : sz/pz : sz}, [px py pz]);
end
u = hta(r{k});
v = hta(r{k});
```

Fig. 7. *mg* - Creation of HTAs

tile. It should be noted that the HTA constructor automatically maps the tiles to the processors according to the specified topology as explained in Section 2.4. The next important step is the communication of the boundary values, shown in Fig. 8. The figure shows the communication along X dimension; the communications along the other dimensions look very similar. The grid operations are implemented as a subroutine with the HTAs as parameters. One such operation, restrict, is shown in the Fig. 9. The above subroutine implemented as such is inefficient, as each addition operation requires the client to send a message to the servers along with the two operands. This is mitigated by the use of parHTAFunc, explained in section 3, as follows - $s = parHTAFunc(@restrict, r, s)$. This requires only one message to be sent to the servers. Thus parHTAFunc, apart from facilitating MIMD-style of programming, also enables optimization. Finally, the program involves computing the sum $\sum r_k{}^2$, which is done using the HTA-overloaded parallel sum and power operators.

```
%dx is the size of the HTA along X dimension
    u{1 : dx − 1, :, :}(n1, 2 : n2 − 1, 2 : n3 − 1) = u{2 : dx, :, :}(2, 2 : n2 − 1, 2 : n3 − 1);
    u{dx, :, :}(n1, 2 : n2 − 1, 2 : n3 − 1) = u{1, :, :}(2, 2 : n2 − 1, 2 : n3 − 1);
    u{2 : dx, :, :}(1, 2 : n2 − 1, 2 : n3 − 1) = u{1 : dx − 1, :, :}(n1 − 1, 2 : n2 − 1, 2 : n3 − 1);
    u{1, :, :}(1, 2 : n2 − 1, 2 : n3 − 1) = u{dx, :, :}(n1 − 1, 2 : n2 − 1, 2 : n3 − 1);
```

Fig. 8. *mg* - Communication of Boundary Regions

```
%i1b,i2b,i2e - begining position in tiles of r along X,Y,Z respectively;
%i1e,i2e,i3e - ending position in tiles of r along X,Y,Z respectively;
%m1j,m2j,m3j - ending position in tiles of s along X,Y,Z respectively;
s{:, :, :}(2 : m1j − 1, 2 : m2j − 1, 2 : m3j − 1) = 0.5D0 * r{:, :, :}(i1b : 2 : i1e, i2b : 2 : i2e, i3b : 2 : i3e)...
    +0.25D0 * (r{:, :, :}(i1b − 1 : 2 : i1e − 1, i2b : 2 : i2e, i3b : 2 : i3e)...
        +r{:, :, :}(i1b + 1 : 2 : i1e + 1, i2b : 2 : i2e, i3b : 2 : i3e)...
        +r{:, :, :}(i1b : 2 : i1e, i2b − 1 : 2 : i2e − 1, i3b : 2 : i3e)...
        +r{:, :, :}(i1b : 2 : i1e, i2b + 1 : 2 : i2e + 1, i3b : 2 : i3e)...
        +r{:, :, :}(i1b : 2 : i1e, i2b : 2 : i2e, i3b − 1 : 2 : i3e − 1)...
        +r{:, :, :}(i1b : 2 : i1e, i2b : 2 : i2e, i3b + 1 : 2 : i3e + 1));
    + several other similar operations, ignored here for brevity
```

Fig. 9. *mg* - Operation `restrict` (Line 3 of Fig. 6)

5.3   NAS Kernel *ft*

NAS kernel *ft* numerically solves certain partial differential equations (PDE) using forward and inverse Fast Fourier Transform. Consider the PDE, $\frac{\partial u(x,t)}{\partial t} = \alpha \nabla^2 u(x,t)$ where x is a position in 3-dimensional space. Now applying FFT on both side we get, $\frac{\partial v(z,t)}{\partial t} = -4\alpha\pi^2|Z|^2 v(z,t)$, where $v(z,t)$ is the Fast Fourier transform of $u(x,t)$. This has the solution $v(z,t) = e^{-4\alpha\pi^2|z|^2 t} v(z,0)$. Thus, the original equation can be solved by applying the FFT to u, then multiplying the result by a certain exponential, and finding the inverse FFT of the result. To implement this algorithm we essentially need to have a forward and inverse FFT operator. Fortunately, MATLAB^{TM} already has this operator.

In the parallel version of FFT for N-Dimensional arrays, one of the dimensions is not distributed. 1D-FFTs are calculated along each non-distributed dimension, one by one. If a dimension is distributed, it is transposed with a non-distributed dimension and the 1-D FFT is applied along that dimension. In the MPI version the programmer has to implement the transpose using `alltoall` communication and cumbersome processor mapping data structures. An implementation of this algorithm for calculating the forward FFT of a 3-D array, 2-D decomposed along Y and Z axes, using HTAs is shown in Fig. 10. The function `fft` is the native MATLAB^{TM} function to calculate the FFT of an array along a specified dimension. The operator `dpermute` permutes the data of the `fft` array without changing its underlying structure. In this kernel, the HTAs are of complex data type.

$$x = hta(complex(nx, ny, nz), \{1, 1 : ny/py, 1 : nz/pz\}, [1 \; py \; pz]);$$
$$x = parHTAFunc(@compute\_initial\_conditions, x);$$
$$x = parHTAFunc(@fft, x, [\,], 1);$$
$$x = dpermute(x, [2 \; 1 \; 3]);$$
$$x = parHTAFunc(@fft, x, [\,], 1);$$
$$x = dpermute(x, [3 \; 2 \; 1]);$$
$$x = parHTAFunc(@fft, x, [\,], 1);$$

Fig. 10. *ft* - Calculating Forward FFT using HTA

6   Analysis of the Results

In this subsection we discuss two aspects of our implementation of NAS bench-mark kernels using HTA - Performance and Programmability. We conducted our experiment in an IBM SP system consisting of two SMP nodes of 8 Power3 processors running at 375 MHz and sharing 8 GB of memory each. In our ex-periments we allocated one processor for the client (master) and either other 4 or 8 additional ones for the servers. In both cases, half of the processors were allocated from each one of the two SMP nodes. The next natural step of ex-perimentation involves 16 servers, but that would require 17 processors. The C files of the toolbox were compiled with the VisualAge C xlc compiler for AIX, version 5.0, while the MPI versions of the NAS benchmarks were compiled with the corresponding xlf compiler from IBM. In both cases the O3 level of optimiza-tion was applied. The computational engine and interpreter for the HTA was MATLAB^{TM} R13, while the MPI programs used the native highly optimized IBM ESSL library to perform their computations. The MPI library and envi-ronment in both cases was the one provided by the IBM Parallel Environment for AIX Version 3.1.

6.1   Performance

Fig. 11 is the execution time and speedup plot using 4 and 8 servers (processors) for both MPI and HTA programs . *ft_1d* and *ft_2d* correspond to *ft* with 1-D and 2-D decomposition respectively. Also shown in the figure is the speedup for *mg* without the use of **parHTAFunc** (*mg_H*). The size of the input for *mg* is a $256 \times 256 \times 256$ array, while for *ft* it is $256 \times 256 \times 128$. For kernel *ep* 536870912 random numbers are generated. All of them correspond to Class A of the NAS benchmark. The raw execution time is considerably larger for HTA - the HTA system is built over MATLAB^{TM} which is a slow interpreted environment. However, the speedup obtained for each kernel is significant.

Kernel *ep* has a perfect speedup, as it is embarrassingly parallel and there is no communication overhead apart from the initial distribution and final reduc-tion. Kernel *ft* has a super-linear speedup for HTA version. In *ft* the timing also includes the initialization of the complex array with random entries. This takes huge time in a serial MATLAB^{TM} program, which we believe is due to overhead

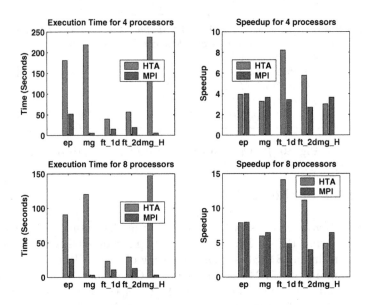

Fig. 11. Execution Time and Speedup

in cache or TLB. For kernel *mg* the speedup of HTA program is slightly lesser than that of MPI program. We discovered two main sources of overhead that are the reasons for this. The first overhead is associated with the interpretation of every command and its broadcast to the servers each time. We plan to have a compiler support to overcome this overhead. The other overhead is caused by the need to make a full copy of the LHS of any indexed HTA assignment operation. This is due to the fact that the (overloaded) indexed assignment operator cannot deal with arguments passed in by reference; it needs arguments to be passed by value. This is a limitation imposed by our need to operate inside the MATLAB^{TM} environment. This overhead is pronounced in *mg*, which has a lot of communication. Readers should note that the NAS benchmark kernels are highly optimized, while our current HTA versions are not that optimized.

6.2   Ease of Programming

The primary goal of our research is to ease the burden of parallel programmers. In order to show the effectiveness of HTA for this purpose, we measure the number of lines of key parts of the HTA and MPI programs. Though the number of lines of code is not a standard metric to measure the ease of programming, it gives a rough idea about the complexity of programs.

Fig. 12 shows the number of lines of code for two main parts of *mg* and *ft* programs - data decomposition/mapping and communication. Kernel *ep* look very similar in both MPI and HTA versions, resulting in equal sized codes in both the cases. In *mg*, the domain decomposition/mapping has almost same number of lines because both the HTA and MPI programs do similar steps to find the

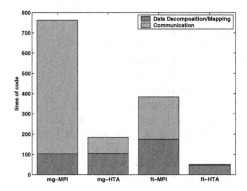

Fig. 12. Lines of code for key sections of *mg* and *ft*

init and limit of each array chunk. However, the MPI version of *ft* does additional computations for the later transpose operation and hence it is bigger than the HTA version. The number of lines consumed by the communication operations is significantly lesser in the HTA programs for both *mg* and *ft*. In the HTA programs, communication consists of simple assignments for *mg* as explained in Fig. 8 and an overloaded HTA-aware **permute** operation for *ft* as explained in Fig. 10. Another metric worth measuring is the degree of similarity of parallel programs to the serial versions. HTA programs look very similar, in style and size, to the serial programs written in MATLAB^{TM} , while MPI programs look drastically different from their serial versions. Readers should note that NAS benchmarks are very well written and are easily readable; programs written by less experienced MPI programmers are more complex.

7   Related Works

Languages for Parallel Programming have been an object of research for very long time. Several experimental languages and compilers have been developed so far. Prominent among them is High Performance Fortran [2]. HPF is an extension to FORTRAN that provides new constructs to define the type of data distribution and mapping of data chunks into processors. However, a key drawback in HPF is the inability to operate on a tile (chunk) as a whole. The programmer must explicitly compute the tile sizes and their indexes for each distributed array for each processor. The second drawback is the lack of transparency in communication of data elements across processors. For instance, the main loop in the matrix multiplication program using cannon's algorithm would look like that in Fig. 13. The code in the figure assumes block distribution along both the dimensions of the matrices.

A more closely related work to ours is ZPL [6]. ZPL defines a **region** of a specified shape and size that can be distributed using any specified **distribution** on any specified **grid**. Using the **indexed sequential arrays**, one can build

```
for i= 1, nprow
  blocksize = n/nprow
  FORALL (j=1:nprow, k=1:npcol)
    j_b = (j-1)*blocksize + 1
    j_e = j_b + blocksize - 1
    k_b = (k-1)*blocksize + 1
    k_e = k_b + blocksize - 1
    c( j_b:j_e, k_b:k_e) = c( j_b:j_e, k_b:k_e) + &
      matmul(a(j_b:j_e, k_b:k_e), b(j_b:j_e, k_b:k_e))
  ENDFORALL
  a = cshift( a, blocksize, 2 )
  b = cshift( b, blocksize, 1 )
enddo
```

Fig. 13. HPF - Main loop in Cannon's algorithm

```
region     R = [1..n, 1..n];
direction  north = [-1, 0]; south = [ 1, 0];
           east  = [ 0, 1]; west  = [ 0,-1];
[R]  repeat
       Temp := (A@north+A@east+A@west+A@south) / 4.0;
       err  := max<< abs(A-Temp);
       A    := Temp;
     until err < tolerance;
     end;
```

Fig. 14. ZPL - Main loop in Jacobi

a structure similar to HTA, with operations on tiles as a whole. However, ZPL is still not transparent to the programmer and it is of higher level than HTA. For instance, in ZPL the programmer never knows where and how the exchange of data occurs, in a case like *jacobi*. Lack of such a transparency might lead to programs that are difficult to debug. Fig 14 shows the main part of *jacobi* implementation in ZPL.

8   Conclusions

In this paper we have presented a novel approach to write parallel programs in object-oriented languages using a class called Hierarchically Tiled Arrays (HTAs). HTAs allow the expression of parallel computation and data movement by means of indexed assignment and computation operators that overload those of the host language. HTAs improve the ability of the programmer to reason about a parallel program, particularly when compared to the code written using SPMD programming model. HTA tiling can also be used to express memory locality in linear algebra routines.

We have implemented our new data type as a MATLAB^{TM} toolbox. We have successfully written three NAS benchmark kernels in the MATLAB^{TM} + HTA environment. The kernels are easy to read, understand and maintain, as the examples shown through our paper illustrate. We discovered two key overheads suffered by HTA codes, both related to details of our current implementation. First, the current implementation combines the interpreted execution of MATLAB^{TM} with the need to broadcast each command to a remote server. This could be mitigated in the future by more intelligent ahead-of-time broadcasting of commands or by the deployment of a compiler. The second cause of overhead is the need to use intermediate buffering and to replicate pieces of data. This is not because of algorithmic requirements, but due to the need to operate inside the MATLAB^{TM} environment. This effect can be improved by more careful implementation.

In summary, we consider the HTA toolbox to be a powerful tool for the prototyping and design of parallel algorithms and we plan to make it publicly available soon along with the benchmark suite.

References

1. Nas Parallel Benchmarks. Website. http://www.nas.nasa.gov/Software/NPB/.
2. High performance fortran forum. *High Performance Fortran Specification Version 2.0*, January 1997.
3. G. Almasi, L. De Rose, B.B. Fraguela, J. Moreira, and D. Padua. Programming for locality and parallelism with hierarchically tiled arrays. In *Proc. of the 16th International Workshop on Languages and Compilers for Parallel Computing, LCPC 2003*, to be published in Lecture Notes in Computer Science, vol. 2958, College Station, Texas, Oct 2003. Springer-Verlag.
4. L.E. Cannon. *A cellular computer to implement the Kalman Filter Algorithm*. PhD thesis, Montana State University, 1969.
5. W. Carlson, J. Draper, D. Culler, K. Yelick, E. Brooks, and K. Warren. Introduction to upc and language specification. Technical Report CCS-TR-99-157, IDA Center for Computing Sciences, 1999.
6. B.L. Chamberlin, S.Choi, E.C. Lewis, C. Lin, L. Synder, and W.D. Weathersby. The case for high level parallel programming in ZPL. *IEEE Computational Science and Engineering*, 5(3):76–86, July–September 1998.
7. Al Geist, Adam Beguelin, Jack Dongarra, Weicheng Jiang, Robert Manchek, and Vaidyalingam S. Sunderam. *PVM: Parallel Virtual Machine: A Users' Guide and Tutorial for Networked Parallel Computing*. MIT Press, Cambridge, MA, USA, 1994.
8. W. Gropp, E. Lusk, and A. Skjellum. *Using MPI (2nd ed.): Portable Parallel Programming with the Message-Passing Interface*. MIT Press, 1999.
9. S. Hiranandani, K. Kennedy, and C.-W. Tseng. Compiling fortran d for mimd distributed-memory machines. *Commun. ACM*, 35(8):66–80, 1992.
10. C. Koelbel and P. Mehrotra. An overview of high performance fortran. *SIGPLAN Fortran Forum*, 11(4):9–16, 1992.
11. R. W. Numrich and J. Reid. Co-array fortran for parallel programming. *SIGPLAN Fortran Forum*, 17(2):1–31, 1998.

A Geometric Approach for Partitioning N-Dimensional Non-rectangular Iteration Spaces

Arun Kejariwal[1], Paolo D'Alberto[1], Alexandru Nicolau[1],
and Constantine D. Polychronopoulos[2]

[1] Center for Embedded Computer Systems,
University of California at Irvine,
Irvine, CA 92697, USA
arun_kejariwal@computer.org
{paolo, nicolau}@cecs.uci.edu
http://www.cecs.uci.edu/
[2] Center for Supercomputing Research and Development,
University of Illinois at Urbana-Champaign,
Urbana, IL 61801, USA
cdp@csrd.uiuc.edu
http://www.csrd.uiuc.edu/

Abstract. Parallel loops account for the greatest percentage of program parallelism. The degree to which parallelism can be exploited and the amount of overhead involved during parallel execution of a nested loop directly depend on partitioning, i.e., the way the different iterations of a parallel loop are distributed across different processors. Thus, partitioning of parallel loops is of key importance for high performance and efficient use of multiprocessor systems. Although a significant amount of work has been done in partitioning and scheduling of rectangular iteration spaces, the problem of partitioning of non-rectangular iteration spaces - e.g. triangular, trapezoidal iteration spaces - has not been given enough attention so far. In this paper, we present a geometric approach for partitioning N-dimensional non-rectangular iteration spaces for optimizing performance on parallel processor systems. Speedup measurements for kernels (loop nests) of linear algebra packages are presented.

1 Introduction

High-level parallelization approaches target the exploitation of regular parallelism at loop-nest level for high performance and efficient use of multiprocessors systems [1,2,3]. For example, one approach is to distribute the iterations of a nested loop across multiple processors, also known as *loop spreading*. The efficiency (and usefulness) of loop spreading depends on the ability to detect and partition the independent iterations in a manner that distributes the load uniformly across different processors. Though partitioning loop nests with rectangular iteration spaces has received a lot of attention [4,5], the problem of

R. Eigenmann et al. (Eds.): LCPC 2004, LNCS 3602, pp. 102–116, 2005.
© Springer-Verlag Berlin Heidelberg 2005

partitioning nested loops with non-rectangular iteration spaces has not been given enough attention so far, except in [6,7]. However, the approaches proposed in [6,7] do not partition the iteration space uniformly across different processors and have several limitations, as discussed in Section 7.

In this paper, we focus on the problem of partitioning parallel loop nests with N-dimensional non-rectangular iteration spaces. [1] We present a geometric approach to partition an iteration space for optimizing performance i.e. achieving minimum execution time on a minimum number of processors and achieving balanced work load among processors. We partition an iteration space along the axis corresponding to the outermost loop and achieve a near-optimal partition. The partition thus obtained consists of *contiguous* sets, unlike the approach discussed in [7], which facilitate exploitation of data locality. Furthermore, our approach obviates the need to remap the index expressions and loop bounds of inner loops, in contrast to linearization-based approaches [8,9]. Thus, our approach provides a simple, practical and intuitive solution to the problem of iteration space partitioning. In this paper, we only consider loop nests with no loop-carried dependences. Discussion about partitioning of loops with loop-carried dependences is beyond the scope of this paper.

The rest of the paper is organized as follows - in Section 2, we present an intuitive idea behind iteration space partitioning with an illustrative example. Section 3 presents the terminology used in the rest of the paper. In Section 4 we present a formal description of the problem. Next, we present our partitioning scheme. Section 6 presents our experimental results. Next, we present previous work. Finally we conclude with directions for future work.

2   Iteration Space Partitioning

Consider the loop nest shown in Figure 1. The corresponding iteration space is shown in Figure 1(b). Note that the loop nest has a *triangular* geometry in the (i_1, i_2) plane and a rectangular geometry in the (i_1, i_3) plane. Assuming 3 processors are available, one can partition the outermost loop into three sets along the i_1-axis, as shown in Figure 2(a). [2] The cardinality of the sets thus obtained is as follows (from left to right in Figure 2(a)): $|S(1,3)| = 18$, $|S(3,5)| = 42$ and $|S(5,7)| = 66$, where $S(x,y) = \{i | x \leq i_1 < y\}$.

However, one can interchange the loops corresponding to the loop indices i_1 and i_3 before partitioning. The sets thus obtained have equal cardinality, i.e., $|S(1,3)| = |S(3,5)| = |S(5,7)|$, as shown in Figure 2(b). Unfortunately, in general, such partitioning may be impossible or impractical due to the following reasons: firstly, an equi-partitionable axis may not exist in a given N-dimensional

---

[1] Naturally, our technique can also handle rectangular loop nests too.

[2] Though an iteration space can be partitioned along an axis corresponding to an inner loop, however, it requires remapping of the index expressions (due to affine loop bounds) which introduces significant overhead. Therefore, we always partition an iteration space along the axis corresponding to the outermost loop.

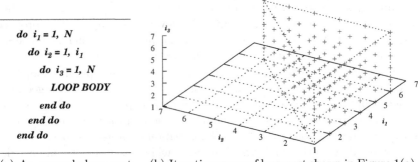

(a) An example loop nest   (b) Iteration space of loop nest shown in Figure 1(a), $N = 6$

Fig. 1. Partitioning non-rectangular iteration space

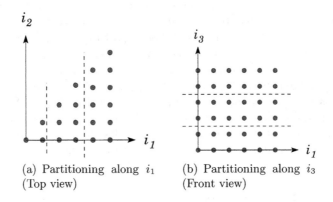

(a) Partitioning along i_1 (b) Partitioning along i_3
(Top view)   (Front view)

Fig. 2. Effect of geometry of an iteration space on partitioning

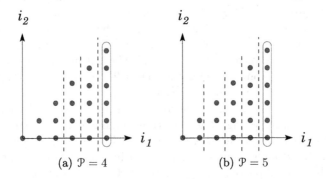

(a) $\mathcal{P} = 4$ (b) $\mathcal{P} = 5$

Fig. 3. Determining the number of processors ($\leq \mathcal{P}$) for optimal performance based on the minimum size of the largest partition

convex polytope; secondly, determining functions for the loop bounds of the permuted loop is non-trivial.

In practice, it is imperative to take into account the iteration space geometry to achieve a balanced work load distribution amongst the different sets of a partition. Also, the number of processors plays an important role in the efficient partitioning of a parallel loop nest. For example, we may partition the iteration space of Figure 1(b) across 4 and 5 processors. The corresponding partitions are shown in Figures 3(a) and 3(b) respectively. We observe that the size of the largest set (represented by boxes in Figures 3(a) and 3(b)) is the same in both the cases, and so is the execution time - if we exclude the scheduling overhead. However, unlike the partition in Figure 3(a), the partition of Figure 3(b) may incur additional scheduling overhead (e.g., communication due to an extra processor and partition) with no performance gain. Thus, efficient processor allocation may also be important during iteration space partitioning.

3   Terminology

Let $\mathcal{L}$ denote a perfect nest of DOALL loops as shown in Figure 4. Without loss of any generality, we assume that the outermost loop is normalized from 1 to N with $s_1 = 1$.[3] The **index variables** of the individual loops are $i_1, i_2, \ldots, i_n$ and they compose an **index vector** $\mathbf{i} = (i_1, i_2, \ldots, i_n)$. An instance of the index vector $\mathbf{i}$ is an **iteration**. The set of iterations of a loop nest $\mathcal{L}$ is an **iteration space** $\Gamma = \{\mathbf{i}\}$. We model an iteration space as a convex polytope in $\mathbb{Z}^n$.

The lower and upper bounds (e.g., f_3 and g_3, respectively) of an index variable (e.g., i_3) are assumed to be affine functions of the outer loop indices (e.g., i_1 and i_2). We assume that $f_j \leq g_j$ for $1 \leq j \leq n - 1$.

---

doall $i_1 = 1,\ N,\ s_1$
  doall $i_2 = f_1(i_1),\ g_1(i_1),\ s_2$
    .
      .
        doall $i_n = f_{n-1}(i_1, i_2, \ldots, i_{n-1}),\ g_{n-1}(i_1, i_2, \ldots, i_{n-1}),\ s_n$
      H(i)
        end doall
      .
  end doall
end doall

Fig. 4. A perfectly nested DOALL loop

---

[3] Note that the lower and upper bound of the outermost loop can be any two real numbers $x, y \in \mathbb{R}$. Loops with real bounds are common in numerical applications [10] such as the Newton-Raphson method and Runge-Kutta method.

The set of hyperplanes, defined by $i_1 = 1, i_1 = N, i_r = f_{r-1}$ and $i_r = g_{r-1}$ for $2 \leq r \leq n$, determine the *geometry* of an iteration space. For example, if $f_r = l_r$ and $g_r = u_r$ where $l_r, u_r \in \mathbb{Z}$ (i.e., constant bounds) for $1 \leq r \leq n - 1$, then the geometry of Γ is a rectangular parallelepiped. In this paper, we consider iteration spaces with complex geometries (e.g. tetrahedral, prismoidal) and with different, but constant, strides along each dimension. Of course, our technique can handle simpler, more regular loops as well.

Definition 1. *For each* $x, y \in \mathbb{R}$ *such that* $x < y$, *an* **elementary set** $S(x, y)$ *in* Γ *is defined as follows :* $S(x, y) = \{i | i \in \Gamma, x \leq i_1 < y\}$.

Let $\beta(\Gamma) = \{\gamma_k, k = 1, 2, \ldots, m\}$ denote a set of **breakpoints** of the outermost loop of $\mathcal{L}$ such that $\gamma_1 < \gamma_2 < \ldots < \gamma_m$, where $\gamma_k \in \mathbb{R}$ and $m \leq \mathcal{P} \leq N$, $\mathcal{P}$ is a set of identical processors. A **boundary set** B_{γ_k} in Γ is a set of iterations $B_{\gamma_k} = \{i | i \in \Gamma, i_1 = \gamma_k, \text{and } \gamma_k \in \beta(\Gamma), \gamma_k \in \mathbb{Z}\}$, i.e. B_{γ_k} is a set of all iterations that lie on a hyperplane corresponding to an integer breakpoint.

Definition 2. *A* **contiguous outermost partition** *of* Γ *is defined as follows:* $Q_{\beta(\Gamma)} = \{S(\gamma_k, \gamma_{k+1}) \mid \bigcup_{\forall k} S(\gamma_k, \gamma_{k+1}) \text{ and } \gamma_k \in \beta(\Gamma)\}$.

4   Problem Statement

The execution time of an elementary set $S(\gamma_i, \gamma_{i+1})$ is proportional to the number of iterations, $|S(\gamma_i, \gamma_{i+1})|$, in the set. Therefore, the **execution time of a contiguous outermost partition** is

$$T(Q_{\beta(\Gamma)}) = \max_{\gamma_i \in \beta(\Gamma)} |S(\gamma_i, \gamma_{i+1})| \times t_{LB} \tag{1}$$

where, t_{LB} is the execution time of the innermost loop body (from hereon, we omit t_{LB}, being a constant,[4] in future discussions). Now, we present a rigorous formulation of the problems we want to solve.

Problem 1 (Minimum execution time). Given an iteration space Γ and $\mathcal{P}$ processors, find a contiguous outermost partition $Q_{\beta(\Gamma)}$ so as to minimize the execution time:

$$\mathcal{T}_{\min}(\Gamma, \mathcal{P}) = \min_{|\beta(\Gamma)| = \mathcal{P} - 1} T(Q_{\beta(\Gamma)}) \tag{2}$$

However, as shown in Figure 3(b), there may exist two (or more) contiguous outermost partitions (e.g., $\beta_1(\Gamma)$ and $\beta_1(\Gamma)$) having a different number of processors (e.g. $\mathcal{P}_1 < \mathcal{P}_2$) but with the same execution time (e.g., $T(Q_{\beta_1(\Gamma)}) = T(Q_{\beta_2(\Gamma)})$). Therefore, we need to find an optimal number of processors so as to minimize the scheduling overhead and maximize efficiency. More precisely, the **processor partition** problem can be stated as follows:

---

[4] We assume that the loop body $H(i)$ has the same execution time in each iteration.

Problem 2 (Minimum processor number). Given a minimum execution time $\mathcal{T}_{\min}(\Gamma, \mathcal{P})$ for $\mathcal{P}$ processors, find the minimum number of processors $\mathcal{P}_{\min} \leq \mathcal{P}$ such that :

$$\mathcal{T}_{\min}(\Gamma, \mathcal{P}_{\min}) \leq \mathcal{T}_{\min}(\Gamma, \mathcal{P})$$

5   The Approach

In this section, we present our algorithm for partitioning an iteration space Γ across $\mathcal{P}$ processors, with an illustrative example.

First, we compute a partial volume, denoted by $\mathcal{V}(x)$ in Algorithm 1, of the convex polytope corresponding to the loop nest $\mathcal{L}$ as a function of the outermost index variable. [5] In presence of affine loop bounds, a closed form of the partial volume can be obtained using mathematical packages like Matlab [30]. Note that $\mathcal{V}(x)$ is a non-linear polynomial. Then we compute the total volume of the convex polytope using Equation (3). Next, we determine the breakpoints, using Equation (4), along the i_1-axis for partitioning Γ across the given processors. Note that Equation (4) is a non-linear equation. In case of a quadratic equation, closed form of the roots may be used to determine the breakpoints. However, it is important to note that the same approach is not viable for higher (> 2) degree polynomials as it is non-trivial to determine the closed form of their roots and is impossible for polynomial equations higher than fourth degree as stated by Abel's Impossibility Theorem [31]. To alleviate this problem, we use binary search to determine the breakpoints. The solution of Equation (4) corresponds to the kth breakpoint γ_k. [6] In contrast, algebraic approaches [6,7,11] solve a system of $\mathcal{P}$ simultaneous equations to determine the breakpoints, which incurs significant overhead. The breakpoints thus obtained define the boundaries of the elementary sets in Γ.

Note that unlike the approach presented in [7], the sets obtained by our approach are contiguous which eliminates the need for multiple loops, required in case of non-contiguous sets. Furthermore, contiguous sets facilitate exploitation of data locality. In contrast, previous approaches [6,7] balance load across different processors at the expense of data locality, as the sets obtained by applying these approaches are non-contiguous.

Next, we eliminate the void sets, i.e., the sets which do not contain any index points and the corresponding breakpoints. The remaining sets are allocated to each processor. Given a minimum size of the largest set, the elimination process reduces the total number of sets which in turn minimizes the scheduling overhead. The (integer) lower and upper bounds of the loops corresponding to each set are determined using the Equations 5 and 6 respectively. The algorithm is formally presented as Algorithm 1 on page 108.

---

[5] Assuming constant loop strides, partial volume is proportional to the number of index points in it.

[6] Note that $\mathcal{V}(x)$ is a monotonically increasing function of x. Therefore, there exists only one real solution of Equation (4).

Algorithm 1. Near-Optimal Partitioning of N-dimensional Non-Rectangular
Iteration Spaces

Input : An N-dimensional non-rectangular iteration space Γ and $\mathcal{P}$ processors.

Output : A near-optimal (w.r.t. load balance amongst the different processors)
partition of the iteration space.

/* Compute the partial volume $\mathcal{V}(x)$ of Γ' */

$$\mathcal{V}(x) = \int_1^x \int_{f_1}^{g_1} \ldots \int_{f_{n-1}}^{g_{n-1}} di_1 di_2 \ldots di_n$$

/* Compute the total volume $\mathcal{V}$ of Γ */

$$\mathcal{V} = \int_1^N \int_{f_1}^{g_1} \ldots \int_{f_{n-1}}^{g_{n-1}} di_1 di_2 \ldots di_n \tag{3}$$

/* Determine the kth breakpoint γ_k. For $1 < k < (\mathcal{P} - 1)$, determine the *
* solution of Equation (4) using binary search */

$$\mathcal{V}(\gamma_k) = \frac{k}{\mathcal{P}} \times \mathcal{V} \tag{4}$$

$\beta(\Gamma) = \{\gamma_1, \gamma_2, \ldots, \gamma_{\mathcal{P}-1}\}$

/* Eliminate void sets */

$i \leftarrow 0, \ E \leftarrow 0$

while $i \neq |\beta(\Gamma)|$ **do**

    if $\lfloor \gamma_i \rfloor = \lfloor \gamma_{i+1} \rfloor$ **then**

        $\beta(\Gamma) \leftarrow \beta(\Gamma) - \{\gamma_i\}$

        $i \leftarrow i - 1, \ E \leftarrow E + 1$

    end if

    $i \leftarrow i + 1$

end while

/* Determine the loop bounds for the remaining $\mathcal{P} - E$ sets */

$$lb_k = \begin{cases} 1, & \text{if } k = 1 \\ ub_{k-1} + 1, & \text{otherwise} \end{cases} \tag{5} \qquad ub_k = \begin{cases} \gamma_k - 1, & \text{if } \gamma_k = \lfloor \gamma_k \rfloor \\ \lfloor \gamma_k \rfloor, & \text{if } \gamma_k \neq \lfloor \gamma_k \rfloor \\ N, & \text{if } k = \mathcal{P} - E \end{cases} \tag{6}$$

where, lb and ub are the integer lower and upper bounds of an elementary set.

Note that, enumeration-based approaches may be used alternatively for computing the volume of a convex polytope. However, such techniques are not applicable in the presence of *ceiling* and *floor* functions in the loop bounds. [7] Furthermore, enumeration-based techniques such as [6,7] are not viable in the presence of non-unit strides. In fact, when the loop is normalized so that all index variables have unit stride, a non-linear constraint may appear in the loop bound. A similar problem is encountered during the data cache interference analysis for scientific computations. The non-linear constraint can be reduced to a linear one but with the introduction of further constraints. The authors of Omega Test and Polylib ([13,14]) formalize this transformation and propose a valid solution for the enumeration of rather complex iteration spaces. Nonetheless, the enumeration may be impractical for non-unit strides. In any case, our volumetric approach provides a simple, integrated and intuitive solution to the partitioning and processor allocation problem.

Let us now examine the behavior of our algorithm on the example shown in Figure 1(a). First, we compute a partial volume of the convex polytope as a function of the outermost index variable. Next, we compute the volume of the convex polytope corresponding to the iteration space Γ. The total and partial volumes are given by:

$$\mathscr{V} = \int_1^N \int_1^{i_1} \int_1^N di_3 \, di_2 \, di_1 \; = \; 62.5$$

$$\mathscr{V}(x) = \int_1^x \int_1^{i_1} \int_1^N di_3 \, di_2 \, di_1 \; = \; (N-1)\frac{(x-1)^2}{2}$$

Notice that alternatively, enumeration-based approaches may apply for the computation of volumes as follows:

$$\Xi = \sum_{i_1=1}^N \sum_{i_2=1}^{i_1} \sum_{i_3=1}^N 1 \; = \; N \cdot \sum_{i_1=1}^N \sum_{i_2=1}^{i_1} 1 \; = \; N \cdot \sum_{i_1=1}^N i_1 \; = \; \frac{N^2(N+1)}{2}$$

Next, assuming 5 processors, we determine the breakpoints for the iteration space of Figure 1(b) are:

$$\frac{(\gamma_1-1)^2}{2}(N-1) = \frac{1}{5}\mathscr{V} \;\; \Rightarrow \; \gamma_1 = 3.2, \qquad \frac{(\gamma_2-1)^2}{2}(N-1) = \frac{2}{5}\mathscr{V} \;\; \Rightarrow \; \gamma_2 = 4.1$$

$$\frac{(\gamma_3-1)^2}{2}(N-1) = \frac{3}{5}\mathscr{V} \;\; \Rightarrow \; \gamma_3 = 4.8, \qquad \frac{(\gamma_4-1)^2}{2}(N-1) = \frac{4}{5}\mathscr{V} \;\; \Rightarrow \; \gamma_4 = 5.4$$

For simplicity, in this example we use the closed form of the roots of a quadratic equation to determine the breakpoints. Next, we eliminate the void

---

[7] Floors and ceilings in loop bounds may arise after applying unimodular transformations [12]. Similarly, in many real applications, rational loop bounds can be found. In such cases, it is essential to convert the loop bounds to integers using the functions *ceiling* and *floor*.

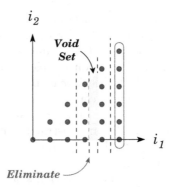

Fig. 5. Elimination of void sets

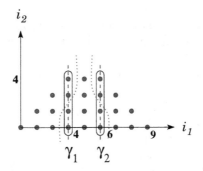

Fig. 6. Iteration space partitioning in presence of integer breakpoints

sets i.e. the sets which do not contain any index points and the corresponding breakpoints, as shown in Figure 5. Next, we determine the lower and upper bounds of the remaining sets using the equations 5 and 6 respectively. The new loop bounds for the partition shown in Figure 5 are given by:

$$(lb_1, ub_1) = (1, 4), \quad (lb_2, ub_2) = (4, 4), \quad (lb_3, ub_3) = (5, 5), \quad (lb_4, ub_4) = (6, 6)$$

In the previous example, we assume that sets with equal volumes contain same number of iterations. It is important to note that the assumption is valid only if $\gamma_i \in \mathbb{R} - \mathbb{Z} \ \forall i$. In presence of integer breakpoints, the iterations belonging to the corresponding boundary set must be allocated to either one adjoining elementary sets. This introduces load imbalance in the resulting partition. In Algorithm 1, we allocate such iterations to the elementary set on the right. For example, consider the iteration space shown in Figure 6. Assuming 3 processors, from Figure 6 we observe that $\gamma_1, \gamma_2 \in \mathbb{Z}$. The cardinality of the contiguous sets obtained from Algorithm 1 is 6, 8 and 10.

Ideally, in this case the iterations in each boundary set must be distributed equally amongst the adjoining elementary sets in order to achieve perfect load balance. The boundaries corresponding to such a (optimal) partition is shown by dotted lines in Figure 6. However, such a distribution is not possible as the iteration space is partitioned only along the axis corresponding to the outer-most loop. In the worst case, one might have to distribute the iterations in a boundary set equally amongst different processors. We now present a bound on performance deviation of the partition obtained by Algorithm 1 from the optimal partition.

Remark 1. Given any contiguous outermost partition $Q_{\beta(\Gamma)}$ determined by Algorithm 1, we have

$$0 \leq \mathcal{T}(Q_{\beta(\Gamma)}) - \mathcal{T}_{\mathrm{opt}}(\Gamma, \mathcal{P}) \leq \max_{\gamma_i \in \beta(\Gamma) \cap \mathbb{Z}} \frac{|B_{\gamma_i}| + |B_{\gamma_{i+1}}|}{\mathcal{P}} \qquad (7)$$

where, $\mathcal{T}_{\mathrm{opt}}(\Gamma, \mathcal{P})$ corresponds to the execution time of the optimal partition.

Any elementary set $S_i \in Q_{\beta(\Gamma)}$ is bounded by at most two hyperplanes $i_1 = \gamma_i$ and $i_1 = \gamma_{i+1}$. In Remark 1, if $\gamma_{i+1} \notin \mathbb{Z}$, then $|B_{\gamma_{i+1}}| = 0$.

So far, we have only considered perfect loop nests. However, our algorithm can be applied to *multiway* loop nests[8] in a similar fashion. Likewise, our approach can be easily extended to handle non-constant strides. Detailed discussion of the above is outside the scope of this paper.

6   Experiments

To illustrate our algorithm's behavior, we experimented with different loop nests taken from linear algebra packages and the literature. Table 1 lists the loop nests - the geometry of their iteration spaces and their source. The loops were partitioned using Algorithm 1. Subsequently, we refer to our approach as *VOL* and the canonical loop partitioning technique as *CAN*.

First, we illustrate the effect of contiguous sets on performance. For the same, we partitioned loop L_1 uniformly across P processors. Since L_1 has rectangular geometry, both our approach and *CAN* result in the same number of iterations per processor. Thus, since both approaches have identical workload on each processor, the difference in performance, refer to Figure 7, can be attributed to data locality effects associated with contiguous sets, as explained in Section 5. Note that, our approach generates contiguous sets even with non-rectangular iteration spaces, thus facilitating exploitation of data locality in such iteration spaces as well.

Next, we illustrate the performance of our algorithm for non-rectangular iteration spaces. For this, we determine the size (cardinality) of the largest set of partitions corresponding to each technique. Note that the size of the largest set in a partition correlates to the performance of that partitioning scheme. Table 2 presents the size of the largest set corresponding to our approach and (for comparison purposes) *CAN*. From Table 2 we observe that our approach results in

---

[8] A loop is *multiway nested* if there are two or more loops at the same level. Note that the loops may be nested themselves[15].

Table 1. Geometries of the loop kernels. For each loop, N=1000

#	Geometry	Source
L_1	Rectangular	SSYRK routine (BLAS3)
L_2	Tetrahedral	[7]
L_3	Trapezoidal	Appendix A [16]
L_4	Rhomboidal	Appendix A [16]
L_5	Parallelepiped	pp. 58 [17]

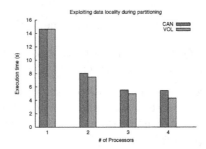

Fig. 7. Impact of data locality on performance of loop nest L_1 (see Table 1)

Table 2. Performance (size of the largest set of a partition) of our geometric approach and canonical loop partitioning

Loop	# of Processors							
	2		4		8		16	
Nest	VOL	CAN	VOL	CAN	VOL	CAN	VOL	CAN
L_2	83368284	83596878	41810044	43807393	21003180	22397760	10738024	11538395
L_3	476000	516000	219900	225037	109500	112056	55000	57232
L_4	200000	-	100000	-	50000	-	25000	-
L_5	25000	-	12500	-	6250	-	3150	-

smaller sizes of the largest set i.e. more uniform distribution of iterations across different processors. The difference in performance can be attributed to the fact that our approach accounts for the geometry of an iteration space during partitioning. We observe that the difference in performance decreases (expectedly) with increasing number of processors, as the volume of each set in a partition also decreases.

As explained earlier, the applicability of *CAN* is restricted to canonical loops only, which explains the presence of dashes for loop nests L_4 and L_5 (non-canonical loop nests) for *CAN*. Furthermore, in case of large number of processors, we also address processor allocation issues which eliminates the communication overhead due to extra processors and ensures efficient use of the processors.

7 Previous Work

It has been shown that loops without dependences among their iterations (traditionally known as DOALLs [18]) are a rich source of parallelism [19]. In addition, several compiler techniques [20] have been proposed to convert loops with inter-iteration dependences to DOALL loops for parallel execution. However, once this is done, the problem is how to partition the iteration space of the DOALLs across a given number of processors so as to minimize execution time and optimize processor utilization.

In [21], Anik et al. discuss several models for parallel execution of nested loops. The simplest model is to execute the outermost loop in parallel and all the inner parallel loops sequentially. Another model involves *collapsing* [22] the nested loops into a single loop using compiler transformations. In another model, the inner loops are executed in parallel and a blocking barrier is used at the end of each parallel loop, which prevents the overlapping between execution of inner loops.

Techniques such as loop concurrentization [23] partition the set of iterations of a loop and assigns a different subset to each processor. Irigoin and Triolet's *supernode partitioning* approach [24] divides an iteration space of a loop nest into nodes with several goals : vector computation within a node, loop tiling for data reuse and parallelism between tiles. In [7], Sakellariou discusses the necessary condition for partitioning a loop nest across different processors with *equal* workload. Based on whether the iterations are distributed among processors before or during run-time, loop partitioning can be classified as *static* or *dynamic*. In *static* partitioning, each processor is assigned a fixed number of iterations such that the distribution among processors is as even as possible. The most common approaches for *static* partitioning are:

- ❏ *Cyclic partitioning (CP)* : It distributes the iterations in a round robin fashion; thus given n iterations and p processors, processor i executes iterations $i + kp$, $k = 0, 1, \ldots, n/p$. However, this approach may deteriorate performance due to *false sharing*.[9]
- ❏ *Block partitioning (BP)* [25] : This approach maps contiguous iterations onto processors in a consecutive manner; thus a processor i executes iterations $in/p + 1$ through $(i + 1)n/p$. The efficiency of BP is governed by the block size. Assuming zero scheduling overhead, the optimal block size is $k = \lceil n/p \rceil$ number of iterations.
- ❏ *Balanced chunk scheduling (BCS)* [26] : BCS attempts to distribute the total number of iterations of the loop body among processors as evenly as possible as opposed to cyclic and block partitioning which distribute only the

---

[9] *False sharing* occurs when multiple processors access data in the same cache line and one of the accesses is a 'write', thus causing the cache line to be exchanged between processors even though the processors access different parts of it.

iterations of the outer loop. An example of the latter is shown in Appendix B of [7]. However, Haghighat and Polychronopolous restrict their discussion to double loops.

☐ *Canonical loop partitioning (CAN)* [7] : Sakellariou introduce a notion of *canonical loop nest* for loop partitioning. CAN assumes that the outermost loop can be equi-partitioned into $2p^{m-1}$ parts, where p is the number of processors and m is the depth of a loop nest. However, this may generate empty sets which leads to load imbalance. Moreover, CAN generates a fragmented partition i.e. each individual set is a collection of non-contiguous subsets. CAN employs an enumeration-based approach to determine the total number of index points in an iteration space. It relies on loop normalization in the presence of non-unit strides. However the introduction of floors and ceilings renders this approach nonviable in practice (see Section 5). Furthermore, determination of the set boundaries in CAN is very cumbersome.

Similarly, Boyle et al. [11] present an approach for load balancing of parallel affine loops using unimodular transformations. Their approach transforms a loop into a load balanced form, i.e. it identifies an index variable i_k, referred to as an invariant iterator, that neither makes any reference to any other index variable in its loop bounds, nor is referenced by any other index variable and reorders the iterations to move i_k as far out as possible. However, this approach relies on the existence of an invariant iterator which restricts it's applicability to rectangular iteration spaces only. Similarly, several techniques have been proposed in [27,28,29] for mapping affine loops on to multiple processors. However, these techniques focus primarily on communication minimization between the processors.

8   Conclusions

In this paper we presented an algorithm for partitioning N-dimensional iteration spaces. Unlike previous approaches [6,7], we follow a geometric approach for partitioning an iteration space. The partition thus obtained consists of contiguous sets, which facilitates exploitation of data locality. Our approach provides an integrated solution to the partitioning and processor allocation problems. Our experiments show that our approach has better performance than the CAN partitioning technique. As future work, we would like to extend our approach to partition iteration spaces at run-time.

Acknowledgments

The first author is highly grateful to Dr. Utpal Banerjee for the discussions, comments and suggestions which helped a lot in preparing the final version of the paper. He would like to thank Rafael Lopez, Carmen Badea and Radu Cornea for their help and feedback.

References

1. D. A. Padua. Multiprocessors: Discussion of theoritical and practical problems. Technical Report 79-990, Dept. of Computer Science, University of Illinois at Urbana-Champaign, November 1979.
2. R. Cytron. Doacross: Beyond vectorization for multiprocessors. In *Proceedings of the 1986 International Conference on Parallel Processing*, St. Charles, IL, August 1986.
3. J. Davies. Parallel loop constructs for multiprocessors. Technical Report 81-1070, Dept. of Computer Science, University of Illinois at Urbana-Champaign, May 1981.
4. C. Polychronopoulos, D. J. Kuck, and D. A. Padua. Execution of parallel loops on parallel processor systems. In *Proceedings of the 1986 International Conference on Parallel Processing*, pages 519–527, August 1986.
5. E. H. D'Hollander. Partitioning and labeling of loops by unimodular transformations. *IEEE Trans. Parallel Distrib. Syst.*, 3(4):465–476, 1992.
6. Mohammad R. Haghighat and Constantine D. Polychronopoulos. Symbolic analysis for parallelizing compilers. *ACM Transactions on Programming Languages and Systems*, 18(4):477–518, July 1996.
7. R. Sakellariou. *On the Quest for Perfect Load Balance in Loop-Based Parallel Computations*. PhD thesis, Department of Computer Science, University of Manchester, October 1996.
8. U. Banerjee. Data dependence in ordinary programs. Master's thesis, Dept. of Computer Science, University of Illinois at Urbana-Champaign, November 1976. Report No. 76-837.
9. M. Burke and R. Cytron. Interprocedural dependence analysis and parallelization. In *Proceedings of the SIGPLAN '86 Symposium on Compiler Construction*, Palo Alto, CA, June 1986.
10. M.K. Iyengar, S.R.K. Jain, and R.K. Jain. *Numerical Methods for Scientific and Engineering Computation*. John Wiley and Sons, 1985.
11. M. O'Boyle and G. A. Hedayat. Load balancing of parallel affine loops by unimodular transformations. Technical Report UMCS-92-1-1, Department of Computer Science, University of Manchester, January 1992.
12. U. Banerjee. *Loop Transformation for Restructuring Compilers*. Kluwer Academic Publishers, Boston, MA, 1993.
13. W. Pugh. The Omega test: A fast and practical integer programming algorithm for dependence analysis. In *Proceedings of Supercomputing '91*, Albuquerque, NM, November 1991.
14. P. Clauss and V. Loechner. Parametric analysis of polyhedral iteration spaces. In IEEE, editor, *Int. Conf. on Application Specific Array Processors*, Chicago, Illinois, August 1996.
15. C. Polychronopoulos. Loop coalescing: A compiler transformation for parallel machines. In S. Sahni, editor, *Proceedings of the 1987 International Conference on Parallel Processing*. Pennsylvania State University Press, August 1987.
16. S. Carr. *Memory-Hierarchy Management*. PhD thesis, Dept. of Computer Science, Rice University, September 1992.
17. U. Banerjee. *Loop Parallelization*. Kluwer Academic Publishers, Boston, MA, 1994.
18. S. Lundstrom and G. Barnes. A controllable MIMD architectures. In *Proceedings of the 1980 International Conference on Parallel Processing*, St. Charles, IL, August 1980.

19. D. Kuck et al. The effects of program restructuring, algorithm change and architecture choice on program performance. In *Proceedings of the 1984 International Conference on Parallel Processing*, August 1984.

20. M. J. Wolfe. *Optimizing Supercompilers for Supercomputers*. The MIT Press, Cambridge, MA, 1989.

21. S. Anik and W. W. Hwu. Executing nested parallel loops on shared-memory multiprocessors. In *Proceedings of the 1992 International Conference on Parallel Processing*, pages III:241–244, Boca Raton, Florida, August 1992.

22. M. J. Wolfe. *High Performance Compilers for Parallel Computing*. Addison-Wesley, Redwood City, CA, 1996.

23. D. A. Padua and M. J. Wolfe. Advanced compiler optimizations for supercomputers. *Communications of the ACM*, 29(12):1184–1201, December 1986.

24. F. Irigoin and R. Triolet. Supernode partitioning. In *Proceedings of the Fifteenth Annual ACM Symposium on the Principles of Programming Languages*, San Diego, CA, January 1988.

25. C. P. Kruskal and A. Weiss. Allocating independent subtasks on parallel processors. *IEEE Transactions on Software Engineering*, 11(10):1001–1016, 1985.

26. M. Haghighat and C. Polychronopoulos. Symbolic program analysis and optimization for parallelizing compilers. In *Proceedings of the Fifth Workshop on Languages and Compilers for Parallel Computing*, New Haven, CT, August 1992.

27. N. Koziris, G. Papakonstantinou, and P. Tsanakas. Mapping nested loops onto distributed memory multiprocessors. In *International Conference on Parallel and Distributed Systems*, pages 35–43, December 1997.

28. M. Dion and Y. Robert. Mapping affine loop nests: new results. In *HPCN Europe 1995*, pages 184–189, 1995.

29. M. Dion and Y. Robert. Mapping affine loop nests. *Parallel Computing*, 22(10):1373–1397, 1996.

30. Matlab. http://www.mathworks.com.

31. Eric W. Weisstein. "Abel's Impossibility Theorem." From MathWorld–A Wolfram Web Resource. http://mathworld.wolfram.com/AbelsImpossibilityTheorem.html.

JuliusC: A Practical Approach for the Analysis of Divide-and-Conquer Algorithms

Paolo D'Alberto and Alexandru Nicolau

School of Information and Computer Science,*
University of California at Irvine
{paolo, nicolau}@ics.uci.edu

Abstract. The development of divide and conquer (D&C) algorithms for matrix computations has led to the widespread use of high-performance scientific applications and libraries. In turn, D&C algorithms can be implemented using loop nests or recursion. Recursion is extremely appealing because it is an intuitive means for the deployment of top-down techniques, which exploit data locality and parallelism naturally. However, recursion has been considered impractical for high-performance codes, mostly because of the inherent overhead of the division process into small subproblems.

In this work, we develop techniques to model the behavior of recursive algorithms in a way suitable for use by a compiler in estimating and reducing the division process overheads. We describe these techniques and JuliusC, a (lite) C compiler, which we developed to exploit them. JuliusC unfolds the application call graph (partially) and extracts the relations among function calls. As a final result, it produces a directed acyclic graph (DAG) modeling the function calls concisely. The approach is a combination of compile-time and run-time analysis and both have negligible complexity.

We illustrate the applicability of our approach by studying 6 test cases. We present the analysis results and we show how our (optimizing) compiler can use these results to increase the efficiency of the division process between 14 to 20 million times, for our codes.

1 Introduction

With the introduction of divide and conquer (**D&C**) algorithms for the solution of matrix computations (e.g., BLAS level 3 [1]), the performance of scientific applications has improved markedly (e.g., Lapack [2]). In practice, D&C computations exploit both spatial and temporal data locality and this data locality results in efficient use of resources in modern uniprocessor and multiprocessor systems. Due to this efficient use of resources, D&C computations can achieve extremely good performance.

* This work has been supported in part by NSF Contract Number ACI 0204028 and by PBK Alumni in Southern California.

R. Eigenmann et al. (Eds.): LCPC 2004, LNCS 3602, pp. 117–131, 2005.
© Springer-Verlag Berlin Heidelberg 2005

D&C algorithms can be *a priori* implemented using either of two language constructs: loop nests or recursion. In this work, we refer to the algorithms implemented using loop nests as **blocked** [3,4], and to those using recursion as **recursive** algorithms [5,6].

Due to the importance of matrix algorithms, practical and efficient solutions of basic matrix computations have been the center of substantial efforts in terms of time (and money) in the last decades. As a result, ready-to-use and highly-tuned libraries for several systems have been proposed and used (e.g., Lapack [2]) and, more recently, self-installing and self-tuning libraries arose as new standards [7,8] delivering astonishingly good performance. Briefly, self-installing and self-tuning libraries extract the parameters of an architecture by profiling; then they tailor the source code to those parameters and, eventually, they tune the application using trial-and-error techniques. These libraries are based on blocked algorithms rather than recursive ones because of two inherent problems of recursive algorithms – which we shall discuss shortly after an brief introduction of recursive algorithms – and because of the following compelling reasons: code legacy (e.g., FORTRAN has no-recursion), small code size (i.e., amenability to traditional aggressive compiler optimizations), negligible overhead and the ability to exploit locality by loop tiling [9].

Recursive algorithms are appealing because of their intuitive formulation and implementation. In fact, they are top-down solutions; they exploit data locality naturally at every level of cache in architectures with deep memory hierarchies [10]; they may present data dependency intuitively and, in turn, they present clear examples for the application of programming constructs driving the practical parallelization along the recursive calls naturally [11]. It is matter of fact, most recursive matrix algorithms, such as matrix multiply and LU-factorization, are *optimal cache oblivious algorithms* [12,13]. That is, they have asymptotically optimal cache reuse at any cache level (without any tuning except for the register file, where some code tuning may further increase performance [14]). Ultimately, recursive algorithms represent an efficient solution using a higher level of abstraction, therefore a more intuitive format, freeing the developer from the details of the architecture on which these applications will run. Despite the above advantages, recursive algorithms have been considered impractical (for high-performance applications) for two reasons.

First, a compiler has a difficult time optimizing at which point the recursion should stop (**leaf computation**). Thus, if only recursion is applied, the leaf computation may have too few instructions leaving little room for optimizations, exploiting little register reuse, and, especially, incurring a high overhead due to the (otherwise avoidable) proliferation of small recursive procedure calls. Otherwise if recursion stops too soon, the leaf computation may be too large to exploit fully cache locality.

Second, any recursive algorithm *inherits* an overhead due to the **division process**, or partitioning, (intrinsic in D&C algorithm) into small subproblems. This overhead is proportional to the number of recursive function calls and to the work involved in computing the actuals of a function call.

Several authors target the solution of the recursive-algorithm problems proposing applications based on both loop nests and recursion [15,14,16]. The division process is implemented by a recursive algorithm, exploiting the *oblivious* data cache locality. The leaf computation is implemented by a blocked algorithm, exploiting aggressive compiler optimizations. These authors propose to stop the recursion at a certain level and then call high-performance non-recursive routines. This is also known as **pruning**. Pruning reduces the number of function calls, and therefore it reduces the overhead (but it does not reduce the work per function call; that is, the computation of the actuals for every function call).

In nowadays-technology scenario where modern systems are always-evolving and, thus, every chip generation is more complex than the previous one, the number of the parameters representing a system must increase (e.g., due to the deployment of several levels of cache). This complexity increase undermines the portability and the efficiency of current self-tuning high-performance applications because probing the parameters, as well as tailoring the source code to an architecture, will become more difficult and then impractical – if not quixotic. In contrast, recursive algorithms assure optimal locality and parallelism with little knowledge of the architecture, therefore recursive algorithms for matrix computations should become increasingly appealing (if only they can be made more efficient by addressing their inherent problems as mentioned previously).

We have previously introduced the concept of a DAG data structure, the **recursion-DAG** (we used the term "**type-DAG**" [14]), to model recursive algorithms; for example, using a hand-coded implementation of the recursion-DAG, we were able to reduce the integer computation – index computation to access matrix elements – by 30% in matrix multiplication [14]. In this paper, we propose an automatic approach for the determination of the recursion-DAG of general recursive algorithms and we have four main contributions:

1. We present techniques to model the run-time unfolding of recursive algorithms concisely and to represent abstractly function calls with the same division work as a single node in a recursion-DAG.

   The recursion-DAG is a concise and precise representation of the computation and we envision its application as support to drive further compiler techniques or optimizations such as dynamic cache mapping [17], automatic parallelization (e.g., using sophisticated abstract data description [18] and in combination with parallelizing techniques or compilers [19]) and leaf size determination (automatic determination of when the recursion should yield control to blocked algorithms).

2. We present **JuliusC** [20], a (lite) C compiler in which we present an implementation of our techniques for the determination of a recursion-DAG. We also show that our implementation, therefore our approach, has practical time complexity and space complexity.

3. We show how the system embodying the above techniques (namely our compiler JuliusC) can be useful as an analysis tool for performance evaluation purposes (profiling) and for software design purposes.

4. To illustrate our techniques and provide a feel for the improvements achievable, we show that we can reduce the division work by 14 or more times for the computation of the binomial coefficients (in fact, the original exponential execution time becomes polynomial) and by 20 millions times for all-pair shortest path of an adjacency matrix (of size 7500×7500). Furthermore, we show that the division-work reduction is a function of: the problem size, the algorithm and the pruning technique.

Notice that in parallel applications on large data sets, the division process constitutes the main overhead and it may be driven by a single processor – in a multiprocessor system. A recursion-DAG may be used to reduce the division work, therefore speeding up the sequential execution of the problem division. Also, a recursion-DAG may assist the parallelization process helping the efficient processor allocation to parallel function calls at run-time; for example, it may help reducing the number of process spawns, therefore reducing initialization time and initialization of communications.

We organize the paper as follows. We start in Section 2 with an example. In Section 3, we introduce the related work mostly on the topic of dynamic programming and partial evaluators of λ-calculus. In Section 4, we show the organization of our compiler. In Section 5, we present a set of linear algebra applications where our approach is applied and we derive statistics useful for compile-time and run-time optimizations.

2   An Example

Briefly, we illustrate the application of JuliusC on the recursive Fast Fourier transform in Fig. 1. Consider that, at run time, JuliusC reaches a function call $fft(*, *, 200, 1)$ (where $*$ is wild, any valid vector pointers). JuliusC then generates a recursion-DAG rooted at the function call $fft(*, *, 200, 1)$. In Fig. 2, we present a graphical representation of the recursion-DAG. Each node in the DAG represents

```
void fft(MATRIX_TYPE *re, MATRIX_TYPE *im, int n, int stride) {
  int p,q,i,prime,k;

  p = find_balance_factorization(n);
  q= n/p;

  /* leaf or n is prime */
  if (n<=LEAF || p==n ) DFT_1(re,im,n,stride,cos(M_PI/n),sin(M_PI/n));
  else {
    for (i=0;i<q;i++) {   // by column
      k = i*stride;
      fft(re+k, im+k,p, stride*q);
    }
    distribute_twiddles(re,im,n,p,q,stride);
    for (i=0;i<p;i++) {   // by row
      k = i*stride*q;
      fft(re+k, im+k,q, stride);
    }
  }

}
```

Fig. 1. Fast Fourier Transform. The factorization is determined at run-time and the recursion stops when n is prime or no larger than $LEAF = 5$

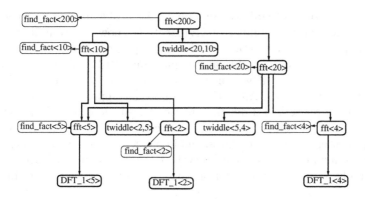

Fig. 2. Recursion-DAG having *fft(*,*,**200**,*)* as root associated with node fft<200>. To simplify the recursion-DAG presentation, **find_fact** stands for *find_balance_factorization* and **twiddle** stands for *distribute_twiddle* as in Fig. 1. Note that every node represents a set of function calls

a function call (of a certain problem size) during the execution of the function call *fft(*,*,**200**,1)*. Embedded in the recursion-DAG, we may recognize a familiar structure: the **plan**, which is used in scientific libraries – e.g., FFTW [16] – to guide the self-installation of recursive algorithms. The only difference is that the recursion-DAG is not a tree (a plan is a binary tree), because of the node fft<5> associated with the function call *fft(*,*,5,*)*. The node fft<5> is a child shared by two nodes-function calls in the recursion-DAG: fft<10> and fft<20>, which are associated with the function calls *fft(*,*,10,*)* and *fft(*,*,20,*)*, respectively.

In Fig. 2, we count only 18 different nodes. Each node is identified by the function name and by an integer summarizing the problem size (i.e., fft<5>). The integer number is determined by the factorization of the problem size of the parent node(s); for example, the number <5> in fft<5> is a factor of both <10> and <20>. So we may store the factorization results in the recursion-DAG, avoiding unnecessary re-computation. For this example, if, in the worst case scenario, the factorization of an integer n takes $O(\sqrt{n})$ operations, the function call *fft(*,*,20,*)* executes $10 * (\sqrt{20}+5\sqrt{2}+4\sqrt{5}) \sim 170$ integer operations for its recursive factorization, and the function call *fft(*,*,10,*)* executes $20 * (\sqrt{10}+2\sqrt{5}+5) \sim 200$ integer operations, for a total of 370 integer operations. Instead, if we compute the factorization of 200, just once, and we store the factors in the recursion-DAG, it takes 14 – i.e., $\sqrt{200}$ – integer operations and 5 store instructions – i.e., 5 factors, respectively.

3   Related Work

Our approach has several similarities with approaches in two very active research areas: one is self-applicable partial evaluation and the other is dynamic programming.

Self-applicable partial evaluation is the problem of optimizing an algorithm when a partial number of arguments is known at compile time and, therefore, specializing a function, or the entire program, to partially compute the result to the extent feasible at compile time [21,22,23]. For example Fibonacci number $F(n)$, [1] if we know that $n = 4$, we may compute the value and substitute $F(4) = 5$. All authors propose an approach composed of two phases: a static phase and a dynamic phase. The static phase determines what can be computed at compile time and what cannot be computed, called **residual**. Object-oriented class templates, and in particular function specialization in C++, are familiar examples of partial evaluations. Some general purpose compilers also apply partial evaluation for optimizations such as dead code elimination [24].

Our approach is also a combination of static and dynamic phases (analyses). The static analysis takes the input program and annotates the formals parameters of function definitions such as to clearly mark the formals involved in the recursive division process only (e.g., in the function defined in Fig. 1, we mark the third formal *int n*). The dynamic analysis execute partially the program, and using the annotations, binds function calls to nodes in the recursion DAG (e.g., the function call *fft(*,*,200,1)* is associated to the node fft<200>, Fig. 2). When no arguments is known at compile time, previous techniques are by definition not applicable, however, our technique is applicable and enables us to compute (at run time) data that will be used during the recursive algorithm execution; in practice, we may specialize the computation of the recursive algorithm at run time.

In **dynamic programming**, there are basically two *philosophies*: function caching and incrementalization. **Function caching** is a top-down approach to solve a problem remembering the result of a function invocation and reusing this result when the function is invoked again with same arguments. For example, Fibonacci numbers $F(4)$ involves the computation of $F(2) + F(1) + F(2)$, the first invocation of $F(2)$ is computed once, and the result is reused for the second invocation [25,26,27,28]. Unfortunately, function caching may require an interpretive overhead to manage and store partial results. In turn, **incrementalization** is a bottom-up approach proposed to reduce or annihilate the overhead typical in function caching [29] reducing the working set of cached function results to a minimum – at any time – and having a fast access to them.

In general, dynamic-programming approaches are not applicable for matrix algorithms, because the final result is highly dependent on the contents of the input matrices (making the *classic* value reuse impossible). However, matrix algorithms have such a regularity in their computation that some of dynamic-programming techniques may be applied, at least in principle. In fact, our technique borrows the same basic ideas of function caching: the recursion-DAG is the collection of all cached function-call results organized in a DAG (even though,

---

[1] $F(n) = F(n-1) + F(n-2)$ with $F(1) = 1$ and $F(2) = 2$.

we do not necessarily store any function return value). Because we need to store all cached results, incrementalization has no better performance and space advantages than function caching has but at expense of a more complex design and implementation.

In addition, our approach is not meant for the conversion of loop nests to recursion [30] or vice versa [31], but it offers a means to speed up the conversion process and a quantitative measure of the overhead due to recursion. A compiler may then be able to make an informed choice between recursion or blocked instantiation. Our approach is not meant to optimize the function call mechanism (e.g., register minimization, solving allocation of the actuals-formals, in-lining or recursion elimination, state elimination) because modern compiler/hardware technology already exists for these tasks and it is orthogonal to (and it could be use in combination with) our approach.

4   JuliusC: An Overview

JuliusC is a (lite) C compiler written in C/C++. To simplify the compiler design, we accept a subset of the C language (e.g., no **struct** and no **union** are handled). For linear-algebra applications, our C-language simplifications have little effect on the design and implementation of D&C algorithms (and were chosen to allow a quick demonstration of our ideas). In the longer run, we will port our techniques into more advanced and robust compilers [32] thus avoiding these limitations.

In different phases of the compilation, we manipulate an intermediate representation (**IR**) of the input program. After lexical and syntactical analysis, we create an abstract syntax tree (**AST**). We perform static type checking and we annotate the result of the analysis on the AST. Using the AST for

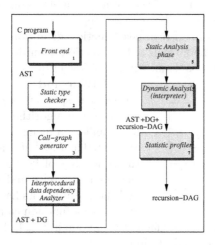

Fig. 3. JuliusC block Diagram. Acronyms: intermediate representation = IR, abstract syntax tree = AST, data dependency graph = DG

each function definition, we determine all function-call expressions. We then determine a call-graph and its all-pair shortest-path matrix closure. Using this analysis, we may mark whether a function definition is explicitly self recursive, recursive, non-recursive or a **leaf** (a leaf is a non-recursive function that has calls to non-recursive functions only). For example, if the closure matrix shows a loop for a function definition, the function is recursive; otherwise it is not recursive.

We employ a simplified inter-procedural data dependency analysis: the data dependency of each function definition is executed in one pass; arrays are considered as monolithic units (we do not need more accurate analysis because we rediscover the array decomposition from the recursive algorithm, which we assume correct); for loops, we perform the data dependency in one pass (i.e., we do not determine the loop carried dependencies) of the loop body. We would benefit from a more powerful data dependency analysis, which we will plan to obtain by using a more sophisticated infrastructure, but this is not necessary to demonstrate the proposed techniques on useful applications. As a result of the data-dependency analysis, we enrich our IR building a data dependency graph structure (**DG**) upon the AST. In the following, there is our original contribution.

4.1   Static Analysis: The Art of Divide et Impera

In this work, we assume that the division process of a recursive algorithm is driven by the values of some specific formal variables (or parameters). This assumption is based on the observation of real codes and, in practice, it simplifies both the implementation and the analysis of recursive algorithms. Thus, our static analysis summarizes the division process by annotating the formal variables of function definitions (composing the application) with three attributes, which stand for different uses of the formal variables. Our attribute-annotation process is composed of the following two steps.

First, the formals of self-recursive function definitions are annotated with **D&C** attributes, and the formals of leaf function definitions are annotated with **MO** and **LO** attributes as defined in the following.

```
int factorial(int N) {
 if (N<=1)
    return 1;
 else
    return N*factorial(N-1);
}
```

Fig. 4. N is a D&C formal

Divide and Conquer (D&C): It is a formal that specifies the size of the problem and how the algorithm divides the problem into smaller problems. In practice, a formal is annotated as D&C, if it is used as operand in the conditions of flow-of-control statements, such as if-then-else and while-do statement, and these statements have an execution path leading to a function call of a recursive function. For example, consider the factorial function in Fig.4, the formal N is a D&C formal. This is an **inherited** attribute.

```
void set(int *m, int n,
         int L ) {
  int i;
  for (i=0;i<n;i++)
    m[i+L] = i;
}
```

Fig. 5. *L* is a LO formal

Location Operand (LO) and **Matrix Operand (MO):** a formal is annotated as LO, if it is used in the index computation of a vector; a formal is annotated as MO, if it is a pointer to a vector. For example, the formal m in Fig. 5 is annotated as MO and formal L as LO. These are **synthesized** attributes. The terms *inherited* and *synthesized* come from the way we annotate–evaluate these attributes in the second, and following, step. In fact, the call graph is an instance of an annotated (parse) tree, and we evaluate the attributes as inherited and synthesized attributes by a syntax-directed translation.

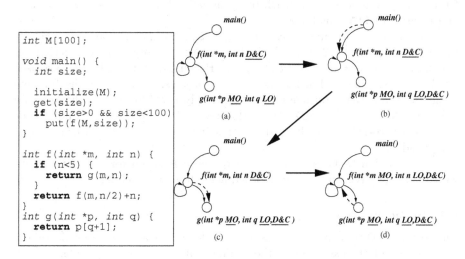

Fig. 6. Example of multiple attributes: *n* is eventually marked as D&C and LO, the evaluation process is schematically represented in Fig. (a), (b), (c) and (d). The procedure *put*() is an I/O call

Second, we determine an in-order left-to-right visit of the call graph (e.g., by a depth-first search) starting from the `main()` function definition. The visit determines a tree: the leaf function definitions correspond to the leaves of the tree. As any syntax-directed translation process (e.g., type checking), we visit the tree and we compute inherited and synthesized attributes using the data dependency among function calls.

Consider the example in Fig. 6. We annotate the formals of the self-recursive function definition *int f(int *m, int n)*: formal n is annotated as D&C. We annotate the formals of leaf function definition *int g(int *p, int q)*: the first formal has attribute MO and the second formal has attribute LO (Fig. 6 (a)). We start the second phase of the annotating process from `main()`, which does not have formals. We then visit `f()`: the second formal q of `g()` inherits an attribute D&C

(Fig. 6 (b)) from the formal n of function definition f(). We then visit g() (Fig. 6 (c)). We then backtrack to f() and we synthesize the attributes from its child g(): the first formal has attribute MO, and the second has attribute LO (Fig. 6 (d)). Eventually, the formals n in f() and p in g() have attributes D&C and LO. For example, n in f() is an operand in the condition of the only if-then-else statement in f() and, indirectly, it is used to access the vector p in function g().

An attribute summarizes the use of a formal in the body of the function definition and, in turn, in the functions called as well. In this paper, we present applications for those recursive algorithms having formals with D&C attributes only.

4.2 Dynamic Analysis: Interpretation and Recursion-DAG

During the dynamic analysis, each function call will be associated with a node in a **recursion-DAG** as follows.

When we reach an function call (e.g., z(i,3,i+3) in a program), we evaluate the actuals (e.g., z(10,3,13)). We look up for the definition of the function call (e.g., *void z(int i, int j, int k /* D&C */)* ...). Because only D&C formals are used by the recursive algorithm for the division process, we consider the function name and the actual values associated with only D&C formals as the **key** of a function call (e.g., f(*,*,13)). Using this key, we look up whether or not a node in the recursive-DAG already exists (with same key). If it does not exist, a new node is added.

The recursion-DAG is an unfolding of the call graph for an initial input, where only the division work is recorded using function caching.

4.3 Static Profiler

The recursion-DAG can be used as a means for a fast and precise collection of statistics about the execution of the recursive algorithm. For example, we may want to compute how many times a function (solving a particular problem size) is called and we just need to exploit the acyclic nature of the recursion-DAG. In fact, we determine a topological sort of the recursion-DAG by a depth-first search. By construction, the function main() is associated with the first node and we set its **count** to 1. For every node in the topological sort v, we consider each child u and we update the child count $u.count+ = v.count$. In this way, while we compute the number of function calls per node visiting each node once, we can compute the total number of function calls and the total number of nodes in the recursion-DAG.

The **reuse ratio**, $\mathcal{R}$, is the ratio between the number of functions calls over the number of nodes in the recursion-DAG. It represents a concise estimate of the work reduction. For example, we may evaluate the common computations and store them in the recursion-DAG, the reuse ratio represents how many time we reuse those precomputed values during the execution of the recursive algorithm.

$$\mathcal{R} = \frac{\#\text{function calls}}{\#\text{nodes in recursion-DAG}}. \tag{1}$$

5   Experimental Results

In this section, we show that our approach is practical; that is, the execution time of static and dynamic analysis is negligible. We show that we may exploit reuse of the division work and we present the reuse ratio for 6 recursive algorithms for various inputs.

Our compiler does not yet fully implement the previously developed optimizations (e.g., register allocation) and thus we cannot present here fully automated results of actual speedups. However, our contribution is to present the automatic derivation of the recursion-DAG. The practicality of the overall approach has been already demonstrated previously [14,33,17].

Static Analysis: The annotation of formal parameters using attributes (e.g., D&C, MO, LO as described in Section 4.1) is based on data-dependency interprocedural analysis and our data-dependency analysis is polynomial in the number of the code instructions.

Dynamic Analysis: At this stage of the project, JuliusC is an interpreter and the recursion-DAG generation is one component of the dynamic analysis (i.e., partial interpretation of the recursive algorithm for some inputs). Therefore, any performance comparisons between the execution time of JuliusC's analysis and the execution time of the recursive algorithm – compiled for the native system – would be inconclusive. For now, we present an asymptotic analysis, which is based only on the recursive algorithm. Ultimately, the recursion-DAG generation time is asymptotically related to the recursion-DAG size. In turn, we may use the reuse ratio to express the relation between recursion-DAG generation – dynamic analysis – and recursive algorithm execution time. Indeed, the execution time of the recursion-DAG generation is $O(1/\mathcal{R})$ of the execution time of the recursive algorithm – see (1).

Reuse Ratio: We apply JuliuC to 6 recursive algorithms (for various inputs); three algorithms are from linear algebra; two algorithms are from number theory and one is a classic graph algorithm. The results presented in Table 1 are a significant excerpt and they can be reproduced running JuliusC on-line [20]. Table 1 reports the reuse ratio for recursive algorithms, the ratio represents the possible work reduction we may achieve. We consider briefly each illustrative example as follows.

Binomial is a straightforward recursive algorithm but its time complexity is exponential. Function caching – in JuliusC – allows the reuse of already computed values so as the final time complexity is just polynomial. For the input $\binom{10}{5}$, the reuse is 14; however, larger reuse ratios are achievable for larger problems.

Integer factorization is used in algorithms such as Cooley-Tookey FFT. Given an integer n, we determine the factors p and q so that $n = pq$ and $\min_{p,q} |p-q|$. We determine the factorization for p and q recursively. We analyze an exact and a heuristic factorization (e.g., integer factorization is important in cryptography [34]).

Table 1. Reuse ratio $\mathcal{R}$ is a function of the problem size, the algorithm definition and the static analysis

Notation	Name	$\mathcal{R}$	Inputs
$\binom{n}{k}$	Binomial	14	$\binom{10}{5}$
		3053	$\binom{20}{10}$
$n = pq$	Integer factorization	93	$n = 65536$
		133	$n = 524288$
FFT_n	Balanced Cooley-Tookey	34	$n = 128$
		2076	$n = 5000$
		12683	$n = 65536$
A^*	All-pair shortest path	60728	$\mathbf{A} \sim 750 \times 750$,
		23967500	$\mathbf{A} \sim 7500 \times 7500$
$\mathbf{A} = \mathbf{LU}$	LU-factorization	16110	$\mathbf{A} \sim 300 \times 300$,
		93757	$\mathbf{A} \sim 500 \times 500$
$\mathbf{C}+ = \mathbf{AB}$	Matrix multiply	1950	size of $\mathbf{C}, \mathbf{A}, \mathbf{B} = 100 \times 100$
		107176	size of $\mathbf{C}, \mathbf{A}, \mathbf{B} = 517 \times 517$
		2765800	size of $\mathbf{C}, \mathbf{A}, \mathbf{B} = 1123 \times 1123$

Balanced Cooley-Tookey is the Cooley-Tookey FFT algorithm using balanced factorizations [35,17].

All-pair shortest path is an algorithm based on matrix multiplication and Wharshall-Floyd algorithm [36,37].

LU-factorization is an algorithm based on matrix multiply with no row pivoting [33,13].

Matrix multiply is matrix multiplication with matrices stored in nonstandard layout [14,5].

This paper is about how to reduce the algorithm work division, which is intrinsic to D&C algorithms. JuliusC implements an approach to extract and reduce such work division, which is the most difficult part of the implementation.

For completeness, in Fig. 7 we show results for a representative example, FFT (the main algorithm is presented in Fig. 1, Section 2). In Fig. 7, we present an excerpt from JuliusC's output, which is reproducible on-line [20] at the native system - Fujitsu HAL 100MHz. The data dependency analysis takes 0.05 seconds and the annotation of the formals using attributes is negligible (static analysis). The interpretation takes 5.4 seconds (dynamic analysis). The collection of the statistics is negligible. The result of the analysis is a text-based recursion-DAG. Each function call has an entry that we can describe using a single line:

```
name< size > [ number of times this function is called ] |Rec| or |LeaF|
```

The problem `fft()` has size `<6>`; it is called 630 times; the last attribute is `|Rec|`, which stands for *Recursive*. The problem `DFT_1()` has problem size `<1260,3>` (stride and problem size); it is called 3780 times; the last attribute is `|LeaF|`, non recursive.

We use a somewhat limited graphical representation for the final recursion-DAG. We use indentation to present the relation among function calls so we

```
Call Graph from Main ....
----------> get time 0 sec<------
Function calls properties ....
----------> get time 0 sec<------
Data Dependency Analysis ...
----------> get time 0.05 sec<------
Data dependecy result ....
----------> get time 0 sec<------
Marking D&C formals ...
----------> get time 0.01 sec<------
Check the formals on the function definitions ...
Interpretation ...
----------> get time 5.4 sec<------
On count
Reuse Ratio 1007.26
----------> get time 0 sec<------
main<> [1] {} |Rec|
    fft<3780> [1] {0} |Rec|
        find_balance_factorization<3780> [1] {60} |LeaF|
        fft<60> [63] {0} |Rec|
            find_balance_factorization<60> [63] {6} |LeaF|
            fft<6> [630] {0} |Rec|
                find_balance_factorization<6> [630] {3} |LeaF|
                fft<3> [3780] {0} |Rec|
                    find_balance_factorization<3> [3780] {3} |LeaF|
                    DFT_1<1260,3> [3780] {0} |LeaF|
```

Fig. 7. JuliusC's output excerpt for Balanced Cooley-Tookey

can identify the root immediately: the node **main**. Using this simplified format, two siblings function calls have same indentation and two function calls with a caller-callee relation have different indentation; for example, *fft(*,*,3,*)* is called by *fft(*,*,6,*)*:

6   Conclusion and Future Work

In this work, we have presented an automatic approach to model the computation of recursive D&C algorithms using a DAG data structure, **recursion-DAG**. We show that the approach is practical and it can be incorporated into a generic compiler. We apply our approach to 6 recursive algorithms and we present an estimation of the potential improvements.

In the near future, we will investigate how to use the recursion-DAG as a run-time support for recursive algorithm parallelization and as an alternative means for collecting data currently obtainable by profiling only.

References

1. Kagström, B., Ling, P., van Loan, C.: Gemm-based level 3 blas: high-performance model implementations and performance evaluation benchmark. ACM Transactions on Mathematical Software **24** (1998) 268–302
2. : (LAPACK – Linear Algebra PACKage) http://www.netlib.org/lapack/.
3. Dongarra, J., Duff, I., D.C.Soransen, van Der Vorst, H.: Numerical Linear Algebra for Performance Computers. SIAM (2000)
4. Golub, G., van Loan, C.: Matrix Computations. Ed. The Johns Hopins University Press (1996)
5. Frens, J., Wise, D.: Auto-blocking matrix-multiplication or tracking blas3 performance from source code. In: Proc. 1997 ACM Symp. on Principles and Practice of Parallel Programming. Volume 32. (1997) 206–216

6. Park, J., Penner, M., Prasanna, V.: Optimizing graph algorithms for improved cache performance. In: In Proceedings of the International Parallel and Distributed Processing Symposium. (2002)
7. Whaley, R., Dongarra, J.J.: Automatically tuned linear algebra software. In: Proceedings of the 1998 ACM/IEEE conference on Supercomputing (CDROM), IEEE Computer Society (1998) 1–27
8. Bilmes, J., Asanovic, K., Chin, C., Demmel, J.: Optimizing matrix multiply using PHiPAC: a portable, high-performance, ANSI C coding methodology. In: Proceedings of the 11th international conference on Supercomputing, ACM Press (1997) 340–347
9. Lam, M., Rothberg, E., Wolfe, M.: The cache performance and optimizations of blocked algorithms. In: Proceedings of the fourth international conference on architectural support for programming languages and operating system. (1991) 63–74
10. Jonsson, I., Kagström, B.: Recursive blocked algorithms for solving triangular systems part i: one-sided and coupled sylvester-type matrix equations. ACM Trans. Math. Softw. **28** (2002) 392–415
11. Szymanski, B.: Parallel functional languages and compilers. ACM Press (1991)
12. Frigo, M., Leiserson, C., Prokop, H., Ramachandran, S.: Cache-oblivious algorithms. In: Proceedings of the 40th Annual Symposium on Foundations of Computer Science, IEEE Computer Society (1999) 285
13. Toledo, S.: Locality of reference in lu decomposition with partial pivoting. SIAM Journal on Matrix Analysis and Applications **18** (1997) 1065–1081
14. Bilardi, G., D'Alberto, P., Nicolau, A.: Fractal matrix multiplication: a case study on portability of cache performance. In: Workshop on Algorithm Engineering 2001, Aarhus, Denmark (2001)
15. Gustavson, F., Henriksson, A., Jonsson, I., Ling, P., Kagström, B.: Recursive blocked data formats and BLAS's for dense linear algebra algorithms. In Verlag, S., ed.: PARA'98 Proceedings. Lecture Notes in Computing Science. Number 1541 (1998) 195–206
16. Frigo, M., Johnson, S.: The fastest fourier transform in the west. Technical Report MIT-LCS-TR-728, Massachusetts Institute of technology (1997)
17. D'Alberto, P., A.Nicolau, Veidenbaum, A.: A data cache with dynamic mapping. In Rauchwerger, L., ed.: Languages and Compilers for Parallel Computing. Volume 2958 of Lecture Notes in Computer Science., Springer Verlag (2003)
18. Hummel, J., Hendren, L., Nicolau, A.: Abstract description of pointer data structures: an approach for improving the analysis and optimization of imperative programs. ACM Lett. Program. Lang. Syst. **1** (1992) 243–260
19. Rugina, R., Rinard, M.: Automatic parallelization of divide and conquer algorithms. In: Proceedings of the seventh ACM SIGPLAN symposium on Principles and practice of parallel programming, ACM Press (1999) 72–83
20. D'Alberto: (JuliusC) http://halps.ics.uci.edu/ paolo/JuliusC.
21. Albert, E., Hanus, M., Vidal, G.: Using an Abstract Representation to Specialize Functional Logic Programs. In: Proc. of 7th International Conference on Logic for Programming and Automated Reasoning, LPAR'2000, Springer LNAI 1955 (2000) 381–398
22. Gomard, C.: A self-applicable partial evaluator for the lambda calculus: correctness and pragmatics. ACM Trans. Program. Lang. Syst. **14** (1992) 147–172
23. Jones, N., Gomard, C., Sestoft, P.: Partial Evaluation and Automatic Program Generation. Soft edn. Prentice Hall International (1993)

24. Knoop, J., Rüthing, O., Steffen, B.: Partial dead code elimination. In: Proceedings of the ACM SIGPLAN 1994 conference on Programming language design and implementation, ACM Press (1994) 147–158
25. Pugh, W., Teitelbaum, T.: Incremental computation via function caching. In: Proceedings of the 16th ACM SIGPLAN-SIGACT symposium on Principles of programming languages, ACM Press (1989) 315–328
26. Pugh, W.: An improved replacement strategy for function caching. In: Proceedings of the 1988 ACM conference on LISP and functional programming, ACM Press (1988) 269–276
27. Heydon, A., Levin, R., Yu, Y.: Caching function calls using precise dependencies. In: Proceedings of the ACM SIGPLAN 2000 conference on Programming language design and implementation, ACM Press (2000) 311–320
28. Abadi, M., Lampson, B., Lévy, J.: Analysis and caching of dependencies. In: Proceedings of the first ACM SIGPLAN international conference on Functional programming, ACM Press (1996) 83–91
29. Liu, Y., Stoller, S.: Dynamic programming via static incrementalization. Higher Order Symbol. Comput. **16** (2003) 37–62
30. Liu, Y., Stoller, S.: From recursion to iteration: What are the optimizations? In: Partial Evaluation and Semantic-Based Program Manipulation. (2000) 73–82
31. Yi, Q., Adve, V., Kennedy, K.: Transforming loops to recursion for multi-level memory hierarchies. In: Proceedings of the ACM SIGPLAN 2000 conference on Programming language design and implementation, ACM Press (2000) 169–181
32. Lam, M.: SUIF (1994-current) http://suif.stanford.edu/.
33. D'Alberto, P.: Performance evaluation of data locality exploitation. Technical report, University of Bologna, Computer Science (2000)
34. Lenstra, A.: The development of the number field sieve. Volume 1554 of Lecture Notes in Math., Springer-Verlag (1993)
35. Cormen, T., Leiserson, C., Rivest, R.: Introduction to Algorithms. MIT Press (1990)
36. Floyd, R.: Algorithm 97: Shortest path. Communications of the ACM **5** (1962)
37. Ullman, J., Yannakakis, M.: The input/output complexity of transitive closure. In: Proceedings of the 1990 ACM SIGMOD international conference on Management of data. Volume 19. (1990)

Exploiting Parallelism in Memory Operations for Code Optimization

Yunheung Paek[1], Junsik Choi[1], Jinoo Joung[2], Junseo Lee[2], and Seonwook Kim[3]

[1] School of Electrical Engineering,
Seoul National University, Seoul 151-744, Korea
ypaek@snu.ac.kr, jschoi@compiler.snu.ac.kr*
[2] Samsung Advanced Institute of Technology Mt. 14-1,
Nongseo-Ri, Giheung-Eup, Yongin-Shi, Gyeonggi-Do 449-712, Korea
{jjoung, junseo.lee}@samsung.com
[3] Department of Electronics and Computer Engineering,
Korea University, Seoul 136-701, Korea
seon@korea.ac.kr

Abstract. Code size reduction is ever becoming more important for compilers targeting embedded processors because these processors are often severely limited by storage constraints and thus the reduced code size can have a positively significant impact on their performance. Various code size reduction techniques have different motivations and a variety of application contexts utilizing special hardware features of their target processors. In this work, we propose a novel technique that fully utilizes a set of hardware instructions, called the *multiple load/store* (MLS) or *parallel load/store* (PLS), that are specially featured for reducing code size by minimizing the number of memory operations in the code. To take advantage of this feature, many microprocessors support the MLS instructions, whereas no existing compilers fully exploit the potential benefit of these instructions but only use them for some limited cases. This is mainly because optimizing memory accesses with MLS instructions for general cases is an NP-hard problem that necessitates complex *assignments of registers and memory offsets* for variables in a stack frame. Our technique uses a couple of heuristics to efficiently handle this problem in a polynomial time bound.

1 Introduction

In general, microprocessors contained in an embedded system are heavily limited by resource constraints such as size, power and cost. In particular, as embedded software grows rapidly complex and large to satisfy diverse demand from the market, efficient use of limited storage resources are ever becoming more important for compilers targeting these processors. To attain a desired performance goal even with such limited storage, the processors are designed assuming software that runs on them would make heavy use of their various special hardware instructions and addressing modes [4,7]. One such example is the MLS instructions, which are often encountered in modern processors such as Motorola Mcore, ARM 7/9/10, Fujitsu FR30 and IBM R6000. The following shows an example of the MLS instructions in an ARM processor:

---

* This work is supported in part by SAIT, KOSEF R08-2003-000-10781-0, the university IT Research Center project.

R. Eigenmann et al. (Eds.): LCPC 2004, LNCS 3602, pp. 132–148, 2005.

$$\texttt{ldmia/stmia } r_{base}, \{r_1, r_2, \cdots, r_m\}$$

where $m \leq 16$ and all the operands (r_{base}, r_1, r_2, ..., r_m) can be any of the ARM general-purpose registers: r0, r1, $\cdots$, r15. These instructions allow large quantities of data to be transferred more efficiently in a single operation between any subset (or all) of the 16 registers and the memory locations starting at the address designated by the register content of r_{base}. For instance, the instruction, ldmia r1, {r3,r4,r8}, loads a block of three words Mem[r1], Mem[r1+4] and Mem[r1+8] respectively into the registers in an increasing order of their numbers, that is, r3, r4 and r8. The order of registers appearing inside the braces does not affect the data transfer result. The main advantages of MLS instructions are two fold:

- code size reduction thru compaction of a number of memory operations into one instruction word, and
- running time reduction thru pipelining of memory accesses.

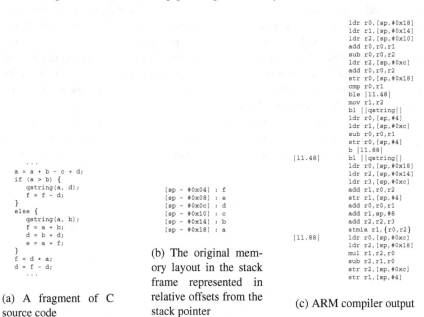

(a) A fragment of C source code

(b) The original memory layout in the stack frame represented in relative offsets from the stack pointer

(c) ARM compiler output

Fig. 1. Benchmark code, and its assemby with the memory layout generated by the ARM native compiler with a -O2 optimization option

To illustrate this, consider the example in Figure 1, which shows the C source code and its assembly translated by a commercial ARM native compiler. The figure also shows the memory offsets the compiler assigns the variables in the stack. From this memory layout, we can see that the ARM compiler, like many other conventional ones, performs memory assignment simply in a declaration or lexicographic order of variables. This naïve approach does not satisfy the above requirements for *registers* and *memory offsets* in an MLS instruction and so impedes the chance to use it in the code. In consequence, even after traditional optimizations such as redundant load and store elimination, the ARM compiler output in Figure 1 (c) still has 17 loads/stores in total, including just a single multiple store generated from *double stores* (i.e., two stores). Furthermore, even this single use of the MLS may not bring any advantage in the code size, because one ALU instruction, add r1,sp,#8, was inserted to initialize the base register r1 for the MLS. This fact implies that the ARM compiler needs a much more aggressive approach for *memory and register assignment* to fully utilize hardware support for the MLS.

In this paper, we report our recent study on a problem, which we name the *MLS problem*, whose goal is to find an optimal register and memory assignment that leads us to fully capitalize on the advantages of MLS instructions. In our example, an ideal memory assignment for this problem would be the one in Figure 2 (a). Reflecting this new memory layout, we may change the original code as listed in Figure 2 (b), where we notice that more neighboring loads/stores are accessing contiguous addresses under this layout. But we also notice that despite this improved memory assignment, they still cannot be converted to MLS instructions. This is of course because without a proper register assignment, a smart memory assignment alone cannot enable neighboring loads/stores to aggregate into an MLS. For instance, although the last two stores in Figure 2 (b) access contiguous addresses (0x10, 0x14), an MLS instruction cannot be generated for them since it stipulates that a lower address be assigned a lower register number in its operand. Thus, in this case, if the address 0x14 is assigned the register r1, then the other one 0x10 must be re-assigned the register r0.

This example convinces us that optimizing a program with MLS instructions is quite a complex memory assignment problem tangled with a register assignment (or we may call *register renaming*) problem. On top of this, when we solve this problem, we must

```
                              ldr r0,[sp,#0xc]
                              ldr r1,[sp,#8]
                              ldr r2,[sp,#4]
                              add r0,r0,r1
                              sub r0,r0,r2                      add r10,sp,#0x10
                              ldr r2,[sp,#0x10]                add r9,sp,#4
                              add r0,r0,r2                     ldmia r9,{r0,r1,r2,r3}
                              str r0,[sp,#0xc]                 add r2,r2,r1
                              cmp r0,r1                        sub r2,r2,r0
                              ble |11.48|                      add r2,r2,r3
                              mov r1,r2                        str r2,[sp,#0xc]
                              bl ||qstring||                   cmp r2,r1
                              ldr r0,[sp,#0x14]                ble |11.48|
                              ldr r1,[sp,#0x10]                mov r0,r2
                              sub r0,r0,r1                     bl ||qstring||
                              str r0,[sp,#0x14]                ldmia r10,{r0,r1}
                              b |11.88|                        sub r1,r1,r0
         |11.48|             bl ||qstring||                   str r1,[sp,#0x14]
                              ldr r0,[sp,#0xc]                 b |11.88|
                              ldr r2,[sp,#8]          |11.48|  bl ||qstring||
                              ldr r3,[sp,#0x10]                add r9,sp,#8
                              add r1,r0,r2                     ldmia r9,{r0,r2,r3}
                              str r1,[sp,#0x14]                add r1,r2,r0
                              add r0,r0,r1                     add r2,r2,r1
                              str r0,[sp,#0x18]                add r0,r0,r3
                              add r2,r2,r3                     stmia r10,{r0,r1,r2}
                              str r2,[sp,#0x10]       |11.88|  add r9,sp,#0xc
         |11.88|             ldr r0,[sp,#0x10]                ldmia r9,{r0,r2}
                              ldr r2,[sp,#0xc]                 mul r1,r0,r2
                              mul r1,r2,r0                     sub r0,r1,r2
                              sub r2,r1,r0                     stmia r10,{r0,r1}
                              str r2,[sp,#0x10]
                              str r1,[sp,#0x14]
```

[sp - #0x04] : c
[sp - #0x08] : b
[sp - #0x0c] : a
[sp - #0x10] : d
[sp - #0x14] : f
[sp - #0x18] : e

(a) Optimal memory assignment for MLSs

(b) Modified ARM code output with the memory assignment in (a)

(c) Optimized code output both after memory and register assignment

Fig. 2. Improving the original code by using MLSs with better memory & register assignment: To obtain (c), local instruction scheduling and other traditional optimizations were applied

also consider *instruction rescheduling* simultaneously because a single large memory transfer formed together from many small ones scattered in the code mostly results in better performance.

Our final code optimized with ldmia/stmia is shown in Figure 2 (c). As compared to the original code, the code size is reduced about 20%. If we only consider memory operations, the number of loads/stores are reduced about 60%. Since memory accesses in an MLS can be overlapped by pipelining when data are actually transferred, we may also expect some significant amount of reduction in the total memory access time.

In the optimized code, there are three MLS instructions, each of which is combined from double loads/stores. At first glance, they seem unprofitable in terms of code size, as we already stated, due to additional ALU operations for base register initialization. But we sometimes found in real cases that these ALU operations are often exposed to conventional optimizations such as common subexpression elimination (CSE) and redundancy elimination, and thereby some of them were removed. In this example, one add was removed since the base address in the register r10 is reused by two of the MLS instructions. In fact, note in the code that one more add was removed for another MLS (converted from triple stores) with r10 as its base register. Due partially to temporal locality embedded in real code, we observed this reuse of base addresses was made possible in our experiments.

To summarize, finding an optimal solution to the MLS problem is an extremely difficult task complicated with several NP-complete optimization subproblems. Therefore, it is not surprising to discover that all the compilers we tested in our experiments fail to utilize the MLS instructions to such a degree as we demonstrated in Figure 2, and only use them for special occasions, such as exception handlers, function prologues/epilogues and context switches, where recognizing block memory copies for MLS instructions are rather trivial. All this inevitably implies that to utilize MLS instructions, the users should hand-optimize their code in assembly, making programming complex and time consuming.

The purpose of this paper is to discuss our heuristic-based algorithm that solves the MLS problem efficiently in a polynomial time bound. Although our algorithm does not guarantee to find an optimal solution to the MLS problem for all cases, our experiment with real benchmark programs exhibits its effectiveness on most cases. In Section 2, we start our discussion by relating our study with previous ones that worked on broadly similar but completely different problems from ours. In Section 3, we describe our algorithm, and in Section 4, present our experimental results. In Section 5, we conclude.

2   Related Work

Memory assignment of scalar variables in a stack frame had hardly been a crucial issue in compiler research until about a decade ago when the utilization of special addressing modes became important for typical embedded processors. Since then, there has been much work on code size reduction through optimal memory assignment for such addressing modes. One of the earliest work was done by Bartley [1] who first addressed the *simple offset assignment* (SOA) problem, the problem of assigning scalar variables to memory such that the number of explicit address arithmetic instructions are minimized by using auto-increment/decrement addressing modes. Later, Liao et al. [4]

formally proved that the SOA problem can be reduced to the *maximum-weighted path cover* (MWPC) problem, and thus that it is NP-complete. Hence, to cope with the SOA problem fast in polynomial time, they proposed a heuristic based on Kruskal's *maximum spanning tree* (MST) algorithm.

Inspired by the previous work, many researchers [3,7,8] extended the work in various aspects. All these previous studies are in some sense related to ours in that they aim at finding optimal memory (offset) assignment for certain hardware instructions or addressing modes. But they are also clearly different from ours in that they all center around only the SOA problem, which varies from our MLS problem in many ways. In fact, our problem subsumes the SOA problem because as discussed in Section 1, ours must find not only optimal memory assignment but at the same time optimal register assignment along with the load/store scheduling that facilitates maximum utilization of MLS instructions. This means that we need a more aggressive approach to handle our problem than previous studies.

To our best knowledge, the only study on code optimization with MLS instructions was published most recently by Nandivada and Palsbergby at Purdue [5]. In their study independent from ours, they investigated the use of SDRAM for optimization of spill code. The core of their problem is to arrange the variables in the spill area such that loading to and storing from the SDRAM is optimized with MLS instructions. Their work differs from ours in two key points.

First, their technique focuses on running time not code size in the sense that, as explained in Section 1, it generates MLS instructions only from double loads/stores. For this reason, we deem their problem to be a special MLS problem for double loads/stores, which is simpler than our general problem. Second, their algorithm is based on *integer linear programming* (ILP). As mentioned above, the MLS problem is composed of several optimization subproblems tightly coupled to each other. So, the ideal strategy for this would be to solve the whole problem in a single, combined phase, where all subproblems are simultaneously considered. In their approach, therefore, they converted their problem to an ILP problem so that they solve it in a *coupled*, single phase. Obviously one critical drawback of such a coupled approach is that it uses an exponential time algorithm as they also did in their work. To avoid this excessively high time complexity, we take a more *decoupled* approach where we apply fast polynomial-time algorithms to solve each subproblem in a sequential, step-by-step manner. In Section 3, we present our algorithm based on this decoupled approach.

3   Solving the MLS Problem

In our approach, the information about memory access patterns is first culled from the code and summarized in a graph form. In the next phase, this form is used to find an optimal schedule for MLSs. Then, this load/store scheduling result is in turn used to determine the best possible offsets of variables in memory. Only after code has been scheduled and compacted by MLSs with all their variables fixed to memory, comes the assignment of physical registers to the variables. In this section, we discuss how the original MLS problem is divided in these phases and how each phase is structured in a decoupled fashion.

3.1   Dividing the Problem in Three Phases

To more formally describe the MLS problem, we define *parallel loads* and *parallel stores* to be respectively a block of loads and stores that can be executed simultaneously. In our approach, they are identified from the code as the first step of generating MLSs. Ideally, each parallel load/store block can be scheduled together and converted directly to an MLS instruction. However, the conversion is not always so straightforward because it stipulates beforehand that all the three constraints below be satisfied.

For the definition of the constraints, we follow the convention of the ARM architectures (see Section 1) to assume our MLS instructions is of the form:

$$\{r_1, r_2, \cdots, r_m\} = \text{Mem}[r_{base}] \quad \textit{// multiple load}$$
$$\text{Mem}[r_{base}] = \{r_1, r_2, \cdots, r_m\} \quad \textit{// multiple store}$$

where $m \leq n$ and n is the number of general-purpose registers on the target machine.

RF-size constraint: This is enforced because the MLS problem involves the instruction scheduling issue. When loads/stores are moved together to form a single MLS, it normally increases the life span of each value associated with them and so the overall register pressure in the code. Therefore, if there exists a point where the register pressure becomes higher than the actual *register file size*, then some of those loads/stores responsible for it may not be executed in the same MLS.

M-sequence constraint: The sequence of the memory locations where the m words, $m \leq n$, are fetched must be contiguous starting from the address specified by the content of r_{base}:

$\text{Mem}[r_{base}], \text{Mem}[r_{base}+4], \cdots, \text{Mem}[r_{base}+4m-4]$.

R-sequence constraint: The number sequence of the m registers where the memory data are transfered may not be contiguous, but the sequence must be strictly increasing.

Simply stated, the MLS problem is of finding optimal blocks of parallel loads/stores subject to these constraints. In our decoupled approach, it is divided and conquered individually in separate three phases. Starting from the graph called *LS-regions*, the initial information about parallel loads/stores is gradually shaped into the final form, called an *mPLS graph*, as each constraint is applied in the subsequent phases. At the end of Phase 3, the parallel loads/stores remaining in an mPLS graph satisfy all the constraints; thus each block of them can now be converted safely to an MLS. In the next subsections, we will detail each phase.

3.2   Computing Parallel Loads and Stores

Figure 3 shows the subroutine **build_PLS** for Phase 1 whose task is to identify all parallel loads and stores in each basic block of the input code. To describe this task, we first define two types of regions in Definitions 1 and 2, where given a block B with size $|B|$, we assume the cycles in B count from 0 up to $|B|-1$.

Definition 1. *Suppose B contains a load $r = v$ at the cycle t that loads the value into the register r from the memory location denoted by the variable v. Then, the Loadable region (**L-region**) of the load is the time interval $int_v=[lb,ub]$ where its lower/upper bounds lb and ub are defined as follows.*

```
build_PLS(P):
    G_PLS ← ∅;  // PLS graph
    for each basic block B in P do
        R_L ← compute_L_regions(B);   // according to Definition 1
        R_S ← compute_S_regions(B);   // according to Definition 2
        R ← R_L ∪ R_S;   // a unified set of L/S-regions
        while R ≠ ∅ do
            select int_v ∈ R such that ∀int_u ∈ R, int_v.ub ≤ int_u.ub;
            I ← {int_v};   // We call int_v the seed interval of I
            if int_v ∈ R_L then   // loadable region
                add to I all the L-regions in R overlapping with int_v;
            else   // storable region
                add to I all the S-regions in R overlapping with int_v;
            // check if register pressure > RF_size at t_vio
            t_vio ← check_RFsize(I, B);
            while (t_vio > 0) do   // RF-size constraint violated
                remove int_w from I such that ∀int_u ∈ I, int_w.ub ≥ int_u.ub;
                int_w.lb ← t_vio + 1;
                t_vio ← check_RFsize(I, B);
            od
            // construct a complete graph with all elements of I as its nodes
            C ← build_complete_graph(I);
            if int_v ∈ R_L then   // loadable region
                C.gen_time ← max   int_u.lb;
                              int_u ∈ I
                C.type ← load;
            else   // storable region
                C.gen_time ← min   int_u.ub;
                              int_u ∈ I
                C.type ← store;
            fi
            add C to G_PLS;
            R ← R − I;
        od
    od
    return G_PLS;
end
```

Fig. 3. Greedy algorithm designed to find PLSs

- *If there occurs the last store into v at some cycle t' in B before the load, then $int_v.lb = t'+1$. Otherwise, $int_v.lb = 0$.*
- *If the value loaded at t is first used at some cycle t'' in B, then $int_v.ub = t''$. Otherwise, $int_v.ub = |B|-1$*

Definition 2. *Suppose B contains a store $v = r$ at the cycle t that stores the value from the register r into the memory location denoted by the variable v. Then, the Storable region (**S-region**) of the store is the time interval $int_v = [lb, ub]$ where its lower/upper bounds lb and ub are defined as follows.*

- *If the register value stored at t was last defined at the cycle t' in B, then $int_v.lb = t'+1$. Otherwise, $int_v.lb = 0$.*
- *If there is the first load from v at the cycle t'' in B after the store, then $int_v.ub = t''$. Otherwise, $int_v.ub = |B|-1$.*

The L- and S-regions respectively represent the maximum ranges within B where the load $r = v$ and the store $v = r$ can move without violating data dependences on the variable v. Examples of the L/S-regions are shown in Figure 4 where the original ARM code (see Figure 1) is translated into 3-address form for better readability. The vertical bars in the figure stand for the L/S-regions of each load/store. For instance, the load

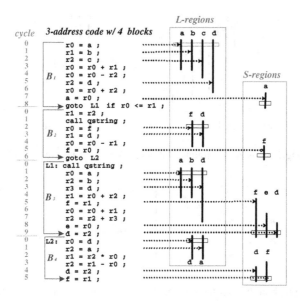

Fig. 4. 4 basic blocks, B_i, of 3-addess code rewritten from Figure 1 (c) and the L/S-regions for loads/stores in each block

from the variable d in the basic block B_1 has the L-region stretching from the cycle 0 to 6 because by definition, there is no store before the load in B_1 and the value loaded to r2 is first used at the cycle 6. Similarly, the S-region for the store into the variable f in the block B_3 stretches from the cycle 5 to 9 since the stored value is defined at the cycle 4 and there is no load from f in B_3 after the store.

The routine build_PLS uses the L/S-regions to identify parallel loads/stores. For this, it first divides the input procedure P into basic blocks, and for each block, computes the L/S-regions R_L and R_S according to Definitions 1 and 2. In principle, any loads/stores are parallel as long as their L/S-regions are overlapped. So in build_PLS, these parallel loads/stores are initially all gathered into the same block I of parallel loads/stores. However, this simple gathering may cause many new register spills in the final code. To explain this with an example, suppose in Figure 4 that we combine a load for d in B_1 to the same I with those for a, b and c. Then, when we generate MLS instructions, we will schedule these four loads into the same MLS so that by definition they can be executed simultaneously. This inevitably means that the load for d should move up from the cycle 5 to 2 or even earlier. This movement would prolong the life time of the value in the register r2, possibly increasing the register pressure as well. This can be a major drawback for us because we might have to generate MLSs with extra spills due to the increased register pressure, and very likely, these spills would offset the gains from our MLS uses in terms of code size and running time. To prevent this potential problem, the subroutine **check_RFsize** invoked inside build_PLS enforces the RF-size constraint when parallel loads/stores are collected to I.

When check_RFsize reports that the current configuration of I violates the RF-size constraint, some L/S-regions – or we may say simply *intervals* by their definitions – are

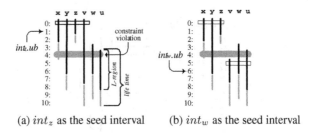

(a) int_z as the seed interval   (b) int_w as the seed interval

Fig. 5. RF-size constraint validity check for register pressue = 4

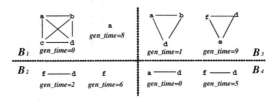

Fig. 6. The PLS graph built from the code in Fig 4: Each node v represents the interval of a load/store for variable v

removed from I until the constraint is satisfied. To explain this, consider Figure 5 where each L-region is extended with a gray line to represent the whole life span of the value loaded from a memory location. Assume that the target machine currently has only four registers available for loads/stores in this part of code. In Figure 5 (a), the block I of L-regions are first formed with four intervals $(int_x, int_y, int_z, int_v)$, begining with int_z as the *seed interval*. However, under the register file size limit (= 4), moving up the two loads for v and y to join I before the cycle 2 would cause the resulting pressure to violate the RF_size constraint by exceeding the limit at the cycle 4. When this violation is reported, build_PLS forbids the load for v to move up before the cycle 5 by eliminating it from I and adjusting its lower bound $int_v.lb = 5$, as shown in Figure 5 (b), where we now see the constraint is no longer violated. We could also prevent the violation by choosing int_y instead of int_v, but we choose the interval with the longest tail since its life span streches longest having more chance overlapping with other intervals.

After int_v is removed, the three intervals remaining in I will form a block of parallel loads, as shown in Figure 5 (b). Then, by definition, the interval int_w will be selected as the next seed, and clustered with the other two intervals, int_v and int_u.

The output of build_PLS is an undirected graph G_{PLS}, called the *parallel load/store* (PLS) graph, which is a collection of disconnected subgraphs. Each subgraph is constructed from a block of parallel loads/stores by turning an interval in the block to one node in the subgraph. Figure 6 shows the PLS graph built from the intervals in Figure 4. Each subgraph forms a complete graph because the edge is designed to represent the parallelism between two loads in the code and parallelism is an equivalence relation.

In Section 3.4, we will see that each subgraph in the PLS graph is given the code generator to emit MLS instructions in the final code. When an instruction is emitted,

---

[1] The interval whose upper bound is the lowest of all in the same block.

the generator must know where in the code it must be scheduled. To supply this information, every subgraph is associated with an integer *gen_time* that records the time just before which an MLS for the graph is inserted in the code. To minimize pipeline hazards, gen_time is set as early as possible to schedule loads and as late as possible to schedule stores. These times are denoted by the horizontal white bars in Figure 4.

When we build a PLS graph in the routine build_PLS, we follow a greedy approach by choosing as a seed interval an interval with the lowest upper bound among all remaining ones. The number of disconnected subgraphs in the PLS graph is proportional to that of loads/stores emitted in the final code. This means that the less subgraphs we produce in build_PLS, the more likely we will have an optimal code in the end. Luckily, Theorem 1 proves that our greedy approach reaches an optimal solution.

Theorem 1. *Given a set of loads/stores in the basic block B, the routine* **build_PLS** *finds the minimum number of parallel loads and stores for B.*

PROOF: The proof is straightforward. Suppose build_PLS produces k blocks of parallel loads/stores. Let S be the set of all seed intervals. The seed intervals are all disjoint since otherwise some of them would be included in the same block of parallel loads/stores. Since $|S| = k$, k is the minimum number of parallel loads/stores. ∎

3.3 Memory Assignment

In Phase 1, we imposed the RF-size constraint on the initial parallel load/store blocks when we summarized them as the disconnected subgraphs in a PLS graph. The task of Phase 2 is to impose the M-sequence constraint on them in an attempt to find an optimal memory layout for variables that can minimize the number of loads/stores emitted in the final code, as depicted in Figure 7.

```
solve_MAM(P, G_PLS)
    G_wPLS ← build_wPLSG(G_PLS);   // according to Definition 5
    mwp ← solve_SOA(G_wPLS);
    // Maximum-weight path algorithm from [4]
    E_np ← get_non_path_edges(G_wPLS, mwp);
    for all complete graphs C = (V_C, E_C) ∈ G_PLS do
        if ∃(u, v) ∈ E_np such that (int_u, int_v) ∈ C then
            remove (int_u, int_v) from E_C;
    od
    for every variable v ∈ P do
        v.offset ← assign_offsets_in_memory(v, mwp);
    return G_PLS;   // return PLS graph as mPLS graph
end
```

Fig. 7. Phase 2 algorithm to solve the MAM problem

In principle, we can simultaneously run any parallel loads/stores in the same block by emitting them in one MLS instruction. However, the M-sequence constraint tells us that the memory locations accessed in an MLS should be contiguous. This means that if parallel loads/stores are referencing variables with non-contiguous memory offsets, they should be scheduled to more than one different MLS instructions, which will certainly result in an increase in code size. So, the ultimate problem we need to solve in

Phase 2 is how to find such memory offsets for variables that satisfy the M-sequence constraint and at the same time, minimize the number of parallel loads/stores that must be scheduled to different MLS instructions. For clarity, this problem, which we call the *memory assignment for MLS* (MAM), can be stated more formally below.

Definition 3. *Given a set of local variables* S, *let* $[v]$ *denote a memory offset of* $v \in S$ *in a local stack. We define* $\prec$ *to denote a relation between* u *and* v *in* S *such that* $u \prec v$ *iff* u *immediately precedes* v *in the stack, that is,* $[v] = [u] + 4$. *From the relation* $\prec$, *we define a reflexive transitive closure* $\prec^*$ *on* S *as follows:*

- $\forall v \in S$: $v \prec^* v$;
- $\forall u, v \in S$: $\exists w \in S$: $u \neq v$, $u \prec^* w$ *and* $w \prec v$ *iff* $u \prec^* v$.

Definition 4. *Given a PLS graph* $G_{PLS} = (N, E)$, *let* U *be a set of all possible partitions* Ψ *of* N *such that* $\forall \psi \in \Psi$, *the block* ψ *satisfies the following conditions:*

1. $\forall int_u, int_v \in \psi$: $(int_u, int_v) \in E$;
2. $\forall int_u, int_v \in \psi$: *either* $v \prec^* u$ *or* $u \prec^* v$.

Then, the MAM is a problem that finds a partition $\Psi \in U$ *such that* $\forall \Phi \in U$, $|\Psi| \leq |\Phi|$.

The first condition in Definition 4 implies that a partition Ψ consists of disjoint subsets of N each of which corresponds to a block of the parallel loads/stores summarized in G_{PLS}. On such a partition Ψ, the second condition imposes the M-sequence constraint. Since the possible number of all partitions of N is $O(2^{|N| log |N|}/\sqrt{log|N|})$ bound by an exponential in $|N|$, it requires an exponential-time algorithm to optimally solve the MAM problem, like other memory assignment problems listed in Section 2. Considering $|N|$ can be several orders of 10 in real code, therefore, we devise a heuristic that solves the problem fast in polynomial time. For this goal, we first transform the MAM problem to an MWPC problem even though the MWPC problem is NP-complete. This is because as discussed in Section 2, the MWPC problem is already well-understood and solved with many powerful algorithms thanks to numerous previous studies. For this transformation, we build a weighted graph, called the *wPLS* graph, as described in Definition 5.

Definition 5. *Let* V *be the set of all variables declared in a procedure* P. *Let* $G_{PLS} = (N', E')$ *be the PLS graph built for* P *by the routine build_PLS. Then, the wPLS graph* $G_{wPLS} = (N, E)$ *is defined as follows.*

- $N = V$
- $\exists e = (u, v) \in E$ *if* $\exists (int_u, int_v) \in E'$.
- *For* $e = (u, v) \in E$, *e.weight, the weight on* e, *is the total number of edges* $e' \in E'$ *such that* $e' = (int_u, int_v)$.

Figure 8 (a) shows the wPLS graph generated from the PLS graph in Figure 6. The weight on an edge (u, v) equals to the number of times the variables u and v can be either loaded or stored in parallel.

After a wPLS graph being constructed, the MAM problem in effect reduces to a simpler, yet still exponential-time MWPC problem. To efficiently solve this problem, therefore, we resort to a widely-known heuristic based on an MST algorithm that has

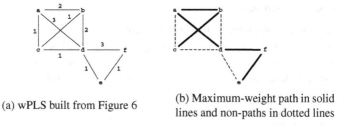

(a) wPLS built from Figure 6

(b) Maximum-weight path in solid lines and non-paths in dotted lines

Fig. 8. wMPLS graph and the maximum-weight path on it

also been used to solve the SOA problem [4]. Figure 8 (b) shows the resulting *maximum-weight path* (MWP) computed by this heuristic. The MWP is constituted by a set of edges in thick solid lines, and all the other edges in dotted lines form what we call a set of *non-paths* (= E_{np} in Figure 7). The rationale for this use of a MST-based heuristic relies on our speculation that assigning contiguous addresses to the variables that can be more often accessed together is more likely to increase the chance better utilizing MLS instructions, thus reducing the overall cost of memory accesses.

The resultant MWP is now used to determine the memory variable offsets (see Figure 9 (a)). It is also used to measure the total number of memory operations required for this program by removing the non-path edges of the wPLS graph from the original PLS graph. We abbreviate this modified PLS graph as an *mPLS* graph. Figure 9 (b) shows that after non-paths are removed, the mPLS graph is no longer a collection of complete graphs, but instead that of connected components. In most cases, the number of those components will become the number of required memory operations in the final code. From Figure 9 (b), we can estimate that the program will probably need eight load/store instructions in total, including both single and multiple loads/stores.

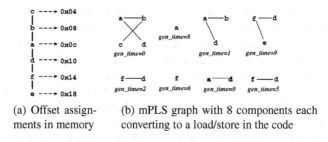

(a) Offset assignments in memory

(b) mPLS graph with 8 components each converting to a load/store in the code

Fig. 9. Offset assignment and the mPLS graph both determined according to the MWP in Figure 8

Although in this example the number of connected graphs does not increase when we modify the PLS graph, in reality we have seen several cases where it actually does. This is of course in part because our heuristic cannot always find an optimal solution. For instance, suppose our algorithm finds the path c-b-a-d-e-f as the result instead of the optimal path c-b-a-d-f-e. Then, the complete graph f-d in Figure 6 would be split into two separate graphs f and d since the edge (f,d) belongs to the non-paths of the wPLS graph. This would result in 10 connected components in the mPLS graph, producing more loads/stores in the code.

3.4   Register Assignment

Every connected component in the mPLS graph corresponds to a block of PLSs accessing contiguous memory locations starting at their base offset m_{base} from the stack pointer. Since the M-sequence constraint is now satisfied, each component with k nodes can be converted to a sequence of code either for a multiple load

$$r_{base} \;=\; \text{sp+\#}m_{base}$$
$$\{r_1, r_2, \cdots, r_k\} \;=\; \text{Mem}[r_{base}],$$

or for a multiple store

$$r_{base} \;=\; \text{sp+\#}m_{base}$$
$$\text{Mem}[r_{base}] \;=\; \{r_1, r_2, \cdots, r_k\}.$$

Of course, if the component has only one node, as in the cases of a and f in Figure 9 (b), then it will be converted to an ordinary single load/store.

As displayed in the algorithm of Figure 10, this whole conversion process is completed in Phase 3 after a valid order of the registers referenced in each MLS instruction is determined by enforcing the R-sequence constraint. The definition of the R-sequence constraint in Section 3.1 can be divided in two parts.

1. All register operands in an MLS instruction must be distinct.
2. The memory words are transferred from/to the registers in an increasing order of the register numbers.

Given a connected component with k nodes, the first part of the constraint implies that at least k registers must be available for the MLS instruction. For instance, in Figure 2 (c), the first MLS instruction generated for the four loads from the variables a,b, c and d requires four registers. But as caln be seen from the original code in Figure 1 (b), c and d were assigned to the same register r2. Therefore, when we generate an MLS for them, we need to allocate one more register (r3 in this case).

Fortunately, the first part of the R-sequence constraint is trivially met in Phase 3 since the RF-size constraint ensures that the register pressure always stays within the register file size. So, as long as we handle load instructions, we will always find as many registers as we need to generate them. To the contrary, when we handle store instructions, we may not find, although not common in practice for several reasons, an enough number of registers that we need to generate them because we need one more register as the base register r_{base} for each multiple store. In case none is available for the base register, we generate an extra store for one of the registers included in the original multiple store, as shown in Figure 10. Then, this register becomes free and can be provided as the base register for the rest of the registers. In the case of a multiple load, we can avoid this additional work by arbitrarily designating the base register to be the one from the registers already allocated for the load.

Once an enough number of registers are allocated for an MLS instruction, the second part of the R-sequence constraint is enforced when these registers are bound to each variable in the instruction. To explain this, consider the example in Figure 1 (b) where the first three loads are accessing contiguous addresses: 0x10 for c, 0x14 for b and 0x18 for a. Even if the loads are satisfying all other constraints, the ARM compiler could not convert them to a multiple load because they still do not satisfy the R-sequence constraint; that is, a was assigned to r2, b to r1 and c to r0.

```
emit_MLSs(P, G_mPLS)
  for each connected component C ∈ G_mPLS do
    Bind ← ∅;  // set of tuples <r,v>: binding register r to variable v
    t ← C.gen_time;  // the cycle just before which an MLS is inserted
    k ← # of nodes in C;  // = # of registers for this MLS instruction
    L_var ← a list of variables v such that int_v ∈ C;
    L_reg ← get_free_registers(k);  // a list of registers
    for all r ∈ L_reg selected in an increasing order of their numbers &
      all v ∈ L_var selected in an increasing order of their offsets do
      insert <r,v> into Bind;
    if C.type = load then
      if k = 1 then  // generate a single load at t in P
        emit_load(P, t, Bind);  // a load: r = v
      else  // k > 1: generate a multiple load at t in P
        r_base ← select_first_reg(Bind);  // select 1^st register ∈ Bind
        m_base ← find_base_offset(L_var);
        emit_base_register(P, t, r_base, m_base);  // r_base=sp+#m_base
        emit_mload(P, t, Bind);  // {r_1,r_2,···,r_k}=Mem[r_base]
      fi
    else  // C.type = store
      if k = 1 then  // generate a single store at t in P
        emit_store(P, t, Bind);  // a store: v = r
      else  // k > 1: generate a multiple store at t in P
        if free register available for base register then
          r_base ← select_free_reg();  // return a free register
          m_base ← find_base_offset(L_var);
          emit_base_register(P, t, r_base, m_base);  // r_base=sp+#m_base
          emit_mstore(P, t + 1, Bind);  // Mem[r_base]={r_1,···,r_k}
        else  // make free the 1^st register r_1 in Bind
          remove <r_1,v_1> from Bind;
          Bind' ← {<r_1,v_1>};  // spill r_1 to use it as r_base
          remove v_1 from L_var;
          emit_store(P, t, Bind');  // a store: v_1 = r_1
          m_base ← find_base_offset(L_var);
          emit_base_register(P, t, r_1, m_base);  // r_1=sp+#m_base
          emit_mstore(P, t + 1, Bind);  // Mem[r_1]={r_2,···,r_k}
          emit_load(P, t + 2, Bind');  // reloading: r_1 = v_1
        fi
      fi
    rename_registers_in(P, Bind);
  od
  eliminate_redundancy_in(P);  // CSE and redundancy elimination
end
```

Fig. 10. Phase 3 algorithm for register (re-)assignment

Since the first part of the R-sequence constraint is already satisfied, finding an binding between variables and registers that satisfies the second part is straightforward in our algorithm. However, after a load/store instruction is inserted in the code, we may need do an extra chore for appropriate register renaming in the code so as to reflect the new binding made in the instruction.

4   Experiment

The effectiveness of our 3-phase algorithm on the MLS problem has been evaluated with a set of benchmarks from the *DSPStone* [9] and *MediaBench* [2] suites. The evaluation was conducted on an ARM 7 processor. Our compiler [6] was used to compare the size of both versions of the code output generated before and after the algorithm is applied to the compiler. In this section, we report our empirical results.

In the experiment, we generated two versions of the ARM assembly code from a set of DSPstone benchmarks. The first version was generated mostly by using single load/store instructions, with the exception of procedure boundaries where MLS instructions were limitedly used to save a few status registers. The second was generated after applying our algorithm to the first version. Figure 11 compares the code size of the two versions, each respectively denoted by *Before* and *After* in the legends. For each benchmark, the upper bar stands for the code size of the first version, and the lower for that of the second one. Each bar is halved in two sections. The dark section represents ALU operations, and the light section represents memory operations (i.e., loads/stores).

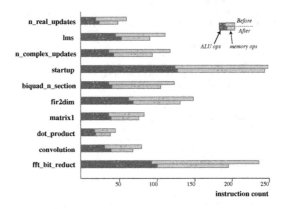

Fig. 11. ARM code size before and after our technique is applied

The amount of code size reduction gained from our MLS generation ranges from 1% to 23%. On average, the overall code size reduction rate is roughly 10%. In the figure, we see that there is a slight increase in the number of ALU instructions for every program. This is certainly because base registers should be initialized before MLS instructions.

For a couple of reasons, we argued in Section 3 that the performance gain with a reduction of loads/stores often outweighs the performance loss with an equal amount of the increase of integer adds for base register initialization. To support this argument, in Figure 12, we single out the effect of load/store reduction and evince the performance benefits we achieve in memory accesses. In the figure, the vertical dashed line denotes the original number of loads/stores in the first version, normalized to one. The horizontal bar represents a reduced code size ratio of loads/stores in the second version against those in the first version. This performance figures reveal to us that the average reduction ratio is approximately 30%, and thus prove that given a set of loads/stores, our technique can reduce the number of loads/stores substantially.

Often many embedded system designers are only allowed limited storage space for their hardware due to stringent resource constraints. Thus, we investigate the effectiveness of our technique on an architecture with a less number of registers than the original ARM processor. For this experiment, the compiler is retargeted to the same ARM ar-

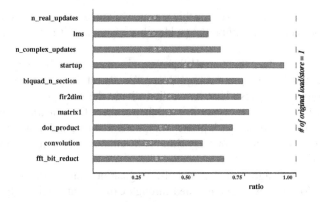

$$\textbf{Fig. 12. } \text{Ratio} = \frac{\text{\# of loads/stores in } 2^{\text{nd}} \text{ version}}{\text{\# of loads/stores in } 1^{\text{st}} \text{ version}}$$

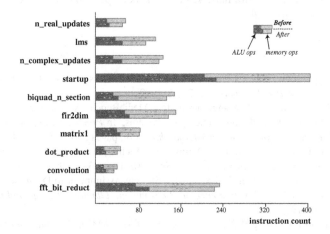

Fig. 13. Code size reduction on a modified ARM with 8 registers

chitecture but with the register file size reduced by half, that is, 8 registers in total. Figure 13 compares the code size of the two versions on this new target machine.

As can be expected, the reduced file size increases register spills, producing more loads/stores in the code. However, except for the code `startup`, the code size has been just slightly increased for all the others. So, for these codes, we achieve almost identical code size reduction ratios in Figure 13 as we did in Figure 11.

5 Conclusion

The work reported here has been motivated by our on-going project to build an optimizing compiler for a commercial media processor under development. In the processor, we found a variety of instructions specifically designed to accelerate media applications, and among them there were MLS instructions. In our efforts to optimize the code with these instructions, we found that no previous compilers had addressed this optimization problem seriously before. For this reason, we opted for pursuing our research to devise a cost-effective algorithm that tackles this exponential-time problem fast and efficiently.

In this paper, we analyze that the MLS problem is an enormously complex problem tangled with several NP-complete subproblems. We, therefore, circumvent this complexity by applying heuristics. That is, we first divide the original problem in three subproblems each defined by a constraint, and then enforce the constraints one-by-one in three different phases. Since each phase is implemented by a polynomial time algorithm, the overall complexity of our algorithm still remains polynomial in the number of input loads/stores.

Our heuristic-based algorithm does not always guarantee an optimal solution to the MLS problem. However, we demonstrated through experiments that it exploits MLS instructions effectively to further reduce the size of code even after the code is fully optimized by existing production-quality compilers. Although our technique cannot reduce the total code size on a dramatic scale, it has been proven to be effective to some extent for most cases after all.

References

1. D. Bartley. Optimizing Stack Frame Accesses for Processors with Restricted Addressing Modes. *Software Practice & Experience*, 22(2), 1992.
2. C. Lee, M. Potkonjak, and W Mangione-Smith. MediaBench: A Tool for Evaluating and Synthesizing Multimedia and Communications Systems. In *Proceedings of the 30th Annaul IEEE/ACM Internation Symposium on Microarchitecture*, pages 330–335, Nov. 1997.
3. R. Leupers and F. David. A Uniform Optimization Technique for Offset Assignment Problems. In *International Symposium on Systems Synthesis*, pages 3–8, 1998.
4. S. Liao, S. Devadas, K. Keutzer, and S. Tjiang. Storage Assignment to Decrease Code Size. *Proceedings of the SIGPLAN Conference on Programming Language Design and Implementation*, pages 186–195, 1995.
5. V. Nandivada and J. Palsberg. Efficient Spill Code for SDRAM. In *International Conference on Compilers, Architectures and Synthesis for Embedded Systems*, Nov. 2003.
6. Y. Paek, M. Ahn, and S. Lee. Case Studies on Automatic Extraction of Target-specific Architectural Parameters in Complex Code Generation. In *Workshop on Software and Compilers for Embedded Systems*, Sep. 2003.
7. A. Rao and S. Pande. Storage Assignment Optimizations to Generate Compact and Efficient Code on Embedded DSPs. In *Proceedings of the SIGPLAN Conference on Programming Language Design and Implementation*, pages 128–138, May 1999.
8. X. Zhuang, C. Lau, and S. Pande. Storage Assignment Optimizations through Variable Coalescence for Embedded Processors. In *Proceedings of the SIGPLAN Conference on Languages, Compilers and Tools for Embedded Systems*, pages 220–231, June 2003.
9. V. Zivojnovic, J.M. Velarde, C. Schager, and H. Meyr. DSPStone - A DSP oriented Benchmarking Methodology. In *Proceedings of International Conference on Signal Processing Applications and Technology*, 1994.

An ILP-Based Approach to Locality Optimization

Guilin Chen[1], Ozcan Ozturk[1], and Mahmut Kandemir[1]

Department of Computer Science and Engineering,
The Pennsylvania State University,
University Park, PA 16802, USA
{guilchen, ozturk, kandemir}@cse.psu.edu

Abstract. One of the most important factors that determine performance of data-intensive applications is data locality. A program with high data locality makes better use of fast, on-chip memories and can avoid large main memory latencies. Although previous compiler research investigated numerous techniques for enhancing locality, we lack of formal techniques, against which the existing heuristics can be compared. Motivated by this observation, this paper presents a fresh look at locality optimization based on integer linear programming (ILP). We formulate the conditions for data locality, and present a system of constraints whose solution gives optimal computation re-ordering and data-to-memory assignment under our objective function and cost model. Our experimental results using three data-intensive applications clearly indicate that the ILP-based approach generates very good results and outperforms a previously proposed heuristic solution to locality.

1 Introduction and Motivation

Performance of today's large-scale, data-intensive applications is dictated by their memory behavior. This is because in many architectures, while executing a CPU operation takes one or two cycles, visiting main memory for a data item can cost tens of cycles. One of the classical approaches to eliminate this memory bottleneck is to use fast on-chip memories that can be accessed in a few cycles. The success of these fast memories depends strongly on the program access pattern, data dependences between the different parts of the embedded application, and the compiler optimizations available.

Locality-enhancing techniques such as compiler-directed data reuse optimizations [20,3,1,17] decrease the number of accesses to memory, thereby reducing both latency and required bandwidth. Although previous compiler research investigated numerous techniques for enhancing locality (e.g., see [21] and the references therein), we lack of formal techniques against which the existing heuristics can be compared. Such formal techniques are not important only because they may allow us rank and classify different heuristics but also because they may indicate how much additional benefits can be expected from adopting sophisticated heuristic techniques in the future.

Motivated by this observation, this paper presents a fresh look at locality optimization based on integer linear programming (ILP). We formulate the conditions for locality and present a system of constraints whose solution gives optimal computation re-ordering and data-to-memory assignment, under our objective function and cost model.

R. Eigenmann et al. (Eds.): LCPC 2004, LNCS 3602, pp. 149–163, 2005.

An important issue to note here is that the ideas presented in this work are not restricted to data cache locality. The locality problem exhibits itself in many different forms in many different contexts such as memory bank locality, communication locality, and instruction locality. Section 2 discusses three locality problems encountered in practice. After introducing the key players in our optimization problem in Section 3, our baseline formulation is presented in Section 4. This baseline formulation is limited in the sense that it operates under several important assumptions. Nevertheless, it forms the basis which one can build upon. We relax our assumptions in Section 5 where we discuss how to handle issues regarding parallelism, data dependences, and memory location reuse. As will be discussed in that section, most of these issues are addressed by either adding some extra constraints to the baseline formulation or by eliminating one or two of the original constraints.

An important question to answer is whether it is possible to use an ILP-based approach in a realistic optimization environment (e.g., an optimizing compiler). Section 6 tries to address this issue. Based on our observations in Section 6, we implemented the first version of our optimization framework, and performed several experiments. The results presented in Section 7 demonstrate that our approach is very successful in optimizing data locality. Our presentation concludes by a discussion of future work (Section 8) and by summarizing our major contributions (Section 9).

2   Practical View: Locality Problem

A number of optimization problems encountered in practice can be cast as locality optimization problems. Examples include cache locality optimization, bank locality optimization, and communication optimization. In the following, we discuss these three popular locality optimization problems in more detail.

- *Cache Locality Optimization.* Manipulation of scalar and array data is an ubiquitous operation in most programs. Rarely do programmers concern themselves with details of memory hierarchy. However, if there is a cache memory (a small, fast on-chip memory) in the architecture, accessing a data item can exhibit a large latency variance depending on where it is found. Typically, the access latency rate between the first level cache, second level cache, and main memory is in the order of 1:10:100, meaning that it is extremely important to find the required data item in the first level of cache [20]. Cache memories have low access latencies because they are small in size and close to the processor datapath (where computation takes place). Consequently, performance of many data-intensive applications critically depends on their data cache behavior. To improve cache behavior (performance), compilers/programmers can use computation re-ordering (i.e., changing the order of computations in the code to reduce the gap between the successive accesses to the same data item/block [11]) and/or data re-layouting (i.e., re-structuring the data layout in memory to place the successively accessed data items in nearby memory locations [10]). Note that the first of these optimizations is in the temporal domain, whereas the second one is in the spatial domain.
- *Bank Locality Optimization.* Breaking large hardware components into smaller ones is beneficial from several perspectives. The most important of these is that

the smaller components can be power-managed at a finer-granularity. For example, dividing a large memory space into two banks allows us to turn off the power to one of the banks if we (i.e., the current computation) are accessing only the other one. In many cases, it is beneficial to increase the inter-access time for a given memory bank [9,5]. This is because doing so allows us to keep a turned off bank in the turned off state for a longer duration of time, thereby offsetting the potential performance (and power) penalty due to frequent turn-on/offs. In addition to this, a current trend in low-power computing is the support for different operating modes (for a given computer architecture), each consuming a different amount of energy. This provision is available in processors (e.g., the mobile Pentium III has five power management modes), memories (e.g., the Rambus technology [16] provides up to seven modes of operation), disks [4,12], and other peripherals. While these energy saving modes are extremely useful during idle periods, one has to pay a cost of exit latency (resynchronization time) when these hardware entities transition back to the fully-operational (active) state. Therefore, typically, there is a tradeoff between the aggressiveness of the power saving mode and the magnitude of resynchronization cost it entails. Improving bank locality by extending the bank idle times (i.e., accumulating accesses in a small set of banks at a given time) may also allow us to use the most aggressive operating modes, thereby maximizing energy savings.

– *Communication Optimization.* Communication optimization is one of the most widely-used optimizations performed by compilers/middleware written for parallel architectures, including embedded on-chip multiprocessors. When a given application is divided into multiple parts, each running on a separate processor, processors may engage communication if they share data [18,2]. This communication may take the form of message-passing. In such a scenario, it is beneficial to minimize the number of inter-processor communications (messages) by reusing the communicated data as much as possible. Failing to do so may necessitate frequent (and unnecessary) inter-processor communication, thereby wasting communication bandwidth and increasing latency. Several communication optimization techniques (e.g., message vectorization, message coalescing, and inter-nest optimizations) try to achieve communication locality by modifying (restructuring) a given application.

These are just three examples where one needs to optimize locality to improve performance. Other examples include memory locality optimizations in multiprocessors, instruction locality enhancement, and register-level data reuse. In the next section, we will abstract out the details of these problems and introduce our key players in optimizing locality. While our presentation is biased towards data (cache) locality, we believe that our results can be extended to most other forms of locality without much difficulty.

3   Abstract View and Key Players

In abstract terms, there are two key players in a locality-sensitive execution environment: "data items" and "computations." Data items represent the data manipulated by an application, and are stored in memory locations which constitute a linear (storage) space. Computations, on the other hand, correspond to the operations (to be performed) on the data stored in memory locations. They are assumed to be expressed at a fine-granular fashion. For example, in a loop-based, array-intensive embedded program, the work done by each iteration of each loop can be considered as a separate computation.

Data items and computations are important because they are the entities that can be controlled (manipulated) by an optimizer. For example, an optimizer can change the execution order of computations to achieve better locality (without breaking any data or control dependences). Similarly, another optimizer can modify the storage order (i.e., the data item–to–memory mapping) for clustering items with temporal affinity together. Yet a third optimizer can combine both these strategies to achieve even better locality behavior.

Below, we define what we mean in this paper by "data items", "memory locations", and "computations":

- $\mathcal{V}$: the set of data items (also called variables). Each $v_i \in \mathcal{V}$ (where $1 \leq i \leq |V|$) corresponds to a variable in the high-level application. It should be observed that each $v_i \in \mathcal{V}$ can have multiple instances in the code. Assuming v_i has n_i instances, the total number of instances (i.e., variable occurrences) in the code is

$$|n| = \sum_{i=1}^{|V|} n_i.$$

  We use notation $v_{i,l}$ to refer to the lth (where $1 \leq l \leq n_i$) instance of v_i.
- $\mathcal{M}$: the set of addressable memory locations (i.e., the place-holders for the variables). In principle, each $m_j \in \mathcal{M}$ (where $1 \leq j \leq |M|$) can hold multiple variables if their lifetimes do not overlap.
- $\mathcal{C}$: the set of computations. Each $c_k \in \mathcal{C}$ (where $1 \leq k \leq |C|$) can be a loop iteration, statement, a block of statements, etc.

Typically, there are two important decisions that need to be performed by a locality optimizer. The first of them is to decide on a mapping from variables to memory locations. This is also called the "variable-to-memory mapping." The second one is to decide on an (execution) order for computations. In other words, it is to assign an execution cycle to each computation. This problem is also called the "scheduling problem."

4 Formulation of the Problem

4.1 Our Goal

Informally, our objective is to optimize locality in embedded applications. When a data item is accessed by different computations, we say that there exists "temporal reuse." Similarly, if different computations access the data in the same neighborhood (e.g., a cache line or a data page), we say that "spatial reuse" occurs. It is important to observe that reuse is an intrinsic property of a given data access (reference) pattern, and is independent of the cache hierarchy organization (i.e., the underlying architecture). In contrast, locality is the actual realization of the potential reuse (by satisfying the accesses from the cache rather than the main memory), and depends on a number of factors including the access pattern, cache topology, and cache space management policy (e.g., LRU vs. LFU). Depending on these factors, the intrinsic reuse exhibited by a data reference can be "converted" into locality if the data item in question can be found in the cache when it is "reused."

This can be achieved in three different ways. First, we can re-order computations in the program such that the computations that access the same set of data are executed immediately one after another. In this way, the chances that the data can be caught in the cache (when reused) are increased dramatically. This is called the computation transformation. Second, instead of computations, we can focus on data and cluster the data items that are accessed by the same computation in the same neighborhood (to take advantage of spatial reuse). This is called data storage (layout) optimization. Third, we can combine computation reordering and storage optimization (in a coordinated way) to take advantage of the both at the same time. In other words, our objective is to convert reuse patterns into locality. However, in the rest of the paper, when there is no confusion, we use the terms "reuse" and "locality" interchangeably.

The approach described in this work constructs a set of linear equalities and inequalities and solves the locality problem optimally using zero-one integer linear programming (ILP). ILP provides a set of techniques that solve those optimization problems in which both the objective function and constraints are linear functions, and the solution variables are restricted to be integers. The zero-one ILP is an ILP problem in which each (solution) variable is restricted to be either zero or one [15]. Our ILP formulation allows us to solve the locality problem optimally. It should be stressed, however, that this optimality is within our objective function and cost model. In particular, as will be discussed later in the paper, there might be multiple ways of defining an objective function for locality, and an objective function suitable for one scenario may not be very preferable in a different one.

4.2 Baseline Formulation

Our baseline implementation works with the following assumptions. First, we assume that each variable will be stored in a single memory location. Second, each memory location will hold a single variable (the same variable) throughout the execution. Third, there are no data or control dependences among the computations; that is, we are dealing with a fully parallel application (i.e., complete flexibility in re-ordering the computations in the application). Fourth, at each execution cycle, only one variable (instance) will be touched (i.e., the memory accesses are sequentialized). Fifth, there is no higher level clustering requirement between the variables; that is, we have complete flexibility in assigning memory locations to data items. Finally, we assume that no (potentially) redundant computation is performed (e.g., prefetching). Let us start by defining a zero-one variable $k_{i,j}$:

$$k_{i,j} = \begin{cases} 1, \text{ if } v_j \text{ is mapped to location } m_i \\ 0, \text{ otherwise} \end{cases} \tag{1}$$

What this definition means is that $k_{i,j}$ will be one if variable v_j (after the locality optimization) is assigned to location m_i; otherwise, $k_{i,j}$ will be zero.

Based on two of our assumptions listed above, we have:

$$\sum_{i=1}^{|M|} k_{i,j} = 1 \quad \forall j : 1 \leq j \leq |V| \tag{2}$$

$$\sum_{j=1}^{|V|} k_{i,j} = 1 \quad \forall i : 1 \leq i \leq |M| \tag{3}$$

The first of these integer conditions states that each variable is stored in only one memory location. The second one, on the other hand, states that each memory location will hold a single variable. These two conditions implement two of our assumptions listed above.

Our next set of conditions are for execution cycles (i.e., the scheduling constraints). Recall that one of our assumptions states that, in each cycle, the execution will touch a single variable (instance). Therefore, we can establish a one-to-one correspondence between the variable instances and the execution cycles. To achieve this, we define the following zero-one variable:

$$s_{i,j,k} = \begin{cases} 1, & \text{if } v_{i,j} \text{ is touched at cycle } k \\ 0, & \text{otherwise} \end{cases} \tag{4}$$

Since we assumed that the execution will touch a single (variable) instance at each cycle, the total number of cycles (i.e., the execution time) is $|N|$. Using this zero-one variable, we can state the following two conditions. Condition (5) indicates that each variable instance will be touched at only one cycle. In a similar vein, condition (6) states that at each cycle only one variable instance will be touched.

$$\sum_{k=1}^{|N|} s_{i,j,k} = 1 \quad \text{for each } v_{i,j} \tag{5}$$

$$\sum_{v_{i,j}} s_{i,j,k} = 1 \quad \forall k : 1 \leq k \leq |N| \tag{6}$$

We can now express the memory location a given variable is mapped to, and the execution cycle at which a variable instance is touched. Specifically, in mathematical terms,

$$Loc(v_j) = \sum_{i=1}^{|M|} i.k_{i,j} \tag{7}$$

$$Sch(v_{i,j}) = \sum_{k=1}^{|N|} k.s_{i,j,k} \tag{8}$$

$Loc(v_j)$ gives the memory location which variable v_j is mapped to, and $Sch(v_{i,j})$ is the cycle at which the variable instance $v_{i,j}$ will be touched. It should be emphasized that determining a $Sch(v_{i,j})$ for each $v_{i,j}$ corresponds to assigning an execution cycle to each computation $c_k \in \mathcal{C}$ (under our assumptions). As will be shown shortly, temporal locality and spatial locality can be stated in terms of $Loc(.)$ and $Sch(.)$ functions.

4.3 Temporal Locality

We say that temporal locality is exhibited when a data item is referenced frequently; that is, the average inter-access time for the variable is low. It should be noticed that temporal locality can be achieved if the instances of a given variable are accessed in close time proximity. Based on this observation, one might write the following optimization objective:

$$minimize \sum_{i=1}^{|V|} \sum_{l=1}^{n_i-1} Sch(v_{i,l+1}) - Sch(v_{i,l}). \tag{9}$$

This expression tries to reduce the time gap between the successive accesses to the instances of a given variable (i.e., the shorter the time gap between the access times of the instances, the smaller the value of sum expression above). However, a closer look may reveal that this objective function may not always be very successful in capturing temporal locality. To see this, let us consider an example scenario where a variable has four instances in a given code. For illustrative purposes, we focus on two cases. In the first case, the instances are touched in cycles 1, 4, 7, and 10. In the second case, they are touched in cycles 1, 2, 3, and 20. According to the objective function above, the cost for the first case is 9, whereas that for the second case is 19. That is, the first case is preferable over the second one. On the other hand, in the second case, three instance accesses occur in consecutive cycles, so it is guaranteed that we will take advantage of data locality (e.g., the requested data will be in the cache at the time of the reuse) during the last two of these accesses. In other words, we are 100% sure that the data will be reused twice from the cache. On the other hand, in the first case, although the reuse distance is short, if another variable happens to map to the same (cache) location between the successive accesses to the variable in question, the locality may not be materialized (i.e., we cannot be sure whether the data reuse will be converted into locality). Therefore, there might exist cases where the objective function considered above may not be the best choice for stating temporal locality.

Based on this observation, we next consider another objective function for temporal locality. Let us first define:

$$m_{i,l} = \begin{cases} 1, \text{ if } Sch(v_{i,l+1}) - Sch(v_{i,l}) = 1 \\ 0, \text{ otherwise} \end{cases} \tag{10}$$

That is, $m_{i,l}$ takes the value of 1 if the two instances of variable v_i are accessed successively; otherwise, $m_{i,l}$ is set to zero. Then, we can define our new objective as:

$$maximize \sum_{i=1}^{|V|} \sum_{l=1}^{n_i-1} m_{i,l} \tag{11}$$

It can be observed that the objective function in (11) tries to maximize the number of instance accesses that occur one after immediately another. Returning to the scenario and the cases discussed earlier, the value of this new objective function for the case one and case two is 0 and 2, respectively (that is, in the second case we reuse the same variable in two successive cycles, whereas in the first case no such reuse occurs). In other words, according to this objective function, the case two is preferable. To sum up, whether objective function (9) or (11) performs better than the other is application (access pattern) and architecture dependent.

At this point, we can state our temporal locality optimization problem formally. Our problem is to optimize (9) (or (11)) subject to the constraints in given in (2), (3), (5), (6), (7), and (8).

An important point to note when one considers objective functions (9) and (11) is that neither of them makes any use of $Loc(.)$ function mentioned above. That is, they are independent of the variable-to-memory mapping. While at first glance this may seem unreasonable, a closer look reveals that modifying the storage layout of variables (i.e., the variable-to-memory mapping) cannot affect temporal locality. Put another way, if we are not having temporal locality with a given variable-to-memory mapping, we "cannot" have temporal locality by changing that variable-to-memory mapping. This is because temporal locality deals with accesses to the same variable (more precisely, to the different instances of the same variable), and this is independent of the memory location of the variable in question. Consequently, in our definition given in the previous paragraph, constraints (2), (3), and (7) can be omitted. However, as discussed in the next subsection, when one considers spatial locality, the situation changes.

4.4 Spatial Locality

In a sense, spatial locality is a relaxed form of temporal locality. In spatial locality, instead of requiring that the successive instance touches should be on the same memory location, we simply demand that such touches occur on the neighboring memory locations. Such memory locations with spatial proximity are said to constitute a "memory block." Without loss of generality, in the following discussion, we assume that a memory block contains L data items. Note that when any one of the data items residing in a given memory block is accessed, the entire block is brought to the cache; i.e., the granularity of transfer is a block.

We start by giving definitions for two zero-one integer variables:

$$g_{i,j,l,l'} = \begin{cases} 1, \text{ if } Sch(v_{i,l}) - Sch(v_{j,l'}) = 1 \\ 0, \text{ otherwise} \end{cases} \tag{12}$$

$$h_{i,j} = \begin{cases} 1, \text{ if } Loc(v_i) - Loc(v_j) < L \text{ and} \\ \quad \exists c_1, c_2, c_3 \text{ such that } \{Loc(v_i) = c_1L + c_2, \\ \quad Loc(v_j) = c_1L + c_3, \text{ and } 0 \le c_2, c_3 < L\} \\ 0, \text{ otherwise} \end{cases} \tag{13}$$

Note that $g_{i,j,l,l'}$ and $h_{i,j}$ can easily be re-written as linear constraints. $g_{i,j,l,l'}$ indicates whether two instances of two variables (not necessarily distinct) are accessed one immediately after another. $h_{i,j}$, on the other hand, says whether two variables belong to the same memory block, or not. Next, we define:

$$gh_{i,j,l,l'} = \begin{cases} 1, \text{ if } (g_{i,j,l,l'} = 1) \text{ and } (h_{i,j} = 1) \\ 0, \text{ otherwise} \end{cases} \tag{14}$$

It is easy to see that $gh_{i,j,l,l'}$ returns 1 if the two variable instances are accessed one after another and the variables are stored in the same memory block. Based on this, we can define an objective of the following form:

$$maximize \sum_{i=1}^{|V|} \sum_{j=1}^{|V|} \sum_{l=1}^{n_i} \sum_{l'=1}^{n_j} gh_{i,j,l,l'} \qquad (15)$$

In formal terms, we can define the problem of optimizing spatial locality as one of satisfying (15) under the constraints expressed in (2), (3), (5), (6), (7), (8), (12), (13), and (14).

4.5 Combined Optimization

It should be emphasized that the objective function given above targets only spatial locality. In the next step, one may want to combine temporal and spatial locality under a unified strategy. Assuming that we are using the temporal locality objective given by (11) and the spatial locality objective expressed in (15), the combined locality objective can be expressed as:

$$maximize \left\{ \alpha.\left(\sum_{i=1}^{|V|} \sum_{j=1}^{|V|} \sum_{l=1}^{n_i} \sum_{l'=1}^{n_j} gh_{i,j,l,l'} \right) + \beta.\left(\sum_{i=1}^{|V|} \sum_{l=1}^{n_i-1} m_{i,l} \right) \right\}. \qquad (16)$$

The first expression here is for spatial locality, whereas the second one is for temporal locality. Constant coefficients α and β help us assign different weights to different types of localities. This is important because, in many cases, exploiting temporal locality and exploiting spatial locality may bring benefits of different magnitudes. For example, as far as cache memories are concerned, exploiting temporal locality might be more beneficial as doing so can eliminate a cache reference altogether, whereas we still incur a cache miss across cache block (memory block) boundaries even if we have optimized spatial reuse [21]. In expression (16), by giving different values to α and β, one can experiment with different optimization strategies. In formal terms, the entire locality optimization problem (which includes both temporal and spatial locality) can be expressed as one of satisfying (16) under (2), (3), (5), (6), (7), (8), (12), (13), and (14).

5   Relaxing Assumptions

Our baseline formulation presented above is limited due to the assumptions discussed at the beginning of Section 4.2. In this section, we discuss how one can relax some of these assumptions, thereby potentially increasing the applicability of the proposed solution.

First, many computations are subject to data dependences. That is, we have some restrictions in re-ordering computations, and not respecting these restrictions can violate the original semantics of the embedded application being optimized. To incorporate data dependences into our framework, we need to formulate a constraint for each data dependent reference pair. Let us suppose that $v_{i,l}$ is data dependent on $v_{j,l'}$. Then, any legal (acceptable) scheduling should satisfy:

$$Sch(v_{i,l}) - Sch(v_{j,l'}) \geq 1. \tag{17}$$

In other words, $v_{i,l}$ should be touched after $v_{j,l'}$. Control dependence constraints [14] can also be expressed in a similar fashion. Another important assumption we made was that each memory location can hold only one variable throughout the execution. It should be noticed that this assumption can (in some cases) result in excessive memory space consumption since, in general, not all variables are alive during the entire execution time of an application [3]. Specifically, if lifetimes of two variables do not overlap with each other, we should be able to use the same memory location for both these variables. We can incorporate this memory location reuse property into our framework by focusing on the variables whose lifetimes do not overlap. In mathematical terms, if $v_{i,last}$ is the last instance of variable v_i and $v_{j,first}$ is the first instance of variable v_j, we have

$$k_{l,i} + k_{l,j} \leq 2 \quad \text{if } Sch(v_{i,last}) < Sch(v_{j,first}), \tag{18}$$

where the zero-one parameter k is as defined in expression (1). This constraint should be written for each such variable pair. The remaining memory location assignments can be governed as indicated in constraint (3).

One of the other assumptions we had was that at each cycle the execution touches only a single variable instance. In a parallel execution environment, on the other hand, it is reasonable to expect that multiple variable references can occur at the same time (i.e., the memory-level parallelism). This can be handled by dropping constraint (6) from consideration.

6   Discussion

One of the potential problems in employing an ILP solver within an optimizing compiler is that it can take large amounts of time to find a solution. This is particularly true if we are dealing with large number of variables and constraints. Unfortunately, such cases occur frequently, especially considering the fact that applications are becoming more data centric and dataset sizes keep continuously increasing. Clearly, adopting an ILP-based strategy when we are dealing thousands of loop iterations will not be feasible.

Our approach to address this problem is based on the following observation. In reordering the computations, an optimizer typically focuses only on the computations that belong to a "temporal neighborhood". For instance, in performing loop optimizations for locality [21], an optimizing compiler typically handles one nest (or a small number of nests) at a time. In fact, in many cases, enlarging the scope of optimizations (i.e., to include far apart computations as well) is not feasible in practice as more distance between computations means more probability for data dependences that could prevent access reordering. Therefore, it is possible to divide a given program into disjoint "computation domains". Each computation domain typically represents a group of computations that can be restructured together using compiler transformations [14], and is optimized in isolation (i.e., separately from the other computation domains). Since our ILP-based optimizer focuses only on a single computation domain at a time, our approach will be applicable to even large programs. However, in such cases, we also need to consider the extra cots that would be incurred due to re-mapping the data layout across the computation domains (this cost is captured in our experimental evaluation).

Another potential problem is that, we are letting our ILP solver to come up with both storage and computation mappings. While in most cases (in fact, in all the cases in our experiments) the resulting computation mappings are regular in the sense that they can be expressed using nested loops, it might be possible to have complex mappings that would require full loop unrolling in the worst case. In such cases, one option would be to use the closest regular mapping to the selected one. Finally, it is to be noted that while our formulation targets at maximizing locality, an optimizer should consider other aspects of the program and other optimizations as well.

7   Experimental Results

In this section, we present preliminary performance results from our implementation for three codes from the embedded image processing domain — "Edge" (an edge detection application), "ObjSearch" (an object search algorithm for color images), and "Vtrack" (a vehicle detection and tracking application). A common characteristic of all these three applications is that the size of the images can be set by the user. This allows us to experiment with different image sizes. Also, all pixel values are represented using a floating-point number. Our experimental results have been obtained using a custom simulation environment for a MIPS 4kp kind of architecture (with a maximum MFLOPS rate of 150). Our simulator allows us change cache parameters, and outputs the number of cache hits/misses and the "MFLOPS" rate (which indicates the performance; the higher, the better). All code modifications to the original codes have been performed using SUIF [19], an experimental compiler from Stanford University. However, in our ILP-based optimization, we also need to find the solution to the integer variables. For this purpose, we use lp_solve [13], a linear programming solver (the zero-one constraints are encoded explicitly). Unless stated otherwise, our default data cache is 8KB, two-way set-associative with a line (block) size of 32 bytes.

We compare the performances of six different versions of each code. "OR" corresponds to the original application without any locality optimization. "HR" is a heuristic based locality optimization that makes use of classical loop-oriented transformations [11] (including iteration space tiling). "TL1" and "TL2" are our temporal locality optimization strategies based on the objective functions given in (9) and (11), respectively. "SL" is the result of the spatial locality optimization strategy based on the objective function given in (15). Finally, "TL2+SL" represents the version obtained using the combined objective function in (16). In this last version, we assumed $\alpha = 1$ and $\beta = 2$; that is, we give higher weight to temporal locality. Later, we also present results obtained using different (α, β) values. The compilation times (which also include the LP solver times) for the TL2+SL version were 58 sec, 137 sec, and 113 sec for Edge, ObjSearch, and Vtrack, respectively. As expected, the other versions took less time to find the solutions.

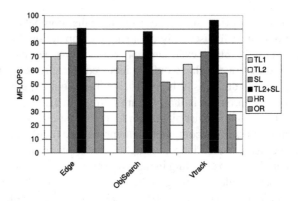

Fig. 1. Performance of different versions with 8KB data cache

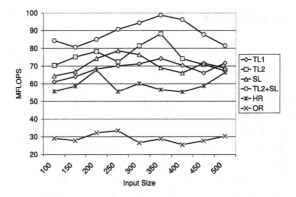

Fig. 2. Performance of Edge with different input sizes

Figure 1 compares the performances of all these six versions for our three codes. One can clearly observe that our ILP-based versions outperform the remaining versions, TL2+SL generating the best performance. Specifically, the average (across all three codes) MFLOPS due to TL1, TL2, SL, TL2+SL, HR, and OR are 67.1%, 69.2%, 73.7%, 91.8%, 57.9%, and 37.6%, respectively. These results clearly illustrate the importance of using ILP for detecting the best computation and layout transformations. To see how our savings vary when input size is changed, we performed another set of experiments. Figure 2 shows how the performance of Edge varies with different input sizes (the default input size is 300, which corresponds to the number of elements used to represent a dimension of the image being processed). One can observe that, for all input sizes, the TL2+SL version generates the best performance results. Another observation is that the difference between TL2+SL and HR is larger around the medium values of the input size. This is because when the input size is very small, there is little pressure on the cache, and, when the input size is very large, the ILP-based approach does not perform very well as it works on computation domain granularity which may not capture sufficient amount of locality with large inputs.

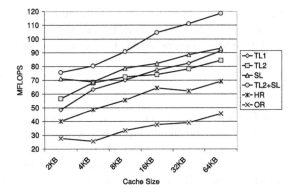

Fig. 3. Performance of Edge with different cache sizes

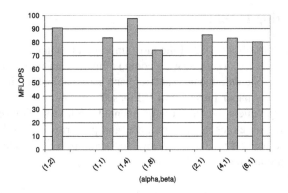

Fig. 4. Performance of TL2+SL with different (α, β) values (Edge)

Recall that so far in our experiments we used a cache size of 8KB. To see the impact of cache size on the effectiveness of our approach, in our next set of experiments, we measured MFLOPS with different cache sizes. The results given in Figure 3 show that while TL2+SL is still the best version, the relative improvements due to TL1 and TL2 change with the cache size. In particular, when the cache size becomes larger, TL1 starts to outperform TL2. This is mainly due to the fact that with large cache sizes we do not need to insist on perfect temporal locality (i.e., the same variable is accessed at the next cycle), as the cache captures most of the locality independent of the access pattern. We also note that, with large cache sizes, SL and TL1 performs similarly. This is also because a large cache size helps to capture locality (to some extent) irrespective of the data access pattern exhibited by the application.

The effectiveness of our TL2+SL strategy also depends on the (α, β) parameters used in expression (16). We also performed experiments with different (α, β) values and plotted the results in Figure 4 for Edge. We can clearly see that the values used for (α, β) have an impact on performance. In particular, giving a large weight to either α or β does not lead to very good results. For this application, $(\alpha, \beta) = (1, 4)$ generates the best performance behavior. However, in general, the best values for α and β are application dependent. Our framework allows making experiments with different (α, β) values, and choosing the most appropriate one for a given platform.

8   Future Work

The work presented in this paper can be extended in several ways. First, we would like to experiment with other potential objective functions for temporal, spatial, and combined locality. Second, we would like to investigate ILP formulation of different locality problems such as instruction locality and memory locality in multiprocessor environments. Third, we would like to perform experiments with different (and a larger set of) benchmarks. And finally, we plan to compare our ILP-based approach to different heuristic solutions, and highlight the strengths and weaknesses.

9   Concluding Remarks

Optimizing data locality is one of the most important problems in data-intensive computing. This is because straightforward coding of many data-intensive applications does no lend itself to good data locality, and in many cases, an optimizing compiler may be of great help. This paper presents an ILP-based formulation of the locality problem and presents experimental data. We implemented the first version of our optimization framework using an experimental compiler, and performed several experiments. The results obtained using three data-intensive applications demonstrate that our approach is successful in optimizing data locality.

Acknowledgement

This work was supported by NSF CAREER Award #0093082.

References

1. B. Aarts et al. OCEANS: optimizing compilers for embedded applications. In *Proceedings of EuroPar,* Lecture Notes in Computer Science, Springer-Verlag, 1997.
2. Z. Bozkus, A. Choudhary, G. C. Fox, T. Haupt, and S. Ranka. Fortran 90D/HPF compiler for distributed memory MIMD computers: design, implementation, and performance results. In *Proceedings of Supercomputing,* November 1993, Portland, OR.
3. F. Catthoor et al. *Data Access and Storage Management for Embedded Programmable Processors.* Kluwer Academic Publishers, 2002.
4. F. Douglas, P. Krishnan, and B. Marsh. Thwarting the power-hungry disk. In *Proceedings of Winter Usenix,* 1994.
5. M. Kandemir, I. Kolcu, and I. Kadayif. Influence of loop optimizations on energy consumption of multi-bank memory systems. In *Proceedings of the International Conference on Compiler Construction,* Grenoble, France, April 6–14, 2002.
6. K. Kennedy and K. McKinley. Optimizing for parallelism and data locality. In *Proceedings of the 1992 ACM International Conference on Supercomputing,* ACM, New York.

7. I. Kodukula, N. Ahmed, and K. Pingali. Data-centric multi-level blocking. In *Proceedings of SIGPLAN Conference on Programming Language Design and Implementation*, June 1997.
8. M. Lam, E. Rothberg, and M. Wolf. The cache performance of blocked algorithms. In *Proceedings of the Fourth International Conference on Architectural Support for Programming Languages and Operating Systems*, April 1991.
9. A. R. Lebeck, X. Fan, H. Zeng, and C. S. Ellis. Power-aware page allocation. In *Proceedings of the Ninth International Conference on Architectural Support for Programming Languages and Operating Systems,* November 2000.
10. S.-T. Leung and J. Zahorjan. Optimizing data locality by array restructuring. *Technical Report TR 95–09–01,* Department of Computer Science and Engineering, University of Washington, September 1995.
11. W. Li. *Compiling for NUMA Parallel Machines.* Ph.D. Thesis, Computer Science Department, Cornell University, Ithaca, NY, 1993.
12. K. Li, R. Kumpf, P. Horton, and T. Anderson. A quantitative analysis of disk drive power management in portable computers. In *Proceedings of Winter Usenix,* 1994.
13. lp_solve. ftp://ftp.es.ele.tue.nl/pub/lp_solve/
14. S. S. Muchnick. *Advanced Compiler Design and Implementation.* Morgan Kaufmann Publishers, 1st edition, July 1997.
15. G. Nemhauser and L. Wolsey. *Integer and Combinatorial Optimization,* Wiley-Interscience Publications, John Wiley & Sons, New York, 1988.
16. Rambus Inc. http://www.rambus.com/.
17. G. Rivera and C.-W. Tseng. Locality optimizations for multi-Level caches. In *Proceedings of SC'99,* Portland, OR, November 1999.
18. C.-W. Tseng. *An Optimizing Fortran D Compiler for MIMD Distributed-Memory Machines.* Ph.D. Thesis, Rice COMP TR93-199, Department of Computer Science, Rice University, January 1993.
19. R. Wilson et al. SUIF: an infrastructure for research on parallelizing and optimizing compilers. SIGPLAN Notices, 29(12):31–37, December 1994.
20. M. Wolf, D. Maydan, and D. Chen. Combining loop transformations considering caches and scheduling. In *Proceedings of the International Symposium on Microarchitecture,* pages 274–286, Paris, France, December 1996.
21. M. Wolfe. *High Performance Compilers for Parallel Computing,* Addison Wesley, CA, 1996.

A Code Isolator: Isolating Code Fragments from Large Programs*

Yoon-Ju Lee and Mary Hall

University of Southern California / Information Sciences Institute,
4676 Admiralty Way, Suite 1001, Marina del Rey, California, 90292
{yoonju, mhall}@isi.edu

Abstract. In this paper, we describe a tool we have developed called a code isolator. We envision such a tool will facilitate many software development activities in complex software systems, but we are using it to isolate code segments from large scientific and engineering codes, for the purposes of performance tuning. The goal of the code isolator is to provide an executable version of a code segment and representative data that mimics the performance of the code in the full program. The resulting isolated code can be used in performance tuning experiments, requiring just a tiny fraction of the execution time of the code when executing within the full program. We describe the analyses and transformations used in a code isolator tool, which we have largely automated in the SUIF compiler. We present a case study of its use with LS-DYNA, a large widely-used engineering application. In this paper, we demonstrate how the tool derives code that permits performance tuning for cache. We present results comparing L1 cache misses and execution time for the original program and the isolated program generated by the tool with some manual intervention. We find that the isolated code can be executed 3600 times faster than the original program, and most of the L1 cache misses are preserved. We identify areas where additional analyses can close the remaining gap in predicting and preserving cache misses in the isolated code.

1 Introduction

In this paper, we describe a tool to support debugging and performance tuning of large scientific computations. Typically, the key computations in such a code comprise only a small fraction of the overall size[1]. Further, the overall program may execute for hours, or sometimes even days. If the developer is focusing on implementation or tuning of a key computation, it would be far more efficient and less cumbersome to run just the key computation, isolated from the rest of the program.

* Work sponsored by the National Science Foundation (NSF) under award ACI-0204040 and by the Department of Energy under contract DE-FG01-03ER25563.

[1] This is often referred to as the 90-10 rule of thumb: a program typically spends 90% of its time in 10% of the code.

R. Eigenmann et al. (Eds.): LCPC 2004, LNCS 3602, pp. 164–178, 2005.
© Springer-Verlag Berlin Heidelberg 2005

For this purpose, we have developed a tool called a *code isolator*. The goal of the code isolator is to automatically produce an isolated version of a key code segment that can be compiled and executed with inputs representative of the original program. If performance tuning is the goal, the isolator must initialize the machine state such that execution of the isolated code segment mimics the performance behavior of the computation when executing in the full program.

We envision several uses of such a tool:

- A programmer could vary the internal algorithms in the isolated code.
- It could be used as a debugging aid.
- It could be used to derive benchmarks of key computations from large application codes, to facilitate research on architectural techniques and software tools that would benefit the code.
- It could be used by a compiler or programmer in the process of performance tuning.

Within our own research, our goal in developing the code isolator is to support *empirical optimization* in the ECO project. Empirical optimization involves generating and executing variants of a computation with representative input data sets on representative hardware so that performance can be measured and compared [3]. Empirical data aids the compiler in navigating the complex search spaces of optimizations for today's increasingly complex architectures. Our approach is related to self-tuning, domain-specific libraries such as ATLAS [16], PhiPAC [4], SPIRAL [17] and FFTW [7], which automatically derive architecture-specific implementations of their libraries through evaluation of a large collection of variants of their implementations. Our goal in ECO is to achieve these results for more general application code, through a combination of user-directed and compiler-directed techniques.

Any number of techniques can be used to determine what code merits isolation; as examples, the user could select and annotate the computation, it could be selected by the compiler as a result of profiling, or it could be triggered by code that failed to meet a user's performance expectations [14]. The focus of this paper is to describe the code isolator implementation and how we are using it for optimizing portions of LS-DYNA, a large engineering application [10]. In the next section, we present in detail the analysis and code transformations used to generate isolated code. In Section 3, we describe the case study with LS-DYNA, and we show implementation and experiments of the code isolator in Section 4. Subsequently, we present related work and a conclusion.

2   A Code Isolator

The goal of the code isolator is to produce an isolated version of the code that can be *compiled* and *executed* with inputs representative of the original program, and initializing the *machine state* such that execution of the isolated code segment mimics the performance behavior of the computation when executing in the full program.

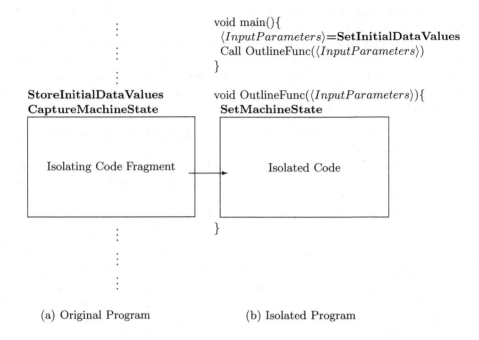

(a) Original Program   (b) Isolated Program

Fig. 1. A code isolator

Figure 1 presents an overview of how the code isolator achieves these results. Let us assume that a core computation has been selected for isolation, either by the programmer or compiler. As is shown in Figure 1(a), the code isolator instruments the original application to capture initial machine state and representative input data values, just prior to executing the code to be isolated. The tool generates a version of the isolated code, as shown in Figure 1(b), with the data set and machine state initialized. The isolated code is encapsulated in a function, which is invoked by a main program.

We have implemented the code isolator in the Stanford SUIF compiler as part of the ECO project [3,6], with some modest manual intervention, and we describe its features in the remainder of this section. We first describe how to generate isolated code that can be compiled, followed by code that can be executed and subsequently describe how to initialize machine state of the isolated code.

2.1   Compilable Isolated Program

The first step of the code isolator is to automatically extract from application programs key code segments, such as a loop nest computation. In Figure 1, a code segment is selected from the original program to make the outline function called $OutlineFunc(\langle InputParameters\rangle)$. The outline procedure is generated by the outline transformation based on the SUIF compiler library. Outlining takes a body of code and forms a function; input data that is live on entry to the code is passed as a parameter. The isolated program consists of two parts; the main procedure and the outlined procedure (see Figure 1(b)). The main procedure calls the outlined procedure and includes all parameter values in local symbol tables.

In general, the outline transformation takes a body of code, forms a new function, and inserts calls to the function in place of the code body. When the outline transformation is used with the code isolator, a main procedure (in C) is created to replace the remainder of the program, which simply initializes parameters and invokes the outlined procedure. The resulting isolated program contains this main function and the outlined procedure.

Input Parameters for Outlined Code. The outline transformation generates $\langle InputParameters \rangle$ to be passed to the outlined procedure. Important goals are to minimize the number of input parameters, and to determine whether parameters should be call-by-value, or call-by-reference.

An analysis of upwards exposed uses is used to identify which variables referenced in a loop body must be passed as input parameters. Upwards exposed uses determine what uses of variables in the outlined code may be reached by definitions outside the loop. More formally, $UE(\text{ß})$ represents the variables that are upwards exposed to the beginning of code segment ß; that is, the set of variables v such that there exists a definition-free control flow path from the beginning of ß to a reference of v. If ß represents the outlined code segment, then

$$\langle InputParameters \rangle = UE(\text{ß})$$

With respect to input parameters, we also distinguish whether to pass scalar variables by value or reference (arrays are always passed by reference). This is because SUIF supports both Fortran and C codes. By default, Fortran is call-by-reference, so when the main C function passes parameters to the isolated code, as an optimization it can pass some of the parameters by value. We use MOD and REF analysis to make this determination, where $MOD(\text{ß})$ is the set of variables that may be modified in the code segment represented by ß and $REF(\text{ß})$ is the set of variables that may be referenced in the code segment ß. If the scalar variable is referenced but not modified in ß, then it can be passed by value; otherwise, it is passed by reference.

$$CBR \in InputParameters \cap MOD(\text{ß})$$
$$CBV \in (InputParameters \cap REF(\text{ß})) - MOD(\text{ß})$$

All input parameters are located in local symbol tables of the main procedure. The set of input parameters of the outline procedure are called Initial Data Values. For all variables in ß that are not input parameters, the isolator creates local variables in the outlined procedure.

2.2   Executable Isolated Program

In the second step, the code isolator creates an executable program. The set $\langle InputParameters \rangle$ must be initialized prior to invoking the outline procedure in the isolated program. First of all, if the isolated code includes undefined sizes of arrays, then the lower and upper bounds of array sizes are determined through instrumenting the original program. Second of all, data values are extracted from the original program, and are initialized in the isolated program. In Figure 1(a), the *StoreInitialDataValues* module saves input parameter data from the original program into a file. In Figure 1(b), the *SetInitialDataValues* module assigns initial data values to the ⟨*InputParameters*⟩ before setting up the call to the outlined procedure in the main procedure of the isolated program, by reading the input data from a file.

Undefined Dynamic Array Size. Code generated by the outline transformation sometimes includes undefined array sizes. For example, if an array is passed by reference, it may not have fixed static bounds. In Fortran, static bounds must be specified on all but the last dimension of the array. The code isolator determines bounds on arrays of undefined sizes through instrumentation, which determines the largest size for each dimension among all executions of the code segment, and for a given input data set. In the following, a represents an array, and d represents a specific dimension of the array. a_lb_d and a_ub_d represent the lower and upper bounds on the d dimension of array a. Then, e represents a specific subscript expression for dimension d, computed at run time.

$$a\_lb\_d = (e < a\_lb\_d) \ ? \ e \ : \ a\_lb\_d; \ a\_ub\_d = (e > a\_ub\_d) \ ? \ e \ : \ a\_ub\_d;$$

In the original program, the code isolator creates the new symbols for upper and lower bounds of each dimension for each array of unknown size in the global symbol table. At each reference to the array, the statement above is inserted into the code. Thus, through these variables, we compute the range of values of the array dimensions. Then, in the outlined procedure, the array is statically declared to be of the largest size in each dimension.

StoreInitialDataValues. The module of StoreInitialDataValues extracts Initial Data Values from the original program. Each type and size of the set of Initial Data Values has been found while generating the outline transformation and determining dynamic array sizes at the previous step. Followed by the order of the set of Initial Data Values, each value is stored into the file immediately before the part of the isolated code in the original program.

SetInitialDataValues. The module of SetInitialDataValues initializes Initial Data Values, which achieved from the module of StoreInitialDataValues, to the isolated program. The code isolator has a library which reads all type of values, such as integer, float, one dimensional array or two dimensional arrays, from the file, and this file is created from instrumenting in the module of StoreInitialDataValues. The code isolator calls to library, followed by the order of the set of Initial Data Values. Finally, the isolated program is able to execute independently after this SetInitialDataValues. We generate this module automatically combined with the step of the compilable isolated program.

2.3   Machine State

In the final step of the code isolator, the state of the machine from the original program is captured through instrumentation, and is set during initialization in the isolated code. The machine state describes all relevant state of the target architecture, including register, cache memory, TLB, and so on, that will impact the performance of the isolated code. In Figure 1(a), the *CaptureMachineState* module executes just prior to the isolated code fragment in the original program.

As a starting point of this research, we focus on achieving comparable cache behavior from the original code, and specifically, L1 cache behavior (other cache levels should be comparable). We combine models with simulation data and execution-time measurements to derive the cache state from the original program. We generate additional code to set the cache state in the isolated program.

Capturing Machine State. To understand the machine state prior to executing the isolated code fragment, the tool must understand the impact of the code that executes prior to the isolated code fragment on the behavior of the isolated code. Since we currently are focusing on cache behavior, this means that the tool must identify what data accessed by the isolated code is already in cache. (Ideally, it is also important to know where the data is located in cache, as will be discussed in Section 4.) For this reason, the tool must capture the relevant behavior of code preceding the isolated code.

For this purpose, we capture an address trace for a small portion of the code that executes immediately prior to the isolated code fragment. Using a cache simulator, we determine which of these addresses remain in cache at the entry of the isolated code. We also capture an address trace for the isolated code, and determine what data accessed by the isolated code will be in cache as a result of executing its preceding code.

A full trace is expensive in terms of memory, disk, and execution time. In addition, it is difficult to get initial memory addresses for all array references, because addresses are not always determined statically, and addresses of local variables are reused for different data structures in different functions. Our current approach reduces the cost of tracing by executing just a fragment of the code preceding the isolated code. In the future, we can reduce this cost further by combining tracing with analytical modeling of cache behavior.

The result of tracing addresses in both preceding and isolated code, we determine the set of cache blocks CB1, that are in cache immediately prior to the isolated code. When tracing the isolated code, we must identify the set of cache blocks CB2, which represent the *first* access to each cache line accessed by the isolated code. Note that recognizing the first access is important since subsequent accesses to a cache line may displace data that was available on entry to the isolated code. Then, the machine state can be determined as follows:

$$\forall m \in CB1 \cap CB2, \ m \text{ is potentially in cache.}$$

To reduce the amount of preceding code that must be traced, we use analysis to identify how much code must be executed to achieve the comparable cache state. Conceptually, we examine the code prior to the isolated code fragment in a reverse traversal. Using an adaptation of the region-based interprocedural array data-flow analysis described in [8], we determine the minimum data footprint of each code region. When analysis can prove that the data footprint of preceding code exceeds the cache capacity, there is no need to traverse the code further. This is the point in the preceding code where address tracing should begin.

To compute the footprint size of the preceding code, we define the footprint size of an array and the footprint size of a hierarchical region (statement, basic block, loop body, loop, procedure, etc.). $FP(x_i)$ is a function of footprint size of an array with subscript expressions, loop bounds, loop nests, and the element size, where x_i represents arrays and summarizes references to the same array in the loop. We formulate footprint analysis as a backward data-flow problem. Let L represent a particular loop nest, and x_0, x_1, $\cdots$, and x_n be different arrays in this loop, defined by L. $FP(L)$ denotes a function of footprint size that is the sum of footprints of all arrays in loop nest L.

$$FP(L) = \quad FP(x_0) + \cdots\cdots\cdots + FP(x_n)$$

Suppose that A and B are loop nests, and B is followed by A. $FP(A \circ B)$ represents footprint size when A loop nest and B loop nest are combined. *Read* is a list of read references within the loop, and *Write* is a list of write references within it with array data-flow analysis [8].

$$FP(A \circ B) = \quad FP(A) + FP(B) -$$
$$FP(\{Read(A) \bigcup Write(A)\} \bigcap \{Read(B) \bigcup Write(B)\})$$
$$FP(Preceding\ Code) > Cache\ Capacity$$

We thus determine the preceding code which has minimum code fragments which is greater than the cache capacity.

Setting Machine State. The module *SetMachineState* initializes the cache to include the cache blocks identified by the analysis to capture the machine state, previously described. To set the machine state in the isolated code, after initializing the data values, we flush the cache. Subsequently, we prefetch into cache the desired cache blocks, which are described as the array index of the first element of the cache line. We insert prefetch instructions into the source code using the SUIF annotation mechanism; which permits adding pragmas that will be passed along to final code generation. On the SGI Origin, our target architecture, we insert a set of *#pragma prefetch_ref* directives, which are supported by the MIPSpro compiler [11].

3   Case Study in LS-DYNA

We used the code isolator to isolate a code segment from LS-DYNA, which is a large, engineering application. LS-DYNA is a general purpose, nonlinear finite element program capable of solving a vast array of engineering and design problems ranging from bioprosthetic heart valve operation to automotive crash

```
                              void main(){
        ⋮                        float l[4096];
        ⋮                        float matrix[ Undefined size ];
        ⋮                        int lp, pl, sl, size, l_len;
        ⋮
        ⋮                        OutlineFunc(&pl, &lp, l, matrix, sl, &l_len, &size);
    do20 j = 1, size          }
      do10 i = 1, l_len
        l(lp+i) = matrix(pl+i)  void OutlineFunc(pl, lp, l, matrix, sl, l_len, size)
10      continue                int *pl, lp; float (*l)[ ], (*matrix)[ ];
        lp = lp + CACHE_BLK     int sl, *l_len, *size; {
        pl = pl + sl            int j, i;
        sl = sl - 1             for (j = 1; j <= *size; j++) {
20continue                        for (i = 1; i <= *l_len; i++) {
                                    (*l)[*lp+i-1] = (*matrix)[*pl+i-1];
        ⋮                         }
        ⋮                        *lp = *lp + 64;
        ⋮                        *pl = *pl + sl;
        ⋮                        sl = sl - 1;
        ⋮                       }
        ⋮                      }
```

(a) Original Program   (b) Isolated Program

Fig. 2. The example of the isolated code in LS-DYNA

and earthquake engineering. LS-DYNA is a commercial derivative of DYNA originally developed at Lawrence Livermore National Laboratory. LS-DYNA is over two million lines of code.

Figure 2 illustrates the isolated program from a real code segment in the original program of LS-DYNA. Small fragments of Figure 2(a) are part of the LS-DYNA program which is written in Fortran. Figure 2(b) shows the isolated program which is built by the outline transformation of the code isolator from code segments of Figure 2(a). This isolated code has been simplified in this paper from the automatically generated code, that is the step of compilable isolated program.

To build the isolated which mimics the original program, we require five steps, which are determining undefined array sizes, StoreInitialDataValues, SetInitial-DataValues, CaptureMachineState and SetMachineState. Figure 3 presents four of these five steps, and Step 4, CaptureMachineState, is described in Figure 4. In Figure 2(b), we have found an undefined dynamic array, *matrix*. Step 1 of Figure 3 depicts how to instrument this undefined dynamic array size in the original program. After instrumenting the lower and upper bounds, we found 2252 to be the window size of bounds, which is from 81 lower bound to 2332 upper bound, for the *matrix* array in the original program. The set of Initial Data Values

```
INTEGER   matrix_lb_1, matrix_ub_1
COMMON    matrix_lb_1, matrix_ub_1

          ⋮

do20 j = 1, size
  do10 i = 1, l_len
```

```
    if (pl+i .lt. matrix_lb_1) then
      matrix_lb_1 = pl+i
    end if
    l(lp+i) = matrix(pl+i)
    if (pl+i .gt. matrix_ub_1) then
      matrix_ub_1 = pl+i
    end if
```

```
10    continue
      lp = lp + CACHE_BLK
      pl = pl + sl
      sl = sl - 1
20continue

          ⋮
```

Step1: Undefined Dynamic Array Size

```
void main(){
    float l[4096], matrix[ 2252 ];
    Undefined array size ↗

          ⋮
```

```
InitializeFile(StoreInitialDataValues);

          ⋮

GetOneDimFloatArray(fp,matrix,2252);
sl = GetInteger(fp);

          ⋮
```

```
    OutlineFunc(&pl, &lp, l, matrix,
        sl, &l_len, &size);
}
```

Step3: SetInitialDataValues

```
          ⋮

    write(fp, *) pl

          ⋮

    do100 tmp_i = 81, 2332
      write(fp,*) matrix(tmp_i)
100continue

          ⋮

    write(fp, *) size
```

```
do20 j = 1, size
  do10 i = 1, l_len
    l(lp+i) = matrix(pl+i)
10    continue
      lp = lp + CACHE_BLK
    pl = pl + sl
    sl = sl - 1
20continue

          ⋮
```

Step2: StoreInitialDataValues

```
void OutlineFunc
        (pl, lp, l, matrix, sl, l_len, size)

          ⋮

{ int j, i;
```

```
#pragma prefetch_ref=matrix[0],···
#pragma prefetch_ref=matrix[56],···

          ⋮

#pragma prefetch_ref=matrix[2128],···
#pragma prefetch_ref=matrix[2248],···
```

```
    for (j = 1; j <= *size; j++) {
      for (i = 1; i <= *l_len; i++) {
        (*l)[*lp+i-1] =
            (*matrix)[*pl+i-81];
      }
      *lp = *lp + 64;
      *pl = *pl + sl;
      sl = sl - 1; } }
```

Step5: SetMachineState

Fig. 3. Processing Steps of the Code Isolator

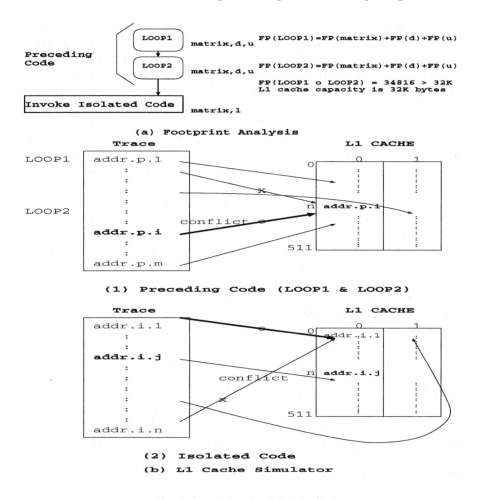

Fig. 4. Step4: CaptureMachineState

which are input parameters of the outlined procedure has five integers and two
float arrays. The integer *sl* is treated as a call-by-value parameter, and other
integers and arrays are call-by-reference parameters. Step 2 of Figure 3 shows
how to store the data values from the original program that will be needed in
the isolated code. Step 3 of Figure 3 describes how to initialize the data for
the isolated code from the file created by Step 2. Functions of the initialization
library appeared in Step 3 of Figure 3 (*e.g.*, GetInteger and GetOneDimFloatAr-
ray.) These library code segments can be compiled and executed on the target
machine.

Capturing and setting the machine state are dependent on both the target
architecture and the particular state that must be preserved. Our focus in the
current work is capturing the state of the caches that is relevant to the isolated code, just prior to its execution. The machine-dependent details of these

steps (Step 4 and 5) are discussed in Section 4 below, in conjunction with the experiments. Generally speaking, to capture machine state, we begin executing the original program at a point prior to the isolated code determined by the footprint analysis in Figure 4(a). The number of footprint size of LOOP1 and LOOP2, which is $FP(LOOP1 \circ LOOP2)$ in Figure 4(a), exceeds L1 cache capacity, thus, we selected preceding code included LOOP1 and LOOP2. These footprint sizes of LOOP1 and LOOP2 are measured with *matrix*, *d*, and *u* arrays. Figure 4(b) shows how to find L1 cache blocks which are potentially the point prior to the isolated code. In Step 4, CaptureMachineState, we traced memory addresses sequence of the preceding code and the isolated code (see left trace boxes in Figure 4(b).) Right boxes of Figure 4(b) describe L1 cache configuration of target machine (*e.g.*, two-way associative cache of 32 Kbytes), as mentioned in Section 2.3. In Figure 4(b), arrows present how to map L1 cache block number from memory addresses of traces. Arrows also describe different mapping between preceding code (see *nth* cache block in Figure 4(b)(1)), and the isolated code (see *0th* cache block in Figure 4(b)(2)), when conflict misses occur. In Step 5 of Figure 3, we first flushed the cache to remove data from cache that may remain from Step 3, SetInitialDataValues. For example, the entire array *matrix* fits in the L1 cache of our target architecture, filling only about 20% of the cache, and thus will be present after Step 3. In Figure 4(b), when we assume that *addr.p.i* (represents the *ith* memory address sequence in preceding code) equals to *addr.i.j* (represents the *jth* memory address sequence in the isolated code) in same cache block, this cache line will be loaded into L1 cache at Step 5, SetMachineState. The CaptureMachineState step identifies that only 14 of these cache lines should be in cache. Associated with these 14 cache lines, we determine the corresponding array indices of the cache lines so that we can subsequently set the machine state appropriately in the source code. Following the cache flush, we then inserted prefetch instructions in the source code to load these blocks into cache, referencing the array indices.

4   Implementation and Experiments

We have implemented the code isolator in the Stanford SUIF compiler. The tool that is described in this paper is partially automated and the remainder of the tool has been designed to use techniques that can be automated in a straightforward way within SUIF. The executable isolated code, as described in Sections 2.1 and 2.2, is generated automatically, with the exception of setting the sizes of dynamic arrays and inserting calls to the data initialization library. Most of the work involved in capturing and setting the machine state, as described in Section 2.3, was performed manually, but modeling of the cache was automated using a simple cache simulator. We use the Performance Application Programming Interface (PAPI) to access the SGI's performance monitoring hardware and derive measurements of machine state during execution.

We performed a series of experiments on the LS-DYNA code described in the previous section. Our goal in these experiments is to validate the isolator

Table 1. A Sampling of 100 times experiments

	Original Program	Isolated Program
L1 cache misses (Avg)	207	184
Running time (hh:mm:ss)	4:37:20	00:00:04

technique, and determine the feasibility of capturing and setting machine state for this application. So far we have focused on cache state of just the L1 cache. The target architecture for the experiment is a single processor of an SGI Origin system, with a 195MHz MIPS R10K CPU with a MIPS R10010 FPU, a main memory of 3 Gbytes, L1 data and instruction caches of 32 Kbytes each and unified instruction/data L2 cache of 4 Mbytes. The L1 data cache is two-way set associative, with 32 byte cache lines. The replacement policy is Least Recently Used (LRU).

Table 1 summarizes our preliminary results. We compare the behavior of the isolated code within the original program (first column), and in the isolated version derived by the approach described in this paper (second column). Results of this table are sampled by running 100 times for the particular isolated code of the case study in LS-DYNA. Cache misses were obtained from PAPI. The row entitled L1 cache misses is the average number of misses across the 100 runs of the code. The row entitled running time is the total execution time for 100 times running samples. We found similar L1 cache misses between the original program and the isolated program – 89% of the cache misses from the original program occur in the isolated code. In contrast, in the absence of the prefetch instructions to set the machine state in the isolated code, the number of L1 misses is 1.6 times that of the corresponding code in the original program.

One reason for the loss of precision in the isolated code has to do with alignment of data to cache line boundaries. Our tools assume that the starting address of an array is aligned with the beginning of a cache line boundary, which is not always true when a point in the middle of an array is passed to an array parameter of a function or procedure. While alignment issues account for a significant fraction of the cache miss differences, there are two remaining issues that impacting preserving the cache state. Conflict misses between arrays are not captured as part of the machine state, and we observed a fairly significant variation in the performance monitoring results returned by PAPI. These issues will be addressed in future work.

The second row shows the value of the code isolator, if it can successfully model code behavior. The isolated code ran for only 4 seconds, while the original program took more than 4 hours, for a *3600X reduction in execution time*.

5   Related Work

In this section we discuss related work in the areas of run-time system, simulation of a large program, and a discussion of our model.

5.1 Run-Time System

Researchers have recognized the lack of adequate programming language support for applications that must react to changing environments. Currently, programmers must intermix their application code with run-time-system calls that implement the desired adaptation or optimization policies. The resulting code is complex and virtually impossible to port and maintain. In ADAPT [15], researchers have defined new languages used exclusively to specify adaptation policies, triggering events and performance metrics. Programmers develop their base application textually independently from their adaptation specification. While attractive from the viewpoint of separation of concerns, this approach suffers from the problems of naming and scoping as well as coherency. An alternative approach extends existing languages to provide hints or directives to the compiler about the dynamic nature of the application. Adve [2] *et. al.* describe an extension to the class hierarchy of an objected-oriented model of computation with three basic concepts - adaptors, metrics and events.

5.2 Large Scale Applications

Other researchers have also focused on performance tools and simulation in large scale application. Sherwood [12] *et. al.* found and exploited the large scale behavior of programs using basic block vectors. Saltz [9,13] *et. al.* modeled the tool for simulating communication and for executing in large scale parallel machines. Adve [1] *et. al.* also worked on performance tools which are program slicing to analyze and to simulate communication in very large scale applications.

5.3 Discussion

We can use more efficient strategies, such as static models (*e.g.,* the model reported in [5]) to predict where in the memory hierarchy data accessed by the isolated code might be based on code executed prior to the isolated code. Alternatively, hardware performance counters can be used to measure and predict such information. Setting the machine state in the isolated program (the module *SetMachineState*) is also a difficult problem. To initialize the L1 cache to contain the appropriate elements, the code isolator must lay out the data in memory in a comparable way to the original program, and touch the data in an appropriate order such that it remains in the cache until the computation is initiated. Efficient mechanisms to capture and set machine state are the subject of future work.

6   Conclusion

In conclusion, this paper has described a code isolator, which we are using to isolate code segments from large programs for the purpose of performance tuning. While our current implementation of the code isolator is fairly straightforward, it does rely on a host of program analyses available in the SUIF compiler. The key challenge in moving forward is to optimize some of the current strategies. For example, we could potentially use range analysis and other symbolic analysis to derive dynamic array sizes in some of the cases where instrumentation is currently used, although instrumentation will always be required when analysis of subscripts becomes too complex. Beyond this, we have only scratched the surface of mechanisms to derive and set machine state for the purposes of locality optimization. We also plan to derive machine state for parallelization, such as data and computation partitioning. The code isolator we have developed is geared towards scientific computations. A number of other interesting issues arise in more general codes, such as for example, deriving a representative data layout of pointer-based data structures.

References

1. V. Adve, R. Bagrodia, E. Deelman, T. Phan and R. Sakellariou. Compiler-Supported Simulation of Highly Scalable Parallel Applications. In Proceedings of SC99, Nov. 1999.
2. V. Adve, V. Lam and B. Ensink. Language and Compiler Support for Adaptive Distributed Applications. In Proc. of the ACM SIGPLAN Workshop on Optimization of Middleware and Distributed Systems (OM 2001) Snowbird, Utah, June 2001.
3. N. Baradaran, J. Chame, C. Chen, P. Diniz, M. Hall, Y. Lee, B. Liu and R. Lucas. ECO: an Empirical-based Compilation and Optimization System. In Proc. of the Workshop on Next Generation Software, held in conjunction with IPDPS '03, April, 2003.
4. J. Bilmes, K. Asanovic, C.-W. Chen, J. Demmel. Optimizing Matrix Multiply using PHiPAC: a Portable High-Performance ANSI-C Coding Methodology. In Proc. of the ACM International Conference on Supercomputing, 1997.
5. S. Chatterjee, E. Parker, P. J. Hanlon, A. R. Lebeck. Exact Analysis of the Cache Behavior of Nested Loops. In Proc. of the 2001 ACM SIGPLAN Conference on Programming Language Design and Implementation (PLDI'01), ACM Press, pp. 286-297, June 2001.
6. P. Diniz, Y. Lee, M. Hall and R. Lucas. A Case Study Using Empirical Optimization for a Large, Engineering Application In Proc. of the Workshop on Next Generation Software, held in conjunction with IPDPS '04, April, 2004.
7. M. Frigo. A Fast Fourier Transform Compiler. In the Proc. of the 1999 ACM SIGPLAN Conference on Programming Language Design and Implementation (PLDI '99), ACM Press, June 1999.
8. M. Hall, S. Amarasinghe, B. Murphy, S. Liao, M. Lam. Interprocedural Parallelization Analysis in SUIF. In ACM Transactions on Programming Languages and Systems, 2004.
9. T. Kurc, M. Uysal, H. Eom, J. Hollingsworth, J. Saltz , A. Sussman. Efficient Performance Prediction for Large-Scale Data-Intensive Applications. The International Journal of High Performance Computing Applications, Volume 14, number 3, pages 216-227, 2000.
10. LS-DYNA User's Manual V. 960. Livermore Software Technology Corporation, http://www.lstc.com, March 2001.

11. MIPSpro C and C++ Pragmas. Document Number 007-3587-003, 1998, 1999 Silicon Graphics, Inc.
12. T. Sherwood, E. Perelman, G. Hamerly, and B. Calder. Automatically Characterizing Large Scale Program Behavior. In Proceeding of the International Conference on Architectural Support for Programming Languages and Operating Systems, Oct. 2002.
13. M. Uysal, T.M. Kurc, A. Sussman, and J. Saltz. A Performance Prediction Framework for Data Intensive Applications on Large Scale Parallel Machines. Lecture Notes in Computer Science, 4th International Workshop on Languages, Compilers, and Run-Time Systems for Scalable Computers, Pages: 243 - 258, 1998.
14. J.S. Vetter and P. Worley. Asserting Performance Expectations. Proceedings of SC 2002, Nov. 2002.
15. M. Voss and R. Eigenmann. High-Level Adaptive Program Optimization with ADAPT. In Proc. of the ACM SIGPLAN Conference on Principles and Practice of Parallel Processing (PPoPP'01), ACM Press, June, 2001.
16. C. Whaley and J. Dongarra. Automatically tuned linear algebra software. In Proc. of Supercomputing (SC'98), 1998.
17. J. Xiong, J. Johnson, R. Johnson and D. Padua. SPL: A Language and Compiler for DSP Algorithms. In Proc. of the ACM 2001 Conference on Programming Language Design and Implementation (PLDI'01), ACM Press, June 2001.

The Use of Traces for Inlining in Java Programs*

Borys J. Bradel and Tarek S. Abdelrahman

Edward S. Rogers Sr. Department of Electrical and Computer Engineering,
University of Toronto, Toronto, Ontario, Canada M5S 3G4
{bradel, tsa}@eecg.toronto.edu

Abstract. We explore the effectiveness of using traces in optimization.
We build a trace collection system for the Jikes Research Virtual Machine
and create traces based on the execution of the SPECjvm98 and Java
Grande benchmarks. We evaluate the use of traces for inlining in Jikes,
and find that the use of traces leads to a decrease in execution time
of 10%, when compared to providing similar information from Jikes's
adaptive system from a previous execution. This increase in performance
is achieved at the expense of a code expansion of 47%. Further, this
performance is slightly better than that achieved when using a greedy
algorithm. We conclude that traces may be used effectively to perform
inlining, although code expansion and trace collection overhead must be
addressed.

1 Introduction

Traditional static compilation has shortcomings in that it cannot take advantage of information available at runtime to produce high-performance executables. Such runtime information includes processor architecture, specific input data characteristics, and control flow patterns within the program. Feedback-directed systems can monitor the execution of a program to collect this runtime information and to use it to improve program performance.

Feedback-directed systems can be divided into two categories: *offline* and *online*. One advantage of online systems is that the feedback loop is shorter, because the collected information is immediately used while a program is executing. The main advantage of offline systems is that they can analyze collected information more thoroughly because they do not compete with the executing program for resources. This may lead to more effective optimizations.

There have been many systems that use both online and offline feedback. These include systems created by Arnold et al [1], Whaley [2], and Suganuma, Yasue, and Nakatani [3]. One common aspect to these feedback directed systems is that they employ counters to collect information regarding which instructions and methods are frequently executed.

In this paper, we explore the effectiveness of using *traces*, which are sequences of unique basic blocks that are executed by a program [4], for optimization in an

---

* This research was supported in part by NSERC.

offline feedback directed system. The use of traces may improve the opportunities for optimization because traces contain detailed inter-procedural information regarding which instructions are frequently executed, thus allowing optimizations to more aggressively focus on a subset of instructions. Specifically, we explore the benefits of traces in performing method inlining in Java programs. We have added a trace collection system, that we call BlueSpot, to the Jikes Research Virtual Machine, and we have evaluated the effectiveness of using the traces collected by BlueSpot to perform method inlining. We find that the use of traces leads to lower execution time, by 10%, compared to providing similar information from Jikes's adaptive system from a previous execution. This is in spite of a code expansion of 47% and the associated potential degradation of cache performance. We also find that using traces to inline leads to slightly better performance compared to a greedy offline algorithm that employs counters [1]. Our trace collection system, however, has a high overhead and may increase execution time by 139% on average. We conclude that using traces is a viable option to explore, although code expansion and trace collection efficiency need to be addressed in the future.

The remainder of this paper is organized as follows. Section 2 describes background material. Section 3 describes our trace collection system. Section 4 describes our trace based inlining strategy. Section 5 presents our experimental results. Section 6 contains related work. The paper ends with some concluding remarks and directions for future work in Section 7.

2   Background

2.1   Traces

A trace is a sequence of n *unique* basic blocks $(b_1, b_2, \ldots, b_n)$ such that basic blocks $b_1, b_2, \ldots, b_n$ are executed in sequential order during the execution of a program [4]. Block b_1 is called the *start* of the trace and b_n is the *end* of the trace. The trace may contain any basic blocks of the program as long as the sequence corresponds to a path on the control flow graph. We use this definition because it expresses the traces that we collect more precisely, although other definitions exist, such as the definition given by Fisher [5].

An example of what traces look like is shown in Figure 1. The figure contains three copies a control flow graph, each with a different valid trace. The traces are (B0,B2,B1), (B1,B2,B3), and (B1,B2). In contrast, the sequence (B1,B2,B1) is not a valid trace because B1 appears twice, making the sequence not unique.

The use of traces may improve the opportunities for optimization in three ways. First, traces can span multiple methods, thus facilitating inter-procedural analysis and extending the scope of analyses. Second, traces contain only the most frequently executed portions of a program and therefore can be used to only optimize frequently executed instructions saving compilation and optimization times. Finally, traces can be used to eliminate infrequently executed instructions from the control flow graph. The resulting control flow graph is simpler and therefore more amenable to optimization. However, since execution may go off

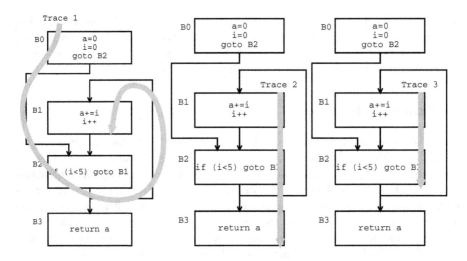

Fig. 1. Traces mapped onto the control flow graph of a loop

trace, *fix-up code* must be added to ensure that when this occurs the program's execution is still correct [6].

2.2   Inlining

Inlining reduces the overhead of invoking and returning from methods. It also allows inter-procedural analysis without a separate framework that performs analyses across multiple methods. However, inlining has to be performed selectively since it usually leads to an increase in code size and register pressure [1].

Approaches to decide where to perform inlining fall into two categories: static and dynamic. Static approaches base these decisions on the analysis of the source code of a program. Dynamic approaches make decisions based on profile information that is collected from the execution of a program. Counters are used at runtime to keep track of how often all the call sites are executed. These counters can then be used to identify which call sites should be inlined both in either an online or an offline feedback-directed system.

An example of inlining in an online system is presented by Suganuma, Yasue, and Nakatani [3]. They sample the executing program periodically to detect frequently executed methods and then instrument these methods to identify the frequently executed call sites. Once these call sites are determined, the system recompiles the appropriate methods using the additional inline information.

An example of inlining in an offline system is the greedy knapsack-type algorithm described by Arnold et al. [1]. The algorithm uses counters to determine the number of invocations of each method. The algorithm selects the best call sites based on the ratio of the number of times that a method is invoked to the number of instructions that the program would increase by if the invoked method is inlined. The call sites are selected one at a time, until a code expansion threshold is reached. Whenever a call site is selected, the ratios are modified to take into account what has already been selected. We compare the performance of this counter based offline feedback-directed system, along with the adaptive system in Jikes, to using traces for inlining.

3   Trace Collection

Traces are generated by a trace collection system (TCS) that monitors a program's execution and collects traces based on this execution. The TCS starts recording a trace when occurrences of certain events exceed a specific threshold. These events are a *backward taken branch*, a *backward taken jump*, and a *trace exit*. These cases capture frequently executed instructions within loops [7]. Another event that we use to start the recording of traces is a *return*[1]. This allows traces to capture execution that uses recursion as well. We use the threshold value of 42, which was chosen arbitrarily, before collecting traces.

The recording stops when a backward branch or jump which corresponds to the end of a loop is taken. Recording also stops when the block that is about to be recorded is the start of a different trace or is already in the trace that is being recorded. These conditions ensure that beginnings of loops will correspond to trace starts and that traces do not overlap each other unnecessarily. Recording also stops if the recorded trace is too long for the recording buffer.

Once recording stops, the newly formed trace is stored in a buffer referred to as a *trace cache*. The TCS keeps track of trace starts that occur when a trace's first basic block is executed and no other trace is executing, and trace exits, which occurs when the block that is executed is not the next block in the sequence of basic blocks on the trace. This allows us to treat trace exits as events that trigger trace recording. It is also possible to only include those returns that do not occur between trace starts and exits as events that can start recording traces. However, we treat all returns as events that can start recording traces.

The traces in the trace cache can be used in several different ways. They can be executed directly, they can be optimized and then executed, an approach taken by HP Dynamo [7], or they can be used to provide information for a feedback-directed system that does not use traces as the unit of compilation. We take this last approach.

3.1   Trace Collection Example

We demonstrate the operation of a TCS with an example. Figure 2 shows a JVM and a TCS. The TCS is linked to a JVM that executes the program shown in Figure 1. The JVM contains the program to execute as well as storage for the program's variables. These variables' values are modified as shown when the program is executed. The lower part of the figure shows the sequence of steps that the JVM performs when executing the program.

---

[1] Alternatively we could have decided not to use returns, or to use invocations instead of returns, or to use both invocations and returns.

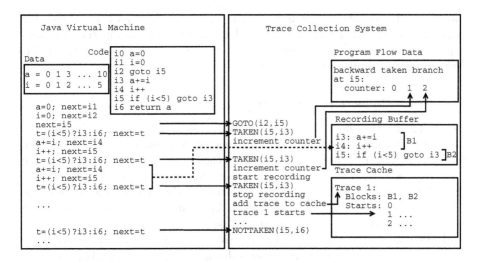

Fig. 2. Example of interaction between a JVM and a TCS

The TCS contains three components: a set of event counters that are used to determine when recording should start, a recording buffer that is used to hold basic blocks as they are recorded, and a trace cache. The TCS knows when the control flow instructions are executed and acts upon the knowledge. In the figure, the left side of the TCS contains the actions of the TCS. Solid arrows show the link between individual control flow instructions and the resulting actions in the TCS. The dotted arrows indicate the recording of a trace. Within the TCS, solid arrows show the updating of the TCS's components.

In Figure 2 the JVM executes basic blocks B1 and B2 repeatedly and the TCS keeps track of how often the backward branch between B2 and B1 is taken. When the backward branch is taken often enough[2], the TCS starts recording a sequence of basic blocks (i.e. a trace). The TCS records the execution of the program until it detects that the next basic block is already in the recorded sequence. After recording is stopped the sequence of basic blocks, (B1,B2), is stored in the trace cache. After the trace (B1,B2) is saved, instruction i3 is executed and the system detects that i3 is in B1, which is the head of Trace 1. The TCS keeps track of this trace's execution until the loop exits. This is shown by incrementing the number of times that the trace starts.

3.2   Jikes

The Jikes Research Virtual Machine (RVM) is an open source just-in-time (JIT) Java Virtual Machine (JVM) developed by IBM [8]. Jikes is a multi-threaded program written in Java. It is designed to deliver performance that is comparable to commercial JVMs. To achieve this, it uses a compile-only strategy and employs two compilers: a baseline compiler that quickly translates Java bytecodes

---

[2] We have set the threshold for the counter to 2 for this example.

into unoptimized native code and an optimizing compiler that takes longer, but generates optimized native code. Jikes has an adaptive system that monitors a program's behaviour and determines which methods should be optimized to reduce overall execution time.

3.3   Trace Collection Within Jikes

We modified Jikes's baseline compiler to enable us to collect traces. We did so by making it produce additional native instructions for each control flow bytecode instruction. When the native code executes, these extra instructions also execute. The purpose of these instructions is to record information regarding the control flow of the program. The information consists of the type and location of the control flow instruction, as well as the location of its target. These locations are the methods and bytecode indices of the instructions.

BlueSpot consists of a *data handler*, a *listener*, and an *organizer thread* in the adaptive system. The data handler stores the information generated by the added native instructions. In Jikes, the program's main thread yields after executing for some period of time, and the adaptive system is then called. The adaptive system calls BlueSpot's listener which then wakes up BlueSpot's organizer thread. The organizer then processes the stored information.

BlueSpot must be able to infer the sequence of bytecode basic blocks that is executed based on the execution of native instructions. There are several problems that need to be addressed when performing this task: the native instructions must contain very specific information, basic blocks must be identified, and the methods that these basic blocks are part of must be identified. The remainder of this section describes how we solve these three problems.

The native instructions are created with no knowledge of what actually happens at run time, and when these instructions are executed they do not have access to any information regarding the original bytecode. Our added native code is therefore created to provide the bytecodes in the form of constant operands. For example, whether a branch is taken cannot be determined at compile time, while the bytecode index of the target is not known at runtime. Therefore we add native instructions that store the bytecode indices of the branch targets such that the correct target index will be stored both when the branch is taken and not taken. Furthermore additional native instructions are added to the beginning of each method so that the data handler contains information regarding each method's invocation, which is not part of the bytecode.

The organizer processes the information in the data handler by inferring the program's control flow from it, and then collecting traces based on the control flow. The data handler contains a list of control flow instruction–target pairs as well as a list of invoked methods. The organizer uses these lists to generate information that is equivalent to a sequence of executed basic blocks [9].

BlueSpot maintains a virtual call stack to keep track of invoke and return bytecodes to make its information as complete as possible. When a return is executed the organizer must identify the corresponding invoke and make the return's target the instruction immediately after the invoke. If there is no matching invoke then the target cannot be identified and any trace recording is stopped [9]. There are several reasons for this virtual call stack to be incomplete: finite storage capacity, loss of information at thread switches and exceptions, arbitrary invocations of Java methods internal to Jikes, and the execution of optimized code that is not instrumented. Only the last leads to a serious degradation of collected trace information. We have addressed this by keeping track of the byte-code that is used to invoke optimized methods, which contains information that, although not completely accurate all the time, is accurate most of the time.

4   Inlining Using Traces

Traces can also be used to perform inlining, either in an offline or an online system. Traces capture frequently executed paths of a program, and thus they contain the frequently executed call sites. These call sites can therefore be extracted from traces and then used to perform inlining. Any invocation and return on a trace should have the corresponding call site inlined.

Before inlining can be performed a base method for compilation must be selected. When selecting the base methods to compile based on traces, we choose the *top methods* of all the traces. The top method is the method whose invocation is placed on the call stack before the invocation of any of the other methods that the trace is on. A trace does not have to start at a top method since the trace can start with several returns and then be in its top method. For the other inlining strategies that we describe in the following section, the base methods are the methods that all the call sites identified by the strategy are located in.

Inlining can result in a large code expansion. One approach of reducing this expansion is to use *inline sequences* [10]. An inline sequence is a list of call sites followed by a method. When a compiler is given a collection of inline sequences, which can be generated from traces, it can use the collection to determine which methods to inline. A method is inlined only if it is the last method in an inline sequence and all the predecessors in the sequence have already been inlined. For example, if a single trace exists that has the inline sequence "a(),b(),c()", then b() and c() will both be inlined into a() when a() is compiled, but c() will not be inlined into b() when b() is compiled. Since b() is already inilined into a(), it will never be called frequently, and spending extra compilation time on b() is not necessary. We do not present the effects of using inline sequences in this paper, although we do so elsewhere [9].

5   Results

In this section we present our evaluation of using traces to perform inlining in an offline feedback-directed system. We explore the use of traces with two types of compilers: a JIT compiler and an ahead-of-time compiler. The JIT compiler decides which methods to optimize; the only information it receives from us identifies the call sites that should be inlined. This information is given to the compiler during initialization of the system. The ahead-of-time compiler performs all the compilation during system initialization, and is given information regarding both what to compile and what to inline. Although we provide both compilers with offline information, JIT compilers can be used both in online and offline feedback-directed systems, while ahead-of-time compilers can be used only in offline feedback directed systems.

We measure the impact of using traces to perform inlining on program execution time, compile time, and code expansion for both types of compilers. In the context of a JIT system, we compare using: traces, the greedy algorithm of Arnold et al. [1], and information provided by the adaptive system. In the context of an ahead-of-time system, we ran out of memory when trying to compile several benchmarks with the greedy algorithm. We therefore only compare using traces with information provided by the adaptive system. We also examine the information provided to the compiler when it performs inlining. Finally, we present the overhead incurred when collecting traces.

5.1   Platform and Methodology

Our experiments are run on a 4 processor Dell PowerEdge 6600 with a 400MHz front-side bus and 2 GB of ECC DDR RAM. Each processor is a 1.4 GHz Pentium 4 Xeon processor with 512KB of L2 cache. The operating system used is RedHat 7.3 using Linux kernel 2.4.18.

We use Jikes RVM 2.0.3, which uses IBM's class libraries version 2.11, and is compiled using gcc 3.0.4, the Sun JDK 1.3.1 bytecode compiler, and the Jikes bytecode compiler 1.13. Jikes is set to use a single processor, have assertions disabled, and have all the required methods precompiled. Furthermore we set the level of all optimizations performed at run-time to be "O1". We have also instrumented Jupiter [11], a Java interpreter, to count the number of times that all call sites are executed. This allows us to collect only application based call sites, and we not have to deal with call sites that are part of Jikes itself. Jupiter is compiled using gcc 3.0.4, and uses both a modified version 0.04 of the classpath libraries and a modified version 6.1 of the Boehm garbage collector.

We use the single threaded programs found in the SPECjvm98 benchmarks as well as the single threaded level 3 Java Grande benchmarks with the smaller data sets. The benchmarks, along with the labels that we use for them in parenthesis, are: _201_compress (201), _202_jess (202), _209_db (209), _213_javac (213), _222_mpegaudio (222), _228_jack (228), MolDyn (2a1), RayTracer (2a2), Euler (2a3), MonteCarlo (2a4), and Search (2a5). The first six benchmarks are part of SPECjvm98 and the latter five are part of the Java Grande benchmarks. All averages or means that we present in our results are arithmetic averages.

5.2   Inlining Using Traces with a Just-in-Time Compiler

We use Jikes with the adaptive system, which identifies the methods to optimize at run-time. We give the adaptive system inline information collected in an offline manner from three different sources: a previous execution of the same program

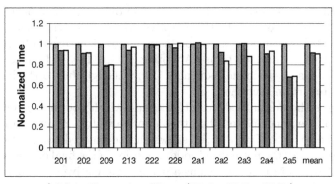

a) Main Execution Time (25.6s, 23.3s, 22.7s)

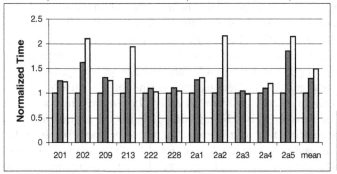

b) Compile Time (0.52s, 0.61s, 0.69s)

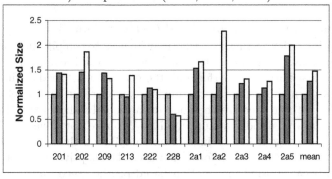

c) Native Code Size (21.3kb, 22.8kb, 27.7kb)

Fig. 3. Inlining using the adaptive system

using the adaptive system, the greedy algorithm presented in Section 2.2[3], and the collected traces. This is a fair evaluation of the relative benefit of using traces when inlining, since all three strategies are used in the same context.

---

[3] We have used a code expansion threshold of 25%.

The inline information consists of call sites for the optimizing compiler to inline. These are used as suggestions by the adaptive system, which may choose not to act on them. The experimental data points on our graph corresponding to the use of these sources are referred to as "Adaptive", "Greedy", and "Trace", respectively. We have also used inline sequences [10], although due to the lack of space, we do not report on them here [9].

Figure 3 (a) shows the normalized execution time—which does not include compilation time—of the benchmarks when the adaptive system is given input from the above three sources. Figure 3 (b) shows the normalized compilation time, and Figure 3 (c) shows the normalized code expansion of the final optimized machine code. All of our data is calculated as a percentage relative to using the information provided by Jikes's adaptive system. Each data point is based on the arithmetic mean of two consecutive runs using identical settings. The label of each graph contains the mean of the non-normalized values over all benchmarks.

Using traces reduces execution time by 10% on average relative to using information from the adaptive system. There is however on average a code expansion and increase in the compilation time of 47% and 49% respectively. In comparison, using the greedy algorithm reduces execution time by 9% with both a code expansion and increase in compilation time of 29%. The observed increased overheads are a result of more call sites being inlined. Since the entire run-time is dominated by the execution time of the program, the overheads, resulting from compilation and increased code size, are insignificant (0.69s on average compared to 22.7s). The results show that both the greedy algorithm and traces perform equally well, and that traces slightly outperform the greedy algorithm.

5.3   Inlining Using Traces with an Ahead-of-Time Compiler

Jikes provides an optimization test harness that may be used to compile methods ahead of time. This allows us to avoid the limitations of a JIT compiler. We use the optimization test harness to perform all the compilation ahead of time. We specify two sets of methods for the optimizing compiler and the baseline compiler to compile. We also increase the code expansion thresholds that the optimizing compiler uses to decide to stop inlining. We have not done this in previous experiments because it has an impact on compilation time and is not feasible for a JIT system. We only use information from the adaptive system and the collected traces because using information based on the greedy algorithm causes the optimization test harness to run out of memory for three benchmarks (_202_jess, _213_javac, and _228_jess). Furthermore, we omit _213_javac because using traces for it also leads to an out of memory error.

Figure 4 (a) shows the normalized execution time[4] of the benchmarks when the adaptive system is given input generated using the adaptive system and traces from Jikes. Figure 4 (b) shows the normalized time used by the optimization test harness, which is computed as the user time used by Jikes minus

---

[4] We execute each benchmark both with and without logging. We take the minimum of the two values collected because for _209_db and 2a5 Search some of the execution with logging take significantly less time than the ones without logging.

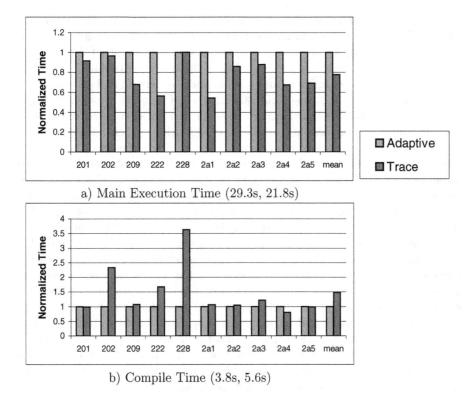

a) Main Execution Time (29.3s, 21.8s)

b) Compile Time (3.8s, 5.6s)

Fig. 4. Inlining with ahead-of-time compilation

the execution time. We refer to this as compile time because it includes time spent compiling using both the baseline compiler and optimizing compiler, even though it also includes the start up and shut down time of Jikes. The label of each graph contains the non-normalized value for the mean over all benchmarks.

Using traces leads to a 22% reduction in execution time on average, with all the benchmarks having some reduction in execution time, except for _228_jack, which exhibits a 0.1% increase in execution time. Furthermore, the majority of the benchmarks have a relatively small increase in compilation overhead, and therefore a reduction in overall program run-time. Nonetheless, two of the benchmarks, _202_jess and _228_jack, stand out; they have an increase in compile time of over 100%, which results in an increase in overall program run-time. These results illustrate that inlining using traces leads to a reduction in execution time, but there are situations where the inlining can be too aggressive.

5.4 Details of the Provided Inline Information

To provide insight into the results that we have presented we have looked at the information that we use as input in our experiments. The information consists of sets of call sites to inline and sets of methods to compile using the optimizing compiler. We present this information for the three different sources that we use: the adaptive system (A), the greedy algorithm (G), and the collected traces (T).

Table 1 (a) contains the number of compilation requests and Table 1 (b) contains the number of inline requests made under different configurations. The adaptive system has on average only 40 compilation requests, which is less than the other configurations. Furthermore the collected traces have 88 requests on average, which is comparable to the greedy algorithm, which has 98 requests. Requests based on the adaptive system are less numerous because the adaptive system acts as a JIT and is therefore limited in the amount of optimization that it can perform. The limits are imposed by internal checks in the system that ensure that only a small amount of time is spent outside of the main execution thread. The traces and greedy algorithm on the other hand are not limited in this way and therefore generate more requests that lead to code expansion.

Different benchmarks also have different numbers of requests. _213_javac has three times more requests than any of the other benchmarks. The large number of requests is the reason for the optimization test harness running out of memory when trying to compile it. Furthermore, we believe that because of the large number of inline requests for _202_jess and _228_jack, these two benchmarks are not optimized effectively and incur large overheads when the optimization test harness is used. Finally, _228_jack's execution is dominated by a single trace [9]. It is likely that all the methods that the trace is on are requested to be inlined by the adaptive system, which only asks for 7 methods to be inlined, and that there is little benefit to optimizing other methods.

Table 1. Requests to direct compilation decisions

	A	G	T
201	12	107	12
202	37	90	105
209	5	85	30
213	207	322	368
222	44	88	130
228	17	138	121
2a1	7	86	17
2a2	32	16	36
2a3	30	77	46
2a4	38	62	87
2a5	13	3	11
mean	40	98	88

	A	G	T
201	15	64	11
202	74	186	190
209	0	58	26
213	547	696	683
222	50	204	164
228	7	177	204
2a1	1	15	22
2a2	63	44	71
2a3	73	48	94
2a4	42	98	99
2a5	10	14	16
mean	80	146	144

a) Total Methods   b) Total Inline Requests

5.5   Trace Collection Overhead

We have not designed BlueSpot with efficiency as a high priority. This is accept-able because we use an offline system, which does not have a direct effect on the run-time performance of a program. Nonetheless, BlueSpot can be used as an online system to both collect traces and optimize the executing program based on them. We therefore present the overheads of BlueSpot since this information may be useful when collecting traces in an online system.

When optimization is disabled (i.e. the adaptive system is not allowed to perform inlining) there is an average increase in the main thread's execution time of 22% associated with collecting information in the data handler, as op-posed to the information that the adaptive system collects. Due to our inefficient implementation, BlueSpot's organizer thread frequently executes just as long as the main execution thread. The time overhead of the entire system is on average approximately 139% larger than that of the adaptive system.

When optimization is enabled the main execution thread takes 14% more time with BlueSpot than with the adaptive system. This increase has three causes. The first is the overhead of storing information in the data handler. The second is that unoptimized methods may execute for a longer period of time before they are optimized, because the trace system is slower and takes longer to make decisions than the adaptive system. The third is that the two systems may select different methods to optimize. When optimization is enabled the time overhead of the organizer thread decreases from 117% to 56%. This decrease is mainly due to the overhead of the organizer thread decreasing to less than 25% for _201_compress, _209_db, 2a1 (MolDyn), 2a2 (RayTracer), and 2a5 (Search)[5].

These results show that an online system based on traces may be effective, since the time spent in the main execution thread increases only 14% when BlueSpot is used. However, the time overhead of the entire system is on aver-age 70%. If traces are to be used in an online system this overhead must be reduced.

6   Related Work

Fisher [5] was the first to introduce traces and to use them for instruction scheduling. His work has been extended by many others including Ellis [6,12], Howland et al [13], Chang and Hwu [14], Hwu et al [15], and Lowney et al [6] at Multiflow. Static trace scheduling involves selecting traces at compile time and scheduling instructions using these traces. Our work differs from this approach in that we collect traces at run time and base our decisions on these traces as opposed to traces created at compile time.

---

[5] The results contain test runs for which the trace system optimized 2a5 (Search) effectively, although we have found that at times the trace system did not optimize this benchmark effectively.

The HP Dynamo [7,4] and DynamoRIO [16,17] systems, which are designed for the PA-RISC architecture and the IA-32 architecture respectively, interpret a program while collecting profile information. When frequently executed traces are detected, they are compiled and optimized. These traces can then be executed instead of interpreted. Mojo is a similar system by Chen et al [18] that uses a similar scheme on Windows 2000. Our work differs from these approaches because our traces are based on Java bytecodes while these systems use traces based on native machine code instructions. This allows us to abstract traces away from a specific architecture.

Whaley differentiates between hot (frequently executed) and cold (infrequently executed) basic blocks to reduce the amount of compilation [2]. Arnold et al [1] have looked at inlining based on static heuristics versus inlining based on a profile based optimum cost/benefit strategy. Suganuma, Yasue, and Nakatani [3] examine the benefits of inlining using imperfect information in a feedback directed online system. Hazelwood and Grove [10] have looked at reducing the code explosion associated with inlining by being selective about where they perform inlining. Krintz looks at using bytecode annotations to perform inlining in a feedback directed offline system [19]. Our work differs from the feedback directed systems in Java because we use a different representation of feedback information, namely traces.

7   Conclusion

We have created a trace collection system for Jikes, and examined the use of traces when performing inlining in an offline feedback-directed manner. We have shown that traces are useful for this purpose. We have compared traces to several different inlining algorithms and shown that they are as good as, and in some cases better than, the alternate inlining algorithms. In particular we have found that using system dependent traces leads to a 10% decrease in execution time in spite of a code expansion of 47% when used in the adaptive system relative to using the information in the adaptive system itself. This performance is even slightly better than that achieved when using a greedy algorithm. Our work is only a starting point that has shown that traces can be used effectively in offline feedback-directed systems.

There are many different directions in which this work can be further expanded in the future. First, code expansion is quite large and needs to be reduced. Second, traces can be used in an online feedback-directed system. It is unclear whether trace collection overhead will make this approach feasible. Although we did not design our TCS with efficiency in mind, the overhead of the TCS is large. Work needs to be performed to efficiently collect and use traces. Third, traces should be applied to different optimizations. The methods that have inlining performed based on traces are a natural basis for the optimizations. One of the challenges that must be addressed is that optimizations are affected by many different factors and that it is hard to quantify the effect of any individual factor.

References

1. Matthew Arnold et al: A comparative study of static and profile-based heuristics for inlining. In: Proceedings of SIGPLAN Workshop on Dynamic and Adaptive Compilation and Optimization. (2000) 52–64
2. Whaley, J.: Partial method compilation using dynamic profile information. In: Conference on Object-Oriented Programming Systems, Languages, and Applications (OOPSLA). (2001) 166–179
3. Suganuma, T., Yasue, T., Nakatani, T.: An empirical study of method inlining for a Java Just-In-Time compiler. In: Proceedings of USENIX 2nd Java Virtual Machine Research and Technology Symposium (JVM'02). (2002) 91–104
4. Bala, V., Duesterwald, E., Banerjia, S.: Transparent dynamic optimization: The design and implementation of dynamo. HP Laboratories Technical Report HPL1999 -78 (1999)
5. Fisher, J.A.: Trace scheduling : A technique for global microcode compaction. IEEE Transactions on Computers **C-30** (1981) 478–490
6. Lowney, P.G.: The multiflow trace scheduling compiler. The Journal of Supercomputing **7** (1993) 51–142
7. Bala, V., Duesterwald, E., Banerjia, S.: Dynamo: a transparent dynamic optimization system. ACM SIGPLAN Notices **35** (2000) 1–12
8. Arnold, M., Fink, S., Grove, D., Hind, M., Sweeney, P.F.: Adaptive optimization in the Jalapeño JVM. ACM SIGPLAN Notices **35** (2000) 47–65
9. Bradel, B.J.: The use of traces in optimization. Master's thesis, University of Toronto (2004)
10. Hazelwood, K., Grove, D.: Adaptive online context-sensitive inlining. In: Proceedings of International Symposium on Code Generation and Optimization. (2003) 253–264
11. Doyle, P.: Jupiter: A modular and extensible Java virtual machine framework. Master's thesis, University of Toronto (2002)
12. Ellis, J.R.: A Compiler for VLIW Architectures. PhD thesis, Yale University (1984)
13. Howland, M.A., Mueller, R.A., Sweany, P.H.: Trace scheduling optimization in a retargetable microcode compiler. In: Proceedings of the 20th Microprogramming Workshop (MICRO-20). (1987) 106–114
14. Chang, P.P., mei W. Hwu, W.: Trace selection for compiling large c application programs to microcode. In: Proceedings of the 21st Annual Workshop on Microprogramming and Microarchitecture. (1988) 21–29
15. Wen-mei W. Hwu et al: The superblock: An effective technique for vliw and superscalar compilation. Journal of Supercomputing **7** (1993) 229–248
16. Bruening, D., Duesterwald, E., Amarasinghe, S.: Design and implementation of a dynamic optimization framework for windows. In: Proceedings of 4th ACM Workshop on Feedback-Directed and Dynamic Optimization (FDDO-4). (2001)
17. Bruening, D., Garnett, T., Amarasinghe, S.: An infrastructure for adaptive dynamic optimization. In: Proceedings of the international symposium on Code generation and optimization. (2003) 265–275
18. Chen, W.K., Lerner, S., Chaiken, R., Gillies, D.M.: Mojo: A dynamic optimization system. In: Proceedings of 3rd ACM Workshop on Feedback-Directed and Dynamic Optimization (FDDO-3). (2000)
19. Krintz, C.: Coupling on-line and off-line profile information to improve program performance. In: Proceedings of International Symposium on Code Generation and Optimization. (2003) 69–78

A Practical MHP Information Analysis for Concurrent Java Programs

Lin Li and Clark Verbrugge

School of Computer Science, McGill University,
Montréal, Canada
{lli31, clump}@sable.mcgill.ca

Abstract. In this paper we present an implementation of *May Happen in Parallel* analysis for Java that attempts to address some of the practical implementation concerns of the original work. We describe a design that incorporates techniques for aiding a feasible implementation and expanding the range of acceptable inputs. We provide experimental results showing the utility and impact of our approach and optimizations using a variety of concurrent benchmarks.

1 Introduction and Motivation

Although specific techniques for handling problems related to compiling multithreaded languages are being actively researched, e.g., synchronization removal [7], and race detection [4], more general techniques that also allow one to compute the impact of concurrency on other compiler analyses or optimizations are still desireable. Such a more general approach for Java is provided by Naumovich et al's *May Happen in Parallel* (MHP) analysis [15]. This analysis only determines which statements may be executed concurrently, but from this information on potential data races and synchronization problems can be derived.

The original MHP algorithm relies on a simplified program structure. All methods need to be inlined, and cloning is necessary to eliminate polymorphism and aliasing. Unfortunately, while these limitations still allow a variety of applications to be analyzed, they cannot be feasibly applied to more complex programs. Whole program inlining is not possible for non-trivial programs, and moreover excludes many recursive programs. Cloning further expands the program size, and even in the presence of good alias resolution is likely to cause space concerns. Thus although Naumovich et al's results are encouraging, it is important to also know how well the analysis would work in a more practical compiler setting.

In this paper we present an implementation of MHP for Java that attempts to address such practical concerns. Our implementation of MHP incorporates several simple analyses as well as modifications to MHP structures in order to reduce many of the practical limitations. We provide experimental results and show how simple optimizations on the MHP internal data structures can make MHP analysis of even moderate size programs quite feasible.

R. Eigenmann et al. (Eds.): LCPC 2004, LNCS 3602, pp. 194–208, 2005.

In the next section we describe the basics of Naumovich et al's MHP analysis and its accompanying *Parallel Execution Graph* data structure. Further details on our implementation and context are given in section 3. Improvements to this implementation are then developed in section 4, and experimental results and analysis are given in section 5. Related work is described in section 6 and we describe future work and conclude in section 7.

2   PEG and MHP Analysis

MHP analysis first requires the construction of a *Parallel Execution Graph* (PEG) data structure, an augmented control flow graph for the input program. The actual analysis is then on the PEG, with a fairly trivial mapping back to the original CFG. We sketch out the major steps and structure definitions here; complete details are of course provided in Naumovich et al's original paper [15]. First, however, we give further details on the practical constraints.

MHP analysis relies on a simplified and constrained input program structure, including limits on thread creation, method and variable aliases and method call structure. Some constraints such as having a known and bounded number of runtime threads represent reduced generality, but have no impact on efficiency. Others however imply significant cost, and severely impact practicality.

One main requirement is that alias resolution be done, and code cloning used to eliminate polymorphism and ensure precise variable and method targets are known. This simplifies the analysis at a potentially very large cost in data size and thus overall running time. More complex programs with larger alias sets cannot be efficiently represented or analyzed under these constraints.

MHP analysis is not defined over most method calls, and requires all methods except specific *communication methods* (`Thread.start()`, `wait()`, `notify()` etc) to be inlined. This eliminates the need to consider issues of disentangling information propagated back from multiple call sites to the same callee (the *calling context problem*). However, recursive programs cannot then be analyzed without prior conversion to iterative forms. More critically, and particularly in conjunction with cloning, the space requirements of this approach can easily be excessive for even moderate programs, and so is not feasible in general.

2.1   Parallel Execution Graph

The *Parallel Execution Graph* or PEG is a superstructure of a normal control flow graph. Special arrows and nodes are incorporated to explicitly represent potential thread communication and synchronization. Since thread bounds are known, the actions of each thread are also uniquely represented in the graph. Figure 1 gives an example of a PEG for a simple program that launches 2 threads (`t1` and `t2`) from a main thread and then attempts to signal them using a global lock and a wait/notify pattern.

Nodes in PEG's are structured as triples; e.g., for *communication methods* the triple *(object, name, caller)* is used, where the field *object* represents the monitor

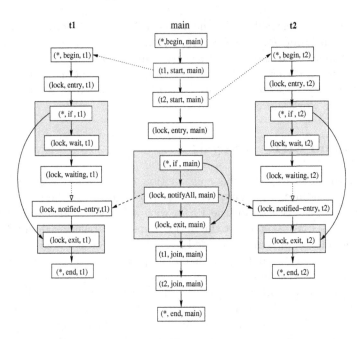

Fig. 1. An example of a PEG, a simplified version of figure 3 in [15]

object controlling the communication, *name* is the method name, and *caller* is the thread name. For nodes that do not represent *communication method*s, a wildcard symbol (*) is used for the object field.

Certain new nodes are added to aid in later analysis. Most simply, *(*,begin,t)* and *(*,end,t)* nodes are inserted to mark the beginning and end of each thread *t*, and *(lock, entry,t)* and *(lock, exit,t)* nodes indicate monitorenter and monitorexit operations for operations by *t* on object *lock*. Condition synchronization is only slightly more complex. A `wait()` method call is broken down into a chain of *wait*, *waiting* and *notified-entry* nodes, representing the substeps of starting the call to `wait()`, actually sleeping after the lock is released, and having been notified and trying to reacquire the lock, respectively.

PEG edges fall into one of four different categories: *local*, *start*, *wait* and *notify* edges. The first three are statically constructed, and the last is created during the analysis. A *local edge* represents normal, intra-thread control flow, not dependent on thread communication. These edges are inherited from the base CFG, and are shown as solid edges in Figure 1. A *start edge* is created to indicate a must-precede relation between a call to `Thread.start()` and the first action of the initiated thread. These edges are shown in Figure 1 as the dotted edges with solid arrowheads between the *(t_i,start,main)* nodes and the corresponding *(*,begin,t_i)* node. A *waiting edge* models the control flow dependent on thread notification. These are inserted between *waiting* nodes and *notified-entry* nodes, and are shown as dotted edges with empty arrowheads in Figure 1.

Notify edges are created dynamically during the analysis process. They allow precedence information to flow from the notifier to the waiting thread, and since they are inserted during analysis, this information flow can be more precise than a static approach. Notify edges are only inserted from an *(object,notify/notifyAll,t1)* node to a *(object,notified-entry,t2)* node if the same object is involved, the threads are distinct, and the analysis has computed that these two events may indeed happen in parallel.

2.2   A Worklist Flow Analysis Algorithm

MHP analysis is performed using a worklist dataflow algorithm. The goal is to find for each PEG node the set of other PEG nodes which may execute concurrently. For each PEG node a set $M(n)$ is initialized to the empty set, and a least fixed-point based flow algorithm propagates set information around the PEG. Although this largely follows the template of a standard dataflow analysis, with special modifications to create notify edges and flow information across and through the various special edges and nodes, the algorithm also includes a "symmetry step" to guarantee that if $m \in M(n)$ then $n \in M(m)$. This non-standard component of the analysis ensures information is accurately maintained as the actions of concurrently executing threads are analyzed. Note that as with most static analyses the computed information is a conservative approximation.

3   MHP Analysis in the Context of Soot

3.1   Soot Framework

Our implementation is based on Soot [22], a free compiler infrastructure written in Java. The Soot framework was designed to provide a common infrastructure for analyzing and transforming Java bytecode, and in particular includes a number of useful analyses, transformations and representations we used to simplify our effort. Major components are described below.

Jimple. The main internal program representation in Soot is *Jimple*. Jimple is a typed, "3-address" code representation of input, stack machine based bytecode, and Soot provides control flow graph construction and various control flow analyses on Jimple. Since a stack-less, CFG form is also convenient for MHP analysis, we based our analysis on Jimple. This also simplifies interaction with other analyses in the Soot framework.

Intra-procedural Analysis. Soot has two built-in intra-procedural analysis schemata: `ForwardFlowAnalysis` and `BackwardFlowAnalysis`. Due to the symmetry step MHP analysis is strictly speaking neither a forward flow analysis nor a backward flow analysis; we implemented our MHP analysis based on the ForwardFlowAnalysis framework, modified to incorporate the symmetry step.

Inter-procedural Analysis. Soot also provides several inter-procedural analyses important to our implementation:

- **Call Graphs** For a multithreaded program, the *CallGraph* must include all the methods that can be reached from the `main` method, as well as the `run` method in a class that implements `java.lang.Runnable`.
- **Class hierarchy analysis (CHA)** *Class hierarchy analysis* [5] conservatively estimates the run-time targets of method calls by using the class-subclass relationships in the type hierarchy.
- **Points-to analysis** *Points-to* analysis [6] computes the set of concrete locations to which each variable may point. Points-to information identifies variable aliasing, and in object-oriented languages like Java, method targets too. Soot includes SPARK [14], a points-to analyzer that provides fast and precise points-to data.

Figure 2 shows how our MHP analysis is integrated with Soot. Java class files are first input into Soot framework, producing Jimple files, the Call Graph, as well as CHA and Spark analysis information. These are all used as input to the MHP module, which computes the may happen in parallel information for each PEG node. MHP information can subsequently be used for further program analyses and optimization.

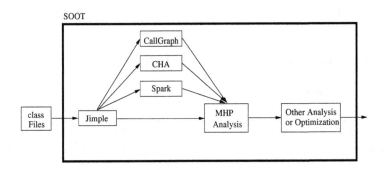

Fig. 2. MHP Analysis in Soot

4   Practical MHP Analysis

Our MHP implementation is composed of a few steps; Figure 3 shows an overview of the process. There are three phases in our MHP analysis. The first phase is a PEG Builder which uses Jimple and takes input from CallGraphs, CHA, and SPARK. We get PEGs after the PEG builder phase, then a PEG Simplifier works on PEGs to get a smaller PEG by aggregating some nodes into one node. The final phase is an MHP analyzer which runs the worklist algorithm based on the simplified PEG. Each of these processes has performance-affecting practical considerations or goals, and we describe the salient features below.

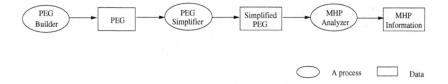

Fig. 3. Overview of our MHP analysis

Note that many of our simplifications are based on the observation (made in [15]) that code not containing synchronization does not need to be explicitly modelled. Here, by *interesting statements* we refer to statements related to modeling execution of threads and synchronization of Java programs, i.e., the communication methods `wait()`, `notify()`, `notifyAll`, `Thread.start()`, and `Thread.join()`, as well as *monitorenter, monitorexit* bytecode operations (including entry/exit of synchronized methods). A method is interesting if it either contains an interesting statement, or any callee is interesting.

4.1   Efficient PEG Construction

Conceptually, building PEG's from a CFG is straightforward. In practice, non-obvious information needs to be computed to make correct decisions. In order to keep the data size manageable, a realistic implementation must also incorporate techniques to limit the size of the resulting data structures.

One obvious way of restricting data size is to focus attention on application code only. Java includes a very large standard class library, and so even for a very small program a complete call graph tends to be quite large. However, in many cases the application itself is of main interest, and so if external actions are assumed safe enough, greater efficiency can be derived by excluding library and startup information. We therefore define a *PegCallGraph* to be a call graph restricted to methods inside application classes, i.e., user defined classes.

Constructing the PEG can involve a lot of duplicated effort, as the same method is inlined in various places. Our strategy is to build small PEGS, one for each method a thread may invoke, and then combine these small PEGs into a PEG for the whole program. This of course doesn't change the final PEG size, and other techniques are necessary for that. Methods without *interesting statements* are good candidates for pruning, and so our PEG construction first proceeds with a simple, fast interprocedural analysis to identify and compact such methods, followed by a standard inlining operation.

Finding Interesting Methods. Clearly methods that will never execute any interesting statements are of little interest to the MHP analysis: any MHP information true on entry to such a method is true at exit, and at all points in between. Since thread communication code is typically a small part of any significant program, restricting the PEG to useful parts of the program is very effective.

Unfortunately, knowing whether a method is interesting is recursively dependent on the status of all callee methods. A precise, flow-sensitive interprocedural analysis would be most effective, but is of course both complex and expensive. We have elected for a more pragmatic flow-insensitive approach, implemented in two stages.

The body of each method in the PegCallGraph is first scanned to see if contains an interesting statement. If so the method node in the PegCallGraph is marked interesting. Once all methods are examined, marks are propagated in the reverse direction of call graph edges, and logically OR'd at each merge point using a depth first search of the PegCallGraph. The result is a conservative overapproximation of interesting methods. During actual PEG construction uninteresting methods are represented by single node placeholders, greater reducing PEG size.

Recursive method calls will result in the failure of inlining, and so naturally must be avoided. The call graph is thus also analyzed to locate recursive cycles, and rejects the input program if so. Of course cycles are only problematic if interesting methods are involved, since uninteresting methods are not actually included in the PEG. Our algorithm ensures any detected call graph cycles involve at least one interesting method before rejecting the program.

Inlining. Actual inlining is straightforward, and proceeds in a bottom up fashion on the PegCallGraph. Each inlining operation involves creating a new local scope for the code and mapping local variable, parameter and return value usage. In the case of Java, care must also be taken to ensure appropriate *monitorenter* and *monitorexit* instructions are inserted in the case of inlining `synchronized` method calls.

Note that because inlining is used in computing MHP information, finding precise method targets is very important. Imprecision in the destination of virtual calls can have a large impact on call graph size. To get a more precise call graph than that provided by CHA alone, we used Spark to help resolve objects used in invocation calls, and hence method polymorphism. In places where the method target was still ambiguous all potential callees must be presumed invoked.

4.2   PEG Simplification

We can proceed to use the MHP algorithms to compute MHP information once the PEG is built. However, even with the above inlining strategy we may still have a large PEG. Further optimization techniques can still be useful to simplify the PEG before running the MHP algorithms, and so we applied two straightforward graph reductions as optimizations: merging lists, and collapsing strongly connected components. Since the MHP analysis manipulates sets of PEG nodes, reductions in PEG size can have a significant effect, and we give some results on the effect of PEG reductions in Section 5.

Merging Strongly Connected Components. This is based on an observation: suppose a *strongly connected component* (SCC) S inside a PEG does not contain *interesting statements*. If a statement A can be concurrently executed with a statement B inside S, it should also be possible for A to be concurrently executed with all the other nodes inside S. Thus, we can merge the nodes inside this SCC and create a new node to represent the entire SCC. The new node is simply a reference to the list containing all the nodes inside the SCC.

After finding SCCs, we check if they contains *interesting statements*. If not, we can merge the nodes in the SCC into one node.

Merging Sequential Nodes. A sequence of nodes with no *interesting statements*, and no branching in or out except at the beginning and end respectively necessarily has the same MHP information at each node in the sequence. We thus locate all maximal chains of this form, and as with SCC's collapse them into a single node. Again, these new nodes are references to lists of the replaced nodes.

4.3   Practical MHP Analysis

The efficient PEG construction described above incorporates inlining, but avoids resolving variable aliases through cloning. The latter technique is quite expensive in an allocation-intensive setting such as Java.

Specifically handling object aliases in the MHP analysis would significantly complicate the algorithm, and certainly increase its actual running time. It is further unclear whether this extra effort is worthwhile, given that even a set of 2 potential object targets for a monitor operation may make a conclusion of success or failure of the operation impossible. We have thus chosen to focus on detecting situations in which precise conclusions can be made rather than on a general inclusion of aliasing. Below we describe our technique for handling this problem.

Finding Runtime Target Objects. MHP analysis relies on knowing the value of the *Object* field in PEG triples for determining lock ownership and monitor-based information flow. In Soot and by using SPARK, it is possible to find the potential textual allocation sites corresponding to a given object reference. Allocation sites are locations in the code, and thus one can easily determine a set of potential types of an object reference, and this is sufficient for many analyses (including call graph refinement).

For MHP analysis, however, decisions as to whether synchronization has occurred requires knowing that an object involved in a *monitorexit* is the same *runtime* object involved in a previously examined *monitorenter*. SPARK computes *may*-alias information, and so even the same singleton allocation site sets for the respective objects are not sufficient for this conclusion, since allocation sites in loops may spawn more than one runtime object. A form of interprocedural value numbering analysis is thus required. Again for simplicity of implementation and as well as asymptotic complexity concerns we have elected for a custom analysis, composed of an intraprocedural analysis and a flow-insensitive interprocedural step.

An allocation site that is only ever executed at most once of course does represent one runtime object. Thus an obvious guarantee that two or more synchronization operations are operating on the same value can be provided if the computed sets of allocation sites are both the same singletons, and the allocation site is only ever executed once.

Intraprocedurally, a statement is surely executed at most once if it is not included in any control flow cycles, and so is the complement of knowing what may be executed more than once. This information is computed for each allocation site of every method in the PegCallGraph. To find out which methods are called more than once interprocedurally, we use a modified depth-first search on the PegCallGraph to detect whether a node is potentially reachable more than once from **main**. Methods that can be called more than once conservatively imply each statement in them can be executed more than once, regardless of internal control flow. Our algorithm actually computes both intra and interprocedural information together, performing intraprocedural analysis as the interprocedural analysis proceeds, and only if required. This allows the conclusions of each analysis to be merged and propagated together.

Finding Monitor Nodes. Computation of MHP information is partially based on knowing which PEG nodes may be contained within a Java monitor lock. However, as well as the need to determine the exact runtime identity of a locked object, an analysis of Java locks must also account for recursive locking—a thread that owns a lock may relock it repeatedly, and is required to unlock it a corresponding number of times in order to release it. Simply identifying nodes dominated by an enter node without reaching an exit node is thus insufficient to determine whether a node outside this region is or is not protected by a monitor—lock level must also be tracked.

To model locking state we have implemented a simple, forward, flow-sensitive analysis on the PEG. This analysis conservatively tracks locking depth for objects used in monitor operations by associating a lock count with each such object. These structures are propagated through the PEG, incrementing the count for the object specified at each *monitorenter* operation and decrementing counts at *monitorexit*'s. Unbounded recursive locking, as in general merge points with unmatched locking depths for corresponding objects (not possible with Java programs) and are not handled, so this is guaranteed to reach a fixed point.

With lock depth information the MHP analysis can make sound judgements as to whether a PEG node is truly in a monitor or not.

5   Experimental Results

5.1   Benchmarks

We collected our benchmarks from several sources. Most of the benchmarks are multithreaded benchmarks from the Java Grande Benchmark Suite [21]:

FORKJOIN, SYNC and BARRIER represent low level benchmarks that test synchronization, SERIES, LUFACT, SOR, CRYPT and SPARSEMULT test specific "kernel" operations, and MONTECARLO, RAYTRACER and MOLDYN are larger, more complete applications. MTRT is the only multithreaded benchmark from the SPECjvm98 [1] suite. In order to fit our input requirements, we modified most of these benchmarks by manually unrolling all the loops containing method calls to *communication methods*.

For comparative purposes we have also attempted to collect some of the same benchmarks used in Naumovich et al's paper. However, most of the code we have been able to acquire is in the form of incomplete program fragments that require a driving main program to analyze in our system. Fine-grained comparisions are thus not likely to be meaningful. We therefore include AUBANKING and PEBANKING, programs based on the examples AutomatedBanking and PessimBankAccount from Doug Lea's book [11]. We have focussed on these two examples since in [15] Naumovich et al's version of these benchmarks had the largest PEG sizes and also had the largest MHP analysis times (by an order of magnitude) of all their benchmarks. CYCLIC is a smaller benchmark from the CyclicBarrier example in the second edition of Lea's book [12]. In each case we added an appropriate main method, modifying them to be complete applications. All tests were run on a Pentium 4 1.8GHz, using the Sun HotSpot VM 1.4.1 (maximum 1500Meg heap) under Debian Linux.

5.2   Results

Tables 1 and 2 present the experimental results of our MHP analysis. In Table 1 the first column gives the names of the benchmarks, the second column gives the number of threads (including the main thread), and the next two columns give the number of nodes and edges in the PEGs representing each program respectively. In the fifth and sixth columns, we specify the average and maximal number of nodes in the computed $M()$ set for each node, i.e., how many nodes were determined may be executed in parallel with each node. This gives some notion of analysis accuracy, at least in the absence of measuring a consuming analysis. The seventh column gives the total number of node pairs found in the entire PEG—as well as the PEG itself, this represents the total space requirements of the analysis.

The remaining columns measure time for the various stages of the analysis. PEG time is the time to build the PEG, MHP is the subsequent analysis time, and Spark time is the total cost of points-to analysis. Total time is greater than the sum of the these stages; the remainder represents time required to load and initialize and shutdown the Soot environment.

The timings and data in Table 1 already represent application of many of the previously discussed simplification and implementation techniques (excessive data sizes prevented computation of totally unoptimized data), we only exclude the PEG node merging techniques of Section 4.2. Note that MTRT contains recursive method calls. Method inlining for such a benchmark would normally fail;

Table 1. Experimental results without PEG simplification

Programs	Threads	Nodes	Edges	$|M()|$ Ave	$|M()|$ Max	Pairs	PEG (s)	MHP (s)	Spark (s)	Total (s)
FORKJOIN	4	308	331	64	173	6105	0.18	4.46	67.2	88.5
SYNC	5	656	712	118	459	28944	0.40	51.51	68.2	136.8
BARRIER	5	561	716	175	339	34651	0.34	72.72	68.7	160.4
CRYPT	5	1025	1061	672	772	297220	0.52	6812.68	67.2	6917.7
MONTECARLO	3	405	433	104	182	11340	0.28	14.15	68.0	102.3
RAYTRACER	3	660	724	125	318	25188	0.37	57.58	67.5	143.42
SERIES	3	315	342	109	130	9660	0.24	8.84	67.8	93.3
LUFACT	3	465	510	202	224	32032	0.23	87.86	68.8	163.08
SOR	3	662	673	289	363	66430	0.29	259.26	68.0	347.9
SPARSEMULT	3	305	329	81	120	6180	0.21	3.98	67.2	88.1
MOLDYN	3	2173	2295	1093	1866	1088392	1.86	44313.44	69.2	44553.9
CYCLIC	5	162	201	69	124	4580	0.14	1.13	67.8	86.2
MTRT	4	188	211	43	108	2819	0.33	1.53	139.7	232.9
AUBANKING	3	170	203	31	92	4114	0.17	1.14	66.5	86.4
PEBANKING	3	154	270	63	137	4414	0.14	1.17	66.4	85.3

however, using the techniques of Section 4.1 we determined that the recursive calls do not involve *interesting statements*, and so we are still able to get results.

For most benchmarks the time to build the PEG is small, and in all but one case well under a second. MHP analysis time clearly dominates PEG construction time. This is unsurprising given the $O(n^3)$ time complexity of MHP analysis, but was considerably less evident in the data presented in [15], where the majority of benchmarks were very small (mostly < 100 PEG nodes) and so PEG time generally appeared to dominate. For larger programs the cubic behaviour of MHP becomes more evident: MOLDYN, the largest benchmark we examined at 2173 nodes takes less than 2 seconds to build the PEG, but over 12 hours to analyze. These running times are clearly still excessive for even moderate programs, and further steps are necessary to reduce PEG size, and thus MHP analysis time.

Table 2 shows similar experimental results when the PEG is optimized using the techniques of Section 4.2. The second and third columns give the PEG size reductions supplied by the two techniques of merging SCCs and merging sequential nodes respectively; the resulting graph size is given in the fourth and fifth columns. In smaller programs sequential node contractions are most effective, but in the bigger programs the volume of modular, synchronization independent sections of code sometimes made SCC merging quite valuable. In every case our PEG optimizations were able to reduce the graph, and in some cases quite dramatically: MOLDYN is reduced from 2173 nodes to 144.

The next two columns give the time in seconds taken to perform the PEG simplifications and run MHP analysis on the smaller PEG. The eighth column shows the total running time including Spark and Soot overhead. The remain-

Table 2. Experimental results after optimization

Programs	Sim.Scc	Sim.Seq.	Nodes	Edges	Sim. (s)	MHP (s)	Total (s)	Total Speedup	PEG+MHP Speedup
FORKJOIN	0	199	109	132	0.02	0.41	84.4	1.05	4.76
SYNC	2	389	255	307	0.07	8.81	94.1	1.45	5.95
BARRIER	12	287	262	411	0.06	21.21	108.8	1.47	3.71
CRYPT	662	240	121	149	0.10	0.93	105.1	65.82	4395.80
MONTECARLO	26	247	132	158	0.03	0.53	88.7	1.15	17.13
RAYTRACER	18	431	211	267	0.07	6.66	92.5	1.55	8.48
SERIES	26	180	109	134	0.03	0.64	85.0	1.09	9.98
LUFACT	166	194	105	130	0.04	0.53	87.9	1.91	110.06
SOR	298	223	101	124	0.04	0.39	89.0	3.91	360.37
SPARSEMULT	55	165	85	104	0.02	0.09	84.5	1.04	12.65
MOLDYN	1482	547	144	174	0.18	1.18	90.0	495.04	13763.80
CYCLIC	0	51	11	150	0.02	0.74	85.8	1.00	1.40
MTRT	3	107	78	95	0.02	0.10	231.8	1.00	3.73
AUBANKING	2	71	97	126	0.02	0.53	85.8	1.01	1.75
PEBANKING	0	66	88	204	0.02	0.62	84.7	1.01	1.68

ing columns give the relative speedup (old-time/new-time) ratio achieved by the optimized version versus the base approach, for both total running time, and the time just to construct and simplify the PEG and run the MHP analysis. Again, MOLDYN speedups were most significant, as running time drops from half a day to just under 2 seconds. As a general rule, larger benchmarks have more nodes, and hence more opportunities for PEG compaction, which is quite encouraging for analysis of reasonable size programs. The benchmarks with the lowest speedup, CYCLIC, AUBANKING and PEBANKING, also have the fewest reductions due to PEG simplification, both in absolute terms and proportionally. These are also all relatively small benchmarks with a high proportion of communication and synchronization statements, and this limits merging opportunities.

SCC and sequential merging has clear benefits, with a fairly minimal cost—even for MOLDYN simplification takes less than 1/5s. Merging in combination with an already efficient initial PEG construction allows reasonable size programs to be analyzed. Interestingly, after optimization efforts, the BARRIER benchmark is the most expensive to analyze, and MOLDYN time is even less than SYNC. With optimization overall analysis cost is related more closely to number and density of communication operations than input program size.

6   Related Work

Obviously, our work here is based most directly on the MHP analysis originally designed by Naumovich et al [15]. There are of course other approaches to analyzing and representing concurrent programs, with a variety of specific and general purposes.

Program Dependence Graphs (PDGs) [8] can be used for general program optimizations where dependency is a concern; for example, detecting medium to fine-grain parallelism for sequential programs. They are however not designed to represent parallel programs. *Parallel Program Graphs* (PPGs) [18, 19] are a generalization of PDGs and CFGs and can be used to fully represent sequential programs and parallel programs. PPGs can be used for program optimization and detecting data races. Srinvasan et al. [10] proposed a *Parallel Flow Graph* (PFG) for optimizing explicitly parallel programs. They provided dataflow equations for the reaching definitions analysis and used a copy-in/copy-out semantics for accessing shared variables in parallel constructs. *Concurrent Control Flow Graphs* (CCFGs) [13] are similar to PPGs and PFGs, with the addition of conflict edges in addition to synchronization and control flow edges. None of these representations are Java-specific.

Specific problems have engendered more specific, and more efficient results. For the purpose of data race detection, Savage et al developed *Eraser*, a race checker in the C, C++ environment. Jong-Deok Choi et al [4] compute relatively precise data race information using *Inter-Thread Control Flow Graphs* (ICFGs). Flanagan and Freund analyze large Java program for race conditions by examining user-provided type annotations for code [9]. Improvements to accuracy and efficiency of data race detection continue to be addressed; e.g., through dynamic techniques [23], and by combining information from multiple analyses [16]. A similar concentration of efforts has looked at synchronization removal [7, 3].

Our implementation and optimization techniques largely depend on a combination of well known approaches. Good quality points-to analysis is one of the more complex and expensive compiler problems, and has been addressed in a variety of settings [6, 20, 17, 2]. Spark [14] produces precise points-to information, and this has been quite crucial to our ability to analyze non-trivial programs. Exclusion and compaction of PEG nodes according to the presence of communication methods was briefly mentioned, though not developed in [15].

7   Future Work and Conclusions

We have presented a more realistic implementation of MHP analysis for Java. Our design makes use of a variety of existing and small custom analyses in order to build a feasible implementation that can analyze programs of a reasonable size, bypassing a number of previous input restrictions. We have presented experimental results from such an implementation, and shown how excessive MHP analysis time can be efficiently handled through simple input compaction techniques.

Our work has clear extensions in a number of ways, including analysis and potential implementation improvements. Certainly accuracy of the resulting information deserves examination. Naumovich et al compare MHP information to precise reachability analyses, but this is not feasible for larger programs. Accuracy could however be judged by assessing how useful the information is to a consumer analysis, such as race detection or synchronization removal.

Internal improvements can of course still be done. Our simple value prediction and interesting method identification algorithms are sufficient to produce results, but are not especially precise. More accurate strategies could be applied, which would allow determination of the relative cost versus benefit for this information. Similarly, further PEG compaction approaches seem worth exploring.

We also aim to expand the range of acceptable input programs. Programs with an unbounded number of threads, use of timed synchronization constructs, and so on could be handled, and this would allow more programs to be analyzed with less manual intervention.

Acknowledgements. This work has been supported by the National Sciences and Engineering Research Council of Canada, and the McGill Faculty of Graduate Studies. We would like to thank Ondřej Lhoták for lots of implementation help and advice.

References

1. SPEC JVM98 Benchmarks. http://wwww.spec.org/jvm98.
2. Marc Berndl, Ondřej Lhoták, Feng Qian, Laurie Hendren, and Navindra Umanee. Points-to analysis using BDDs. In *Proceedings of the ACM SIGPLAN 2003 conference on Programming language design and implementation*, pages 103–114. ACM Press, 2003.
3. J. Bogda and U.Holzle. Removing unnecessary synchronization in Java. In *Proceedings of the ACM SIGPLAN 1999 Conference on Object-Oriented Programming, Systems, Languages, and Application*, pages 35–46, November 1999.
4. Jong-Deok Choi, Keunwoo Lee, Alexey Loginov, Robert O'Callahan Vivek Sarkar, and Manu Sirdharan. Efficient and precise datarace detection for multithreaded object-oriented programs. In *Proceedings of the ACM SIGPLAN 2002 Conference on Programming language design and implementation*, Berlin, Germany, June 2002.
5. Jeffrey Dean, David Grove, and Craig Chambers. Optimization of object-oriented programs using static class hierarchy analysis. In Walter G. Olthoff, editor, *ECOOP'95—Object-Oriented Programming, 9th European Conference*, volume 952 of *Lecure Notes in Computer Science*, pages 77–101, Åarhus, Denmark, 7-11 August 1995. Springer.
6. Maryam Emami, Rakesh Ghiya, and Laurie J. Hendren. Context-sensitive interprocedural points-to analysis in the presence of function pointers. In *Proceedings of the ACM SIGPLAN'94 Conference on Programming Language Design and Implementation*, pages 242–256, 1994.
7. E.Ruf. Effective synchronization removal for Java. In *Proceedings of the ACM SIGPLAN 2000 Conference on Programming language design and implementation*, pages 208–218, June 2000.
8. Jeanne Ferrante, Karl J.Ottenstein, and Joe D. Warren. The program dependence graph and its uses in optimization. In *ACM Transactions on Programming Languages and Systems*, July 1987.
9. Cormac Flanagan and Stephen N. Freund. Type-based race detection for Java. In *Proceedings of the ACM SIGPLAN 2000 conference on Programming language design and implementation*, pages 219–232. ACM Press, 2000.

10. Ferrante J, K.Ottenstein, and J. Warren. Compile-time analysis and optimization of explicitly parallel programs. In *Journal of Parallel algorithms and applications*, 1997.

11. Doug Lea. *Concurrent Programming in Java Design Principles and Patterns*. Addison-Wesley, Reading, Massachusetts, 1997.

12. Doug Lea. *Concurrent Programming in Java Design Principles and Patterns*. Addison-Wesley, Reading, Massachusetts, second edition, 1999.

13. Jaejin Lee. *Compilation techniques for explicitly parallel programs*. PhD thesis, University of Illinois at Unbana-Champaign, 1999.

14. Ondřej Lhoták. Spark: A flexible points-to analysis framework for Java. Master's thesis, McGill University, December 2002.

15. Gleb Naumovich, George S.Avrumin, and Lori A.Clarke. An efficient algorithm for computing MHP information for concurrent Java program. In *Proceedings of the 7th European engineering conference held jointly with the 7th ACM SIGSOFT international symposium on Foundations of software engineering*, Toulous, France, 1999.

16. Robert O'Callahan and Jong-Deok Choi. Hybrid dynamic data race detection. In *Proceedings of the ninth ACM SIGPLAN symposium on Principles and practice of parallel programming*, pages 167–178. ACM Press, 2003.

17. Atanas Rountev, Ana Milanova, and Barbara G. Ryder. Points-to analysis for Java using annotated constraints. In *Proceedings of the 16th ACM SIGPLAN conference on Object oriented programming, systems, languages, and applications*, pages 43–55. ACM Press, 2001.

18. Vivek Sarkar. Analysis and optimization of explicitly parallel programs using the parallel program graph representation. In *Proceedings of the 10th International Workshop on Languages and Compilers for Parallel Computing, LNCS Springer-Verlag*, Minneapolis, MN, August 1997.

19. Vivek Sarkar and Barbara Simons. Parallel program graphs and their classification. In *Proceedings of ACM SIGPLAN-SIGSOFT workshop on Program analysis for software tools and engineering*, Montreal, Quebec, Canada, 1998.

20. Bjarne Steensgaard. Points-to analysis in almost linear time. In *Proceedings of the 23rd ACM SIGPLAN-SIGACT symposium on Principles of programming languages*, pages 32–41. ACM Press, 1996.

21. Java Grande Benchmark Suite. http://www.epcc.ed.ac.uk/javagrande/javag.html.

22. Raja Vallée-Rai, Laurie Hendren, Vijay Sundaresan, Patrick Lam, Etienne Gagnon, and Phong Co. Soot - a Java optimization framework. In *Proceedings of CASCON 1999*, pages 125–135, 1999.

23. Christoph von Praun and Thomas R. Gross. Object race detection. In *Proceedings of the 16th ACM SIGPLAN conference on Object oriented programming, systems, languages, and applications*, pages 70–82. ACM Press, 2001.

Efficient Computation of Communicator Variables for Programs with Unstructured Parallelism

Christoph von Praun*

IBM T. J. Watson Research Center,
Yorktown Heights, NY

Abstract. We present an algorithm to determine communicator variables in parallel programs. If communicator variables are accessed in program order and accesses to other shared variables are not reordered with respect to communicators, then program executions are sequentially consistent. Computing communicators is an efficient and effective alternative to delay set computation. The algorithm does not require a thread and whole-program control-flow model and tolerates the typical approximations that static program analyses make for threads and data. These properties make the algorithm suitable to handle multi-threaded object-oriented programs with unstructured parallelism. We demonstrate on several multi-threaded Java programs that the algorithm is effective in reducing the number of fences at memory access statements compared to a naive fence insertion algorithm (the reduction is on average 28%) and report the runtime overhead caused by the fences (between 0% and 231%, average 81%).

1 Introduction

The reordering of seemingly independent memory access in individual threads of a parallel program can lead to violations of sequential consistency (SC). This phenomenon can be prevented by the selective insertion of memory fences into a parallel program. Algorithms that insert memory fences to maintain SC basically proceed along three steps:

1. *May-happen-in-parallel analysis* identifies statements that are executed concurrently by different threads [8]. *Static data race analysis* goes a step further and identifies those concurrent statements that operate on the same shared data [2,14].
2. Given statements that execute concurrently, *delay-set analysis* [10,5,6,1] determines the set of pairs of object access statements that should occur in program order. If all such ordering constraints are met at runtime, the execution SC [10].

---

* This work was done, in part, while the author was working at the Laboratory for Software Technology, ETH Zürich, 8092 Zürich, Switzerland.

R. Eigenmann et al. (Eds.): LCPC 2004, LNCS 3602, pp. 209–223, 2005.

```
initially: x, y, z, r1, r2, r3 = 0

    thread1              thread2
  a1: r1 = z;          a2: x = 1;
  b1: r2 = x;          b2: y = 1;
  c1: r3 = y;          c2: z = 1;
```

Fig. 1. Scenario with a communicator variable

3. *Fence-insertion* implements the ordering constraints (delays) through the placement of memory fences. Specific properties of memory ordering of a computer architecture and its fence model can be exploited to combine and to reduce the number of memory fences [3].

The three steps build on one another, i.e., the results of one are the input to the next. The first and second step are machine-independent and account only for programming language properties, e.g., the ordering semantics of synchronization features. The third step is machine-specific. The overall goal of a the fence insertion is to place a sufficient number of fences to ensure correctness with respect to the memory model (SC) and at the same time to minimize the number of executed memory fences.

This paper presents a novel procedure for the second phase of the algorithm. Instead of a *delay set*, we compute a set of so called *communicator variables*. Intuitively, a variable acts as a communicator if it allows one thread to determine the progress made by another thread. In the program in Figure 1, variable z, e.g., acts as communicator: if thread1 observes a value of 1 at statement $a1$, then thread2 must have made progress at least till statement $c2$, and hence the effects of $a2$ and $b2$ must also observable by thread1, i.e., $r2$ and $r3$ must receive a value of 1. If communicator variables are accessed in program order and accesses to other shared variables occur in program order with respect to communicators, then program executions are SC. The novel aspect of our approach is that it is effective for the most general, i.e., MIMD-style, object-oriented programs; unlike previous algorithms for delay set computation that have polynomial complexity (for SPMD programs), the runtime of our algorithm is mostly linear in the size of the program.

1.1 Background

The fundamental principles of computing the delay set for a given parallel program execution has been first described in [10]. Since then, several algorithms have been designed that approximate the delay set for parallel programs. The general procedure followed by these algorithms is to compute an abstract model for possible program executions from the program and then apply a variant of the delay set analysis proposed in [10] to this abstract execution model. For realistic programs, however, there are several aspects that complicate this procedure; we describe these difficulties in the following paragraphs.

The algorithm in [10] assumes a precise model of threads and shared variables. In practice, a static analysis is faced with the ambiguity in the distinction of variables through aliasing and a relatively coarse model of threads that may leave the multiplicity of threads unspecified.

Krishnamurthy and Yelick [5] showed that the computation of delays according to the original algorithm of Shasha and Snir [10] is NP hard for general MIMD programs. The same authors present an algorithm with polynomial worst case complexity for a restricted class of programs, namely SPMD programs [5] $(O(n^3)$, n is program length). The efficiency of this algorithm is further improved by recent work in [6,1], yet these algorithms have polynomial complexity $(O(n^2)$, n is program length).

The problem of computing delay sets for general MIMD parallel programs has been addressed by Midkiff, Sura, Lee, and Padua in [7,12]. Their model of multi-threaded programs [7] is based on `cobegin/coend` (MIMD) and `parallel do` (SPMD) constructs that precisely capture the extent of parallelism with respect to the program scope – this is however uncommon for many multi-threaded object-oriented programs such as the Java programs that we use in Section 3. In [12] the authors present the architecture of an optimizing compiler with fence-insertion for general Java programs. The approach is based on a comprehensive set of techniques for the analysis of multi-threaded object-oriented programs such as thread-based escape analysis, MHP analysis, and synchronization analysis. Some of the implementation is elaborated in more detail in [3]. The proposed delay set analysis, however, is still performed on a 'traditional' control-flow model based on `cobegin/coend` and `parallel do`.

1.2   Approach

Our work differs from previous approaches in that it does not try to capture the control flow and thread structure of the overall program. This makes the approach suited for programs with unstructured parallelism. Instead of the program structure, we build a model of those shared variables that may not behave sequentially consistent. A static analysis approximates the order in which individual methods access these variables and determines from that ordering those variables that act as 'communicators' between threads. The algorithm is efficient because each method is treated once and individually.

1.3   Contributions

Algorithm. We present the concept of communicator variables and specify an algorithm for the computation of communicator variables in unstructured parallel programs. This algorithm provides information for the sparse insertion of memory fences (for SC) and is more efficient than previous algorithms that compute delay sets.

Evaluation. We demonstrate the effectiveness of communicator information for fence insertion on a number of common multi-threaded Java programs and compare the results to a naive fence insertion procedure. Moreover, we combine the computation of communicators with a powerful conflict analysis [14] and quantify the total runtime overhead of the resulting programs after fence insertion.

2 Algorithm

2.1 Preliminaries

SC is violated through the reordering of memory accesses inside individual threads. According to Shasha and Snir [10], explicitly enforcing an order among *some* memory accesses can provide SC. Naturally, only accesses to shared memory need to be considered; more precisely, only those accesses to shared memory that participate in a data race. A *data race* occurs, if several threads access the same variable without order, i.e., ordering is not established through explicit means of synchronization such as locks, and if at least one access is a write [9].

Ultimately, a compiler has to establish access order among statements and hence we need to convey the notion of a data race to a concept that is available to a static analysis: For short we say that a statement is *conflicting* if it may issue an access that participates in a data race.

2.2 Overview

Naive Algorithm. A naive delay set computation requires that all memory accesses that may participate in data races (i.e., conflicting accesses) occur in program order at each processor. The delays required in the naive scheme can be enforced by consistently inserting a memory fence either before, or after each conflicting statement.

Ideal Algorithm. Shasha and Snir describe an algorithm that determines a minimal set of delays based on a program execution trace; the algorithm is NP complete and does not easily map to general parallel programs with loops, and procedures. Some papers report the results of an algorithm with ideal precision and effectiveness as 'manual', because the escape information, conflicting statements, and fence instructions are determined through manual program inspection and not through an automated algorithm [8,3]. We do not attempt to determine such an 'ideal' setting as a lower boundary. Our recent work on data race detection [13,14] has shown that there are typically no or very few actual data races in correct multi-threaded programs and hence an ideal tool would, for most programs, not need to insert any fences at all.

Our Approach. Our approach to selectively establish access ordering is different from previous delay set analyses that determine the necessity of a delay pairwise for conflicting statements. We determine communicator variables and ensure that access to communicators is associated with a memory fence. The property of a communicator is a whole program property and hence unnecessary delays may be enforced if a variable is used as a communicator in some context and in other contexts as 'ordinary' shared variable. The fence insertion based on communicators should however be comparable to approaches that are based on a delay set analysis and also result in fewer fences than the naive algorithm.

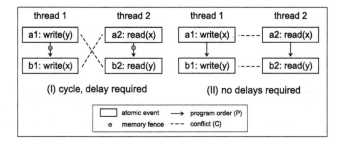

Fig. 2. Program order / conflict relation and required delays

2.3 Conflict Analysis

We use a static whole program analysis for multi-threaded Java programs to determine a conservative set of statements that are conflicting. The analysis is based on a flow-insensitive symbolic execution on an abstract thread and heap domain and tracks the thread, lock, and heap context when analyzing methods and their access to shared objects. The conflict analysis is tuned to recognize monitor-style and fork-join synchronization idioms. As it will be reported in Section 3, the effectiveness of the analysis is quite good, i.e., few or no statements are reported as conflicting for correctly synchronized programs. This is important because it narrows the scope of the communicator computation (Section 2.6). Details of the conflict analysis are discussed in [14].

2.4 Intra-thread Variable Access Ordering

A variable acts as a *communicator* if it may communicate the occurrence of updates to another thread. In Figure 2 (I), e.g., the update of x in statement $b1$ communicates the information that y has been updated (at statement $a1$) to thread2 that first reads x and then y. Hence, if access of shared variable y occurs in program order with respect to the communicator x, then executions are guaranteed to be SC; this is achieved by the memory fences in the scenario (I). The scenario (II) in Figure 2 is different, namely all threads access variables in a specific global order: first variable x, then y. Although there are conflicts, there is no cycle in the P/C relation, there are no communicator variables and hence no fences are necessary for SC.

In the following, we abstract from the read/write property of memory accesses and discuss the issue of intra-thread variable access ordering in more detail. We present a data structure that captures the intra-thread variable access ordering (Section 2.5) and finally show how that information is used to determine communicator variables (Section 2.6).

Absolute access order (AO): The execution in Figure 3 (I) exhibits critical accesses to variable z that occur after (in program order) the accesses to x and y in *all threads*.[1] Hence, no delay is necessary to enforce this ordering

---

[1] In Section 2.5, we describe a technique that allows to treat every method like a different thread. This allows to define absolute access order as "order in *all methods*".

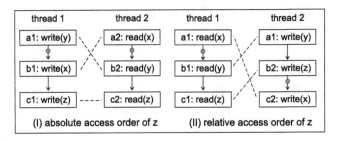

Fig. 3. Scenarios of conflicting accesses that do not require delays (for SC)

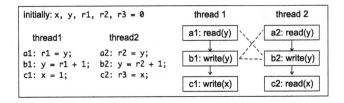

Fig. 4. Implicit ordering due to a data hazard

because the values of z will appear consistent to thread2 even if access to z is hoisted above or between the x, y access sequence. This means that for the observations of z, the effects of access reordering and different thread interleaving are equivalent.

Relative access order (RO): Figure 3 (II) resembles a scenario presented in [10]: The delays required in this scenario are $\{(a1, b1), (a1, c1), (a2, c2), (b2, c2)\}$. These delays are enforced by two memory fences that are specified in the figure. Intuitively, variable x acts as a *communicator* between threads. It is sufficient to ensure that access to shared variables occurs in program ordered with respect to the access to the communicator variable. We observe that there is a relative access order, i.e., access to z consistently occurs after access to y; hence access to y and z can be reordered among each other without changing the the memory semantics that a different thread interleaving would have also allowed.

Implicit access order due to hazard (IO): Figure 4 shows an execution with a P/C relation that is cyclic due to accesses to shared variable y. The procedure in [10] breaks the cycle through a delay between accesses $a1, b1$ and $a2, b2$. In this case, the WAR (write after read) hazard does, however, prevent reordering anyway and hence no explicit delay (fence) is necessary. Note that hazards are a program property and affect ordering independently of the compiler and machine architecture. SC executions allow all combinations of values in $(r1, r2, r3)$ except $(1, 1, *)$. The accesses to x can be reordered arbitrarily without changing this semantics (there is an absolute access order between y and x).

2.5   Variable-Order Graph

The principal idea of the algorithm is to compute a relation between shared conflicting variables that expresses ordering (absolute (AO), relative (RO), and implicit ordering (IO)) constraints that *should* be met by the program when accessing theses variables (program order). The relation is recorded in the so called *variable-order graph* that is presented in this section.

Nodes in the variable-order graph stand for shared variables. Edges in the graph represent *possible reordering* that may let actual variable access order deviate from the program order at runtime. An edge between nodes corresponding to field f_s and f_t means: in some thread, access to f_s occurs immediately before f_t in program order; however, these accesses might be reordered at runtime. To facilitate the computation of the graph at compile-time, we make the following abstractions:

- First, instead of individual variables, we only distinguish different fields; the analysis makes the conservative assumption that two variables are the same if they are the same field although the fields may belong to different object instances at runtime. While a compiler could use points-to information to distinguish object instances in certain cases, we chose to distinguish just fields to facilitate the description and also the implementation of the analysis.
- We assume that each method behaves as if it would run in its own thread. To establish any ordering that might be necessary, we require a fence at the beginning and the end of a method if necessary (Section 2.7).
- The edges in the graph correspond to a partial order of object access program order in each method. Assume that s, t are object access statements in the same method to fields f_s, f_t; both access statements are conflicting (not necessarily with statements in the same method). Then, s, t will lead to an edge $f_s \longrightarrow f_t$ in the variable-order graph if s may immediately precede t in the program order specified by the method. A loop is treated like a series of method invocations that call the loop body. Hence, a special node `meth/loop` precedes the first critical object access(es) in a loop body (or method). During the analysis of the graph, this special node expresses uncertainty about previously accessed variables and leads to a conservative placement of fences (Section 2.7).

  If s and t access the same variable and s is a read and t is a write, then no edge is created in the graph due to the WAR hazard that guarantees ordering (recall that an edge expresses a potential deviation from the program order).

Examples. Figure 5 shows two methods, their control flow, and the variable-order graph; the program corresponds to the execution in Figure 3 (II); all statements/variables in method1 and method2 are conflicting. The variable-order graph in Figure 5 (III) reflects the immediate successor relation of the basic blocks of the two methods. The nodes for x and y have the special node `meth/loop` as predecessor because those variables are accessed at the beginning of the methods.

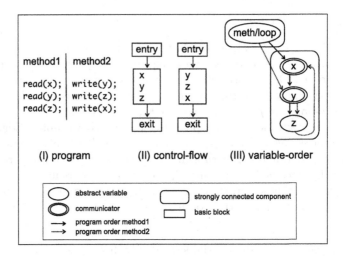

Fig. 5. Two methods, their control flow and variable-order graph

Figure 6 illustrates the variable-order graph for a complex control flow with branches and loops. The graph records the immediate program order relation among object accesses, in this case across basic block boundaries. Note that the control-flow back-edge from block 5 to block 1 is not considered when creating the variable-order graph. Hence, edge $d \longrightarrow b$ is not due to the loop, but due to the access sequence in block 6 and 7.

Algorithm. The computation of the variable-order graph starts with the creation of nodes: there is one node for every field that may be subject to a data race and additionally the special node `meth/loop`. Then, edges are established through the analysis of every method with conflicting accesses: If critical access s may be immediately followed by access t, i.e., there is no other critical access in between, then an edge is established between field f_s and f_t. In this context, the notion of "followed" considers only forward edges in the control flow.[2] No edge is created if s and t access the same variable (same field and same object) and s is a read and t is a write (reordering not permissible, see case IO in Section 2.4).

2.6   Determining Communicator Variables

A communicator variable is characterized by the fact that the variable is accessed in contexts that do not consistently provide guarantees about absolute ordering (AO) or relative ordering (RO) with respect to other shared variable accesses.

Examples. In Figure 5 (III), variable x is marked as a communicator because z occurs as an immediate predecessor of x (method2), there is however no absolute

---

[2] If s and t occur inside the same loop, then reordering along the back-edge of the loop is generally prevented by a fence at loop boundaries (Section 2.7).

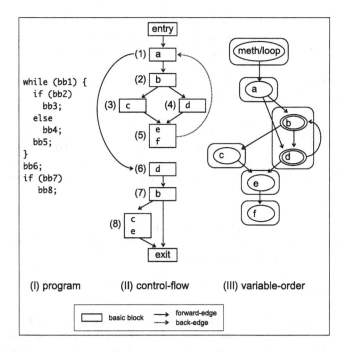

Fig. 6. Variable-order graph for control flow with branches and loops

ordering between access **z** and **x** because **z** is also reachable as a (transitive) successor of **x** (method1). There is no relative order between **z** and **x** either, because **x** has node **meth/loop** as predecessor and hence any shared variable access could immediately precede (in program order) and be reordered with access of **x**; the access that is reordered with **x** could occur in a different method or loop iteration. Similarly, variable **y** is marked as a communicator.

Algorithm. The algorithm starts with the computation of the acyclic components (ACG) of the variable-order graph. All nodes (except the special node **meth/loop**) are potential candidates for communicators; some of the nodes can be excluded from being communicators by determining the absolute and relative ordering of the accesses to the variables that these nodes stand for:

Absolute ordering (AO): Accesses to variable f are absolutely ordered in all methods with respect to other accesses if all of the following hold: (1) the node corresponding to field f is the sole node in its SCC of the variable-order graph; (2) there is no self-edge $f \longrightarrow f$.[3]
Relative ordering (RO): Accesses to variable f are relatively ordered with respect to accesses to some other variable g if all of the following hold: (1) the

---

[3] A self-edge means that accesses to the same variable or to the same field on different object instances might be reordered.

node corresponding to field f falls into an SCC with several other nodes; (2) the node corresponding to f has only one predecessor, namely the one representing field g, which should be inside the same SCC.

Variables that do not enjoy absolute or relative ordering in the variable-order graph are designated as communicators.

Further Examples. In Figure 6 (III), a, c, e, and f are not communicators because they enjoy *absolute ordering*, i.e., they occur strictly after (c, e, f) or before (a) accesses to b and d. In Figure 5 (III), field z is not a communicator because all accesses to this field enjoy *relative ordering*, i.e., they occur always after an access to y.

Note that it is always correct to insert additional edges in the variable-order graph, as those edges might lead to larger SCCs and hence additional – not fewer – variables are designated as communicators.

2.7   Fence Insertion

Memory fences implement the ordering of variable accesses that is required for (1) access to communicator variables, (2) method boundaries, and (3) loop boundaries. We use a simple model for a memory fence: the occurrence of a fence ensures that all preceding memory accesses complete and that no subsequent memory access starts before the fence completes. In our model, a fence affects all memory accesses independently of the type of access (read/write) and the target location.

Algorithm. The algorithm processes every method that accesses conflicting variables in three steps:

Fence due to communicator: A fence is inserted before every statement that accesses a communicator variable. In case of a read immediately followed by a write to the same variable, a fence is only inserted before the read; the following write is implicitly ordered (IO) with respect to the read.

Fence at loop boundary: A fence is inserted at the beginning of the loop header if there are accesses to conflicting variables in the loop that are not communicators. The fence is repeated at every loop iteration.

Fence at method boundary: A fence is inserted at the beginning and the end of every method that accesses conflicting variables that are not communicators. The insertion at method begin is omitted if an already inserted fence postdominates the method begin.

Handling of Methods. Figure 7 shows two programs that access variables a and b. In scenario (I), the accesses occur in the run method and the corresponding variable-order graph designates a as a communicator variable; the resulting fence instructions occur before the read access statements of a in method run.

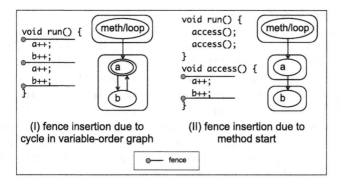

Fig. 7. Handling of methods

Scenario (II) is similar, however the access sequence a,b is factored out into method access. Although the resulting variable-order graph is different, i.e., there is no communicator because there is an absolute order in the accessed variables in each method, a fence is inserted at the beginning of method access, resulting in a runtime delay structure that is equivalent to the delays created in scenario (I).

2.8 Complexity

The construction of the variable-order graph treats each method once and individually. The worst case complexity *per method* is quadratic because ordering may need to be determined for all pairs of conflicting statements inside a method; for typical control flows, however, the complexity is almost linear. Note that the worst case quadratic complexity here applies only to the statements in the scope of a method. The delay set analysis in, e.g., [6,1], has polynomial, more precisely quadratic worst case complexity that applies to all statements of the program.

The analysis of the variable-order graph requires the computation of the ACG, which is linear in the size of nodes and edges. Overall, we observe the the cost of the graph construction and the computation of communicators is linear in the program size (number of conflicting statements in the program); the execution time of the overall analysis is in the order of hundreds of milliseconds on a Pentium IV 1.4 MHz system for the programs we use in Section 3.

3 Experience

We applied the communicator analysis to the following multi-threaded programs: philo is a simple dining philosopher application. elevator is a real-time discrete event simulator that is used as an example in a course on concurrent programming. jvm98_mtrt is a multi-thread raytracer from the JVM98 benchmark suite [11]. sor and tsp are data- and task-parallel applications. The jgf_xxx programs are scientific application kernels from the multi-threaded Java Grande benchmark suite [4].

We have implemented the communicator analysis in a Java-X86 way-ahead compilation environment that we used in earlier work to study static and dynamic race detection for object-oriented programs [14]. The runtime system is based on GNU libgcj version 2.96. On the Intel Pentium III architecture that we used for the study, the bidirectional memory fence described in Section 2.7 is implemented by an add operation with memory operand and lock prefix.

Table 1 specifies the number of nodes in the variable-order graph and its ACG. Due to the special node meth/loop, this number amounts to the total number of conflicting fields + 1. The conflicting fields are partitioned in rows *fields*, into communicators (*comm*), absolutely (*AO*), and relatively (*RO*) ordered.

The conflict analysis is quite precise for most programs and hence few field variables are specified as conflicting; for some programs that operate on shared arrays however, e.g., sor and jgf_lufact, most accesses target a single conceptual field that represents all slots of the shared arrays. Thus, for these programs a large number of access statements are classified as conflicting (they all target the same conceptual field). For jgf_raytracer, the conflict analysis is not able to determine a significant part of the application data as thread-local and hence, also for this benchmark, the imprecision of the conflict analysis is significant.

The number of nodes in the ACG show that, perhaps surprisingly, not all fields are lumped together into a single SCC without ordering; for jgf_moldyn, where this effect is especially pronounced, relative ordering can be determined for a number of field accesses. For other benchmarks, e.g., elevator, several fields enjoy absolute access ordering.

Table 2 compares the results of the naive fence insertion with the fence insertion that is guided through communicator information. The number of fences inserted by the naive strategy corresponds to the number of conflicting statements in the program. For some programs, the communicator analysis reduces this number considerably, e.g., for jgf_moldyn. Column *[% naive]* specifies the number of fences inserted due to access to communicator variables relative to

Table 1. Number of nodes in the variable-order graph and classification of fields

program	nodes	acg	comm	AO	RO
philo	2	2	1	0	0
elevator	11	9	3	6	1
jvm98_mtrt	3	3	1	1	0
sor	2	2	1	0	0
tsp	5	4	3	1	0
jgf_crypt	2	2	1	0	0
jgf_lufact	4	3	3	0	0
jgf_series	4	2	2	0	1
jgf_sor	3	2	2	0	0
jgf_sparsematmult	2	2	0	1	0
jgf_montecarlo	2	2	0	1	0
jgf_moldyn	68	3	52	0	15
jgf_raytracer	12	4	10	1	0

Table 2. Number of fences inserted by the *naive* algorithm and according to our *communicator analysis*

program	naive	communicator analysis				
		stmt	[% naive]	loop	begin	end
philo	9	9	100.0	0	1	3
elevator	97	75	77.3	1	12	23
jvm98_mtrt	10	5	50.0	0	2	5
sor	42	42	100.0	0	3	3
tsp	62	47	75.8	0	7	11
jgf_crypt	16	16	100.0	0	0	1
jgf_lufact	43	39	90.7	0	9	11
jgf_series	18	11	61.1	0	4	6
jgf_sor	32	27	84.4	0	3	3
jgf_sparsematmult	2	0	50.0	1	1	1
jgf_montecarlo	2	0	0.0	0	0	0
jgf_moldyn	744	397	53.4	0	1	11
jgf_raytracer	103	88	86.4	1	5	20
average			**71.5**			

the naive insertion strategy. The static reduction of inserted fences relative to the naive strategy is on average 28.5%. Besides the naive strategy, there are more precise algorithms to determine the delay set, e.g., [1,6,12]. A comparison of our communicator analysis to these analyses (some of which are restricted to SPMD style programs) is not done here and is left for future work.

The number of fences inserted at at loop boundaries (column *loop*), at method begin (column *begin*), and at method end (column *end*) is moderate for most benchmarks; these numbers are not included in the relative comparison with the naive fence insertion strategy (column *[% naive]*). Note that the insertion of fences at method boundaries is not due to an inherent property of the computation of the program (e.g. conflicting access to shared variables) but merely due to the structure of the implementation.

Table 3 reports the runtime of the *original* and instrumented benchmarks, both with moderate optimization (copy-propagation, partial redundancy elimination, no inlining). The numbers specify the average duration of three program runs. The effective cost of the memory fences is very high, especially for programs where the conflict analysis is unnecessarily conservative, i.e., for sor, tsp, jgf_lufact, jgf_moldyn, and jgf_raytracer. The static difference in the number of inserted fences between the naive and the communicator approach affects the runtime situation only in part: there is a significant benefit for jgf_sparsematmult and jgf_lufact, not for jgf_moldyn and jgf_raytracer however. In some situations, the naive approach of fence insertion yields better performance than the communicator analysis, e.g., for tsp, jgf_moldyn, and jgf_raytracer. Such a situation can occur, if the naive approach places fences in the body of a conditional branch that is rarely taken at runtime, while the communicator-based approach requires a fence at method start and end.

Overall, the reduction of fences inserted at memory access statements (Table 2, *communicator* vs. *naive* on avg. 28%), does not necessarily imply a re-

Table 3. Execution times for different fence insertion algorithms on a Pentium III 933 MHz system (average of three runs). The programs philo and elevator are not CPU-bound and hence omitted from the reporting. The absolute times are rounded to tens of seconds, the percentage numbers are computed from precise values

program	orig [s]	naive total	[% orig]	communicator analysis [s]	[% orig]	[% naive]
jvm98_mtrt	19.8	20.1	1.7	19.8	0.2	-1.5
sor	2.4	7.6	218.2	7.6	218.2	0.0
tsp	7.6	12.0	57.3	12.6	65.1	5.0
jgf_crypt	3.5	4.0	14.1	4.0	14.3	0.2
jgf_lufact	3.4	8.7	156.8	8.2	141.1	-6.1
jgf_series	25.8	25.8	0.1	25.8	0.0	0.0
jgf_sor	31.9	46.9	47.0	46.8	46.7	-0.2
jgf_sparsematmult	17.4	25.0	43.4	19.3	11.2	-22.5
jgf_montecarlo	23.7	23.8	0.4	23.8	0.4	0.0
jgf_moldyn	23.1	57.9	150.8	60.6	162.4	4.6
jgf_raytracer	42.0	118.7	182.7	139.2	231.4	17.2
average			79.3		**81.0**	-0.3

duction of fences that are executed at runtime. Although we have not studied the frequency of executed fences at runtime in detail, the execution times in Table 3 (on average, there is almost no difference between *communicator* vs. *naive*) reflect this observation. There are basically two reasons for this behavior: First, the communicator analysis may allow to remove fences that are "rarely" executed, not those that are critical to the execution time. Second, the overhead due to fences at method boundaries can outweigh the benefit of fences removed by the communicator analysis.

4   Conclusions

We have presented an algorithm to determine communicator variables in parallel programs. If communicator variables are accessed in program order and access to other shared variables is not reordered with respect to communicators, then program executions are sequentially consistent. Computing communicators is an efficient and effective alternative to delay set computation, especially for object-oriented multi-threaded programs with unstructured parallelism.

We have applied the analysis in combination with a powerful conflict analysis [14] to a number of multi-threaded Java programs. Using communicators as a guide for the fence insertion yield on average about 28% fewer fences at memory access statements than a naive fence insertion algorithm. The total runtime overhead due to the fences is however still considerable (81% on average). For programs with significant overhead, we observe that this overhead is mainly due to conservatism in the automated conflict analysis (especially for programs that mainly operate on shared arrays), not due to the inability of the communicator analysis to reduce the number of fences.

Acknowledgments

We thank Thomas Gross for his support and comments on the paper. We thank the anonymous referees, Rajkishore Barik, and Zehra Sura for their comments and insightful discussions. We thank Matteo Corti for his contributions to the compiler infrastructure.

References

1. W.-Y. Chen, A. Krishnamurthy, and K. Yelick. Polynomial-time algorithms for enforcing sequential consistency in SPMD programs with arrays. In *Proceedings of the International Workshop on Compilers for Parallel Computing (LCPC'03)*, Oct. 2003.
2. J.-D. Choi, A. Loginov, and V. Sarkar. Static datarace analysis for multithreaded object-oriented programs. Technical Report RC22146, IBM Research, Aug. 2001.
3. X. Fang, J. Lee, and S. Midkiff. Automatic fence insertion for shared memory multiprocessing. In *Proceedings of the International Conference on Supercomputing (ICS'03)*, pages 285–294, June 2003.
4. Java Grande Forum multi-threaded benchmark suite. `http://www.epcc.ed.ac.uk/javagrande/`.
5. A. Krishnamurthy and K. Yelick. Analyses and optimizations for shared address space programs. *Journal of Parallel and Distributed Computing*, 38(2):130–144, Nov. 1996.
6. M. Kurhekar, R. Barik, and U. Kumar.exit An efficient algorithms for computing delay set in SPMD programs. In *Proceedings of the International Conference on High Performance Computing (HiPC'03)*, Oct. 2003.
7. S. Midkiff, J. Lee, and D. Padua. A compiler for multiple memory models. In *Rec. Workshop Compilers for Parallel Computers (CPC'01)*, June 2001.
8. G. Naumovich, G. Avrunin, and L. Clarke. An efficient algorithm for computing MHP information for concurrent Java programs. In *Proceedings of the European Software Engineering Conference and Symposium on the Foundations of Software Engineering*, pages 338–354, Sept. 1999.
9. R. Netzer and B. Miller. What are race conditions? Some issues and formalizations. *ACM Letters on Programming Languages and Systems*, 1(1):74–88, Mar. 1992.
10. D. Shasha and M. Snir. Efficient and correct execution of parallel programs that share memory. *ACM Trans. on Programming Languages and Systems*, 10(2):282–312, Apr. 1988.
11. SPEC JVM98 Benchmarks. `http://www.spec.org/osg/jvm98`.
12. Z. Sura, C.-L. Wong, X. Fang, J. Lee, S. Midkiff, and D. Padua. Automatic implementation of programming language consistency models. In *Record of the Workshop on Compilers for Parallel Computers (CPC'03)*, Jan. 2003.
13. C. von Praun and T. Gross. Object race detection. In *Proceedings of the Conference on Object-Oriented Programming, Systems, Languages, and Applications (OOPSLA'01)*, pages 70–82, Oct. 2001.
14. C. von Praun and T. Gross. Static conflict analysis for multi-threaded object-oriented programs. In *Proceedings of the Conference on Programming Language Design and Implementation (PLDI'03)*, pages 115–129, June 2003.

Compiling High-Level Languages for Vector Architectures

Christopher D. Rickett[1,2], Sung-Eun Choi[2],
and Bradford L. Chamberlain[3]

[1] South Dakota School of Mines & Technology, Rapid City, SD 57701
Christopher.Rickett@gold.sdsmt.edu
[2] Los Alamos National Laboratory, Los Alamos, NM 87545
{crickett, sungeun}@lanl.gov
[3] Cray Inc., Seattle, WA 98104
bradc@cray.com

Abstract. In this paper, we investigate the issues of compiling high-level languages for vector architectures. Vector architectures have regained popularity in recent years, from simple desktop computers with small vector units motivated by multimedia applications to large-scale vector multiprocessing machines motivated by ever-growing computational demands. We show that generating code for various types of vector architectures can be done using several idioms, and that the best idiom is not what a programmer would normally do. Using a set of benchmark programs, we also show that the benefits of vectorization can be significant and must not be ignored. Our results show that high-level languages are an attractive means of programming vector architectures since their compilers can generate code using the specific idioms that are most effective for the low-level vectorizing compiler. This leads to source code that is clearer and more maintainable, has excellent performance across the full spectrum of vector architectures, and therefore improves programmer productivity.

1 Introduction and Motivation

Vector architectures have regained popularity in recent years. Traditional vector architectures such as the Cray X1 have again caught the attention of the high performance computing community due to their effectiveness in hiding the memory latency gap. In fact, number one on the Top 500 is the NEC-built Japanese Earth Simulator, a vector machine, that was able to achieve 98% efficiency on the LinPack benchmark. In addition, even simple desktop computers have and will continue to have small vector units motivated by multimedia applications. For example, Intel's next generation vector instruction set, SSE3, provides instructions which will effectively enable hardware support for sum reductions and cross products [1]. These architectures are currently used in small- to tera-scale commodity clusters, the most popular high performance computer platform today. Thus vector architectures are again making their way into the parallel computing realm, but this time from both ends of the computing spectrum.

R. Eigenmann et al. (Eds.): LCPC 2004, LNCS 3602, pp. 224–237, 2005.

Application programmers can leverage vectorizing capabilities with little effort using libraries written in hand-tuned assembly, such as the Cray Bioinformatics Library (BioLib). In the absence of an appropriate library (and the patience to write assembly code), a programmer can carefully write code that may be automatically vectorized by the native compilers. Pragmas and other directives can also be used to guide the compiler to proper vectorization.

Another alternative is to use a higher level programming language. High-level parallel programming languages are being promoted now more than ever as a means of increasing productivity as well as performance of high end applications. Examples of such languages include UPC [2], Co-Array Fortran [3], ZPL [4,5], Titanium [6], and Chapel [7]. Implementations of these and other such languages often compile to a lower level language such as C or Fortran which is then compiled with a native, back-end compiler. Using a language like C as an intermediate format has many advantages: it eases initial development, aids portability, and leverages the most up-to-date and best-performing native compilers. However, it can also create several challenges. As we will explain in the next section, the high-level language compiler may have to jump through a few extra hoops to get good performance from the back-end compiler, especially for vector architectures.

In this paper, we investigate the issues of compiling high-level languages for vector architectures ranging from narrow vector width architectures used in clustered systems to traditional wide vector width machines like the Cray X1. We show that the benefits of automatic vectorization can be significant and that these benefits are specific to particular "idioms" of code generation. More importantly, we show that generating vectorizable, and more importantly, good performing code requires an idiom that is a tedious and error prone task—one that a programmer would rather not have to wrestle with. Our results also suggest that using a high-level language is better than lower-level languages in the high-performance computing field, as the compilers for high-level languages are able to generate code using the best performing idiom for a given platform however obfuscated it may be.

The remainder of the paper is organized as follows. In Section 2, we give background on compiling high-level languages and previous work in the area of vectorizing compilers. In Section 3, we present our results that show that vectorizability is essential for good application performance on modern architectures. We conclude in Section 4.

2   Background and Previous Work

In this section, we describe background on compiling a high-level language and previous work in vectorizing compilers.

2.1   Compiling High-Level Languages

The most convenient and practical way to compile a high-level language is to translate it to a lower-level language like C or Fortran. Experience has shown

```
for (i = 0; i < m; i++) {
    for (j = 0; j < n; j++) {
        A[i][j] = B[i][j] + C[i][j];
}
```

```
for (i = 0; i < info->m; i++) {
    for (j = 0; j < info->n; j++) {
        A->data[i*jhi+j] = B->data[i*jhi+j] +
                           C->data[i*jhi+j];
}
```

(a)   (b)

Fig. 1. Simple differences between human-written and compiler-generated C code

that a high-level language compiler must jump through a few extra hoops to get good performance from the back-end compiler [5]. For obvious reasons, C compilers are very good at optimizing *human-written* code, but less good at optimizing *compiler-generated* code. For example, a common feature among the previously named high-level languages is support for multi-dimensional arrays as first class citizens. Since C does not have rich support for arrays, such arrays are implemented using a record (*array descriptor* or *dope vector*) with a pointer to the heap-allocated memory that will hold data for the array. The descriptors typically contain information on data type, array rank, array bounds, etc. Even if the lower-level language does have good support for multi-dimensional arrays, the match between the high-level language and lower-level language is typically not exact and might require similar descriptors.

Figure 1 illustrates a few simple differences between human-written and compiler-generated code. The operation implemented by both loop nests adds corresponding elements of arrays B and C, assigning the result into the corresponding element in array A. The human-written code (Figure 1(a)) has simple loop bounds (m and n) and accesses array elements directly via square brackets. The compiler-generated code (Figure 1(b)) has loop bounds embedded in a structure (info->m and info->n) and accesses the array elements through a pointer dereference as a flat piece of memory. These small differences can thwart most compilers from performing induction variable elimination which in turn requires each array element access to require two memory accesses (pointer to the data field) as well as the arithmetic (one multiply and one addition) to offset from the pointer to data. One solution to this problem is to copy the loop bounds and the pointers to the array data into local scalar variables. This will typically enable a compiler to produce much more efficient code. Note that if the human-written code uses statically allocated arrays (the only way to declare true multi-dimensional arrays in C), performance of the sample compiler-generated code may never match the human-written code since the semantics of most high-level languages is often richer than those of C's static arrays (*e.g.*, dynamically sized multidimensional arrays).

2.2   Previous Work on Vectorizing Compilers

Vector machines have gone in and out of fashion since the 1970's, and they have recently regained popularity with the Cray X1 and the Japanese Earth Simulator. As was true back in the 1970's, the key to getting performance out of vector machines is writing vectorizable code, or perhaps more accurately, the ability for the compiler to recognize code as vectorizable. This will be particularly impor- tant for a compiler for a high-level language (HLL) so that it can generate code that is automatically vectorizable by the low-level language (LLL) compiler.

A large body of work has been done in the past on compiler techniques for exploiting the abilities of vector architectures (*e.g.*, [8], [9], [10], [11]). In addi- tion, accurate data dependence analysis is typically required for the necessary optimizations and transformations that enable vectorization. Some of the more useful optimizations include scalar expansion, loop interchanging, loop fission, strip-mining, and loop collapsing.

Vectorization has also become a part of desktop architectures, such as the Intel Xeon and the AMD Opteron. While the vectorization abilities of these architectures is significantly limited in comparison to more traditional vector machines like the Cray X1, vectorization can still be beneficial. For example, it has been shown that the Intel Xeon, which supports 128-bit vectors (two doubles, four floats or integers, eight short integers), can achieve nearly linear speed-up when utilizing the vector SSE2 instructions [12]. Until fairly recently, much of the work on vectorization with the SSE2 instructions has been done by hand.

The Cray compiler performs many optimizations, including those listed above, in an attempt to vectorize loops either fully or partially. Some of these op- timizations include conditionally vectorizing a loop, generating both a scalar and vector version. A runtime test is used to determine which to execute. Further, a loop can be vectorized for a safe vector length, or fully vectorized if the safe vector length is greater than or equal to the maximum vector length. Vectorized loops with a low trip count can be further optimized by removing the branch to the top of the loop if the count is less than the maximum vector length. Some other optimizations performed by the Cray compiler include pattern matching, which could allow a loop to be replaced by an optimized library routine, loop unrolling, and transforming reduction loops.

The Intel compiler attempts vectorization on loops with unit-stride and memory-references of the same type, though certain mixed-type loops can still be vectorized [12]. It also implements some of the aforementioned techniques, such as scalar expansion and strip-mining. Strip-mining is used as the technique for vectorizing a loop, with the block-size equal to the vector length (*e.g.*, 2 in the case of a double). Additionally, the Intel compiler can generate dynamic data dependence testing and create multiple forms of a loop, allowing the decision about vectorization to be made at runtime. Loop transformations such as loop interchange and distribution are possible, along with some idiom recognition (re- ductions or MAX/MIN/ABS operators).

The Portland Group compiler for Parallel Fortran, C, and C++ also performs automatic vectorization, including the use of SSE/SSE2 instructions. Many of the optimizations performed by the PGI are the same as those done by the Intel compiler, including loop transformations such as loop splitting and loop interchange.

3   Experimental Results

In this section we present experimental results on an Intel Xeon and an AMD Opteron system, narrow vector width architectures that are typical cluster node architectures, and the Cray X1, a traditional vector machine.

Table 1. Platform vital statistics. Note that use only used a single streaming processor (SSP) for the experiments on the Cray X1

machine	clock speed	memory	compiler	vector width	timer
Intel Xeon (P4)	2.6 GHz	2 GB	icc/ifc 8.0	128 bits	rdtsc
AMD Opteron (K8)	1.8 GHz	2 GB	pgcc/pgf90 5.1	128 bits	rdtsc
Cray X1 (1 SSP)	800 MHz 400 MHz	16 GB	cc 5.2.0.0/ftn 5.2.0.0	4K bits	_rtc

Table 1 shows vital statistics for the experimental platforms used in the remainder of this section, an Intel Xeon-based machine (P4) using the Intel compiler (`icc/ifc`), an AMD Opteron-based system (K8) using the Portland Group (PGI) x86-64 compiler (`pgcc/pf90`), and a Cray X1. We used cycle-accurate timers on all three platforms. Programs on the K8 were run in 64-bit mode. For our Cray X1 results, we ran our programs on one single-streaming processor (SSP) using the X1 compiler's SSP mode. An SSP is comprised of a vector unit running at 800 MHz and a scalar unit running at 400 MHz. The fundamental processor in an X1 system is the multi-streaming processor (MSP), composed of four SSPs. However, we chose to restrict our studies to a single SSP in order to ignore the effects of multistreaming since it is not the primary focus of our study and does not have an analogue on the other vector processors in our experiments. It is worth noting, however, that running our experiments on an MSP resulted in execution time improvements of 20% to an order of magnitude.

3.1   Microbenchmarks

For our first experiment, we ran a suite of simple microbenchmarks written in various ways that would be representative of code generated by a HLL compiler. The loop nest performs a simple, element-wise addition of two arrays and stores the result in a third. The arrays are two dimensional. For example, HLL code that could be the source of such generated loop nests in Co-Array Fortran would look like:

```
A(:) = B(:) + C(:)
```

Similarly, in ZPL:

```
[R]    A := B + C;
```

In UPC:

```
upc_forall (i = 0; i < N; i++; i)
  for (j = 0; j < M; j++)
    A[i][j] = B[i][j] + C[i][j];
```

In Titanium:

```
for (i = 1; i <= N; i++)
  for (j = 1; j <= M; j++)
    A[i,j] = B[i,j] + C[i,j];
```

For any given compiler-generated code, we assume that arrays will be dynamically allocated. Since C does not have direct support for dynamically-allocated multidimensional arrays, we assume two alternative ways to generate code. The first is to allocate an array of arrays, or rather an array of pointers to arrays. This technique is inconvenient for allocation (more calls to `malloc`) and requires more memory, but is more convenient for code generation (simple indexing with square brackets can be used) and typically requires three memory accesses for two dimensional arrays, though this can be optimized to only two in the inner loop. The other way to generate code for multidimensional arrays is to use a flattened, one dimensional array with all accesses linearized (as shown in Figure 1). This technique is more convenient for allocation, and more efficient in space and time, but requires more complex indexing.

As mentioned earlier, array accesses using standard indexing typically require two memory accesses—one to load the base address and the other to add the offset and load the actual data. With standard analysis, a LLL compiler can optimize array accesses to use only a single memory access. This *array access optimization* replaces each array access with a reference to a pointer, which we will call the *walker*, which is initialized to the first array element accessed in the loop. At the bottom of the loop, the walker is *bumped* to point to the next element that will be accessed. The loop from Figure 1 would then look something like:

```
walkerA = &(A[0]);
walkerB = &(B[0]);
walkerC = &(C[0]);
for (i = 0; i < ihi; i++) {
  for (j = 0; j < jhi; j++) {
    *walkerA = *walkerB + *walkerC;
    walkerA++;
    walkerB++;
    walkerC++;
  }
}
```

Note that if not all elements of the array will be accessed, the walkers must be bumped at the end of the outer loop as well. The walkers can be of the appropriate data type (*e.g.*, double) or a byte-sized type (void or char), which can ease code generation but requires type casting and non-unit incrementing (the *bump* increments). We call the use of the byte-sized type *byte walkers*. Type casting and complicated indexing schemes can thwart vectorization of this optimized code, which we will see in the following experiments. Fortran compilers can perform this optimization readily on arrays. In C, the optimization is more difficult to perform as pointers and thus potential aliasing are involved.

For the C loops, we used four different types of HLL compiler loop code generation idioms.

1. **AOA.** Array of arrays.
2. **ACC.** Flattened one dimensional arrays with standard accessing (*i.e.*, accessing technique typically used by programmers).
3. **TWB.** Flattened one dimensional arrays with typed walkers and array access optimizations.
4. **BWB.** Flattened one dimensional arrays with byte walkers and array access optimizations.

Whenever possible, the `restrict` keyword was used, to indicate to the compiler that the pointers would not alias.

For the Fortran loops, we used six different HLL compiler code generation idioms.

1. **2D.** Two dimensional arrays with regular indexing.
2. **2DA.** Two dimensional array using Fortran 90 array notation.
3. **2DAS.** Two dimensional array using Fortran 90 array slice notation.
4. **1D.** Flattened one dimensional arrays with regular indexing.
5. **1DA.** Flattened one dimensional array using Fortran 90 array notation.
6. **1DAS.** Flattened one dimensional array using Fortran 90 array slice notation.

Table 2 shows how well each compiler vectorized the loop nests. The Intel compiler was able to vectorize three of four loop nests written in C and all six Fortran loops. The PGI compiler was not able to vectorize any of the C loops, but was able to vectorize five of the six Fortran loops; the indexing in the Fortran *1D* case proved to be too complex for analysis. The Cray compiler was able to vectorize three of the four C loops and all of the Fortran loops. Note that the Cray compiler was only able to partially vectorize the AOA loop.

Figure 2 shows the performance improvement due to automatic vectorization. Two problem sizes were run: one that fits comfortably in cache (35x35) and one

Table 2. Results from compiling microbenchmarks. v indicates the compiler was able to vectorize the inner-most loop nest. Note that for the AOA case on the X1, the compiler was only able to partially vectorize the loop

	C loops				Fortran loops					
compiler	*AOA*	*ACC*	*TWB*	*BWB*	*2D*	*2DA*	*2DAS*	*1D*	*1DA*	*1DAS*
Intel		v	v	v	v	v	v	v	v	v
PGI					v	v	v		v	v
Cray	v*	v	v		v	v	v	v	v	v

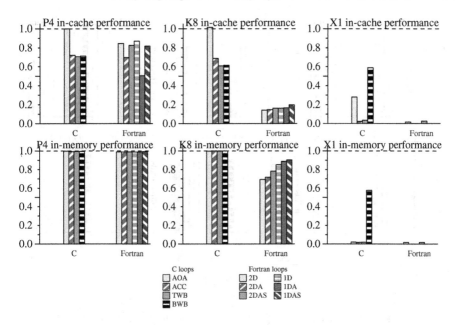

Fig. 2. Performance improvement due to automatic vectorization for the P4, K8, and X1. Each bar is normalized to the performance of the unvectorized version of the same benchmark, if one could be obtained

that fits comfortably in memory (5000x5000). Each bar represents performance of a loop generation idiom normalized to that of the non-vectorized versions of the same loop, *i.e.*, a lower bar means that there was more improvement due to vectorization. Note that this is not necessarily a straightforward task. Specifically, even though the PGI compiler was not able to vectorize any of the C loops, it did perform optimizations in the process such as unrolling which improved performance; the same is true for the *BWB* case on the X1. Also, on the Cray X1 we were unable to disable vectorization for *2DA*, *2DAS*, *1DA*, and *1DAS*, because vectorization is always enabled for Fortran 90 array and array slice notation.

For the in-cache versions on the P4, the benefits for vectorization range from 0–30% for the C loops and 14–50% for the Fortran loops. In-cache performance on the K8 result in improvements from 0–40% despite the fact that the PGI compiler did not actually vectorize any of the loop nests; the Fortran performance improved by 80–86%. In the case of the Cray X1, the improvements for most cases were approximately two orders of magnitude for all loops (excluding the ones named above as not having been able to disable vectorization). The *BWB* suffered since it was not automatically vectorized, as did the *AOA* case which was only partially vectorized. The X1 is a very aggressive vector machine with aggressive optimizing compilers. Thus the scalar processors are not the main focus (running at half the clock speed of the vector processors) and scalar performance is much worse relative to vector performance.

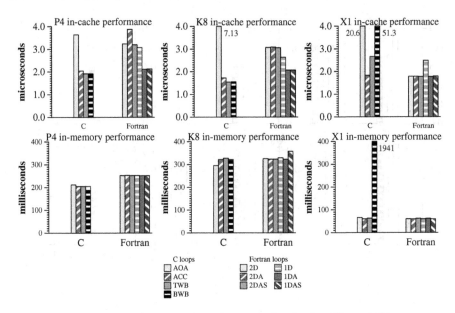

Fig. 3. Microbenchmark performance for the P4, K8, and X1

For the in-memory case, the C loops saw less than 1% improvement due to vectorization on both the P4 and the K8. The Fortran loops benefited less than 1% for the P4 and from 10–31% for the K8. Again, for the X1, improvements due to vectorization were over two orders of magnitude, except in the case of *BWB* which saw about a 43% improvement in performance despite the fact that the loop was not automatically vectorized.

Figure 3 shows performance of the C and Fortran loops on P4, K8, and X1. For the in-cache C benchmarks on the P4 and K8, the version with byte walkers and access optimizations (*BWB*) performed best and the array of arrays (*AOA*) performed the worst. For the X1, the best performing versions were *ACC* and *TWB*. The best in-cache idiom on the P4 (*BWB*) performed worst on the X1 (an order of magnitude worse).

For the in-cache Fortran loops on the P4 and K8, the best performance was obtained by the flattened one dimensional case using array notation (*1DA*) and array slice notation (*1DAS*). Notice that the one dimensional version with regular indexing (*1D*) performed better than any of the two dimensional versions even though it was not vectorized. For the in-memory case, all loops performed nearly identically. On the X1, the best idiom was *2DAS* by a small percentage.

For the in-memory cases on the P4 and K8, performance is not affected by vectorization too much. Notice that here the array of arrays idiom performed the best, even though it performed worst for the in-cache case. The reason for this is that when the arrays are very large, the overhead for the additional array access (for the first dimension) is amortized over the accesses for the second dimension. Because we used the `restrict` attribute, the compilers were able to generate the best code possible for the inner loop nest. For the X1, the *AOA* idiom which was not fully vectorized performed only slightly worse than the *ACC* and *TWB* cases, while the *BWB* idiom, which was not vectorized at all, performed significantly wors e than the rest.

What is also interesting is that the performance of the loops written in C is comparable to those written in Fortran. It is often assumed that Fortran array codes outperform similar codes written in C, but these results show that using C as an intermediate format for array-based languages does not necessarily result in a significant performance hit over using Fortran.

3.2 Application Performance

In this section, we examine the performance of seven benchmark applications. All applications are written in ZPL. The ZPL compiler translates code into low level C code which is compiled with a native C compiler, in this case Intel's icc or Cray's cc. The ZPL compiler is able to generate loops using three of the techniques described in the previous section: *ACC*, *TWB*, and *BWB*. The applications, problem sizes, and number of vectorized loops are summarized in Table 3. The performance of the applications is shown in Figure 4; the top row shows results for the P4, the bottom row for the X1. For each platform, we show the normalized performance (as described in the previous section) and the absolute performance.

The *TWB* and *BWB* versions of the applications performed very similar on both architectures, with the *TWB* often performing slightly better. While the Cray compiler could vectorize the applications for each generation technique, the Intel compiler vectorized more if *TWB* or *BWB* was used. The ability to vectorize was due to the simpler array expressions for the compiler to analyze.

Vectorization on the X1 was much more significant than on the P4, as expected. The Cray compiler was able to vectorize all of the applications, with the exception of the *ACC* and *TWB* forms of EP. Vectorization drastically improved the performance of all the applications, except Summa, Jacobi, and EP. Cannon showed the most improvement. As with the P4, the *TWB* and *BWB* versions performed similar on the X1, with the exception of the Jacobi. Contrary to the

Table 3. Number of vectorized loops for each application

application	description	problem size	ACC		TWB		BWB	
			P4	X1	P4	X1	P4	X1
Cannon	matrix multiply	1000x1000	0	6	4	6	4	7
Summa	matrix multiply	500x500	0	2	2	2	2	2
Jacobi	iterative solver	257x257	3	3	3	3	0	3
NAS CG	conjugate gradient	class A (14000)	1	16	1	15	1	15
NAS EP	random number generator	class A	3	2	5	2	5	2
NAS FT	Fourier transform	class A (128x256x256)	0	20	0	18	0	18
NAS MG	multigrid	class A (256^3)	2	14	2	16	3	16

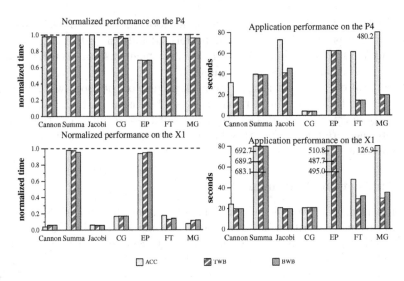

Fig. 4. Application benchmark performance for the P4 and X1

finding in the previous section, the *TWB* version performed best on the X1, not *ACC*.

Secondary effects of ACC. The performance of the applications is dependent on both the ability of the compilers to automatically vectorize the generated code, and the work involved in the technique. The *ACC* version uses an array access technique that requires array offsets to be recomputed each iteration of a loop. Note that these computations could be hoisted out of the loop by the LLL compiler, but in the case of our HLL compiler-generated code, these expressions proved too difficult to optimize. The number of operations is thus a function of the number of array accesses in the loop. In the case of MG, the arrays are 3D and strided (adding an additional division and addition), therefore, there are three multiplies, divides, and additions per access. One of the triply-nested loops from MG contains 23 array accesses in the inner most loop and accounts for approximately half of the overall program runtime. For the *ACC* version, there is a total of 69 multiplies, divides, and additions performed every iteration of the loop. The total runtime of the program in the *TWB* version is approximately 4-5% of that for the *ACC* version. We also found that this percentage holds as the problem size varies, showing that the cost of *ACC* is not dependent on the problem size. The performance cost of *ACC* is also visible on the P4 in the Jacobi and FT applications. As with the MG, the *TWB* version of Jacobi (for varying problem sizes) executes in approximately 60% of the time of *ACC*. The cost on the X1 is also worse for the applications using the *ACC* method.

Secondary effects of SSE2 instructions on the P4. Vectorization on the P4 did not significantly improve most of the applications. However, Jacobi improved by approximately 20%, EP by over 30%, and FT by over 10%. The improvement in

Jacobi could be expected, since the main computation is vectorizable. EP had a large number of vectorized loops, but the loops vectorized were not the ones that provided the gain. This anomaly is the same with FT, which had no loops vectorized, but still saw a performance improvement. The improvements for FT and EP were both due to these alternative uses of SSE2 instructions by the Intel compiler. The SSE2 instructions allowed the use of the vector registers, even by scalars, and simplified the instructions for the loops, causing the improvement. This improvement is very obvious in the case of EP where the use of SSE2 instructions allowed one of the loops to run in approximately half the time, and the other in 84%.

3.3 Summary

For the microbenchmarks, the best idioms for the P4 and K8 were *BWB* for the C loops and the flattened one dimensional case using array notation (*1DA*) or array slice notation (*1DAS*). For the X1, the best idioms were *ACC* and *2DAS*. Recall that *ACC* most closely resembles the technique that would be used by a programmer if they were to write the loops directly. The results for P4 and K8 argue for the use of the best in-cache loop generation idioms when performing optimizations such as tiling, where the data set matches to the cache size. Preliminary experiments with tiling on the Jacobi application showed up to a 25% improvement in overall performance when tiling and vectorization were performed.

The application benchmarks told a different story. The *TWB* was clearly the best idiom. The Cray compiler's superior analysis showed in its ability to vectorize nearly the same number of loops in each version of the benchmarks, but the secondary affects of *ACC* resulted in worse performance than the *TWB* idiom, contrary to the microbenchmark findings.

While we were unable to obtain the advertised linear speed ups for P4 due to vectorization [12], we did see significant improvements (as much as 50%) due to vectorization for the microbenchmarks; for the applications, the measurable improvements were due to alternative uses of the SSE2 instruction set. The overall speed ups were most significant for small (in-cache) problem sizes; vectorization helped very little for the in-memory microbenchmarks.

4 Conclusions

In this paper, we examined the effects of code generation techniques of HLL compilers for vector architectures. We found that for commodity vector architectures such as the Intel Xeon (P4) or the AMD Opteron (K8), vectorization did not significantly improve whole application performance as advertised. For the benchmark applications, alternative uses of the SSE2 instruction set on the P4 lead to the biggest performance improvements. The best idiom for the Cray X1 found using the microbenchmarks, was not the best for the applications due to the computational overhead of that technique which grows with the number of array accesses in the loop. Finally, the best overall idiom, *TWB* is quite tedious and error prone and thus something that a programmer should not write directly.

Our results also suggest that it may be time for HLL compilers to make the same transition that LLL compilers made decades ago. Just as LLL compilers have made assembly programming all but obsolete, HLL compilers may need to do the same for low-level language programming for high-performance computing. HLL compilers can generate code that is better optimized than an application programmer would typically be willing to extend. The lifetime of today's production codes lasts several machine generations and maintaining both performance and portability over this lifetime is difficult for codes written in low-level languages. High-level languages lead to source code that is clearer and more maintainable, and that can have excellent performance across the full spectrum of vector architectures, and thus results in improved programmer productivity.

Acknowledgments. This work was supported in part by a grant of HPC resources from the Arctic Region Supercomputing Center at the University of Alaska Fairbanks as part of the Department of Defense High Performance Computing Modernization Program. Los Alamos National Laboratory is operated by the University of California for the National Nuclear Security Administration of the United States Department of Energy under contract W-7405-ENG-36. LA-UR-04-3951.

References

1. Intel Corporation: Using Streaming SIMD Extensions 3 in Algorithms with Complex Arithmetic. (2004)
2. Carlson, W.W., Draper, J.M., Culler, D.E., Yelick, K., Brooks, E., Warren, K.: Introduction to UPC and language specification. Technical Report CCS-TR-99-157, Center for Computing Sciences, Bowie, MD (1999)
3. Numrich, R.W., Reid, J.K.: Co-Array Fortran for parallel programming. Technical Report RAL-TR-1998-060, Rutherford Appleton Laboratory, Oxon, UK (1998)
4. Snyder, L.: Programming Guide to ZPL. MIT Press, Cambridge, MA, USA (1999)
5. Chamberlain, B.L.: The Design and Implementation of a Region-Based Parallel Language. PhD thesis, University of Washington (2001)
6. Yelick, K., Semenzato, L., Pike, G., Miyamoto, C., Liblit, B., Krishnamurthy, A., Hilfinger, P., Graham, S., Gay, D., Colella, P., Aiken, A.: Titanium: A high-performance Java dialect. In: ACM 1998 Workshop on Java for High-Performance Network Computing. (1998)
7. Callahan, D., Chamberlain, B.L., Zima, H.P.: The Cascade High Productivity Language. In: Workshop on High-Level Parallel Programming Models and Supportive E nvironments (HIPS '04). (2004)
8. Allen, R., Kennedy, K.: Automatic translation of FORTRAN programs to vector form. ACM Transactions on Programming Languages and Systems **9** (1987) 491–542
9. Bacon, D.F., Graham, S.L., , Sharp, O.J.: Compiler transformations for high-performance computing. ACM Computing Surveys **26** (1994) 345–420

10. Eigenmann, R., Hoeflinger, J.: Parallelizing and vectorizing compilers. Technical Report ECE-HPCLab-99201, Purdue University School of ECE, High-Performance Computing Lab (2000)
11. Padua, D.A., Wolfe, M.J.: Advanced compiler optimizations for supercomputers. Communications of the ACM **29** (1986) 1184–1201
12. Bik, A.J.C., Girkar, M., Grey, P.M., Tian, X.: Automatic intra-register vectorization for the intel architecture. International Journal of Parallel Programming **30** (2002) 65–98

HiLO: High Level Optimization of FFTs*

Nick Rizzolo and David Padua

University of Illinois at Urbana-Champaign,
201 N. Goodwin Ave., Urbana, IL 61801-2302
{rizzolo, padua}@cs.uiuc.edu
http://polaris.cs.uiuc.edu

Abstract. As computing platforms become more and more complex,
the task of optimizing performance critical codes becomes more challenging. Recently, more attention has been focused on automating this optimization process by making aggressive assumptions about the algorithm.
Motivated by these trends, this paper presents HiLO, the high-level optimizer for FFT codes. HiLO blends traditional optimization techniques
into an optimization strategy tailored to the needs of FFT codes and
outputs C code ready to be further optimized by the native compiler. It
has already been shown that such high-level transformations are important to coax the native compiler into doing its job well. HiLO provides a
more appropriate platform for researching these phenomena, suggests an
optimization strategy that improves on previous approaches, and shows
that even software pipelining at the C level can improve the final binary's
performance.

1 Introduction

As computing platforms become more and more complex, the task of optimizing performance critical codes becomes more challenging. It is seldom feasible
anymore to hire a software engineer who is an expert both in the algorithm that
needs to be optimized and the target architecture to write assembly code. Thus,
more concerted efforts are now being expended in the research community to
automate this process. Automatic tuning systems such as SPIRAL [1], FFTW
[2], and ATLAS [3] are devoted to the optimization of codes in a specific domain.
As such, they can make assumptions about their input from information that
general purpose compilers just don't have available to them, reaping significant
performance benefits.

In particular, SPIRAL [1] automatically generates finely tuned DSP transforms by searching through the space of formula decompositions to find an implementation of the transform that can be tuned well on the host architecture.
Once a formula decomposition is selected, its optimization and translation to

---

* This work was supported in part by the National Science Foundation under
grants CCR 01-21401 ITR and 03-25687 ITR/NGS; by DARPA under contract
NBCH30390004; and by gifts from INTEL and IBM. This work is not necessarily
representative of the positions or policies of the Army or Government.

R. Eigenmann et al. (Eds.): LCPC 2004, LNCS 3602, pp. 238–252, 2005.

C is carried out by the SPL compiler [4]. As shown by [4], classical optimizations (the most significant of which was array scalarization) performed at the C source level enable native compilers on several platforms to produce more efficient object code. This result is interesting because it shows that algorithm specific performance improvements can be realized in a platform independent manner. In addition, it shows that although native compiler designers are not necessarily experts in the particular domain we are interested in, their expert knowledge about their architecture is manifested in their compiler, and it can be utilized fruitfully.

Motivated by these ideas, this paper presents HiLO, the high level optimizer for FFT codes. HiLO can, in fact, be viewed as a framework for studying domain specific optimization, although it has only been tested on FFT codes thus far. It is written modularly, each optimization pass in its own source file, adhering to the concept of separation of concerns. The order in which optimization passes will be executed and any parameters those passes might take can be specified on the command line. These characteristics facilitate research concerning the optimizations' interaction as well as lending themselves toward an automatic tuning environment in which some search is being performed over the optimizations themselves.

Furthermore, HiLO is a domain specific compiler that produces C code that competes with and sometimes outperforms that produced by SPL. HiLO blends traditional optimization techniques into an optimization strategy tailored to the needs of FFT codes and outputs C code that is more conducive to further optimization by the native compiler. In addition to exposing new ways to make optimizations work better with each other, HiLO adds software pipelining to the list of optimizations that can yield performance benefits at the C source level. The addition of software pipelining with the right parameters to a pre-existing HiLO optimization strategy that had been applied to all FFT formulas of size 32 yielded an execution time for the best behaved formula that was 35% faster than the time of the previous best formula. This is not to be misconstrued as a 35% improvement on the state of the art, but instead a very good indicator that high level software pipelining is a promising direction for further study.

The rest of this paper is organized as follows: Section 2 discusses some of the decisions we made while implementing HiLO. Section 3 mentions the analysis techniques employed in our compiler. Section 4 talks about how we tailored our optimization passes to the needs of FFT codes and our overall optimization strategy. In section 5, we describe our experimental setup and results. Finally, in section 6, we conclude and discuss future research directions.

2   Implementation Considerations

HiLO was designed with the goal of easing the development process and bolstering the research process. Its design is organized by separation of concerns, and its accepted language includes only what is necessary. Its internal representation and optimization passes are implemented in Java. Java was chosen because it is object oriented, it garbage collects, and its extensive data structure and algorithm libraries seem more standardized and user friendly than C++'s STL. In addition, stack traces including line number information make debugging easier.

2.1   Command Line Interface

HiLO's command line options are used to control the selection, ordering, and parameters of optimization algorithms, none of which are executed by default. Thus, the entire machinery of the compiler is exposed both to the researcher who can easily automate his experiments, and to the automatic tuning system that incorporates HiLO as its back-end compiler and can then include those parameters in its search space. In addition, there is an argument used to include any number of optimization passes in a loop that continually applies them in order until none make any changes to the internal representation of the program in an entire pass through the loop. This utility proved quite useful in discovering the symbiotic nature of certain optimizations, as described further in section 4.7. HiLO's output is C code sent to standard output.

2.2   Front End and Accepted Language

HiLO's front end is implemented with the automatic scanner generator JLex[1] and the automatic parser generator CUP[2]. The language that it accepts is a small subset of C. Only assignment statements, return statements, for and while loops, and function calls are supported. Function calls are assumed to be calls to external functions that don't have side effects. The int and double data types and single dimensional arrays of those are supported. Pointers are allowed as arguments to functions and are assumed to point to arrays in mutually exclusive memory at run-time, freeing def-use and dependence analysis to compute more precise information. Any compiler directives in the input are preserved in the output, but are otherwise ignored.

This setup is specifically designed to accept as input the C code that the SPL compiler produces as output. This code is iterative, and it operates on an array of size $2n$ interpreted as n complex values. SPL and its companion FFT formula generator program splse are used to provide HiLO with all of the codes it optimizes. The appropriate command line parameters are given to SPL so that its internal optimizations are turned off.

2.3   Internal Representation

HiLO represents a source program internally with a simple abstract syntax tree (AST). The visitor pattern [5] enables the detachment of the algorithms that traverse the AST and operate on it from the code that implements the AST. Thus, debugging of an optimization pass is confined to a single source file.

---

[1] JLex was written by C. Scott Ananian.
   http://www.cs.princeton.edu/~appel/modern/java/JLex
[2] CUP was written by Scott E. Hudson.
   http://www.cs.princeton.edu/~appel/modern/java/CUP

3 Analysis

As shown in [4], the handling of arrays is one of the biggest shortcomings of general purpose compilers. When arrays cannot be converted to scalars, care must be taken in the analysis of FFT codes to glean as much information as possible from subscripted array references. Fortunately, the subscripts in FFT codes are always simple linear functions of the induction variables of enclosing loops. As such, the heavy duty analysis in HiLO is based on induction variable recognition. There is nothing unusual about HiLO's induction variable recognition; see [6] for a description of it. Building from that point, HiLO's dependence and def-use analyses can be as precise as needed. Below are descriptions of how these two analyses have been engineered to suit FFT codes. For introductions to them, again, see [6].

3.1 Dependence Analysis

As mentioned above, the subscripts in FFT codes are always simple linear functions of induction variables. Furthermore, the references to any given array within the scope of a specific nested loop have subscripts that differ only by the coefficient on the induction variable of the immediately enclosing loop and the constant if they differ at all. In addition, it is frequently the case that most indices of a given array are written to no more than once in the entire program. When an index is written to more than once, it almost always happens that each write is either in different loops or in the same loop with precisely the same subscript expression. Finally, and most importantly, HiLO's software pipelining algorithm requires only same-iteration dependence information.

Thus, a very obvious dependence test is sufficient to prove the independence of every pair of memory accesses that are in fact independent within a given loop iteration. HiLO simply checks to see if there is any single integer value that the induction variable of the immediately enclosing loop can take that will make a given pair of subscripts equivalent.

3.2 Def-use Analysis

Links in the def-use and use-def chains of subscripted variables are established whenever the GCD dependence test[3] fails to prove independence. We have not witnessed any SPL produced FFT codes in which this weak test doesn't prove sufficiently strong.

4 Optimization

We have implemented the following optimization passes in HiLO: array scalarization, algebraic simplification, common subexpression elimination (CSE), constant and copy propagation, dead code elimination, induction variable elimination, induction variable strength reduction, loop unrolling, register renaming,

---

[3] Again, see [6] for a description of the GCD dependence test.

basic block scheduling, and software pipelining. Those that have a significant impact on FFT or that have been tailored for FFT in some way are discussed in turn below.

4.1   Array Scalarization

The more loops are unrolled, the bigger benefit array scalarization will have on the generated code. Of course, when loops are fully unrolled, the subscripts in FFT codes all turn to constants, and then entire arrays can be replaced. But HiLO also checks for any definition of a subscripted variable for which all uses are defined exclusively by that definition. In such cases, the defined subscripted variable and all its uses can be replaced with the same scalar.[4]

4.2   Algebraic Simplification

Standard algebraic simplifications including constant folding and combining additive operators (for example, $-x + y \rightarrow y - x$) need to be performed, mainly to support the efforts of the other optimization passes. For instance, constant folding can create new constant and copy propagation opportunities.

Another important goal that this pass achieves is the canonicalization of constants to non-negative values. This technique was shown to improve performance in [7], and we have seen the same improvement. When a negative constant is discovered, it is translated to a unary negation operator applied to a positive constant. Unary operators can then combine with additive operators in the surrounding context and be simplified away. Since the majority of constants in FFT codes appear in both their positive and negative forms, this optimization nearly cuts both the size of the compiled program's constant table and the number of constant loads performed by the compiled program in half.

Expressions can also be canonicalized in a similar fashion. Expressions of the form $-x - y$ can be translated to $-(x + y)$. In a multiplicative context, unary negation is expanded to contain the entire multiplicative operation rather than just one of its factors (i.e., $(-x) * y \rightarrow -(x * y)$). Along with constant canonicalization, these translations reduce the number of forms a given expression can be represented in, thus creating previously unavailable opportunities for CSE to further simplify the code. The translation $(-x) * y \rightarrow -(x * y)$ is also useful when combined with the augmented behavior of copy propagation, discussed next.

4.3   Common Subexpression Elimination

When allowed free reign over the AST, CSE often has a detrimental affect on codes with loops. That's because, as mentioned in section 3, the majority of the expressions in subscripts turn out to be common. Pulling these expressions out

---

[4] If the array in question happens to be passed to the function as an argument, then HiLO will choose not to make this replacement unless it can also be proven that the given definition is not the last assignment to that index in the array.

into separate assignments to newly declared variables makes dependence analysis more complicated, and tends to add to the native compiler's confusion. With this in mind, HiLO has been endowed with a command line parameter that instructs CSE not to search for common subexpressions inside subscripts.

4.4 Copy Propagation

Copy propagation replaces occurrences of the variable on the left hand side of a given "simple" assignment statement with the right hand side of that assignment statement. In the context of FFT optimization, we consider an assignment statement simple when its left hand side is comprised of either a scalar variable or a subscripted array reference with either a constant or scalar subscript, and its right hand side is either a constant, a scalar, or a unary negation expression.

Recall that unary negation expressions are often created during algebraic simplification because of constant and expression canonicalization. They are then propagated during copy propagation so that they can combine with additive operators in the new context during further algebraic simplification.

Table 1. Simulated hardware parameters and their default settings

Parameter	Default
integer addition latency	1
integer multiplication latency	2
floating point addition latency	2
floating point multiplication latency	4
load latency	6
store latency	7
integer ALUs	2
floating point units	2
load issue slots	8
store issue slots	8

4.5 Basic Block Scheduling

HiLO's basic block scheduler applies one of two algorithms to every function and loop body. First, it can use the list scheduling algorithm with a reservation table as described in [6]. In order to use this algorithm, the input program must be translated to three-address form and instruction latencies and other hardware parameters must be assumed. Table 1 lists these simulated hardware parameters and their default settings. All of them can be overridden on the command line. So, in the absence of software capable of automatically detecting appropriate values for these parameters, a search can easily be performed over them. The latter is our chosen experimental method, as discussed in section 5.

The second algorithm simply tries to put uses as close to definitions as possible. This alternative was inspired by [7], which shows good performance with a scheduler that provably minimizes register spills no matter how many registers the target architecture has, provided that the size of the FFT transform is a power of 2. That algorithm is not implemented here; we investigated another algorithm that still tries to take other simulated hardware parameters into account, as described below.

First, the dependence DAG for the block is constructed, and the roots of the DAG are added to a queue in decreasing order of their delay to the end of the block (as would be calculated by the list scheduling algorithm, traversing the DAG to the leaves and adding instruction latencies along the way). The instructions in the queue are those instructions that need not wait for any other instructions in the block to be scheduled before they can be correctly scheduled. Next, the first instruction is taken from the queue and scheduled. In keeping with the reservation table, this instruction now occupies a particular hardware component for a particular latency, as determined by the type of operation being performed. Counters associated with every DAG child of every instruction that has already been scheduled are then incremented. If the most recently scheduled instruction has any children that can now be correctly scheduled (because all of their parents in the dependence DAG have already been scheduled), those children are then added to the queue such that the queue remains sorted by decreasing counter value from now on.

From this point further, the next instruction to be scheduled will always be the instruction in the queue with highest counter value that can also be scheduled legally given the simulated hardware's availability. The process of selecting an instruction for scheduling, incrementing counters, and adding newly schedulable children from the dependence DAG to the queue is repeated until all instructions are scheduled.

4.6   Software Pipelining

The software pipelining algorithm implemented in HiLO is called circular scheduling [8], and it is applied only to the bodies of the innermost loops. In circular scheduling, we reason that the instructions in a given loop can be viewed as a circular list, and that instructions from the top of the list (the roots of the dependence DAG, more precisely) can be circled to the bottom of the list, where they represent themselves one iteration later. Instructions moved in this way are also added to the prolog of the software pipeline, and all those that were not moved are added to the epilog. Now, the loop can be re-analyzed to determine if the basic block scheduler can produce a better schedule. If more improvement is desired the process can then be repeated.

In our implementation, we execute this circular code motion only once, reasoning that after loop unrolling, the basic block scheduler should already have enough instructions available to produce a good schedule. However, the number of dependence DAG roots that are circled can be specified as a percentage of the total DAG roots available on the command line. Thus, we give the user the option to circle fewer instructions instead of more. The typical FFT code loop can have many dependence DAG roots already, and at some point, it's possible to circle too many instructions. As pointed out in [8], if we circle more and more instructions, we will eventually end up back at the same schedule we started with.

4.7   Engineering FFT Optimization

The preceding subsections described the classical optimizations we implemented along with some tweaks. Those tweaks were designed with an overall optimization strategy in mind. That strategy is based on the mutually beneficial relationships that different optimization passes can have. For instance, we have already seen the ways that algebraic simplification can bolster copy propagation and the ways that copy propagation can then create new opportunities for algebraic simplification in return.

Alternating between these two optimization passes, the code will eventually reach a form where no further changes can be made. This can be seen easily by noting that each new opportunity created by one pass for another makes the code smaller in some way. Algebraic simplification creates newly propagatable constants by folding them and scalar variables by stripping away a multiplication by one or an addition of zero. The propagation of constants and scalars may not make the code smaller, but algebraic simplification will not reverse the effect either, and it will use the effect to further reduce the size of the code. Lastly, the propagation of unary expressions leads to the elimination of extraneous additive operators. Since the code can only get smaller, the process of alternating between the two passes must eventually terminate.

Common subexpression elimination and copy propagation enjoy the same mutually beneficial relationship. For example, let's say two additions $b + c$ and $y + z$ are calculated, and then both the addition expressions as well as the variables their results were stored in appear later in the code, as in the upper left hand box in Figure 1. A single CSE pass will extract the addition expressions, resulting in the upper right hand box of Figure 1. Note that the variables a and x now have copies that are ready to be propagated. After a copy propagation pass, it is clear that the code in the lower left hand box can benefit from another CSE pass, which can make more variables ready for copy propagation.

In both optimization iteration scenarios described above, the code will eventually reach a form where no further progress can be made. Furthermore, there is no finite number of iterations of such "optimization loops" for which all codes will reach their fully reduced form. An arbitrary code can require an arbitrary (but finite) number of iterations of each loop, but that number can be bounded with regard to the optimization loops described here.

In the case of algebraic simplification and copy propagation, we can only say that the number of iterations applied to a given basic block in three address form is bounded by the number of instructions in that block. Now consider CSE and copy propagation applied in a loop to a basic block in three address form. What is the requirement for a piece of code to necessitate more than one iteration of the optimization loop? At a minimum, one expression must be extracted by CSE so that two new copies are ready for propagation. Those copies can then

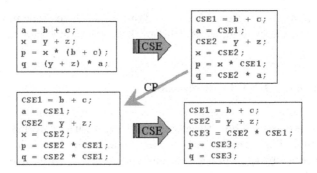

Fig. 1. The mutually beneficial relationship of CSE and copy propagation

combine alternately in two later instructions that involve a common second argument, and another CSE pass will be necessitated for those two instructions. In fact, every successive pair of instructionsIII can involve one common argument and one argument that represents a copy of a common expression discovered by the previous iteration. Therefore, the number of iterations of this optimization loop applied to a basic block in three address form is no greater than $\lfloor \frac{i}{2} \rfloor$, where i is the number of instructions in that block.

5   Experiments

FFT codes are at their fastest when all their loops are fully unrolled. However, for larger formulas, the size of the resulting code can become prohibitive, so loops are preserved. Hence, the following experiments pit HiLO against SPL in both the straight-line and loop code settings. The results will then be indicative of HiLO's ability to simplify when only simplification makes a difference, as well has HiLO's scalability to large formulas when loop based optimizations are also important.

Table 2. Experimental platforms, compilers, and compiler arguments

ISA	SPARC	MIPS	x86
CPU	UltraSparcIII	MIPS R12000	Pentium IV
Clock speed	750 Mhz	300 Mhz	3 Ghz
OS	Solaris 7	IRIX64 6.5	Linux kernel 2.4.21-15EL
Compiler	Forte Developer 7	MIPSpro 7.3.1.1m	gcc 3.2.3
Compiler arguments	-fast -x05	-03	-03

Table 2 describes the platforms used in our experiments. These platforms will hereafter be referred to by their ISA names. A collection of 45 FFT algorithms were selected to test HiLO's performance against SPL's. For each formula in each experiment, the C codes produced by HiLO and SPL were each sent the same back-end compiler with the same command line arguments, whatever was appropriate for the target platform as listed in table 2. The execution time of the resulting program was then plotted as a function of the algorithm number. All execution times were averaged over 10,000 trials.

5.1 Straight-Line Code

To test HiLO's performance on straight line code, SPL was set to generate both optimized and unoptimized versions of the 45 FFT algorithms of size 32 after fully unrolling them. Then, HiLO performed its optimizations on the unoptimized versions, and we then compare the resulting performance against the performance of the optimized versions. This experiment was repeated on the three target architectures. In each experiment, HiLO was invoked with the following optimization schedule: (1) array scalarization, (2) register renaming, (3) "optimization loop" over algebraic simplification and copy propagation, (4) "optimization loop" over common subexpression elimination and copy propagation, (5) dead code elimination, (6) algebraic simplification.

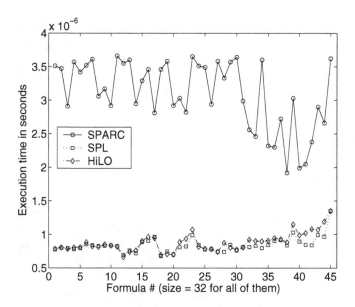

Fig. 2. Straight-line FFT performance on SPARC

In figures 2, 3, and 4, the execution times for each of the 45 selected formulas are depicted as compiled by the native compiler alone, SPL and then the native

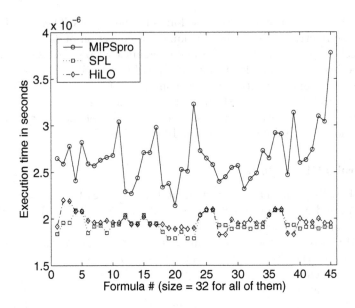

Fig. 3. Straight-line FFT performance on MIPS

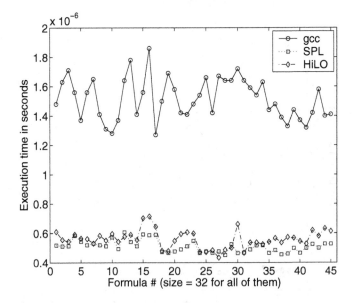

Fig. 4. Straight-line FFT performance on x86

compiler, and finally HiLO and then the native compiler. The best execution times achieved by HiLO on SPARC, MIPS, and x86 were 6.61×10^{-7}, 1.83×10^{-6}, and 4.33×10^{-7} seconds respectively. SPL's best times were 6.76×10^{-7},

1.79×10^{-6}, and 4.51×10^{-7} seconds respectively. We also experimented with FFTW 3.0.1 using its exhaustive search option. FFTW's times were 8.66×10^{-7}, 1.91×10^{-6}, and 4.28×10^{-7} seconds respectively. All three systems achieve significant performance increases and HiLO is competitive with or better than both SPL and FFTW on all three platforms.

5.2   Loop Code

To test HiLO's performance on codes with loops, SPL was set to generate both optimized and unoptimized versions of the 45 FFT algorithms *without* first fully unrolling their loops. Of course, doing *some* unrolling is the only way to get good results out of software pipelining. So, when generating the optimized versions, SPL was allowed to unroll the innermost loops in each algorithm to the same degree that HiLO did before doing its software pipelining.

HiLO then compiled the algorithms with the following optimization schedule: (1) array scalarization, (2) register renaming, (3) "optimization loop" over algebraic simplification and copy propagation, (4) dead code elimination, (5) induction variable elimination, (6) "optimization loop" over CSE and copy propagation, (7) dead code elimination, (8) loop unrolling with factor 4, (9) "optimization loop" over algebraic simplification and copy propagation, (10) array scalarization, (11) register renaming, (12) copy propagation, (13) dead code elimination, (14) software pipelining, (15) copy propagation.

Table 3. Simulated hardware parameter settings used in HiLO's search

Parameter	Settings included in search				
integer ALUs	1	2			
floating point units	1	2			
CSE preserves subscripts	no	yes			
scheduling algorithm	list	HiLO's own			
pipelining	0.25	0.5	0.75	1.0	just scheduling

Then, for each of the 45 algorithms, HiLO searched over several of the simulated hardware parameters, the CSE subscript preservation option (see section 4.3), and the software pipelining parameter (see section 4.6) by repeating the above optimization schedule with different settings and re-measuring the resulting performance. Table 3 lists some of the parameters that are searched over and the values those parameters are allowed to take. For every possible combination of parameter settings from table 3, we tried setting the latencies to their default values and setting them all equal to 1. In addition, we included in the search an optimization schedule identical to the one given above but with software pipelining removed entirely.

This entire search process was then repeated on all three target architectures. The results are depicted in figures 5, 6, and 7, and they show HiLO gains a clear performance advantage when performing software pipelining on both the

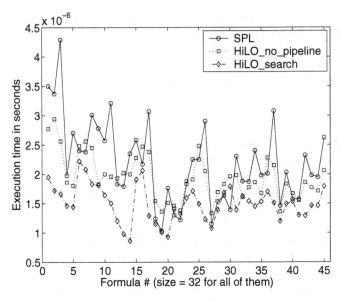

Fig. 5. Pipelined FFT performance after parameter search on SPARC

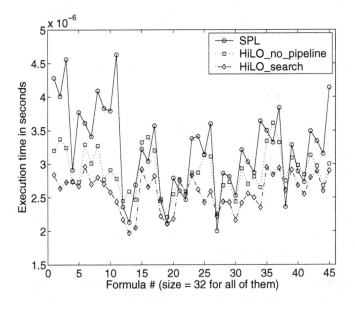

Fig. 6. Pipelined FFT performance after parameter search on MIPS

SPARC and MIPS architectures. On the x86 architecture, HiLO remains competitive. When viewing these results, it should be kept in mind that the initial loop unrollings performed by SPL are very similar, but not identical to those

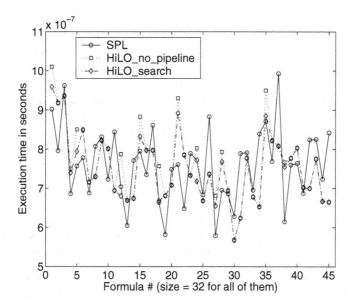

Fig. 7. Pipelined FFT performance after parameter search on x86

performed by HiLO. In some instances, it may be the case that an extra unrolled loop in HiLO accounts for extra performance benefits when compared with SPL.

Solid conclusions about software pipelining can be reached by comparing the two HiLO generated data sets on these graphs. The data labeled "HiLO no pipeline" depict HiLO's performance when using the afore mentioned optimization schedule with the pipelining pass removed. Therefore, it is pipelining with some simulated hardware parameter settings that accounts for the significant improvements seen in almost every formula on both SPARC and MIPS when compared against the non-pipelining HiLO optimization strategy. And the actual values used by different formulas for the parameters in table 3 to achieve the improved performance are quite varied from formula to formula, except for CSE's subscript preserving parameter, which stayed on consistently.

It is also interesting to note that x86 did not respond well to software pipelining. The search process almost always settled on a configuration that involved no pipelining or scheduling on this architecture. Together, all of these results lead us to believe that imprecision of dependence analysis and the difficulty of finding good instruction schedules lie at the heart of native compilers' struggles with FFT codes.

6 Conclusion

We have presented the HiLO high level optimizer and shown that it is a good framework for researching and applying the effects of high level optimizations on domain specific codes. Following in the tradition of domain specific compilers such as SPL and FFTW, we have shown originally that native compilers can be coaxed to produce even more efficient code through software pipelining. Finally, we believe the trends discovered in our experience with searching for a good software pipelining are further evidence that arrays, dependence analysis, and instruction scheduling are the keys high performance in FFT.

In the near future, we plan to expand the domain on which HiLO is applicable to other DSP transformation algorithms. If our techniques prove effective on these related codes, they can be integrated into the SPIRAL automatic tuning system where they will be of greater value.

References

1. Püschel, M., Moura, J., Johnson, J., Padua, D., Veloso, M., Singer, B., Xiong, J., Franchetti, F., Gacic, A., Voronenko, Y., Chen, K., Johnson, R.W., Rizzolo, N.: Spiral: Code generation for dsp transforms. In: to appear in Proceedings of the IEEE special issue on "Program Generation, Optimization, and Adaptation". (2005)
2. Frigo, M., Johnson, S.G.: Fftw: An adaptive software architecture for the fft. In: Proceedings of the IEEE International Conference on Acoustics, Speech, and Signal Processing. Volume 3. (1998) 1381–1384
3. Whaley, R.C., Petitet, A., Dongarra, J.J.: Automated empirical optimizations of software and the atlas project. Parallel Computing **27** (2001) 3–35
4. Xiong, J., Johnson, J., Johnson, R., Padua, D.: Spl: A language and compiler for dsp algorithms. In: Proceedings of the ACM SIGPLAN Conference on Programming Language Design and Implementation, ACM Press (2001) 298–308
5. Gamma, E., Helm, R., Johnson, R., Vlissides, J.: Design Patterns: Elements of Reusable Object-Oriented Software. Addison-Wesley Longman Publishing Co., Inc. (1995)
6. Muchnick, S.S.: Advanced Compiler Design and Implementation. Morgan Kaufmann Publishers, Inc (1997)
7. Frigo, M.: A fast fourier transform compiler. In: Proceedings of the ACM SIGPLAN Conference on Programming Language Design and Implementation, ACM Press (1999) 169–180
8. Jain, S.: Circular scheduling: A new technique to perform software pipelining. In: Proceedings of the ACM SIGPLAN Conference on Programming Language Design and Implementation, ACM Press (1991) 219–228

Applying Loop Optimizations to Object-Oriented Abstractions Through General Classification of Array Semantics

Qing Yi and Dan Quinlan

Lawrence Livermore National Laboratory, Livermore, CA 94550, USA

Abstract. Optimizing compilers have a long history of applying loop transformations to C and Fortran scientific applications. However, such optimizations are rare in compilers for object-oriented languages such as C++ or Java, where loops operating on user-defined types are left unoptimized due to their unknown semantics. Our goal is to reduce the performance penalty of using high-level object-oriented abstractions. We propose an approach that allows the explicit communication between programmers and compilers. We have extended the traditional Fortran loop optimizations with an open interface. Through this interface, we have developed techniques to automatically recognize and optimize user-defined array abstractions. In addition, we have developed an adapted constant-propagation algorithm to automatically propagate properties of abstractions. We have implemented these techniques in a C++ source-to-source translator and have applied them to optimize several kernels written using an array-class library. Our experimental results show that using our approach, applications using high-level abstractions can achieve comparable, and in cases superior, performance to that achieved by efficient low-level hand-written codes.

1 Introduction

As modern computers become increasingly complex, compilers must extensively optimize user applications to achieve high performance. One important class of such optimizations includes loop transformations, such as loop blocking and fusion/fission, which have long been applied to Fortran scientific applications.

Most loop optimizations, however, have been applied only to loops operating on primitive types in Fortran or C. To illustrate this, consider Figure 1, a C++ fragment that uses a high-level array class library. Here the user-defined types, *floatArray* and *Range*, have similar semantics to the Fortran90 array and subscript triplet respectively.

If Figure 1 were written in Fortran90 using the primitive array types, most Fortran compilers would be able to translate the array operations into explicit loop computations and then apply loop optimizations. However, as the same computation is written in C++ using abstractions, a C++ compiler will likely consider all the array operations as opaque function calls, and apply no optimizations.

R. Eigenmann et al. (Eds.): LCPC 2004, LNCS 3602, pp. 253–267, 2005.
© Springer-Verlag Heidelberg 2005

```
void interpolate1D (floatArray& fineGrid, floatArray& coarseGrid) {
  int fineGridSize = fineGrid.getLength(0), coarseGridSize = coarseGrid.getLength(0);
  Range If (2,fineGridSize-2,2), Ic (1,coarseGridSize-1,1);
  fineGrid(If) = coarseGrid(Ic);
  fineGrid(If-1) = (coarseGrid(Ic-1) + coarseGrid(Ic)) / 2.0;
}
```

Fig. 1. Example: 1D interpolation

To avoid this performance penalty for using object-oriented abstractions, programmers are often forced to write low level code and unnecessarily expose many implementation details. This practice discourages code reuse and thus leaves good programming styles in conflict with high performance. The problem is especially acute in scientific applications where performance is critical.

We propose an approach which encourages programmers write high-level object-oriented programs by allowing them to explicitly communicate with the compiler. Our work does not apply to just-in-time compilation techniques, but can apply to Java in a source-to-source manner similar to the way which we apply it to C++. Specifically, we present the following new results.

- We have designed an annotation language specifically for classifying the semantics of user-defined types and operators.
- We have developed a new algorithm, adapted from the traditional constant-propagation algorithm, to propagate semantic properties of object-oriented abstractions. The extracted properties are then used to drive the optimization of user-defined abstractions.
- Based on our annotation interface, we have applied loop optimizations directly to general user-defined array operations. In contrast, traditional loop optimizations only addressed loops operating on primitive language constructs, and not on user-defined abstractions.
- We have implemented the above techniques in a C++ source-to-source translator and have applied them to optimize several kernels written using an array-abstraction library. These results were not possible using traditional techniques for Fortran applications. Our results show that using our approach, applications using high-level abstractions can achieve comparable or even better performance than that achieved by lower-level codes.

Although we promote communication between programmers and compilers, we do not exclude automating the process. Our future work includes at least partially automating the generation of annotations. Section 2 describes our extended loop optimization algorithm. Section 3 and 4 then present our annotation language and overall optimization framework respectively. Finally, Section 5, 6 and 7 present our experimental results, discuss related work, and draw conclusions.

2   Extended Loop Transformation

Figure 2 summarizes our extended loop transformation algorithm, which implements three loop optimizations: interchange, fusion and blocking. The algorithm

```
loop-transformation(C, A)
    C: input code;   A: array abstraction interface
    Dep = construct-dependence-graph(C,A);
    distribute-loop-nests( C, Dep);
    for (each loop nest l ∈ C )
        apply-loop-interchange(l, Dep);
    apply-loop-fusion( C, Dep);
    for (each loop nest l ∈ C)
        apply-blocking( l, Dep)

construct-dependence-graph(C, A)
    C: input code;   A: array abstraction interface
    for (each pair of statements s₁ and s₂)
        (mod₁,use₁) = get-side-effects(A,s₁);
        (mod₂,use₂) = get-side-effects(A,s₂);
        if ( mod₁ or mod₂ contains unknown side-effect)
            create-dependence(s₁, s₂); continue;
        for (each (a₁, a₂) ∈ {(mod₁, use₂) or (use₁, mod₂)
                        or (mod₁, mod₂) })
            if (is-var(a₁) and is-var(a₂) and identical(a₁,a₂))
                create-dependence(s₁, s₂);
            else if (((arr₁,sub₁) = is-array-elem(A, a₁))
                and ((arr₂, sub₂) = is-array-elem(A,a₂))
                and identical(arr₁,arr₂))
                compute-array-dependence(sub₁, sub₂);
            else if (may-alias(A,a₁, a₂))
                create-dependence(s₁,s₂);
```

```
is-array-elem(A, a₁)
    A: array abstraction interface;
    a₁: memory access expression;
    return: array and subscripts of the access
    if ((obj, subs) = A.is-access-array-elem(a₁))
        return (obj, subs);
    else if ((pntr,subs)=is-pntr-array-access(a₁))
                and is-constant-pointer(pntr))
        return (pntr, subs);
    else return ∅

may-alias(A, a₁, a₂)
    A: array abstraction interface;
    a₁,a₂: memory references to be analyzed;
    return : whether a₁ and a₂ may be aliased;
    if ((arr₁, sub₁)=A.is-access-array-elem(a₁))
        return may-alias(arr₁, a₂);
    if ((arr₂, sub₂)=A.is-access-array-elem(a₂))
        return may-alias(a₁, arr₂);
    if (A.is-known-array(a₁) and
        A.is-known-array(a₂))
        return A.is-aliased-array(a₁, a₂);
    if (a₁ and a₂ are both local variables)
        return is-aliased-local-var(a₁, a₂);
    else
        return is-type-alias-compatible(a₁,a₂);
```

Fig. 2. Loop transformation algorithm

is an extension to previous work by Yi, Kennedy and Adve [22], which optimized loops in Fortran applications. We have extended their dependence analysis algorithm with an interface, *array abstraction interface*, to facilitate the optimization of loops operating on user-defined array classes [1].

2.1 Dependence Analysis

In Figure 2, function *construct-dependence-graph* computes the reordering constraints between each pair of statements (s_1, s_2). Specifically, a transformation is safe if it never reorders any iterations of s_1 and s_2 that are connected by dependences.

In the algorithm, we first collect all the memory references modified (mod_1 and mod_2) or used (use_1 and use_2) by s_1 and s_2 respectively. We then create dependence edges to connect each pair of iterations, $I_1(s_1)$ (iteration I_1 of statement s_1) and $I_2(s_2)$, when both $I_1(s_1)$ and $I_2(s_2)$ may access a common memory store *loc*, and at least one of them may modify *loc*.

Given two arbitrary memory references, a_1 and a_2, if they access memory through an identical scalar or array variable[2], we compute their reordering constraints using traditional dependence analysis algorithms for Fortran [1,19,3], as

---

[1] The array abstraction interface is also used in the profitability analysis of applying loop optimizations, which is omitted in this paper.

[2] Here the variable could be a class variable concatenated with a list of non-pointer field names.

encoded by functions *create-dependence* and *compute-array-dependence* respectively. Note that function *is-array-elem(A,a_1)* uses the array-abstraction interface A to determine whether a_1 accesses the element of some array arr_1 using subscripts sub_1. Section 2.2 describes this function in more detail.

If a_1 or a_2 indirectly access memory through dereferencing unknown address pointers, or if they refer to different variables, we perform aliasing analysis to determine whether a_1 and a_2 may reach a common memory store. Unless a_1 and a_2 can be proved to never alias to each other, we connect them with a dependence edge to disable optimizations that attempt to reorder them.

2.2 Array Abstraction Interface

In object-oriented languages such as C++, programmers can define their own array classes. As the addresses of class objects cannot be redefined, these array classes can be treated as if they are Fortran arrays, and their aliasing relations can be determined more easily than C pointers.

We use an array-abstraction interface to communicate the semantics of user-defined array types with our loop optimizer. In Figure 2, we use this array-abstraction interface to both recognize user-defined array objects and to determine the aliasing relations between array objects.

We use function *is-array-elem(A,a_1)* to query the array-abstraction interface A whether a_1 is a subscripted array element access. If yes, we return both the array object *obj* and a list of integer subscripts *subs* (multi-dimensional array is allowed). Otherwise, we determine whether a_1 is the subscript operator for C pointers and whether the address of the pointer is never changed within the optimization scope. If neither cases apply, we conclude that a_1 does not access array elements and return $\emptyset$.

We use function *may-alias(A, a_1,a_2)* to determine the aliasing relations between two memory references a_1 and a_2. First, if either a_1 or a_2 is a subscripted array element access, we examine the corresponding arrays for aliasing relations. Second, if both a_1 and a_2 are array class objects, we query the array-abstraction interface for their aliasing relations. Third, if both a_1 and a_2 are local variables, we use a simple context-insensitive algorithm (*is-aliased-local-var* in Figure 2) to determine whether the input code C has performed operations that might cause a_1, a_2 to reach to a common memory store. Finally, if none of the above cases apply, as long as the types of a_1 and a_2 are compatible, we conservatively assume that they might be aliased.

3   Annotating Semantics of Abstractions

Figure 3(a) shows the grammar of our annotation language. Figure 3(b) shows some example annotations for the 1D interpolation code in Figure 1. Section 3.1, 3.2, and 3.3 will describe the semantics of these annotations in more detail. Section 3.4 then will discuss the inheritance of these annotations. Although we currently require programmers to explicitly annotate all the abstractions, our

<annot> ::= <annot1> | <annot1>;<annot>
<annot1> ::= **class** <cls_annot>
 | **operator** <op_annot>
<cls_annot> ::= <clsname>:<cls_annot1>;
<cls_annot1>::=
   <cls_annot2> | <cls_annot2> <cls_annot1>
<cls_annot2>::= <arr_annot>
 | **inheritable** <arr_annot>
 | **has-value** { <val_def> }
<arr_annot>::= **is-array**{ <arr_def>}
 | **is-array**{**define**{<stmts>}<arr_def>}
<op_annot> ::= <opdecl> : <op_annot1> ;
<op_annot1> ::=
   <op_annot2> | <op_annot2> <op_annot1>
<op_annot2> ::= **modify** <namelist>
 | **new-array** (<aliaslist>){<arr_def>}
 | **modify-array** (<name>) {<arr_def>}
 | **restrict-value** {<val_def_list>}
 | **read** <namelist>
 | **alias** <nameGrouplist>
 | **allow-alias** <nameGrouplist>
 | **inline** <expression>
<arr_def> ::=
   <arr_attr_def> | <arr_attr_def> <arr_def>
<arr_attr_def> ::= <arr_attr>=<expression>;
<arr_attr> ::= **dim** | **len** (<param>)
 | **elem**(<paramlist>)
 | **reshape**(<paramlist>)
<val_def> ::= <name>;| <name>;<val_def>
 | <name> = <expression> ;
 | <name> = <expression> ; <val_def>

(a) grammar

(1) **class floatArray:**
inheritable is-array { dim = 6;
      len(i) = this.getLength(i);
      elem(i$x:0:dim-1) = this(i$x);
      reshape(i$x:0:dim-1) = this.resize(i$x); };
has-value {dim; len$x:0,dim-1=this.getLength(x); }
(2) **operator floatArray::operator =**
(const floatArray& that):
modify-array (this) {
      dim = that.dim; len(i) = that.len(i);
      elem(i$x:1:dim) = that.elem(i$x); };
(3) **operator +(const floatArray&** a_1**,double** a_2**):**
new-array () { dim = a_1.dim; len(i) = a_1.len(i);
      elem(i$x:1:dim) = a_1.elem(i$x)+a_2; };
(4) **operator floatArray::operator ()**
(const Range& I):
restrict-value { this = { dim = 1; } };
      result = {dim = 1; len(0) = I.len;}; };
new-array (this) { dim = 1; len(0) = I.len;
      elem(i) = this.elem(i*I.stride + I.base); };
(5) **class Range:** has-value {stride; base; len; };
(6) **operator Range::Range(int** _l**,int** _s**):**
modify none; read {_b,_l,_s}; alias none;
restrict-value { this={base =_b;len=_l;stride=_s;};};
(7) **operator floatArray::operator() (int index)** :
inline { this.elem(index) };
restrict-value { this = { dim = 1; };};
(8) **operator + (const Range& lhs, int x)** :
modify none; read {lhs,x}; alias none;
restrict-value { result={stride=lhs.stride;
      len = lhs.len; base = lhs.base + x; };};

(b)example

Fig. 3. Annotation language

future work will target developing compiler techniques to automate the process. Section 3.5 discusses the automation issues in more detail.

3.1 Array Annotation

We provide three annotations, *is-array*, *modify-array*, and *new-array*, to describe the array abstraction semantics of both user-defined types and operations.

The declaration(1) in Figure 3(b) uses *is-array* to declare that the class *floatArray* satisfies the pre-defined array semantics. Specifically, it has at most 6 dimensions, with the length of each dimension i obtained by calling member function $getLength(i)$, and with each element of the array accessed through the "()" operator. Here $i\$x : 0 : dim - 1$ denotes a list of parameters, $i_1, i_2, ..., i_{dim-1}$.

In Figure 3(a), the *is-array* annotation also allows a optional "*define* <stmts>*" phrase to define loop-invariant operations that should be executed before enumerating array elements. Further, programmers can use *inheritable* to specify that the annotation is preserved by class inheritance.

The declaration(2) in Figure 3(b) uses *modify-array* to declare that the operator "*floatArray::operator= (const floatArray& that)*" performs element-wise modification of the current array (the "this" argument of the C++ member function call). Specifically, the operator first modifies the current array to have the same shape as the input array *that*. It then modifies each element of the current array to be a copy of the corresponding element in *that*.

The declaration(3) in Figure 3(b) uses *new-array* to declare that the operator "*+(const floatArray& a_1, double a_2)*" constructs a new array with the same shape as that of a_1, and each element of the new array is the result of adding a_2 to the corresponding element of a_1. Similarly, the declaration(4) declares that the operator "*floatArray::operator()(const Range& I)*" constructs a new array that is aliased to the current one, by selecting only those elements that are within the iteration range I.

3.2   Property Annotation

We use two annotations, *has-value* and *restrict-value*, to describe properties of user-defined abstractions. These properties are described using symbolic values.

The annotation *has-value* declares that a user-defined type has certain properties that can be represented as symbolic values. For example, the declaration(1) in Figure 3(b) uses *has-value* to declare that the class *floatArray* has two properties: the array dimension and the length of each dimension i (if the length cannot be statically determined, *this.getLenth(i)* will be used in place). Similarly, the declaration(5) declares that the *Range* class (which selects a subset of elements in an array) has three properties, *base*, *len* and *stride*.

The annotation *restrict-value* describes how properties of user-defined types can be implied from function calls. For example, the declaration(6) in Figure 3(b) declares that if "*floatArray::operator()(int index)*" is used to access the element of a *floatArray* object *arr*, the array object *arr* must have a single dimension, and it will remain single-dimensional until some other operator modifies its shape.

3.3   Side-Effect Annotation

We provide four annotations, *mod*, *read*, *alias*, and *inline*, to describe the general side-effects of user-defined operators.

The *mod* annotation declares a list of memory references that might be modified by a function. Similarly, the *read* annotation declares the list of the references being used, and the *alias* annotation declares the groups of references that might be aliased to each other. These annotations communicate with our alias and side-effect analysis algorithms in resolving semantics of function calls. The declaration(8) in Figure 3(b) shows an example of using these annotations.

The *inline* annotation declares the high-level semantic interpretations of user-defined functions. As example, the declaration(7) in Figure 3(b) declares that "*floatArray::operator()(int)*" is semantically equivalent to a subscripted element access of the current *floatArray* object.

3.4   Inheritance of Semantic Annotations

We have provided two class annotations, *is-array* and *has-value*, to describe the properties of user-defined types. Since the *has-value* annotation does not make implicit assumptions about the declared properties, the annotation is preserved

apply-optimization(*C*, *A* **)**
    C: input code fragment; *A*: annotation interface
(1) translate element-wise array operations
    (1.1) rewrite-inline-operators(*C*, *A*)
    (1.2) *valmap* = ∅;   property-propagate(*C*, *A*, *valmap*);
    (1.3) rewrite-modify-array(*C*, *A*, *valmap*);   rewrite-new-array(*C*, *A*, *valmap*);
(2) loop-transformation(*C*, *A*);
(3) rewrite-array-access(*C*, *A*);

Fig. 4. Steps of optimizing array abstractions

property-propagate(C, A, *vmap***)**
    C: input code fragment; *A*: annotation interface;
    vmap: map from objects to their property values
    wklist = ∅; *defUse* = build-dataflow-graph(*C*);
    find-restr-op(*C*,*A*,*vmap*,*wklist*);
    while (*wklist* ≠ ∅)
      cur = pop(wklist); *curval* = vmap(*cur*);
      if (*cur* is a def-node in *defUse*)
      for (each *cur*'s unique use-node *n*)
      if (vmap(*n*).merge-with(*curval*) changes)
        find-restr-op(*stmt*(*n*),*A*,*vmap*,*wklist*);
      else if (*cur* has a unique def-node *n* and
             vmap(*n*).merge(*curval*) changes)
      find-restr-op(*stmt*(*n*),*A*,*vmap*,*wklist*);
      add *n* to *wklist*

find-restr-op(C, A, *vmap*, *wklist***)**
    C: input code fragment;
    A: annotation interface;
    vmap: map from objects to their property values
    wklist: working list of object references;
    for (each expression *exp* ∈ *C*)
      if (*desc* =*A*.is-value-restr-op(*exp*, *vmap*))
      for (each (*ref*, *value*) ∈ *desc*))
        if (*vmap*(*ref*).merge(*value*) changes)
        add *ref* to *wklist*;

Fig. 5. Property propagation algorithm

by class inheritance. However, the *is-array* annotation assumes that elements of an array object cannot be aliased, an assumption which can be violated by the derived classes. Consequently, we decide that the derived classes do not automatically inherit the *is-array* annotations unless programmers explicitly specify otherwise (using the *inheritable* annotation). For pointer variables of non-inheritable array types, we first try to precisely determine their types, and if not successful, conservatively assume that their semantics are unknown.

Similar situations arise for virtual functions, whose side-effect annotations (*modify-array, new-array, restrict-value, mod, read, alias,* and *inline*) should not be inherited. Consequently, we assume that the semantics of virtual function calls are unknown unless their implementations can be statically determined.

3.5 Automatic Extraction and Verification of Annotations

Our annotation language serves as an interface between program analyses and transformations. Though currently annotations can only be manually produced by programmers, our future work will try to automate the process. Automatically extracting semantic annotations is in general a hard problem, which cannot yet be solved satisfactorily through existing techniques. Specifically, the implementation details of user-abstractions (e.g., book-keeping, performance optimizations, parallelization considerations) can easily obscure the real semantics and force compilers to conservatively assume non-existing dependences.

To illustrate the complexity, consider a smart-object class that performs reference-counting and copy-on-write. The objects of this class are conceptually independent of each other, but any global aliasing analysis algorithm would see the internal sharing of data and would conclude that all such objects can potentially be aliased. To figure out that each modification applies uniquely to a single object, the algorithm must know that data sharing happens only when the reference count of a smart-object has value > 1, a piece of context information mostly ignored by existing algorithms. If the programmer chooses to annotate the smart-object assignment as having no aliasing side-effect, it would be rejected by a verifier. However, if an optimizer chooses to trust the programmer, it will always produce correct code because the annotation conveys precisely the external semantics of smart-objects. Other implementation details can produce similar effects. We are investigating techniques to overcome these issues.

4   Optimizing Array Abstractions

Figure 4 summarizes the overall steps of our optimizer. Given both the input code and the annotations, we first translate all the collective array operations into an intermediate form of explicit loop computations. Then, we apply the loop optimization algorithm in Figure 2 to the intermediate form. Finally, we translate the output code into efficient low-level implementations.

As shown in Figure 4, we further separate the first step into three sub-steps. First, we replace all the function calls with *inline* annotations with their semantic definitions. Then, we apply an adapted constant propagation algorithm to derive the properties of all objects annotated with *has-value* declarations. Specifically, we try to precisely determine the shapes of all array objects. Finally, we translate all the operations annotated with *modify-array* and *new-array* declarations into explicit loop computations.

It is important that we apply loop optimizations to an intermediate form instead of to the final low-level implementations. An example of the intermediate form is shown in Figure 7, where all the array accesses are explicitly represented as member function calls, and all object properties are readily available. In contrast, after the final step (3) in Figure 4, multi-dimensional arrays are translated into single-dimensional, and C pointers are used in place of the array objects. These implementation details would obscure the original high-level semantics and disable profitable loop optimizations.

4.1   Property Propagation Algorithm

Figure 5 presents our property propagation algorithm. Given an input fragment and the annotations, this algorithm first builds the data-flow graph (def-use chain) and then propagates the properties of user-defined objects on the data-flow graph. The collected properties are stored in *vmap*, which maps object references to their corresponding property values.

Our algorithm relies on a lattice that is nearly identical to that of the traditional constant-propagation algorithm. The depth of the property lattice is three: $top \rightarrow value \rightarrow bottom$, so each property can change its value twice.

Our algorithm is different from constant propagation in three aspects. First, we propagate symbolic values instead of constants. Second, we imply properties

```
rewrite-modify-array(C, A, vmap)
    C: input code fragment; A:array annotation;        rewrite-new-array(C, A, vmap)
    vmap: map from objects to their property values        C: input code fragment; A:array annotation;
for (each statement s ∈ C s.t. A.is-mod-arr(s))            vmap: map from objects to their property values
  arr = A.get-mod-arr-obj(s)                            for (each expression exp ∈ C )
  (dim,lens) = get-array-shape(vmap,arr)                  if ((arr,subs) = A.is-access-arr-elem(exp))
  ivars = create-new-intvars(dim);                          if (A.is-new-arr(arr))
  if (reshape-arr(A,vmap,arr))                                replace exp with A.get-new-arr-elem(arr,subs);
    ns = create-member-fcall("reshape",arr,lens);        else if (! is-variable(arr) )
    insert ns before s;                                      (tmp, ns) = copy-array-to-tmp(arr);
  rhs = A.get-mod-arr-elem(s,ivars);                        insert ns before exp; replace arr with tmp
  lhs = create-member-fcall("elem", arr, ivars);       else if ((arr,i) = A.is-access-arr-len(exp))
  ns = create-assignment( lhs, rhs);                      if (A.is-new-arr(arr))
  for (i = 0; i < ivars.size(); + + 1))                     (dim,lens)=get-array-shape(vmap,arr)
    ns = create-loop( ivars[i], 0, lens[i], ns );           repl = evaluate(lens, i);
  for (each memory reference a ∈ rhs)                       replace exp with repl;
    if ( loop-dependent(lhs, a))                         else if (! is-variable( arr))
      (tmp, ns1) = copy-array-to-tmp(a);                    (tmp, ns) = copy-array-to-tmp(array);
      insert ns1 before s; replace a with tmp              insert ns before exp; replace arr with tmp;
  replace s with ns;
```

Fig. 6. Array operation translation algorithm

from both the modification and usage of an object, so the propagation is bi-directional. Third, because *restrict-value* annotations are independent of control-flow, the result is always correct even before completion.

In Figure 5, we use a working list (*wklist*) to keep track of the object references whose properties need to be propagated. First, we invoke *find-restr-op* to collect the initial known properties for all objects. Each object is added to the working list if its property collection changes. Since each object has a limited number of different properties, and each property can change its value twice, eventually the working list becomes empty and the iteration terminates.

Each object reference *cur* in *wklist* is processed as follows. If *cur* is a definition node in the data-flow graph, we examine each use-node *n* connected with *cur*. If *n* does not have any other definition point, we update *n* to have the same properties as *cur*. Alternatively, if *cur* is a use-node of the data-flow graph and if *cur* has a single definition point *n*, we update *n* to have the same properties as *cur*, and then add *n* to *wklist* to propagate the properties to other use-nodes connected to *n*. Whenever the property collection of *n* changes, we invoke *find-restr-op* to accumulate new properties that depend on the updated properties of *n*. The process iterates until no more updates are necessary.

4.2   Translating Array Operations

In Figure 6, we use functions *rewrite-modify-array* and *rewrite-new-array* to translate collective array operations into explicit loop computations.

The function *rewrite-modify-array* rewrites each operation *s* that has *modify-array* semantics. First, by querying the annotation interface *A*, we determine both the array object *arr* being modified and the new value of each array element. We then determine the new shape of *arr* (by querying *vmap*) and insert a new statement to reshape *arr* if necessary. Next, we create a loop nest that assigns each element of *arr* with the correct new value, and if these new values are

```
void interpolate1D (floatArray& fineGrid, floatArray& coarseGrid ) {
  int fineGridSize = fineGrid.getLength(0), coarseGridSize = coarseGrid.getLength(0);
  Range If (2,fineGridSize-2,2), Ic (1,coarseGridSize-1,1);
  for (int _i = 0; _i < (fineGridSize - 3) / 2; _i += 1)
    (fineGrid.elem)(_i * 2 + 2) = coarseGrid.elem(_i + 1));
  for (int _j = 0; _j < (fineGridSize - 3) / 2; _j += 1)
    (fineGrid.elem)(_j * 2 + 1) = (coarseGrid.elem(_j) + coarseGrid.elem(_j + 1)) / 2.0;
}
```

Fig. 7. Example of translating array operations

```
rewrite-array-access(C, A)
    C: input code fragment;  A:array annotation;
  for (each array declaration decl in C)
    insert A.get-pre-def(decl) after decl;
  for (each statement s in C s.t. A.is-reshape-arr(s) )
    insert A.get-pre-def(s) after s; replace s with A.get-reshape-def(s);
  for (each expression exp in C s.t. A.is-access-arr-elem(exp) or A.is-access-arr-len(exp))
    replace exp with A.get-arr-elem-def(exp) or A.get-arr-len-def(exp);
```

Fig. 8. Code generation for array abstractions

dependent on the old values of arr, we insert a new statement before s to save the old values into a new temporary array. Note that although $copy\text{-}array\text{-}to\text{-}tmp(a)$ is inside a loop, array arr is copied at most once, and loop dependence analysis is used to determine the necessity of copying. Finally, we replace statement s with the new loop computation.

After applying $rewrite\text{-}modify\text{-}array$, we now further apply $rewrite\text{-}new\text{-}array$ to rewrite each expression that creates a new array arr, accesses an individual element or reads the shape of arr, and then discards arr. If arr is created by an operator annotated with the $new\text{-}array$ declaration, we avoid creating arr by evaluating the information access directly based on the element and shape definitions of the $new\text{-}array$ annotation. Otherwise, if the semantics of the operator that creates arr is unknown, we create a new variable tmp to remember the created temporary array and then replace all the other creations of arr with tmp. By saving the temporary array into a new variable, we create arr only once, instead of creating the same array multiple times in the original code.

Figure 7 shows the result of rewriting the 1D interpolation code in Figure 1. Here the array assignment operators, having $modify\text{-}array$ semantics, are translated into explicit loops. Further, the array $plus$ and $division$ operators, having $new\text{-}array$ semantics, are translated into operations on individual elements.

4.3   Generating Low-Level Implementations

Figure 8 describes the final step of our algorithm, where we replace array abstraction operations with low-level implementation details. First, as each array abstraction is associated with a list of loop-invariant statements, we insert these statements immediately after the declaration of each array variable and immediately after each operation that reshapes the array variable. Second, we replace all operations that read or modify array objects with low-level implementations.

5   Experimental Results

This section presents our results from optimizing kernels written using the A++/P++ Library [14,12], an array class library that supports both serial and parallel array abstractions with a single interface. We selected our kernels from the Multigrid algorithm for solving elliptic partial differential equations. The Multigrid algorithm consists of three phases: relaxation, restriction, and inter-polation, from which we selected both interpolation and relaxation(specifically red-black relaxation) on one, two, and three dimensional problems.

Our experiments aim to validate two conclusions: our approach can signifi-cantly improve the performance of numerical applications, and our approach is general enough for optimizing a large class of applications using object-oriented abstractions. The kernels we used, though small, use a real-world array abstrac-tion library and are representative of a much broader class of numerical compu-tations expressed using sequences of array operations. All six kernels (one, two and three-dimensional interpolation and relaxation) benefited significantly from our optimizations.

```
void Five_Point_Stencil ( Index & i , Index & j ) {
    Solution (i,j) = ( Mesh_Size * Mesh_Size * Right_Hand_Side (i,j) + Solution (i+1,j)
                     + Solution (i-1,j) + Solution (i,j+1) + Solution (i,j-1) ) / 4.0;
}
void Red_Black_Relax (int gridSize) {
    Index Black_Odd(1,(gridSize - 1) / 2,2),  Black_Even(2,(gridSize - 2) / 2,2);
    Index Red_Odd(1,(gridSize - 1) / 2,2),  Red_Even(2,(gridSize - 2) / 2,2);
    Index Odd_Rows(1,(gridSize - 1) / 2,2),  Even_Rows(2,(gridSize - 2) / 2,2);
    Five_Point_Stencil ( Black_Odd , Odd_Rows );   Five_Point_Stencil ( Black_Even , Even_Rows );
    Five_Point_Stencil ( Red_Even , Odd_Rows );   Five_Point_Stencil ( Red_Odd , Even_Rows );
}
```

Fig. 9. Two-dimensional red-black relaxation

Figures 1 and 9 present the original versions of the single-dimensional inter-polation and the two-dimensional red-black relaxation[3] respectively, both using array abstractions. The optimized versions are similar to the 1D interpolation code in Figure 7, except that all the loops are fused and that the final code uses low-level C implementations.

We measured the performance of three versions for each kernel: the original version (*orig*) using array abstractions, the *translate-only* version auto-optimized by translating array operations into low level C implementations, and the *trans-late+fusion* version auto-optimized both with array translation and loop fusion. We measured all versions on a Compaq AlphaServer DS20E. Each node has 4GB memory and two 667MHz processors. Each processor has L1 instruction and data caches of 64KB each, and 8MB L2 cache. We used the Compaq vendor C++ compiler with the highest level of optimization, and measured the elapsed-time of each execution.

---

[3] In our experiment, the *Five_Point_Stencil* function is inlined within *Red_Black_Relax*.

Table 1. Interpolation results (different numbers of iterations were run for different problem sizes)

array size	Interp1D				Interp2D				Interp3D			
	orig (sec)	transla te only	translate + fusion	fusion only	orig (sec)	transla te only	translate + fusion	fusion only	orig (sec)	transla te only	translate + fusion	fusion only
50	4.833	1.915	2.131	1.113	7.000	3.034	3.932	1.296	9.166	2.497	3.184	1.275
75	5.000	4.142	4.519	1.091	7.000	2.766	3.131	1.132	9.333	3.021	3.813	1.262
100	5.333	2.593	2.899	1.118	7.000	2.753	3.247	1.179	9.333	2.929	3.767	1.286
125	7.666	2.853	4.228	1.482	9.833	3.304	3.882	1.175	10.666	3.214	4.442	1.382
150	9.166	2.390	4.214	1.763	11.166	2.897	4.542	1.568	12.333	2.871	4.189	1.459
175	11.366	2.630	4.618	1.756	12.833	2.893	4.964	1.716	15.766	3.403	5.264	1.547
200	11.000	2.419	4.289	1.773	14.799	3.161	5.348	1.692	13.799	2.514	4.211	1.675

Table 2. Red-Black Relaxation Results (different numbers of iterations were run for different problem sizes)

array size	RedBlack1D				RedBlack2D				RedBlack3D			
	orig (sec)	transla te only	translate + fusion	fusion only	orig (sec)	transla te only	translate + fusion	fusion only	orig (sec)	transla te only	translate + fusion	fusion only
50	11.500	2.178	5.338	2.451	17.166	1.650	3.344	2.026	22.499	3.260	3.445	1.057
75	14.999	1.728	6.692	3.872	16.666	1.627	3.280	2.016	27.332	3.938	3.776	0.959
100	26.166	3.540	11.852	3.348	32.165	2.672	5.146	1.926	35.665	4.744	4.176	0.880
125	32.499	1.960	12.327	6.289	41.498	2.418	4.421	1.828	45.998	4.685	3.895	0.831
150	35.165	2.865	13.885	4.847	46.665	2.134	4.643	2.176	53.498	5.272	4.440	0.842
175	38.132	2.344	15.270	6.513	52.065	2.514	5.378	2.140	64.531	6.238	5.701	0.914
200	38.598	3.125	15.117	4.838	53.398	2.501	6.117	2.446	67.797	6.703	5.384	0.803

Tables 1 and 2 present our measurements using multiple array sizes. Here column *orig* lists the elapsed time spent executing the original versions written using array abstractions; column *translate-only* lists the speedups from translating array abstractions into low-level C implementations (obtained by dividing execution time of the *orig* with that of *translate-only*); column *translate+fusion* lists the speedups from both array translation and loop fusion; column *fusion-only* lists the results from dividing *translate+fusion* columns with *translate-only* columns, i.e., the speedups from applying loop fusion alone.

From Table 1, in nearly all cases the translation of the array abstractions results in significant improvements. Applying loop fusion improves the performance further by 20%-75%. This validates our belief that loop optimization is a significant step toward fully recovering the performance penalty for using high-level array abstractions.

From Table 2, the dominate performance improvements come from translating array abstractions into low-level implementations(*translate-only*). Loop fusion can further improve performance by the factor of 2.3-6.5 for one and two-dimensional relaxation kernels, but for three-dimensional relaxation, it showed only slight improvement (5%) for small arrays(50) and degraded performance (up to 20%) for large arrays. Here the performance degradation is due to increased register pressures from the much larger fused loop bodies. We are working on better algorithms to selectively apply loop fusion and avoid overly aggressively loop fusion.

The final codes generated by our optimizer are similar to the corresponding C programs that programmers would manually write. Consequently, we believe that their performance would also be similar. Further, because programmers usually don't go out-of-the-way in applying loop optimizations, our techniques can sometimes perform better than hand-written code. This is especially true for the red-black relaxation kernels, where the original loops need to be re-aligned before fusion and a later loop-splitting step is necessary to remove conditionals inside the fused loop nests. Such complex transformations are much more easily and more reliably applied automatically by compilers than manually by programmers.

6   Related Work

Prior research has developed a rich set of loop transformation techniques [18,11,13,8,6] for optimizing scientific applications. However, most of these techniques target only explicit loop computations operating on primitive array types, such as the arrays in Fortran or *restrict* pointers in C. In contrast, we target extending these techniques to optimize high-level user-defined types, whose semantics are obscured from the compiler. Our approach could be sufficient for optimizing general object-oriented array abstractions such as the C++ *valarray* and containers in STL, though we do not yet have results for these abstractions.

Previous work has also attempted to apply high-level optimizations to user-defined abstractions. Specifically, Wu, Midkiff, Moreira and Gupta [20] proposed *semantic inlining*, which allows their compiler to treat user-defined abstractions as primitive types in Java. Artigas, Gupta, Midkiff and Moreira [2] devised an *alias versioning* transformation that creates alias-free regions in Java programs so that loop optimizations can be applied to Java primitive arrays and the array abstractions from their library. Quinlan and Schordan [15] developed a C++ compiler infrastructure and used it to translate abstractions from the A++/P++ array library into lower level loops. Wu and Padua [21] investigated automatic parallelization of loops operating on user-defined containers, but assumed that their compiler knew about the semantics of all operators. All the above approaches apply compiler techniques to optimize library abstractions. However, by encoding the knowledge within their compilers, these specialized compilers cannot be used to optimize abstractions in general other than those in their libraries. In contrast, we target optimizing general user-defined array abstractions by allowing programmers to explicitly communicate with the compiler.

Several other compiler projects have placed significant emphasis on optimizing libraries, especially in the general context of *Telescoping Languages* [5]. The SUIF compiler [16], MPC++ (OpenC++) and *MPC++* [10,7] each provided a programmable level of control over the compilation of applications in support of library optimizations. Other approaches, such as the Broadway compiler [9], uses more general *annotation languages* to guide source code optimizations. However, these frameworks have not focused on applying loop optimizations to object-oriented abstractions.

Template Meta-Programming[17,4] can also optimize user-defined abstractions, but is effective only when optimizations are isolated within a single statement. Loop fusion across statements, which requires dependence analysis, is beyond the capabilities of template meta-programming.

7   Conclusions

Through the classification of array semantics, this paper develops techniques for applying aggressive loop optimizations to general user-defined abstractions. This work shows promise in significantly raising the level of abstraction while eliminating the associated performance penalty. Although we have only demonstrated our approach on C++ array abstractions, which are similar to F90 array constructs, the approach extends to more general object-oriented abstractions.

References

1. R. Allen and K. Kennedy. *Optimizing Compilers for Modern Architectures*. Morgan Kaufmann, San Francisco, October 2001.
2. P. V. Artigas, M. Gupta, S. Midkiff, and J. Moreira. Automatic loop transformations and parallelization for Java. In *Proceedings of the 2000 International Conference on Supercomputing*, May 2000.
3. U. Banerjee. *Dependence Analysis for Supercomputing*. Kluwer Academic Publishers, Boston, 1988.
4. F. Bassetti, K. Davis, and D. Quinlan. A comparison of performance-enhancing strategies for parallel numerical object-oriented frameworks. In I. et al., editor, *International Scientific Computing in Object-Oriented Parallel Environments, IS-COPE 97*, volume 1343 of *LNCS*. Springer, 1997.
5. B. Broom, K. Cooper, J. Dongarra, R. Fowler, D. Gannon, L. Johnsson, K. Kennedy, J. Mellor-Crummey, and L. Torczon. Telescoping languages: A strategy for automatic generation of scientific problem-solving systems from annotated libraries. *Journal of Parallel and Distributed Computing*, 2000.
6. S. Carr and K. Kennedy. Improving the ratio of memory operations to floating-point operations in loops. *ACM Transactions on Programming Languages and Systems*, 16(6):1768–1810, 1994.
7. S. Chiba. Macro processing in object-oriented languages. In *TOOLS Pacific '98, Technology of Object-Oriented Languages and Systems*, 1998.
8. S. Coleman and K. S. McKinley. Tile size selection using cache organization. In *Proceedings of the SIGPLAN Conference on Programming Language Design and Implementation*, La Jolla, CA, June 1995.
9. S. Z. Guyer and C. Lin. An annotation language for optimizing software libraries. *ACM SIGPLAN Notices*, 35(1):39–52, Jan. 2000.
10. e. a. Ishikawa, Y. Design and implementation of metalevel architecture in c++ - mpc++ approach -. April 1996. San Francisco, USA.
11. M. Lam, E. Rothberg, and M. E. Wolf. The cache performance and optimizations of blocked algorithms. In *Proceedings of the Fourth International Conference on Architectural Support for Programming Languages and Operating Systems (ASPLOS-IV)*, Santa Clara, Apr. 1991.
12. M. Lemke and D. Quinlan. P++, a C++ virtual shared grids based programming environment for architecture-independent development of structured grid applications. In *LNCS*. Springer Verlag, 1992. Proceedings of CONPAR/VAPP V.

13. K. S. McKinley, S. Carr, and C.-W. Tseng. Improving data locality with loop transformations. *ACM Transactions on Programming Languages and Systems*, 18(4):424–453, July 1996.
14. D. Quinlan and R. Parsons. A++/p++ array classes for architecture independent finite difference computations. In *Proceedings of the Second Annual Object-Oriented Numerics Conference*, April 1994.
15. D. Quinlan, M. Schordan, B. Philip, and M. Kowarschik. The specification of source-to-source transformations for the compile-time optimization of parallel object-oriented scientific applications. In H. G. Dietz, editor, *Languages and Compilers for Parallel Computing, 14th International Workshop, LCPC 2001, Revised Papers*, volume 2624 of *Lecture Notes in Computer Science*, pages 570–578. Springer Verlag, 2003.
16. M. S. L. S. P. Amarasinghe, J. M. Anderson and C. W. Tseng. The suif compiler for scalable parallel machines. In *in Proceedings of the Seventh SIAM Conference on Parallel Processing for Scientific Computing*, Feb 1995.
17. T. Veldhuizen. Expression templates. In S. Lippmann, editor, *C++ Gems*. Prentice-Hall, 1996.
18. M. E. Wolf and M. Lam. A data locality optimizing algorithm. In *Proceedings of the SIGPLAN Conference on Programming Language Design and Implementation*, Toronto, June 1991.
19. M. J. Wolfe. *Optimizing Supercompilers for Supercomputers*. The MIT Press, Cambridge, 1989.
20. P. Wu, S. P. Midkiff, J. E. Moreira, and M. Gupta. Improving Java performance through semantic inlining. In *Proceedings of the Ninth SIAM Conference on Parallel Processing for Scientific Computing*, Mar 1999.
21. P. Wu and D. Padua. Containers on the parallelization of general-purpose Java programs. In *Proceedings of International Conference on Parallel Architectures and Compilation Techniques*, Oct 1999.
22. Q. Yi, K. Kennedy, and V. Adve. Transforming complex loop nests for locality. *The Journal Of Supercomputing*, 27:219–264, 2004.

MSA: Multiphase Specifically Shared Arrays

Jayant DeSouza and Laxmikant V. Kalé

University of Illinois, Urbana IL 61801, USA
jdesouza@uiuc.edu, kale@cs.uiuc.edu

Abstract. Shared address space (SAS) parallel programming models have faced difficulty scaling to large number of processors. Further, although in some cases SAS programs are easier to develop, in other cases they face difficulties due to a large number of race conditions. We contend that a multi-paradigm programming model comprising a distributed-memory model with a disciplined form of shared-memory programming may constitute a "complete" and powerful parallel programming system. Optimized coherence mechanisms based on the specific access pattern of a shared variable show significant performance benefits over general DSM coherence protocols. We present MSA, a system that supports such specifically shared arrays that can be shared in **read-only**, **write-many**, and **accumulate** modes. These simple modes scale well and are general enough to capture the majority of shared memory access patterns. MSA does not support a general **read-write** access mode, but a single array can be shared in **read-only** mode in one phase and **write-many** in another. MSA coexists with the message-passing paradigm (MPI) and the processor virtualization-based message-driven paradigm(Charm++). We present the model, its implementation, programming examples and preliminary performance results.[1]

1 Introduction

Parallel programming remains a complex task, even though parallel machines and their use in applications has spread widely, especially with deployment of thousands of clusters. The predominant programming paradigm used is message-passing among independent processes (each with its own address space), as embodied in MPI. It is often argued that shared address space (SAS) is an easier method of programming. Although quantitative empirical support for such a statement is lacking, their probably is an intuitive basis for this belief among a section of researchers.

Our experience with a number of parallel applications over the years indicates that there are distinct programming situations where SAS is an easier programming model whereas there are equally distinct situations where it is not. E.g. when there are data races, shared memory paradigm, which allows for a much larger number of distinguishable interleavings of executions of multiple threads,

---

[1] This work was supported in part by the National Institute of Health under Grant NIH PHS 5 P41 RR05969-04 and the local Department of Energy ASCI center under Grant DOE B341494.

R. Eigenmann et al. (Eds.): LCPC 2004, LNCS 3602, pp. 268–282, 2005.

tends to be a difficult paradigm. In contrast, in a computation such as matrix multiply, where the data in input matrices is only read, and data in the output matrix is only written, is relatively easier to express in SAS. Further, since SAS views all data as uniformly accessible, it does not lend itself to locality-conscious programming, which is needed for efficiency.

We suggest that the problems with SAS are due to trying to do everything (i.e. all kinds of information exchange between processes) with SAS. It may be more productive to incorporate SAS as a *part* of a programming model that also allows private data for each thread, and mechanisms for synchronization and data-exchange such as message-passing or method-invocations. This frees us to support only those SAS access modes that can be efficiently and scalably supported on distributed memory machines including clusters, without being encumbered by having to support a "complete" programming model.

Which access modes can be efficiently supported? `read-only` accesses, `write-many` accesses (where each location is updated by at most one thread), and `accumulate` accesses (where multiple threads may update a single location, but only via a well-defined commutative associative operation) seem to be the obvious candidates. The idea of distinguishing between access patterns was studied in Munin[2] and also in Chare Kernel[8,21] (the precursor to Charm[13,14]) and is used in TreadMarks/NOW[16]. The generalized notion of accumulate accesses (see Section 1) is relatively new, although compiler research (e.g. Polaris[4]) has often focused on identifying commutative-associative operations.

Another observation stemming from our application studies is that the access pattern for the same data changes distinctly between computation phases. For example, a matrix multiply operation (C = AxB) may calculate a C matrix in Phase I of the computation (where A and B matrices are accessed in read-only manner, and C is written-only or accumulated), whereas in the phase II, C matrix may be used in a read-only manner while A and B may be updated. These phases may then iterate.

This suggests the idea of *multi-phase shared arrays*. For each array, the programmer specifies its access mode, and may change it between phases. The phases may be separated by array-specific synchronizations such as barrier (as in release consistency).

The restricted set of operations simplifies the consistency protocol and traffic associated with that: no invalidations are needed, all writes can be buffered, etc. For all other operations not covered, one is free to use other mechanisms such as message passing.

One of the original motivations for this work was computations performed at initialization, where efficiency is less important, and coding productivity is the dominant consideration. However, it quickly became clear that the method is useful more broadly beyond initialization. Of course, such broad use requires more serious consideration of efficiency issues. With "prefetch" calls (See Section 2) , we provide efficiency comparable to that of local array accesses. Further, one of the costs of DSM systems is the long latency on "misses". Processor virtualization techniques that we have been exploring in Charm++ and Adaptive

MPI (AMPI)[9] allow many user-level (lightweight) threads per processor, which help tolerate such latencies.

The MSA abstraction has been implemented as a library in Charm++ and AMPI, and as a language-level feature in a compiler-supported parallel language called Jade [7]. Compiler support enables us to automatically do optimizations which have to be done manually by MSA users (such as inserting prefetches).

2   MSA Description

Conceptually, an MSA is an array of data elements that can be globally accessed in an MIMD program in one of several dynamically chosen global access modes and in units of a user-defined page size. The modes are not expected to be fixed for the lifetime of an array, but for a phase of execution of the program. MSA's are implemented as a templated, object-oriented C++ class. Currently 1D and 2D MSA arrays are supported.

The elements of an MSA can be one of the standard C++ built-in types, or a user-defined class with certain operations. The number of elements in the MSA is specified in the constructor when the MSA is created. Currently, an MSA cannot be resized once created.

For complicated element types (such as linked lists), a `pup()` method must be defined by the user for the element type: this is used to pack and unpack the element when pages are shipped around. This allows each element to be a linked list or other variable sized data structure. (More details of the *PUP* framework can be found in [12].)

Internally, the MSA array is split up into "pages" of a user-defined size. The page size is user specified for each MSA at the time the MSA is created. The page size is specified as a number of elements and can range from one element to the total number of elements in the array. For 2D MSA arrays, the data layout can also be specified at creation time. Currently, row-major and column-major data layouts are supported, and we plan to support block partitioned layout.

The array of "pages" is implemented as a Charm++ `ChareArray` object. `ChareArray` objects are managed by the Charm++ runtime system (RTS); they can be migrated across processors under the control of the RTS and can participate in system-wide load-balancing based on communication patterns, computational load, etc.[15]

The MSA runtime system on each processor fetches and replicates remote pages into local memory on demand, or instantiates blank local copies of remote pages when needed, based on the mode (described below) of the MSA. The amount of local memory so used (the *local cache*) on each processor can be constrained by the user for each MSA. When the local cache fills up, pages are flushed out using a user-defined page replacement policy. A default policy is provided that keeps track of a few most recently used pages and flushes out any page not listed there.

The MSA is globally accessed in one of several *access modes*, which can be changed dynamically over the life of the program. The mode of an MSA is set implicitly by the first operation (read, write, or accumulate) on it after a `sync` or `enroll`. Each phase of execution in a particular mode is terminated by running a `sync` operation on the array.

The modes supported are `read-only`, `write-many` and `accumulate`, and have been chosen for simplicity and efficient implementation.

In the `read-only` mode, the elements of the array are only read by the worker threads. `read-only` is efficiently implemented by replicating pages of the array on each processor on demand. Reading a page that is not available locally causes the accessing thread to block until the page is available. User-level or compiler-inserted explicit `prefetch` calls can be used to improve performance. Since the page is read-only, no invalidates or updates need to be propagated.

In the `write-many` mode, all threads are permitted to write to the elements of an MSA, but to different elements, i.e. at most one thread is permitted to write to any particular index. `write-many` is efficiently implemented by instantiating a blank local copy of an accessed page on all processors that need the page. No page data and no page invalidates or updates need to be communicated during the phase. The MSA runtime on each processor keeps track of which elements of the page are written, in a local bit-vector. At the end of the phase, the changed data in the local cache are forwarded to the above-mentioned `ChareArray` page object, where they are merged.

In the `accumulate` mode, multiple threads can perform an accumulate operation on any given element. `accumulate` is implemented by accumulating the data into a local copy of the page on each processor, (instantiated on first access), and combining these local values at the end of the phase. Once again, no page data or coherence traffic is transmitted during the phase.

The commutative-associative operation to be used in an `accumulate` is specified at creation of the MSA. In addition, it can be changed at any time by invoking a method of the MSA. Accumulation using the common addition, product and max operations is provided via built-in types. For the general case, setting the `accumulate` operation involves passing in a class that contains `accumulate()` and `getIdentity()` methods. This allows the user to define the accumulate operation. In combination with the `pup` framework, `accumulate` can handle complex operations such as set union, appending to a hash table in which each element is a linked list, and so on.

The user is responsible for correctness and coherence; e.g., if an array is in `write-many` mode, the user must ensure that two processors do not write to the same location. The system assists by detecting errors at run-time.

At startup, the threads accessing an MSA must perform an `enroll` operation for the system to detect the number of worker threads on each processor.

When accessing data, the user does not need to check if data is available in the local cache or not. Unlike DSM, MSA does not use VM hardware page faults to detect whether a local copy of the data exists. Thus, MSA page sizes are not tied to the VM page size but can be controlled by the user as described above. In principle, every MSA access is checked for whether the data is local or remote with an `if`. Since this is expensive, using compiler support in Jade we strip-mine *for* loops and use local (non-checked) accesses within a page.

3   Example Programs

3.1   Matrix Multiplication

The pseudocode for a matrix-matrix multiplication using a straighforward row-wise decomposition is as follows (assuming $N * N$ matrices and P processors):

```
for i=1..N/P       // Rows of A matrix
  for j=1..N       // Columns of B matrix
    for k=1..N
      result += A[i][k] * B[k][j]
    C[i][j] = result
```

The i dimension is shared among the worker threads. Thus in this case, each thread will request a subset of the rows of A and C, and the entire B matrix. If all matrices are $N * N$ matrices, the required number of elements required by each of P processors works out to $N^2 + 2N^2/P$.

Relevant sections of the corresponding MSA program are shown in Fig. 1. 2D MSA arrays are used in this example. We use row-major data layout for the A and C matrices, and column-major for the B matrix. The page size for each MSA (i.e. the minimum number of elements fetched) is specified when defining the MSA (lines 1–2). In this case we set it to 5000, in order to fetch an entire row of A or C, or column of B. (We could set B's page size to the number of elements in B, and that would fetch the entire B matrix into local memory upon the first access to it.) The page size is often a crucial parameter for performance. The per processor cache size is specified when instantiating the MSA (lines 5–7). We set the cache size to hold at least the number of elements calculated above, unless it is too large a number to fit in the available memory. (The MSA API has not been finalized yet, and it is likely that the template parameters will be reduced.)

Next, consider the following pseudocode for a block decomposition matrix product:

```
for i= subsection of size N/sqrt(P) // Rows of A matrix
  for j= subsection of size N/sqrt(P)  // Columns of B matrix
    for k=1..N
      result += A[i][k] * B[k][j]
    C[i][j] = result
```

Here too, one thread is solely responsible for an element of C and **write-many** mode suffices. The number of elements required by each processor is $2N^2/\sqrt{P}$.

Finally, consider the case where we decompose in the k-dimension as well.

```
for i=subsection of size N/cuberoot{P}     // Rows of A matrix
  for j=subsection of size N/cuberoot{P}     // Columns of B matrix
    for k=subsection of size N/cuberoot{P}
      result += A[i][k] * B[k][j]
    C[i][j].accumulate(result);
```

Here, the MSA **accumulate** mode comes in useful. An *Add* accumulator class can be specified as the default when creating the C MSA. MSA also provides templated *Null*, *Product*, *Max* and *Min* Accumulators.) The number of elements required by each processor reduces from the previous case to $2N^2/P^{2/3}$.

```
1    typedef MSA2D<double, MSA_NullA<double>, 5000,MSA_ROW_MAJOR>
2    MSA2DRowMjr; typedef MSA2D<double, MSA_SumA<double>,
3    5000,MSA_COL_MAJOR> MSA2DColMjr;
4
5    // One thread/process creates and broadcasts the MSA's
6    MSA2DRowMjr arr1(ROWS1, COLS1, NUMWORKERS, cacheSize1); // row
7    major MSA2DColMjr arr2(ROWS2, COLS2, NUMWORKERS, cacheSize2); //
8    column major MSA2DRowMjr prod(ROWS1, COLS2, NUMWORKERS,
9    cacheSize3); //product matrix
10
11   // broadcast the above array handles to the worker threads.
12   ...
13
14   // Each thread executes the following code
15   arr1.enroll(numWorkers); // barrier arr2.enroll(numWorkers); //
16   barrier prod.enroll(numWorkers); // barrier
17
18   while(iterate) {
19       for(unsigned int c = 0; c < COLS2; c++) {
20           // Each thread computes a subset of rows of product matrix
21           for(unsigned int r = rowStart; r <= rowEnd; r++) {
22
23               double result = 0.0;
24               for(unsigned int k = 0; k < cols1; k++)
25                   result += arr1[r][k] * arr2[k][c];
26
27               prod[r][c] = result;
28           }
29       }
30
31       prod.sync();
32       // use product matrix here
33   }
```

Fig. 1. MSA Matrix Multiplication Code in Jade

3.2   Molecular Dynamics

In classical molecular dynamics based on cut-off distance (without any bonds, for this example), forces between atoms are computed in each timestep. If two atoms are beyond a cutoff distance the force calculation is not done (to save computational cost, since force drops as a square of the distance). After adding forces due to all atoms within the cutoff radius, one calculates new positions for each atom using Newtonian mechanics.

The pseudocode for a particular molecular dynamics algorithm using MSA is shown below. The key data structures used are:

- coords [i]: a vector of coordinates (x,y,z values) for each atom i.
- forces [i]: a vector containing forces (x,y,z values) on atom i.
- atomInfo [i]: a struct/class with basic read-only information about each atom such as its mass and charge.
- nbrList: nbrList [i][j] is true if the two atoms are within a cutoff distance (neighbors).

There are three phases in each timestep. The atomInfo array is read-only in all phases. During the force computation phase, the forces array is write-many whereas the coords array is read-only; while during the integration phase, this is reversed. Every 8 steps (here) we recalculate the `nbrList` in phase III, where `nbrList` is `write-many` and `coords` is `read-only`. The code assumes a block partitioning of the force matrix as suggested by Saltz[10] or Plimpton[19], for example.

```
1   // Declarations of the 3 arrays
2   class XYZ; // { double  x; double y; double z; }
3   typedef MSA1D<XYZ, MSA_SumA<XYZ>, DEFAULT_PAGE_SIZE> XyzMSA;
4   class AtomInfo;
5   typedef MSA1D<AtomInfo, MSA_SumA<AtomInfo>,
6                     DEFAULT_PAGE_SIZE> AtomInfoMSA;
7   typedef MSA2D<int, MSA_NullA<int>,
8                     DEFAULT_PAGE_SIZE, MSA_ROW_MAJOR> NeighborMSA;
9
10  XyzMSA coords;
11  XyzMSA forces;
12  AtomInfoMSA atominfo;
13  NeighborMSA nbrList;
14
15  //broadcast the above array handles to the worker threads.
16  ...
17
18  // Each thread executes the following code
19  coords.enroll(numberOfWorkerThreads);
20  forces.enroll(numberOfWorkerThreads);
21  atominfo.enroll(numberOfWorkerThreads);
22  nbrList.enroll(numberOfWorkerThreads);
23
24  for  timestep = 0 to Tmax {
25    /**************** Phase I ****************/
26    // for a section of the interaction matrix
27    for i = i_start to i_end
28      for j = j_start to j_end
29        if (nbrlist[i][j]) { // nbrlist enters ReadOnly mode
30          force = calculateForce(coords[i], atominfo[i],
31                            coords[j], atominfo[j]);
32          forces[i] += force; // Accumulate mode
33          forces[j] += -force;
34        }
35    nbrlist.sync(); forces.sync();  coords.sync(); atominfo.sync();
36
37    /**************** Phase II ****************/
38    for k = myAtomsbegin to myAtomsEnd
39      coords[k] = integrate(atominfo[k], forces[k]); // WriteOnly mode
40    coords.sync(); atominfo.sync(); forces.sync();
41
42    /**************** Phase III ****************/
43    if (timestep %8 == 0) { // update neighbor list every 8 steps
44      // update nbrList with a loop similar to the force loop above
45      ... nbrList[i][j] = distance(coords[i], coords[j]) < CUTOFF;
46
47      nbrList.sync(); coords.sync();
48    }
49  }
```

3.3 FEM Graph Partitioning

As an example of the power of the generalized `accumulate` operation, we present a part of a program that deals with an unstructured mesh for a finite-elemment method (FEM) computation. Here, the mesh connectivity data is available at input in the `EtoN` array: for each element i, the `EtoN` [i] contains 3 node numbers (we assume triangular elements). The objective is produce `EtoE` array, where

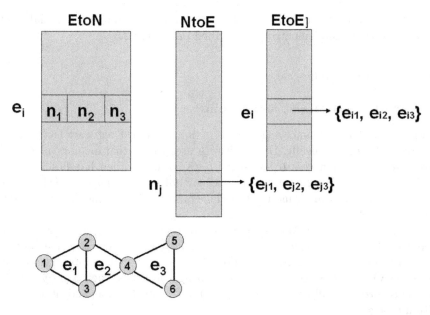

Fig. 2. FEM Graph Partitioning Example

EtoE [i] contains all element (numbers) that are neighbors of E. E_1 is said to be a neighbor of E_2 if they share a common node. So, e2 and e3 are neighbors because they share Node 4.

The algorithm for doing this using MSA proceeds in two phases. In the first phase, an intermediate array NtoE is created by accumulation: NtoE [j] contains all elements that have n_j as their node. To construct this, each thread processes a section of the EtoN array. In the second phase, $e_1, e_2 \in NtoE[j]$ are set to be neighbors of each other.

```
1   // Phase I: EtoN: RO, NtoE: Accu
2   for i=1 to EtoN.length()
3     for j=1 to EtoN[i].length()
4       n = EtoN[i][j];
5       NtoE[n] += i; // Accumulate
6   EtoN.sync(); NtoE.sync();
7
8   // Phase II: NtoE: RO, EtoE: Accu
9   for j = my section of j
10    //foreach pair e1, e2 elementof NtoE[j]
11    for i1 = 1 to NtoE[j].length()
12      for i2 = i1 + 1 to NtoE[j].length()
13        e1 = NtoE[j][i1];
14        e2 = NtoE[j][i2];
15        EtoE[e1] += e2; // Accumulate
16        EtoE[e2] += e1;
17  EtoN.sync(); NtoE.sync();
```

Note that the `accumulate` operations in lines 5, 15 and 16 are actually set-union operations, implemented as described in Section 2.

4   Related Work

4.1   DSM, TreadMarks, and Munin

Distributed Shared Memory (DSM) is a much-studied software-level shared memory solution. Typically, DSM software uses the virtual memory page fault hardware to detect access to non-local data, which it then handles. It works at the page level, fetching and delivering virtual memory pages. DSM uses relaxed consistency memory models to reduce false sharing overheads and improve performance.[11,1]

Munin[2,3] and TreadMarks[16] are DSM implementations. TreadMarks implements the *release consistency* memory model, which typically does not require any additional synchronization over a general shared memory (sequential consistency) program. To reduce false sharing overheads, their *multiple-writer* coherence protocol allows multiple threads to write to independent locations within a page.

Munin takes such coherence optimizations further, and identifies several access modes with correspondingly efficient coherence protocols, as follows:

- *Synchronization:* Global locks were optimized by using a local proxy to minimize global communication.
- *Private:* No coherence.
- *Write-once* These are read-only after initialization. Optimized by replication.
- *Result:* Read by only one thread. Optimized by maintaining a single copy and propagating updates to it.
- *Producer-Consumer:* Optimized by eager update of copies.
- *Migratory:* Optimized by migrating the object.
- *Write-many:* Optimized by a multiple-writer protocol.
- *Read-mostly:* Optimized by replication.
- *General Read-Write:* Uses standard coherence protocol.

Their study of several shared memory programs and their performance results relative to message-passing are impressive and appear to validate their idea of "adaptive cache coherence"[5].

Munin's modes were applied on both a per-object and a per-variable basis. While TreadMarks attempts to maintain the illusion of a general shared address space, Munin requires the programmer to specify the mode for each variable. This was done at compile time and so a variable's mode could not change during the program, and only statically allocated memory was supported. Munin put each shared variable on a separate page of virtual memory.

Comparison: Munin is designed to be a complete shared memory programming model rather than the blended model of MSA. MSA supports Munin's Private and Write-many modes, and introduces a new `accumulate` mode and prefetching commands. Munin's Write-once, Result, and Read-Mostly modes seem to be of limited use, since synchronization will be required at the application level before accessing the updated data; which leads us to believe that these modes are an artifact of Munin's static style of specifying modes. MSA accomplishes these modes by dynamically specifying a `write-many` mode followed by a `read-only` mode. Munin's Producer-Consumer mode with its eager update offers unique features, but, again, given the need for synchronization, a message send might be more efficient. MSA does not support the General Read-Write or the Read-mostly modes.

Specifying portions of an array to be in different modes is not supported in MSA, but this cannot be done in Munin either because of the static specification. Munin's granularity for data movement is the size of a VM page; whereas MSA works physically on a user-defined page size. MSA's user-defined physical page size allows the "page" to be as small as one element, or as large as several rows of a matrix allowing the user (or Jade compiler) to optimize for the expected access pattern. Munin's modes are static, whereas MSA arrays can change their mode dynamically over the life of the program, which leads to needing fewer modes. Furthermore, MSA supports row-major, column-major, and (in the future) other array layouts, which can further improve performance.

DSM systems suffer considerable latency on "misses" and provide no latency tolerance mechanisms since control transfers to the DSM software in kernel space. MSA is implemented in user space, and Charm++'s virtual processors (user level threads) can tolerate latency by scheduling another virtual processor when one thread suffers a "page" miss.

DSM uses page fault hardware to detect non-local access; MSA checks each data access (similar to Global Arrays) and we need to study the cost of this detection mechanism. MSA also has operations that work on data that is known to be available locally (e.g. using `prefetch`), and the Jade compiler can generate code for some such cases. When combined with MSA's prefetch feature, we expect that the efficiency of array element access will approach that of sequential programs.

4.2   Specifically Shared Variables in Charm

Charm (and its earlier version, the Chare Kernel) supported a disciplined form of shared variables by providing abstractions for commonly used modes in which information is shared in parallel programs. [13,14]. The modes were readonly (replicated on all processors), writeOnce, accumulator, monotonic variable (useful in branch-and-bound, for example), and distributed tables (basically, read-only or writeonce, with distributed storage and caching). However, unlike MSA, it does not support the notion of phases, nor that of pages. Further, the original version did not have threads, and so supported only a split phase interface to distributed tables.

4.3   Global Arrays

The Global Arrays project[18], like ours, attempts to combine the portability and efficiency of distributed memory programming with the programmability of shared memory programming. It allows individual processes of an MIMD program to "asynchronously access logical blocks of physically distributed matrices" without requiring the application code on the other side to participate in the transfer. GA typically uses RDMA[6] and one-sided communication primitives to transfer data efficiently. GA coexists with MPI.

Each block is local to exactly one process, and each process can determine which block is local. GA provides get, put, accumulate (float sum-reduction), and int read-increment operations on individual elements of the array. The GA *synchronization* operation completes all pending transfers. *fence* completes all transfers this process initiated. Global Arrays does not implement coherence. It is the user's responsibility to guard shared access by using synchronization operations.

In GA one-sided communication is used to access a block owned by a remote processor: there is no automatic replication or caching of remote data. The user explicitly fetches remote data for extended local access and then directly accesses the data. This mode of access reduces programming simplicity when using GA's, especially if accessing data irregularly across the entire GA. GA RDMA operations are provided to access data remotely in such cases without fetching a block of data, but at the cost of reduced performance, since every data access is then checked (with an if) and redirected to a local or non-local version of the operation.

Comparison: In shared-memory terminology, it appears that GA maintains a single copy of each "page" and either requires the user to fetch the page for efficient local access, or propagates updates to the remote page quickly using RDMA. For the former case, MSA's prefetch operation provides the same benefits, and for amenable access patterns the strip-mining compiler optimization allows the user to skip using prefetch; and for the latter case, MSA's modes allow optimizations that GA cannot support. Like MSA, GA does not tie the "page" size to the VM page size. It allows the "page" to migrate to be closer (i.e. local) to an accessing process. GA seems well-suited to certain access patterns, but, for example, implementing write-many on GA would involve a lot of unnecessary RDMA operations, and the lack of replication makes reading of elements on a "page" by many threads inefficient. The GA accumulate does not support variable-sized elements/pages.

4.4   HPF and Others

Other approaches that deal with similar issues include implementation strategies for HPF. For example, the inspector-executor idea [20,17] allows one to prefetch data sections that are needed by subsequent loop iterations.

Titanium[22] translates Java into C. It adds a global address space and multi-dimensional titanium arrays to Java and is especially suited to grid-structured computations. Each processor on a distributed memory machine maintains its data in a local demesne, and variables can be declared to limit access to only the local demesne of data, or to have unrestricted global access. Several compiler analyses are performed, including identifying references to objects on the local processor. Barriers and data exchange operations are used for global synchronization.

5   Performance Study

As a preliminary performance study, we present results for the row-wise decomposition matrix multiplication program shown in Section 3.1.

Figure 3 shows the speedup for a 2000x5000x300 matrix multiplication on NCSA's Tungsten cluster. When there are 8 threads per processor, the latency of page misses by one thread is better hidden by overlapping with computations for another thread. This effect (the benefit of processor virtualization) can be clearly seen by comparing results for 1 and 8 threads per processor. With a much larger number of threads per processor (32 or 64) the scheduling overhead and fine-grained communication lead to worse performance, although a more detailed study is needed to ascertain that. It should be noted that raw performance is currently unoptimized. With further optimizations, we expect the times to decrease but possibly speedups may decrease.

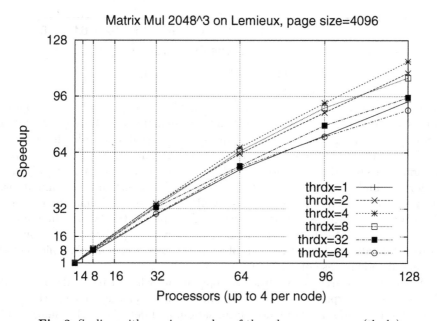

Fig. 3. Scaling with varying number of threads per processor (thrdx)

Figure 4 shows the effect of limiting cache size: with a smaller cache, the time is almost twice as large as that with an adequately large cache. Smaller caches reduce the reuse of fetched data.

6   Summary and Future Work

We described a restricted shared address space programming model called multiphase shared arrays (MSA), its implementation and its use via examples. MSA is not a complete model, and is intended to be used in conjunction with other

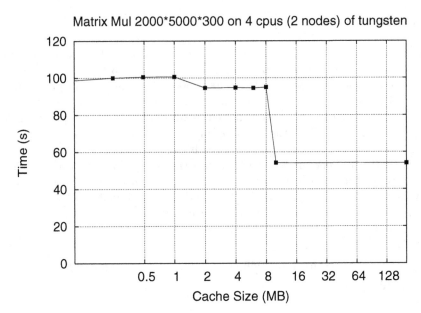

Fig. 4. Effect of MSA software cache size

information-exchange paradigms such as message passing. It currently supports only 3 modes: read-only, write-many and accumulate. One important idea in MSA is that the modes for each array can change dynamically in different phases of the program separated by synchronization points. The generalized `accumulate` operation supported by MSA is powerful, and is especially useful for accumulating sets, in addition to the more common use in summations. MSA is implemented in Charm++ and AMPI, which support many light-weight threads (virtual processors) per processor. As a result, the latency inherent in page misses is better tolerated. Further, we provide a prefetch operation and correspondingly specialized versions of array accesses, which attains efficiency of sequential code in case of prefetched data.

We plan to search for additional applications where this model is useful. Further, we will explore and support additional access modes beyond the three supported currently. Performance optimization, and detailed performance studies are also planned. We hope that a mixed mode model such as MSA will lead to substantial improvement in programmer productivity, and bridge the current divide between SAS and distributed memory programming styles. Further, compiler support is crucial to simplifying use of MSA, which we plan to explore in the context of the ongoing Jade programming language.

Acknowledgements

The authors wish to acknowledge the work of Rahul Joshi on implementing an initial version of MSA, and Orion Lawlor for improving the MSA API and performance.

References

1. S. V. Adve and K. Gharachorloo. Shared memory consistency models: A tutorial. *IEEE Computer*, 29(12):66–76, 1996.
2. J. K. Bennett, J. B. Carter, and W. Zwaenepoel. Munin: Distributed shared memory based on type-specific memory coherence. In *Proc. of the Second ACM SIGPLAN Symp. on Principles and Practice of Parallel Programming (PPOPP'90)*, pages 168–177, 1990.
3. J. K. Bennett, J. B. Carter, and W. Zwaenepoel. Adaptive software cache management for distributed shared memory architectures. In I. Tartalja and V. Milutinovic, editors, *The cache coherence problem in shared memory multiprocessors: software solutions.* IEEE Computer Society Press, 1995.
4. W. Blume, R. Eigenmann, K. Faigin, J. Grout, J. Hoeflinger, D. Padua, P. Petersen, B. Pottenger, L. Rauchwerger, P. Tu, and S. Weatherford. Polaris: Improving the effectiveness of parallelizing compilers. In *Proceedings of 7th International Workshop on Languages and Compilers for Parallel Computing*, number 892 in Lecture Notes in Computer Science, pages 141–154, Ithaca, NY, USA, August 1994. Springer-Verlag.
5. J. B. Carter, J. K. Bennett, and W. Zwaenepoel. Techniques for reducing consistency-related communications in distributed shared memory systems. *ACM Transactions on Computers*, 13(3):205–243, Aug. 1995.
6. A. Cohen. RDMA offers low overhead, high speed. *Network World*, March 2003. URL http://www.nwfusion.com/news/tech/2003/0324tech.html.
7. J. DeSouza and L. V. Kalé. Jade: A parallel message-driven Java. In *Proc. Workshop on Java in Computational Science, held in conjunction with the International Conference on Computational Science (ICCS 2003)*, Melbourne, Australia and Saint Petersburg, Russian Federation, June 2003.
8. W. Fenton, B. Ramkumar, V. Saletore, A. Sinha, and L. Kale. Supporting machine independent programming on diverse parallel architectures. In *Proceedings of the International Conference on Parallel Processing*, pages 193–201, St. Charles, IL, Aug. 1991.
9. C. Huang, O. Lawlor, and L. V. Kalé. Adaptive MPI. In *Proceedings of the 16th International Workshop on Languages and Compilers for Parallel Computing (LCPC 03)*, College Station, Texas, October 2003.
10. Y.-S. Hwang, R. Das, J. Saltz, M. Hodoscek, and B. Brooks. Parallelizing Molecular Dynamics Programs for Distributed Memory Machines. *IEEE Computational Science & Engineering*, 2(2):18–29, Summer 1995.
11. L. Iftode and J. P. Singh. Shared virtual memory: Progress and challenges. *Proc. of the IEEE, Special Issue on Distributed Shared Memory*, 87(3):498–507, 1999.
12. R. Jyothi, O. S. Lawlor, and L. V. Kale. Debugging support for Charm++. In *PADTAD Workshop for IPDPS 2004*, page 294. IEEE Press, 2004.
13. L. Kalé and S. Krishnan. CHARM++: A Portable Concurrent Object Oriented System Based on C++. In A. Paepcke, editor, *Proceedings of OOPSLA'93*, pages 91–108. ACM Press, September 1993.
14. L. V. Kale and S. Krishnan. Charm++: Parallel Programming with Message-Driven Objects. In G. V. Wilson and P. Lu, editors, *Parallel Programming using C++*, pages 175–213. MIT Press, 1996.

15. L. V. Kale and S. Krishnan. Charm++: Parallel Programming with Message-Driven Objects. In G. V. Wilson and P. Lu, editors, *Parallel Programming using C++*, pages 175–213. MIT Press, 1996.
16. P. Keleher, S. Dwarkadas, A. L. Cox, and W. Zwaenepoel. Treadmarks: Distributed shared memory on standard workstations and operating systems. In *Proc. of the Winter 1994 USENIX Conference*, pages 115–131, 1994.
17. C. Koelbel and P. Mehrotra. Compiling global name-space parallel loops for distributed execution. *IEEE Trans. on Parallel and Distributed systems*, 2(4):440–451, 1991.
18. J. Nieplocha, R. J. Harrison, and R. J. Littlefield. Global arrays: A non-uniform-memory-access programming model for high-performance computers. In *Journal of Supercomputing*, volume 10, pages 169–189, 1996.
19. S. J. Plimpton and B. A. Hendrickson. A new parallel method for molecular-dynamics simulation of macromolecular systems. *J Comp Chem*, 17:326–337, 1996.
20. J. Saltz, K. Crowley, R. Mirchandaney, and H. Berryman. Run-time scheduling and execution of loops on message passing machines. *Journal of Parallel and Distributed Computing*, 8:303–312, 1990.
21. A. Sinha and L. Kalé. Information Sharing Mechanisms in Parallel Programs. In H. Siegel, editor, *Proceedings of the 8th International Parallel Processing Symposium*, pages 461–468, Cancun, Mexico, April 1994.
22. K. A. Yelick, L. Semenzato, G. Pike, C. Miyamoto, B. Liblit, A. Krishnamurthy, P. N. Hilfinger, S. L. Graham, D. Gay, P. Colella, and A. Aiken. Titanium: A high-performance Java dialect. *Concurrency: Practice and Experience*, 10(11–13), September – November 1998.

Supporting SQL-3 Aggregations on Grid-Based Data Repositories

Li Weng*, Gagan Agrawal*, Umit Catalyurek[†], and Joel Saltz[†]

* Department of Computer Science and Engineering
[†] Department of Biomedical Informatics,
Ohio State University, Columbus OH 43210

Abstract. There is an increasing trends towards distributed and shared repositories for storing scientific datasets. Developing applications that retrieve and process data from such repositories involves a number of challenges. First, these data repositories store data in complex, low-level layouts, which should be abstracted from application developers. Second, as data repositories are shared resources, part of the computations on the data must be performed at a different set of machines than the ones hosting the data. Third, because of the volume of data and the amount of computations involved, parallel configurations need to be used for both hosting the data and the processing on the retrieved data.

In this paper, we describe a system for executing SQL-3 queries over scientific data stored as flat-files. A relational table-based virtual view is supported on these flat-file datasets. The class of queries we consider involve data retrieval using Select and Where clauses, and processing with user-defined aggregate functions and group-bys. We use a middleware system STORM for providing much of the low-level functionality. Our compiler analyzes the SQL-3 queries and generates many of the functions required by this middleware. Our experimental results show good scalability with respect to the number of nodes as well as the dataset size.

1 Introduction

One of the major recent developments in the areas of scientific and high-end computing is the emergence of *data-driven* applications. Scientific simulations and increasing numbers of high precision data collection instruments (e.g. sensors attached to satellites or medical imaging modalities) are creating very large datasets. The emergence of grid computing and other technological trends are enabling storage, sharing, and processing of very large scientific datasets. Key to this vision are remote and shared data repositories, which store large scientific datasets, and can allow retrieval and even processing of this data. However, realizing this vision also involves a number of challenges.

The first challenge is that scientific datasets are typically stored as binary or character flat-files. Such *low-level* layouts enable compact storage and efficient processing. The use of relational or other database technologies typically involves significant overheads, which may not be justified for scientific datasets that are updated only very infrequently. Therefore, they have typically not been very popular in most scientific communities. The use of low-level and specialized data formats, however, makes the specification of processing much harder. Clearly, it is very desirable to support high-level abstractions of the datasets for the application developers.

R. Eigenmann et al. (Eds.): LCPC 2004, LNCS 3602, pp. 283–298, 2005.

The second challenge arises because of the shared nature of the data repositories. The processing of the data should preferably be carried out at a different set of machines than the ones hosting the data. Thus, the data processing application needs to be broken into a phase that executes on site(s) hosting the data, and phase(s) that execute on other machines.

The third challenge arises because of the scale of the data and the associated computations. The size of scientific datasets can easily be in tera-bytes. Medium and large scale clusters are already being used for hosting large scientific repositories. Similarly, it is desirable to use parallel and/or distributed configurations for carrying out the processing associated with these applications.

This paper describes a compilation-based system addressing the above challenges for a class of applications. We support a relational table abstraction of complex multi-dimensional scientific datasets. Using this abstraction, data subsetting and processing applications can be specified using SQL-3. We can support applications for which data subsetting could be specified using SQL's Select and Where clauses, and processing could be specified with user-defined aggregate functions and group-bys.

Starting from such queries, we retrieve data hosted in a low-level layout on a cluster, and perform the computations on another parallel configuration. This is achieved through a combination of techniques. The low-level layout of the data is described to the compiler using a meta-data description language. The compiler parses these descriptors and generates efficient data subsetting and access functions. By analyzing the SQL-3 code, we also generate aggregation functions that carry out the desired processing. Much of the low-level functionality is provided by a middleware, called STORM [8,7]. We have evaluated our system using two scientific data processing applications. Our results show good scalability with respect to number of nodes as well as the dataset size.

The rest of the paper is organized as follows. Section 2 gives an overview of our system, and also describes motivating applications and example queries. Section 3 describes the meta-data description language that we use. Compiler analysis and code generation is the focus of Section 4. Experimental evaluation is presented in Section 5. We compare our work with related research efforts in Section 6 and conclude in Section 7.

2   Overview of the System and Motivating Applications

In this section, we give an overview of our system. We also describe some of the applications that have motivated this work, and give details of the STORM runtime system we use.

2.1   System Overview

Scientific applications frequently involve large multi-dimensional datasets. Particularly, the data generated by scientific simulations or the data collected from scientific instruments involves spatial and temporal coordinates. Scientists are typically interested in processing a subset of a dataset. The criteria used for subsetting can include one or more of the following: 1) range of spatial and/or temporal coordinates, 2) parameters used for a specific simulation, 3) the set of attributes that are of interest, and 4) value of one or more of the attributes of interest.

CREATE FUNCTION < *func* > (< *AGG_status* >, < *Dataset Name* >) RETURNS < *rettype* > AS '
        < *SQL statementlist* >
' LANGUAGE SQL;

CREATE AGGREGATE < *AGG_name* > (BASETYPE = < *Dataset Name* > ,
        SFUNC = < *sfunc* > ,
        STYPE = < *state_type* > ,
        [, FINALFUNC = < *ffunc* > ,]
        [, INITCOND = < *initial_condition* >])

SELECT < *attributelist* > , < *AGG_name(Dataset Name)* >
        FROM < *Dataset Name* >
        WHERE < *Expression* >
        GROUP BY < *group-by attributelist* >

Fig. 1. Canonical Query Structure

If a dataset is stored as a flat-file or a set of flat-files, a user will need to have a detailed understanding of the layout to be able to select the values of interest. The first premise of our work is that a virtual relational table view and SQL queries with Select and Where clauses on such a virtual view provide a very convenient yet powerful mechanism for specifying subsets of interest. The second premise of our work is that processing of interest can often be specified through user-defined *aggregate* functions and group-bys in SQL-3.

Figure 1 shows the canonical structure of the queries we target. Initially, let us focus on the Select clause. The *attributelist* as part of the *Select* clause is used for specifying the attributes of interest. The use of *Where* further extends the subsetting ability. The use of aggregate function *AGG_name* , which is based on a user-defined function, allows derived values to be computed. The use of *group-by* enables an aggregate value to be computed for each combination of values of attributes from the *group-by attributelist*.

The aggregate function we compile is part of SQL-3 versions supported by many databases, including the PostgreSQL system, Informix system, Oracle 9i, and IBM DB2. The specification of an aggregate function includes the dataset on which aggrega-

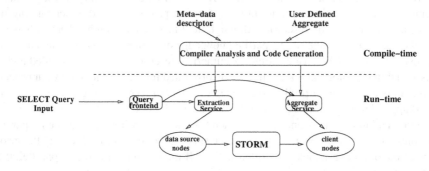

Fig. 2. Overview of Our System

tion is carried out, a user-defined function *sfunc* that is applied on each tuple of interest, the type of the *aggregate status variable*, a finalization function, and an initial value of the aggregate status variable. The semantics of an aggregate function are as follows. A list of tuples of interest is collected and the aggregate status variable is initialized. Then, we process each tuple in the list and update the aggregate status variable by applying the function *sfunc*. In the end, the finalization function *ffunc* is applied. The function *sfunc* must be associative and commutative, i.e., must produce the same result irrespective of the order in which the tuples are processed.

A high-level overview of our system is shown in Figure 2. The data is hosted by a set of *data source* nodes. A potentially different set of nodes, *client nodes*, are used for processing. The underlying runtime system we use, STORM, is described later in this section. As a quick summary, the STORM system requires an extraction service to be implemented for data retrieval, and an aggregate service with a data partitioning strategy to be implemented for data processing. Our compiler analyzes the metadata descriptor and the user-defined aggregate functions that are available to be used with Select queries. It generates the extraction and aggregate services by this analysis.

We assume that SQL-3 queries can be written and submitted by a user who is interested in interactive responses. However, these queries can only use the user-defined aggregate functions that were analyzed and compiled earlier. Because our goal is to minimize the time required for responding to these queries, we do not perform extensive analysis or code generation after these queries are submitted. Our query front-end extracts the attributes of interest and provides them as parameters to the extraction service. Similarly, the parameters on which group-by is carried-out are provided to the aggregate service.

2.2 Target Applications and Example Queries

This work is motivated by data-driven applications from science, engineering, and biomedicine. These applications include simulation-based studies for oil reservoir management, water contamination studies, cancer studies using Magnetic Resonance Imaging (MRI), telepathology with digitized slides, and analysis of satellite data. Here, we describe two applications that are used as case studies in this paper.

Oil Reservoir Management: Cost-effective and environmentally safer production of oil from reservoirs is only possible with effective oil reservoir management. A management strategy should integrate into the decision process a good understanding of physical properties of the reservoir. Although field instrumentation has been enhanced over the years, most of the time a partial knowledge of critical parameters such as rock permeability is available. Thus, complex numerical reservoir models are needed and it is essential that geological uncertainty be incorporated into these models. An approach is to simulate alternative production strategies (number, type, timing and location of wells) applied to realizations of multiple geostatistical models [9]. Simulations are carried out on a three-dimensional grid. At each time step, the value of seventeen separate variables and cell locations in 3-dimensional space are output for each cell in the grid. Each of the output variables are written to files. If the simulation is run in parallel, the data for different parts of the domain can reside on separate disks or nodes.

```
CREATE FUNCTION ipars_func(int, IPARS) RETURNS int AS '
   SELECT CASE WHEN $2.SOIL > 0.7 AND
        1/($2.OILX * $2.OILX + $2.OILY * $2.OILY + $2.OILZ * $2.OILZ) < 30.0
      THEN $1&1
      ELSE 0
   END;
 ' LANGUAGE SQL;

CREATE AGGREGATE ipars_bypass_sum ( BASETYPE = IPARS,
      SFUNC = ipars_func, STYPE = int, INITCOND = '1' );

SELECT X, Y, Z, ipars_bypass_sum(IPARS) FROM IPARS
   WHERE REL in (0,5,10) AND TIME≥1000 AND TIME≤1200
   GROUP BY X, Y, Z;
```

Fig. 3. Ipars: Query and Aggregation Function

Large scale simulations can generate tens of Gigabytes of output per realization, resulting in Terabytes of data per study. Analysis of this data is key to achieve a better understanding and characterization of oil reservoirs. Many interesting analyses involve the computation of *bypassed* oil cells or regions. An expression involving several attributes can be used to determine if a grid cell is bypassed for a particular time-step. The query we consider in this paper specifies a spatial region and a range of time-steps, and requires the computation of grid cells within that spatial region that are bypassed for every time-step within the given range. The SQL-3 representation of this query is shown in Figure 3. This query and the associated dataset are referred to as *Ipars* query and dataset, respectively, in the rest of this paper.

Satellite Data Processing: Analysis of data acquired by earth-orbiting satellites can provide valuable information about regional and global changes. A satellite dataset consists of a number of measurements by a satellite orbiting the earth continuously [3]. While the satellite passes over a region, its sensors record readings from the surface. Each measurement is a data element and is associated with a location (latitude, longitude) on the surface and the time of recording. Five sensor values are stored with each data element. Therefore, a data element in a satellite dataset can be viewed as having 8 attributes (two spatial, one time dimension, and five sensors).

A typical query specifies a rectangular region and a time period. The query can also choose a subset of sensor readings. A typical analysis processes the data for up to a year and generates one or more composite images of the area under study. Generating a composite image requires projection of the globe onto a two dimensional grid; each pixel in the composite image is computed by selecting the "best" sensor value that maps to the associated grid point. The SQL-3 representation of this query is shown in Figure 4.

2.3   The STORM Runtime System

STORM is a middleware designed to support data selection, data partitioning, and data transfer operations on flat-file datasets hosted on a parallel system [8,7]. STORM is

CREATE FUNCTION titan_func(float, TITAN) RETURNS float AS '
  SELECT CASE
    WHEN $1 < (($2.BAND1 - $2.BAND0)/($2.BAND1 + $2.BAND0) + 1) * 512
    THEN (($2.BAND1 - $2.BAND0)/($2.BAND1 + $2.BAND0) + 1) * 512
    ELSE $1
  END;
' LANGUAGE SQL;

CREATE AGGREGATE ndvi_max (BASETYPE = TITAN,
        SFUNC = titan_func, STYPE = float, INITCOND = '0');

SELECT X, Y, ndvi_max(TITAN) FROM TITAN
  WHERE X$\geq$0 AND X$\leq$46080 AND Y$\geq$0 AND Y$\leq$20479 AND Z$\geq$0 AND Z$\leq$175
  GROUP BY X, Y;

Fig. 4. Satellite Data Processing: Query and Aggregation Function

designed as a suite of loosely coupled services. The *query service* is the entry point for clients to submit queries to the database middleware. The *data source* service provides a view of a dataset to other services. It provides support for implementing application-specific *extraction* function. An extraction function returns an ordered list of attribute values for a tuple in the dataset, thus effectively creating a virtual table. The *indexing service* encapsulates indexes for a dataset, using an index function provided by the user. The *filtering service* is responsible for execution of user-defined filters. After the set of tuples that satisfy the query has been determined, the data should be partitioned among the processing units of the client program and transferred from the server to those processors. The purpose of the *partition generation service* is to make it possible for an application developer to implement the data distribution scheme employed in the client program at the server. The *data mover* service is responsible for transferring selected data elements to destination processors based on the partitioning description generated by the partition generation service.

Our compiler focuses on generating two high-level modules for using the STORM system. The *extraction service* denoted in Figure 2 is responsible for retrieving and filtering the tuples of interest. The *aggregate service* in the same figure is responsible for the processing required on the client nodes, and partitioning the data and computations to use a parallel client.

3   Metadata Descriptors

This section gives an overview of the metadata descriptor that is used for exposing the low-level layout of data to the compiler. Our goal was to have a metadata description language which is very expressive, and particularly, can allow description of: 1) dataset physical layout within the file system of a node, 2) dataset distribution on nodes of one or more clusters, 3) the relationship of the dataset to the virtual schema that is desired, and 4) the index that can be used to make subsetting more efficient. In addition, we also

Component I: Dataset Schema Description

```
[IPARS]        // { * Dataset schema name *}
REL = short int  // { * Data type definition *}
TIME = int
X = float
Y = float
Z = float
SOIL = float
SGAS = float
```

Component II: Dataset Storage Description

```
[IparsData]     // { * Dataset name *}
// { * Dataset schema for IparsData *}
DatasetDescription = IPARS
DIR[0] = osu0/ipars
DIR[1] = osu1/ipars
DIR[2] = osu2/ipars
DIR[3] = osu3/ipars
```

Component III: Dataset Layout Description

```
DATASET "IparsData" { // { * Name for Dataset *}
DATATYPE { IPARS } // { * Schema for Dataset *}
DATAINDEX { REL TIME }
DATA { DATASET ipars1 DATASET ipars2 }
DATASET "ipars1" {
 DATASPACE {
  LOOP GRID ($DIRID*100+1):(($DIRID+1)*100):1{
   X Y Z
  }
 }
 DATA { $DIR[$DIRID]/COORDS $DIRID = 0:3:1 }
} // end of DATASET "ipars1"
DATASET "ipars2" {
 DATASPACE {
  LOOP TIME 1:500:1 {
   LOOP GRID($DIRID*100+1):(($DIRID+1)*100):1{
    SOIL SGAS
   }
  }
 }
 DATA { $DIR[$DIRID]/DATA$REL
   $REL = 0:3:1 $DIRID = 0:3:1 }
} // { * end of DATASET "ipars2" *}
}
```

Fig. 5. The Meta-data Descriptor for the IPARS Dataset

wanted the language to be easy to use for data repository administrators, and to serve as a convenient basis for our code generation tool.

Our metadata descriptor comprises three components.

1. Dataset Schema Description: states the virtual relational table view that is desired.

2. Dataset Storage Description: lists the nodes and the directories on the system where the data is resident.

3. Dataset Layout Description: describes the actual layout of the data within and across different files.

To further explain the three components of our description language, we use a running example based upon the Ipars dataset [9] that was described in the previous section. Here, the dataset comprises several simulations on the same grid, each involving a number of time-steps. These simulations are identified by a realization identifier (REL). The X, Y, and Z coordinates of each point in the grid is stored explicitly. For each realization, each time-step, and each grid point, a number of attributes or variables are stored in the dataset.

The physical layout we consider is as follows. We have a 4 node cluster. The grid is divided into four partitions, and each node stores values of all attributes for all time-steps and all realizations for one partition. The X, Y, and Z coordinates for the grid points are stored only once and in a separate file, called COORDS, as they do not change over time and realizations. For storing the values of attributes, a separate file is used for each realization. In each such file, the data is ordered by time-steps. Suppose for simplicity, the dataset has only two other attributes (SOIL and SGAS) for each grid-point and time-step. The spatial coordinates of grid points are not stored explicitly in each file, instead, the values of attributes SOIL and SGAS are stored in the same order in which coordinates are stored in the file COORDS.

The metadata description is shown in Figure 5. The first two components, the dataset schema and dataset storage, are quite simple. We focus our discussion on the dataset layout. This description is based upon the use of six key-words: DATASET, DATATYPE, DATAINDEX, DATASPACE, DATA, and LOOP. A DATASET is a nested structure, which can comprise of one or more other DATASETs. A DATASET can be described by using DATATYPE, DATAINDEX, DATASPACE, and DATA. DATATYPE can be used for relating a DATASET to a schema (as shown in Figure 5), or for defining new attributes that are not part of the schema. DATAINDEX is used for stating the attributes that can be used for indexing the data. DATASPACE is used for the leaf nodes in the structure, i.e., for DATASETs that do not comprise other DATASETs. It describes the layout associated with each file in the DATASET. For non-leaf nodes in the description, DATA is used for listing the DATASETs that are nested. For leaf nodes, DATA is used for listing the files.

In Figure 5, "IparsData" comprises "ipars1" and "ipars2". "ipars1" comprises a single file on each node, which stores the X, Y, and Z coordinates for the grid-points in the partition. Within a DATASPACE, the key-word LOOP is used for capturing the repetitive structure within a file. The variable $DIRID is used for identifying the directory. Thus, the clause "LOOP GRID ($DIRID*100+1):(($DIRID+1)*100):1" implies that we store X, Y, and Z coordinates for grid-points 1 through 100 in the file residing on directory 0 (DIR[0]), grid-points 101 through 200 in the file residing on directory 1 (DIR[1]), and so on. (The number of grid points on each node is identical in this example). The DATA field as part of "ipars1" shows that four different files are associated with this dataset, corresponding to the four different directories listed earlier.

Now, let us consider the "ipars2" dataset. Each file associated with this dataset stores the attributes SOIL and SGAS for 500 time-steps and 100 grid-points. The use of the same loop identifier GRID implies that values for these 100 grid-points are stored in the same order as in the file COORDS. This dataset comprises 16 files, corresponding to the four directories and four different RELs.

4   Compiler Analysis and Code Generation

In this section, we describe the compiler analysis, transformations, and code generation tasks that are handled by our system.

4.1   Overview of the Compilation Problem

Consider the aggregate functions and the declarative queries with group-by operators shown in Figures 3 and 4. They specify the subset of the dataset that is of interest and the aggregation computations that need to be performed. We have a one or more data source nodes hosting a large volume of distributed scientific dataset and one or more client nodes available as computing units. The data is stored in a low-level layout, and not as a relational table. Given such a query, data source, and the processing environment, our goal is to generate code for processing the query.

TempDataset = SELECT $<$ *All attributes* $>$ FROM $<$ *Dataset Name* $>$
        WHERE $<$ *Expression* $>$;
SELECT $<$ *attributelist* $>$, $<$ *AGG_name(Dataset Name)* $>$
    FROM TempDataset GROUP BY $<$ *group-by attributelist* $>$;

Fig. 6. Canonical Query After Transformation

We start from the canonical query that was shown earlier in Figure 1. The first transformation on this query is shown in Figure 6. Here, we are creating two queries. The first involves retrieving the data subsetting, and the second involves aggregation operations on the data subset. These two steps correspond to the Data Extraction and Aggregation Computations of our target STORM system. Thus, by generating Extraction and Indexing functions corresponding to the first query, and the Partitioning and Aggregation functions corresponding to the second query, we can execute such query using the runtime functionality of the STORM system.

However, a number of challenges arise in this process. First, the compiler needs to analyze the meta-data descriptor for generating code to perform data retrieval. Second, the aggregation query needs to be supported on a different set of nodes than the data subsetting query. Therefore, it is important to minimize the data transfer between the nodes. It is also important to pipeline the execution of the two queries. Finally, both the queries need to be executed in a parallel environment. While the layout of data gives a natural way for parallelizing the data retrieval query, we need to decide on a way for parallelizing the aggregation query.

The next two subsections describe the code generation for these two queries.

4.2   Code Generation for Data Extraction

We now describe the key aspects of how we generate the extraction service. Using the meta-data and the query, the key data-structure we try to compute at runtime is the set of *aligned file chunks* (AFC), each of which comprises

$$\{num\_rows, \{File_1, Offset_1, Num\_Bytes_1\}, \ldots,$$

$$\{File_m, Offset_m, Num\_Bytes_m\}\}$$

Here, num_rows denotes the number of rows of the table that can be computed using these file chunks. m is the number of chunks involved. A given set of AFCs contain only one chunk from each file, though there may be multiple sets of AFCs from the same set of files. Thus, m is also equal to the number of files that are required to generate the table rows. For each file chunk, we store the file name, the offset at which we will start reading, and the number of bytes to be read from the file to create one row. By reading the m files simultaneously, with Num_Bytes_i bytes from the file $File_i$, we create one row of the table. Starting from the offset $Offset_i$, $num\_rows \times Num\_Bytes_i$ bytes are read from the file $File_i$.

An important concept in our algorithm is *implicit attributes* associated with a tuple, file chunk, or the file itself. These are attributes which are not stored explicitly, but whose value could be determined from the file name and/or the offset of the chunk or the tuple.

The main steps in our algorithm are as follows. Initially, all files in the dataset are matched against the range query. It is determined if a file has data corresponding to the given query. Next, we *group* the files on the basis of the attributes whose value they store. Using the concept of implicit attributes, our algorithm now determines the sets of files which can jointly contribute towards rows of a table. For each set of files belonging to different groups, we check if the value of the implicit parameters are consistent or not. A set of files is of interest only if the value of implicit parameters is consistent. The next step in our algorithm involves determining aligned file chunks from the sets of files. Given a set of files, our goal is to find file sections from each of these files, which meet two criteria. First, their layouts must be identical. Second, the value of any implicit attributes should also be identical. Finally, we determine the file offsets, number of bytes to be read, and the number of rows that can be computed.

In our implementation, this algorithm is executed in two phases. First, our tool parses the available meta-data and generates code for extraction function. At runtime, these functions take the query as input and compute and read the set of AFCs. The advantage of this design is that the expensive processing associated with the meta-data does not need to be carried out at runtime. At the same time, no code generation or expensive runtime processing is required when a new query is submitted.

4.3   Code Generation for Aggregation

We now discuss how the compiler generates code for the aggregation part of the query. There are four main steps involved. The first two are transformations that we refer to as *projection pushdown* and *aggregation decomposition*, respectively. The third step involves data partitioning, and the final step is code generation.

TempDataset = SELECT < *useful attributelist* > FROM < *Dataset Name* >
     WHERE < *Expression* > ;
SELECT < *attributelist* >, < *AGG_name(Dataset Name)* >
FROM TempDataset GROUP BY < *group-by attributelist* >;

Fig. 7. Canonical Query Structure after Projection Push-down

The motivation for the first transformation is as follows. Consider the query in Figure 6. It selects all attributes from the dataset on which subsetting and retrieval is done.

This is because the argument of the aggregation function is the name of the dataset, and not a specific list of attributes. However, it is likely that the aggregation function would only require a subset of all attributes in the dataset. Therefore, our compiler analyzes the code of the aggregation function and determines the attributes that are required for the computation. Further, we add the attributes on which group-by is carried out. We transform the query to only retrieve these attributes from the dataset. The canonical query after this transformation is shown in Figure 7. We refer to this transformation as *projection pushdown*, based on a similar transformation frequently applied in relational databases.

This transformation reduces the volume of data that needs to be retrieved and communicated. For example, in the Ipars application and the query we have considered, only 7 of the 22 attributes are actually needed. Therefore, the volume of data to be retrieved and communicated is reduced by 66%.

```
CREATE FUNCTION ipars_func(int, IPARS) RETURNS int AS '
    SELECT CASE WHEN $2.TempAttr = 1
        THEN $1&1
        ELSE 0
    END;
' LANGUAGE SQL;
```
(a) Ipars

```
CREATE FUNCTION titan_func(float, TITAN) RETURNS float AS '
    SELECT CASE
        WHEN $1 < $2.TempAttr
        THEN $2.TempAttr
        ELSE $1
    END;
' LANGUAGE SQL;
```
(b) Satellite Data Processing

Fig. 8. Aggregate Functions after Decomposition

The second transformation we apply, *aggregation decomposition*, has a similar goal, but is based on more aggressive analysis. Here, the aggregation computation is divided into two steps. The first step involves computations that can be applied independently on each tuple. The second step updates the *aggregate status* variable. By such decomposition, the first step can be applied on each tuple soon after it is retrieved. The second step still needs to be applied as part of the aggregation function. Such transformation can often eliminate the communication for many attributes.

Our compiler does the following analysis to extract computations that can be applied independently on each attribute. We create an abstract syntax tree for the user-defined function *sfunc*. By definition, the first argument of this function is the aggregate status variable. Currently, we extract only a single expression to be used in the first step. So, we find the largest and/or the most frequently occurring expression that does not involve the first variable ($1) of this function. Once such expression is identified, all occurrences of this expression are replaced by $TempAttr$.

The compiler generates another function for computing the value of $TempAttr$ from a tuple. The attributes which were used for computing $TempAttr$ and are not needed for any other computations need not be communicated any more. $TempAttr$ is added to the list of attributes to be communicated.

In Figure 8 , we show the transformed aggregation functions after this optimization. In the Ipars application, this transformation further reduces the number of attributes to be communicated from 7 to 4.

The next step is partitioning of computation and data for using a parallel configuration for aggregation. We use the following simple scheme in our current implementation. We choose one of the attributes on which the query performs group-by, and divide its range of values into equal-sized partitions. A tuple is directed to a specific node based upon its value of that attribute. Because all attributes that need to be aggregated together are processed on the same node, no further communication is needed for finalizing the computations. In the queries we have considered so far, the range of values of attributes on which group-by was done was quite large, which allowed this simple scheme to work effectively.

The final phase of the algorithm is the actual code generation for aggregation computations. With the partitioning scheme described above, the final code generation becomes quite simple. We maintain a hash-table, whose key is the values of the attributes used in group-by. The values of the aggregate status variables are stored in this hash-table. After a tuple is received by a node, it is mapped to a particular hash-table entry using the hash-key. The compiler generates a function that updates the value of the aggregate status variable using one such tuple.

5   Experimental Results

This section presents the results from the evaluation studies we have carried out so far. We focused on the following four factors in our experiments: 1) scalability of the system as the number of nodes for hosting data and performing the computations is increased, 2) performance as the amount of the data retrieved and processed is increased, and 3) differences in performance of hand-written and compiler generated codes, and 4) the impact of the aggregation decomposition optimization.

The datasets and queries we use correspond to two applications, oil reservoir management (Ipars) and satellite data processing (Titan). The queries we use for our experiments were described earlier in Section 2.2. Our experiments were carried out on a Linux cluster where each node has a PIII 933MHz CPU, 512 MB main memory, and three 100GB IDE disks. The nodes are inter-connected via a Switched Fast Ethernet.

Our first experiment evaluated the parallel performance for Ipars. The results are presented in Figures 9. The number of nodes hosting the data was scaled from 1 to 8. A different set of nodes were used for processing the data. The number of nodes for processing the data was always identical to the number of nodes hosting the data. The total volume of data that had to be scanned was 1.9 GB. However, because not all attributes were needed for the queries, the amount of data actually retrieved and

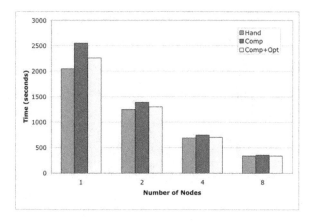

Fig. 9. Parallel Performance, Ipars, 1.9 GB data

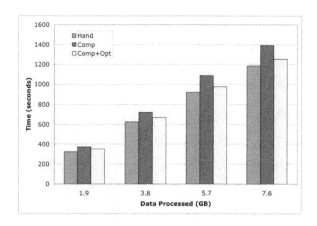

Fig. 10. Scaling the Amount of Data Processed, Ipars, 8 nodes

processed was 640 MB. We compared three versions: Hand uses manually written functions for the STORM system, Comp uses compiler generated functions for data extraction, indexing, and client-side processing, and finally Comp+Opt includes the aggregation decomposition optimization. The projection push-down transformation had been used for all versions.

All three versions show good speedups. The relative speedups on 8 nodes for these three versions are 6.03, 7.17, and 6.61, respectively. The difference between Hand and Comp version is between 6% and 20%. This difference mainly arises because of the more generic processing structure used in the compiler generated code. The use of the aggregation decomposition optimization reduces this difference to be between 1% and 10%.

Our second experiment evaluated the system's ability to scale to larger datasets. For the same query, we used four different dataset sizes. The amount of data that had to be scanned was 1.9 GB, 3.8 GB, 5.7 GB, and 7.6 GB, respectively. The amount of

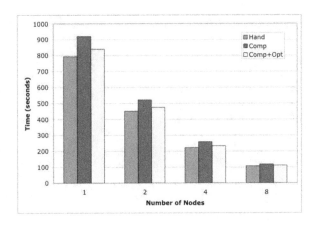

Fig. 11. Parallel Performance, Titan, 456 MB data

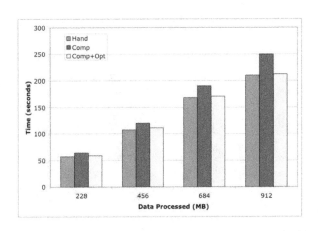

Fig. 12. Scaling the Amount of Data Processed, Titan, 8 nodes

data retrieved and processed for these cases was 649 MB, 1.28 GB, 1.92 GB, and 2.56 GB, respectively. The results are presented in Figure 10. 8 nodes were used for hosting the data and another 8 nodes were used for processing the data. The results show that the execution times for different version stay proportional to the amount of data that is retrieved and processed. The differences between the different versions are quite similar to what was observed in the previous experiments.

We repeated the above two experiments for the Titan application. Figure 11 presents the results from parallelization of data retrieval and processing for Titan. Again, the number of nodes used for processing were identical to the number of nodes used for hosting the data. The query we executed scans 456 MB data size. Because all attributes are not needed, the amount of data retrieved and processed is 228 MB. All three versions scale quite well. The relative speedups with 8 nodes are 7.38, 7.73, and 7.56 for the

Hand, Comp and Comp+Opt versions, respectively. The difference between Hand and Comp versions is at most 17%, and the difference between Hand and Comp+Opt versions is at most 6%.

Finally, in Figure 12, we examine the performance of different versions of Titan as the amount of data processed is scaled. The four different cases we consider correspond to 228, 456, 684, and 912 MB of data being scanned, and 114, 228, 342, and 456 MB being retrieved and processed. We used 8 nodes for hosting the data and another 8 nodes for processing. The results show that the performance of all versions is quite proportional to the amount of data retrieved and processed.

6   Related Work

Parallelization of SQL-based aggregations and reductions has been researched in the database community. For example, Shatdal and Naughton [12,11] have evaluated algorithms for the parallel implementation of the relational queries with group-by and aggregation functions. The key difference in our work is that data is not actually stored in relational databases, and processing is performed on a different set of nodes. Reductions on disk-resident datasets have also been examined in parallelizing compilers community [4,5]. Our work is distinct in considering a higher-level language and virtual view of the datasets. Kurc *et al.* have examined different runtime strategies for supporting reductions in a distributed environment [6]. We focus on supporting a high-level language, but currently have implemented only a single strategy.

There has been a lot of work on parallel, distributed, and grid-based databases, including support for multi-dimensional or spatio-temporal datasets. Sarawagi and Stonebraker showed how array chunks could be described and accessed as objects in an object-relational database [10]. The more recent work in database community treats multi-dimensional data as data cubes [13]. RasDaMan [2,1] is a commercially available domain-independent DBMS for multi-dimensional arrays of arbitrary size and structure. Our work is distinct in supporting an abstract view of array-based datasets. The support for *external tables* as part of Oracle's recent implementation allows tables stored in flat-files to be accessed from a database[1]. The data must be stored in the table format, or an *access driver* must be written. Also, there is no support for indexing such data.

7   Conclusions

This paper has described a compiler-based system for supporting SQL-3 queries on flat-file scientific datasets. There are two main components of our work. First, our compiler analyzes a meta-data descriptor that describes the layout of flat-file scientific datasets and generates functions for data extraction. Second, we analyze the user-defined aggregate functions and generate code for executing them in a parallel environment.

Several interesting observations can be made from our work. First, our experience has shown that for many applications, processing of scientific datasets can be expressed with user-defined aggregate functions and group-by operations. The declarative and

---

[1] See www.dbasupport.com/oracle/ora9i/External_Tables9i.shtml

high-level nature of SQL can greatly simplify the specification of processing, especially when used in conjunction with a virtual relational table view of the low-level dataset. Second, we have shown that program analysis on user-defined functions in SQL-3 can enable additional optimizations.

References

1. P. Baumann, A. Dehmel, P. Furtado, R. Ritsch, and N. Widmann. The multidimensional database system rasdaman. In *Proceedings of the 1998 ACM SIGMOD international conference on Management of data*, pages 575–577. ACM Press, 1998.

2. Peter Baumann, Paula Furtado, and Roland Ritsch. Geo/environmental and medical data management in the RasDaMan system. In *Proceedings of the 23rd International Conference on Very Large Data Bases (VLDB97)*, pages 548–552, August 1997.

3. Chialin Chang, Renato Ferreira, Alan Sussman, and Joel Saltz. Infrastructure for building parallel database systems for multi-dimensional data. In *Proceedings of the Second Merged IPPS/SPDP Symposiums*. IEEE Computer Society Press, April 1999.

4. Renato Ferreira, Gagan Agrawal, and Joel Saltz. Compiling object-oriented data intensive computations. In *Proceedings of the 2000 International Conference on Supercomputing*, May 2000.

5. Renato Ferreira, Gagan Agrawal, and Joel Saltz. Compiler supported high-level abstractions for sparse disk-resident datasets. In *Proceedings of the International Conference on Supercomputing (ICS)*, June 2002.

6. T. Kurc, F. Lee, G. Agrawal, U. Catalyurek, R. Ferreira, and J. Saltz. Optimizing Reduction Computations in a Distributed Environment. In *Proceedings of SC 2003*, Nov 2003.

7. Sivaramakrishnan Narayanan, Umit Catalyurek, Tahsin Kurc, Xi Zhang, and Joel Saltz. Applying database support for large scale data driven science in distributed environments. In *Proceedings of the Fourth International Workshop on Grid Computing (Grid 2003)*, pages 141–148, Phoenix, Arizona, Nov 2003.

8. Sivaramakrishnan Narayanan, Tahsin Kurc, Umit Catalyurek, and Joel Saltz. Database support for data-driven scientific applications in the grid. *Parallel Processing Letters*, 13(2):245–271, 2003.

9. J. Saltz, U. Catalyurek, T. Kurc, M. Gray, S. Hastings, S. Langella, S. Narayanan, R. Martino, S. Bryant, M. Peszynska, M. Wheeler, A. Sussman, M. Beynon, C. Hansen, D. Stredney, , and D. Sessanna. Driving scientific applications by data in distributed environments. In *Dynamic Data Driven Application Systems Workshop, held jointly with ICCS 2003*, Melbourne, Australia, June 2003.

10. Sunita Sarawagi and Michael Stonebraker. Efficient organizations of large multidimensional arrays. In *Proceedings of the Tenth International Conference on Data Engineering*, February 1994.

11. Ambuj Shatdal. Architectural considerations for parallel query evaluation algorithms. Technical Report CS-TR-1996-1321, University of Wisconsin, 199.

12. Ambuj Shatdal and Jeffrey F. Naughton. Adaptive parallel aggregation algorithms. In *Proceedings of the 1995 ACM SIGMOD International Conference on Management of Data (SIGMOD95)*, pages 104–114, San Jose, CA, May 1995.

13. C. Stolte, D. Tang, and P. Hanrahan. Polaris: a system for query, analysis, and visualization of multidimensional relational databases. *IEEE Transactions on Visualization and Computer Graphics*, 8(1):52–65, Jan/Mar 2002.

Supporting XML Based High-Level Abstractions on HDF5 Datasets: A Case Study in Automatic Data Virtualization

Swarup Kumar Sahoo and Gagan Agrawal

Department of Computer Science and Engineering,
Ohio State University, Columbus OH 43210,
{sahoo, agrawal}@cis.ohio-state.edu

Abstract. Recently, we have been focusing on the notion of *automatic data virtualization*. The goal is to enable automatic creation of efficient data services to support a high-level or virtual view of the data. The application developers express the processing assuming this virtual view, whereas the data is stored in a low-level format. The compiler uses the information about the low-level layout and the relationship between the virtual and the low-level layouts to generate efficient low-level data processing code.

In this paper, we describe a specific implementation of this approach. We provide XML-based abstractions on datasets stored in the Hierarchical Data Format (HDF). A high-level XML Schema provides a logical view on the HDF5 dataset, hiding actual layout details. Based on this view, the processing is specified using XQuery, which is the XML Query language developed by the World Wide Web Consortium (W3C). The HDF5 data layout is exposed to the compiler using low-level XML Schema. The relationship between the high-level and low-level Schemas is exposed using a Mapping Schema.

We describe how our compiler can generate efficient code to access and process HDF5 datasets using the above information. A number of issues are addressed for ensuring high locality in processing of the datasets, which arise mainly because of the high-level nature of XQuery and because the actual data layout is abstracted.

1 Introduction

Development of applications that process large datasets is often complicated by complex and specialized data storage formats. In view of this, there has been recent interest in *data virtualization*, and *data services* to support such virtualization. In the mailing list of Global Grid Forum's DAIS working group, the following definitions were presented[1] *"A Data Virtualization describes an abstract view of data. A Data Service implements the mechanism to access and process data through the Data Virtualization"*.

Using data virtualization and data services, low-level, compact, and/or specialized data formats can be hidden from the applications analyzing large datasets. However, supporting data virtualization can require significant effort. For each dataset layout and

---

[1] Please see http://www-unix.gridforum.org/mail_archive/dais-wg/Archive/msg00215.html

R. Eigenmann et al. (Eds.): LCPC 2004, LNCS 3602, pp. 299–318, 2005.

abstract view that is desired, a set of data services need to be implemented. Moreover, when the datasets are large or disk-resident, understanding the layout and maintaining high locality in accessing them is crucial for obtaining a reasonable performance. This further complicates the task of implementing data services.

Recently, we have been focusing on the notion of *automatic data virtualization* [16,26]. As the name suggests, the goal is to enable automatic creation of efficient data services to support data virtualization. The application developers express the processing assuming a high-level or virtual view of the dataset, whereas the data is stored in a low-level format. The information about the low-level layout and the relationship or mapping between the virtual and low-level layouts is exposed to the compiler. The compiler uses this information to generate efficient low-level data processing code.

In this paper, we describe a specific implementation of this approach. We provide XML-based abstractions on datasets stored in the Hierarchical Data Format (HDF) [12]. A high-level XML Schema provides a logical view on the HDF5 dataset, hiding actual layout details. Based on this view, the queries are specified using XQuery [4], which is the XML Query language developed by the World Wide Web Consortium (W3C). The HDF5 data layout is exposed to the compiler using low-level XML Schema. The relationship between the high-level and low-level Schemas is exposed using a Mapping Schema.

We describe how our compiler can generate efficient code to access and process HDF5 datasets using the above information. A number of issues are addressed in ensuring high locality in processing of the datasets, which arise because of the high-level nature of XQuery and because the actual data layout is abstracted. Particularly, we present a new algorithm for data-centric transformation, which improves on our previous work [9,16] in two ways. First, it can handle the cases when disk-resident chunks from multiple datasets needs to be retrieved to carry out the computations. Second, by assuming a different kind of mapping information, we do not need to invert the data access functions.

We believe that our system can offer the following advantages:

- Provide simple and high-level descriptions of the complex scientific datasets to the users interested in analyzing the data.
- Ease the development of scientific data processing applications, by supporting high-level abstractions, allowing the use of high-level language (XQuery), and making the application independent of a particular physical layout.
- Provide efficiency, by allowing compact storage of data, allowing processing on the actual layout of data (i.e, not requiring copying of data to other formats), and using compiler transformations to achieve high-locality in processing.

The rest of this paper is organized as follows. Section 2 gives background information on XML, XML Schemas, and XQuery. Overview of our system is presented in Section 3. This section also describes the high-level, low-level, and mapping schemas that are used in our system. Compiler analysis and code generation is presented in Section 4. Experimental results are presented in Section 5. We compare our work with related research efforts in Section 6 and conclude in Section 7.

2   Background: XML, XML Schemas, and XQuery

This section gives background on XML, XML Schemas, and XQuery.

2.1   XML and XML Schemas

XML provided a simple and general facility which is useful for data interchange. Though the initial development of XML was mostly for representing structured and semi-structured data on the web, XML is rapidly emerging as a general medium for exchanging information between organizations. XML and related technologies form the core of the web-services model [10] and the Open Grid Services Architecture (OGSA) [11].

XML models data as a tree of *elements*. Arbitrary depth and width is allowed in such a tree, which facilitates storage of deeply nested data structures, as well as large collections of records or structures. Each element contains *character data* and can have *attributes* composed of *name-value* pairs. An XML document represents elements, attributes, character data, and the relationship between them by simply using angle brackets.

```
< student >
< firstname > Darin < / firstname >
< lastname > Sundstrom < /lastname >
<DOB > 1974-01-06 < / DOB >
< GPA > 3.73 < / GPA >
< / student >
...
```

(a) XML example

```
    Schema Declaration
< xs:element name="student" >
< xs:complexType >
  < xs:sequence >
      < xs:element name="lastname" type="xs:string"/ >
      < xs:element name="firstname" type="xs:string"/ >
      < xs:element name="DOB" type="xs:date"/>
      < xs:element name= "GPA" type="xs:float"/ >
  < /xs:sequence >
< /xs:complexType >
< /xs:element >
```

(b) XML Schema

Fig. 1. XML and XML Schema

Applications that operate on XML data often need guarantees on the structure and content of data. XML Schema proposals [1,3] give facilities for describing the structure and constraining the contents of XML documents. The example in Figure (a) shows an XML document containing records of students. The XML Schema describing the XML document is shown in Figure (b). For each student tuple in the XML file, it contains two string elements to specify the last and first names, one date element to specify the date of birth, and one element of float type for the student's GPA.

2.2   XML Query Language: XQuery

As stated previously, XQuery is a language recently developed by the World Wide Web Consortium (W3C). It is designed to be a language in which queries are concise and easily understood, and to be flexible enough to query a broad spectrum of information sources, including both databases and documents.

XQuery is a functional language. The basic building block is an *expression*. Several types of expressions are possible. The two types of expressions important for our discussion are:

- FLWR expressions, which support iteration and binding of variables to intermediate results. FLWR stands for the keywords *for*, *let*, *where*, and *return*.
- Unordered expressions, which use the keyword *unordered*. The unordered expression takes any sequence of items as its argument, and returns the same sequence of items in a nondeterministic order.

```
unordered(
    for $d in document("depts.xml")//deptno
    let $e := document("emps.xml")//emp[deptno = $d]
        where count($e) >= 10
    return
        <big-dept>
        {
            $d,
            <headcount> { count($e) } </headcount>,
            <avgsal> {avg($e/salary)} </avgsal>
        }
        </big-dept>
)
```

Fig. 2. An Example Using XQuery's FLWR and Unordered Expressions

We illustrate the XQuery language and the *for*, *let*, *where*, and *return* expressions by an example, shown in Figure 2. In this example, two XML documents, *depts.xml* and *emps.xml* are processed to create a new document, which lists all departments with ten or more employees, and also lists the average salary of employees in each such department.

In XQuery, a *for* clause contains one or more variables, each with an associated expression. The simplest form of *for* expression, such as the one used in the example here, contains only one variable and an associated expression. The evaluation of the expression typically results in a sequence. The *for* clause results in a loop being executed, in which the variable is bound to each item from the resulting sequence in turn. In our example, the sequence of distinct department numbers is created from the document *depts.xml*, and the loop iterates over each distinct department number.

A *let* clause also contains one or more variables, each with an associated expression. However, each variable is bound to the result of the associated expression, without iteration. In our example, the *let* expression results in the variable $e being bound to the set or sequence of employees that belong to the department $d. The subsequent operations on $e apply to such sequence. For example, $count(\$e)$ determines the length of this sequence.

A *where* clause serves as a filter for the tuples of variable bindings generated by the *for* and *let* clauses. The expression is evaluated once for each of these tuples. If the resulting value is true, the tuple is retained, otherwise, it is discarded. A *return* clause is used to create an XML record after processing one iteration of the *for* loop. The details of the syntax are not important for our presentation.

The last key-word we explain is *unordered*. By enclosing the *for* loop inside the *unordered* expression, we are not enforcing any order on the execution of the iterations in the *for* loop, and in generation of the results. Without the use of *unordered*, the departments need to be processed in the order in which they occur in the document *depts.xml*. However, when *unordered* is used, the system is allowed to choose the order in which they are processed, or even process the query in parallel.

3   Overview of Our Approach and System

Scientific datasets are typically stored as binary or character flat-files. Because the underlying data is often multi-dimensional, chunked multi-dimensional layout [24] or

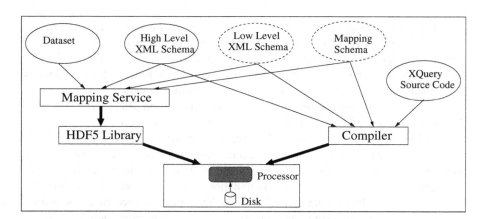

Fig. 3. Overview of the System Architecture

standards like HDF5 [12] and NetCDF [22] are quite popular. Such *low-level* layouts enable compact storage and efficient processing. The use of low-level and specialized data formats, however, makes the specification of processing much harder. Consider an application that needs to access and process data from remote data repositories. The application developer needs to completely understand the data layout in each repositories and incorporate this knowledge in the application. Moreover, for large datasets, the application or an application component needs to be carefully optimized to analyze the data in a particular format efficiently.

The goal of our work is to alleviate the above problems. An overview of our system is shown in Figure 3. A *high-level* XML Schema is used as a virtual view of the dataset. Such Schemas are independent of the physical layout of dataset. An application developer will specify the desired processing using the XML query language XQuery [5]. The physical storage of the data is still be in compact and low-level formats. The particular format we focus on in this paper is Hierarchical Data Format (HDF).

A *low-level* XML Schema file is provided reflecting the actual physical layout in HDF5 data format and metadata information. The mapping between each element of the high-level XML Schema and corresponding element in low-level XML Schema is described by a *Mapping Schema*. Our compiler generates C code which uses HDF5 library for efficient processing of large disk-resident datasets.

3.1 Example Application

We use the *Oil Reservoir Management* application [23] for describing the notion of high-level, low-level, and mapping Schemas, and XQuery representation of the processing. The compiler analysis for generating efficient code is presented in the next Section.

The Oil Reservoir Management is an application to support cost-effective and environmentally safer production of Oil from reservoirs [23]. Using complex numerical models, simulations are carried out on a three dimensional grid. At each time step, the value of 17 variables and cell locations in 3-dimensional space are output for each cell in the grid. Analysis of such simulation data can provide very useful information to the scientists.

The high-level XML Schema for the simulation dataset is shown in Figure 4. As a logical view, the data can be thought as being a simple collection of tuples, where each tuple corresponds to one grid-cell for one time-step. The x, y, z, and $time$ values are stored explicitly along-with other attributes whose value is generated. For simplicity, the attributes we consider are $velocity$, $mom - x$, $mom - y$ and $mom - z$.

Many interesting analyses involve the computation of *bypassed* oil cells or regions. An expression involving several attributes can be used to determine if a grid cell is bypassed for a particular time-step. The query we consider in this paper specifies a spatial region and a range of time-steps, and requires the computation of grid cells within that spatial region that are bypassed for every time-step within the given range.

XQuery code for performing this computation is shown in Figure 5. The code iterates over the three-dimensional space for which the output is desired. Since the order in which the points are processed is not important, we use the directive *unordered*. Within an iteration of the nested for loop, the *let* statement is used to create a sequence of all

```
< xs:element name="data" maxOccurs="unbounded" >
  < xs:complexType >
    < xs:sequence >
      < xs:element name="x" type="xs:integer"/ >
      < xs:element name="y" type="xs:integer"/ >
      < xs:element name="z" type="xs:integer"/ >
      < xs:element name="time" type="xs:integer"/ >
      < xs:element name="velocity" type="xs:float"/ >
      < xs:element name="mom-x" type="xs:float"/ >
      < xs:element name="mom-y" type="xs:float"/ >
      < xs:element name="mom-z" type="xs:float"/ >
    < /xs:sequence >
  < /xs:complexType >
< /xs:element >
```

Fig. 4. High-Level XML Schema for Oil Reservoir Simulation Data

cells that correspond to the particular spatial coordinates and the range of time values. The query involves finding out if the defined condition evaluates to true for all the time periods within the time interval.

We believe that high-level nature of XQuery and the use of high-level schemas can simplify the specification of the processing. However, the simulation output is typically not stored in such a format. Converting the original format to XML format corresponding to the high-level Schema will involve very high storage overheads. Besides the overhead of XML tags, storing x, y, , and z coordinates repetitively for each time-step in the 3-dimensional space is not necessary.

3.2   HDF5 Storage Format

We consider the possibility that dataset is stored in HDF5, which is widely used in many scientific communities. HDF5 is a new Hierarchical Data Format consisting of a data format specification and a supporting library implementation. HDF5 files are organized in a hierarchical structure, with two primary structures: *groups* and *datasets*. HDF5 group is a structure containing instances of zero or more groups or datasets, together with supporting metadata. The metadata contains group name and a list of *group attributes*. A HDF5 dataset is a multidimensional array of data elements, together with supporting metadata. The metadata contains name of the object, its data-type, rank (number of dimensions), actual sizes of the dimensions of the array, and some information regarding the storage layout to speed up access to the dataset. There are small named datasets called *Attributes* that are attached to primary datasets and groups. Attributes can be used for storing small amount of information regarding the primary data object which can be either a dataset or group. The HDF5 library implementation provides functions for accessing member objects belonging to a group, reading and writing any part of a dataset or an attribute, and reading any metadata information associated with a group, dataset, or attribute. HDF5 also supports *chunking*. Here,

```
unordered(
    for $i in ($x1 to $x2)
        for $j in ($y1 to $y2)
            for $k in ($z1 to $z2)
                let $p := document("OilRes.xml")/data[(x=$i)
                    and (y = $j) and (z = $k) and (time ≥ $tmin) and (time ≤ $tmax) ]
                return
                <info>
                    <x-coord> {$i} </x-coord>
                    <y-coord> {$j} </y-coord>
                    <z-coord> {$k} </z-coord>
                    <summary> { analyze($p)} </summary>
                </info>
)

define function analyze (element data $p )
        as boolean
{
    if (empty($p) )
    then true
    else
        let $result:= analyze (subsequence($p,2) )
        let $q:= item-at($p,1)
        return
            if ($q/velocity > 0.7) and
                ( $q/mom-x * $q/mom-x + $q/mom-y * $q/mom-y + $q/mom-z * $q/mom-z < 50.0)
            then $result
            else false
}
```

Fig. 5. Oil Reservoir Data Analysis Using XQuery

multi-dimensional datasets are divided into chunks, which are rectilinear sections of a specified size. HDF5 library functions store chunks in a fashion that their access is optimized.

3.3   Low-level and Mapping Schema

In our system, a *low-level* XML Schema file is provided to the compiler to specify the actual layout of the data in the HDF5 format. The low-level XML Schema for our example is shown in Figure 14. As we can see, the file *coord* stores the spatial coordinate values and the file *info* stores the variables associated with the spatial coordinates for different time-steps. The x, y, and z coordinates are stored as 3 separate datasets in file *coord*. Each dataset stores the coordinate values consecutively as one-dimensional array. The variables velocity and momentum along x, y, and z directions are stored as 4 separate datasets in file *info*. Again, this data is stored consecutively as a one-dimensional array where the index of one data point is the same as the index of its corresponding spatial coordinate. The datasets of all variables for a particular time-step are stored as one group, and there is a separate group for each time-step. Each group contains an attribute stating the time-step.

In our system, we also provide a *Mapping Schema*. This Schema describes the correspondence between high-level and low-level Schemas. The Mapping Schema for the Oil Reservoir Management example is shown in Figure 6.

//high/data/velocity $\rightarrow$ //low/info/data/velocity
//high/data/time $\rightarrow$ //low/info/data/time
//high/data/mom-x $\rightarrow$ //low/info/data/mom-x[index(//low/info/data/velocity, 1)]
//high/data/mom-y $\rightarrow$ //low/info/data/mom-y[index(//low/info/data/velocity, 1)]
//high/data/mom-z $\rightarrow$ //low/info/data/mom-z[index(//low/info/data/velocity, 1)]
//high/data/x $\rightarrow$ //low/coord/x[index(//low/info/data/velocity, 1)]
//high/data/y $\rightarrow$ //low/coord/y[index(//low/info/data/velocity, 1)]
//high/data/z $\rightarrow$ //low/coord/z[index(//low/info/data/velocity, 1)]

Fig. 6. XML Mapping Schema

As we discussed above, x, y, and z coordinates of the 3-dimensional space are stored only once, and not repetitively for each time-step. The spatial coordinates corresponding to a data point in each dataset can be computed using the Mapping Schema. According to the Mapping Schema, the velocity attribute of a tuple in high-level Schema is mapped to a data element of the one-dimensional array of the velocity dataset, which is contained in the group *data* in the file *info*. The x coordinate for this data point in the high-level Schema is the value of dataset x, at the same offset as that of the corresponding data element of the velocity dataset, along the 1st dimension. The time value of this data element is the time value of the group *data*. We use a special construct *index* to specify the above features in the mapping Schema. In the mapping Schema,

$$index(//low/info/data/velocity, i)$$

implies the position of one data element of the dataset velocity, along the ith dimension.

The low-level XML Schemas and mapping Schemas are expected to be invisible to the programmer writing the XQuery code. The goal is to provide a simplified view of the dataset to the application programmers, thereby easing the development of correct data processing applications. The compiler translating XQuery codes obviously has the access low-level XML Schemas and mapping Schemas, which enables it to generate efficient code.

4   Compiler Analysis

In this section, we describe the various analysis, transformations, and code generation issues that are handled by our compiler.

4.1   Overview of Compilation Challenges

The XQuery code shown in Figures 5 operates on high level data abstractions and is called *high-level XQuery* code. Our compiler has to generate efficient low-level code. This code should operate on HDF5 file(s), as described by the low-level Schema, and should use HDF5 library calls. A number of issues need to be considered for this transformation. We initially list these issues, and describe which have been addressed in our previous work. Then, we focus on the issues that are new.

```
unordered(
    for $i in ($x1 to $x2)
        for $j in ($y1 to $y2)
            for $k in ($z1 to $z2)
                let $p := document("OilRes.xml")/data
                    where ($p/x=$i) and ($p/y = $j) and ($p/z = $k)
                            and ($p/time ≥ $tmin) and ($p/time ≤ $tmax)
                return
                <info>
                    <x-coord> {$i} </x-coord>
                    <y-coord> {$j} </y-coord>
                    <z-coord> {$k} </z-coord>
                    <summary> { analyze($p)} </summary>
                </info>
)

define function accumulate (element data $p ) as boolean
{
    $output = true
    foreach element $e in $p
        {
        if ($e/velocity > 0.7) and
        ( $e/mom-x * $e/mom-x + $e/mom-y * $e/mom-y $e/mom-z * $e/mom-z < 50.0)
            $output = $output
        else
            $output = false
        }
}
```

Fig. 7. Results of Recursion Transformations

Consider the XQuery code in Figure 5. Suppose, we translate this code to an imperative language like C/C++, ignoring the *unordered* directive, and preserving the order of the computation otherwise. The mapping schema can be used for accessing data from low-level layout. It is easy to see that the resulting code will be very inefficient. Each execution of the *let* expression will involve a complete scan over the dataset, since we need to find all data-elements that will belong to the sequence. Moreover, significant lookup cost will be associated with translation from high-level to low-level schema.

Our goal is to be able to operate on the dataset as described by the low-level Schema, and perform the computations associated with a portion of the dataset after it is retrieved. The computation in Figure 5 involves accessing portions of the *coordinate*, *velocity*, and *momentum* datasets together. As shown by the low-level Schema in Figure 14, these values are stored separately. Thus, we need to analyze the XQuery code, the low-level Schema, and the mapping schema together to be able to transform the code and access all datasets efficiently.

The first step in the transformation is to recognize the computation in the recursive loop is a reduction operation involving associative and commutative operators only. This means that instead of creating a sequence and then applying the recursive function on it, we can initialize the output, process each element independently, and update the output using the identified associative and commutative operators. This can be done using an algorithm presented in our previous work [17]. In Figure 7, we show the outline of the code after replacing recursion by iteration. Within the nested *for* loops, the function in which recursion has been replaced with iteration is invoked with the sequence obtained from the *let* statement.

The code in Figure 5 is still very inefficient. This is because it iterates over the entire HDF5 file a large number of times. Thus, our goal is to transform it to access a portion of the HDF5 file only once. The transformation algorithm we apply is based upon the general class of transformations known as *data-centric transformations* [9,15]. However, the details of algorithm are quite different, because of the need for analyzing XQuery code, low-level Schema, and mapping schema together.

4.2 Data-Centric Transformation Approach

The overall idea in our algorithm is to iterate over each data element in the low-level Schema. We find out the iterations of the original loop in which they are accessed. Then, the computations corresponding to these iteration instances are executed. Clearly, this idea needs to be extended to the cases when different datasets or portions of the file(s) need to be accessed together for performing the computations.

We create an iteration space corresponding to the high-level XQuery code. Let us suppose that a mapping function $\mathcal{T}$ exists from the iteration space to the high-level Schema, denoting the data elements from the high-level Schema that are accessed in a given iteration. As we will show, this could be computed from analysis of the XQuery code. Similarly, suppose the function $\mathcal{C}$ gives the mapping from the high-level Schema to the low-level Schema. This function will be based upon the mapping schema. Then, the function $\mathcal{M}$ mapping the iterations to the low-level Schema can be computed as

$$\mathcal{M} = \mathcal{C} \cdot \mathcal{T}$$

Our goal is to be able to compute the function $\mathcal{M}^{-1}$, which will map the data elements in the low-level Schema to the iterations. Once such a mapping can be computed, we can directly operate on the low-level Schema and perform the computation.

However, an additional challenge arises when multiple datasets or file portions need to be accessed together. Let there be n datasets. We choose one of the datasets as the

Algorithm DataCentricTransformation
  (Source Code, Low-level schema, High-level schema, mapping schema)
{

    Create an abstract iteration space using Source code.
    Allocate and initialize an array of output element corresponding to iteration space.
    Create the structural tree for all input files.
    Determine the base dataset S_1, which will be accessed first
    Determine the mapping from low-level schema to iteration space and
        mapping from iteration space to low-level schema for each Dataset.
    Determine the expression for iteration instance when an data
        element of dataset S_1 is accessed by applying the mapping.
    For each of the other datasets $S_2, \ldots, S_n$
        Determine the required data elements of the dataset S_i to be accessed by applying the mapping.
    Implement the XQuery code following the "Generated_Query" template
        using the previously computed information.

}
Generated_Query
{

    For $k = 1, \ldots NO\_OF\_CHUNKS$
    {

        Read k^{th} chunk of dataset S_1 using HDF5 functions and structural tree.
        For each of the other datasets $S_2, \ldots, S_n$
        access the required chunk of the dataset.
        For each data element in the chunks of data
        {

            compute the iteration instance.
            apply the reduction computation and update the output.
        }

    }

}

Fig. 8. Algorithm for Data-Centric Transformation

base dataset and denote it by S_1. The other datasets are denoted by $S_2, \ldots S_n$. Let the corresponding mapping functions be $\mathcal{M}_1, \ldots, \mathcal{M}_n$. We can take a portion of the dataset S_1 and apply the function $\mathcal{M}_1^{-1}$ to compute the set of iterations. Then, the portions of the datasets $S_2, \ldots S_n$ we need to access can be computed as $\mathcal{M}_2 \cdot \mathcal{M}_1^{-1}, \ldots, \mathcal{M}_n \cdot \mathcal{M}_1^{-1}$, respectively. The choice of the *base* datasets could impact the locality we might achieve in accessing the other datasets. We discuss this issue in more details later in this section.

4.3 Algorithm Details

The steps in our algorithm are summarized in Figure 8. In this subsection, we describe our approach in details.

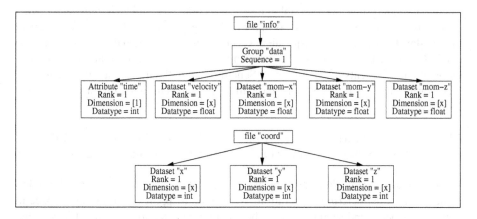

Fig. 9. Structural tree for the low-level Schema in the Oil Reservoir example

We first create an abstract iteration space, corresponding to the nested *for* loops within the *unordered* construct of the XQuery code. An array of output elements corresponding to the iteration space is allocated and initialized in the beginning.

We need to access the required data points from each of the datasets in later steps. For this purpose, we build a *structural tree* from the low-level Schema. In the structural tree, each node represents either a group, a dataset, or an attribute. Each node has child nodes corresponding to each member object. The object members can be groups, datasets, or attributes. Each node is annotated with the metadata information such as name, data-type, rank, and size of each dimension. If a sequence of any member object exists, then the corresponding node is annotated with a special flag to indicate this. The structural tree corresponding to the low-level Schema of Oil Reservoir example is shown in Figure 9.

Now, the structural tree can be traversed in a top-down manner. Appropriate HDF5 library functions are inserted to access data objects depending upon whether a group, dataset,or an attribute is being accessed. If any node is annotated as a sequence, then appropriate HDF5 function is called to determine the number of objects during the runtime and a *for* loop is inserted to access the sequence of objects.

Let us assume that we have already determined the choice of the *base* dataset. We begin with the base dataset. Each element in this dataset is accessed using HDF5 library functions according to the low-level Schema. The elements are read in chunks of a chosen *chunk-size*. For each element in the dataset, the function $\mathcal{M}_1^{-1}$ is applied to determine the zero or more iterations in the abstract space. Our compiler performs static analysis on low-level Schemas, high-level Schemas, mapping Schemas and the XQuery code to compute the mapping function. Specifically, this analysis is done in two steps. First, we extract the conditional statements in the XQuery code which relate iteration numbers with data elements being accessed. These statements can be processed to find out an expression for iteration number(s) involving data elements in high-level Schema. In our example code, the expressions will be "$i = coord/x", "$j = coord/y", and "$k = coord/z".

In the second step, we search the mapping schema. We find the *equivalent expressions*, which relate the data-elements in the high-level Schema with the data elements in the low-level Schema. These equivalent expressions are substituted in the expressions computed in the previous step. Thus, we find out expressions for iteration numbers in terms of data elements in the low-level Schema. In our example, assuming we use velocity or momemtum datasets as the base, the expressions for iteration for the loop over i will be

```
$i = //low/coord/x[index(//low/info/data/velocity, 1)]
$i = //low/coord/x[index(//low/info/data/mom-x, 1)]
```

Next, we determine data elements of all other datasets and attributes which need to be accessed in the determined iteration. We use the mappings from iteration space to low level Schema and search through the mapping Schema to determine the required data elements of all other datasets. In our example, assuming that the velocity dataset is accessed first, the required data element of mom-x dataset will be

```
//low/info/data/mom-x[index(//low/info/data/velocity, 1)]
```

The final step is code generation. Here, we need to insert any additional constraints in the XQuery code. We again use the mapping Schema to substitute the data elements in the high-level Schema with equivalent ones in the low-level Schema. In our example, some of the additional constraints code will be

```
//low/info/data/time >= tmin
//low/info/data/time <= tmax
```

The result of performing data-centric transformation and low-level code generation on our example query code is shown in Figure 10. This is the code if x, y, or z datasets are accessed first.

Finally, we describe how we choose the *base* dataset. We consider each of the n datasets as the base dataset. We compute the mappings we would achieve with each of these. Then, we analyze the I/O behavior of the resulting code. Ideally, we will like to choose the mapping with the lowest execution time. However, this is hard to model, especially because I/O is performed using HDF5 library functions. So, we can use one of the many possible strategies. One strategy we consider is *Min-IO-Volume*. Here, the goal is to choose the base dataset which results in fewest repeated accesses to any other dataset. Another possible strategy is *Min-Seek-Time*. Here, the goal is to minimize any discontinuity in accesses to any dataset.

Consider our example. The Min-IO-Volume strategy gives us x, y, or z as the base dataset. With this strategy, we access a chunk from x, y, or z, then get corresponding chunks for all time-steps for velocity and momentum. Each portion of the file is accessed only once. However, as long as there are multiple chunks for each time-step, the accesses to the velocity and momentum datasets are not contiguous. Using velocity or momentum as the base dataset is optimal with the Min-Seek-Time strategy. This is because we have contiguity in accesses to velocity and momentum dataset. However,

```
For i in ($x1 to $x2)
    For j in ($y1 to $y2)
        For k in ($z1 to $z2)
            Initialize output[i,j,k]
For n = 1,...NO_OF_CHUNKS
    Read nth chunk of datasets x, y, z in file coord using HDF5 library
    For each group "data" in file info
        Read time value using HDF5 library
        Read nth chunk of datasets mom-x, mom-y, mom-z using HDF5 library
        Read nth chunk of dataset velocity using HDF5 library
        For each data element in the chunks of data
            index = offset of data element in the dataset
            i = x[index]; j=y[index]; k=z[index];
            if (i ≥ $x1) and (i ≤ $x2) and
               (j ≥ $y1) and (j ≤ $y2) and
               (k ≥ $z1) and (k ≤ $z2)
                   Apply the reduction function and update output[i,j,k]
```

Fig. 10. Results of Data-Centric Transformations

portions of x, y, and z datasets need to be accessed multiple times, which means higher I/O volume.

The relative performance of two strategies depends upon the system characteristics and the implementation of the library functions used for data accesses. We will experimentally evaluate these two strategies in the next section.

5   Experimental Results

We have conducted a number of experiments to evaluate the generated code that uses HDF5 library functions. Our main goal was to evaluate the impact of choice of strategy and chunk-size on performance. We used two applications, *oil reservoir simulation*, which was also used as the running example in this paper, and *virtual microscope* [16]. All our experiments were carried out on a 700 MHz machine with PIII processor.

We initially describe the results from the *oil reservoir simulation* application. As explained in the previous section, code with significantly different I/O properties are generated with the use of *Min-Seek-Time* and *Min-IO-Volume* strategies. Further, a number of different chunk-sizes could be used with each of these.

We used two different datasets for our experiments with this application. The Dataset 1 has a $200 \times 200 \times 200$ grid with 10 time-steps. The total size of the data is 1.28 GB. The chunks used for storing the data, referred to as the *storage chunks*, comprise $50 \times 50 \times 50$ elements. The Dataset 2 has a $50 \times 50 \times 50$ grid with 200 time-steps. The total size of the data is 400 MB and each storage chunk comprises $25 \times 25 \times 25$ elements.

The results from the *Dataset 1* are presented in Figure 11. We compared the codes corresponding to *Min-Seek-Time* and *Min-IO-Volume* strategies with 6 different chunk-sizes for reading and processing the data. These chunk-sizes are 1K, 5K, 15K, 31K, 62K, and 125K, elements, respectively. In the last case (125K), the chunk-size for reading the data matches the storage chunk-size. The overall minimum execution time is achieved with the *Min-IO-Volume* strategy and the 125K chunk-size. The execution time with the *Min-Seek-Time* strategy is higher. This is because the total I/O volume with this strategy is higher, and moreover, HDF5 storage and access mechanisms allow chunks to be accessed randomly. However, the execution time with the *Min-IO-Volume* strategy is very sensitive to the chunk-size. With smaller chunk-sizes, the execution time increases rapidly. This is because HDF5 reads an entire storage chunk, even if only a part of it is actually required. With the *Min-IO-Volume* strategy, the accesses to chunks are not consecutive, which means that successive I/O requests involve different storage chunks. In the *Min-Seek-Time* strategy, if smaller chunk sizes are used, the consecutive requests are to the same storage chunk. The HDF5 libraries are designed to cache and reuse data from the same storage chunk in these cases. Therefore, the net I/O volume does not increase, and the execution is almost the same with the use of different chunk-sizes for reading the data.

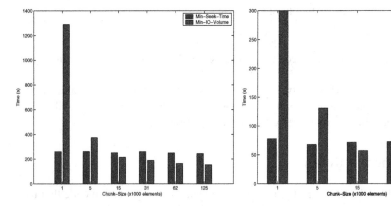

Fig. 11. Impact of Strategy and Chunk-Size, Dataset 1

Fig. 12. Impact of Strategy and Chunk-Size, Dataset 2

The results from the *Dataset 2* are presented in Figure 12. We used 5 different chunk-sizes for reading and processing the data, which are 1K, 5K, 15K, 31K, and 62K elements, respectively. In the 15K case, the chunk-size for reading matches the storage chunk-size. Again, the overall minimum execution time is achieved with the *Min-IO-Volume* strategy and the chunk-size that matches the storage chunk-size. Similar to the previous experiment, the performance of *Min-IO-Volume* strategy is very sensitive to the chunk-size. The execution with *Min-Seek-Time* remains almost unchanged with chunk-size.

The second application we used was *virtual microscope* [16]. Because only a single dataset is involved in this application, the issue of choosing the *base* dataset does

Chunk-size	1000×1000	500×500	500×250	250×250	200×100	100×100
Execution Time (Sec.)	64.18	59.62	61.46	76.76	109.51	93.73

Fig. 13. Impact of Chunk-Size on Virtual Microscope Application

not arise. Our experiment focused on evaluating the impact of chunk-size on the performance. We used a 400 MB dataset with a storage chunk comprising 500×500 elements.

Figure 13 presents the results with 6 different chunk-sizes used for reading and processing the data. Consistent with what we observed for the previous experiments, the lowest execution time is achieved when the size of the chunk for reading the data matches the storage chunk size. Smaller chunk sizes results in higher execution times, as data is always read as storage chunks. A larger chunk size also can increase the execution time.

6   Related Work

Our work is related to, and in part motivated by, the work on automatically synthesizing sparse computations from dense codes [2,19,21]. Our contribution is to show how XML Schemas can be systematically used by the compiler to support high-level abstractions. Thus, our work is not limited to supporting a fixed number of sparse data layouts. However, we are limited to transforming only a limited class of computations.

Our work on data-centric transformations derives from the original work in this area by Pingali *et al.* [15]. Our focus is on supporting such transformations on disk-resident datasets, and applying these transformations on XQuery codes written with high-level view of the datasets. As compared to the data-centric transformations presented in our earlier work [9,16], the algorithm presented in this paper is quite different. First, it can handle the cases when chunks from multiple datasets needs to be retrieved to carry out the computations. Second, by assuming a different kind of mapping information, we do not need to invert the *getData* functions. This paper also deals with issues specific to HDF5.

Compiler optimizations for out-of-core data-structures have been considered by several projects [14,20,6]. Our particular contribution has been the application of XML technologies for supporting high-level abstractions, as well as the new compiler techniques for supporting them.

XQuery compilation is an active area of research in the database community. Significant attention has been paid to integrating and querying XML over relational databases [7,25,27,18] and various approaches for supporting XQuery [13,8]. We are not aware of any other efforts on supporting XQuery over scientific or flat-file datasets.

The NCSA HDF group is developing a suite of tools for using XML together with HDF-5[2]. This includes tool that can output HDF-5 datasets in XML, or can read XML and create HDF-5 datasets. Our focus is quite different, as we support XML as a virtual view of HDF-5 datasets. Our compiler transforms the queries to execute on HDF-5 datasets, and does not involve the overhead of transforming data from one format to another.

---

[2] See http://hdf.ncsa.uiuc.edu/HDF5/XML

```
<file name="coord">
   <dataset name="x">   <datatype> integer </datatype>
    <dataspace>  <rank> 1 </rank> <dimension> [x] </dimension>  </dataspace>
   </dataset>
   <dataset name="y">   <datatype> integer </datatype>
    <dataspace>  <rank> 1 </rank> <dimension> [x] </dimension>  </dataspace>
   </dataset>
   <dataset name="z">   <datatype> integer </datatype>
    <dataspace>  <rank> 1 </rank> <dimension> [x] </dimension>  </dataspace>
   </dataset>
</file>

<file name="info">
 <sequence>
  <group name="data">

    <attribute name="time">   <datatype> integer </datatype>
     <dataspace>  <rank> 1 </rank> <dimension> [1] </dimension>  </dataspace>
    </attribute>

    <dataset name="velocity">   <datatype> float </datatype>
     <dataspace>  <rank> 1 </rank> <dimension> [x] </dimension>  </dataspace>
    </dataset>
    <dataset name="mom-x">   <datatype> float </datatype>
     <dataspace>  <rank> 1 </rank> <dimension> [x] </dimension>  </dataspace>
    </dataset>
    <dataset name="mom-y">   <datatype> float </datatype>
     <dataspace> <rank> 1 </rank> <dimension> [x] </dimension> </dataspace>
    </dataset>
    <dataset name="mom-z">   <datatype> float </datatype>
     <dataspace>  <rank> 1 </rank> <dimension> [x] </dimension>  </dataspace>
    </dataset>

  </group>
 </sequence>
</file>
```

Fig. 14. Low-Level XML Schema for Oil Reservoir Simulation Data

7 Conclusions

This paper has described an implementation of our overall approach of automatic data virtualization. The basic idea is that compiler techniques can be used to create a light-weight, but efficient, layer on top of complex datasets stored in a low-level format. The particular implementation here provides XML-based abstractions on HDF5 datasets. We have presented a new algorithm for data-centric transformation to support code generation and efficient execution.

Our results have shown that it is important for the compiler to understand the performance aspects of the low-level library functions it automatically generates. Our future work will focus on evaluating the overall efficiency of the code generated by the compiler. Other directions for future work include parallelizing the data processing, and further generalizing our data-centric transformation algorithm.

References

1. D. Beech, S. Lawrence, M. Maloney, N. Mendelsohn, and H. Thompson. XML Schema part 1: Structures, W3C working draft. Available at http://www.w3.org/TR/1999/xmlschema-1, May 1999.

2. Aart Bik and Harry A. G. Wijshoff. Compilation techniques for sparse matrix computations. In *Proceedings of International Conference on Supercomputing (ICS)*, pages 416–424. ACM Press, July 1993.

3. P. Biron and A. Malhotra. XML Schema part 2: Datatypes, W3C working draft. Available at http://www.w3.org/TR/1999/xmlschema-2, May 1999.

4. S. Boag, D. Chamberlin, M. F. Fernandez, D. Florescu, J. Robie, and J. Simeon. XQuery 1.0: An XML Query Language. W3C Working Draft, available from http://www.w3.org/TR/xquery/, November 2002.

5. Byron Choi, Mary Fernandez, and Jerome Simeon. The XQuery Formal Semantics: A Foundation for Implementation and Opitmization. May 2002.

6. Daniel Cociorva, Gerald Baumgartner, Chi-Chung Lam, P. Sadayappan, J. Ramanujam, Marcel Nooijen, David E. Bernholdt, and Robert Harrison. Space-time trade-off optimization for a class of electronic structure calculations. In *Proceedings of the ACM SIGPLAN 2002 Conference on Programming Language Design and Implementation (PLDI-02)*, pages 177–186, 2002.

7. David DeHaan, David Toman, Mariano P. Consens, and M. Tamer Ozsu. A Comprehensive XQuery to SQL Translation Using Dynamic Interval Coding. In *Proceedings of the ACM SIGMOD*. ACM Press, June 2003.

8. Mary F. Fernandez, Jerome Simeon, Byron Choi, Amelie Marian, and Gargi Sur. Implementing XQuery 1.0: The Galax Experience. In *Proceedings of the 29th International Conference on Very Large Data Bases (VLDB)*, pages 1077–1080, 2003.

9. Renato Ferreira, Gagan Agrawal, and Joel Saltz. Compiler supported high-level abstractions for sparse disk-resident datasets. In *Proceedings of the International Conference on Supercomputing (ICS)*, June 2002.

10. Chris Ferris and Joel Farrell. What are Web Services. *Communications of the ACM (CACM)*, pages 31–35, June 2003.

11. Ian Foster, Carl Kesselman, Jeffrey M. Nick, and Steven Tuecke. The Physiology of the Grid: An Open Grid Services Architecture for Distributed Systems Integration. In *Open Grid Service Infrastructure Working Group, Global Grid Forum*, June 2002.

12. HDF Group at NCSA. Introduction to HDF5 Release 1.4. Available at http://hdf.ncsa.uiuc.edu/HDF5/doc/H5.intro.html, 2003.

13. H. V. Jagadish, S. Al-Khalifa, A. Chapman, L. V. S. Lakshmanan, A. Nierman, S. Paparizos, J. M. Patel, D. Srivastava, N. Wiwatwattana, Y. Wu, and C. Yu. TIMBER: A native XML database. *The VLDB Journal*, 11(4):274–291, 2002.

14. M. Kandemir, A. Choudhary, J. Ramanujam, and M. A.. Kandaswamy. A unified framework for optimizing locality, parallelism, and comunication in out-of-core computations. *IEEE Transactions on Parallel and Distributed Systems*, 11(9):648–662, 2000.

15. Induprakas Kodukula, Nawaaz Ahmed, and Keshav Pingali. Data-centric multi-level blocking. In *Proceedings of the SIGPLAN '97 Conference on Programming Language Design and Implementation*, pages 346–357, June 1997.
16. Xiaogang Li and Gagan Agrawal. Supporting XML-Based High-level Interfaces Through Compiler Technology. In *Proceedings of Languages and Compilers for Parallel Computing (LCPC)*, October 2003.
17. Xiaogang Li, Renato Ferreira, and Gagan Agrawal. Compiler Support for Efficient Processing of XML Datasets. In *Proceedings of the International Conference on Supercomputing (ICS)*, pages 67–77. ACM Press, June 2003.
18. Ioana Manolescu, Daniela Florescu, and Donald Kossmann. Answering XML Queries on Heterogeneous Data Sources. In *Proceedings of the 27th International Conference on Very Large Data Bases*, pages 242–250, 2001.
19. Nikolay Mateev, Keshav Pingali, Paul Stodghill, and Vladimir Kotlyar. Next-generation generic programming and its application to sparse matrix computations. In *Proceedings of International Conference on Supercomputing (ICS), 2000*, pages 88–100. ACM Press, May 2000.
20. Todd C. Mowry, Angela K. Demke, and Orran Krieger. Automatic compiler-inserted i/o prefetching for out-of-core applications. In *Proceedings of the Second Symposium on Operating Systems Design and plementation (OSDI '96)*, Nov 1996.
21. William Pugh and Tatiana Shpeisman. Generation of efficient code for sparse matrix computations. In *Proceedings of the Eleventh Workshop on Languages and Compilers for Parallel Computing, Lecture Notes in Computer Science (LNCS)*, August 1998.
22. R. K. Rew and G. P. Davis. NetCDF: An Interface for Scientific Data Access. *IEEE Computer Graphics and Applications*, 10(4):76–82, 1990.
23. J. Saltz, U. Catalyurek, T. Kurc, M. Gray, S. Hastings, S. Langella, S. Narayanan, R. Martino, S. Bryant, M. Peszynska, M. Wheeler, A. Sussman, M. Beynon, C. Hansen, D. Stredney, , and D. Sessanna. Driving scientific applications by data in distributed environments. In *Dynamic Data Driven Application Systems Workshop, held jointly with ICCS 2003*, Melbourne, Australia, June 2003.
24. Sunita Sarawagi and Michael Stonebraker. Efficient organizations of large multidimensional arrays. In *Proceedings of the Tenth International Conference on Data Engineering*, February 1994.
25. Igor Tatarinov, Stratis D. Viglas, Kevin Beyer, Jayavel Shanmugasundaram, Eugene Shekita, and Chun Zhang. Storing and querying ordered XML using a relational database system. In *Proceedings of the 2002 ACM SIGMOD international conference on Management of data*, pages 204–215, 2002.
26. Li Weng, Gagan Agrawal, Umit Catalyurek, Tahsin Kurc, Sivaramakrishnan Narayanan, and Joel Saltz. An Approach for Automatic Data Virtualization. In *Proceedings of the Conference on High Performance Distributed Computing (HPDC) (to appear)*, June 2004.
27. Xin Zhang, Mukesh Mulchandani, Steffen Christ, Brian Murphy, and Elke A. Rundensteiner. Rainbow: mapping-driven XQuery processing system. In *Proceedings of the 2002 ACM SIGMOD international conference on Management of data*, page 614, 2002.

Performance of OSCAR Multigrain Parallelizing Compiler on SMP Servers

Kazuhisa Ishizaka[†], Takamichi Miyamoto[†], Jun Shirako[†], Motoki Obata[‡], Keiji Kimura[†], and Hironori Kasahara[†]

[†] Department of Computer Science,
Advanced Chip Multiprocessor Research Institute, Waseda University,
3-4-1 Ohkubo, Shinjuku-ku, Tokyo, 169-8555, Japan
{ishizaka, miyamoto, shirako, kimura, kasahara}@oscar.elec.waseda.ac.jp
[‡] System Development Laboratory, Hitachi Co.Ltd.
m-obata@sdl.hitachi.co.jp

Abstract. This paper describes performance of OSCAR multigrain parallelizing compiler on various SMP servers, such as IBM pSeries 690, Sun Fire V880, Sun Ultra 80, NEC TX7/i6010 and SGI Altix 3700. The OSCAR compiler hierarchically exploits the coarse grain task parallelism among loops, subroutines and basic blocks and the near fine grain parallelism among statements inside a basic block in addition to the loop parallelism. Also, it allows us global cache optimization over different loops, or coarse grain tasks, based on data localization technique with inter-array padding to reduce memory access overhead. Current performance of OSCAR compiler is evaluated on the above SMP servers. For example, the OSCAR compiler generating OpenMP parallelized programs from ordinary sequential Fortran programs gives us 5.7 times speedup, in the average of seven programs, such as SPEC CFP95 tomcatv, swim, su2cor, hydro2d, mgrid, applu and turb3d, compared with IBM XL Fortran compiler 8.1 on IBM pSeries 690 24 processors SMP server. Also, it gives us 2.6 times speedup compare with Intel Fortran Itanium Compiler 7.1 on SGI Altix 3700 Itanium 2 16 processors server, 1.7 times speedup compared with NEC Fortran Itanium Compiler 3.4 on NEC TX7/i6010 Itanium 2 8 processors server, 2.5 times speedup compared with Sun Forte 7.0 on Sun Ultra 80 UltraSPARC II 4 processors desktop workstation, and 2.1 times speedup compare with Sun Forte compiler 7.1 on Sun Fire V880 UltraSPARC III Cu 8 processors server.

1 Introduction

Currently, multiprocessor architectures are widely used for chip multiprocessors to desktop workstations, mid-range servers and high-end servers. However, the gap between peak and effective performance of a multiprocessor system is getting larger with the increase of the number of processors. Although, efficient parallel programs are important to improve effective performance, software development on a multiprocessor requires special knowledge and experience in parallel programming and the long duration. To improve effective performance,

R. Eigenmann et al. (Eds.): LCPC 2004, LNCS 3602, pp. 319–331, 2005.

cost-performance and software productivity of multiprocessor systems , strong automatic parallelizing compilers are required.

So far, in automatic parallelizing compilers for multiprocessor systems, the loop parallelization techniques have been used. For the loop parallelization, various data dependence analysis techniques[1,2,3] such as GCD, Banerjee's inexact and exact tests, OMEGA test[4], symbolic analysis[5] and dynamic dependence test and program restructuring techniques have been researched and also employed in compiler products available in the market. As research compilers, Polaris compiler[3] exploits loop parallelism by using inline expansion of subroutine, symbolic propagation, array privatization[6], run-time data dependence analysis[7] and interprocedural access region test[8] and SUIF compiler uses strong inter-procedure analysis[9] unimodular transformation and data locality optimization[10] including affine partitioning[11]. However, by those research efforts, the loop parallelization techniques are reaching maturity.

In light of this fact, new generation parallelization techniques like multigrain parallelization are needed to overcome the limitation of loop parallelization. NANOS compiler[12] based on Parafrase2 has been trying to exploit the multi-level parallelism including the coarse grain parallelism by using extended OpenMP API. The OSCAR multigrain parallelizing compiler[13] exploits the coarse grain task parallelism among loops, subroutines and basic blocks[14], and the near fine grain parallelism among statements inside a basic block[15] in addition to the conventional loop parallelism among iterations.

The OSCAR compiler has been developed as a core module of Japanese Millennium Project IT21 "Advanced Parallelizing Compiler project". The advanced parallelizing compiler project is a three years project started in FY 2000 to develop an automatic parallelizing compiler to improve effective performance, cost-performance and software productivity for shared memory multiprocessor architectures used for chip multiprocessors to high-end servers.

This paper describes the OSCAR multigrain parallelizing compiler and its performance on off-the-shelf SMP servers, such as IBM pSeries 690 24 way Power4 high-end SMP server and Sun Fire V880 8 UltraSPARC III Cus server, Sun Ultra80 4 UltraSPARC IIs desktop workstation, NEC TX7/i6010 8 way Itanium 2 server, SGI Altix 16 way Itanium 2 server using OSCAR compiler's OpenMP platform-free backend.

2   OSCAR Multigrain Parallelizing Compiler

The OSCAR compiler exploits multigrain parallelism, namely, coarse grain parallelism, loop level parallelism and near fine grain parallelism from the whole source program. As shown in Figure 1, the OSCAR compiler consists of the Fortran frontend, middle path for multigrain parallelization and several backends for different target machines such as the OSCAR chip multiprocessor[16], SMP servers supporting OpenMP and cluster systems supporting MPI. In the multigrain parallel processing for SMP servers treated in this paper, the compiler generates coarse grain tasks called "macro-tasks" such as loops, subroutines

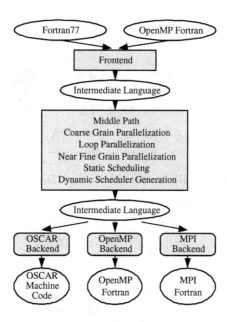

Fig. 1. Flow of OSCAR Multigrain Compiler

and basic blocks, analyzes parallelism among the macro-tasks by the earliest executable condition analysis based on control and data dependence analysis, decomposes macro-tasks and data for cache or distributed shared memory optimization by loop aligned decomposition, schedules macro-tasks to threads or thread groups statically or dynamically considering data locality, generates parallel code with OpenMP API using "One-time single level thread generation".

2.1 Macro-task Generation

In the multigrain parallelization, a source program is decomposed into three kinds of coarse grain tasks, or macro-tasks, namely block of pseudo assignment statements(BPA) repetition block(RB), subroutine block(SB).

Also, macro-tasks are generated hierarchically inside of a sequential repetition block and a subroutine block as shown in Figure 2.

2.2 Earliest Executable Condition

After the generation of macro-tasks, compiler analyzes data flow and control flow among macro-tasks in each layer or each nested level. Next, to extract parallelism among macro-tasks, the compiler analyzes Earliest Executable Condition(EEC)[13] of each macro-task. EEC represents the conditions on which macro-task may begin its execution earliest.

EEC of macro-task is represented in macro-task Graph (MTG) as shown in Figure 3. In macro-task graph, nodes represent macro-tasks. A small circle inside nodes represents conditional branches. Solid edges represent data dependencies.

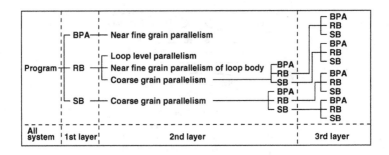

Fig. 2. Hierarchical Macro Task Definition

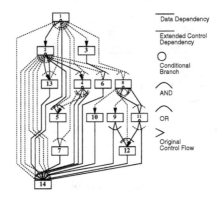

Fig. 3. An Example of Macro-Task Graph

Dotted edges represent extended control dependencies. Extended control dependency means ordinary control dependency and the condition on which a data dependent predecessor macro-task is not executed. A solid arc represents that edges connected by the arc are in AND relationship. A dotted arc represents that edges connected by the arc are in OR relation ship.

2.3 Macro-task Scheduling

In the coarse grain task parallel processing, static scheduling and dynamic scheduling are used for an assignment of macro-tasks to threads.

If a macro-task graph has only data dependencies and is deterministic, static scheduling is selected. In the static scheduling, an assignment of macro-tasks to threads is determined at compile time by the scheduler in the compiler. Static scheduling is useful since it allows us to minimize data transfer and synchronization overhead without runtime scheduling overhead.

If a macro-task graph has control dependencies, the dynamic scheduling is selected to handle runtime uncertainties like conditional branches. The scheduling routines for the dynamic scheduling are generated by the compiler and inserted into a parallelized program with macro-task code.

2.4   Global Cache Optimization

In the coarse grain task parallel processing, macro-tasks can begin its execution when Earliest Executable Condition is satisfied without regard for the program order in the original source code. Therefore, the compiler decides the execution order of macro-tasks so that macro-tasks accessing the same data can be executed on the same processor consecutively to optimize cache usage among the tasks.

Loop Aligned Decomposition
To avoid cache misses among the macro-tasks, Loop Aligned Decomposition (LAD) [17] is applied to the loops that access data larger than cache size. LAD divides the loops, or macro-tasks, into partial loops with the smaller number of iterations so that data size accessed by the divided loops is smaller than cache size.

The partial loops are defined as coarse grain tasks and the Earliest Executable Condition analysis is applied again. The partial loops connected by data dependence edge on the macro task graph are grouped into "Data Localizable Group(DLG)". The macro-tasks inside a DLG are assigned to the same processor as consecutively as possible statically or dynamically.

In the macro-task graph of Figure 4(a), it is assumed that macro-tasks 2, 3 and 7 are parallel loops accessing the same shared array variables exceeding cache size. In this example, the loops are divided into four partial loops by the LAD technique. For example, the macro-task 2 in Figure 4(a) is divided into the macro-tasks 2_A through 2_D shown in Figure 4(b). Also, the DLGs like DLG_A composed of macro-task 2_A, 3_A, 7_A are defined.

Consecutive Execution of Data Localizable Group
In the original program, macro-tasks are executed in the increasing order of the node number on the macro-task graph. For example, the execution order of macro-tasks 2_A to 3_D is 2_A, 2_B, 2_C, 2_D, 3_A 3_B, 3_C, 3_D. In this order, macro-tasks in the same DLG are not executed consecutively.

However, the earliest executable condition shown in Figure 4(b) means that macro-task 3_B, for example, can be executed immediately after macro-task 2_B because macro-task 3_B depends on macro-task 2_B only.

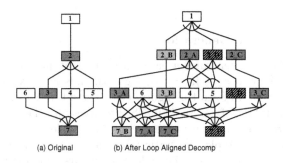

(a) Original   (b) After Loop Aligned Decomp

Fig. 4. Example of Loop Align Decomposition

Fig. 5. Consecutive Execution of Data Localizable Group

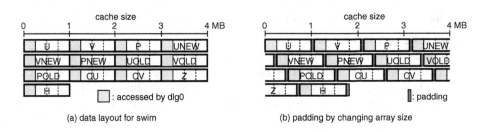

(a) data layout for swim   (b) padding by changing array size

Fig. 6. Padding to Reduce Conflict Messes

In the proposed cache optimization scheme, the task scheduler assigns macro-tasks inside a DLG to the same processor as consecutively as possible[18] in addition to the "critical path" priority used by the both static and dynamic scheduling. Figure 5 shows a schedule when the proposed cache optimization is applied to macro-task graph in Figure 4(b) for a single processor. As shown in Figure 5, the macro-task 2_B, 3_B, 8_B in DLG_B and the macro-task 2_C, 3_C, 7_C in DLG_C are executed consecutively to use the data on cache optimally.

Reduction of Cache Conflict Misses

The Loop Aligned Decomposition and The Consecutive Execution of a DLG enable the shared data to be reused before cache line replacement. However, if the data accessed by the macro-tasks in a DLG share the same cache line on a cache as shown in Figure 6(a), the data may be removed from the cache before reuse because of line conflict misses even though the amount of data accessed in a DLG is smaller than the cache size. To reduce conflict misses, the OSCAR compiler analyzes data layout on the cache and applies inter-array padding to remove line conflicts among data in a DLG on the cache as shown in Figure 6(b)[19].

2.5   OpenMP Code Generation

The OSCAR compiler generates a parallelized Fortran program with OpenMP directives. A generated code image for eight threads is shown in Figure 7 for the macro-task graph in 8. In this figure, eight threads are generated only once by the OpenMP PARALLEL SECTIONS directives and the generated threads join at the end of program by using the "One-time single level thread generation scheme"[13]. In this example, the static scheduling is applied to the 1st layer of MTG in Figure 8. In this case, the eight threads are grouped into two thread groups each of which has four threads as shown in Figure 7 to process MTG1 having parallelism of "2" estimated by the compiler in Figure 7. MT1_1 and

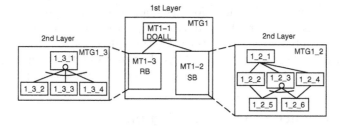

Fig. 7. Sample Macro Task Graph having 3 Layers

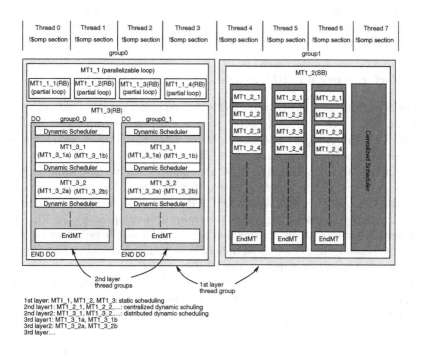

Fig. 8. Generated Code Image using OpenMP (8 threads)

MT1_3 are assigned to thread group0 composed of four threads and MT1_2 is assigned to thread group1. When static scheduling is applied like this program layer, the compiler generates different program codes for each OpenMP SECTION according to the static schedule as shown in Figure 8. The macro-tasks assigned to each thread groups are processed in parallel by threads inside each thread group by using static scheduling or dynamic scheduling hierarchically. In this example, MT1_2 in Figure 7 assigned to thread-group1 in Figure 8 is processed by four threads in parallel using the centralized dynamic scheduling scheme. In Figure 8, threads 5, 6 and 7 execute some of sub macro-tasks like MT1_2_1, MT1_2_2 and so on, which are generated inside MT1_2 in Figure 7, assigned by thread 4 working as the centralized dynamic scheduler. Also, MT1_3 in Figure 7 shows a code image for distributed dynamic scheduling in which scheduling codes are inserted before and after task codes. In this case, MT1_3 is decomposed into sub macro-tasks 1_3_1 through 1_3_4 as shown in Figure 7 and assigned to thread group0_0 and 0_1 defined inside thread group0. In this example, the thread group0_0 and 0_1 consists of two threads respectively.

3   Performance of OSCAR Compiler

This section describes the performance evaluation of the OSCAR multigrain parallelizing compiler on different multiprocessor servers available on the market using popular benchmark programs such as, tomcatv, swim, su2cor hydro2d, mgrid, applu, turb3d from SPEC CFP95 Benchmarks.

3.1   Performance on IBM pSeries 690 24 Way SMP Server

Figure 9 shows the performance of OSCAR compiler on the IBM pSeries 690 high-end UNIX server with 24 processors, or 12 Power4 chips. Left bars show speedups by automatic parallelization of the IBM XL Fortran compiler version 8.1 against sequential executions of the XLF compiler.

Right bars show speedups by OSCAR compiler against the same sequential executions of the XLF compiler. The speedup by OSCAR compiler was mesured using the OpenMP backend of the OSCAR compiler. The generated OpenMP parallelized programs from sequential programs were compiled by the XL Fortran compiler and executed on pSeries 690 server. The numbers above bars show parallel execution times and the numbers below the benchmark program names are sequential execution times by the XLF compiler.

For tomcatv, the sequential execution time was 23 seconds and the fastest parallel execution time up to 24 processors by XLF compiler was 19 seconds and OSCAR compiler was 2.9 seconds. In other words, OSCAR compiler gave

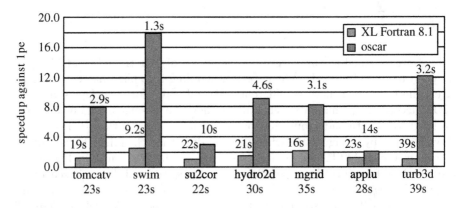

Fig. 9. Performance on IBM pSeries 690 24 Processors Server

us 7.9 times speedup against sequential execution, 6.6 times speedup compared with the XLF compiler. Also, OSCAR gave us 17.8 times speedup compared with sequential execution (7.2 times compared with XLF compiler automatic parallelization) for swim, 3.0 times (3.0 times) for su2cor, 9.2 times (6.4 times) for hydro2d, 8.3 times (3.9 times) for mgrid, 2.0 times (1.7 times) for applu, 12.2 times (11.5 times) for turb3d.

In the average of the above 7 programs, the XLF compiler gave us 1.5 times speedup against sequential execution and OSCAR gave us 8.6 times speedup against sequential execution, namely 5.7 times compared with the parallel execution of the XLF.

3.2   Performance on SGI Altix 3700 16 Itanium 2 SMP Server

This section shows the performance of OSCAR compiler on SGI Altix 3700 server with 16 Itanium 2 processors. Figure 10 shows the performance of Intel Fortran Itanium compiler revision 7.1 and OSCAR compiler using up to 16 processors.

OSCAR compiler gave us 5.7 times speedup against sequetial execution (5.7 times speedup against Intel compiler automatic parallelization) for tomc atv, 8.0 times (2.1 times) for swim, 1.4 times (1.4 times) for su2cor, 3.2 times (3.2 times) for hydro2d, 2.6 times (1.7 times) for mgrid, 1.2 times (1.1 times) for applu, 5.5 times (5.4 times) for turb3d and 3.9 times (2.6 times) in the average for the above 7 programs.

3.3   Performance on NEC TX7/i6010 8 Itanium 2 SMP Server

This section shows the performance of OSCAR compiler on NEC TX7/i6010 server with 8 Itanium 2 processors.

Figure 11 shows the performance of NEC Fortran Itanium Compiler revision 3.4 and OSCAR compiler.

OSCAR compiler gave us 4.4 times speedup against sequetial execution (3.3 times speedup against NEC Compiler automatic parallelization) for tomcat v,

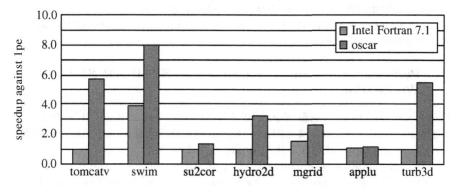

Fig. 10. Performance on Altix 3700 16 Processors Server

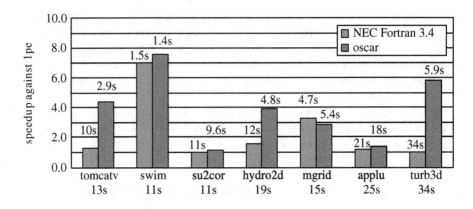

Fig. 11. Performance on NEC TX7/i6010 8 Processors Server

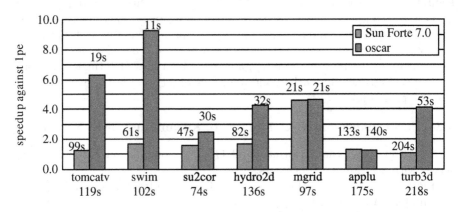

Fig. 12. Performance on Sun Ultra 80 4 Processors Workstation

7.6 times (1.1 times) for swim, 1.1 times (1.1 times) for su2cor, 3.9 times (2.5 times) for hydro2d, 2.9 times (0.9 times) for mgrid, 1.4 times (1.2 times) for applu, 5.8 times (5.8 times) for turb3d and 3.9 times (1.7 times) in the average for the above 7 programs.

3.4   Performance on Sun Ultra 80 4 UltraSPARC II SMP Workstation

This section shows the performance of OSCAR compiler on Sun Ultra 80 desktop workstation with 4 UltraSPARC II. Figure 12 shows the performance of Sun Forte 7.1 compiler and OSCAR compiler on Ultra 80.

OSCAR compiler gave us 6.3 times speedup against sequetial execution (5.2 times speedup against Forte compiler automatic parallelization) for tomcatv, 9.2 times (5.5 times) for swim, 2.5 times (1.6 times) for su2cor, 4.3 times (2.6 times) for hydro2d, 4.7 times (1.0 times) for mgrid, 1.2 times (0.9 times) for applu,

4.1 times (3.8 times) for turb3d and 4.6 times (2.5 times) in the average for the above 7 programs.

3.5 Performance on Sun Fire V880 8 UltraSPARC III Cu SMP Server

This section shows the performance of OSCAR compiler on Sun Fire V880 server with 8 UltraSPARC III Cu processors. Figure 13 shows speedups and execution times of benchmark programs compiled by Sun Forte 7.1 compiler and OSCAR compiler on the V880.

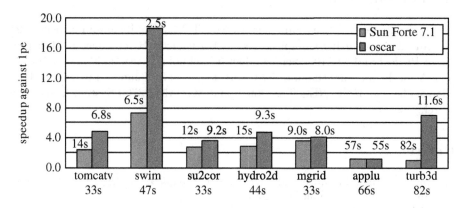

Fig. 13. Performance on Sun Fire V880 8 Processors Server

OSCAR compiler gave us 4.9 times speedup against sequetial execution (2.1 times speedup against Forte compiler automatic parallelization) for tomcatv, 18.6 times (2.5 times) for swim, 3.6 times (1.3 times) for su2cor, 4.7 times (1.6 times) for hydro2d, 4.1 times (1.1 times) for mgrid, 1.2 times (1.0 times) for applu, 7.1 times (7.1 times) for turb3d and 6.3 times (2.1 times) in the average for the above 7 programs.

4   Conclusions

This paper has described the current performance of OSCAR multigrain parallelizing compiler that has been developed as a Japanese Government Millennium Project IT21 Advanced Parallelizing Compiler (APC). The OSCAR compiler exploits the coarse grain task parallelism, the loop parallelism and the near fine grain parallelism hierarchically with "one-time single level thread generation technique" and global cache optimization with padding data layout transformation for various SMP servers such as IBM pSeries 690 24 way Power4 SMP server, Sun Fire V880 8 UltraSPARC III server, Sun Ultra 80 4 UltraSPARC II desktop workstation, NEC TX7/i6010 8 Itanium 2 server, SGI Altix 3700 16 Itanium 2 server.

It currently gives us 5.7 times speedup compared with IBM XL Fortran compiler 8.1 on the IBM pSeries 690 in the average of 7 programs, such as SPEC CFP95 tomcatv, swim, su2cor, hydro2d, mgrid, applu and turb3d. Also it gives us 2.6 times speedup compared with Intel Fortran Itanium Compiler 7.1 on SGI Altix 3700, 1.7 times speedup compared with NEC Fortran Itanium Compiler 3.4 on NEC TX7/i6010, 2.5 times compared with Sun Forte 7.0 on Sun Ultra 80, and 2.1 times speedup compare with Sun Forte compiler 7.1 on Sun Fire V880.

Acknowledgments

A part of this research was supported by METI/NEDO millennium project IT21 "advanced Parallelizing Compiler", NEDO Advanced Heterogeneous Multiprocessor Project and STARC (Semiconductor Technology Academic Research Center). Also, the auhours thank to NEC soft, Ltd. and SGI Japan, Ltd. for the kind offer of the use of the NEC TX7/i6010 and SGI Altix 3700 System for this research.

References

1. Randy Allen and Ken Kennedy. *Optimizaing Compilers for Modern Architectures.* Morgan Kaufmann Publishers, 2001.
2. Michel Wolfe. *High performance compilers for parallel computing.* Addison-Wesley, 1996.
3. R. Eigenmann, J. Hoeflinger, and D. Padua. On the automatic parallelization of the perfect benchmarks. *IEEE Trans. on parallel and distributed systems*, 9(1), Jan. 1998.
4. W. Pugh. The omega test: A fast and practical integer programming algorithm for dependence analysis. In *Proc. of Super Computing '91*, 1991.
5. M. R. Haghighat and C. D. Polychronopoulos. *Symbolic analysis for parallelizing compilers.* Kluwer Academic Publishers, 1995.
6. P. Tu and D. Padua. Automatic array privatization. *Proc. 6th Annual Workshop on Languages and Compilers for Parallel Computing*, 1993.
7. L. Rauchwerger, N. M. Amato, and D. A. Padua. Run-time methods for parallelizing partially parallel loops. *Proceedings of the 9th ACM International Conference on Supercomputing, Barcelona, Spain*, pages 137–146, Jul. 1995.
8. Jay Hoeflinger and Yunheung Paek. Unified interprocedural parallelism detection. *International Journal of Parallel Processing*, 2000.
9. M. W. Hall, B. R. Murphy, S. P. Amarasinghe, S. Liao, , and M. S. Lam. Interprocedural parallelization analysis: A case study. *Proceedings of the 8th International Workshop on Languages and Compilers for Parallel Computing*, Aug. 1995.
10. J. M. Anderson, S. P. Amarasinghe, and M. S. Lam. Data and computation transformations for multiprocessors. *Proc. of the Fifth ACM SIGPLAN Symposium on Principles and Practice of Parallel Processing*, Jul. 1995.
11. A. W. Lim, G. I. Cheong, and M. S. Lam. An affine partitoning algorithm to maximize parallelism and minimize communication. *Proc. of the 13th ACM SIGARCH International Conference on Supercomputing*, Jun. 1999.

12. X. Martorell, E. Ayguade, N. Navarro, J. Corbalan, M. Gonzalez, and J. Labarta. Thread fork/join techniques for multi-level parallelism exploitatio in numa multi-processors. *Proc. of the 1999 International Conference on Supercomputing*, June 1999.

13. H. Kasahara, M. Obata, and K. Ishizaka. Automatic coarse grain task parallel processing on smp using openmp. *Proc. of 13 th International Workshop on Languages and Compilers for Parallel Computing 2000*, Aug. 2000.

14. H. Kasahara, H. Honda, M. Iwata, and M. Hirota. A macro-dataflow compilation scheme for hierarchical multiprocessor systems. In *Proc. Int'l. Conf. on Parallel Processing*, Aug. 1990.

15. H. Kasahara, H. Honda, and S. Narita. Parallel processing of near fine grain tasks using static scheduling on oscar.

16. K. Kimura and H. Kasahara. Near fine grain parallel processing using static scheduling on single chip multiprocessors. *Proc. of International Workshop on Innovative Architecture for Future Generation High-Performance Processors and Systems*, Nov. 1999.

17. H. Kasahara A. Yhoshida, K. Koshizuka. Data-localization using loop aligned decomposition for macro-dataflow processing. *Proc. of 9th Workshop on Languages and Compilers for Parallel Computing*, Aug. 1996.

18. K. Ishizaka, M. Obata, and H. Kasahara. Coarse grain task parallel processing with cache optimization on shared memory multiprocessor. In *Proc. of 14th International Workshop on Languages and Compilers for Parallel Computing*, Aug. 2001.

19. K. Ishizaka, M. Obata, and H. Kasahara. Cache optimization for coarse grain task parallel processing using inter-array padding. In *Proc. of 16th International Workshop on Languages and Compilers for Parallel Computing*, Oct. 2003.

Experiences with Co-array Fortran on Hardware Shared Memory Platforms*

Yuri Dotsenko, Cristian Coarfa, John Mellor-Crummey, and Daniel Chavarría-Miranda

Rice University, Houston TX 77005, USA

Abstract. When performing source-to-source compilation of Co-array Fortran (CAF) programs into SPMD Fortran 90 codes for shared-memory multiprocessors, there are several ways of representing and manipulating data at the Fortran 90 language level. We describe a set of implementation alternatives and evaluate their performance implications for CAF variants of the STREAM, Random Access, Spark98 and NAS MG & SP benchmarks. We compare the performance of library-based implementations of one-sided communication with fine-grain communication that accesses remote data using load and store operations. Our experiments show that using application-level loads and stores for fine-grain communication can improve performance by as much as a factor of 24; however, codes requiring only coarse-grain communication can achieve better performance by using an architecture's tuned `memcpy` for bulk data movement.

1 Introduction

Co-array Fortran (CAF) [1] has been proposed as a practical parallel programming model for high-performance parallel systems. CAF is a global address space model for single-program-multiple-data (SPMD) parallel programming that consists of a small set of extensions to Fortran 90. To explore the potential of this programming model, we are building `cafc`—a multiplatform compiler for CAF. Our goal for `cafc` is to achieve *performance transparency*, namely, to deliver the full power of the hardware platform to the application on a wide range of parallel systems.

In this paper, we investigate how to generate efficient code for microprocessor-based scalable shared-memory multiprocessors with non-uniform shared memory access (NUMA). Such machines are organized as a set of nodes with each node containing one or more processors and memory. Nodes are connected using a low-latency, high-bandwidth interconnect. Each processor can access the memory on its node with low latency and memory on other nodes with higher latency. This class of systems includes platforms such as the SGI Altix [2], the SGI Origin [3]. Communication in

---

* This work was supported in part by the Department of Energy under Grant DE-FC03-01ER25504/A000, the Los Alamos Computer Science Institute (LACSI) through LANL contract number 03891-99-23 as part of the prime contract (W-7405-ENG-36) between the DOE and the Regents of the University of California, Texas Advanced Technology Program under Grant 003604-0059-2001, and Compaq Computer Corporation under a cooperative research agreement. This research was performed in part using the Molecular Science Computing Facility (MSCF) in the William R. Wiley Environmental Molecular Sciences Laboratory, a national scientific user facility sponsored by the U.S. Department of Energy's Office of Biological and Environmental Research and located at the Pacific Northwest National Laboratory. Pacific Northwest is operated for the Department of Energy by Battelle.

R. Eigenmann et al. (Eds.): LCPC 2004, LNCS 3602, pp. 332–347, 2005.
© Springer-Verlag Berlin Heidelberg 2005

these systems occurs via cache line data transfers. Access to a data element on a remote node causes the cache line containing the data element to be fetched into the cache of the requesting node. On such systems, coarse-grain communication is accomplished by moving a group of cache lines individually.

`cafc` uses a source-to-source translation approach to code generation, transforming CAF into a Fortran 90 node program augmented with communication operations. This enables a separation of concerns: `cafc` can leave the details of back-end code optimization to a Fortran 90 compiler and focus on managing parallelism, communication and synchronization.

When transforming CAF into SPMD Fortran 90 node programs for shared-memory multiprocessors, there are several possible ways of representing and manipulating co-array data at the Fortran 90 language level. We explore several choices for representing shared data for co-arrays and accessing both local and remote co-array data. We evaluate the performance implications of these choices for several different codes including CAF variants of the STREAM [4], Random Access [5], Spark98 [6], and NAS MG & SP benchmarks [7]. We also compare the performance of the CAF versions against implementations of the same benchmarks written using MPI [8] and OpenMP [9], the most widely used parallel programming models.

In the next section, we briefly review the Co-array Fortran language and communication libraries used by our generated code. In Section 3, we describe the alternative code shapes that we investigate in this study. In Section 4, we describe the benchmark codes that we study and our experimental results comparing different strategies for representing and accessing shared data. We summarize our findings in Section 5.

2   Background

Co-array Fortran. CAF is a global address space model for SPMD parallel programming that consists of a small set of extensions to Fortran 90. An executing CAF program consists of a static collection of asynchronous process images. CAF programs explicitly manage data locality and computation distribution. CAF supports distributed data using a natural extension to Fortran 90 syntax. For example, the declaration `integer :: x(n,m)[*]` declares a shared co-array with $n \times m$ integers local to each process image. The dimensions inside brackets are called co-dimensions. Co-arrays may also be declared for user-defined types as well as primitive types. A local section of a co-array may be a singleton instance of a type rather than an array of type instances. Instead of explicitly coding message exchanges to obtain data belonging to other processes, a CAF program can directly reference non-local values using an extension to Fortran 90 syntax for subscripted references. For instance, process p can read the first column of data in co-array x from process p+1 with the right-hand side reference to `x(:,1)[p+1]`. CAF also includes synchronization primitives. Since both remote data access and synchronization are language primitives, they are amenable to compiler optimization. A more complete description of the CAF language can be found elsewhere [1].

Shared Memory Access Library (SHMEM). The SHMEM library [10], developed by SGI, provides an application programming interface (API) for NUMA machines such as the SGI Altix and Origin. For SPMD programs, SHMEM supports remote access to symmetric data objects—arrays or variables that exist with the same size, type and relative address in all processes. Examples of symmetric data objects include Fortran COMMON block or SAVE variables and objects allocated from the symmetric heap [10]. The SHMEM API contains routines for data transfer using either contiguous or strided reads and writes, collective operations such as broadcast and reductions, barrier synchronization and atomic memory operations. SHMEM also supports remote pointers, which enable direct access to data objects owned by another process.

Aggregate Remote Memory Copy Interface. The `cafc` compiler generates code that uses the Aggregate Remote Memory Copy Interface (ARMCI) [11]—a multi-platform library for high-performance one-sided (get and put) communication—as its implementation substrate for global address space communication. One-sided communication separates data movement from synchronization; this can be particularly useful for simplifying the coding of irregular applications. ARMCI provides both blocking and split-phase non-blocking primitives for one-sided communication. ARMCI supports non-contiguous data transfers. The latest version of ARMCI performs NUMA-aware memory allocation on the SGI Altix and Origin platforms using the SHMEM library's `shmalloc` primitive.

3   Implementing CAF on Shared Memory Architectures

The `cafc` compiler translates CAF programs into Fortran 90 node programs augmented with communication operations. In previous work [12], we described a translation strategy for generating portable code and performed a preliminary evaluation of the code's performance on several cluster architectures. The portable code we generate allocates memory for co-array data outside the Fortran 90 runtime system, initializes Fortran 90 pointers so that the node program can use them to access local co-array data, and performs communication using ARMCI PUT and GET operations.

As we experimented with `cafc`-generated code on more parallel architectures [13], we found that our generated code was not meeting our goal of performance transparency across the range of architectures and codes. While generating code to use Fortran 90 pointers to access local co-array data is a natural and portable approach, we found that in many cases the node performance of `cafc`-generated code using Fortran 90 pointers was often significantly slower than Fortran 90 code using arrays. Our experiments led us to conclude that performance irregularities we observed were a result of insufficient optimization of pointer-based codes by node compilers.

In [13], we described generating communication using ARMCI PUT and GET primitives. Though this approach is well-suited to cluster architectures, it fails to fully exploit the capabilities of shared-memory architectures. In contrast to clusters, shared memory architectures provide the ability to access remote memory directly via load and store instructions, which makes fine-grain remote accesses much more efficient. On shared-memory multiprocessors, Fortran 90 references can be used to access remote data directly, avoiding the overhead of calling library primitives for communication.

In this paper we compare Fortran 90 representations of COMMON block and SAVE co-arrays on scalable shared-memory multiprocessors to find the one that yields superior performance for both local computation and access to remote data. We report our findings for two NUMA SGI platforms (Altix 3000 and Origin 2000) and their corresponding compilers (Intel and SGI MIPSPro Fortran compilers). An important conclusion of our study is that no single Fortran 90 co-array representation and code generation strategy yields the best performance across all architectures and Fortran 90 compilers. Moreover, two co-array representations can be used profitably together (one for effective local accesses, the other for effective remote accesses) to achieve the best results. An appealing characteristic of CAF is that a CAF compiler can automatically tailor code to a particular architecture and use whatever co-array representations, local data access methods, and communication strategies are needed to deliver the best performance.

3.1   Representing Co-arrays for Efficient Local Computation

To achieve the best performance for CAF applications, it is critical to support efficient computation on co-array data. Because `cafc` uses source-to-source translation into Fortran 90, this leads to the question of what is the best set of Fortran 90 constructs for representing and referencing co-array data. There are two major factors affecting the decision: (i) how well a particular back-end Fortran 90 compiler optimizes different kinds of data references, and (ii) hardware and operating system capabilities of the target architecture.

Most Fortran compilers effectively optimize references to COMMON block and SAVE variables, but fall short optimizing the same computation when data is accessed using Cray or Fortran 90 pointers. The principal stumbling block is alias analysis in the presence of pointers. COMMON block and SAVE variables as well as subroutine formal arguments in Fortran 90 cannot alias, while Cray and Fortran 90 pointers can. When compiling a CAF program, `cafc` knows that in the absence of Fortran EQUIVALENCE statements COMMON block and SAVE co-arrays occupy non-overlapping regions of memory; however, this information is not conveyed to a back-end compiler if `cafc` generates code to access local co-array data through pointers. Conservative assumptions about aliases cause back-end compilers to forgo critical performance optimizations such as software pipelining and unroll-and-jam, among others. Some, but not all, Fortran 90 compilers have flags that enable users to specify that pointers do not alias, which can ameliorate the effects of analysis imprecision.

Besides the aliasing problem, using Fortran 90 pointers to access data can increase register pressure and inhibit software prefetching. The shape of a Fortran 90 pointer is not known at compile time; therefore, bounds and strides are not constant and thus occupy extra registers, increasing register pressure. Also a compiler has no knowledge whether the memory pointed to by a Fortran 90 pointer is contiguous or strided, which complicates generation of software prefetch instructions.

The hardware and the operating system impose extra constraints on whether a particular co-array representation is appropriate. For example, on a shared-memory system a co-array should not be represented as a Fortran 90 COMMON variable if a COMMON block cannot be mapped into multiple process images. Below we discuss five possible Fortran 90 representations for the local part of a co-array variable `real a(10,20)[*]`.

```
type t1
  real, pointer :: local(:,:)
end type t1
type (t1) ca
```

(a) Fortran 90 pointer representation.

```
type t2
  real :: local(10,20)
end type t2
type (t2), pointer :: ca
```

(b) Pointer to structure representation.

```
real :: a_local(10,20)
pointer (a_ptr, a_local)
```

(c) Cray pointer representation.

```
real :: ca(10,20)
common /ca_cb/ ca
```

(d) COMMON block representation.

```
subroutine foo(...)
  real a(10,20)[*]
  common /a_cb/ a
  ...
end subroutine foo
```

(e) Original subroutine.

```
! subroutine-wrapper
subroutine foo(...)
  ! F90 pointer representation of a
  ...
  call foo_body(ca%local(1,1),...)
end subroutine foo

! subroutine-body
subroutine foo_body(a_local,...)
  real :: a_local(10,20)
  ...
end subroutine foo_body
```

(f) Parameter representation.

Fig. 1. Fortran 90 representations for co-array local data

Fortran 90 Pointer. Figure 1(a) shows the representation of co-array data first used by cafc. At program launch, cafc's run-time system allocates memory to hold 10×20 array of double precision numbers and initializes the ca%local field to point to it.

This approach enabled us to achieve performance roughly equal to that of MPI on an Itanium2 cluster with a Myrinet2000 interconnect using the Intel Fortran compiler v7.0 (using a "no-aliasing" compiler flag) to compile cafc's generated code [12]. Other compilers do not optimize Fortran 90 pointers as effectively. Potential aliasing of Fortran 90 or Cray pointers inhibits some high-level loop transformations in the HP Fortran compiler for the Alpha architecture. The absence of a flag to signal the HP Alpha Fortran compiler that pointers don't alias forced us to explore alternative strategies for representing and referencing co-arrays. Similarly, on the SGI Origin 2000, the MIPSPro Fortran 90 compiler does not optimize Fortran 90 pointer references effectively.

Fortran 90 Pointer to Structure. In contrast to the Fortran 90 pointer representation shown in Figure 1(a), the *pointer-to-structure* shown in Figure 1(b) conveys constant array bounds and contiguity to the back-end compiler.

Cray Pointer. Figure 1(c) shows how a Cray pointer can be used to represent the local portion of a co-array. This representation has similar properties to the pointer-to-structure representation. Though the Cray pointer is not a standard Fortran 90 construct, many Fortran 90 compilers support it.

COMMON Block. On the SGI Altix and Origin architectures, the local part of a co-array can be represented as a COMMON variable in each SPMD process image (as shown in Figure 1(d)) and mapped into remote images as symmetric data objects using SHMEM library primitives. References to local co-array data are expressed as references to COMMON block variables. This code shape is the most amenable to back-end compiler optimizations and results in the best performance for local computation on COMMON and SAVE co-array variables (see Section 4.1).

Subroutine Parameter Representation. To avoid pessimistic assumptions about aliasing, a *procedure splitting* technique can be used. If one or more COMMON block or SAVE co-arrays are accessed intensively within a procedure, the procedure can be split into wrapper and body procedures (see Figures 1(e) and 1(f)). The wrapper procedure passes all (non-EQUIVALENCEd) COMMON block and SAVE co-arrays used in the original subroutine to the body procedure as explicit-shape arguments[1]; within the body procedure, these variables are then referenced as routine arguments. This representation enables cafc to pass bounds and contiguity information to the back-end compiler. The procedure splitting technique proved effective for both the HP Alpha Fortran compiler and the Intel Fortran compiler.

3.2   Code Generation for Remote Accesses

In CAF, communication events are expressed at the language level by using the bracket notation for co-dimensions to reference remote data. The CAF programming model is explicit enough that a user can perform communication optimizations such as vectorization or aggregation at the source level. To facilitate retargetability while enabling code to be tailored to a particular target system, cafc uses an abstract interface for instantiating one-sided communication operations. Currently, cafc does not vectorize communication and communication is placed adjacent to the statement in which a non-local reference appears.

Here we describe several candidate code shapes for co-array communication; these range from library-based platform-independent communication to several strategies for expressing fine-grain load/store communication on shared memory systems.

Communication Generation for Generic Parallel Architectures. To access data residing on a remote node, cafc generates ARMCI calls. Unless the statement causing communication is a simple copy, temporary storage is allocated to hold non-local data.

Consider the statement a(:) = b(:)[p] + ..., which reads co-array data for b from another process image. First, cafc allocates a temporary, b_temp, just prior to the statement to hold the value of b(:) from image p. cafc adds an ARMCI GET operation to retrieve the data from image p, rewrites the statement as a(:) = b_temp(:) + ... and inserts code to deallocate b_temp after the statement. For a statement containing a co-array write to a remote image, such as c(:)[p] = ..., cafc inserts allocation of a temporary c_temp prior to the statement. Then, cafc rewrites the statement to store its result in c_temp, adds an ARMCI PUT operation after the statement to perform the non-local write and inserts code to deallocate c_temp.

Communication Generation for Shared Memory Architectures. Library-based communication adds unnecessary overhead for fine-grain communication on shared memory architectures. Loads and stores can be used to directly access remote data more efficiently. Here we describe several representations for fine-grain load/store access to remote co-array data.

---

[1] Fortran 90 argument passing styles are described in detail elsewhere [14].

```
DO J=1, N                      DO J=1,N
  C(J)=A(J)[p]                   call CafGetScalar(A_h, A(J), p, tmp)
END DO                           C(J)=tmp
                               END DO
```

(a) Remote element access

(b) General communication code

Fig. 2. General communication code generation

```
DO J=1,N                       ptrA=>A(1:N)
  ptrA=>A(J)                    call CafSetPtr(ptrA,p,A_h)
  call CafSetPtr(ptrA,p, A_h)   DO J=1,N
  C(J)=ptrA                       C(J)=ptrA(J)
END DO                         END DO
```

(a) Fortran 90 pointer to remote data

(b) Hoisted Fortran 90 pointer initialization

Fig. 3. Fortran 90 pointer access to remote data

```
POINTER(ptr, ptrA)             POINTER(ptr, ptrA)
...                            ...
DO J=1,N                       ptr = shmem_ptr(A(1), p)
  ptr = shmem_ptr(A(J), p)     DO J=1,N
  C(J)=ptrA                      C(J)=ptrA(J)
END DO                         END DO
```

(a) Cray pointer to remote data

(b) Hoisted Cray pointer initialization

Fig. 4. Cray pointer access to remote data

Fortran 90 Pointers. With proper initialization, Fortran 90 pointers can be used to directly address non-local co-array data. The CAF runtime library provides the virtual address of a co-array on remote images; this is used to set up a Fortran 90 pointer for referencing the remote co-array. An example of this strategy is presented in Figure 3(a). The generated code accesses remote data by dereferencing a Fortran 90 pointer, for which Fortran 90 compilers generate direct loads and stores. In Figure 3(a), the procedure CafSetPtr is called for every access; this adds significant overhead. Hoisting pointer initialization outside the loop as shown in Figure 3(b) can substantially improve performance. To perform this optimization automatically, cafc needs to determine that the process image number for a non-local co-array reference is loop invariant.

Vector of Fortran 90 Pointers. An alternate representation that doesn't require pointer hoisting for good performance is to precompute a vector of remote pointers for all the process images per co-array. This strategy should work well for parallel systems of modest size. Currently, all shared memory architectures meet this requirement. In this case, the remote reference in the code example from Figure 2(a) would become:
C(J) = ptrArrayA(p)%ptrA(J).

Cray Pointers. We also explored a class of shared-memory code generation strategies based on the SHMEM library. After allocating shared memory with shmalloc, one can use shmem_ptr to initialize a Cray pointer to the remote data. This pointer can then be used to access the remote data. Figure 4(a) presents a translation of the code in Figure 2 using `shmem_ptr`. Without hoisting pointer initialization as shown in Figure 4(b), this code incurs a performance penalty similar to the code shown in Figure 3(a).

4 Experiments and Discussion

Currently, `cafc` generates code that uses Fortran 90 pointers for references to local co-array data. To access remote co-array elements, `cafc` can either generate ARMCI calls or initialize Fortran 90 pointers for fine-grain load/store communication. Initialization of pointers to remote co-array data occurs immediately prior to statements referencing non-local data; pointer initialization is not yet automatically hoisted out of loops. To evaluate the performance of alternate co-array representations and communication strategies, we hand-modified code generated by `cafc` or hand-coded them. For instance, to evaluate the efficiency of using SHMEM instead of ARMCI for communication, we hand-modified `cafc`-generated code to use `shmem_put`/`shmem_get` for both fine-grain and coarse-grain accesses.

We used two NUMA platforms for our experiments: an SGI Altix 3000[2] and an SGI Origin 2000[3]. We used the STREAM benchmark to determine the best co-array representation for local and remote accesses. To determine the highest-performing representation for fine-grain remote accesses we studied the Random Access and Spark98 benchmarks. To investigate the scalability of CAF codes with coarse-grain communication, we show results for the NPB benchmarks SP and MG.

4.1 STREAM

The STREAM [4] benchmark is a simple synthetic benchmark program that measures sustainable memory bandwidth in MB/s (10^6 bytes/s) and the corresponding computation rate for simple vector kernels. The top half of Figure 5 shows vector kernels for a Fortran 90 version of the benchmark. The size of each array should exceed the capacity of the last level of cache. The performance of compiled code for the STREAM benchmark also depends upon the quality of the code's instruction stream[4].

We designed two CAF versions of the STREAM benchmark: one to evaluate the representations for local co-array accesses, and a second to evaluate the remote access code for both fine-grain accesses and bulk communication. Table 1 presents STREAM bandwidth measurements on the SGI Altix 3000 and the SGI Origin 2000 platforms.

Evaluation of local co-array access performance. To evaluate the performance of local co-array accesses, we adapted the STREAM benchmark by declaring A, B and C as co-arrays and keeping the kernels from the top half of Figure 5 intact. We used the Fortran 90 version of STREAM with the arrays A, B and C in a COMMON block as a

---

[2] Altix 3000: 128 Itanium2 1.5GHz processors with 6MB L3 cache, and 128 GB RAM, running the Linux64 OS with the 2.4.21 kernel and the 8.0 Intel compilers

[3] Origin 2000: 16 MIPS R12000 processors with 8MB L2 cache and 10 GB RAM, running IRIX 6.5 and the MIPSpro Compilers version 7.3.1.3m

[4] On Altix, we use `-override_limits -O3 -tpp2 -fnoalias` for the Intel 8.0 compiler. On the Origin, we use `-64 -O3` for the MIPSpro compiler.

```
DO J=1, N              DO J=1, N              DO J=1, N                  DO J=1, N
  C(J)=A(J)              B(J)=s*C(J)            C(J)=A(J)+B(J)             A(J)=B(J)+s*C(J)
END DO                 END DO                 END DO                     END DO

(a) Copy               (b) Scale              (c) Add                    (d) Triad

DO J=1, N              DO J=1, N              DO J=1, N                  DO J=1, N
  C(J)=A(J)[p]          B(J)=s*C(J)[p]         C(J)=A(J)[p]+B(J)[p]       A(J)=B(J)[p]+s*C(J)[p]
END DO                 END DO                 END DO                     END DO

(e) CAF Copy           (f) CAF Scale          (g) CAF Add                (h) CAF Triad
```

Fig. 5. The STREAM benchmark kernels (F90 & CAF)

baseline for comparison The results are shown in the local access part of the Table 1. The results for the COMMON block representation are the same as the results of the original Fortran 90. The Fortran 90 pointer representation without the "no-aliasing" compiler flag yields only 30% of the best performance for local access; it is not always possible to use no-aliasing flags because user programs might have aliasing unrelated to co-array usage. On both architectures, the results show that the most efficient representation for co-array local accesses is as COMMON block variables. This representation enables the most effective optimization by the back-end Fortran 90 compiler; however, it can be used only for COMMON and SAVE co-arrays; a different representation is necessary for allocatable co-arrays.

Evaluation of remote co-array access performance. We evaluated the performance of remote reads by modifying the STREAM kernels so that A,B,C are co-arrays, and the references on the right-hand side are all remote. The resulting code is shown in the bottom half of Figure 5. We also experimented with a bulk version, in which the kernel loops are written in Fortran 90 array section notation. The results presented in the Table 1 correspond to the following code generation options (for both fine-grain and bulk accesses): the library-based communication with temporary buffers using ARMCI calls, Fortran 90 pointers, Fortran 90 pointers with the initialization hoisted out of the kernel loops, library-based communication using SHMEM primitives, Cray pointers, Cray pointers with hoisted initialization without the no-aliasing flag, Cray pointers with hoisted initialization, and a vector of Fortran 90 pointers to remote data. The next result corresponds to a hybrid representation: using the COMMON block representation for co-array local accesses and Cray pointers for remote accesses. The last result corresponds to an OpenMP implementation of the STREAM benchmark coded in a similar style to the CAF versions; this is provided to compare the CAF versions against an established shared memory programming model.

The best performance for fine-grain remote accesses is achieved by the versions that use Cray pointers or Fortran 90 pointers to access remote data with the initialization of the pointers hoisted outside loops. This shows that hoisting initialization of pointers to remote data is imperative for both Fortran 90 pointers and Cray pointers. Using the vector of Fortran 90 pointers representation uses a simpler strategy to hoist pointer initialization that requires no analysis, yet achieves acceptable performance. Using a function call per each fine-grain access incurs a factor of 24 performance degradation on Altix and a factor of five on the Origin.

Table 1. Bandwidth for STREAM in MB/s on the SGI Altix 3000 and the SGI Origin 2000

Program representation	SGI Altix 3000				SGI Origin 2000			
	Copy	Scale	Add	Triad	Copy	Scale	Add	Triad
Fortran, COMMON block arrays	3284	3144	3628	3802	334	293	353	335
Local access, F90 pointer, w/o no-aliasing flag	1009	929	1332	1345	323	276	311	299
Local access, F90 pointer	3327	3128	3612	3804	323	277	312	298
Local access, F90 pointer to structure	3209	3107	3629	3824	334	293	354	335
Local access, Cray pointer	3254	3061	3567	3716	334	293	354	335
Local access, split procedure	3322	3158	3611	3808	334	288	354	332
Local access, vector of F90 pointers	3277	3106	3616	3802	319	288	312	302
Remote access, general strategy	33	32	24	24	11	11	8	8
Remote access bulk, general strategy	2392	1328	1163	1177	273	115	99	98
Remote access, F90 pointer	44	44	34	35	10	10	7	7
Remote access bulk, F90 pointer	1980	2286	1997	2004	138	153	182	188
Remote access, hoisted F90 pointer	1979	2290	2004	2010	294	268	293	282
Remote access, shmem_get	104	102	77	77	72	70	57	56
Remote access, Cray pointer	71	69	60	60	26	26	19	19
Remote access bulk, Cray ptr	2313	2497	2078	2102	346	294	346	332
Remote access, hoisted Cray pointer, w/o no-aliasing flag	2310	2231	2059	2066	286	255	283	275
Remote access, hoisted Cray pointer	2349	2233	2057	2073	346	295	347	332
Remote access, vector of F90 pointers	2280	2498	2073	2105	316	291	306	280
Remote access, hybrid representation	2417	2579	2049	2062	350	295	347	333
Remote access, OpenMP	2397	2307	2033	2052	312	301	317	287

For bulk access, the versions that use Fortran 90 pointers or Cray pointers perform better for the kernels Scale, Add and Triad than the general version (1.5-2 times better on Altix and 2.5-3 times better on Origin), which uses buffers for non-local data. Copying into buffers degrades performance significantly for these kernels. For Copy, the general version does not use an intermediate buffer; instead, it uses memcpy to transfer the data directly into the C array and thus achieves high performance.

We implemented an OpenMP version of STREAM that performs similar remote data acesses. On Altix, the OpenMP version delivered performance similar to the CAF implementation for the Copy, Add, and Triad kernels, and 90% for the Scale kernel. On Origin, the OpenMP version achieved 86-90% of the performance of the CAF version.

In conclusion, for top performance on the Altix and Origin platforms, we need distinct representations for co-array local and remote accesses. For COMMON and SAVE variables, local co-array data should reside in COMMON blocks or be represented as subroutine dummy arguments; for remote accesses, cafc should generate communication code based on Cray pointers with hoisted initialization.

4.2   Random Access

To evaluate the quality of the CAF compiler generated code for applications that require fine-grain accesses, we selected the Random Access benchmark from the HPC Challenge benchmark suite [5], which measures the rate of random updates of memory, and implemented a CAF version.

The serial version of the benchmark declares a large main array Table of 64-bit words and a small substitution table stable to randomize values in the large array. The Table has the size TableSize = 2^n words. After initializing Table, the code performs a number of random updates on Table locations. The kernel of the serial benchmark is shown in Figure 6 (a).

```
do i = 0, 4*TableSize
  pos = <random number in
         [0,TableSize-1]>
  pos2 = <pos shifted to index
          inside stable>
  Table(pos) = Table(pos) xor
         stable(pos2)
end do
```

```
do i = 0, 4*TableSize
  gpos = <random number in
          [0, GlobalTableSize-1]>
  img = gpos div TableSize
  pos = gpos mod TableSize
  pos2 = <pos shifted to index
          inside stable>
  Table(pos)[img] = Table(pos)[img] xor
         stable(pos2)
end do
```

(a) Sequential Random Access   (b) CAF Random Access

Fig. 6. Random Access Benchmark

In the CAF implementation, the global table is a co-array. `TableSize` words reside on each image, so that the aggregate size is `GlobalTableSize = TableSize * NumberOfImages`. Each image has a private copy of the substitution table. All images concurrently generate random global indices and perform the update of the corresponding locations. No synchronization is used for concurrent updates (errors on up to 1% of the locations due to race conditions are acceptable). The kernel for all of our CAF variants of the benchmark is shown in Figure 6 (b).

A parallel MPI version [5] is available that uses a bucket sort algorithm to cache a number of remote updates locally. Compared to the CAF version, the bucket version improves locality, increases communication granularity and decreases TLB misses for modest numbers of processors.

Our goal is to evaluate the quality of source-to-source translation for applications where fine-grain accesses are preferred due to the nature of the application. Previous studies have shown the difficulty of improving the granularity of fine-grain shared memory applications [15]. We use the Random Access benchmark as an analog of a complex fine-grain application. For this reason, we did not implement the bucket sorted version in CAF, but instead focused on the pure fine-grain version presented above.

The results of Random Access with different co-array representations and code generation strategies are presented in Table 2 for the SGI Origin 2000 architecture and in Table 3 for the SGI Altix 3000 architecture. The results are reported in MUPs, 10^6 updates per second, per processor for two main table sizes: 1MB and 256MB per image, simulating an application with modest memory requirements and an application with high memory requirements. All experiments were done on a power of two number of processors, so that we can replace `div`s and `mod`s with fast bit operations.

Table 2. Random Access performance on the Origin 2000 in MUPs per processor

Version	size per proc = 1MB					size per proc = 256 MB				
# procs.	1	2	4	8	16	1	2	4	8	16
CAF vect. of F90 ptrs.	10.06	1.04	0.52	0.25	0.11	1.12	0.81	0.57	0.39	0.2
CAF F90 pointer	0.31	0.25	0.2	0.16	0.15	0.24	0.23	0.21	0.18	0.12
CAF Cray pointer	12.16	1.11	0.53	0.25	0.11	1.11	0.88	0.58	0.4	0.21
CAF shmem	2.36	0.77	0.44	0.25	0.11	0.86	0.65	0.53	0.36	0.19
CAF general comm.	0.41	0.31	0.25	0.2	0.09	0.33	0.3	0.28	0.23	0.14
OpenMP	18.93	1.18	0.52	0.32	0.17	1.1	0.81	0.62	0.45	0.23
MPI bucket 2048	15.83	4.1	3.25	2.49	0.1	1.15	0.85	0.69	0.66	0.1

Table 3. Random Access performance on the Altix 3000 in MUPs per processor

Version	size per proc = 1MB						size per proc = 256 MB					
# procs.	1	2	4	8	16	32	1	2	4	8	16	32
CAF vect. of F90 ptrs.	47.66	14.85	3.33	1.73	1.12	0.73	5.02	4.19	2.88	1.56	1.17	0.76
CAF F90 pointer	1.6	1.5	1.14	0.88	0.73	0.55	1.28	1.27	1.1	0.92	0.74	0.59
CAF Cray pointer	56.38	15.60	3.32	1.73	1.13	0.75	5.14	4.23	2.91	1.81	1.34	0.76
CAF shmem	4.43	3.66	2.03	1.32	0.96	0.67	2.57	2.44	1.91	1.39	1.11	0.69
CAF general comm.	1.83	1.66	1.13	0.81	0.63	0.47	1.37	1.34	1.11	0.81	0.73	0.52
OpenMP	58.91	15.47	3.15	1.37	0.91	0.73	5.18	4.28	2.96	1.55	1.17	—
MPI bucket 2048	59.81	21.08	16.40	10.52	5.42	1.96	5.21	3.85	3.66	3.36	3.16	2.88

Each table presents results in MUPs per processor for seven variants of Random Access. *CAF vector of F90 ptrs.* uses a vector of Fortran 90 pointers to represent co-array data. *CAF F90 pointer* uses Fortran 90 pointers to directly access co-array data. *CAF Cray pointer* uses a vector of integers to store the addresses of co-array data. A Cray pointer is initialized in place to point to remote data and then used to perform an update. *CAF shmem* uses shmem_put and shmem_get functions called directly from Fortran. *CAF general comm.* uses the ARMCI functions to access co-array data. *MPI bucket 2048* implements a bucket sorted algorithm with a bucket size of 2048 words. *OpenMP* uses the same fine-grained algorithm as the CAF versions; it uses a private substitution table and performs first-touch initialization of the global table to improve memory locality.

The best representations for fine-grain co-array accesses are the Cray pointer and the vector of Fortran 90 pointers. The other representations, which require a function call for each fine-grain access, yield inferior performance. The MPI bucket 2048 row is presented for reference and shows that an algorithm with better locality properties and coarser-grain communication clearly achieves better performance. It is worth mentioning that the bucketed MPI implementation is much harder to code compared to a CAF version. The OpenMP version of the benchmark performs as well as the best CAF version, due to similar fine-grained access patterns.

4.3 Spark98

To evaluate the performance of more realistic fine-grain applications, we selected CMU's Spark98 [6] benchmark. This benchmark computes a sparse matrix-vector product of a symmetric matrix stored in compressed sparse row format, and is available in several versions: a sequential version, a highly tuned shared-memory threaded version (denoted as *hybrid* in [6]) and an MPI version. The original versions are written in C, we translated their computational kernels into Fortran 90 and derived a CAF version from the original MPI version.

All parallel versions of Spark98 use a sophisticated data partitioning which has been computed offline, to improve load balance between processors. The core of the benchmark computes a partial sparse matrix-vector product locally and then assembles the result across processors.

Our experimental results were collected on an Altix 3000 and an SGI Origin 2000. On the Altix 3000 architecture, we considered two different placements of a parallel job

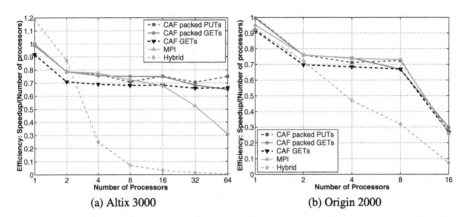

Fig. 7. Comparison of parallel efficiencies (per iteration) for Spark98 (sf2 trace) for CAF, MPI and hybrid versions on an SGI Altix 3000 and an SGI Origin 2000

to the processors. The *single* placement corresponds to running one process per dual-processor node; in the *dual* placement two processes are run on both CPUs of a node, sharing the local memory bandwidth. To eliminate variations in local performance introduced by the backend Fortran or C compilers, the CAF and MPI versions use Fortran kernels for the local computation and result assembly. The threaded shared-memory version uses the original C kernels.

We evaluate three different CAF alternatives: the first (CAF packed PUTs) uses manual data packing and PUTs for communication, the second (CAF packed GETs) uses manual data packing and GETs for communication, the third version (CAF GETs) uses the Fortran 90 array section vector subscript notation to access remote data in place through a Cray pointer (during the assembly phase), but this notation is not currently handled automatically by our CAF compiler. We consider the third version to be written in a more natural style for CAF programs.

Figure 7 shows results for the Spark98 benchmark for the versions described previously for *dual* placement executions on the Altix 3000; similar results were observed for a *single* placement. The CAF and MPI versions have similar performance for a small number of processors (8-16). On the Altix 3000, for larger numbers of processors, the CAF versions outperform the MPI implementation. We observed that the time spent for the result assembly stage is 2.5 times higher on 32 processors and 5 times higher on 64 processors. While we do not know the implementation details of the proprietary MPI library, it appears that the single copy ARMCI data transfers are more efficient. In the hybrid version, a single thread allocates all data structures, thus reducing memory locality for the other threads resulting in poor load balance and non-scalable performance. The CAF GETs version suffers up to a 13% performance penalty for the Altix 3000 and up to a 9% penalty on the Origin 2000 compared to the fastest CAF version (packed PUTs). This shows that this more natural programming style only has a small abstraction overhead.

4.4   NAS MG and SP

To evaluate our code generation strategy for hardware shared memory platforms for codes with coarse-grain communication, we selected two benchmarks, MG and SP, from the NAS Parallel Benchmarks [7,16], widely used for evaluating parallel systems.

We compare four versions of the benchmarks: the standard 2.3 MPI implementation, two compiler-generated CAF versions based on the 2.3 distribution *CAF-cluster*, which uses the Fortran 90 pointer co-array representation and the ARMCI functions that rely on an architecture-optimized memory copy subroutine supplied by the vendor to perform data movement, and *CAF-shm*, which uses the Fortran 90 pointer co-array representation, but uses Fortran 90 pointers to access remote data, as well as the official 3.0 OpenMP [16] versions of SP and MG. The OpenMP version of SP incorporates structural changes made to the 3.0 serial version to improve cache performance on uniprocessor machines, such as fusing loops and reducing the storage size for temporaries; it also uses a 1D strategy for partitioning computation that is better suited for OpenMP.

In the CAF versions, all data transfers are coarse-grain communication arising from co-array section assignments. We rely on the back-end Fortran 90 compiler to scalarize the transformed copies efficiently. Sequential performance measurements used as a baseline were performed using the NPB 2.3-serial release.

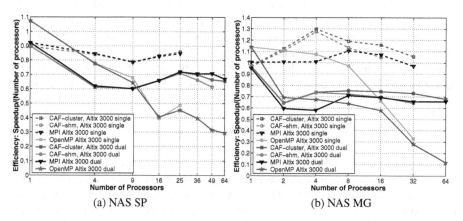

(a) NAS SP   (b) NAS MG

Fig. 8. Comparison of parallel efficiencies for NAS SP and NAS MG for MPI, CAF with general communication and CAF with shared memory communication, as well as OpenMP versions on an SGI Altix 3000

For each benchmark, we present the parallel efficiency of the MPI, CAF and OpenMP implementations [5]. On an Altix, we evaluate these benchmarks for both the *single* and *dual* processor configurations (see Section 4.3). The experimental results for

---

[5] For each parallel version ρ, the efficiency metric is computed as $\frac{t_s}{P \times t_p(P,\rho)}$. In this equation, t_s is the execution time of the original sequential version; P is the number of processors; $t_p(P,\rho)$ is the time for the parallel execution on P processors using parallelization ρ. Perfect speedup would yield efficiency 1.0 for each processor configuration.

problem size class C are shown on the figure 8. For SP, both CAF versions achieve similar performance—comparable to the standard MPI version. For MG, the CAF-cluster version performs better than the CAF-shm version. Since both versions use coarse-grain communication, the performance difference shows that the architecture-tuned memory copy subroutine performs better than the compiler scalarized data copy; it effectively hides the interconnect latency by keeping the optimal number of memory operations in flight. The CAF cluster version outperforms the MPI version for both the single and dual configurations. The results for the OpenMP versions are not directly comparable since they are based on the 3.0 source base, but they are known to be well designed and tuned for OpenMP execution. The OpenMP performance is good for a small number of processors (up to 8-9) but then tails off compared to the MPI and CAF versions.

5   Conclusions

We investigated several implementation strategies for efficiently representing, accessing and communicating distributed data in Fortran 90 source code generated by a CAF compiler for scalable shared memory systems. Generating fine-grain communication that uses direct loads and stores for the STREAM benchmark improved the performance by a factor of 24 on the Altix and a factor of five on the Origin. We found that for benchmarks requiring fine-grain communication, such as Random Access, a tailored code generation strategy that takes into account architecture and back-end compiler characteristics, provides better performance. In contrast, benchmarks requiring only coarse-grain communication deliver better performance by using an architecture's tuned memcpy routine for bulk data movement. Our current library-based code generation already enables us to achieve performance comparable to or better than that of hand-tuned MPI for benchmarks such as SP and MG, which use coarse-grain communication. The Spark98 experiments showed that programming in a natural CAF style by using remote data in place incurs an acceptable performance penalty compared to the fastest CAF version, which manages buffers explicitly.

Based on our study, we plan to develop suport for automatic shared memory code generation using the COMMON block representation for local co-array accesses and using a pointer-based representation for remote accesses in conjunction with pointer initialization hoisting. We will add support for automatic recognition of contiguous remote data transfers and implement them using calls to optimized system primitives. These strategies will enable cafc to generate code with high performance for both local and remote accesses on scalable shared-memory systems.

Acknowledgments

We thank J. Nieplocha and V. Tipparaju for their collaboration on ARMCI. We thank F. Zhao for her work on the compiler and K. Feind for his insights about the Altix.

References

1. Numrich, R.W., Reid, J.K.: Co-Array Fortran for parallel programming. ACM Fortran Forum **17** (1998) 1–31
2. Silicon Graphics, Inc.: The SGI Altix 3000 Global Shared-Memory Architecture. `http://www.sgi.com/servers/altix/whitepapers/tech_papers.html` (2004)
3. Laudon, J., Lenoski, D.: The SGI Origin: a ccNUMA highly scalable server. In: Proceedings of the 24th Intl. Symposium on Computer Architecture, ACM Press (1997) 241–251
4. McCalpin, J.D.: Sustainable Memory Bandwidth in Current High Performance Computers. Silicon Graphics, Inc., MountainView, CA. (1995)
5. HPC Challenge Developers: HPC Challenge Benchmark. `http://icl.cs.utk.edu/projectsdev/hpcc` (2003)
6. O'Hallaron, D.R.: Spark98: Sparse matrix kernels for shared memory and message passing systems. Technical Report CMU-CS-97-178, School of Computer Science, Carnegie Mellon University (1997)
7. Bailey, D., Harris, T., Saphir, W., van der Wijngaart, R., Woo, A., Yarrow, M.: The NAS parallel benchmarks 2.0. Technical Report NAS-95-020, NASA Ames Research Center (1995)
8. Snir, M., Otto, S.W., Huss-Lederman, S., Walker, D.W., Dongarra, J.: MPI: The Complete Reference. MIT Press (1995)
9. Dagum, L., Menon, R.: OpenMP: An Industry-Standard API for Shared-Memory Programming. IEEE Comput. Sci. Eng. **5** (1998) 46–55
10. Silicon Graphics, Inc.: MPT Programmer's Guide, mpi man pages, intro_shmem man pages. `http://techpubs.sgi.com` (2002)
11. Nieplocha, J., Carpenter, B. In: ARMCI: A Portable Remote Memory Copy Library for Distributed Array Libraries and Compiler Run-Time Systems. Volume 1586 of Lecture Notes in Computer Science. Springer-Verlag (1999) 533–546
12. Coarfa, C., Dotsenko, Y., Eckhardt, J., Mellor-Crummey, J.: Co-array Fortran Performance and Potential: An NPB Experimental Study. Number 2958 in LNCS, Springer-Verlag (2003)
13. Dotsenko, Y., Coarfa, C., Mellor-Crummey, J.: A Multiplatform Co-Array Fortran Compiler. In: Proceedings of the 13th Intl. Conference of Parallel Architectures and Compilation Techniques, Antibes Juan-les-Pins, France (2004)
14. Adams, J.C., Brainerd, W.S., Martin, J.T., Smith, B.T., Wagener, J.L.: Fortran 90 Handbook: Complete ANSI/ISO Reference. McGraw Hill (1992)
15. Woo, S.C., Ohara, M., Torrie, E., Singh, J.P., Gupta, A.: The SPLASH-2 programs: Characterization and methodological considerations. In: Proceedings of the 22th International Symposium on Computer Architecture, Santa Margherita Ligure, Italy (1995) 24–36
16. Jin, H., Frumkin, M., Yan, J.: The OpenMP implementation of NAS parallel benchmarks and its performance. Technical Report NAS-99-011, NASA Ames Research Center (1999)

Experiments with Auto-parallelizing SPEC2000FP Benchmarks

Guansong Zhang, Priya Unnikrishnan, and James Ren

IBM Toronto Lab,
Toronto ON, L6G 1C7, Canada

Abstract. In this paper, we document the experimental work in our attempts to automatically parallelize SPEC2000FP benchmarks for SMP machines. This is not purely a research project. It was implemented within IBM's software laboratory in a commercial compiler infrastructure that implements OpenMP 2.0 specifications in both Fortran and C/C++. From the beginning, our emphasis is on using simple parallelization techniques. We aim to maintain a good trade-off between performance, especially scalability of an application program and its compilation time. Although the parallelization results show relatively low speed up, it is still promising considering the problems associated with explicit parallel programming and the fact that more and more multi-thread and multi-core chips will soon be available even for home computing.

Keywords: automatic parallelization, parallelizing compiler, SMT machine, OpenMP, parallel do.

1 Introduction

Automatic parallelization or auto-parallelization involves automatically identifying and translating serial program code into equivalent parallel code to be executed by multiple threads. Both OpenMP parallelization and auto-parallelization try to exploit the benefits of shared memory, multiprocessor systems. But the main difference between OpenMP and auto-parallelization is that, for OpenMP, the user has complete knowledge of the program behavior and is aware of all the code segments that can benefit from parallelization. For auto-parallelization, however, the challenge is to pick the right parallelizable code from the limited information available within the compiler without any modification to the original source program.

1.1 Motivation

It is widely accepted that automatic parallelization is difficult and less efficient than explicit parallel programming. For years, people have been seeking better parallel programming models that can expressively describe the parallelism in an application. The existing models include, just to name a few, HPF[1], MPI[2], OpenMP[3], UPC[4], etc. It is also a known fact that parallel programming is difficult. No matter what kind of parallel programming model is used, creating efficient, scalable parallel code still requires a significant degree of expertise. Parallelization tools can be used as an expert system

R. Eigenmann et al. (Eds.): LCPC 2004, LNCS 3602, pp. 348–362, 2005.

to help users to find potential parallelizable code. However, to use the tools effectively, an understanding of dependence analysis and the application code is still needed.

On the other hand, more and more multi-thread and multi-core chips are becoming available in the market and parallel programming is no longer a privilege available only for high-performance computing. If not now, in the near future, parallel architecture will be a common feature in *desktop* and even *laptop computing*. Keeping this growing trend in mind, auto-parallelization looks like an irresistible option. Auto-parallelization relieves the user from having to analyze and modify the source program with explicit compiler directives. The user is shielded from low-level details of iteration space partitioning, data sharing, thread scheduling and synchronization. Auto-parallelization also saves the user the burden of ensuring correct parallel execution.

However, providing compiler support for automatic parallelization is not easy or straightforward. The biggest critique is that the resultant performance gain is typically limited, particularly in terms of scalability. In addition, accurate analysis can be restricted by the time constraints a compiler must meet for commercial acceptability, where in-depth analysis may be sacrificed to allow rapid operation. Taking these factors into account, we believe that using auto-parallelization is still justified by the following considerations:

- For parallel machines with a small number of node processors, scalability is not a big concern. While auto-parallelization may not give us the speedup that a massively parallel processing (MPP) application can achieve, it can still be used to take advantage of the extra silicon available.
- Even an MPP machine is most likely multi-layered where each node is a tightly coupled SMP machine, as in a cluster. Explicit message passing parallel programs, such as MPI, will still benefit from a nested automatic parallel execution.
- Most of the time-consuming applications are data parallel applications. With the growing problem size outpacing the improvements in hardware, data parallel applications can benefit from simple parallelization techniques.
- As more and more desktop parallel machines are available, users will be willing to try a parallel approach to solve their computational problems, if only for a small speedup as long as the effort to achieve that is reasonable.
- As hardware performance keeps improving, more complicated analysis will be tolerable in the compilation process.

1.2 Organization of the Paper

The rest of the paper is organized as follows. In Section 2 we introduce our existing compilation and runtime environment and also briefly describe the structure of the auto-parallelizer. Section 3 and 4 describes in detail some optimization techniques used by the parallelizer to enhance the parallel performance of the application code. Section 5 looks at a few challenging parallelization cases that we encountered during the course of our work. Finally, in Section 6 we summarize our results and future work.

2   Parallelizer Structure and Position

The auto-parallelization work done here is based on the available OpenMP compilers, i.e. IBM®XL Fortran and VisualAge®C/C++. Our auto-parallelizer is essentially a loop parallelizer. For simplicity, the auto-parallelizer avoids complicated parallelization constructs and focuses on identifying and parallelizing expensive loops in the program. The parallelizer simply marks parallelizable loops as OpenMP `parallel do` constructs. The compiler then generates code similar to parallel loops marked by the user. Our auto-parallelizer does not support nested parallelization of loops unlike OpenMP. Auto-parallelization can also be done on an OpenMP program. In this case the auto-parallelizer skips the loop nests with OpenMP constructs and scans for other loops that can potentially benefit from parallelization.

2.1   Compilation and Runtime Infrastructure

A typical compiler and runtime structure to support OpenMP is shown in Figure 1 [5]. Figure 2 shows the Compile and Link phases of the compiler. *IR* is the intermediate representation. The parallelizer is delayed until the link phase of the compiler to make maximum utilization of the inter-procedural analysis available during linking. This is shown by the dashed lines in Figure 2.

SPEC2000 CPU benchmark suite was used to evaluate our techniques, as it is one of the best indicators of the performance of the processor, memory and compiler. Our tests focus on Spec2000FP, considering that it is where most of the data parallel processing exists. The hardware system used for testing in this paper is 1.1GHz POWER4™ system, with 1 to 8 nodes available.

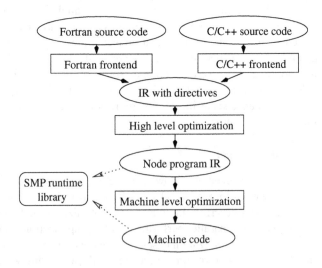

Fig. 1. Compile and runtime environment

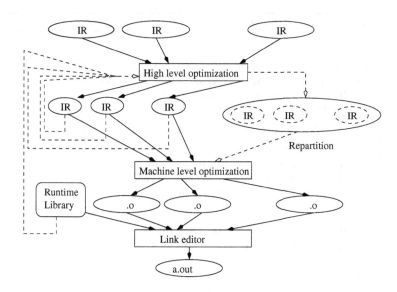

Fig. 2. Compile and link phase optimization

2.2 Basic Parallelizer Structure

Dependence analysis is a core part of the parallelizer. Data *dependence vectors*[6] are still our principal tools to analyze and verify the transformation applied on a loop nest. Suppose $\delta = \{\delta_1 \ldots \delta_n\}$ is a hybrid distance/direction vector with the most precise information derivable.

If we have

```
L₁      DO i₁ = 1, U₁ L₂        DO
i₂ = 1, U₂
            . . .
Lₙ          DO iₙ = 1, Uₙ S₁
A(f₁(i₁,...,iₙ),...,fₘ(i₁,...,iₙ))=···
S₂
···=A(g₁(i₁,...,iₙ),...,gₘ(i₁,...,iₙ))
T₁
B(u₁(i₁,...,iₙ),...,uₘ(i₁,...,iₙ))=···
T₂
···=B(v₁(i₁,...,iₙ),...,vₘ(i₁,...,iₙ))
            END DO
            . . .
        END DO
      END DO
```

as a loop nest from L_1 to L_n, we may have two dependences δ_A and δ_B characterizing the nested loops, which were caused by S_1/S_2 and T_1/T_2, where f, g, u, v are linear functions of the loop induction variables. *Dependence matrix*, denoted as $\mathcal{D}$, includes δ_A and δ_B as two rows.

Algorithm 1: Basic loop parallelizer

---

begin
   for *each loop nest in a procedure* **do**
      for *each loop in the nest in the depthfirst order (outer first)* **do**
         if *the loop is user parallel* **then**
            └ **break**

         if *the loop is marked sequential, has side-effects etc* **then**
            └ **continue**

         if *the loop has loop carried dependence* **then**
            try splitting the loop to eliminate dependence
            if *dependence not eliminated* **then**
               └ **continue**

         if *loop cost is known at compile time* **then**
            if *the loop has not enough cost* **then**
               └ **break**
         else
            └ Insert code for run-time cost estimate

         Mark this loop auto parallel
         └ **break**
end

The Algorithm 1 shows the basic structure of the parallelizer. The parallelizer scans through all the loop nests in a procedure looking for parallelizable loops. Nested parallelism is avoided by parallelizing only one loop in every nest. The loops in a nest are scanned from outer to inner as outer loops have a greater benefit from parallelization than inner loops. As a first step, loops that are not normalized and loops that are explicitly marked as sequential or have residuals, side-affects or with loop carried dependences are discarded by the parallelizer at compile time. For loops with loop carried dependences, the parallelizer tries to split the loop to eliminate the dependences. The loops are then parallelized independently. This preliminary step eliminates all non-parallelizable loops. However, naively executing all the parallelizable loops in an application may not be a good idea as we will soon discover. Parallelization is a very expensive operation with high overhead and the compiler has to be very judicial in identifying loops that can benefit from parallelization.

This paper omits discussions about basic techniques of computing dependence matrix, privatizing scalar variables in a loop, finding reduction variables, peeling or splitting the loop to eliminate the loop carried dependence, etc. which are all parts of the preparation phase for the parallelizer. We focus instead on the advanced techniques used by the parallelizer to intelligently select loops for parallelization and the optimizations that can be done after identifying a parallelizable loop. Section 3 deals with loop transformation techniques that can enhance the parallel performance of loops selected for parallelization. Section 4 explores the use of loop cost as an advanced loop selection technique for parallelization.

3 Balancing Coarse-Grained Parallelism and Locality

There are many loop transformation techniques that exists today[7]. And almost all of them can be applied to more than one kind of code optimizations. For example, loop interchange is widely used to improve data locality in cache management. Meanwhile, it also can be used to exploit parallelism, such as vectorization, and even coarse-grained parallelism. Unfortunately, the transformations for different optimization purposes do not always work in harmony.

For instance, in a loop nest, maximum spatial cache reuse can be achieved by moving the loop with stride-one access of the references to the innermost position. So a loop permutation algorithm will try to calculate such a loop order while keeping the dependence constraints of the original loop nest. On the other hand, in an automatic parallelizing compiler, one would like to parallelize the outermost loop to reduce the parallel region setup overhead, and leave more code in the inner loop for other optimization opportunities.

There has been significant research to study different approaches to solve this problem. A well known technique is *Unimodular transformation* [8,9,10], a compound loop transformation algorithm aiming at integrating different loop transformations for a specific goal and target machine, thereby reducing the problem of finding the best transformation combination to finding the best unimodular matrix. Another technique is *Loop selection*[7], which parallelizes all the parallelizable loops, then uses heuristics to select the next one as sequential, expecting to find more parallelizable loops after that. This is easier to implement when compared to unimodular transformation.

Our work is based on the idea of loop selection, but is different from the original one in two aspects: a) given our target is an OpenMP node program, we only need to find one parallelizable loop per nest, to avoid generating code with nested parallelism; b) our heuristics are directly linked to data locality, unlike the original loop selection technique which picks a loop with most "<" directions to parallelize.

3.1 Analyzing Model

Using the notation in Section 2, we introduce two theorems.

Theorem 1 (C-level interchangeable). *Loop L_c and L_{c-1} is interchangeable if and only if $\forall \delta \in \mathcal{D}$, $\delta \neq (=^{(c-2)} <> \ldots)$, where "$=^{(c-2)}$" indicates that there are $(c-2)$ directions as "=" before the first "<".*

Theorem 1 and its variant forms can be found in [11] and other literatures. We will not prove it here, but use it directly for our theorem later.

Theorem 2 (P-level parallelizable). *Loop L_p can be parallelized as a parallel do if and only if $\forall \delta \in \mathcal{D}$, $\delta \neq (=^{(p-1)} < \ldots)$.*

The proof for Theorem 2 is trivial. By the definition of parallel do, it cannot carry any dependence.

Next, we define a *multiply* operation on a dependence vector. Let $\sigma = \sigma_a \times \sigma_b$, where $\forall \sigma_j \in \sigma, \sigma_j = \sigma_{a_j} \times \sigma_{b_j}$. The multiplication of the two dependence distances is defined as following. It is unknown if one of the distances is unknown. Otherwise, it will be the regular multiplication on two integers. If one of the distances is only a direction, it is treated as 1 or -1, and after the multiplication, converted back to a direction .

Let σ_p and σ_{p-1} be the pth, $(p-1)^{th}$ column vector of dependence matrix $\mathcal{D}$, then we have

Theorem 3 (Keeping it parallelizable). *A p-level parallelizable loop L_p can be interchanged to L_{p-1} and becomes (p-1)-level parallelizable if and only if $\forall \sigma_j \in \sigma$, where $\sigma = \sigma_{p-1} \times \sigma_p$, either*

- *$\sigma_j = 0$ or*
- *the jth dependence in $\mathcal{D}$ is not carried by L_{p-1}*

Proof

We start by proving the "*if*" part of the theorem.

Suppose $\forall \sigma_j = 0$.

First, we can assert that L_{p-1} and L_p is interchangeable. Otherwise, according to Theorem 1 there is a dependence vector δ that has the form of $(=^{(p-2)} <> \ldots)$. This will conflict with the fact that all σ_j is zero. Secondly, we prove that the L_p will become $(p-1)$-level parallelizable after interchanging with L_{p-1}. Otherwise, from Theorem 2, there will a dependence vector δ, of the format $(=^{(p-2)} < \ldots)$, in the dependence matrix preventing it from being parallelized after the interchange. Considering the format of the δ before the interchange, given that all σ_j is zero, it should be in the form of $(=^{(p-1)} < \ldots)$. This conflicts with the fact that L_p is parallelizable according to Theorem 2.

If $\exists \sigma_j \neq 0$, we let δ be the dependence vector on the jth row of the matrix. It should have one of the following formats $(\cdots^{(p-2)} << \ldots)$, $(\cdots^{(p-2)} <> \ldots)$, $(\cdots^{(p-2)} >< \ldots)$, $(\cdots^{(p-2)} >> \ldots)$, where $\cdots^{(p-2)}$ is the leading $(p-2)$ positions. Since L_{p-1} does not carry any dependences as in the given condition, $\cdots^{(p-2)}$ has to be in the format of $(= \ldots =< \ldots)$, in order for the δ to be valid. Therefore, L_p can be interchanged with L_{p-1} and still be kept parallelizable.

Similarly, the "*only if*" part of the theorem can be proved. This is not important in our algorithm, so we will omit it here.

End of Proof

Theorem 4 (Outermost parallelizable). *Loop L_o can be parallelized at the outermost level if and only if $\sigma = 0$, where σ is the oth column vector of dependence matrix $\mathcal{D}$.*

This is a direct conclusion from Theorem 3. It is actually used in [7] for loop selection.

3.2   Loop Permutation with Examples

Based on our discussion in the previous section, we try to find a permutation favoring both data locality and parallelism. To do this, we first assign each loop induction variable with a weight in terms of memory access. We will favor those having maximum memory spatial reuse. A more comprehensive way of evaluating the weights is called profitability-based methods, introduced in [7], which has a cache model to estimate cache misses. Either way, a memory ordering $O = (L_1, L_2, ..., L_n)$ of the nested loops is calculated, where L_1 has the least reuse and L_n the most.

Next we build up a nearby legal permutation in P by first testing to see if the loop L_1 is legal in the outermost position. If it is legal, it is added to P and removed from O. If it is not legal, the next loop in O is tested. Once a loop L_i is positioned, the process is repeated starting from the beginning of $O - \{L_i\}$ until O is empty. P is considered as having the best data locality for the loop nest. The algorithm is summarized in [12].

Finally, we can adjust the other loops further, based on the following conditions to decide if L_i can be moved before L_j,

- The interchange should be legal,
- L_i is still parallelizable after moving, and
- The amount of data locality we are willing to sacrifice.

The first two questions are answered by Theorem 3. We will use heuristics including the induction variable weights calculated previously to control how aggressive the parallelizer should be. Apart from estimating the cache miss, a good heuristic could also include estimations of the loop cost and parallel setup overhead. The topics deserve some discussions on their own, and will not be included here. *Strip-mining* can also be considered, if no loop can be moved at all.

We illustrate the benefits of using our loop permutation algorithm using a simple example. Loop permutation for data locality will transform the Fortran code shown below to K loop as the outermost and I loop as the innermost in the nest. This will lead to the middle J loop getting parallelized. With our loop permutation algorithm we can have the J loop moved to the outermost position, thus striking a balance between locality and the desired coarse-grained parallelism.

```
DO I = 1, N
  DO J = 1, N
    DO K = 1, N
      A(I,J,K)=A(I,J,K+1);
    END DO
  END DO
END DO
```

Figure 3 shows the performance difference of the generated code on the POWER4 system for both the cases discussed. N is set to 100 and the loop nest is executed 100 times. In the figure, "Baseline" and "Improved" use exactly the same compiler, with the only difference being that the parallel loop is in the middle for the "Baseline" case and the outermost for the "Improved" case. We can see that the parallel setup overhead completely offsets the gain from parallelization in the first case, while the improved version sees reasonable speedup even for a loop with small computation cost (the loop body has a single assignment statement).

In the SPEC2000FP suite, mgrid was negatively affected by this transformation, further experiments are being carried out to derive better heuristics.

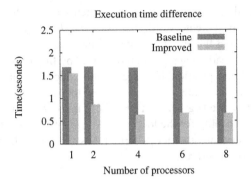

Fig. 3. Performance difference

4   Restricting Parallelization Using Cost Estimation

After a preliminary filtering out of loops unsuitable for parallelization using Algorithm 1, the auto-parallelizer evaluates the cost of a loop to further refine the selection of parallel loops.

4.1   Loop Cost Model

The cost of a loop is the approximate execution time of the loop and is given by

$$LoopCost = (IterationCount * ExecutionTimeOfLoopBody)$$

The loop cost algorithm is a recursive algorithm that computes the approximate execution time of the loop including all nested loops inside the current loop. To evaluate loops based on the loop cost, we define a set of *Threshold* values as the basis for comparison. The threshold values are carefully chosen values based on heuristics and take into account the number of processors, overhead arising from the setup required for parallelization, etc.

For loops whose cost can be estimated at compile-time, the parallelizer simply compares the cost against the precomputed threshold value and rejects loops with low costs. However for loops whose cost cannot be determined at compile-time (which is mostly the case), the auto-parallelizer computes a cost expression for the loop in terms of the values known only at runtime. This expression is then evaluated at runtime to determine whether the loop is worth parallelizing. The runtime cost expression is kept as lightweight as possible because of the overhead incurred in computing the expression at runtime. The auto-parallelizer also has a mechanism to limit the number of threads used to parallelize a loop depending on the cost of the loop. Table 1 shows the parallel loops selected at different stages of filtering.

Figure 4 shows the effectiveness of using the Loop Cost Model to restrict parallelization. The results show that careful restriction and appropriate selection of loops for parallelization is extremely crucial for parallel performance. Evaluation of our auto-parallelization techniques for Spec2000FP benchmarks indicate that the auto-parallelizer

Table 1. Stages of Loop Selection for Auto-parallelization of Spec2000 FP Benchmarks

Benchmark	#Input Loops	#Loops Processed	#After Stage1	#After Stage2/	#After Stage3
Stage1: Preliminary compile-time filtering					
Stage2: Compile-time loop cost filtering					
Stage3: Runtime loop cost filtering					
swim	23	18	9	9	5
wupwise	58	58	6	6	4
mgrid	47	30	11	11	7
applu	180	104	27	27	11
galgel	642	538	280	280	36
lucas	123	123	16	16	4
mesa	777	777	118	118	0
art	83	83	18	18	5
equake	62	64	0	0	0
ammp	283	282	18	18	0
apsi	303	284	92	92	5
sixtrack	1157	1135	347	347	11
fma3d	1648	1635	272	272	33
facerec	202	133	69	69	9

Table 2. Evaluation of Loop Selection for Auto-parallelization of Spec2000 FP Benchmarks

Benchmark	#HighCostLoops from PDF	#Parallelizable HighCostLoops from PDF	#HighCostLoops selected by Parallelizer	#LowCostLoops selected by Parallelizer
swim	8	5	5	0
wupwise	7	4	4	0
mgrid	9	7	7	0
applu	41	11	11	0
galgel	84	49	36	0
lucas	47	4	4	0
mesa	74	3	0	0
art	37	5	5	0
equake	8	0	0	0
ammp	31	0	0	0
apsi	28	11	5	0
sixtrack	44	13	11	0
fma3d	61	33	33	0
facerec	43	25	9	0

is quite precise in selecting high-cost loops for parallelization as shown by Table 2.
The Spec2000FP benchmarks were analyzed using Profile Directed Feedback techniques
[13] [14] to identify the high-cost loops in the program. The loops selected by the auto-
parallelizer are then compared with the list of expensive loops obtained from profile
directed feedback. From Table 2 we can see that the auto-parallelizer is quite accurate

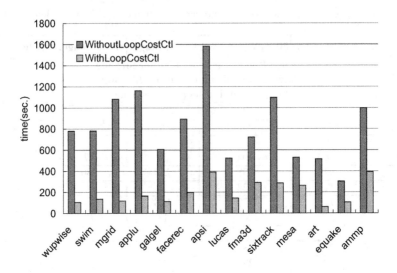

Fig. 4. Benchmark performance with and without Loop Cost using two CPU's

within a small error margin. Column 4 of Table 2 indicates the number of loops incorrectly picked by the parallelizer, i.e., loops that have a low cost and hence are not worth parallelizing. It is important to keep this number a minimum as selecting the wrong loop can adversely impact the parallel execution performance. The zero values in Column 4 indicate that the parallelizer never picks the wrong loops.

4.2 Runtime Profiling

In addition to using loop cost for restricting parallel loops, the auto-parallelizer employs runtime profiling[15] to further filter out loops at a finer granularity. The runtime profiling is a more accurate way of measuring the execution time of a chunk of code. The execution time of a chunk of a loop executed in parallel (as measured by the runtime profiler) is compared with selected *serial* and *parallel* thresholds. If the execution time of the chunk is less than the serial threshold, the next chunk of the loop is serialized disregarding the decision from the runtime loop cost evaluation. The decision to parallelize or serialize changes dynamically depending on previous executions of the loop.

5 Missed Parallelization Opportunities

As expected, the performance improvements from auto-parallelization are limited (refer to Section 6 for the actual data). To understand the auto-parallelization results, we compare our results with the SPECOMP benchmarks. For an SMP machine with a small number of processors, SPECOMP achieves relatively good performance and scalability. With this comparison, we hope to understand the reasons for the disparity in the results between explicit and auto parallelization and also expose opportunities missed by the auto-parallelizer.

Among the 14 SPEC2000FP benchmarks, 10 of them are also included in SPECOMP test suite. The two versions of the benchmarks were compared on a loop-to-loop basis. This analysis exposes limitations in the auto-parallelizer and also led to some very interesting observations. We list here some of the cases where the auto-parallelizer failed to parallelize a loop that was explicitly parallelized in the SPECOMP version. We believe that improvements to the auto-parallelizer to handle these cases can result in significant performance improvements for at least some of the benchmarks. To prove this, we try to manually parallelize loops that were explicitly parallelized in SPECOMP and compare the performance gain (manual parallelization is not possible in all cases).

5.1   Case 1: Loop Body Contains Function Calls

The auto-parallelizer fails to parallelize loops that have function calls in the loop body. Function calls could result in side-effects; the current auto-parallelizer is not capable of handling such loops. Shown here is a code snip found in *wupwise* where the loop body has function calls. *wupwise* has four such case, two in muldeo.f and two in muldoe.f. Manual parallelization of such loops shows good speedup. To manually parallelize the loops, array's AUX1 and AUX3 were privatized. The execution time is about 114 seconds with one thread, 61.8 seconds for two threads and 46.5 seconds with four threads, i.e., a 46% improvement with 2 threads and 59% improvement with 4 threads over using 1 thread. More complicated forms of this case exists in *apsi*, *galgel* and *applu*

```
COMPLEX*16    AUX1(12),AUX3(12)
. . . .

DO 100 JKL = 0, N2 * N3 * N4 - 1
  L = MOD (JKL / (N2 * N3), N4) + 1
  LP=MOD(L,N4)+1
  K = MOD (JKL / N2, N3) + 1
  KP=MOD(K,N3)+1
  J = MOD (JKL, N2) + 1
  JP=MOD(J,N2)+1
  DO 100 I=(MOD(J+K+L,2)+1),N1,2
    IP=MOD(I,N1)+1
    CALL GAMMUL(1,0,X(1,(IP+1)/2,J,K,L),AUX1)
    CALL SU3MUL(U(1,1,1,I,J,K,L),'N',AUX1,AUX3)
    CALL ZCOPY(12,AUX3,1,RESULT(1,(I+1)/2,J,K,L),1)
100   CONTINUE
```

5.2   Case 2: Array Privatization

Several loops in SPECOMP benchmarks have arrays that are explicitly marked as private, enabling the loops to be parallelized. Array privatization analysis is not yet implemented in our parallelizer preventing it from exploiting these opportunities. The code snip in Case 1 illustrates an example where array privatization is required in order to parallelize the loop. 3 such nested loops can be found in subroutine *rhs* of *applu*. Manual parallelization of such loops resulted in a 12% performance gain for *applu*. Similar situations exist in *galgel* and apsi

5.3   Case 3: Zero Trip Loops

Zero trip loops are loops in which the number of iterations calculated from the parameters of the loop is less than 1. There are 8 such loops in *apsi*, one of which is shown below. There exists loop carried dependence on the induction variable L, which the compiler tries to eliminate by rewriting the induction variable in terms of the loop parameters. However, in the case shown here, the parallelizer cannot identify L as an induction variable because of the possibility that the value of NX or NY is zero, thereby preventing the outer loop from getting parallelized. By manually parallelizing the outermost loop of such loops, the performance of *apsi* was improved by 3%.

```
        DO 30 K=1,NZTOP
          DO 20 J=1,NY
            DO 10 I=1,NX
              L=L+1
              DCDX(L)=-(UX(L)+UM(K))*DCDX(L)-(VY(L)+VM(K))*DCDY(L)
     *                   +Q(L)
10          CONTINUE
20        CONTINUE
30    CONTINUE
```

6   Summary and Future Work

We measured the performance of both the sequential and the auto-parallel versions of SPEC2000FP benchmarks. The results are shown in Figure 5[1].The figure shows three execution times for each benchmark,

- *Sequential* : sequential execution time of the benchmark code compiled by our compiler at the highest optimization level.
- *Parallel* : parallel (2 threads) execution time of the benchmark parallelized by the auto-parallelizer for SMP machines.
- *Improved* : parallel (2 threads) execution time with manual changes to the source code as described in Section 5

We also emphasize that for simplicity, the modification to individual benchmarks for the *Improved* results address only one specific problem among the 3 identified in Section 5. For instance, apsi is affected by zero trip loops, function calls in the loop body as well as array privatization. However, the source modification includes only source changes for zero trip loops. Among those 10 benchmarks in the SPECOMP test suite, swim, mgrid, applu, galgel and wupwise see reasonable speedup, with improvement up to 40%.

The results from auto-parallelization as shown by Figure 5 are not very impressive, especially considering that the hardware resource has actually doubled. However, we argue that the focus in this paper has been the utilization of simple techniques to achieve parallelization with minimal impact on the compilation time. This paper has also shown that much better performance is obtainable using sophisticated techniques

---

[1] The numbers shown here are based on a snap shot of our development compiler.

One CPU vs. two CPU runs

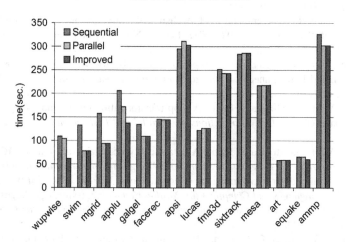

Fig. 5. Performance of auto-parallelization

at the cost of increased compilation time. In addition, this paper also presents a simple loop permutation algorithm to balance data locality and coarse-grained parallelism on SMP machines.

Our auto-parallelizer has several limitations as shown in Section 5. Implementing array privatization analysis and improving the existing dependence analysis are part of the planned future work. We also plan to fine-tune several heuristics and guidelines used in the parallelizer. With all these improvements, we hope that the auto-parallelizer will be able to detect inherent parallelism in the application code on par with explicit parallelization if not better.

7 Trademarks and Copyright

IBM, POWER4, and VisualAge are trademarks or registered trademarks of International Business Machines Corporation in the United States, other countries, or both. Other company, product and service names may be trademarks or service marks of others. [2]

References

1. Charles H. Koelbel, David B. Loveman, and Robert S. Schreiber. *The High Performance Fortran Handbook*. MIT Press, 1993.
2. Peter Pacheco. *Parallel Programming with MPI*. Morgan Kaufmann, 1996.
3. Rohit Chandra et al. *Parallel programming in OpenMP*. Morgan Kaufmann Publishers, 2001.

---

[2] The opinions expressed in this paper are those of the authors and not necessarily of IBM.

4. Tarek A. El-Ghazawi, William W. Carlson, and Jesse M. Draper. Upc language specification (v 1.1.1), 2003. http://upc.gwu.edu.
5. Guansong Zhang, Raul Silvera, and Roch Archambault. Structure and algorithm for implementing OpenMP workshare. In *WOMPAT*, Lecture Notes in Computer Science. Springer, 2004.
6. U. Banerjee. *Dependence Analysis for Supercomputing*. Boston MA: Kluwer, 1988.
7. Randy Allen and Ken Kennedy. *Optimizing compilers for modern architectures*. Morgan Kaufmann Publishers, 2002.
8. Michael E. Wolf and Monica S. Lam. A loop transformation theory and an algorithm to maximize parallelism. *IEEE Transactions on Parallel and Distributed Systems*, 2(4):452–471, 1991.
9. Michael E. Wolf and Monica S. Lam. A data locality optimizing algorithm. *ACM SIGPLAN'91 Conference on Programming Language Design and Implementation*, 1991.
10. U. Banerjee. Unimodular transformations of double loops. In *Proc. of the 3rd Workshop on Programming Languages and Compilers for Parallel Computing*, Irvine, CA, August 1990.
11. Hans Zima and Barbara Chapman. *Supercompilers for Parallel and Vector Computers*. Addison-wesley, 1990.
12. K.S.Mckinley, S.Carr, and C.-W Tseng. Improving data locality with loop transformations. *ACM Trans. on Programming Language and Systems*, 18(4), 1996.
13. Robert Cohn and P. Geoffrey Lowney. Feedback directed optimization in Compaq's compilation tools for Alpha. 2nd ACM Workshop on Feedback-Directed Optimization, 1999.
14. W. J. Schmidt et. al. Profile-directed restructuring of operating system code. In *IBM Systems Journal, 37(2)*, 1998.
15. Sagnik Nandy, Xiaofeng Gao, and Jeanne Ferrante. TFP: Time-sensitive, Flow-specific Profiling at Runtime. In *LCPC 2003*, 16th Workshop on Languages and Compilers for Parallel Computing, 2003.

An Offline Approach for Whole-Program Paths Analysis Using Suffix Arrays

G. Pokam and F. Bodin

IRISA
Campus Universitaire de Beaulieu,
35042, Rennes Cedex, France
{gpokam, bodin}@irisa.fr

Abstract. Software optimization techniques are highly reliant on program behavior to deliver high performance. A key element with these techniques is to identify program paths that are likely to achieve the greatest performance benefits at runtime. Several approaches have been proposed to address this problem. However, many of them fail to cover larger optimization scope as they are restricted to loops or procedures. This paper introduces a novel approach for representing and analyzing complete program paths. Unlike the whole-program paths (WPPs) approach that relies on a DAG to represent program paths, our program trace is processed into a *suffix-array* that can enable very fast searching algorithms that run with time $O(\ln(N))$, N being the length of the trace. This allows to process reasonable trace sizes offline, avoiding the high runtime overhead incurred by WPPs, while accurately characterizing hot paths. Our evaluation shows impressive performance results, with almost 48% of the code being covered by hot paths. We also demonstrate the effectiveness of our approach to optimize for power. For this purpose, an adaptive cache resizing scheme is used that shows energy savings in the order of 12%.

1 Introduction

The increasing processor complexity makes the optimization process a compelling task for software developers. These latter usually face the difficult problem of predicting the impact of a static optimization at runtime. One approach used to meet this challenge is to rely on path profiling to collect statistics about dynamic program control flow behavior. While this has proved to be very effective to assist program optimization [12,20], the way this information is recorded fails to reveal much insight about dynamic program behavior. One main concern with current path profiling techniques is that they are often restricted to record intra-procedural paths only [4].

More recently, Larus [14] has proposed an efficient technique for collecting path profiles that cross procedure boundaries. In his proposed approach, an input stream of basic blocks is compacted into a context-free grammar using SEQUITUR [16] to produce a DAG representation of a complete program. SEQUITUR, however, is a compression algorithm that proceeds online; hence, the

R. Eigenmann et al. (Eds.): LCPC 2004, LNCS 3602, pp. 363–378, 2005.

grammar production rules are far from being minimal such that in practice, the achieved compression ratio is likely to incur a high runtime overhead. In addition, as each grammar rule is processed into a DAG, the information pertaining to a particular dynamic path is lost since all dynamic instances of a given path are fused into a unique DAG node.

In this paper, we propose to collect and analyze whole-program paths offline. In this way, we make it possible to manage reasonable trace sizes, while shifting the cost of online processing off-line. Since, however, the relatively large sizes of the trace may render the path analysis cumbersome, an approximation of the trace is needed which also can enable efficient path analysis techniques. We introduce a novel program trace representation to deal with path analysis in an efficient way. In particular, our approach stems from the fact that the data retrieval nature of the path analysis problem makes it very tempting to consider pattern-matching algorithms as a basis for path identification. One such approach is given by *suffix-arrays* [15], which have already proved to be a very efficient data structure for analyzing biological data or text. Conceptually, looking for DNA sequences in biological data, or patterns in a text, is an analogous problem to searching for hot paths in a trace; thus making *suffix-array*-based searching techniques appropriate for path analysis. In addition, in contrast to a DAG representation, a *suffix-array* provides the advantage of treating each dynamic sub-path differently from one other.

This paper makes two contributions. The first and the foremost contribution of this paper is to demonstrate the effectiveness of using *suffix-array*-based techniques for analyzing hot program paths. More specifically, we show the appropriateness of suffix arrays to represent program paths, and to identify and characterize the exact occurrences of hot sub-paths in a trace. One particular strength of suffix arrays which make them very attractive for this purpose is their low computational complexity, which usually requires $O(\ln(N))$ time, N being the length of the input trace. The second contribution of this paper is to indeed illustrate the effectiveness of the proposed path analysis technique to guide power-related compiler optimizations. For this purpose, an adaptive cache resizing strategy is used and its potential benefits evaluated at the hot program paths frontiers.

The remainder of this paper is organized as follows. Section 2 introduces the background on suffix arrays. The profiling scheme used to collect paths is described in Section 3. In Section 4, we introduce the offline algorithm used to identify the sequences of basic blocks that appear repeated in the trace, while in Section 5 we show how these sequences can be qualified as hot paths. In Section 6, we present our experimental results and discuss a practical application of our scheme to reducing power consumption. Related work is presented in Section 7, while Section 8 concludes.

2   Suffix Arrays Background

Suffix arrays have been intensively used in several research areas such as genome analysis or text editing to look for DNA or text patterns. However, despite their widespread use in these domains, we are not aware of any attempt to use this technique in the context of program path analysis. In this section, we briefly introduce the background of suffix arrays and discuss why they may be an efficient data structure for analyzing a whole-program trace.

Given an N-length character string S, the suffix array of S, denoted by Pos in the remainder of this paper, is defined as the sorted array of the integer indices corresponding to all the N suffices of S. Hence, $Pos[i]$ denotes the string starting at position i in S which extends until the end of the string. Figure 1 illustrates a simple example representing a program execution trace T which is first processed into an initial suffix array data structure and then sorted according to a lexicographical ordering.

One key characteristic of suffix arrays is that they can enable computation of search queries in time complexity $O(p + \ln(N))$, where p is the length of the searched pattern and N the length of the string; making it very convenient to implement very fast searching algorithms. The query computation principally undergoes a binary search phase on the sorted suffix array, taking advantage of the fact that every substring is the prefix of some suffix. In addition to matching the searched query, suffix arrays also permit to compute the frequency of the queried pattern along with the exact positions of all of its occurrences in the string. As for instance, in the given example shown in Figure 1, the basic block sequence *geabc* appears 2 times in the trace, respectively at position $i = 16$ and $i = 17$ in the sorted suffix array Pos. By generalizing this concept on variable length substrings, several interesting items of information pertaining to dynamic program behavior can be efficiently retrieved. These include, for instance:

1. finding the longest repeated sequence of basic blocks in a trace, *lmax*;
2. finding all n-length repeated sequences of basic blocks in a trace, $n \leq lmax$;
3. determining the distribution frequency of each specific n-length basic blocks sequence in a trace;

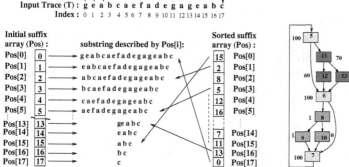

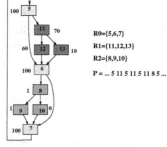

Fig. 1. Processing of an input trace T into an initial suffix array Pos

Fig. 2. Example of a sub-path

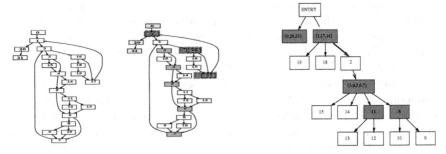

Fig. 3. CFG   **Fig. 4.** CFG with three   **Fig. 5.** CDG with instrumented nodes
                        strong regions

4. identifying the positions of each different n-length basic blocks sequence in
   a trace.

Many of the above items may be of interest for several program optimizations. For instance, item 4 can be used for grouping hot sub-paths together to drive the formation of ILP regions. In addition, if two neighbor hot paths have associated distinct dynamic profiles, this information can be used to decide if their respective profile can be merged or not. This may be helpful for inferring a common configuration to adjacent hot paths in case of an adaptive compilation strategy scheme.

Although suffix arrays present very interesting properties regarding program path analysis, they still have some drawbacks. The most noticeable of them is the memory space required to construct the suffix array, which is linear with the size of the processed trace. This latter issue has since been the subject of intensive studies and some compression algorithms have already emerged that significantly reduce the amount of memory space required [10]. While this work can also be accommodated with such a compression scheme, this is not our main concern in this study.

3   Profiling Scheme

In this section, we describe our general profiling scheme. In particular, we describe how the whole-program path trace is collected, and what kind of dynamic information is recorded together with the trace.

3.1   Collecting the Trace

Profiling can be used in a straightforward manner to collect a whole-program trace by instrumenting each basic block of the CFG. This approach is however very costly in terms of memory space. A more efficient approach is to instrument only a subset of the executed basic blocks to capture nearly the same amount of control flow information.

We use Ball's definition of a *strong region* [5] to reduce the amount of basic blocks that need to be instrumented. Given a directed control flow graph, CFG, with nodes set V and edges set $E \subseteq V \times V$, a *strong region* identifies the set of basic blocks S in which any two nodes $v, w \in S$ occur the same number of time in any complete control flow path. Strong regions are actually computed as part of the loop analysis phase. The computation relies on a generalized notion of dominance information to identify nodes of a *strong region*. Simply stated, given a loop region L with entry node h, set of exit nodes E and set of backedge sources B, two nodes $(v, w) \in L$ are in the same *strong region* iff:

$$h = loophead(v) = loophead(w) \text{ and } (v \text{ } \mathbf{dom} \text{ } w, \text{ } w \text{ } \mathbf{pdom} \text{ } v \text{ } with \text{ } respect \text{ } to \text{ } B+E)$$

The definition of the *strong region* given above allows us to identify regions in the CFG in which all basic blocks execute with nearly the same dynamic frequency, whatever the taken control flow path is. In this respect, any node belonging to such a region can be used to capture the dynamic control flow path induced by the other nodes of that region. This drastically reduces the number of instrumented basic blocks, as illustrated in Figure 4. The figure shows three strong regions, two of them are composed of 3 basic blocks while the last one has 4 nodes. The amount of instrumented basic blocks reduces from 22 to 14 because in each strong region we need to instrument only one basic block.

In some cases, however, the remaining number of instrumented basic blocks can still be large. Of most concern here are the strong regions composed of a single-node. Figure 4 shows for instance that these regions can represent almost half of the nodes. To reduce this number further, we also consider the control dependence relation [8] on the CFG induced by the strong regions. The idea is to reduce the number of such instrumented single-node regions by selecting only those that are actually control condition block. In this way, we can make sure that the number of instrumented regions with one node get reduced as we only need to keep track of the execution frequency of single-node regions of same control condition rather than of the execution count of each such individual region. This is illustrated in Figure 5. As shown in the example, the number of instrumented nodes reduces from 22 to 5 overall, providing up to 80% reduction of the total number of instrumented basic blocks.

We applied another compression technique to further reduce the size of the trace. This technique principally targets cyclic regions such as loops in which basic blocks execute repeatedly. In such a case, it is not necessary to record all the back-to-back dynamic occurrences of the same region. Instead of that, we can choose to record in the trace the last such dynamic occurrence with all attached information updated accordingly. Combined with our profiling scheme, this shows a real improvement in the compression ratio, typically up to 47%, on average, for our benchmark sets.

3.2 Control-Flow Information Accuracy

The profiling approach presented in the previous section makes it difficult to rebuild a copy of the control flow path. This, however, is of less a concern since we are merely interested of knowing which *regions* are executed more often than others, rather than knowing exactly the execution count of each basic block. Such a region-directed path profiling approach is at the advantage of the program optimizer since it may permit him to focus the analysis only on the predominant paths in the trace. In an another phase, however, each *region* can be investigated more closely to identify individual hot basic blocks.

Consider for instance the example shown in Figure 2. Three *regions* are identified: the strong region $R0$ and the regions of same control condition $R1$ and $R2$. Assuming that only nodes 5, 11 and 8 get executed in each of these regions respectively, the corresponding dynamic execution trace is shown with name P in the figure. This simple example indicates that sub-path 5, 11 is predominant. In the figure, we also show the cumulated execution count of each node. It is then straightforward to derive from the sub-path 5, 11 the exact set of the most representative basic blocks by excluding those which execute less frequently, i.e. node 13. In our abstraction, nodes 12, 13, 9, 10 are subsumed by the control dependence relation. While this effectively reduces the space, it also emphasizes the rapid identification of the main sub-path 5, 11. This is central to our program sub-path detection technique.

3.3   BBWS Signature

When a sequence of basic blocks appears repeated in the trace, we denote by *basic block working set* (BBWS) the set of static basic blocks that constitutes this sequence. The annotation attached to each such sequence is called a basic block working set signature. This annotation can be used to describe such a sequence in a unique manner, depending on the kind of dynamic information that is appended to it. For our experiments, we have considered the region id, *reg-id*, which identifies each instrumented *region*, the performance parameters *cyc, dyn, dmiss, imiss* which represent the number of elapsed cycles, the dynamic instructions count, the number of data and instruction cache misses attached to each region, respectively. This information will become more apparent during the formation of the hot program sub-paths, to determine the pertinence of a candidate hot region.

4   Identifying BBWS

The key idea to search for BBWS is to rely on the suffix array data structure to implement an efficient suffix sorting algorithm. We employ an adapted version of the KMR [13] algorithm used in genetic and text querying systems to achieve this.

4.1   KMR Algorithm

The KMR (for Karp, Miller and Rosenberg) algorithm is a well known algorithm for computing the occurrence of repeated patterns in a string. The idea is dictated by the observation that each suffix in P can be defined as the k-length suffix of another suffix starting at position i. This implies that, at the j-th stage of the sorting algorithm, $j \geq 1$, the suffix array indices $i + 2^{j-1}$ computed at stage $j - 1$ are used to initially sort each suffix i obtained at stage j. This technique allows to double the suffix length at each stage, requiring only $O(\log(N))$ processing time. The ordering relation used in the KMR sorting algorithm is based on the definition of an equivalence relation over the suffix positions of the path P. Given a path $P = p_1 p_1 p_2 ... p_n$, two suffices starting at positions i and j in P are said to be k-equivalent, $k < n$, denoted by $i \; E_k \; j$, if and only if the path of length k starting at these positions are the same.

4.2 Sorting Algorithm Description

We can easily make an analogy between the suffix array $Pos_k^{(j)}$ obtained at the j-th stage of the sorting algorithm described in the previous section and a partition of all E_k equivalent integer indices obtained from $Pos_k^{(j)}$, k being the length of the expanded suffix at that stage. Interestingly, the number of elements in the partition gives the actual number of BBWS of length k, whereas their integer indices in the suffix array $Pos_k^{(j)}$ gives their position in the trace P. Hence, it becomes straightforward to identify a BBWS according to its size (i.e length k), its dynamic frequency of occurrence (i.e cardinal of the partition E_k) as well as its dynamic coverage time (i.e start position in the trace until the position where a new BBWS is encountered).

The algorithm used to sort the suffix array Pos is shown in Algorithm 4. The alphabet is composed of the set of *regions* encountered in each CFG. The input search space P represents the execution trace. In line 6 of the algorithm, we first build the partition E_n corresponding to the set of BBWS with maximal repeated occurrence of length n. As each element of the partition is identified, it is hashed into a table of BBWS partitions with the hash key featuring the length of the BBWS. This is done for E_n as well as for the other partition elements used to iteratively compute it (see Algorithm 3). In lines 8-10 of the algorithm, the program terminates as soon as the set of BBWS identified so far is representative enough of the whole trace P. This issue is addressed in the next section. If this is not the case, i.e. the set of BBWS is not representative enough of the trace, then the algorithm undergoes a binary search to look for other BBWS, as shown in lines 11-19. The idea is to incrementally add new BBWS until the condition of the trace representativeness is met. At the end of the algorithm, the partition table T contains, for each valid entry k, the set of all k-length BBWS that appear repeated in the trace. The processing time for this algorithm is quite feasible. For instance, a 40MB trace size requires less than a few minutes to process, whereas for trace sizes ranging from several hundreds of MB to a GB, the processing time is within the order of hours.

4.3 Sorting Example

Let us consider the example shown in Figure 6. We illustrate next the different processing steps involved when searching for the longest repeated BBWS. Step

---

Algorithm 1 Initialization

Require: P : control flow path defined over Σ^m
1: Construct the suffix array $Pos_{k=1}^{(0)}$
2: Add class elements E_1 to $T[1]$

Algorithm 2 Construct suffix array $Pos_k^{(j)}$ from $Pos_{k'}^{(j-t)}$

1: **repeat**
2:    Use $Pos_{k'}^{(j-t)}$ to construct $Pos_{k'+1}^{(j-t+1)}$
3:    Add class elements $E_{k'+1}$ to $T[k'+1]$
4:    $k' := k' + 1$
5: **until** $k' < k$

Algorithm 3 Construct suffix array $Pos_{k=max}^{(N)}$ and E_{max}, N number of processing steps

---

1: Use Algorithm 1 to initialize the suffix array $Pos_{k=1}^{(0)}$
2: **repeat**
3:    $r = r' + 2^{j-1}$
4:    Construct $Pos_{k=r}^{(j)}$ from $Pos_{k=r'}^{(j-1)}$
5:    Add class elements E_r to $T[r]$
6: **until** $Pos_{k=r}^{(j)}$ is unchanged
7: **return** r

Algorithm 4 Basic block working set partitioning

1: n, k : Integer := 0
2: T : BBWS partition table
3: $\Sigma := \{$Set of reg-id$\}$, $|\Sigma| = m$
4: $P : p_1\ p_2\ p_3\ ...\ p_m \in \Sigma^m$
5:
6: Use Algorithm 3 to suffix sort the array Pos, obtaining n, the longest repeated BBWS
7:
8: **if** all BBWS are representative of P **then**
9:    stop here
10: **end if**
11: **for** $k = n - 1$ to 2 **do**
12:    **if** $T[k]$ is empty **then**
13:       Find $T[d]$ such that $d < k$, d is a power of 2 and $T[d] \neq \emptyset$
14:       Use Algorithm 2 to iteratively construct E_k from E_d
15:    **end if**
16:    **if** all BBWS are representative of P **then**
17:       stop here
18:    **end if**
19: **end for**

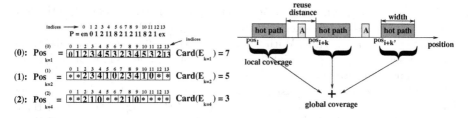

Fig. 6. Example of BBWS identification   **Fig. 7.** Hot path characteristics

0 shows the suffix array $Pos_{k=1}^{(0)}$ that corresponds to the initial sorting stage with suffix length $k = 1$. The partition elements of the equivalent class $E_{k=1}$ are deduced directly from $Pos_{k=1}^{(0)}$. The cardinal of the partition gives the number of BBWS of length $k = 1$. At the next iteration step, the array $Pos_{k=2}^{(1)}$ is computed from the array $Pos_{k=1}^{(0)}$ in the following way. The suffix positions of P that correspond to the integer indices in $Pos_{k=1}^{(0)}$ are sorted into buckets of same equivalent class. For instance, suffix positions $2, 7, 12$ in P will belong the same bucket since their integer indices in $Pos_{k=1}^{(0)}$ are identical (i.e. 2). Note that, at this stage, the number of elements in each bucket yields the dynamic execution frequency of the considered BBWS in P. From here, each bucket is sorted according to the b-equivalent relation, where $b = k^{(j)} - k^{(j-1)}$, i.e. $b = 1$ at stage 1. The result of this sorting is a new set of buckets where two suffix positions belong the same bucket iff they are E_b equivalent with regard to their integer indices in $Pos_{k=1}^{(0)}$. For instance, suffix positions $2, 7$ belong the same bucket because they are E_1 equivalent with respect to $Pos_1^{(0)}$. The array $Pos_k^{(j)}$ is obtained by renumbering the integer indices of the suffix positions contained in a bucket list with a same equivalent class number if they satisfy to the b-equivalent relation. Note that BBWS that appear only once are systematically discarded from the suffix array since we are only interested in identifying those that appear at least twice in the trace. This explains the stars in the arrays $Pos_{k=2}^{(1)}$ and $Pos_{k=4}^{(2)}$.

5   Qualified BBWS for Hot Sub-paths

Not all BBWS that are identified with the algorithm described in the previous section are of interest. Of course, there are some BBWS that effectively appear repeated in the trace but which inherently bring no value for the optimization. To distinguish among the BBWS those who are the most representative, we apply three selection criteria, as illustrated in Figure 7.

The first criterion is the *local coverage*. This metric is an indication of the number of elapsed cycles in the region, or the dynamic instructions count of that region, before a transition to another region occurs. Either one of the number of cycles or the dynamic instructions count can be directly obtained from the trace, as indicated in Section 3.3.

The second criterion is the *global coverage*. This metric is related to the *local coverage* by the dynamic execution frequency of a BBWS, *global_coverage = frequency × local_coverage*. With respect to the overall program execution, this metric assigns to each potential hot path a global cycle weight or a dynamic instructions count weight.

The last criterion is the *reuse distance*, measured in number of dynamic basic blocks. The reuse distance is an approximation of the temperature of a BBWS. As the reuse distance gets larger, the probability that the underlying BBWS is a hot path lowers. This can be mainly attributed to the fact that, although the BBWS appears repeated in the trace, it is not too often executed to infer a hot temperature. In contrast, tighter reuse distances indicate a high probability that the considered BBWS is a hot path. A consequence of this is that cold blocks in the vicinity of a hot path may also be inferred a hot temperature since the heat may propagate to them indirectly. In Figure 7 for instance, if the reuse distance of the highlighted hot path is below a given threshold, block A can be included in the BBWS induced by the nodes of the hot path to form a coarser region. Assuming *Position* designates the set of all consecutive, non-overlapping positions of a BBWS in the trace, the average reuse distance $\overline{D}$ is computed as shown in Equation (1), where *width* refers to the size of the BBWS (number of basic blocks) and % represents the modulo function.

$$\overline{D} = \frac{\sum (pos_{i-1} + width) \ \% \ pos_i}{|Position|} \tag{1}$$

Note that, since a *region* is represented with a single basic block, the computation of $\overline{D}$ must actually consider all basic blocks encountered in that *region*. Hence, the expression of $\overline{D}$ provides only an approximation of the reuse distance value. A hot path candidate is then formed by selecting BBWS with a relatively high local coverage and low reuse distance. The global coverage serves as an indication of the hot paths weight in the program.

6   Experimental Evaluation

This section presents an evaluation of the proposed approach. We first introduce the simulation platform and the benchmarks used in Section 6.1. Then, in Section 6.2, we evaluate and discuss our results.

6.1   Experimental Methodology

We conducted our experiments using applications collected from MiBench [11] as illustrated in Table 1. The applications are first compiled with the PISA compiler from the SimpleScalar [7] tool suite, with optimization level 3, to obtain an input assembly file. Each assembly file is then processed by SALTO [6], which is a general, compiler-independent tool that makes the manipulation of the assembly code at the CFG level easier. SALTO is used essentially to instrument the code, using the SimpleScalar annotation feature, and to add new compiler optimization

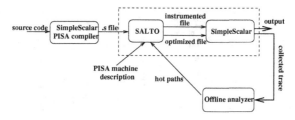

Fig. 8. Simulation framework

passes. The produced executable is processed by SimpleScalar to extract the compressed trace which is then fed to the offline analyzer. After the hot paths have been identified, this information can be re-injected into SALTO to drive the various compiler-dependent optimization passes. An overview of the different processing stages is shown in Figure 8.

Our measurements were performed with SimpleScalar, which we use to model a 5-stage in-order issue processor such as those encountered in the embedded computing domain, e.g. the Lx processor [9]. Details on the processor configuration parameters used in this study are shown in Table 2.

6.2   Evaluation

This section presents the evaluation results of using our scheme on the set of benchmarks described in the previous section. The evaluation consisted to measuring the relative compression ratio achieved by our approach and to analyzing the quality of the detected hot paths with respect to the criteria introduced in Section 5.

Trace size. The last column of Table 1 gives an estimate of the compression ratio achieved with our approach. Note that the size of the trace depends strongly on the information encoded with each trace line. For this experiment, we used 20 bytes for each trace line, one byte each for recording the region id, the number of cycles, the number of dynamic instructions, the number of data and instruction cache misses associated with each region respectively. More elaborate trace line

Table 1. Benchmark

Bench.	size (MB)	compr. ratio
dijkstra	110	65%
adpcm	148	67%
bf	55	74%
fft	6	85%
sha	11	77%
bmath	6	78%
patricia	21	77%

Table 2. Machine parameters

Issue	in-order 4-issue
Integer ALU	4
Mult. units	2
Load/Store unit	1
Branch unit	1
instr. cache	32K 1-way
data cache	32K 4-way
cache access latency	1 cycle
data cache replacement policy	LRU
memory access latency	100 cycles

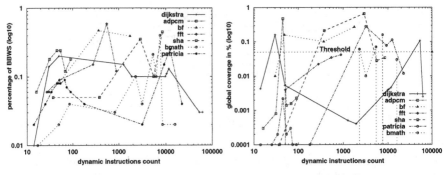

Fig. 9. Local coverage   **Fig. 10.** Global coverage

representations can be imagined to reduce further the trace size; however, this is not the scope of this paper. The column labeled *trace size* shows the original size of the trace. As it can be seen from the table, the trace size can be reduced by up to 74% on average. This compression ratio includes the compaction of back-to-back occurrences of loop paths (see Section 3.1), which accounts for about 47% of the trace reduction.

Local coverage. This metric measures the time spent in a BBWS, or the number of dynamic instructions executed within that BBWS. Figure 9 shows the distribution of the local coverage for some representative BBWS when considering the dynamic instructions count. As it can be observed from the figure, some applications have their BBWS which extend from a few tens of instructions to a few hundreds or more, e.g. *adpcm, fft, bf, dijkstra, patricia, bmath*. These applications are therefore best candidates for local optimizations such as instruction coalescence that reduces a region's critical path, or local strength reduction which replaces expensive operations with cheaper ones. In the figure, some BBWS whose sizes extend beyond a few thousand of instructions are also distinguishable, e.g. *bmath, dijkstra, patricia, sha*. As these applications tend to spend a large amount of their execution time within a single region, they may best benefit from memory re-layout techniques such as cache-conscious placements or resizing. The local coverage is however not sufficient enough for deciding on the pertinence of a BBWS.

Global coverage. The local coverage must be interpreted in the light of global coverage to yield a fair understanding of the pertinence of a BBWS. Such a comprehensive reading can be provided with help of Figure 10. For this experiment, we have fixed an arbitrary threshold at 5% of the total instructions count as indicated in the figure with the *threshold* line. With regard to the local coverage of each BBWS, all the points above the threshold line are therefore these that are likely to provide substantial performance benefits across the whole program run. Of most concern are all the applications at the exception of *fft*, which has a global coverage value slightly below the threshold. Some applications such as

Table 3. Qualified BBWS as hot paths

Table 4. Energy ratio

Bench	BBWS (%)	local cov. (%)	glob. cov. (%)	reuse (avg)
dijkstra	2.81	0.09	47	1.74
adpcm	5.88	< 0.005	90	0.00
bf	27.01	0.06	24	85.00
fft	11.7	< 0.005	7	4.21
sha	20.0	0.06	72	0.75
bmath	15.22	0.05	37	19.21
patricia	5.85	0.15	65	24.84

config	energy/access
32K4W	1.00
32K2W	0.58
32K1W	0.37
16K2W	0.55
16K1W	0.35
8K1W	0.35

sha and *patricia* exhibit BBWS whose sizes extend from a few hundreds to a few thousands of instructions, with a fairly good distribution among the two. This is an indication that these BBWS are good candidates for both local and global optimizations.

Reuse distance. The last criterion that qualifies a BBWS as a hot path is the reuse distance. This metric measures the heat of a BBWS by estimating the average number of accesses to different basic blocks between non-overlapping occurrences of this BBWS. Clearly, the larger is the reuse distance, less is the probability that it is a hot path. This trend can be well observed in Figure 11 where we show the cumulative distribution of the reuse distance for our benchmarks set. Applications with BBWS whose sizes extend to a few tens of instructions tend to have reuse distance values distributed among a few tens (e.g. *bmath, fft, bf*) to a few hundreds (e.g. *dijkstra, bmath, fft, sha, adpcm*) and thousands (e.g. *patricia, dijkstra, adpcm*) of basic blocks. Medium sized BBWS which extend from a few hundreds to a few thousands of instructions constitute the other category with reuse distance values less than a thousand, at the exception of *patricia, dijkstra* and *bmath*. Finally, as it is to be expected, very large BBWS tend to have also poor reuse distance values as evidenced with *patricia* and *dijkstra*. Tough, an exception with *dijkstra* is to be noted as a few number of these BBWS exhibit very good reuse distance value with $\overline{D} \approx 1$.

We summarize our experimental results in Table 3. The values were computed with a global threshold at 5%. This table presents results obtained by combining all the selection criteria together in order to qualify a BBWS as a hot path. As illustrated in the table, from 7% to 90% of the program dynamic instructions can be covered using our approach, with only as much as 0.15% of the dynamic instructions being executed within a single region.

6.3   Application Example: Adaptive Cache Reconfiguration

The cache hierarchy is the typical example where the power/performance trade-off plays a central role. While a large cache permits significant improvements in performance, only a small fraction of it is usually accessed during a program run. Henceforth, to address this source of inefficiency, much recent work has focused on the design of configurable caches [2,21]. A key point with such work is

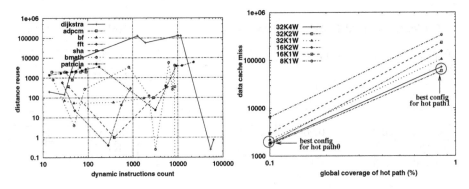

Fig. 11. Reuse distance

Fig. 12. Hotpath d-cache miss distribution for *dijkstra* (baseline config is 32K4W)

deciding when to perform such a reconfiguration. With general purpose processors, this can be done dynamically with some mean of hardware, or at software following procedure boundaries [2]. With embedded systems, this is often done once on a per-application basis [21].

In this section, we examine the possibility of reconfigurating a cache at hot path boundaries. To do so, we assume a scheme similar to that presented in [21] in which the associativity of a cache can be modified while still preserving the whole cache capacity. Furthermore, we also assume an extension of this scheme, proposed in [18], in which the associativity as well as the size of a cache can be adapted at runtime with the help of a reconfiguration instruction. Because of space convenience, we will only discuss one result, namely *dijkstra* which is that having the best BBWS profiles with larger local and global coverage and low reuse distance. Figure 12 shows the cumulative distribution of the number of data cache misses, using varying cache configurations, for the two most representative hot paths of *dijkstra* with global coverage at 10% and 83%, respectively. As indicated in the figure, each hot path has a set of cache configuration candidates which vary according to either of the selection criteria introduced in Section 5. The first hot path, for instance, has a reuse distance of ≈ 0 and a local coverage of 0.09%, whereas the second occurs practically each 4 blocks with a relative low local coverage ($\approx 0.004\%$). The first hot path is therefore more regular than the second, which could explain the larger choice for the former. Table 4 shows the relative energy per access obtained by means of CACTI [19] for each cache configuration. Each $xKyW$ stays for a cache of size x and associativity y. The best configuration for *hot path0* is given by 32K1W which is from far more energy-efficient than the 32K4W case. On the other hand, for *hot path1*, 32K2W yields the best energy-performance ratio. However, although both hot paths yield substantial energy savings, only the first one may be of interest because it has a near 0 reuse distance value, which infers that reconfiguration will take place very infrequently. This is crucial for performance as each reconfiguration instruction consumes extra cycles and energy. The energy savings obtained in this way is in the order of 12% with almost no performance slowdown (less than 1%).

7 Related Work

Many work have been proposed to collect profiling information. In [3], Ball and Larus propose to collect profile information via edges profiling. They extended their work in [4] to include path profiling information that are restricted to intra-procedural paths. Bala [1] then augmented the intra-procedural path profiling scheme to capture inter-procedural paths as well. A similar work has been proposed by Larus [14] which relies on a online compression scheme, SEQUITUR [16], to produce a compact representation of a whole-program paths. Our scheme is to some extent similar to [14] in that we also provide a representation of a whole-program paths. However, unlike the DAG representation used in [14], we rely on a suffix array representation that permits the implementation of very fast searching algorithms, allowing quick offline processing; thereby offsetting the high runtime overhead of Larus's scheme. In addition, this also permits us to treating each dynamic path distinctly from one other and consider large trace sizes. The performance of the proposed scheme can be rather significantly improved, namely by using other compression techniques which are complementary to that proposed in this paper. For instance, a direct improvement can be obtained by encoding the suffix array compression scheme described in [10]. Compression techniques such as that describe in [17] can also be used to further reduce the size of the trace to less than a fraction of a bit per reference.

8 Conclusions

While suffix arrays (SAs) have been widely used in biological data analysis or text editing, we are not aware of any prior published work that shows its application to compiler optimization. In this paper, we presented a first attempt to apply suffix array to the compiler domain. In particular, we showed how a SA can be used to represent a whole-program paths and to accurately identify hot program paths. Our evaluation results revealed that up to 48% of the code can be covered by hot paths, each one representing at most 0.15% of the total instructions count. Practical application of our approach has confirmed its effectiveness to reduce power consumption. We showed that up to 12% energy savings can be obtained with a hot-path-directed adaptive cache resizing strategy that used our technique. Because of its power to precisely model program paths (reuse distance, local+global coverage), we believe that SAs can be of a crucial aid to assist a programmer during the optimization process.

References

1. Bala, V. Low overhead path profiling. Technical Report HPL-96-87, Hewlett Packard Labs, 1996.
2. Balasubramonian, R., Albonesi, D.H., Buyuktosunoglu, A., and Dwarkadas, S. Memory hierarchy reconfiguration for energy and performance in general purpose processor architectures. In *Proc. of the 33th Int'l Conf. on Microarchitecture*, pages 245–257, Dec. 2000.

3. Ball, T., and Larus, J.R. Optimally profiling and tracing programs. *ACM Transactions on Programming Languages and Systems*, 16(4):1319–1360, July 1994.
4. Ball, T., and Larus, J.R. Efficient path profiling. In *Proc. of the 29th Annual Int'l Symposium on Microarchitecture*, Dec. 1996.
5. Ball, Thomas. What's in a Region? or computing control dependence regions in near-linear time for reducible control flow. *ACM Letters on Programming Languages and Systems*, 2(1-4):1–16, March-Dec. 1993.
6. Bodin, F., Rohou, E., and Seznec, A. Salto: System for Assembly-Language Transformation and Optimization. In *Proc. of the 6th Workshop on Compilers for Parallel Computers*, 1996 Dec.
7. Burger, D., and Austin, T. The SimpleScalar Tool Set, Version 2.0. *Computer Architecture News*, pages 13–25, 1997.
8. Cytron, R., Ferrante, J., Rosen, B.K., Wegman, M.N., and Zadeck, K. Efficiently Computing Static Single Assignment Form and the Control Dependence Graph. *ACM Transactions on Programming Languages and Systems*, 13(4):451–490, 1991.
9. Faraboschi, P., Brown, G., Fisher, J.A., Desoli, G., and Homewood, F. Lx: A Technology Platform for Customizable VLIW Embedded Processing. In *Proc. of the 27th Int'l Symposium on Computer Architecture*, June 2000.
10. Grossi, R., and Vitter, J.S. Compressed Suffix Arrays and Suffix Trees with Applications to Text Indexing and String Matching. In *Proc. of the ACM Symposium on the Theory of Computing*, 2000.
11. Guthaus, M.R., Ringenberg, J.S., Ernst, D., Austin, T.M., Mudge, T., and Brown, R.B. MiBench: A Free, Commercially Representative Embedded Benchmark Suite. In *Proc. of the 4th IEEE Int'l Workshop on Workload Characterization*, pages 3–14, Dec. 2001.
12. Jacobson, Q., Rotenberg, E., and Smith, J. Path-Based Next Trace Prediction. In *Proc. of the 30th Int'l Symposium on Microarchitecture*, Nov. 1997.
13. Karp, R.M., Miller, R.E., and Rosenberg, A.L. Rapid Identification of Repeated Patterns in Strings, Arrays and Trees. In *Proc. of the 4th ACM Symposium on Theory of Computing*, 1972.
14. Larus, J.R. Whole Program Paths. In *Proc. of the ACM SIGPLAN Conf. on Programming Language Design and Implementation*, May 1999.
15. Manber, U., and Myers, G. Suffix Arrays: A New Method for on-line String Searches. In *Proc. of 1st ACM-SIAM SODA*, pages 319–327, 1990.
16. Nevill-Manning, C.G. and Witten, I.H. Identifying Hierarchical Structure in Sequences. *Journal of Artificial Intelligence Research*, 7:67–82, 1997.
17. Plezkun, A.R. Techniques for compressing program address traces. In *Proc. of the 27th Int'l Conf. on Microarchitecture*, pages 32–40, 1994.
18. Pokam, G., and Bodin, F. Energy-efficiency potential of a phase-based cache resizing scheme for embedded systems. In *Proc. of the 8th Int'l Worskhop on Interaction between Compilers and Computer Architectures*, Feb. 2004.
19. Shivakumar, P., and Jouppi, N. Cacti 3.0: An integrated cache timing power, and area model. Technical report, DEC Western research Lab, 2002.
20. Young, Cliff., and Smith, Michael. Better Global Scheduling Using Path Profiles. In *Proc. of the 30th Int'l Symposium on Microarchitecture*, Dec. 1998.
21. Zhang, C., Vahid, F., and Najjar, W. A highly configurable cache architecture for embedded systems. In *Proc. of the 30th Int'l Symposium on Computer Architecture*, June 2003.

Automatic Parallelization Using the Value Evolution Graph*

Silvius Rus, Dongmin Zhang, and Lawrence Rauchwerger

Parasol Laboratory,
Department of Computer Science,
Texas A&M University
{silviusr, dzhang, rwerger}@cs.tamu.edu

Abstract. We introduce a framework for the analysis of memory reference sets addressed by induction variables without closed forms. This framework relies on a new data structure, the *Value Evolution Graph* (VEG), which models the global flow of scalar and array values within a program. We describe the application of our framework to array dataflow analysis, privatization, and dependence analysis. This results in the automatic parallelization of loops that contain arrays indexed by induction variables without closed forms. We implemented this framework in the Polaris research compiler. We present experimental results on a set of codes from the PERFECT, SPEC, and NCSA benchmark suites.

1 Introduction

The analysis of memory reference sets is crucial to important optimization techniques such as automatic parallelization and locality enhancement. This analysis gives information about data dependences within or across iterations of loops, about potential aliasing of variable names and, most importantly about the flow of values stored in program memory. The analysis of memory references reduces to an analysis of the addresses used by the program, or, more specifically in the case of Fortran programs, an analysis of the indices used to reference arrays. A large body of research has been devoted to this field yielding significant achievements. When index functions are relatively simple expressions of the loop induction variables and the array references are not masked by a complex control flow, then the analysis is relatively straight forward. Current compilers can easily answer questions such as "what is the array region written first in a loop".

Unfortunately, arrays are not always referenced in such a simple manner. Sometimes the values of the addresses used are not known during compilation, e.g., when the values of the addresses are read from an input file or computed within the program (use of indirection arrays). In other situations although the addresses are expressed as a simple function of the loop induction variable, the

---

* Research supported in part by NSF CAREER Award CCR-9734471, NSF Grant ACI-9872126, NSF Grant EIA-0103742, NSF Grant ACI-0326350, NSF Grant ACI-0113971, DOE ASCI ASAP Level 2 Grant B347886.

R. Eigenmann et al. (Eds.): LCPC 2004, LNCS 3602, pp. 379–393, 2005.

control flow that masks the actual references makes it impossible to compute a closed form of the index variable and thus very difficult to perform any meaningful analysis.

Some of these difficulties have been addressed in the recent past by using runtime analysis and speculative optimizations on loops that cannot be analyzed statically, e.g., loops with input dependent reference patterns [21]. Recently, Hybrid Analysis [22] has improved the accuracy and performance of optimizations by bridging the gap between static and run-time analysis (compile-time analysis partial results can be saved and used at run-time, when all statically unknown values are available).

However, despite recent progress, memory reference analysis and subsequent loop parallelization cannot be performed with sufficient accuracy when the arrays are indexed by functions that cannot be expressed as a closed form of the primary loop induction variable.

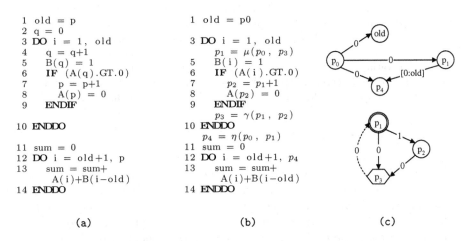

```
1  old = p
2  q = 0
3  DO i = 1, old
4      q = q+1
5      B(q) = 1
6      IF (A(q).GT.0)
7          p = p+1
8          A(p) = 0
9      ENDIF
10 ENDDO

11 sum = 0
12 DO i = old+1, p
13     sum = sum+
           A(i)+B(i−old)
14 ENDDO
```

(a)

```
1  old = p0
3  DO i = 1, old
       p1 = μ(p0 , p3)
5      B(i) = 1
6      IF (A(i).GT.0)
7          p2 = p1+1
8          A(p2) = 0
9      ENDIF
       p3 = γ(p1 , p2)
10 ENDDO
       p4 = η(p0 , p1)
11 sum = 0
12 DO i = old+1, p4
13     sum = sum+
           A(i)+B(i−old)
14 ENDDO
```

(b)

(c)

Fig. 1. (a) Arrays A and B are indexed with values from recurrences without and with closed forms respectively. (b) The same code after closed form substitution and in GSA. (c) Value Evolution Graphs for the recurrence on p

Recurrences with closed forms are those in which the i-th term can be written as an algebraic formula of i. References to arrays using recurrences with closed forms can be meaningfully expressed using systems of inequations [25,20,13] or triplet-based notations [14,9] containing the closed form terms and other symbolic values such as loop bounds. When a recurrence that has no closed form is used to index an array, the corresponding memory reference set cannot be summarized using an algebraic formula. For example, the algebraic expressions for the index of array A at line 8 in Fig. 1(a) for iterations k and $k+1$ are identical, p, but their values always differ. Hence, we need to develop an alternative analysis technique because we cannot use the symbolic calculus algebra we use with closed form recurrences.

We propose to model the data flow of the recurrences without closed form using a new data structure, the *Value Evolution Graph* (VEG) and use it to extract parallelization information. Array B in Fig. 1 (a) is accessed through a recurrence with closed form $q(i) = i$, which was substituted in Fig. 1(b). It is easy to prove that there are no loop carried dependences on B because it is indexed by an analytical function of the loop index. However, there is no such function for p (the index of A), which is defined by a recurrence without a closed form. Fortunately, data dependence analysis does not require the existence of closed form solutions, but rather proofs of relations between the index sets corresponding to different iterations. For instance, in order to prove array A independent, we need to show that statements 6 and 8 are independent. At statement 6 we read from A at offsets between $[1 : old]$, and at 8 we write based on all the values of the recurrence on p. We prove that the set of all the values of the recurrences does not intersect $[1 : old]$ by means of graph search operations on the VEG displayed in Fig. 1(c).

Our Contribution

(a) We propose the *Value Evolution Graph* that can represent the flow of scalar and array values within a program. The Value Evolution Graph is pruned based on control dependence and predicate extraction, and produces tighter value ranges than abstract interpretation methods.

(b) Unlike the previous efforts of looking for patterns in the code text, we can analyze partially aggregated and classified memory descriptors. This single generic approach both extends and unifies in a single framework most cases which were previously solved using various, different, pattern matching techniques. It allows for the parallelization of important classes of memory reference patterns, e.g., pushbacks.

(c) By integrating the VEG in our memory classification analysis we have been able to accurately classify memory access sequences and use them to improve the coverage of important analysis techniques, e.g., data dependence analysis, privatization.

(d) The presented technology is implemented and fully functional as a module in the Polaris compiler and was crucial in further parallelizing a larger number of benchmark codes.

2   The Value Evolution Graph (VEG)

Finite recurrences are usually described by an initial value, a function to compute an element based on the previous one[1] (an *evolution* function), and a limiting condition. Depending on the evolution function's formula, in certain cases we can evaluate important characteristics even for recurrences without closed forms: the *distance* between two consecutive elements, the *image* of the recurrence, i.e. the set of all values it may take, and the *last element* in the sequence.

---

[1] We only address first order recurrences in this paper.

We introduce the *Value Evolution Graph (VEG)*, a compiler representation for the flow of values across arbitrarily large and complex program sections, including, but not limited to, recurrences without closed forms. Consider the loop at line *3* in Fig. 1. It performs a repeated conditional push to a stack array A. The stack pointer is stored in variable p. Due to the fact that p is incremented conditionally, there is no closed form for the recurrence that defines its value. We represent values as *Gated Static Single Assignment (GSA)* [2] names. In GSA, there are three types of ϕ-nodes. γ nodes merge two values on different forward control flow paths. μ nodes merge a loop back value with the loop incoming value. η nodes merge the outcome of a loop with the value before the loop. We extended the GSA representation to interprocedural contexts in a way similar to [16]. While this helps to discern between the values of p on the left and right hand side of the assignment at line *7* respectively, it does not differentiate between the value of p at line *8* in successive iterations. However, it makes it easy to determine that the stack array is written only at position p_2, and that p_2 is always the result of an addition of 1 to p_1. The subgraph consisting of $\{p_1,$ $p_2, p_3\}$ (in Fig. 1(c)) represents the value flow between different GSA names for p in a single iteration of the loop. Each edge label represents the value added to its source to obtain its destination. The dashed edge carries values across iterations, but is not part of the VEG as it does not contribute to the flow of values within an iteration. We can employ well-known graph algorithms to prove that the distance between two consecutive values of p_2 is always *1*, which makes the write to $A(p_2)$ be a stack push operation.

We will show how we construct the VEG in general, and how we run queries on it to compute recurrence characteristics over complex program constructs, such as loop nests, complex control flow, and subprogram calls.

2.1 Formal Definition

We define a *value scope* to be either a loop body (without inner loops), or a whole subprogram (without any loops). Immediately inner loops and call sites are seen as simple statements. We treat arrays as scalars and assume that programs have been restructured such that control dependence graph contains no cycles other than self-loops at loop headers. We have implemented such a restructuring pass in our research compiler.

Definition. Given a value scope, the Value Evolution Graph is defined as a directed acyclic graph in which the nodes are all the GSA names defined in the value scope and the edges represent the flow of values between the nodes.

Nodes. In addition to the nodes defined in the value scope, we add, for every immediately inner loop, the set of GSA names that carry values outside the inner loop. An example is p_1 in Fig. 1. Such nodes appear both in their current value scope graph as well as in the immediately outside value scope graph. They are called μ nodes in the context of the graph corresponding to the inner value scope and are displayed as double circles. Nodes representing variables assigned values defined outside their scope are called *input* nodes and are labeled with the assigned value (they are displayed as rectangles). The μ and *input* nodes are the only places where values can flow into a VEG. Values can flow out of the VEG through μ nodes only. *Back* nodes represent the last value within a VEG (shown as hexagons). They are used to solve recurrences.

Edges. An edge between two variables p and q represents the *evolution* from p to q, defined as the function f, where $q = f(p)$. The evolution belongs to a scope if p and q are defined within the scope, and all symbolic terms in f are defined outside it. We represent four types of evolutions, additive and multiplicative for integer values and *or* and *and* for logical values. We represent an evolution by its type and the value of the free term. Certain evolutions can be composed along a path symbolically. For instance, the evolution along path $p_1 \rightarrow p_2 \rightarrow p_3$ is an additive evolution with value $1 + 0 = 1$. Instead of keeping a single value for an evolution, we store a range of possible values. This allows us to define an aggregated evolution from a node p to a node q as the union of the evolutions along all paths from p to q. For example, the aggregated evolution from p_1 to p_3 is $[0 : 1]$, which represents the union of the evolution $[0 : 0]$ along path $p_1 \rightarrow p_3$ and the evolution $[1 : 1]$ along path $p_1 \rightarrow p_2 \rightarrow p_3$. Each edge is also labeled with a predicate extracted from the associated GSA gate. For instance, edge $p_1 \rightarrow p_2$ is labeled with predicate $A(i).GT.0$. If no GSA gate is associated with an edge, we label it $.TRUE.$. Predicates are not displayed in to improve the clarity of the presentation.

Complexity. VEGs are as scalable as the GSA representation of the program since the number of nodes in all VEGs is at most twice the number of GSA names in the program and every node corresponding to a ϕ definition has the same number of incoming edges as the number of ϕ arguments. All other nodes have at most one incoming edge.

2.2   Value Evolution Graph Construction

Table 1 shows how we create edges from their corresponding statements. For now, we support only one evolution type per VEG. This evolution type is given by the first evolution we encounter, and is called the default type of the graph. If a value is computed in a way different from the ones shown in the table, we conservatively transform it into an *input* node and label it with $[-\infty : +\infty]$ (or $[.FALSE. : .TRUE.]$). If it is computed in an assignment statement, then we try to find a closer range for the right hand side of the statement. We compute the aggregated evolution of an entire recurrence as the aggregated evolution, over all iterations, from the μ node to all nodes that may carry evolutions to the next iteration. We draw an edge from the value of the μ node to the corresponding value on the left hand side of the corresponding η definition, and we label it with the aggregated evolution of the inner recurrence. Fig. 1(c) shows such an edge between p_1 (a μ node in the inner recurrence $\{p_1, p_2, p_3\}$) and p_4. The range $[0 : old]$ is a result of multiplying the range of the aggregated evolution from p_1 to p_3, $[0 : 1]$, with the iteration count of the loop, *old*. When values are obtained as a result of a subprogram call, we add edges to represent the aggregated value evolutions of the *OUT* actual arguments (and global variables) as functions of *IN* actual arguments (and global variables). In the last line in Table 1, b_2 and b_1 are the *OUT* and *IN* arguments respectively.

Table 1. Extracting evolutions from the program

Statement	Edge	Ev. Type	Label
$b_1 = a + \exp$	$a \to b_1$	$+$	exp
$b_1 = a$ .OR. exp	$a \to b_1$	$\vee$	exp
$b_1 = a * \exp$	$a \to b_1$	$*$	exp
$b_1 = a$ .AND. exp	$a \to b_1$	$\wedge$	exp
$b_1 = a$	$a \to b_1$	Default	Identity
$b_1 = \exp$	no edge, mark *input* node		
$b_2 = \gamma(b_0, b_1)$	$b_1 \to b_2$	Default	Identity
	$b_0 \to b_2$	Default	Identity
$b_2 = \mu(b_0, b_1)$	no edge, mark μ node		
$b_2 = \eta(b_0, b_1)$	$b_1 \to b_2$	Default	Loop effect
	$b_0 \to b_2$	Default	Identity
CALL sub$(b_1 \to b_2)$	$b_1 \to b_2$	Default	*sub* effect

The VEGs are built in a single bottom-up traversal of the whole program. We precompute the shortest and longest paths between every μ and *input* node and every other node and use these measures to solve queries such as recurrence *step* in $O(1)$ time. If every node is reachable from exactly one μ node and there are no *input* nodes, the complexity of the algorithm is linear in the number of GSA names + the number of arguments in all the ϕ nodes in the program. If more than one μ node can reach one same other node (coupled recurrences), the complexity may increase by a factor of at most the number of coupled recurrences.

2.3   Queries on Value Evolution Graphs

We obtain needed information about the values taken by induction variables by querying the VEG. All our queries are implemented using shortest path algorithms. Since all VEGs are acyclic, these algorithms have linear complexity.

Distance between two values in two consecutive iterations of a loop. Given two GSA variables (possibly identical) and a loop, we can compute the range of possible values for the difference between the value of the second variable in some iteration $i+1$, and the value of the first variable in iteration i. For recurrences without closed forms, this computes the *distance* between two consecutive elements. In the example in Fig. 1, the distance between p_2 in iteration i and p_2 in iteration $i+1$ is exactly *1*. This information can be used to prove that the write pattern on array A at statement *8* cannot cause any cross-iteration dependences. The value of the distance between a source node and a destination node across two consecutive iterations of a loop can be used for comparisons only if the destination node is not reachable from an *input* node.

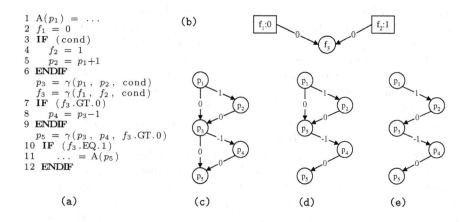

```
1  A(p₁)  =  ...
2  f₁ = 0
3  IF  (cond)
4      f₂ = 1
5      p₂ = p₁+1
6  ENDIF
     p₃ = γ(p₁, p₂, cond)
     f₃ = γ(f₁, f₂, cond)
7  IF  (f₃.GT.0)
8      p₄ = p₃−1
9  ENDIF
     p₅ = γ(p₃, p₄, f₃.GT.0)
10 IF  (f₃.EQ.1)
11     ...  = A(p₅)
12 ENDIF
```

(a)   (c)   (d)   (e)

Fig. 2. (a) Sample code in GSA, (b) VEG for f_1, f_2, f_3; VEG for p_1, p_2, p_3, p_4, p_5 – (c) before pruning, (d) after pruning based on GSA Paths, and (e) based on range tracing

Range of a variable over an arbitrarily complex loop nest. Given a GSA variable and a loop, we can compute the range of values that the variable may take over the iteration space of the loop. For recurrences without closed forms, this computes their *image* and can be used to evaluate the *last element*. In the example in Fig. 1, the range for variable p_2 over the loop is $[p_0 + 1 : p_0 + old]$. This information is crucial for proving that the write pattern on array A at statement *8* cannot have cross-iteration dependences with the read pattern at statement *6* (they are contained in disjoint ranges $[p_0 + 1 : p_0 + old]$ and $[1 : p_0]$ respectively). This information is computed in $O(d)$ time, where d is the depth of the loop nest between the given loop and the definition site of the given variable.

Global value comparison. Given two GSA variables in the same subprogram, we can compare their values even if they are not in the same value scope, by comparing their ranges in a larger common scope. This information can be used to prove either an order between their values or their equality and which in turn can be used in many compiler analysis techniques.

2.4   VEG Logic Inference and Conditional Pruning

We can prune a VEG by removing certain edges that cannot be taken based on the truth value of a condition. The shortest path algorithms used to compute aggregated evolutions will then produce tighter ranges. Consider the code shown in Fig. 2 (a). Because we do not know anything about the value of *cond*, we cannot compare the values of p_1 and p_5, information that is needed to determine if the memory read at offset p_5 in array A is always covered by the write at offset p_1. Based on its corresponding VEG (Fig. 2 (c)), we can only infer that $p_5 \in [p_1\text{-}1 : p_1 + 1]$.

The GSA path technique [26] describes how control dependence relations can be used to disambiguate the flow of values at γ gates. It can infer that at line 11 condition $f_3.EQ.1$ holds true, which implies also $f_3.GT.0$ holds true. To the VEG, this means that value p_5 comes from p_4 and not directly from p_3. With the VEG pruned using this information (Fig. 2 (d)), we have $p_5 \in [p_1\text{-}1{:}p_1]$.

We have improved on [26] by using the VEG to trace back ranges extracted from control dependence predicates. The read from array A at line 11 is guarded by condition $f_3.EQ.1$. This implies $f_3.EQ.1$ holds true. From this predicate, we extract the range $[1 : 1]$ for f_3. In Fig. 2 (b), we trace this range for f_3 backward to see where it could have come from. Since the initial value for *input* node f_1 is *0*, and the edge $f_1 \rightarrow f_3$ has weight *0*, the only range that can be produced on the path $f_1 \rightarrow f_3$ is *0+0=0*. The GSA gate $f_3 = \gamma(f_1, f_2, cond)$, associates the pair (f_1, f_3) with condition *.NOT.cond*. Since f_3 cannot come from f_1, *.NOT.cond* must be false, thus *cond* must be true. The same predicate, *cond*, controls the other gate, $p_3 = \gamma(p_1, p_2, cond)$. Since *cond* holds true, p_3 must have come from p_2, and not from p_1. So the edge $p_1 \rightarrow p_3$ cannot be taken. This leads to the graph in Fig. 2 (e). On the pruned graph in Fig. 2 (e), $p_5 = p_1 + 1 + 0 \text{-} 1 + 0 = p_1$, which proves the read at line 11 covered by the write at line 1.

This method improves on [26], leads to more accurate ranges than the abstract interpretation method used in [3], and can solve classes of problems that [27] cannot.

3   VEG Enabled Memory References Analysis

Memory Reference Classification. Memory Classification Analysis (MCA) [14] is a general dataflow technique used to perform data dependence tests and privatization analysis, but which is also usable in any optimization that requires dataflow information, such as constant propagation. For a given program context – a statement, loop, or subroutine body – MCA classifies all memory locations accessed within the context in *Read Only (RO)*, *Write First (WF)* and *Read Write (RW)*.[2] We perform MCA in a single bottom-up traversal of the program by applying simple rules that aggregate and classify memory locations across larger and larger program contexts. For instance, if a variable is *RO* in a statement and *WF* in the following statement, it is classified as *RW* for the block of two statements. The symbolic manipulation within MCA relies on the existence of closed forms for induction variables. We will show that in certain cases we can perform MCA even in the absence of closed forms.

Memory Reference Sequences. The write to A in Fig 1, although indexed by a recurrence without closed forms, can be described by $[1 : p_4]$ since it is written contiguously within these bounds. A memory reference sequence is *contiguous in a loop* if it is contiguous within every iteration and, for any iteration i, its image

---

[2] The RO set records all memory locations that are only read (never written); the WF set records all memory locations that are first written, then possibly read and/or written again; the RW set includes all other memory locations.

Table 2. Uses of sequence classification to the parallelization at the outer level of a nest of two loops

	Sequence	Context	Benefit
1	Contiguous	Inner	Privatization
2	Increasing	Outer	Independence
3	Contiguous	Outer	Efficient parallel code

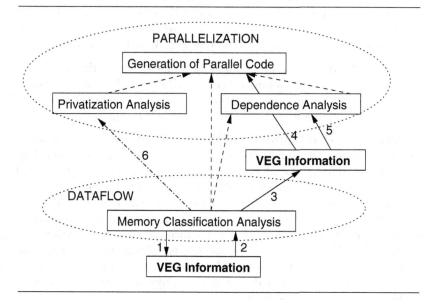

Fig. 3. Integration of the information produced by the VEG in a parallelizing compiler

over iterations $1-i$ is contiguous. It is *increasing in a loop* if every access index in iteration $i+1$ is strictly larger than any index in iterations $1-i$. It is *consecutive in a loop* if it is both contiguous and increasing in the loop. These definitions can be extended to strided memory access. To prove a sequence contiguous, we show that *on all control flow paths within each iteration*, the step of induction variable is smaller or equal to the span of the memory reference. To prove a sequence increasing, we show that *on all control flow paths within each iteration*, the step of induction variable is larger or equal to the span of the memory reference.

3.1 Applications: Compiler Optimizations

Fig. 3 presents a general view of the use of VEG information to various analysis crucial to effective automatic parallelization. Table 2 presents the use of memory reference sequence classification to the parallelization at the outer level of a loop nest containing two loops.

Dataflow Analysis. We can use the WF, RO, and RW sets to prove general dataflow relations. For instance, a WF followed by a RO represents a def-use edge with weight $WF \cap RO$. This information can be used in transformations such as constant propagation. In the example in Fig. 1, we can prove that there is a def-use edge between lines 8 and 13 on array A, with weight $[old + 1 : p_4]$. We can therefore propagate all constant array values at offsets within this range.

Privatization. The privatization transformation benefits from memory reference sequence classification indirectly. The refined WF, RO, and RW sets for Inner will result in refined RO_i, WF_i, and RW_i sets for Outer. This leads to more opportunities for removing memory related dependences through privatization. This corresponds to edges 2 and 6 in Fig. 3, and to row 1 in Fig. 2.

Dependence Analysis. Let us assume that we have the descriptors RO_i, WF_i, and RW_i for Outer. If we can find a memory sequence d that includes them and is increasing in Outer, then no cross iteration data dependences can exist. This corresponds to edges 3 and 5 in Fig. 3, and to row 2 in Fig. 2.

Recognition and Parallelization of Pushbacks. When a loop contains array references through inductions variables, its parallelization is conditioned by: (i) there should be no data dependences between iterations of the loop except those involving the induction variable, (ii) it must be possible to compute the values taken on by the induction variable in parallel. Two cases in which the induction values can be computed in parallel are when the induction recurrence has a closed form solution or when it is associative; in the former case parallelization is trivial and in the latter case it can be done using a parallel prefix type computation [15]. [18] presents the parallelization of loops that contain the pattern $p = p+1;$ $A(p) = ...$ and where p and A do not appear anywhere else in the loop body, using the "array-splitting" technique.

In this work, we use the VEG to extend the applicability of the parallel prefix parallelization to more general types of loops that cannot be analyzed using pattern matching techniques alone. We define a *pushback sequence* as a sequence of consecutive WF reference sets. WF is more general than *write* (covered reads are allowed). The WF set is computed accurately by the VEG improved MCA and thus qualifies more loops for parallelization. By working on aggregated reference sets, we can qualify more loops as pushbacks through the VEG-enhanced MCA, while previous approaches are bound to statement-level pattern recognition.

4   Implementation Details and Experimental Results

Integration with Hybrid Analysis in Polaris. The Hybrid Analysis framework [22] integrates compile-time and run-time analysis of memory reference patterns. It performs dataflow analysis by implementing the MCA algorithm using partially aggregated RT_LMAD memory reference descriptors, and uses its results to parallelize loops (Fig. 4). Privatization, data dependence, and parallel code generation problems such as copy-in and last value assignment are mapped into equations containing the RO, WF, and RW per-iteration descriptors (as

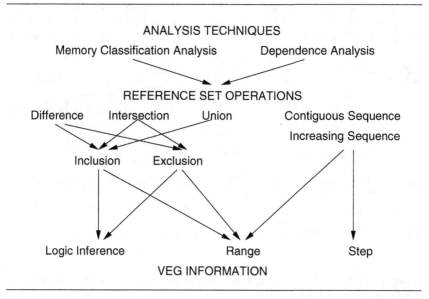

Fig. 4. Implementation of memory reference analysis using the VEG

RT_LMADs). These operations rely heavily on VEG information, such as step, range, or logical inferences. The RT_LMAD operations: $\cap$, $-$ and $\cup$ (Fig. 4) rely on two relational operators, set inclusion and set exclusion. In addition to the range information, the more accurate GSA paths produced while pruning the VEG are used to prove predicate implication, which is used extensively in the inclusion and exclusion operators. For instance, in the case in Fig.1(b), in order to classify the references on array A across statements 6–8, we use the VEG to intersect the RO descriptor i with the WF descriptor p_2. The VEG produces the range $[1 : old]$ for i and $[old + 1 : 2 * old]$ for p_2. Since these ranges are found disjoint (exclusive), the intersection (RW) is empty.

Table 3 presents a set of loops parallelized using VEG-based memory reference analysis. The third column shows the percentage of the total sequential execution of the program spent in the loop. The parallelization of these loops is crucial to the overall performance improvement in *TRACK, BDNA, ADM, P3M,* and *MDLJDP2.* Although our VEG-based analysis can also parallelize a large number of loops in which memory is referenced based on recurrences with closed forms, we only show here the loops that contain recurrences without closed forms and thus could not be solved previously.

Seven out of the eleven parallelized loops are *conditional pushbacks.* The cases in *TRACK* are the most difficult as the arrays are not used as a stack at statement level, but only at the whole loop body level [23]. We are not aware of any other static analysis that can parallelize any of these three loops. Six out of eleven loops required privatization analysis based on either *contiguous writes* or VEG information directly (value ranges).

Table 3. Loops parallelized using the VEG. ADM, BDNA, DYFESM, QCD, and TRACK are from the PERFECT benchmark suite, MDLJDP2 and HYDRO2D from SPEC92, and P3M from NCSA. CP = Conditional Pushback, CW = Contiguous Write

Program	Loop	Seq. %	Description
TRACK	EXTEND_do400	15-65	CP, CW, stack lookup/update in inner loop
	FPTRAK_do300	4-50	CP, stack lookup in inner loop
	GETDAT_do300	1-5	CP, CW, stack lookup/update in inner loop
P3M	PP_do100	52	CW in inner loops – privatization
	SUBPP_do140	9	CW in inner loops – privatization
BDNA	ACTFOR_do240	29	Index array range using VEG – privatization
MDLJDP2	JLOOPB_do20	12	CP
ADM	DKZMH_do60	6	CW in inner loops – privatization
QCD	QQQLPS_do21	< 1	CP
DYFESM	SETCOL_do1	< 1	CP
HYDRO2D	WNFLE_do10	< 1	CP

Loop *BDNA/ACTFOR_do240* contains an inner loop that fills an index array *ind* with values within range $[1 : i]$, where i is the index of the outer loop. Then, these values index a read operation on an array *xdt*. Since array *xdt* is first written in every iteration of the outer loop from 1 to i, this write covers all successive reads from *xdt(ind(:))*. The read pattern *ind(:)* is found to be completely contained in $[1 : i]$ based on the VEG range approximation for *ind*, which proves *xdt* privatizable. This pattern also appears in *P3M/PP_do100*.

5   Related Work

Automatic recognition and classification of general recurrences was discussed extensively in [1,24,27,7], and their parallelization was presented in [5,4,6]. [12,19,8,11] extend the analysis of memory indexed by irregular recurrences, but do not address most of the cases we focus on. Let us follow (Table 4) a comparison between our framework and the most recent work on the parallelization of loops that reference memory through recurrences without closed forms [10,17,28,29].

1, 2. We introduce a single technique that covers all the problems solved by [17,28,29], has wider applicability, and, additionally, builds generic array dataflow information. [10] uses monotonic information to improve memory reference set operation accuracy in a generic way, but does not recognize contiguous sequences. [28,29] do not address privatization and [17] does it only based on specific algorithm recognition.

3, 4, 5, 6. [10] extracts ranges from array indices as well as from predicates based on affine expressions. [28,29] introduced the idea of evolution and a recurrence model that produces distance ranges. We believe that the VEG paths represent the evolution and control information more explicitly. The VEG can model recurrences defined using multiple variables, unlike previous representa-

Table 4. Comparison to recent work on memory referenced through recurrences without closed forms

		Gupta et al [10] PACT'99	Lin, Padua [17] CC'00
		Wu, Padua [28,29] ICS'01-LCPC'01	Our Framework
1	**Problems Solved**	Privatization, Data Dependence	Privatization, Some Data Dependence
		Data Dependence	Privatization, Data Dependence, Dataflow
2	**Method**	Memory Reference Analysis	Algorithm recognition (3)
		Monotonic evolution	Memory Reference Sequence Classification
3	**Recurrence Model**	Implicit	Implicit: DDG
		Explicit: evolution	Explicit: evolution graph
4	**Multi-variable**	Not specified	No
		No	Yes
5	**Distance Ranges**	Yes	No
		Yes	Yes
6	**Conditional Ranges**	Range extraction	No
		No	Range extraction and tracing
7	**Mem. Ref. Type**	Generic	Single indexed
		Not defined	Generic
8	**Interprocedural**	Yes	No
		No	Yes
9	**Pushback Parallelization**	No	Yes (restrictive)
		No	Yes (more general)

tions that rely on the statement-level pattern $i = i + exp$. The VEG conditional pruning is a new feature.

7, 8. Previous approaches generally require that arrays be unidimensional and that the index expression consist of exactly the recurrence variable. The recurrence variable cannot appear in the loop text except for the recurrence statements and as an array index. Our framework is more flexible: we analyze partially aggregated generic memory descriptors that represent the reference pattern in a single statement, an inner loops or a whole subprogram uniformly.

9. We can parallelize *pushback sequences* in a more general case than [17]. None of the other techniques could parallelize the loops from *TRACK* in Table 3.

6 Limitations and Future Work

At this point we only support one evolution type within a single graph. This allows us to compose evolutions along paths by performing simple range arithmetic. We are planning to investigate the need for an evolution graph that contains multiple types of evolutions and the algorithmic complications involved.

For now, we treat arrays as scalars. We are planning to investigate the use of array dataflow information produced by MCA to create more expressive value evolution graphs.

We are also looking into further applications of value evolution graphs to the GSA path technique. Preliminary results show that, with minor improvement, we could solve more complex problems such as the parallelization of loop *INTERF_do1000* in code *MDG* from the *PERFECT* suite.

References

1. Z. Ammarguellat and W. L. Harrison, III. Automatic recognition of induction variables and recurrence relations by abstract interpretation. In *ACM SIGPLAN '90 Conference on Programming Language Design and Implementation*, pages 283–295, White Plains, N.Y., June 1990.
2. R. A. Ballance, A. B. Maccabe, and K. J. Ottenstein. The Program Dependence Web: A representation supporting control-, data-, and demand-driven interpretation of imperative languages. In *ACM SIGPLAN '90 Conference on Programming Language Design and Implementation*, pages 257–271, White Plains, N.Y., June 1990.
3. W. Blume and R. Eigenmann. Symbolic Range Propagation. Technical Report 1381, Univ of Illinois at Urbana-Champaign, Cntr for Supercomputing R&D, 1994.
4. D. Callahan. Recognizing and parallelizing bounded recurrences. In *1991 Workshop on Languages and Compilers for Parallel Computing*, number 589 in Lecture Notes in Computer Science, pages 169–185, Santa Clara, Calif., Aug. 1991. Berlin: Springer Verlag.
5. S.-C. Chen and D. J. Kuck. Time and parallel processor bounds for linear recurrence systems. *IEEE Transactions on Computers*, 24(7):701–717, 1975.
6. A. L. Fisher and A. M. Ghuloum. Parallelizing complex scans and reductions. In *Proceedings of the ACM SIGPLAN 1994 conference on Programming language design and implementation*, pages 135–146. ACM Press, 1994.
7. M. P. Gerlek, E. Stolz, and M. Wolfe. Beyond induction variables: Detecting and classifying sequences using a demand-driven SSA form. *ACM Transactions on Programming Languages and Systems*, 17(1):85–122, 1995.
8. A. M. Ghuloum and A. L. Fisher. Flattening and parallelizing irregular, recurrent loop nests. In *Proceedings of the fifth ACM SIGPLAN symposium on Principles and practice of parallel programming*, pages 58–67, Santa Barbara, CA, 1995. ACM Press.
9. J. Gu, Z. Li, and G. Lee. Symbolic array dataflow analysis for array privatization and program parallelization. In *Proceedings of the 1995 ACM/IEEE conference on Supercomputing (CDROM)*, page 47. ACM Press, 1995.
10. M. Gupta, S. Mukhopadhyay, and N. Sinha. Automatic parallelization of recursive procedures. *International Journal of Parallel Programming*, 28(6):537–562, 2000.
11. R. Gupta. Optimizing array bound checks using flow analysis. *ACM Letters on Programming Languages and Systems*, 2(1–4):135–150, 1993.
12. M. R. Haghighat and C. D. Polychronopoulos. Symbolic analysis for parallelizing compilers. *ACM Transactions on Programming Languages and Systems*, 18(4):477–518, 1996.

13. M. Hall, J. Anderson, S. Amarasinghe, B. Murphy, S.-W. Liao, E. Bugnion, and M. Lam. Maximizing Multiprocessor Performance with the SUIF Compiler. *IEEE Computer*, 29(12):84–89, December 1996.

14. J. Hoeflinger. *Interprocedural Parallelization Using Memory Classification Analysis*. PhD thesis, University of Illinois, Urbana-Champaign, August, 1998.

15. J. JàJà. *An Introduction to Parallel Algorithms*. Addison–Wesley, Reading, Massachusetts, 1992.

16. S.-W. Liao, A. Diwan, R. P. B. Jr., A. M. Ghuloum, and M. S. Lam. SUIF explorer: An interactive and interprocedural parallelizer. In *Principles Practice of Parallel Programming*, pages 37–48, 1999.

17. Y. Lin and D. Padua. Analysis of irregular single-indexed array accesses and its application in compiler optimizations. In *International Conference on Compiler Construction*, pages 202–218, 2000.

18. Y. Lin and D. A. Padua. On the automatic parallelization of sparse and irregular fortran programs. In *Poceedings of the 1998 Workshop on Languages, Compilers, and Run-TimeSystems for Scalable Computers (LCR98)*, pages 41–56, 1998.

19. W. Pottenger and R. Eigenmann. Parallelization in the presence of generalized induction and reduction variables. Technical Report 1396, Univ. of Illinois at UrbanaChampaign, Center for Supercomp. R&D, January 1995.

20. W. Pugh. The Omega test: A fast and practical integer programming algorithm for dependence analysis. In *Supercomputing '91*, pages 4–13, Albuquerque, N.M., Nov. 1991.

21. L. Rauchwerger and D. A. Padua. The LRPD Test: Speculative Run-Time Parallelization of Loops with Privatization and Reduction Parallelization. *IEEE Transactions on Parallel and Distributed Systems*, 10(2):160–180, 1999.

22. S. Rus, J. Hoeflinger, and L. Rauchwerger. Hybrid analysis: static & dynamic memory reference analysis. *International Journal of Parallel Programming*, 31(3):251–283, 2003.

23. S. Rus, D. Zhang, and L. Rauchwerger. The value evolution graph and its use in memory reference analysis. In *13th Conference on Parallel Architecture and Compilation Techniques*, pages 243–254. IEEE Computer Society, 2004.

24. M. Spezialetti and R. Gupta. Loop monotonic statements. *IEEE Transactions on Software Engineering*, 21(6):497–505, 1995.

25. R. Triolet, F. Irigoin, and P. Feautrier. Direct parallelization of Call statements. In *ACM '86 Symp. on Comp. Constr.*, pages 175–185, Palo Alto, CA., June 1986.

26. P. Tu and D. Padua. Gated SSA–based demand-driven symbolic analysis for parallelizing compilers. In *Proceedings of the 9th ACM International Conference on Supercomputing, Barcelona, Spain*, pages 414–423, January 1995.

27. M. Wolfe. Beyond induction variables. In *ACM SIGPLAN '92 Conference on Programming Language Design and Implementation*, pages 162–174, San Francisco, Calif., June 1992.

28. P. Wu, A. Cohen, J. Hoeflinger, and D. Padua. Monotonic evolution: An alternative to induction variable substitution for dependence analysis. In *2001 ACM International Conference on Supercomputing*, pages 78–91, Sorrento, Italy.

29. P. Wu, A. Cohen, and D. Padua. Induction variable analysis without idiom recognition: Beyond monotonicity. In *2001 Workshop on Lang. and Compilers for Par. Computing*, pages 427–441, Cumberland Falls, KY.

A New Dependence Test Based on Shape Analysis for Pointer-Based Codes*

A. Navarro, F. Corbera, R. Asenjo, A. Tineo, O. Plata, and E.L. Zapata

Dpt. of Computer Architecture, University of Málaga,
Campus de Teatinos, PB: 4114, E-29080. Málaga, Spain
{angeles, corbera, asenjo, tineo, oscar, ezapata}@ac.uma.es

Abstract. The approach presented in this paper focus on detecting data dependences induced by heap-directed pointers on loops that access dynamic data structures. Knowledge about the shape of the data structure accessible from a heap-directed pointer, provides critical information for disambiguating heap accesses originating from it. Our approach is based on a previously developed shape analysis that maintains topological information of the connections among the different nodes (memory locations) in the data structure. Basically, the novelty is that our approach carries out abstract interpretation of the statements being analyzed, and let us annotate the memory locations reached by each statement with read/write information. This information will be later used in order to find dependences in a very accurate dependence test which we introduce in this paper.

1 Introduction

Optimizing and parallelizing compilers rely upon accurate static disambiguation of memory references, i.e. determining at compiling time if two given memory references always access disjoint memory locations. Unfortunately the presence of alias in pointer-based codes makes memory disambiguation a non-trivial issue. An alias arises in a program when there are two or more distinct ways to refer to the same memory location. Program constructs that introduce aliases are arrays, pointers and pointer-based dynamic data structures.

Over the past twenty years powerful data dependence analysis have been developed to resolve the problem of array aliases. The problem of calculating pointer-induced aliases, called pointer analysis, has also received significant attention over the past few years [12], [10], [2]. Pointer analysis can be divided into two distinct subproblems: stack-directed analysis and heap-directed analysis. We focus our research in the latter, which deals with objects dynamically allocated in the heap. An important body of work has been conducted lately on this kind of analysis. A promising approach to deal with dynamically allocated structures consists in explicitly abstracting the dynamic store in the form of a bounded graph. In other words, the heap is represented as a storage shape graph and the

---

* This work was supported in part by the Ministry of Education of Spain under contract TIC2003-06623.

R. Eigenmann et al. (Eds.): LCPC 2004, LNCS 3602, pp. 394–408, 2005.

analysis tries to capture some shape properties of the heap data structures. This type of analysis is called *shape analysis* and in this context, our research group has developed a powerful shape analysis framework [1].

The approach presented in this paper focus on detecting data dependences induced by heap-directed pointers on loops that access pointer-based dynamic data structures. Particularly, we are interested in the detection of the loop-carried dependences (henceforth referred as LCDs) that may arise between the statements in two iterations of the loop. Knowledge about the shape of the data structure accessible from heap-directed pointers, provides critical information for disambiguating heap accesses originating from them, in different iterations of a loop, and hence to provide that there are not data dependences between iterations.

Until now, the majority of LCDs detection techniques based on shape analysis [3], [8], use as shape information a coarse characterization of the data structure being traversed (Tree, DAG, Cycle). One advantage of this type of analysis is that it enables faster data flow merge operations and reduces the storage requirements for the analysis. However, it also causes a loss of accuracy in the detection of the data dependences, specially when the data structure being visited is not a "clean" tree, contain cycles or is modified along the traverse.

Our approach, on the contrary, is based on a shape analysis that maintains topological information of the connections among the different nodes (memory locations) in the data structure. In fact, our representation of the data structure provides us a more accurate description of the memory locations reached when a statement is executed inside a loop. Moreover, as we will see in the next sections, our shape analysis is based on the symbolic execution of the program statements over the graphs that represent the data structure at each program point. In other words, our approach does not relies on a generic characterization of the data structure shape in order to prove the presence of data dependences. The novelty is that our approach symbolically executes, at compile time, the statements of the loop being analyzed, and let us annotate the real memory locations reached by each statement with read/write information. This information will be later used in order to find LCDs in a very accurate dependence test which we introduce in this paper.

Summarizing, the goal of this paper is to present our compilation algorithms which are able to detect LCDs in loops that operate with pointer-based dynamic data structures, using as a key tool a powerful shape analysis framework. The rest of the paper is organized as follows: Section 2 briefly describes the key ideas under our shape analysis framework. With this background, in Section 3 we present our compiler techniques to automatically identify LCDs in codes based on dynamic data structures. Next, in Section 4 we summarize some of the previous works in the topic of data dependences detection in pointer-based codes. Finally, in Section 5 we conclude with the main contributions and future works.

2   Shape Analysis Framework

The algorithms presented in this paper are designed to analyze programs with dynamic data structures that are connected through pointers defined in languages like C or C++. The programs have to be normalized in such a way that each statement dealing with pointers contains only simple access paths. This is, we consider six simple instructions that deal with pointers:

```
x = NULL; x = malloc; x = y; x->field = NULL; x->field = y; x = y->field;
```

where x and y are pointer variables and field is a field name of a given data structure. More complex pointer instructions can be built upon these simple ones and temporal variables. We have used and extended the ANTLR tool [11] in order to automatically normalize and pre-process the C codes before the shape analysis.

Basically, our analysis is based on approximating by graphs (Reference Shape Graphs, RSGs) all possible memory configurations that can appear after the execution of a statement in the code. By *memory configuration* we mean a collection of dynamic structures. These structures comprise several memory chunks, that we call *memory locations*, which are linked by references. Inside these memory locations there may be several fields (data or pointers to other memory locations). The pointer fields of the data structure are called *selectors*. In Fig. 1 we can see a particular memory configuration which corresponds with a single linked list. Each memory location in the list comprises the val data field and the nxt selector (or pointer field). In the same figure, we can see the corresponding RSG which capture the essential properties of the memory configuration by a bounded size graph. In this graph, the node $n1$ represent the first memory location of the list, $n2$ all the middle memory locations, and $n3$ the last memory location of the list.

Basically, each RSG is a graph in which nodes represent memory locations which have similar reference patterns. To determine whether or not two memory locations should be represented by a single node, each one is annotated with a set of properties. Now, if several memory locations share the same properties, then all of them will be represented (or summarized) by the same node ($n2$ in our example). These properties are described in [1], but two of them are sketched here because they are necessary in the following sections: (i) the **Share Information** can tell whether at least one of the locations represented by a node is referenced more than once from other memory locations. We use two kinds of attributes for each node: (1) $SHARED(n)$ states if any of the locations repre-

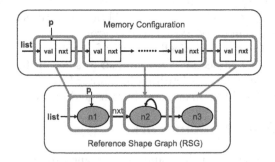

Fig. 1. Working example data structure and the corresponding RSG

S1: l=malloc()				
S2: p=l				
while() {	Iteration 1	Iteration 2	Iteration 3	Iteration 4
S3: a=malloc();				
S4: p->nxt=a;				
S5: p=a; }				

Fig. 2. Building an RSG for each statement of an example code

sented by the node n can be referenced by other locations by different selectors (e.g. *SHARED(n2)=FALSE* in the previous figure); (2) *SHSEL(n, sel)* points out if any of the locations represented by n can be referenced more than once by following the same selector *sel* from other locations. For instance, *SHSEL(n2, nxt)= FALSE* captures the fact that following selector *nxt* you always reach a different memory location; and (ii) the **Touch Information** is taken into account only inside loop bodies to avoid the summarization of already visited locations with non-visited ones. The touch information will be also the key tool in order to automatically annotate the nodes of the data structure which are written and/or read by the pointer statements inside loops.

Each statement of the code may have associated a set of RSGs, in order to represent all the possible memory configuration at each particular program point. In order to generate the set of RSGs associated with each statement (or in other words, to move from the "memory domain" to the "graph domain" in Fig. 1), a **symbolic execution** of the program over the graphs is carried out. In this way, each program statement transforms the graphs to reflect the changes in memory configurations derived from statement execution. The **abstract semantic** of each statement states how the analysis of this statement must transform the graphs [1]. The abstract interpretation is carried out iteratively for each statement until we reach a fixed point in which the resulting RSGs associated with the statement does not change any more. All this can be illustrated by the example of Fig. 2, where we can see how the statements of the code which builds a single linked list are symbolically executed until a fixed point is reached.

3   Loop-Carried Dependence Detection

As we have mentioned, we focus on detecting the presence of LCDs on loops that traverse heap-based dynamic data structures. Two statements in a loop induce a LCD, if a memory location accessed by one statement in a given iteration, is accessed by the other statement in a future iteration, with one of the accesses being a write access.

Our method tries to identify if there is any LCD in the loop following the algorithm that we outline in Fig. 3. Let's recall that our programs have been normalized such that the statements dealing with pointers contain only simple access paths. Let's assume that statements have been labeled. The set of the loop body simple statements (named SIMPLESTMT) is the input to this algorithm.

Summarizing, our algorithm can be divided into the following steps:

1. Only the simple pointer statements, S_i, that access the heap inside the loop are annotated with a **Dependence Touch**, DepTouch, directive. A Dependence Touch directive is defined as DepTouch(AccPointer, AccAttrS$_i$, AccField). It comprises three important pieces of information regarding the access to the heap in statement S_i: i) The **access pointer**, AccPointer: is the stack declared pointer which access to the heap in the statement; ii) The **access attribute**, AccAttS$_i$: identifies the type of access in the statement (ReadS$_i$ or WriteS$_i$); and iii) The **access field**, AccField: is the field of the data structure pointed to by the access pointer which is read or written. For instance, an S1: aux = p->nxt statement should be annotated with DepTouch(p, ReadS1, nxt), whereas the S4: aux3->val = tmp statement should be annotated with DepTouch(aux3, WriteS4, val).

2. The **Dependence Groups**, are created. A Dependence Group, $DepGroup_g$, is a set of access attributes fulfilling two conditions:
   - all the access attributes belong to Dependence Touchs with the same access field (g) and access pointers of the same data type, and
   - at least one of these access attributes is a WriteS$_i$.

```
fun LCDs_Detection (SIMPLESTMT)
1. ∀ Sᵢ ∈ SIMPLESTMT that accesses the heap
        Attach(Sᵢ, DepTouch(AccPointer,AccAttSᵢ,AccField));
2. DEPGROUP = Create_Dependence_Groups(DEPTOUCH);
     ∀ DepGroupg ∈ DEPGROUP
     AccessPairsGroupg = ∅ ;
3. ACCESSPAIRSGROUP = Shape_Analysis(SIMPLESTMT, DEPTOUCH, DEPGROUP);
4. ∀ AccessPairsGroupg ∈ ACCESSPAIRSGROUP
        Depg = LCD_Test(AccessPairsGroupg);
   if ∀ g, Depg == NoDep then
        return(NoLCD);
   else
        return(Depg);
   endif;
end
```

Fig. 3. Our dependences detection algorithm

```
fun Create_Dependence_Groups(DEPTOUCH)
 DEPGROUP = ∅;
 ∀ DepTouch(AccPointer_i,AccAttS_i,AccField_i) ∈ DEPTOUCH
     if [(AccAttS_i == WriteS_i) or
     ∃ DepTouch(AccPointer_j,AccAttS_j,AccField_j) being j ≠ i /
     (AccField_i == AccField_j) and (TYPE(AccPointer_i) == TYPE(AccPointer_j)) and
     (AccAttS_i == WriteS_i or AccAttS_j == WriteS_j)] then
         g = AccField_i;
         if ∄ DepGroup_g ∈ DEPGROUP then
             DepGroup_g = {AccAttS_i}; DEPGROUP = DEPGROUP ∪ {DepGroup_g};
         else
             DepGroup_g = DepGroup_g ∪ {AccAttS_i};
         endif;
     endif;
 return(DEPGROUP);
```

Fig. 4. Create_Dependence_Groups function

In other words, a $DepGroup_g$ is related to a set of statements in the loop that may potentially lead to a LCD, which happens if: i) the analyzed statement makes a write access (WriteS$_i$) or ii) there are other statements accessing to the same field (g) and one of the accesses is a write. We outline in Fig. 4 the function Create_Dependence_Groups. It creates Dependence Groups, using as an input the set of Dependence Touch directives, DEPTOUCH. Note that it is possible to create a Dependence Group with just one WriteS$_i$ attribute. This Dependence Group will help us to check the output dependences for the execution of S_i in different loop iterations. As we see in Fig. 4 the output of the function is the set of all the Dependence Groups, named DEPGROUP. Associated with each $DepGroup_g$, our algorithm initializes a set called $AccessPairsGroup_g$ (see Fig. 3). This set is initially empty but during the analysis process it may be filled with the pairs named **access pairs**. An access pair comprises two ordered access attributes. For instance, a $DepGroup_g$ = {ReadS$_i$, WriteS$_j$, WriteS$_k$} with an $AccessPairsGroup_g$ comprising the pair <ReadS$_i$,WriteS$_j$> means that during the analysis the same field, g, of the same memory location may have been first read by the statement S_i and then written by statement S_j, clearly leading to an anti-dependence. The order inside each access pairs is significant for the sake of discriminating between flow, anti or output dependences. The set of all $AccessPairsGroup$'s is named ACCESSPAIRSGROUP.

3. The shape analyzer is fed with the instrumented code. As we have mentioned, the shape analyzer is described in detail in [1] and briefly introduced in Section 2. However, with regard to the LCD test implementation the most important idea to emphasize here is that our analyzer is able to precisely identify at compile time the memory locations that are going to be pointed to by the pointers of the code. Basically, the task of the analyzer is to sym-

```
fun Shape_Analysis(SIMPLESTMT, DEPTOUCH, DEPGROUP)
 . . .
 ∀ Sⱼ ∈ SIMPLESTMT
    . . .
    if DepTouch(AccPointer,AccAttSⱼ,AccField) attached to Sⱼ then
        AccessPairsGroupₘ = TOUCH_Updating(TOUCHₙ, AccAttSⱼ, DepGroupₘ);
    endif;
    . . .
return(ACCESSPAIRSGROUP);
```

Fig. 5. Shape_Analysis function extension4

bolically execute each statement updating the graphs. At the same time, with the information provided by the DepTouch directive, the node pointed to by the access pointer of the statement, is "touched". This means, that the memory location is going to be marked with the access attribute of the corresponding DepTouch directive. In that way, we annotate in the memory location, that a given statement has read or written in a given field comprised in the location. In this step, our algorithm call to the Shape_Analysis function whose inputs are the set of simple statements SIMPLESTMT, the set of DepTouch directives, DEPTOUCH, and the set of Dependence Groups, DEPGROUP. The output of this function is the final set ACCESSPAIRS-GROUP. In Fig. 5 we outline the necessary extension to our shape analysis presented in [1] in order to deal with the dependence analysis.

Let's see more precisely how the Shape_Analysis function works. The simple statements of the loop body are executed according to the program control flow, and each execution takes the graphs from the previous statement and modifies it (producing a a new set of graphs). When a statement S_j, belonging to the analyzed loop and annotated with a DepTouch directive, is symbolically executed the access pointer of the statement, AccPointer, points to a node, n, that has to represent a single memory location. Each node n of an S_j's RSG graph, has a **Touch Set** associated with it, $TOUCH_n$. The DepTouch directive is also interpreted by the analyzer leading to the updating of that $TOUCH_n$ set.

This TOUCH set updating process can be formalized as follows. Let be DepTouch=(AccPointer,AccAttS$_j$,AccField) the Dependence Touch directive attached to sentence S_j. Let's assume that AccAttS$_j$ belongs to a Dependence Group, $DepGroup_g$. Let n be the RSG node pointed to by the access pointer, AccPointer, in the symbolic execution of the statement S_j. Let be $\{AccAttS_k\}$ the set of access attributes which belongs to the $TOUCH_n$ set, where k represents all the statements S_k, which have previously touched the node. $TOUCH_n$ could be an empty set. Then, when this node is going to be touched by the above mentioned DepTouch directive, the updating process that we show in Fig. 6 takes place.

```
fun TOUCH_Updating(TOUCHₙ, AccAttSⱼ, DepGroup_g)
  if TOUCHₙ == ∅ then /* The Touch set was originally empty */
     TOUCHₙ = {AccAttSⱼ}; /* just append the new access attribute */
  else /* The Touch set was not empty */
     AccessPairsGroup_g = AccessPairsGroup_Updating(TOUCHₙ, AccAttSⱼ, DepGroup_g);
        /* update the access pairs group set */
     TOUCHₙ = TOUCHₙ ∪ {AccAttSⱼ}; /* append the new access attribute */
  endif;
return(AccessPairsGroup_g);


fun AccessPairsGroup_Updating(TOUCHₙ, AccAttSⱼ, DepGroup_g)
  ∀ AccAttS_k ∈ TOUCHₙ
     if AccAttS_k ∈ DepGroup_g then /* AccAttS_k and AccAttSⱼ ∈ DepGroup_g */
        AccessPairsGroup_g = AccessPairsGroup_g ∪ {<AccAttS_k,AccAttSⱼ>};
           /* A new ordered pair is appended */
     endif;
return(AccessPairsGroup_g);
```

Fig. 6. TOUCH and AccessPairsGroup updating functions

As we note in Fig. 6, if the Touch set was originally empty we just append the new access attribute $AccAttS_j$ of the DepTouch directive. However, if the Touch set does already contains other access attributes, $\{AccAttS_k\}$, two actions take place: first, an updating of the $AccessPairsGroup_g$ associated with the $DepGroup_g$ happens; secondly, the access attribute $AccAttS_j$ is appended to the Touch set of the node, $TOUCH_n = TOUCH_n \cup \{AccAttS_j\}$. The algorithm for updating the $AccessPairsGroup_g$ is shown in Fig. 6. Here we check all the access attributes of the statements that have touched previously the node n. If there is any access attribute, $AccAttS_k$ which belongs to the same $DepGroup_g$ that $AccAttS_j$ (the current statement), then a new access pair is appended to the $AccessPairsGroup_g$. The new pair is an ordered pair $<AccAttS_k, AccAttS_j>$ which indicates that the memory location represented by node n has been first accessed by statement S_k and later by statement S_j, being S_k and S_j two statements associated with the same dependence group, and so a conflict may occur. Note that in the implementation of an $AccessPairsGroup_g$ there will be no redundancies in the sense that a given access pair can not be stored twice in the group.

4. In the last step, our LCD_Test function will check each one of the $AccessPair\ Group_g$ updated in step 3. This function is detailed in the code of Fig. 7. If an $AccessPairGroup_g$ is empty, the statements associated with the corresponding $DepGroup_g$ does not provoke any LCD. On the contrary, depending on the pairs comprised by the $AccessPairsGroup_g$ we can raise some of the dependence patterns provided in Fig. 7, thus LCD is reported. We note that the LCD_Test function must be performed for all the $AccessPair\ Group$s updated in step 3. When we verify for all the $AccessPairGroup$s,

```
fun LCD_Test(AccessPairGroup_g)
  if <WriteS_i,ReadS_j> ∈ AccessPairGroup_g
    then return(FlowDep); /* Flow dep. detected between S_i and S_j */
  if <ReadS_i,WriteS_j> ∈ AccessPairGroup_g
    then return(AntiDep); /* Anti dep. detected between S_i and S_j */
  if <WriteS_i,WriteS_j> ∈ AccessPairGroup_g
    then return(OutputDep); /* Output dep. detected between S_i and S_j */
  if <WriteS_i,WriteS_i> ∈ AccessPairGroup_g
    then return(OutputDep); /* Output dep. detected between S_i and S_i */
  endif
return(NoDep); /* no LCD detected */
```

Fig. 7. LCD test

that none of the dependence patterns is found, then our algorithm informs that the loop does not contain LCD dependences (NoLCD) due to heap-based pointers.

3.1 An Example

Let's illustrate via a simple example how our approach works. Fig. 8(a) represents a loop that traverses the data structure of Fig. 1. This is, this loop is going to be executed after the building of the linked list data structure due to the code of Fig. 2. In the loop, the statement tmp = p->val read a memory location that has been written by p->nxt->val = tmp in a previous iteration, so there is a LCD between both statements.

In order to automatically detect this LCD, we use an ANTLR-based preprocessing tool that atomizes the complex pointer expressions into several simple pointer statements which are labeled, as we can see in Fig. 8(b). For instance, the statement p->nxt->val = tmp; has been decomposed into two simple statements: S2 and S3. After this step, the SIMPLESTMT set will comprise four simple statements.

```
p = list;                          p = list;
while (p->nxt != NULL)             while (p -> nxt != NULL)
{                                  {
  tmp = p->val;                      S1: tmp = p->val; DepTouch(p, ReadS1, val);
  p->nxt->val = tmp;                 S2: aux = p->nxt; DepTouch(p, ReadS2, nxt);
  p = p->nxt;                        S3: aux->val = tmp; DepTouch(aux, WriteS3, val);
}                                    S4: p = p->nxt; DepTouch(p, ReadS4, nxt);
                                   }
            (a)                                    (b)
```

Fig. 8. (a) Loop traversal of a dynamic data structure; (b) Instrumented code used to feed our shape analyzer

Next, by applying the first step of our algorithm to find LCDs, the DepTouch directive is attached to each simple statement in the loop that accesses the heap, as we can also appreciate in Fig. 8(b). For example, the statement S2: aux = p->nxt has been annotated with the DepTouch(p, ReadS2, nxt), stating that the access pointer is p, the access attribute is ReadS2 (which means that the S2 statement makes a read access to the heap) and finally, that the read access field is nxt. This first step of our method have been also implemented with the help of ANTLR.

Next we move on to the second step in which we point out that statements S1 and S3 in our code example meet the requirements to be associated with a dependence group: both of them access the same access field (val) with pointers of the same type (p and aux), being S3 a write access. We will define this dependence group as $DepGroup_{val}$={ReadS1, WriteS3}. Besides, the associated $AccessPairsGroup_{val}$ set will be, at this point, empty. Therefore, after this step, DEPGROUP = {$DepGroup_{val}$} and ACCESSPAIRSGROUP = {$AccessPairsGroup_{val}$}.

Let's see now how step 3 of our algorithm proceeds. As we have mentioned, Fig. 1 represents the only RSG graph of the RSGs set at the loop entry point. Remember that our analyzer is going to symbolically execute each of the statements of the loop iteratively until a fixed point is reached. This is, all the RSG graphs in the RSGs set associated with the statements will be updated at each symbolic execution and the loop analysis will finish when all the graphs in the RSGs do not change any more.

Now, in the first loop iteration, the statements S1, S2, S3 and S4 are executed by the shape analyzer. The resultant RSG graphs when these statements are symbolically executed, taking into account the attached DepTouch directives, are shown in Fig. 9. Executing S1 will produce that the node pointed to by p (n_1) is touched by ReadS1. When executing S2, aux = p->nxt will produce the materialization of a new node (the node n_4), and the node pointed to by p will be touched by ReadS2. Next, the execution of S3 will touch with a WriteS3 attribute, the node pointed to by aux (n_4). Finally, the execution of S4 will touch with a ReadS4 attribute the node n_1, and then p will point to node n_4.

In the second loop iteration, when executing S1 over the RSG graph that results from the previous symbolic execution of S4, we find that the nodes pointed to by p (now node n_4) is touched by ReadS1. When touching this node, the TOUCH_Updating function detects that the node has been previously touched because $TOUCH_{n4}$ ={WriteS3}. Since the set is not empty, the function will call to the AccessPairsGroup_Updating function. Now, this function will check each access attribute in the $TOUCH_{n4}$ set, and it will look for a dependence group for such access attribute. In our example, WriteS3 is in the $DepGroup_{val}$. In this case, since the new access attribute that is touching the node (ReadS1) belongs to the same dependence group, a new access pair is appended to the $AccessPairsGroup_{val}$= {<WriteS3, ReadS1>}. This fact is indicating that the same memory location (in this case the field val in node n_4) has been reached by a write access from statement S3, followed by a read access from statement S1.

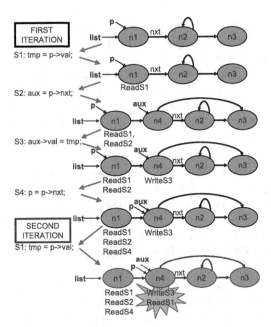

Fig. 9. Initial RSG at the loop entry and the resultant RSG graphs when executing S1, S2, S3 and S4 in the first loop iteration, and when S1 is executed in the second loop iteration

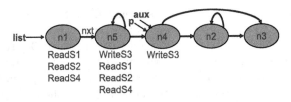

Fig. 10. Resultant RSG when the fixed point is reached

The shape analyzer follows, iteratively, the symbolic execution of statements in the loop until a fixed point is reached. The resultant RSG graph is shown in Fig.10. We also get at the end of the analysis that $AccessPairsGroup_{val}=$ {<WriteS3, ReadS1>}.

Our algorithm applies now the fourth step: the LCD test (Fig. 7). Our LCD test reports a `FlowDep` (flow dependence), because the only access pair group, $AccessPairGroup_{val}$ in the ACCESSPAIRSGROUP set, contains a <WriteS3, ReadS1> pair. As we see, our dependences detection algorithm accurately captures the LCD that appears in the loop.

3.2   Some Preliminary Results

We have applied our dependences detection algorithm to some sample codes, which we show in Fig. 11. The goal of these preliminary experiments is to illus-

trate the accuracy of our method in the detection of data dependences in codes
that traverse (and/or modify) complex data structures. In each code, the sen-
tences have been atomized and annotated with the corresponding directives (for
simplicity, we do not display them) in step 1. The code from Fig. 11(a) traverses
a DAG data structure, which is shown in Fig. 12(a) and whose RSG at the loop
entry is shown in the same figure. Note that in the RSG, the dotted edges reaching $n4$ means that SHSEL($n4$,ch)=true, which captures the fact that a memory
location represented by $n4$ can be reached from different memory locations by
following the ch selector. We assume that there is only one RSG graph in the
RSGs set at this program point. The write statement that may induce an LCD
is S3 (S1 access the same "i" field but using an access pointer of a different data
type). Therefore a dependence group is created: $DepGroup_i=\{<\text{WriteS3}>\}$. The
associated $AccessPairsGroup_i$ is empty at this point. At the end of step 3, our
algorithm returns $AccessPairsGroup_i=\{\text{WriteS3, WriteS3}\}$. This is due to the
fact that we can write the same p->ch->i location in several iterations of the
loop. Applying the step 4, our LCD test function reports an output dependence
(OutputDep) for such access pair group.

Another case is illustrated in the code of Fig. 11(b). The cyclic data structure
and the corresponding RSG at the loop entry are shown in Fig. 12(b). Although
this RSG is similar to the one of the previous example, now SHSEL($n4$,ch)=false,
accurately capturing the new topology of this data structure. In the step 2 of
our algorithm, a dependence group $DepGroup_i=\{\text{WriteS4}\}$ is created and the
associated $AccessPairsGroup_i$ is initially set to the empty set. At the end of step
3, our algorithm reports that $AccessPairsGroup_{val}$ is still empty because our
shape analysis does not touch twice the same node with the WriteS4 attribute.
Thus now, the LCD test function in step 4 reports a no dependence (NoDep). As
there is not another access pair group, our test informs that there is not LCDs
due to heap-based pointers (NoLCD).

Finally, a new case is illustrated in the code of Fig. 11(c). The data structure
and the corresponding RSG at the loop entry are shown in Fig. 12(c). In this case,

```
p = list;
while (p->nxt != NULL)
{
S1: tmp = p->i;
S2: aux1 = p->ch;
S3: aux1->i = tmp;
S4: p = p->nxt;
}

            (a)
```

```
p = list;
while (p != NULL) {
S1: tmp = p->val;
    if (p->prv != NULL){
S2:     aux2 = p->prv;
S3:     aux3 = aux2->ch;
S4:     aux3->i = tmp;}
S5:   p = p->nxt;
    }

            (b)
```

```
p = list;
while (p->nxt != NULL)
{
S1: tmp = p->num;
    if (cond){
S2:     aux4 = p->nxt;
S3:     aux4->num = tmp;}
    else{
S4:     aux5 = p->prv;
S5:     aux5->num = tmp;}
S6: p = p->nxt;
}

            (c)
```

Fig. 11. (a) Traversal of a DAG data structure; (b) Cyclic access in a Cyclic data
structure; (c) Conditional cyclic access in a Cyclic data structure

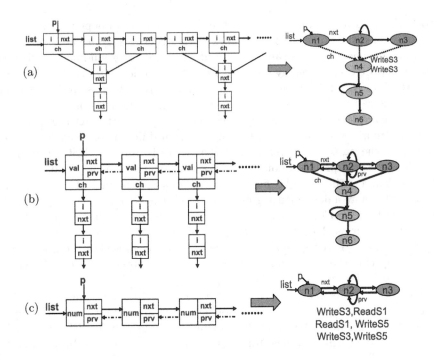

Fig. 12. Data structures and the corresponding RSG: (a) DAG; (b) Cyclic; (c) Cyclic

the statement S1 read a field memory location (given by *num*) that may be written conditionally by statements S3 or S5. Thus some dependence may arise. Now, some traversal of the data structure may contain a cycle (due to the (*nxt, prv*) selectors). In step 2 the dependence group is defined as $DepGroup_{num}=\{ReadS1, WriteS3, WriteS5\}$. At the end of step 3, our algorithm reports that the pairs <WriteS3, ReadS1>, <ReadS1, WriteS5> and <WriteS3, WriteS5> are in the $AccessPairsGroup_{num}$. Thus, our LCD test function accurately detects a flow dependence (`FlowDep`), an anti-dependence (`AntiDep`) and an output dependence (`OutDep`).

4 Related Works

Some of the previous works on dependences detection on pointer-based codes, combine dependence analysis techniques with pointer analysis [4], [5], [9], [6], [3], [7]. Horwitz et al. [5] developed an algorithm to determine dependences by detecting interferences in reaching stores. Larus and Hilfinger [9] propose to identify access conflicts on alias graphs using path expressions to name locations. Hendren and Nicolau [4] use path matrices to record connection information among pointers and present a technique to recognize interferences between computations for programs with acyclic structures. The focus of these techniques is on identifying dependences at the function-call level and they do not consider the detection in the loop context, which is the focus in our approach.

More recently, some authors [3], [7], [8] have proposed dependence analysis tests based on shape analysis in the context of loops that traverse dynamic data structures, and these approaches are more related to our work. For instance, Ghiya and Hendren [3] proposed a test for identifying LCDs that relies on the shape of the data structure being traversed (Tree, DAG or Cycle), as well as on the computation of the access paths for the pointers in the statements being analyzed. In short, their test identifies dependences in programs with Tree-like data structure or loops that traverse DAG/Cycle structures that have been asserted by the programmer as acyclic and where the access paths do not contain pointer fields. Note that the manual assertion of loops traversing DAG or cyclic data structures is a must in order to enable any automatic detection of LCDs. For instance, even asserting as acyclic the loop example from Fig.11(b), this method would have detected a LCD in the code (due to the `prv` and `ch` pointer fields in the access path of statement S4), while our method can successfully proves that there is no dependences. Another limitation of this approach is that data structures must remain static during the data traversal inside the analyzed loops.

In order to solve some of the previous limitations, Hwang and Saltz proposed a new technique to identify LCDs in programs that traverse cyclic data structures [7], [8]. This approach automatically identifies acyclic traversal patterns even in cyclic (Cycle) structures. For this purpose, the compilation algorithm isolates the traversal patterns from the overall data structure, and next, it deduces the shape of these traversal patterns (Tree, DAG or Cycle). Once they have extracted the traversal-pattern shape information, dependence analysis is applied to detect LCDs. Summarizing, their technique identifies LCDs in programs that navigate cyclic data structures in a "clean" tree-like traverse. For instance, in the code example from Fig.11(b), this method would detect a LCD due to a cycle in the traversal pattern (due to the `prv` and `nxt` selectors). On the other hand, their analysis can overestimate the shape of the traverse when the data structure is modified along the traverse, and in these situations, the shape algorithm detect DAG or Cycle traversal patterns, in which case dependence is reported.

We differ from previous works in that our technique let us annotate the memory locations reached by each heap-directed pointer with read/write information. This feature let us analyze quite accurately loops that traverse and modify generic heap-based dynamic data structures. Our algorithm is able to identify accurately the dependences that appears even in loops that navigate (and modify) cyclic structures in traversals that contain cycles, as we have seen in the code examples from Fig. 11. Besides we can successfully discriminate among flow, anti and output dependences.

5   Conclusions and Future Works

We have presented a compilation technique that is able to identify LCDs in programs which work with general pointer-based dynamic data structures. We base our algorithms in a powerful shape analysis framework that let us analyze quite accurately loops that traverse and modify heap-based dynamic data structures. Our algorithm is able to identify precisely dependences even in loops that navigate (and modify) cyclic structures in traversals that contain cycles. Our main contribution is that we have designed a LCD test that let us extend the scope of applicability to any program that handle any kind of dynamic data structure. Moreover, our dependence test let us discern accurately the type of dependence: flow, anti, output.

We have a preliminary implementation of our compilation algorithms and we have checked the success in the LCDs detection in several synthetic small codes. We are planning to conduct a large set of experiments based on C benchmarks, in order to demonstrate the effectiveness of our method in real applications.

References

1. F. Corbera, R. Asenjo, and E.L. Zapata. A framework to capture dynamic data structures in pointer-based codes. *Transactions on Parallel and Distributed System*, 15(2):151–166, 2004.
2. R. Ghiya and L. J. Hendren. Putting pointer analysis to work. In *Proc. 25th Annual ACM SIGPLAN-SIGACT Symposium on Principles of Programming Languages*, pages 121–133, San Diego, California, January 1998.
3. R. Ghiya, L. J. Hendren, and Y. Zhu. Detecting parallelism in c programs with recursive data strucutures. In *Proc. 1998 International Conference on Compiler Construction*, pages 159–173, March 1998.
4. L. J. Hendren and A. Nicolau. Parallelizing programs with recursive data structures. *IEEE Transactions on Parallel and Distributed Systems*, 1:35–47, January 1990.
5. S. Hortwitz, P. Pfeiffer, and T. Repps. Dependence analysis for pointer variables. In *Proc. ACM SIGPLAN'89 Conference on Programming Language Design and Implementation)*, pages 28–40, July 1989.
6. J. Hummel, L. J. Hendren, and A. Nicolau. A general data dependence test for dynamic, pointer-based data structures. In *Proc. ACM SIGPLAN'94 Conference on Programming Language Design and Implementation)*, pages 218–229, June 1994.
7. Y. S. Hwang and J. Saltz. Identifying parallelism in programs with cyclic graphs. In *Proc. 2000 International Conference on Parallel Processing*, pages 201–208, Toronto, Canada, August 2000.
8. Y. S. Hwang and J. Saltz. Identifying parallelism in programs with cyclic graphs. *Journal of Parallel and Distributed Computing*, 63(3):337–355, 2003.
9. J. R. Larus and P. N. Hilfinger. Detecting conflicts between structure accesses. In *Proc. ACM SIGPLAN'88 Conference on Programming Language Design and Implementation)*, pages 21–34, July 1988.
10. M. Shapiro and S. Horwitz. Fast and accurate flow-insensitive points-to analysis. In *Proc. 24th Annual ACM SIGPLAN-SIGACT Symposium on Principles of Programming Languages*, pages 1–14, Paris, France, January 1997.
11. T.J.Parr and R.W. Quong. ANTLR: A predicated-LL(k) parser generator. *Journal of Software Practice and Experience*, 25(7):789–810, July 1995.
12. R. P. Wilson and M. S. Lam. Efficient context-sensitive pointer analysis for C programs. In *Proc. ACM SIGPLAN'95 Conference on Programming Language Design and Implementation*, pages 1–12, La Jolla, California, June 1995.

Partial Value Number Redundancy Elimination

Rei Odaira and Kei Hiraki

University of Tokyo, Bunkyo-ku, Tokyo, Japan
{ray, hiraki}@is.s.u-tokyo.ac.jp

Abstract. When exploiting instruction level parallelism in a runtime optimizing compiler, it is indispensable to quickly remove redundant computations and memory accesses to make resources available. We propose a fast and efficient algorithm called Partial Value Number Redundancy Elimination (PVNRE), which completely fuses Partial Redundancy Elimination (PRE) and Global Value Numbering (GVN). Using value numbers in the data-flow analyses, PVNRE can deal with data-dependent redundancy, and can quickly remove path-dependent partial redundancy by converting value numbers at join nodes *on demand* during the data-flow analyses. Compared with the naive combination of GVN, PRE, and copy propagation, PVNRE has a maximum 45% faster analyses speed, but the same optimizing power on SPECjvm98.

1 Introduction

Redundancy elimination is an optimizing technique that removes instructions that compute the same value as previously executed instructions, so that it can shorten the critical path and make resources available for instruction level parallelism. When using redundancy elimination in runtime optimizing compilers, which have recently gained widespread use in Java and other execution environments, we need to make it as powerful as possible, and at the same time, keep its analysis time short. In this paper, we aim to manage both optimizing power and analysis speed of redundancy elimination.

So far, the most widely used redundancy elimination methods have been Partial Redundancy Elimination (PRE) [1,2,3,4] and Global Value Numbering (GVN) [5,6,7]. PRE can eliminate redundancy on at least one, but not necessarily all execution paths leading to an instruction. It deals with lexically identical instructions between which there is no store for any of their operand variables. To remove the redundancy it has to solve three data-flow equations for availability (*AVAIL*) and anticipatability (*ANTIC*) of instructions.

On the other hand, GVN can remove instructions that compute the same value on all paths even when they are lexically different. GVN uses value numbering, which is an algorithm to detect redundancy by assigning the same *value number* to a group of instructions that can be proved to compute the same value by static analysis. One GVN variants called *the bottom-up method* uses a hash table to assign value numbers to instructions [8]. It first transforms the whole program into the Static Single Assignment (SSA) form [9] and then searches

R. Eigenmann et al. (Eds.): LCPC 2004, LNCS 3602, pp. 409–423, 2005.

the hash table, using an operator for each instruction and the value numbers of its operands as a key to the table. If the key has already been registered, a redundant instruction is then found. If not, it generates a new value number and registers it to the table together with the key. After value numbering, GVN performs dominator-based or availability-based redundancy elimination, which removes instructions dominated by ones with the same value numbers, or instructions whose value numbers are available.

Because of their complementary power, most modern optimizing compilers perform both GVN and PRE [8]. They first perform GVN, then convert the program back into the non-SSA form, and finally execute PRE.

In reality, we need to perform PRE and copy propagation (CP) iteratively after GVN[10], because otherwise there remain many redundancies in a program as described in Section 2. We propagate copy instructions generated by the previous PRE to get as many instructions lexically identical as possible. We then make the next PRE remove the now-lexically-identical instructions. In other words, from the upper stream of data dependency, we must perform both PRE and CP for each depth level of the dependency, because PRE cannot deal with data dependency in one pass. Therefore, this algorithm suffers from an overhead due to the iteration, which a runtime optimizing compiler cannot ignore.

In this paper, we propose Partial Value Number Redundancy Elimination (PVNRE), which fuses GVN and PRE, and removes the need for the iteration of PRE and CP. PVNRE performs PRE-like data-flow analyses, in which it uses not the lexical appearances of instructions but rather their value numbers as GVN does. In contrast to PRE, PVNRE can deal with data dependency between value numbers during data-flow analyses, and avoid the iteration of PRE and CP. Thus, it is as powerful as, and faster than the combination of GVN and the iteration of PRE and CP.

The main contributions of our work are as follows.

- PVNRE is the first redundancy elimination algorithm that tackles the iteration of PRE and CP, and succeeds in managing both optimizing power and analysis speed.
- To allow PVNRE to include the powerful features of PRE, we developed a new algorithm to convert value numbers at join nodes *on demand* during data-flow analyses.
- We present the effectiveness of PVNRE by implementing it in our just-in-time compiler and conducting experiments using real benchmarks.

The rest of the paper is organized as follows. Section 2 presents the types of redundancy we deal with in this paper, and explains the inefficiencies of the existing algorithms to remove such redundancies. Section 3 describes the algorithm of PVNRE and Section 4 shows the experimental results. Section 5 reviews related work, and Section 6 sets out the conclusion.

2   Background

We categorize the redundancy we deal with in this paper into eight types (Type I – VIII) as shown in Table 1. We also show in the table which types of redundancy PRE and GVN can detect and eliminate.

Table 1. Eight types of redundancy

	data independent		data dependent	
	path independent	path dependent	path independent	path dependent
total	(I): PRE, GVN	(II): PRE	(V): GVN	(VI)
partial	(III): PRE	(IV): PRE	(VII)	(VIII)

2.1   Type I – IV

Figure 1 illustrates the four types of redundancy PRE can detect. PRE removes the computations of Instructions 3, 7, 12, 15, and 19 by using a temporary variable "t" as exemplified in Type IV(b) of the figure.

In contrast, GVN can detect Types I and V. Precisely speaking, availability-based GVN can detect both (1) and (2) of Type I in Fig. 1, while dominator-based GVN can detect only (1).

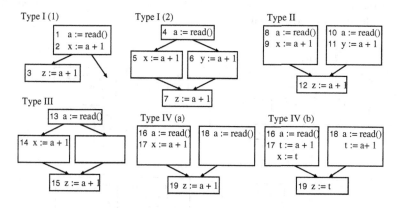

Fig. 1. Examples of optimization by PRE

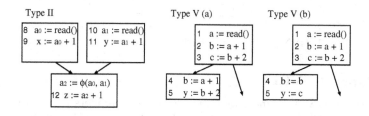

Fig. 2. Examples of optimization by GVN

GVN cannot detect Type II because of the path-dependent redundancy; depending on the execution path that leads to it, Instruction 12 computes different values, since "a" refers to the different definitions (Instructions 8 and 10). The path-dependency becomes clearer if we convert the program into the SSA form as in Fig. 2 Type II. The newly inserted ϕ function is a pseudo function that merges more than one definitions of a variable at a join node. Thus, Instructions 8, 10, and the ϕ function are assigned distinct value numbers, and so are Instructions 9, 11, and 12, which makes it impossible to detect the redundancy among them.

The reason GVN cannot detect Type III is that Instruction 14 does not dominate 15, nor make the value number of "a + 1" available at 15 due to its partial redundancy. Type IV in Fig. 1 is a combination of Types II and III, so that it also cannot be detected by GVN.

2.2 Type V

Figure 2 Type V illustrates the type of redundancy GVN can remove but PRE cannot. Instructions 2 and 4, and 3 and 5 are assigned the same value numbers; hence, we can eliminate the redundancy by using the transformation shown in (b). In particular, although 3 and 5 are lexically identical, their redundancy cannot be removed by PRE because there is a store for the operand between them (Instruction 4), or in other words, because they are data-dependent on different instructions (2 and 4). Therefore, we call this type of redundancy between 3 and 5 a data-dependent redundancy.

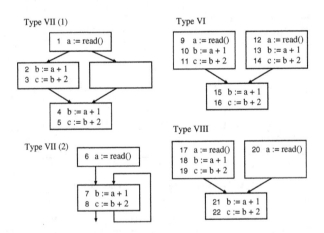

Fig. 3. GVN+PRE cannot optimize these types of redundancy

2.3 Type VI – VIII

As described in Sect. 1, most modern optimizing compilers perform both GVN and PRE; but other types of redundancy (Fig. 3), which neither of them can eliminate, can also be encountered in real programs. For example, a data-dependent chain of loop invariants, which can frequently be found in address computations of loop-invariant array loads, is one of the variants of Type VII as shown in Fig. 3 Type VII (2).

Thus, after GVN, we have to perform PRE and copy propagation (CP) iteratively to completely eliminate such redundancies [1]. For example, in Fig. 4, (a) is the same as Type VII (2) in Fig. 3. The first PRE moves Instruction 7 out of the loop (b). It cannot move Instruction 8 because this is data-dependent on 7. The generated copy instruction is then propagated to 8 (c). Finally, since the data dependency has been removed, the second PRE can move 8 out of the loop (d). The redundancies of Types VI and VIII in Fig. 3 can be eliminated in the same manner.

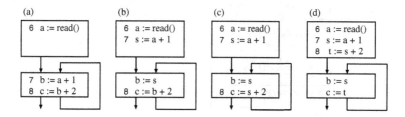

Fig. 4. Sequence of optimization by iteration of PRE and CP

The diagram of the resulting algorithm, which we call GVN+PRECP, is shown in the left-hand side of Fig. 5. However, the inefficiencies in the algorithm are as follows.

- To collect the local information of instructions in PRE, a hash table is used to number each lexical appearance of instructions. This operation is similar to value numbering in GVN.
- In spite of the fact that copy propagation is trivial in the SSA form, we cannot perform it in that form during PRECP because PRE is based on a non-SSA form.
- For each iteration of the loop, we must set up data structures and collect information for all instructions in the program, although most of them might be unaffected by that iteration.

In the next section, we describe PVNRE, a redundancy elimination algorithm which overcomes these inefficiencies of GVN+PRECP.

3   PVNRE Algorithm

PVNRE aims to provide equal or better optimizing power with faster analysis speed than GVN+PRECP. In this section, we give an overview of PVNRE and

---

[1] In fact, if we iterate PRE and CP, we need not perform GVN from the point of view of optimizing ability. However, we should perform GVN first because it can eliminate Type V much faster than the iteration of PRE and CP.

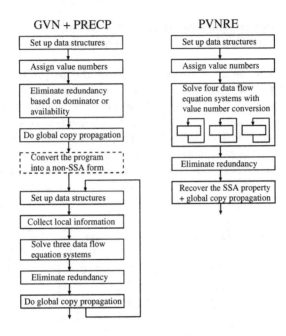

Fig. 5. GVN+PRECP and PVNRE algorithms

explain its intuitive behavior, using examples. Due to space limitations, we omit the formalization of its algorithm and the proof of correctness; these can be found in our technical report[11]. Without loss of generality, we make the following assumptions about a program.

- The program has already been transformed into the SSA form.
- The control flow graph is reducible.
- The nesting relationship of the loops has already been analyzed.
- The critical edges have already been removed.
- All instructions including ϕ functions are binary, except for function calls.

The overview of the algorithm is shown on the right-hand side of Fig. 5. In fact, PVNRE can remove redundancies beyond the ones listed in Table 1, but such types of redundancy are rarely found in real programs.

3.1 Value Numbering

The value numbering in PVNRE shown in Fig. 6 is the same as that for GVN, except that (1) it computes backedges (*Backedges*) and transparency (*UnTransp*), and (2) it must assign incremental value numbers (Line 7 and 18). *Operator*, *Left*, and *Right* in the figure represent the operator and the left and right operand instructions, respectively. *GEN* is used as local information in the following data-flow analyses. Backedges and transparency are described in Sect. 3.3.

Incremental value numbers ensure that Instruction x is assigned a greater number than Instruction y if x is data-dependent on y. This is because in value

```
 1  for each edge e do UnTransp(e) := ∅ end
 2  VN := 0
 3  for each basic block N in reverse post order do
 4    GEN(N) = ∅
 5    for each instruction n in N in pre-order do
 6      if Operator(n) is φ or function call then
 7        VN := VN + 1; Num(n) := VN
 8        Backedges(VN) := the set of the enclosing backedges of N
 9      else
10        α := call Hash(Operator(n), Num(Left(n)), Num(Right(n)))
11        Num(n) := α; GEN(N) := GEN(N) ∪ {α}
12      end
13    end
14  end
15
16  Hash(op, l, r) {
17    If ⟨op, l, r⟩ is registered, returns the corresponding VN. If not,
18    VN := VN + 1; Register VN with ⟨op, l, r⟩.
19    Backedges(VN) := Backedges(l) ∪ Backedges(r)
20    for each b in Backedges(VN) do
21      UnTransp(b) := UnTransp(b) ∪ {VN}
22    end
23    return VN
24  }
```

Fig. 6. Algorithm for value numbering

numbering we must number instructions in the data dependency order (the reverse post order in Line 3 and the pre-order in Line 5), so that we can use the value numbers of the left and right operands as a key to the hash table. PVNRE utilizes this numerical order in the following data-flow analyses to process value numbers in data dependency order.

3.2 Data-Flow Analyses

Using value numbers in PRE-like data-flow analyses, PVNRE can detect not only the redundancies of Types I and V like GVN, but also partial redundancies, particularly Types III and VII.

PVNRE solves four equation systems for $AVAIL^{all}$, $AVAIL^{some}$, $ANTIC^{all}$, and $AVAIL^{Msome}$. These are the framework for PRE proposed by Bodik et al. [2]. $AVAIL^{all}$ and $AVAIL^{some}$ represent the availability on all paths and some paths respectively, while $ANTIC^{all}$ denotes the anticipatability on all paths. $AVAIL^{Msome}$ is akin to $AVAIL^{some}$, but a condition is added to prevent speculative insertion of instructions. Because of space limitations, we refer readers to the paper by Bodik et al. [2] for details about these predicates. Here, we focus on the differences between their work and PVNRE, namely, transparency and value number conversion.

3.3 Transparency

Transparency is a condition that determines whether or not data-flow information is valid beyond a block or an edge in data-flow analysis. In traditional PRE, the propagated information ($AVAIL$ or $ANTIC$) of an instruction is invalidated if a block contains a store for an operand variable of the instruction. PVNRE, on the other hand, does not need such kind of condition because it can deal with data-dependent redundancy as illustrated in Fig. 2 Type V.

In PVNRE, however, we need special treatment for backedges. For example, in Fig. 7(1), if we allowed the $AVAIL$ of the value numbers of Instructions 3 and 4 to flow through the backedge, the information would reach 3 and 4 again; hence, we would consider them to be loop invariants. However, since these instructions are induction variables, this does not happen and they return different values for each iteration of the loop.

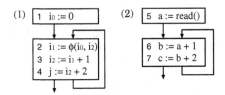

Fig. 7. Examples of backedge and transparency

Thus, we define transparency for value numbers and back-edges: the value numbers of instructions that may compute different values for each iteration of a loop are invalidated at the backedge of the loop. The reason an instruction computes different values for each iteration is that it is data-dependent on a ϕ function or a function call inside the loop. Therefore, during value numbering, PVNRE computes the enclosing backedges for ϕ functions and function calls (Fig. 6 Line 8). Other instructions inherit backedges from the data-dependent instructions (Line 19), and register themselves to $UnTransp$ (the complementary set of the transparency) for the backedges (Line 20 – 22). For example, in Fig. 7(2), even if Instructions 6 and 7 are inside the loop their value numbers are transparent through the backedge, so that PVNRE can detect their partial redundancy (Types III and VII, respectively).

3.4   Conversion of Value Numbers

If we only propagate value numbers on PRE-like data-flow analyses, we cannot detect path-dependent redundancies (Types II, IV, VI, and VIII) as we described in Sect. 2. To solve the problem, we convert value numbers at join nodes on demand during data-flow analyses, using ϕ functions. It is worth noting that the reason GVN cannot detect the path-dependent redundancy is the existence of ϕ functions in the SSA form.

PVNRE uses two sets, $JT(N)$ and $JT'(N)$, which are defined for each join node N. Their elements are of the form $\langle t, l, r \rangle$, which means "value number l and r join at N, and are converted into t." $JT(N)$ is initialized by the ϕ

functions in N in the original program, and $JT'(N)$ is set to $\emptyset$. PVNRE uses and adds elements to JT and JT' while solving $AVAIL^{all}$ and $AVAIL^{some}$. To solve $ANTIC^{all}$ and $AVAIL^{Msome}$, it just uses JT', adding no more elements.

Types II and VI (Path-Dependent Total Redundancy). We use the example in Fig. 8. Value numbers (italic numbers $1 - 9$) are already assigned as the hash table shows. Assume that we are now processing basic block 3 (BB3) for the first time while we are computing the maximum fixed points for $AVAIL^{all}$ and $AVAIL^{some}$. JT is initialized as $\{\langle 7, 1, 4\rangle\}$ by the ϕ function (Instruction 7).

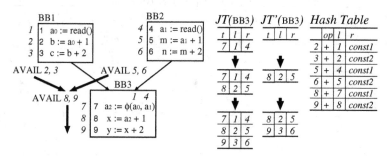

Fig. 8. Example of value number conversion for Type II and VI

Now we have to compute $AVAIL^{all}_{in}(BB3)$ and $AVAIL^{some}_{in}(BB3)$. 2 and 3 are available from the left, so that we process 2 first, utilizing the constraints between the numerical order and the data dependency described in Sect. 3.1. We search the "l" column of JT for 1 (the left operand of 2). We need not search for the right operand, because it is constant 1, and is not subject to conversion. We find an element in JT^2, which indicates that 1 merges with 4 and is converted into 7. Now we search the hash table for "$4 + const1$" and "$7 + const1$," finding 5 and 8. Thus we add a new element $\langle 8, 2, 5\rangle$ to JT and JT'. In the same manner, we process 3 and add another element $\langle 9, 3, 6\rangle$. Note that if we process 3 first, we cannot convert either 2 or 3. Then we process 5 and 6 from the right, but we need not add any more elements. Consequently, $AVAIL^{all}_{in} = \{8, 9\}$, $AVAIL^{some}_{in} = \{2, 3, 5, 6, 8, 9\}$. We propagate them into BB3, and finally detect the redundancy of Instructions 8 (Type II) and 9 (Type VI), because their value numbers are available. When we process BB3 again during the computation of the maximum fixed points, we need not repeat the process again for 2, 3, 5, and 6, but just use JT'. In the same way, we also use JT' to compute $ANTIC^{all}$ and $AVAIL^{Msome}$.

Indeed, it is not mandatory to compute $AVAIL^{some}$, but we do so in order to speed up the analyses that follow; if not, we would have to update JT', even during the computation of $ANTIC^{all}$. This is because the number of propagated value numbers in $AVAIL^{all}$ is so small that the resulting JT' would not have enough elements to convert value numbers backward for $ANTIC^{all}$.

---

[2] If we could not find any, then 2 would not be converted at BB3.

Types IV and VIII (Path-Dependent Partial Redundancy). For the path-dependent partial redundancy, we must generate new value numbers during the conversion. For example, in Fig. 9, when we process *2*, we cannot find "*4 +* const1" in the hash table. Then we generate a new value number *8*, and register it to the hash table[3]. The same goes for *3*, and *9* is generated. Consequently, $AVAIL_{in}^{all} = \emptyset$, $AVAIL_{in}^{some} = \{2, 3, 6, 7\}$, so that we can detect the partial redundancy of Instructions 6 (Type IV) and 7 (Type VIII).

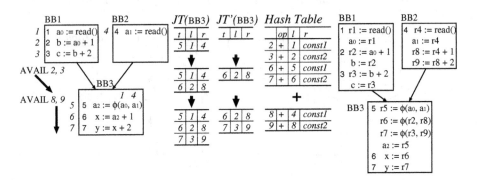

Fig. 9. Example of value number conversion for Type IV and VIII, and the result of redundancy elimination

In summary, instead of iterating PRE and CP for all instructions, PVNRE uses iterations for only the essential subset of the instructions; it iterates the value number conversion at the innermost loop of data-flow analyses to detect Types VI and VIII. In addition, by using the on-demand conversion, it need not construct any special representation of redundancy such as a *Value Flow Graph* [12] in advance of the analyses.

Data-Flow Equation System. The resulting data-flow equation system for $AVAIL^{all}$ is as follows.

$$AVAIL_{in}^{all}(\alpha, N) = \bigwedge_{\forall M \in Pred(N)} \Big((AVAIL_{out}^{all}(\alpha, M) \wedge \alpha \notin UnTransp(M \rightarrow N))$$

$$\vee (AVAIL_{out}^{all}(\beta, M) \text{ s.t. } \beta \text{ is converted to } \alpha \text{ along } M \rightarrow N \text{ by } JT'(N)) \Big)$$

$$AVAIL_{out}^{all}(\alpha, N) = AVAIL_{in}^{all}(\alpha, N) \vee \alpha \in GEN(N)$$

The equation systems for $AVAIL^{some}$, $ANTIC^{all}$, and $AVAIL^{Msome}$ are similar to the one above [11].

---

[3] If we cannot find a conversion target (in this case, "*5 +* const1"), we generate another value number, and let it propagate down.

3.5   Redundancy Elimination

After the computation of $AVAIL^{all}$, $AVAIL^{some}$, $ANTIC^{all}$, and $AVAIL^{Msome}$, we insert new instructions into edges and remove all redundancies as in [2]. We show an example of redundancy elimination in the right-hand side of Fig. 9. We use a new variable "rn" for a value number n. For a non-redundant instruction, the value is stored into "rn," For a redundant instruction, the expression is replaced with "rn." For each element in JT', a new ϕ function is inserted. To make partially redundant instructions totally redundant, new instructions are inserted at certain edges to join nodes [2]. For example, we must insert instructions to compute 8 and 9 at the tail of BB2. Thus, consulting the hash table, "r8 := r4 + 1" and "r9 := r8 + 1" are inserted in the data dependency order, or the numerical order of the value numbers.

After redundancy elimination, we must recover the SSA property because "rn" can be assigned at more than one place. We use the algorithm proposed by Cytron et al. [9], and at the same time perform copy propagation.

3.6   Complexity

Let p and n be the number of ϕ functions and the other instructions, respectively, in the original program. The complexity of PVNRE is $O(n^2 + np^{2^n})$ in the worst case. However, in practice we can expect the complexity to be $O((1 + p)n^2)$. Details can be found in our technical report[11].

4   Experimental Results

We implemented PVNRE in a Java just-in-time (JIT) compiler that we are now developing, called RJJ. RJJ is invoked from kaffe-1.0.7 [13], a free implementation of a Java virtual machine. This time, we used RJJ only for counting the *dynamic* number of redundancies eliminated and measuring analysis time; we delegated the generation of execution code to a JIT compiler in kaffe.

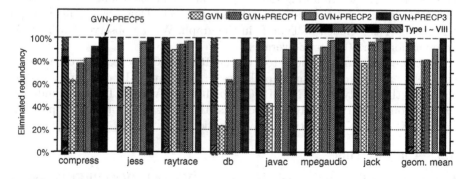

Fig. 10. Dynamic counts of eliminated redundancies (PVNRE = 100%)

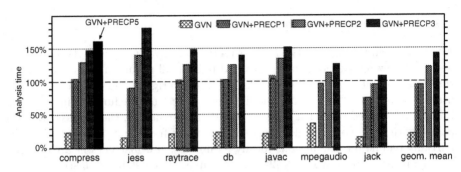

Fig. 11. Analysis time (PVNRE = 100%)

We also implemented dominator-based GVN and GVN+PRECP. We refer to algorithms that execute both PRE and CP exactly once, at most twice, and at most three times as GVN+PRECP1, GVN+PRECP2, and GVN+PRECP3, respectively. GVN+PRECP2 and GVN+PRECP3 stop iteration when further improvement cannot be achieved.

We eliminated redundancy not only in arithmetic but also in load instructions. We assumed a new memory model for Java (JSR-000133), so that we aggressively eliminated redundant loads. To measure the intrinsic power of PVNRE, we did not preserve the exception order before and after optimization.

As benchmarks, we used SPECjvm98 [14]. All measurements were collected on Linux 2.4.18 with a 2.20 GHz Xeon and 512 MB main memory.

4.1 Effectiveness of Redundancy Elimination

We calculated the *dynamic* counts of reduced instructions for all the executed methods. Figure 10 shows the results. Each bar corresponds to PVNRE, GVN, GVN+PRECP1, GVN+PRECP2, and GVN+PRECP3 from left to right, except that we also show the result of GVN+PRECP5 for "compress." Further iteration of PRE and CP made no improvement. The bars are normalized to PVNRE = 100%, and the breakdown of PVNRE represents Types I – VIII from bottom to top. Note that GVN = Type I + V, and GVN+PRECP1 = Type I + II + III + IV + V. It is also worth noting that Types I and V in the results represent only the redundancies dominator-based GVN can detect. Thus, for example, Type I(2) in Fig. 1 is included in Type II in the graph. We can observe that Type V accounts for over 50% on an average.

In these programs, we need to iterate PRE and CP at least three times to completely remove redundancies of Types VI, VII, and VIII, or in other words, to match the ability of GVN+PRECP to that of PVNRE. Those redundancy types account for 19% in dynamic counts, thus it is not sufficient to perform only GVN, or GVN and PRE with no iteration.

4.2 Analysis Time

Figure 11 shows the total analysis time of GVN and GVN+PRECPs for all the executed methods in comparison with that of PVNRE. We did not include the time to convert the program into a non-SSA form in GVN+PRECPs. Note that the analysis time of GVN+PRECPs does not increase proportionally to the number of iterations because iteration is stopped when further improvement cannot be achieved. GVN+PRECP3, which has almost the same ability to eliminate redundancy as PVNRE, is 82% slower than PVNRE for "jess," and 42% slower on an average. That means PVNRE achieves a 45% maximum speedup over GVN+PRECP3, and a 30% speedup on an average.

5   Related Work

Several approaches [10,12] that are as powerful as PVNRE have been proposed, but actual data have never been presented concerning their analysis speed compared with traditional algorithms. In contrast, we measured the analysis time of PVNRE on real benchmarks and showed that it is faster than GVN+PRECP. Moreover, we estimate that the existing approaches are slower than PVNRE as follows. Rosen et al.[10] proposed an algorithm that converts the lexical appearance of instructions through ϕ functions. It first assigns an integer called *rank* to each instruction that represents the depth of data dependency. It then performs copy propagation, code motion and redundancy elimination separately for each class of instructions with the same rank. Therefore it is essentially as slow as PRECP. Steffen et al.[12] proposed a two-phased algorithm that first computes *Herbrand equivalences* of instructions represented by a *Value Flow Graph*. It then performs PRE on that graph. In comparison, our value numbering is much faster than its equivalence computation. In addition, our work relies solely on the traditional SSA form and on-demand value number conversion at join nodes, while their algorithm suffers from an overhead due to a necessary conversion of the whole-program graph representation.

Bodik et al.[4] proposed "Path-Sensitive Value-Flow Analysis," which extends the optimizing power of GVN and PRE by using symbolic back-substitution at the cost of analysis time. Actually, PVNRE also includes part of the extended ability, but we did not encounter such a situation in SPECjvm98 where this kind of ability is of use. Rather, the emphasis of our work is on providing the power of GVN+PRECP in a shorter analysis time.

Bodik et al.[2] also proposed the framework for PRE that we utilize in PVNRE. Its optimizing power is the same as that of the existing frameworks for PRE, hence, is weaker than that of PVNRE. Chow et al.[15] proposed PRE on the SSA form. The goal of their work was to speed up analysis by exploiting sparse data structures. Thus, its optimizing ability is just the same as that of the traditional PRE algorithms.

Alpern et al.[5] proposed GVN using a partitioning algorithm, and Rüthing et al.[16] extended it to detect *Herbrand equivalences*. PVNRE cannot use partitioning because it has to assign value numbers even while it is solving data-flow equations. Click [6] proposed an algorithm combining GVN and aggressive code motion. It first performs hash-table-based GVN, and then moves instructions out of loops using dominator relationship. It can eliminate partial redundancy, but cannot detect path-dependent redundancy. Cooper et al.[7] proposed an algorithm that first performs GVN using a hash table and then performs PRE on value numbers. It is similar to PVNRE in that it propagates value numbers in data-flow analyses, but it does not convert them using ϕ functions. Thus, it cannot remove path-dependent redundancy. VanDunen et al.[17] proposed "Value-based Partial Redundancy Elimination", but it cannot eliminate part of Type I, II, V, and VI. In addition, their approach cannot use efficient bit-vector implementation in data-flow analyses.

6   Conclusion

We proposed PVNRE, a redundancy elimination algorithm that manages both optimizing power and analysis time. Using value numbers in data-flow analyses, PVNRE can deal with data-dependent redundancy. It can also detect path-dependent partial redundancy by converting value numbers through ϕ functions on demand. It represents data dependency by the numerical order between value numbers; therefore it can quickly process data-dependent redundancy during data-flow analyses, and avoid the overhead due to the iteration of PRE and CP.

We implemented PVNRE in a Java JIT compiler and conducted experiments using SPECjvm98. The results showed that PVNRE has the same optimizing power but has a maximum 45% faster analysis speed than algorithms that iterate PRE and CP. These results show that PVNRE is an outstanding algorithm to exploit instruction level parallelism in a runtime optimizing compiler, where both optimizing power and analysis time are important.

We are currently integrating PVNRE with redundant exception elimination in Java. We expect that all redundancy eliminations that preserve exception orders can be performed in one pass.

References

1. Knoop, J., Rüthing, O., Steffen, B.: Lazy code motion. ACM SIGPLAN Notices **27** (1992) 224–234
2. Bodik, R., Gupta, R., Soffa, M.L.: Complete removal of redundant expressions. In: SIGPLAN Conference on Programming Language Design and Implementation. (1998) 1–14
3. Briggs, P., Cooper, K.D.: Effective partial redundancy elimination. ACM SIGPLAN Notices **29** (1994) 159–170
4. Bodik, R., Anik, S.: Path-sensitive value-flow analysis. In: Symposium on Principles of Programming Languages. (1998) 237–251
5. Alpern, B., Wegman, M.N., Zadeck, F.K.: Detecting equality of variables in programs. In: Conference Record of the Fifteenth Annual ACM Symposium on Principles of Programming Languages, San Diego, California (1988) 1–11
6. Click, C.: Global code motion: global value numbering. ACM SIGPLAN Notices **30** (1995) 246–257
7. Cooper, K., Simpson, T.: Value-driven code motion. Technical report, CRPC-TR95637-S, Rice University (1995)

8. Muchnick, S.S.: Advanced Compiler Design & Implementation. Morgan Kaufmann Publishers (1997)

9. Cytron, R., Ferrante, J., Rosen, B.K., Wegman, M.N., Zadeck, F.K.: Efficiently computing static single assignment form and the control dependence graph. ACM Transactions on Programming Languages and Systems **13** (1991) 451–490

10. Rosen, B.K., Wegman, M.N., Zadeck, F.K.: Global value numbers and redundant computations. In: Proceedings of the 15th ACM SIGPLAN-SIGACT symposium on Principles of programming languages, ACM Press (1988) 12–27

11. Odaira, R., Kei, H.: Partial value number redundancy elimination. Technical report, TR 04-01, University of Tokyo (2004) http://www-hiraki.is.s.u-tokyo.ac.jp/members/ray/pvnre_tr.ps.gz.

12. Steffen, B., Knoop, J., Rüthing, O.: The value flow graph: A program representation for optimal program transformations. In: European Symposium on Programming. (1990) 389–405

13. Kaffe.org: (Kaffe Open VM) http://www.kaffe.org/.

14. Standard Performance Evaluation Corporation: (SPEC JVM98 Benchmarks) http://www.spec.org/osg/jvm98/.

15. Chow, F., Chan, S., Kennedy, R., Liu, S.M., Lo, R., Tu, P.: A new algorithm for partial redundancy elimination based on ssa form. In: Proceedings of the 1997 ACM SIGPLAN conference on Programming language design and implementation, ACM Press (1997) 273–286

16. Rüthing, O., Knoop, J., Steffen, B.: Detecting equalities of variables: Combining efficiency with precision. In: Static Analysis Symposium. (1999) 232–247

17. VanDrunen, T., Hosking, A.L.: Value-based partial redundancy elimination. In: Compiler Construction (CC). (2004) 167–184

Overflow Controlled SIMD Arithmetic*

Jiahua Zhu, Hongjiang Zhang, Hui Shi, Binyu Zang, and Chuanqi Zhu

Fudan University, Computer Science Department,
Handan Rd. 220, Shanghai, China
{jhzhu, hjzhang, byzang, cqzhu}@fudan.edu.cn

Abstract. Although the "SIMD within a register" parallel architectures
have existed for almost 10 years, the automatic optimizations for such
architectures are not well developed yet. Since most optimizations for
SIMD architectures are transplanted from traditional vectorization techniques, many special features of SIMD architectures, such as packed operations, have not been thoroughly considered. As operands are tightly
packed within a register, there is no spare space to indicate overflow. To
maintain the accuracy of automatic SIMDized programs, the operands
should be unpacked to preserve enough space for interim overflow. By
doing this, great overhead would be introduced. Furthermore, the instructions for handling interim overflows can sometimes prevent other
optimizations. In this paper, a new technique, OCSA (overflow controlled
SIMD arithmetic), is proposed to reduce the negative effects caused by
interim overflow handling and eliminate the interference of interim overflows. We have applied our algorithm to the multimedia benchmarks
of Berkeley. The experimental results show that the OCSA algorithm
can significantly improve the performance of ADPCM-Decoder (110%),
MESA-Reflect (113%) and DJVU-Encoder (106%).

1 Introduction

In 1994, HP introduced MAX-1, the first SIMD instruction set, into the general-
purpose processor PA-7100LC. Since then, more and more SIMD architectures
have been integrated into general-purpose processors to improve their ability to
run multimedia applications. [9] As one of the latest-delivered SIMD instruction
sets, Intel imported SSE3 into Pentium IV processor in 2004.

During 10 years of architecture development, many useful patterns have been
integrated into SIMD extensions. However, it is not an easy task to make full use
of the hardware supports to speed up applications. Hand-coded SIMD intrinsic
functions, libraries and assemblies built into applications [7] might be the major
approaches for these applications. Actually, it is difficult for software developers
who are not familiar with the SIMD architecture or library interfaces to adopt
those approaches, and this could affect the portability of the application code as

* Supported by the National Natural Science Foundation of China under Grant No.
60273046; Shanghai Science and Technology Committee of China Key Project Fund-
ing (02JC14013).

R. Eigenmann et al. (Eds.): LCPC 2004, LNCS 3602, pp. 424–438, 2005.

well. Moreover, the hand-coding programs for SIMD architectures do not achieve as acceptable performances as programmers expect. Therefore, people hope that compilers could play a more effective role in exploiting the capabilities of SIMD architectures for user applications. A compiler can automatically replace the user code with SIMD intrinsic functions and instructions wherever it is applicable, thereby improving the performance of the code running on SIMD architectures. Developers could code with the standard languages and rely on a compiler to tune their programs for SIMD hardware.

Actually, much effort has been spent in past decade on developing compilers to automatically optimize user codes for SIMD extension. Cheong and Lam[1] developed an optimizer for the SUN SIMD extension VIS. Krall and Lelait[7] applied traditional vectorization to the code for VIS. Sreraman and Govindarajan [3] developed a vectorizer based on SUIF for the Intel MMX. Larsen and Amerasinghe[4] developed SLP analysis technique to detect potential super word- level parallelism to utilize the SIMD extensions of general-purpose processors. Performance has been improved for small and simple kernels through applying these techniques. However, there are still few successful stories of optimizing real-life applications.

One difficulty that people could encounter in optimizing complicated, real-life applications with SIMD extension is the conflict between the data type in SIMD instructions and the data type rules into program language standard. Specifically, many multimedia applications work on 8-bit or 16-bit data sets. Hence, SIMD extension works most efficiently on the short length data set. However, several independent 8-bit (or 16-bit) operations cannot be optimized into 8-bit (or 16-bit) SIMD instructions directly if the data overflow problem is taken into consideration. C language standard requires the integer promotion semantics [18]. It means that if an operation on two 8-bit integers or two 16-bit integers could cause overflow, the short length integer data should be automatically promoted into the long length INT type, which is usually 32 or 64 bits, to deal with the overflow. To comply with this standard, the SIMD transformation has to take the conservative assumption and extend the 8-bit (or 16-bit) integer into a 32-bit (or 64-bit) integer wherever an overflow might occur, which could decrease the efficiency of SIMD instruction and introduce extra overhead.

In this paper, we propose an algorithm, OCSA(Overflow Controlled SIMD Arithmetic), to eliminate the overhead of cases in which the overflowed data is an intermediate result of the expression and the overall result is sensitive to these overflows. OCSA algorithm consists of two sub-algorithms, the overflow controlled wraparound SIMD arithmetic and the overflow controlled saturation SIMD arithmetic. We applied this algorithm to the applications from the Berkeley Multimedia Workload. The experimental results show that the OCSA algorithm significantly reduces the overhead by eliminating the overflow-guarded calls in the SIMD code and thereby improving the performance.

The remainder of this paper is organized as follows: Section 2 gives a more detailed analysis for the overflow problem in SIMD programs and provides some background information. Section 3 and Section 4 describe the detailed OCSA algorithm for handling the overflow problem. The overflow controlled wraparound arithmetic is introduced in Section 3, while the overflow controlled saturation arithmetic is introduced in Section 4. The experimental results are shown in Section 5. In Section 6, we discuss the related work. We then end this paper with Section 7 in which our conclusion is given.

2   Overflow in SIMD Programs

To clarify the problem more explicitly, we will first describe in this section the parallelism within the register and the integer promotion rule. Next, we will describe the problem we are going to solve in this paper. The parallelism within a register is the most effective way to implement SIMD architecture as it can perform SIMD operations within the register. The integer promotion is a rule defined in C99. It insures that the overflow of shorter data types can be kept during the computation.

SIMD–Parallelism within a register: The data paths of general-purpose microprocessors are 32-bit or 64-bit in width, while multimedia applications operate on data that is typically 8-bit or 16-bit in width. To utilize the spare data path and computation capability, hardware designers introduced the SIMD (Single Instruction Multiple Data) architectures to implement the parallelism within a register. For example, Intel introduced 128-bit wide registers for SIMD instructions that can operate on four 32-bit data, eight 16-bit data or sixteen 8-bit data simultaneously.

Furthermore, some special instructions are introduced in SIMD extensions to meet the special requirements of multimedia applications. For example, the Intel SSE2 instruction set consists of Minimum, Maximum and Saturation operations. However, such instructions are only performed on special data types (the MaxMin and Saturation of SSE2 are based on 16 bits wide data type only).

Integer promotion and overflow: The latest version of ANSI C standard requires computations to use INT data type if some shorter integer-type values, signed or unsigned, might overflow during the computing. It means that the overflows of the shorter integer-typed data should be kept during computation. To general-purpose processors, when a shorter data-type computation is performed, the data size will be expanded to meet the rule naturally.

SIMD program with overflow: When computations are performed with SIMD extensions, the shorter data-typed operands are packed into a register. These operands are arranged one by one, each one takes as many bits as its data-type requires. There are no spare bits left for keeping the potential overflow. The overflow would be clipped, possibly causing an incorrect result.

An example shows how a potentially overflowed program is translated with SIMD extension.

```
foo (unsigned short * a, unsigned short * b) {
  for (int j = 0; j<8; j++)
  a[j] = (a[j]+b[j])>>1;
```

```
}
_mm_foo (__m128i * va, __m128i * vb) {
*va = _mm_add_epi16(*va,*vb);
*va = _mm_srai_epi16(*va,1);
}
```

(The intrinsic functions used in this example have been included in Appendix A.)

The serial function foo coded with standard C loops and the parallel function _mm_foo coded with Intel SIMD calls are of the same functionality without considering the overflow problem. However,when we call them in the following program, one of the output is "Vector a is: 32768 32768 32768 32768 32768 32768 32768 32768" when we pass foo to the function Overflow_check, the other is "Vector a is: 0 0 0 0 0 0 0 0" when we pass _mm_foo instead.

```
Overflow_check(void (*f)()) {
  short a[8] = {1,1,1,1,1,1,1,1};
  short b[8] = {65535,65535,65535,65535,65535,65535,65535,65535};
  f(a,b);
  printf("Vector a is:");
  for (int j=0;j<8;j++)    printf("\t %d",a[j]);
}
```

The result shows how overflow affects the correctness of _mm_foo and causes it to give a different result from the one given by foo.

Let us see how the function foo and function _mm_foo work differently. For foo, when it is computed with general-purpose units, all computations are implemented in 32-bit registers and are not clipped before the values are assigned. That means the results of a[j] plus b[j] (j = 0...8) is preserved in 32 bits. In this case, the result is 65536 (at least 17 bits are required). When 65536 is shifted right by 1 bit, we get 32768 (16 bits are enough for representing this value). Therefore, the result of foo is a vector of 32768. On the other hand, when computed with SIMD architecture, the interim result of the addition would be clipped. Therefore, the 17 bits summation 65536 would be clipped to zero. As a result, vector a is a vector of zero.

Instead of _mm_foo, _mm_foo_1 is a correction compilation of foo. And _mm_foo is a correction compilation of foo_1. If we abide by the C standard strictly, we must spend many cycles packing, unpacking and sign extracting (if the data is of signed type) operations, as the function _mm_foo_1 does. The overhead of these operations would counteract the benefits coming from SIMD, even leading to negative speedup.

```
foo_1 (unsigned short * a, unsigned short * b) {
  for (int j=0; j++; j<8){
    a[j] = a[j]+b[j];
    a[j] = a[j]>>1;
  }
```

```
}
_mm_foo_1 (__m128i * va, __m128i * vb) {
 __m128i va_hi,va_lo,vb_hi,vb_lo;
 va_hi = _mm_unpackhi_epi16(*va, vzero);
 va_lo = _mm_unpacklo_epi16(*va, vzero);
 vb_hi = _mm_unpackhi_epi16(*vb, vzero);
 vb_lo = _mm_unpacklo_epi16(*vb, vzero);
 va_hi = _mm_add_epi16(va_hi,vb_hi);
 va_hi = _mm_srai_epi16(va_hi,1);
 va_lo = _mm_add_epi16(va_lo,vb_lo)
 va_lo = _mm_srai_epi16(va_lo,1);
 *va = _mm_packs_epi32 (va_hi,va_lo);
}
```

After reviewing the operations supported by Intel SIMD extension, we find that not every expression is sensitive to the overflow. Therefore, in this paper, we will discuss only those cases in which some interim results would overflow. Meanwhile, the overall results are sensitive to these overflows as some operations make the overflow live during computation. We will provide an efficient method: overflow controlled SIMD arithmetic (OCSA), to reduce the overhead of these cases while optimized for SIMD architectures.

Obviously, the right shift is an operation that makes the overflow live, because the right shift operation might move some overflow bits to regular bits. The saturation arithmetic is another operation that makes the overflow live during the computation, since the overflow will determine whether the result is a saturated value or not. Although only these two operations will introduce sensitivity to the overflow, they are frequently used in multimedia applications and are essential to the performance. In the next two sections, we will provide the methods to improve performance for these two cases.

3   Overflow Controlled Wraparound SIMD Arithmetic

In this section, we are going to provide a transformation to reduce the overhead due to living overflow introduced by right shift. The approach consists of the five following steps:

> Pattern mattch
> Overflow analysis
> Transformation
> Overflow checking
> Simplification

Pattern Match: Pattern match is widely used in traditional optimization and vectorization to find the potential optimizable and vectorizable fragment of programs. We use it to find the fragment that might be beneficial from overflow controlled wraparound SIMD arithmetic (OCWSA). We perform a bottom-up search recursively on the syntax tree for the node that matches the pattern of (SubExp)≫N. In this pattern, N is a constant and the other operand of shift in right, SubExp is an expression that may generate interim overflow.

Overflow Analysis: OCWSA tends to reduce the overhead and boost the performance through controlling the overflow during the computation. The second step is to determine if the interim results would overflow during the computation.

We use the bitwidth analysis method provided by Stephenson and Amarasinghe [8] to detect the overflow. This method is based on the following knowledge:

1. The valid bits of result are affected by the valid bits of the operands.
2. The valid bits of operands are affected by the valid bits of result.

For example, the valid-bits of the sum of two 16-bits operands are bits 0–16. On the other hand, if the result is assigned to an 8-bit variable, the valid bits of the operands are bits 0–7.

To extract the valid bits of each interim result precisely, we perform a two-pass analysis. The first pass calculates the valid bits of each interim result according to the valid bits of operands with a bottom-up approach. The second pass calculates the valid bits of each operand according the valid bits of the results.

Since the valid bit analysis is out of the scope of this paper, we will not describe the detailed method of this analysis.

Transformations: Transformation is the pivotal part of OCWSA. Since the overhead is caused by the sensitivity of the right shift operation to the overflow of its sub-expression, it is natural to consider promoting the priority of shift in right operations. If the right shift operation is performed before the overflow is generated, it would be unnecessary to have an extra bit to keep the overflow during the computing. That means we can perform optimization for SIMD architecture without expanding the integer values to INT size or packing them before assignation.

The SubExp found in the pattern match step could be an expression of addition, subtraction, multiplication, division, or any bit operations, such as &, $|, \ll, \gg$ etc. We consider addition and subtraction the same kind of operation since they are analogous. The transformation for $(E_1 - E_2) \gg n$ is also analogous to that of $(E_1 + E_2) \gg n$. The division and the bit operation and will not cause the increase of data width, so we will not consider them as the causes of potential overflow. The shift operations $' \ll '$ and $' \gg '$ can be simplified as Eq. 1 and 2, which have no interim value to be overflowed. Therefore, in this section, we will focus on solving the cases of addition and multiplication.

$$
(E \gg m) \gg n = \begin{cases} E \gg (n+m) & (if\ n+m>0) \\ E \ll (n+m) & (if\ n+m<0) \\ E & (if\ n+m=0) \end{cases} \tag{1}
$$

$$
(E \ll m) \gg n = \begin{cases} E \gg (n-m) & (if\ n-m>0) \\ E \ll (n-m) & (if\ n-m<0) \\ E & (if\ n-m=0) \end{cases} \tag{2}
$$

First, consider the cases in real domain. If the data type of E_1 and E_2 is real and the operation result is real as well, Eq. 3 and 4 are true.

$$\frac{E_1 + E_2}{2^n} = \frac{E_1}{2^n} + \frac{E_2}{2^n} \tag{3}$$

$$\frac{E_1 \times E_2}{2^n} = \frac{E_1}{2^n} \times E_2 \tag{4}$$

In integer domain, divided by 2^n can be replaced by the operations of shift in right by n bits. Take the impact of the last n bits of E_1 and E_2 into consideration, we get the Eq. 5 and 6 that are true in integer data domain. In these two equations, the overhead due to living overflow could be avoided by performing a right shift operation before the overflow comes into being.

$$(E_1 + E_2) \gg n = E_1 \gg n + E_2 \gg n + (E_1 \& (2^n - 1) + E_2 \& (2^n - 1)) \gg n \tag{5}$$

$$(E_1 \times E_2) \gg n = (E_1 \gg n) \times E_2 + (E_1 \& (2^n - 1)) \times E_2 \gg n \tag{6}$$

Overflow Checking: To control the overflow in SIMD arithmetic, we hope the computation of remediation part of the Eq. 5 and 6 will not overflow. So we append the following two restrictions:

1. If and only if $(E_1 \& (2^n - 1)) + (E_2 \& (2^n - 1))$ will not overflow, is Eq.5 applicable.
2. If and only if $(E_1 \& (2^n - 1)) \times E_2 \gg n$ will not overflow, is Eq.6 applicable.

Complicated Cases and Simplification: In real life applications, we may have more complicated expressions than the cases above. For these complicated cases, we need to perform OCWSA recursively and the computation would be expanded exponentially. For example, when applying OCWSA recursively, the expression $(a + b + c) \gg 4$ would be transformed to Expr. 7. Obviously, the expression is so complex that it would take a lot of CPU time even if it were vectorized.

$$a \gg 4 + b \gg 4 + c \gg 4 + ((a\&0xf) + (b\&0xf)) \gg 4 +$$
$$(((a + b)\&0xf) + (c\&0xf)) \gg 4 \tag{7}$$

To reduce the complexity caused by the recursive use of OCWSA, we focus on a series of Expr. 8, 9 and 10, to simplify the result expressions. Other complicated cases can be simplified recursively.

$$((E_1 + E_2) + E_3) \gg n \tag{8}$$

$$((E_1 + E_2) \times E_3) \gg n \tag{9}$$

$$((E_1 \times E_2) + E_3) \gg n \tag{10}$$

When applying OCWSA recursively, Expr. 8 would be transformed to Expr. 11.

$$E_1 \gg n + E_2 \gg n + E_3 \gg n + (E_1 \& (2^n - 1) + E_2 \& (2^n - 1)) \gg n +$$
$$((E_1 + E_2)\&(2^n - 1) + E_3 \& (2^n - 1)) \gg n \tag{11}$$

Notice that expression $(E_1 \& (2^n - 1) + E_2 \& (2^n - 1)) \gg n$ is the carry of $E_1 \& (2^n - 1)$ plus $E_2 \& (2^n - 1)$, expression $(E_1 + E_2) \& (2^n - 1)$ is the result of $E_1 \& (2^n - 1)$ plus $E_2 \& (2^n - 1)$ clipped by n bits. Therefore, through some ordinary arithmetic we can get Eq. 12.

$$[E_1 \& (2^n - 1) + E_2 \& (2^n - 1)] \gg n + [(E_1 + E_2) \& (2^n - 1) + E] \gg$$
$$= [E_1 \& (2^n - 1) + E_2 \& (2^n - 1) + E] \gg n \quad (12)$$

Similarly, another two simplification equations can be derived for Expressions 9 and 10. They are Eq. 13 and 14

$$((E_1 \& (2^n - 1) + E_2 \& (2^n - 1)) \gg n) \times E +$$
$$(((E_1 + E_2) \& (2^n - 1)) \times E) \gg n$$
$$= E \times [(E_1 \& (2^n - 1)) + (E_2 \& (2^n - 1))] \gg n \quad (13)$$

$$(E_1 \& (2^n - 1) \times E_2) \gg n + ((E_1 \times E_2) \& (2^n - 1) + E) \gg n$$
$$= ((E_1 \& (2^n - 1)) \times (E_2 \& (2^n - 1)) + E) \gg n \quad (14)$$

With these simplification equations, the Expressions 8, 9 and 10 are equal to the Expr. 15, 16 and 17. After simplification, the computation amount of these expressions is reduced significantly.

$$E_1 \gg n + E_2 \gg n + E_3 \gg n + (E_1 \& (2^n - 1) +$$
$$E_2 \& (2^n - 1) + E_3 \& (2^n - 1)) \gg n) \quad (15)$$

$$(E_1 \gg n + E_2 \gg n) \times E_3 + ((E_1 \& (2^n - 1) + E_2 \& (2^n - 1)) \times E_3) \gg n) \quad (16)$$

$$(E_1 \gg n) \times E_2 + E_3 \gg n + ((E_1 \& (2^n - 1)) \times E_2 + E_3 \& (2^n - 1)) \gg n) \quad (17)$$

With these simplification equations, OCWSA would be much more effective to handle the complicated cases of real applications.

Discussion: With OCWSA, the pack and unpack operations and the operations to extract sign bits (if the operands are of signed data-type) are replaced by shift and mask operations. Since the pack and unpack operations require many more CPU cycles than shift and mask operations, OCWSA can reduce the overhead due to the optimization for SIMD architecture with interim overflows. Meanwhile, because of the doubled parallelity, the expanded computation requirement of OCWSA will not lead to additional penalty.

4   Overflow Controlled Saturation SIMD Arithmetic

Saturation SIMD Arithmetic: Saturation is one of the typical operations in multimedia applications. It limits the out-of-range results to the range that 8/16/32 bits singed/unsigned integers can represent. Instead of clipping the operands to the desired size as wraparound arithmetic does, saturation operation saturates the positive overflow to the largest representable value or negative overflow to the minimum representable value. With saturation, the result of multimedia applications could be much more natural.

The saturation operation can be combined with arithmetic operations in SIMD architectures. The results of arithmetic computation can be saturated before being written back. This kind of arithmetic is called saturation arithmetic. For example, Intel's instruction set provides addition and subtraction operations combined with saturation (throughout the remainder of this paper, saturation arithmetic means saturation addition or saturation subtraction). These operations can improve the performance of multimedia applications significantly. Related research, such as automatic detection [6] for the saturation pattern, has been well documented and exciting results have been reported.

Different Data-Types of Operands and their Results: Since Intel integrates the saturation arithmetic into the SIMD architecture, only if the operand and result are of the same data-type the saturation SIMD arithmetic is applicable. Whenever one of the operands is not representable by the data-type of result, it is hard for the saturation arithmetic to be applied.

For example, the code has a typical saturation arithmetic.

```
for(i= 0, i<n,i++) {
 short a[], b[],c[],d[];
 ...
 if ((b[i]+c[i]+d[i])<-32768) a[i] = -32768;
 else if ((b[i]+c[i]+d[i])>32767) a[i] = 32767;
 else a[i] = b[i]+c[i]+d[i];
}
```

Ignoring overflow, the if-then, if-then statement can be transformed to Expr. 18. The symbol $\oplus$ stands for saturation addition.

$$a[i] = b[i] \oplus (c[i] + d[i]) \tag{18}$$

To apply the expression with SIMD architecture, the overflow introduced by c[i]+d[i] has to be considered. However, if the operands were expanded to INT data-type, the operands and result would be of different data-type and no corresponding saturation arithmetic could be applied.

Abstract Problem: To generalize the various cases in real applications, the problem can be summarized as follows:
Both $E_1 \oplus E_2$ and $E_1 \ominus E_2$ are saturation arithmetics that limit the results in m bits. (the symbols $\oplus$ and $\ominus$ stand for saturation addition/subtraction).
Any possible results of expression E_1 are represented by the m bits integer.
Any possible results of expression E_2 are represented by m + p bits integer.
How could we optimize the expression with m-bit saturation arithmetic?

In this section we are going to provide an efficient method, overflow controlled saturation SIMD arithmetic (OCSSA), to apply saturation SIMD arithmetic for the above cases and exert the saturation arithmetic's power.

Since only addition and subtraction are combined with saturation and the features of saturation addition and saturation subtraction are similar to each other, we will present the OCSSA with saturation addition. The method for saturation subtraction is the same.

Process: Like the OCWSA, overflow controlled saturation arithmetic is performed in four steps, while OCSSA need not be simplified.

> Pattern mattch
> Valid bits analysis
> Transformation
> Range checking

The first step is well-studied [6] as we mentioned before. The second step is similar to that of the OCWSA, but the valid bits analysis of OCSSA requires the detailed valid bits instead of the brief judgment about overflow. In the rest of this section, we will introduce the conditional associative law first as it is the foundation for OCSSA, then we will introduce transformation and rang-checking with the simplest case. Finally, we are going to generalize the method.

Conditional Associative Law: Unlike wraparound arithmetic, the saturation arithmetic operation is not relative. Consider the expression $a \oplus b \oplus c$. Variable a, b, and c are of the signed short integer type, and a=0x7FF5, b = 0x14, c = 0xFFEC. In this case, $(a \oplus b) \oplus c$ is 0x7FEB while $a \oplus (b \oplus c)$ is 0x7FFF.

As a compromise substitute when the addends/subtracts $e_i(i = 2 \cdots n)$ are of the same sign except for some zero elements, Eq. 19 and 20 are true. We call these two equations the conditional associative law.

$$E_1 \oplus E_2 \oplus E_3 \oplus \cdots \oplus E_n = E_1 \oplus (E_2 + \cdots + E_n) \tag{19}$$

$$E_1 \ominus E_2 \ominus E_3 \ominus \cdots \ominus E_n = E_1 \ominus (E_2 + \cdots + E_n) \tag{20}$$

Transformation: In this section, we present the OCSSA from the simplest case, which is p = 1.

> $E_1 \oplus E_2$, is saturation arithmetic that limits the result in m bits.
> Any possible result of expression E_1 is represented by m bits integer.
> The result of expression E_2 should be represented by m +1 bits integer.

Any m+1 bits integer E2 can be represented as a sum of two $E_2 \gg 1$ and one $E_2 \& 0x1$. Thus $E_1 \oplus E_2$ can be translated into $E_1 \oplus ((E_2 \gg 1) + (E_2 \gg 1) + (E_2 \& 1))$. According to the conditional associative law, Eq. 21 is true if $E_2 \gg 1$ and $E_2 \& 0x1$ are of the same sign or one of them is zero.

$$E_1 \oplus E_2 = E_1 \oplus (E_2 \gg 1) \oplus (E_2 \gg 1) \oplus (E_2 \& 1) \tag{21}$$

As $E_2 \& 0x1$ will not be a negative value, the equation is true only when $E_2 \geq 0$. To real applications, such a constraint is unacceptable since in most cases we cannot ensure E_2 is not less than zero. We have to abandon these cases due to this constraint. Therefore, it is necessary to refine the method to extend the applicable range. Combining the $E_2 \gg 1 + (E_2 \& 1)$ together, we will get the Equation (13). Whenever $E_2 \gg 1 + (E_2 \& 1)$ and $E_2 \gg 1$ are of the same sign, or one of them is zero, Eq. 22 is true.

$$E_1 \oplus E_2 = E_1 \oplus (E_2 \gg 1) \oplus ((E_2 \gg 1) + (E_2 \& 1)) \tag{22}$$

Let us next examine the possible value of $E_2 \gg 1 + (E_2 \& 1)$ and $E_2 \gg 1$. In this equation, when $E_2/2 \geq 0$, $E_2/2 + (E_2 \& 1)$ must be no smaller than zero, so the equation is true. When $E_2/2 < 0$, the value of $E_2/2 + (E_2 \& 1)$ is shown in Table 1.

Table 1 shows that if E_2 is a negative number, $(E_2 \gg 1) + (E_2 \& 1)$ is no larger than zero, so Eq. 22 is true no matter what the value of E_2 is.

Range Check: When E_2 reaches its peak value $2^{m+1} - 1$, the value of $E_2/2 + (E_2 \& 1)$ is 2^m. This cannot be represented by m bits integer. Using the OCSSA again to solve the problem would be costly. Therefore, we compute the possible range that E_2 might be to determine in which cases the value of E_2 would never be $2^{m+1} - 1$. We use the method similar to the bitwidth analysis to check whether E_2 will reach peak value or not. We will not describe it in detail.

p=2 and Other Cases: To generalize the method, we consider the cases that E_2 is represented by m+2 bits integer. The general idea described above is adoptable as well. We have Eq. 23 for p=2 cases.

Table 1. The value of $(E_2 \gg 1) + (E_2 \& 1)$ and $E_2 \gg 1$

E_2	$E_2 \gg 1$	$E_2 \& 1$	$(E_2 \gg 1) + (E_2 \& 1)$
-1	-1	1	0
-2	-1	0	-1
< -2	< -1	0 or 1	< 0

$$E_1 \oplus E_2 = E_1 \oplus [(E_2 \gg 2) + (E_2 \& 2 \oplus 1)] \oplus [(E_2 \oplus 2) + \\ (E_2 \& 2 \oplus 1)] \oplus [(E_2 \oplus 2) + (E_2 \& 1)] \oplus (E_2 \oplus 2) \tag{23}$$

Similar to the p=1 cases, each operand of the expression is of the same sign or zero, and when the value of E_2 is larger than $2^{m+2} - 4$, the operands may be out of the range of m bits integer, we should check the value range of E_2 to ensure the transformation is effective. Otherwise, we can apply the transformation recursively to solve this problem by exponential cost. The solution can also be extended to the cases in which E_2 is represented by m + p bits integer, but the cost of such transformations increases exponentially with the increase of p.

5   Experiment Result

To prove the effectiveness of OCSA, some experiments would be described in this section. In these experiments, we select Berkeley Multimedia Workload (BMW) as benchmark and Pentium IV NetBurst as hardware platform (Appendix C). Before the experiments being carried out, we find that there are eight fixed pointed programs in the BMW. And four of them involve shift right or saturation arithmetic in their hot spots. Further more, when optimized with SIMD architecture, three of them are prevented by overflow from achieving acceptable performance (Appendix B).

In the experiments, we optimize the three programs in four ways and compare the performance of the optimized programs. The optimizing methods are:
1. Automatic optimization of ICC without automatic vectorization: As the IA-32 compiler developed by Intel Corporation, it is reasonable to believe that ICC is one of the best C compilers for Pentium IV series computer. We compile the programs with '-xW' and '-vec-' options. '-xW' option means optimizing for Pentium IV processors, '-vec-' means turn off the automatic vectorization of ICC.
2. Automatic vectorization of ICC: we also compile the programs with ICC and '-xW' option turned on to inspect the effectiveness of ICC automatic vectorization.
3. Manually Vectorization with OCSA: we also optimize the programs for SIMD architecture with ICC intrinsic functions manually, and compile the optimized programs with ICC, -xW option turned on. While optimizing the programs manually, we perform if-conversion, scalar-extension, const propagation, dispersed data gathering, OCSA and so on to implement the SIMD optimization.
4. Manually Vectorization without OSCA: To clarify the effectiveness of OCSA we also try to optimize the programs without OCSA technique, use pack and unpack to treat potential overflow.

Fig 1 shows the execution time of programs optimized by different optimizing method, and the speedups compared with the programs optimized automatically by ICC without automatic vectorization. It seems that the automatic vectorization of ICC could do nothing to these programs although the manually optimized programs are benefited from the SIMD architecture. Further more the optimizing with OCSA could achieve a higher performance than that without OCSA. Table 2 shows the speedup due to OCSA.

6   Related Work

Verctorizing techniques for SIMD architecture have been researched since the 1990's. Most research is based on the SUIF compiler for different architectures. [1] Cheong and Lam implement an optimizer for VIS instruction sets. To optimize for the SIMD architecture, they focus on the code generation and memory alignment. [2] Larsen and Amarasinghe realize the superword level parallelizing for Ativec, the SIMD instruction set of Motorola MPC 740. With the optimizer, some scientific computation applications and some small kernels of multimedia applications achieve a significant increase in speed. [4] Sreraman and Gobindarajan also implement a MMX optimizer based on the SUIF compiler. Beside these, the SIMD optimizer based on SUIF, [3] Sreraman and Govindarajan developed a prototype for an MMX instruction set as well. Nevertheless, most of these works can only provide the results for small components such as dot products and so on.

Furthermore, as the most powerful compiler for Intel architecture, ICC also provided with an automatic verctorizor [5][6]. The recently delivered ICC 8.0, was not only verctorizor, but also had the saturation arithmetic detector implemented. The results of the dot product and gzip experiments are reported, but to the benchmarks used in this paper, the verctorizor of ICC 8.0 can almost do nothing about them.

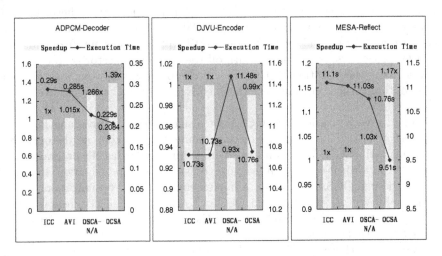

Fig. 1. Experiment Results. ICC: Automatic optimization of ICC without automatic vectorization AVI: Automatic vectorization of ICC OSCA-N/A: Manually Vectorization without OSCA OCSA: Manually Vectorization with OCSA

Table 2. Speedup due to OSCA

	ADPCM-Decoder	DJVU-Encoder	MESA-Reflect
Speedup of OCSA	1.10x	1.06x	1.13x

Although, many experiments have been done regarding the automatic optimization for SIMD architecture, the overhead due to the interim overflow has not yet been researched.

7   Conclusion

In this paper, we provided a new technology, overflow controlled SIMD arithmetic, to improve the performance of multimedia applications for SIMD architectures. The new approach improves the performance through reducing the overhead caused by the overflow of interim results and avoiding obstacles caused by the unequal size of destination operands and source operands in saturation SIMD arithmetic. OCSA significantly improves the performance of ADPCM-Decoders and MESA-Reflects. Meanwhile, it reduces the negative speedup for the DJVU-Encoder and almost eliminates all the penalties stemming from SIMD optimization.

Now, we are implementing our automatic vectorizor for the Intel SIMD architecture based on Gcc-3.4, and this work would be completed in two months.

References

1. Gerald Cheong and Monica Lam. An Optimizer for Multimedia Instruction Sets. Second SUIF Compiler Workshop, Stanford January. (1996)
2. Randall J. Fisher and Henry G. Dietz. Compiling for SIMD Within Register. Workshop on Language and Compiler for Parallel Computing, University of North Carolina at Chapel Hill, North Carolina. (1998)
3. N. Sreraman and R.Govindarajan. A Vectorizing Compiler for Multimedia Extensions. International Journal of Parallel Programming, Vol. 28 No.4, (2000) 363–400
4. Samuel Larsen and Saman Amarasinghe. Exploiting Superword Level Parallelism with Multimedia Instruction Sets. Proceeding of SIGPLAN Conference on Programming Language Design and Implementation, Vancouver B.C. (2000)
5. Aart J.C. Bik, Milind Girkae, Paul M. Grey, Xinmin Tian. Automatic Intra-Register Vectorization for Intel Architecture. International Journal of Parallel Programming, Vol. 30 No. 2 (2002) 65–98
6. Aart J.C. Bik, Milind Girkae, Paul M. Grey, Xinmin Tian. Automatic Detection of Saturation and Clipping Idioms. Proceedings of the 15th International Workshop on Languages and Compilers for parallel computers. (2002).
7. Andreas Krall and Sylvain Lelait. Compilation Techniques for Multimedia Processor. International Journal of Parallel Programming, Vol. 18, No. 4. (2000) 347-361.
8. Mark Stephenson, Jonathan Babb and Saman Amarasinghe. Bitwidth Analysis with Application to Silicon Compilation, ACM SIGPLAN conference on Programming Language Design and Implementation, Vancouver, British Columbia, June 2000
9. Keith Diefendorff and Pradeep K. Dubey. How Multimedia Workloads Will Change Processor Design. IEEE Computer, Vol. 30, No 9, 43-45, (1997).

Appendix A: ICC Intrinsic Description

__mm128i _mm_add_epi8(__m128i a, __m128i b)
Adds the 16 signed or unsigned 8-bit integers in a to the 16 signed or unsigned 8-bit integers in b.
__m128i _mm_srai_epi16(__m128i a, int count)
Shifts the 8 signed 16-bit integers in a right by count bits while shifting in the sign bit.
__m128i _mm_unpacklo_epi16(__m128i a, __m128i b) Interleaves the lower 4 signed or unsigned 16-bit integers with the lower 4 signed or unsigned 16-bit integers in b.
__m128i _mm_unpackhi_epi16(__m128i a, __m128i b)

Interleaves the upper 4 signed or unsigned 16-bit integers with the upper 4 signed or unsigned 16-bit integers in b.

__m128i _mm_packs_epi16(__m128i a, __m128i b)

Packs the 16 signed 16-bit integers from a and b into 8-bit integers and saturates.

Appendix B: Pattern Matched Code Fragments

1. ADPCM_Decoder (OCSSA)

```
void adpcm_decoder(...) {...
       for ( ; len > 0 ; len-- ) {...
          if ( sign )
            valpred -= vpdiff;
          else
            valpred += vpdiff;
          if ( valpred > 32767 )
            valpred = 32767;
          else if ( valpred < -32768 )
            valpred = -32768;
       ...}...}
```

2. DJVU_Encoder (OCSWA)

```
forward_filter(...) {...
       while (n+s3 < e) {...
          x = (9*(bb+cc)-(aa+dd)+8) >> 4;
       ...}...}
```

3. MESA_Reflect (OCSWA)

```
persp_textured_triangle(...){ ...
for (i=0; i < n; i++) { ...
 dest[0] = ffr * (tr + 1) >> (11 + 8);
 dest[1] = ffg * (tg + 1) >> (11 + 8);
 dest[2] = ffb * (tb + 1) >> (11 + 8);
 dest[3] = ffa * (ta + 1) >> (11 + 8);
 ... } ... }
```

Appendix C: Hardware Platform And OS

CPU: Pentium IV 2.0G
Mem: 512M DDR400
Os: RedHat 9.0

Branch Strategies to Optimize Decision Trees for Wide-Issue Architectures

Patrick Carribault[1,2,3], Christophe Lemuet[1],
Jean-Thomas Acquaviva[1], Albert Cohen[2], and William Jalby[1]

[1] PRiSM, University of Versailles
[2] ALCHEMY group, INRIA Futurs, Orsay
[3] Bull Les Clayes-sous-Bois
William.Jalby@prism.uvsq.fr

Abstract. Branch predictors are associated with critical design issues for nowadays instruction greedy processors. We study two important domains where the optimization of decision trees — implemented through switch-case or nested if-then-else constructs — makes the precise modeling of these hardware mechanisms determining for performance: compute-intensive libraries with versioning and cloning, and high-performance interpreters. Against common belief, the complexity of recent microarchitectures does not necessarily hamper the design of accurate cost models, *in the special case of decision trees*. We build a simple model that illustrates the reasons for which decision tree performance is predictable.

Based on this model, we compare the most significant code generation strategies on the Itanium2 processor. We show that *no strategy dominates in all cases*, and although they used to be penalized by traditional superscalar processors, *indirect branches regain a lot of interest* in the context of predicated execution and delayed branches. We validate our study with an improvement from 15% to 40% over Intel ICC compiler for a Daxpy code focused on short vectors.

1 Introduction

Due to the increasing depth of pipelines and wider instruction fetch, branch prediction becomes more and more crucial. Consequently, large hardware structures supporting branch prediction and acceleration are ubiquitous on modern microarchitectures. To supply the pipeline with a continuous stream of instructions, branch predictors have to forecast the outcome of the branch — *taken* or *not taken* — and the target address. In control-intensive codes, multiple kinds of branches occur at a very high rate, hence wide issue processors need to issue and predict multiple branches every cycle.

On the compilation side, many optimization strategies have been proposed [1], to expose more instruction-level parallelism in branch-intensive codes, or to circumvent the limitations of the branch predictor and instruction fetch engine.

We study two important domains where decision trees are responsible for a significant part of the computation time: optimized libraries with versioning and cloning, and high-performance interpreters. Decision trees are implemented through switch-case or nested if-then-else constructs. Generic strategies in general-purpose compilers are often sub-optimal, because they are not well suited to the size of the decision trees (from

R. Eigenmann et al. (Eds.): LCPC 2004, LNCS 3602, pp. 439–454, 2005.

tens up to hundreds of leaf nodes). In addition, optimizing decision trees is a problem due to the dependence on input data, but it should be emphasized that most of the complexity is brought by the large variety of code generation options.

Versioning and cloning. When optimizing high-performance libraries, decision trees are often produced by the specialization of loops with small iteration counts, e.g., vector operations (for the BLAS or FFT), memory copying routines (important for I/O routines), or sorting networks (QuickSort libraries, adaptive sort [5]): a standard strategy consists in generating specialized code for 1, 2,... up to k iterations, using a `switch` instruction to select the right version. Procedure specialization and cloning is also common practice when performing context-sensitive interprocedural optimizations or partial evaluation. The resulting decision trees are based on interval tests in general, implemented as nested `if-then-else` structures.

High-performance interpreters. Bytecode interpreters and processor emulators also rely on decision trees for their computation kernel [2]. These trees are generally implemented as `switch-case` structures spanning over a hundred cases. Such kernels consist of a loop iterating over a decision tree, and two orthogonal optimization directions exist: one may either minimize the latency of the decision tree itself (on average, in the worst case, based on frequency or cost of each leaf, etc.), or restructure the loop such that global correlations can be better exploited. The latter scheme is explored in great detail by Ertl and Gregg in [2]. However, this scheme performs poorly on large decision trees whose global history overflows the hardware prediction tables. Also, it may not fit the constraints (memory capacity, performance predictability) of embedded systems.

After introducing decision trees in Section 2, and our experimental platform, — the Itanium 2 —, in Section 3 we provide details on branch implementation. Section 4 is focused one *one-way* branches, while Section 5 depicts more advanced features of *multiway* branches. Section 6 is dedicated to indirect branch. Experimental results and in-depth comparisons are provided in Section 7, at last Section 8 concludes and gives several openings.

2   Domain-Specific Optimization for Decision Trees

2.1   Decision Tree Patterns at the Source Level

Two code patterns are dominant: the nested tree of `if-then-else` tree conditionals and the linear `switch-case` selector. Nested conditionals are often restructured at intermediate compilation steps, leading to linear sequences of `else if` branches, see Figure 1. These linear sequences are more general than `switch` selectors whose case-distinction is based on integer constants only. However the `switch` selector deserves a specific treatment because it enables additional optimizations and is pervasive in interpreters [2] and codes optimized through versioning or cloning.

In this generic form, the code fragments after each `else if` or `case` may contain further branches. We will only deal with *one-level* `else if` *structures* and *one-level* `switch` *structures*, abstracting away the nested branches (i.e., handling them separately at each

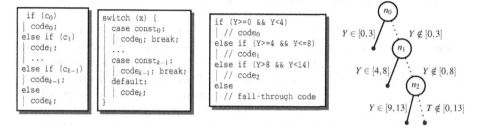

Fig. 1. Code patterns

Fig. 2. Graphical representation of a decision tree (dotted lines correspond to fall-through)

nesting depth). Notice complex nests of conditionals can be often linearized by control-flow restructuring passes.

For the sake of simplicity, expressions in `else if` conditions must be integer *interval checks* — strict or not. These checks neither have to be exclusive nor to involve the same variable throughout the one-level structure.

2.2 Representation of Decision Tree Implementations (Assembly Level)

For both `else if` and `switch` structures, we use a tree abstraction to study code generation strategies. Since we consider one-level structures, there is no a priori restriction on the shape of the tree: all leaves can be reorganized in any possible fashion — except when dependence constraints on non-exclusive conditions require the preservation of the original execution order. Notice that, in a more general setting, identical leaves may be reachable through separate branches; this is not a real problem since the following discussion could easily be extended to a directed acyclic graph.

- *Internal nodes* correspond to the evaluation of the condition associated with an `else if` or `case` construct. The latter pattern restrictions guarantee that `switch` conditions can be evaluated by a single operation (comparison to a constant) and that `else if` conditions require exactly two operations.
- *Leaves* represent the code that has to be executed after the correct branch decision is made; it may be arbitrarily complex, but we may have to make some assumptions about its execution time in several of the proposed optimization strategies.
- *Directed edges* are labeled with the condition of the branch or its negation. Edges have an additional attribute to tell whether they correspond to taken branches — solid lines — or fall-through — dotted lines. Notice dotted-lines correspond to the predicted case in general [10].

A one-level `else if` structure and its associated decision tree are shown in Figure 2. Such a figure is named a *one-way comb* in the remainder of the paper. In fact, a *comb* refers to any list of internal nodes, where the *one-way* or *multi-way* (introduced in next section) prefix is added to characterize the number of extra edges for every node in addition of the fall-through edge (in dotted line on the figure).

3   Description of the Target Architecture

Optimizing decision trees for the Itanium architecture is interesting because the platform provides the programmer or compiler with many opportunities to "drive the processor to the correct path". It is also representative of the modern mechanisms implemented in wide-issue architectures, including the IBM Power4 and Power5 (multiway branches), as well as embedded VLIW processors like the Philips TriMedia [9] and the HP Lx alias ST-Micro 2x0 series [3] (predication, delay slots). This section quickly surveys the Itanium2 branch mechanisms from a programmer perspective [4,6,8].

3.1   Itanium Instruction Set for Branches

First of all, traditional conditional branches are implemented as predicated branches. Typically, a compare instruction evaluates a relation and sets accordingly a pair of mutually exclusive 1-bit predicate registers. Any instruction guarded by a predicate register (called the qualifying predicate) is "nullified" if this predicate is false; thus, a predicated branch behaves exactly like a conditional branch.

Like in any pipelined processor, there is a delay between the issue cycle of the branch and the cycle when the qualifying predicate is known. If a misprediction occurs the associated penalty corresponds to the pipeline re-steer.

Branch instructions fields descriptions are given in [4]. One of these fields provides a guess on branch outcome (*taken* or *not taken*) either statically or dynamically. The others for example allow to determine how many instructions should be prefetched or to avoid the pollution of predictors tables with information relative to the branch. The ISA also supports indirect branch through the storage of target address within a set of dedicated branch registers.

In addition to this fairly complex branch instruction, the Itanium instruction set provides a specific instruction (brp) for controlling instruction prefetch.

The Itanium instructions are grouped by chunks of three instructions called *bundles*. A bundle can contain, one, two or three branch instructions. While up to two bundles can be issued every cycle, only three branches can be dispersed to branch functional units per cycle. Interestingly, branches do not have to be mutually exclusive: their relative ordering matters when resolving the correct path.

3.2   Itanium2 Branch Hardware

The branch prediction algorithm used in the Itanium2 is based on the two-level prediction scheme proposed by Yeh and Patt [10] combining local prediction (branch history tables) and global predictions (pattern history tables). On the Itanium2, a large amount of hardware resources have been dedicated to branch prediction mechanisms, for instance tables keeping track of several thousands of branches.

For minimizing the impact of instruction cache misses, the Itanium2 provides an instruction streaming engine which can be controlled by the compiler through branch hints. We will always assume a perfect locality in the L1 instruction cache in this paper (thanks to compact code or smart usage of brp instructions).

Overall branch penalties (assuming no instruction miss) are given below:

- 0 cycle for correctly predicted branch (both outcome and target);
- 1 cycle for branches for which the outcome has been correctly predicted but the predicted address is incorrect (making use of dedicated address calculation units);
- 6 cycles for branches whose outcome has been incorrectly predicted (the pipeline has to be drained).

Indirect (or delayed) branches behave slightly differently: they take 2 cycles to execute, and there is a 7-cycle delay corresponding to the length of the pipeline, between the assignment of the branch register (b0 to b7) and the beginning of instruction fetch at this target address. During these 7 cycles, any code can be executed (provided the branch register is not overwritten) like in traditional delay slots of many in-order issue processors. Unlike VLIW processors, delay slots do not have to be filled with nops, a pipeline flush will occur if the delay is not satisfied. In addition, the assignment to a branch register triggers a prefetch stream, and one may want to wait for a few more cycles to let this stream operate.

3.3 Experimental Settings

Throughout this paper, we use ICC version 8, choosing the best result from -O2 and -O3. The target platform is a NovaScale 4020 server from Bull featuring two Itanium2 1.5GHz (Madison) processors.

We used both "regular" and "random" data input to study the effects of our optimizations on the prediction hardware. While for the sake of results stability we used a surrounding loop, predictor learning effectiveness is tested by using data input either completely random or exhibiting regular patterns.

Special care was taken to randomize branch histories without flushing the caches, given the large prediction tables and their integration in the L1 and L2 caches.

4 Generating a Tree of One-Way Conditional Branches

An intuitive algorithm to order a decision tree is a balanced binary tree (built by dichotomy), with a logarithmic distance between each leaf. In practice, a balanced tree has a very poor performance since most branches are locally unpredictable and lead to strong penalties.

Conversely, a comb shape has a better branch behavior due to its bias towards the fall-through path. [1] Over a few tenths of branches, some dichotomy is needed to achieve a logarithmic complexity. An optimization framework should consider this strategy as an option.

4.1 Code Motion and Hoisting

Partially redundant expression elimination (PRE) and invariant code motion can bring significant performance benefits for decision trees. The reason is not specific to the

---

[1] By default, branches are thus predicted *not taken*; only those with a recent *taken* history occupy hardware prediction structures.

Itanium: if an expression is common to several leaves, it can be moved up to a common branch, filling some unused issue slots into the tree of conditional branches itself.

Thanks to predicated execution, hoisting can be even more aggressive on the Itanium, allowing to fill more issue slots with speculative computations coming from the leaves. ICC and Open64/ORC [7] implement both PRE and this hoisting strategy.

Alternatively, code motion can be used to fill issue slots with instructions ahead of the decision tree (if the decision is not control-dependent on them). This requires less speculation than hoisting, but increases code size by duplicating code along several branches of the tree.

4.2   Node Reordering

The order in which internal nodes are visited can often be changed, permuting the else if or case leaves at the source level. There are several motivations for this.

- When optimizing for the average-case on a distribution of decisions, leaves with the highest probability of being executed can be moved closer to the root of the tree. This type of optimization is typically interesting for high-performance interpreters.
- When optimizing the performance of a versioned computation kernel, it is more important to take the *relative execution time of the leaves* into account. Indeed, the decision tree overhead is only significant when executing short leaves, i.e., when the versioned kernel is run on small data-sets. Typical short-vector or memory copying operations are of this kind.
- Code motion and hoisting can be more profitable when grouping together leaves with similar or partially redundant expressions.

4.3   Cost Evaluation of the One-Way Comb Approach: Definition

First, we define a performance metric, the *Number of Mispredictions per Decision (MpD)*, as the number of mispredicted branches per taken decision, i.e. per traversal of the decision tree. In addition to input data, *MpD* depends on the decision tree structure.

Cost evaluation for else if structures.   We recall that the conditions of else if constructs are assumed to be interval tests requiring two integer comparisons per cycle, and that the cost of a branch misprediction is 6 cycles (length of the back-end of the pipeline). An extra one cycle overhead is needed to pipeline predicate computations (comparisons) ahead of their qualified branches. The cycle costs for a one-way comb implementation, for the last leaf (worst latency) and for the median one are displayed in Table 1. The *last leaf* corresponds to the case where the targeted leaf is the last one in the comb therefore yielding to the maximum number of branch predictions for this decision tree. Accordingly the *median leaf* corresponds to the case where the targeted leaf is the median one in the comb.

Per cycle, three instruction slots are consumed by the branch and the two compare instructions. This leaves three slots for hoisting instructions of each leaf, or for moving code that precedes the decision tree.

Cost evaluation for `switch` *structures.* Compared to the previous evaluation, the only difference is the number of integer comparisons per node, reduced to one. The cycle costs for a one-way comb implementation, are given in Table 1. Every cycle, only two slots are consumed, leaving four available slots for hoisting.

Table 1. Cost model in cycle for one-way comb implementation in the case of `else if` and `switch` structures. *MpD* depends on the decision tree structure, furthermore it is not a fixed constant for each cost function.

Cost model	Last Leaf	Median Leaf
One-Way `else if`	$c_{oneway,last} = 1 + L + 6MpD$	$c_{oneway,median} = 1 + \lceil \frac{L}{2} \rceil + 6MpD$
One-Way `switch`	$c_{oneway,last} = 1 + L + 6MpD$	$c_{oneway,median} = 1 + \lceil \frac{L}{2} \rceil + 6MpD$

4.4   Cost Evaluation of the One-Way Comb Approach: Analytical

Considering a tree representation, we call L the number of leaves and $\overline{MpD}$ the average *MpD*. Of course, $\overline{MpD}$ depends on the input data; yet we show that the *strongly biased predictions in the comb-shaped implementation makes it almost impossible to find a sequence of decisions leading to bad* average *branch prediction performance.*

Indeed considering a dumb branch predictor always predicting each branch as *not taken*, $\overline{MpD}$ will be equal to 1 on a one-way comb because all branches will always be correctly predicted except the last one. Notice this result is independent of input data.

Consider a more representative branch predictor based on the *2-bit saturating up-down counter* [10] shown in Figure 3; computing $\overline{MpD}$ is more difficult. For a comb, whatever is its initial state, we are going to demonstrate that the average number of mispredictions per decision (i.e bad leaves improperly called due to branches predicted as *taken* or the good leaf not called due to the branch in *not taken* predicted state) is bounded by 1.

We will denote $MpD(i)$ the number of mispredictions for the ith decision, $tk(i)$ the number of 2-bit counters in a *taken* state and $TK(i)$ the number of potential mispredictions considering that the *strongly taken* state allows two possible consecutive mispredictions:[2]

$$0 \leq MpD(i) \leq tk(i)+1 \quad TK(i+1) \leq TK(i) - MpD(i)+1 \quad MpD(i) \leq TK(i)$$

The maximal number of mispredictions per decision is equal to number of branch in *taken* state in the comb plus 1 corresponding to the called leaf potentially in *not taken* state. The counter associated to this called leaf is incremented so the maximal number of possible consecutive mispredictions is decremented by the previous mispredictions and incremented by 1. By induction, one may deduce the following inequality:

$$TK(n+1) \leq n - \sum_{i=1}^{n} MpD(i) \Rightarrow \sum_{i=1}^{n} MpD(i) \leq n - TK(n+1) \leq n$$

For n decisions, the total number of mispredictions is less or equal to n so $\overline{MpD}$ is at most 1 whatever the input data.

---

[2] $TK(i)$ counts predictors in a *weakly taken* state plus twice those in a *strongly taken* state.

4.5   Cost Evaluation of the One-Way Comb Approach: Experimental

However, the previous reasoning does not easily extend to more precise models of the predictor, due to state-space explosion. In some unfortunate cases, it is expected that false sharing and history patterns may actually degrade the prediction rate beyond the 1 misprediction per decision limit. For example, Table 2 shows experimental results on multiple decision tree sizes and on practical distributions (for a one-way comb implementation): the $\overline{MpD}$ varies between 0 and 1.1.

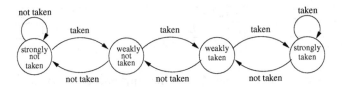

Fig. 3. 2-bit Saturating Up-down Counter

Although the mispredict ratio can be significant — up to 26% — on small decision trees, these experiments confirm that the comb shape keeps the number of mispredictions per decision under control. This result is a good indication that it is possible to design an accurate cost function which does not suffer from input data variability.

Table 2. Branch predictor experimental performance on a one-way comb implementation.

Distribution (sequence of leaf selections)	Correct predictions			Mispredictions per Decision		
	4 leaves	8 leaves	16 leaves	4 leaves	8 leaves	16 leaves
Random	74 %	82 %	88 %	0.9	1.0	1.1
Upwards $(0, 1, \ldots, n)$	99 %	83 %	89 %	0.0	0.9	1.1
Downwards $(n, \ldots, 1, 0)$	99.9 %	88 %	89 %	0.0	0.6	1.1
Up-and-Down $(0, 1, \ldots, n, \ldots, 1, 0)$	96 %	82 %	92 %	0.1	0.8	0.8
Custom (3 *identical then up*)	82 %	85 %	90 %	0.6	0.8	0.9

Notice the highest prediction rates (96 % to 99.9 %) come from the global predictor, which only succeeds in capturing history patterns on small decision trees. The local predictor can act too on the deeper nodes predictions. Because these nodes are called a few times compared to the total number of decisions, this predictor could recognize a period and, therefore, make correct predictions.

5   Generating a Tree of Multiway Conditional Branches

We now detail the additional strategies offered by *multiway conditional branches*. Of course, hoisting, code motion, node reordering and rebalancing can be generalized from the one-way strategies.

Table 3. Cost model in cycle for two-way comb implementation in the case of `else if` and `switch` structures and three-way comb in case of a `switch` structure. MpD value depends on the cost model.

Cost model		Last Leaf	Median Leaf
Two-Way	`else if`	$c_{twoway,last} = 1 + \lceil \frac{L}{2} \rceil + 6MpD$	$c_{twoway,median} = 1 + \lceil \frac{L}{4} \rceil + 6MpD$
Two-Way	`switch`	$c_{twoway,last} = 1 + \lceil \frac{L}{2} \rceil + 6MpD$	$c_{twoway,median} = 1 + \lceil \frac{L}{4} \rceil + 6MpD$
Three Way	`switch`	$c_{threeway,last} = 1 + \lceil \frac{L}{3} \rceil + 6MpD$	$c_{threeway,median} = 1 + \lceil \frac{L}{6} \rceil + 6MpD$
Three Way	`else if`	$c_{threeway,last} = 1 + \lceil \frac{L}{3} \rceil + 6MpD$	$c_{threeway,median} = 1 + \lceil \frac{L}{6} \rceil + 6MpD$

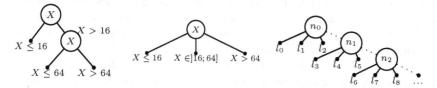

Fig. 4. Merging Nodes in a Decision Tree. (left: not merged, right: merged)   **Fig. 5.** Comb of multiway branches

5.1 Dealing with Multiway Branches

Starting from a binary decision tree, using multiway branches is equivalent to merge internal nodes. Node merging can be combined with hoisting, code motion and modifications of node ordering, see Figure 4; Figure 5 shows a three-way comb.

5.2 Cost Evaluation of the Multiway Comb Approach

Using multi-way branches makes the combs shorter, the MpD is experimentally kept below 1.1, reinforcing the ability to build an accurate cost function. *MpD* depends on the decision tree structure, furthermore it is not a fixed constant for each cost function.

Cost evaluation for `else if` structures. We recall that the conditions of `else if` constructs are assumed to be interval tests requiring two integer comparisons per cycle.

The cycle costs for a two-way comb implementation, for the last leaf and for the median one are displayed in Table 3. Hoisting is not possible because the branches and the four comparison instructions are already using all of the available slots. For the same reason, using three-way branches will yield to the same cost function (but requires two thirds of the predictions of the two-way implementation).

Cost evaluation for `switch` structures. Compared to the previous evaluation, the only difference is the number of integer comparisons per node, which is reduced to one. For a two-way comb implementation, two slots are available for hoisting. In the case of a three-way comb no hoisting is possible. Costs models are detailed in Table 3.

6 Generating Indirect Branches

Indirect branches have not been popular in recent compilers due to the overhead and high unpredictability of such instructions on superscalar processors. Exploring alternative implementations, we show that the delayed branch and predicted execution capabilities of the Itanium make indirect branches very attractive.

6.1   The Basics on a Simple Example

On the Itanium2, an indirect branch implies computing the target address and storing it in one of the branch registers. The execution of this indirect branch is an unconditional jump to the target address. This is a convenient way to implement Fortran `goto`s.

For sake of simplicity, let us start with the simple one-level `switch` structure with four leaves in Figure 6. Assume that the code size of each leaf is less than $64B$ and starts at base address a. First the code for each leaf is allocated to a very specific address: namely $code_k$ is allocated to address $a + k \times 64B$. Such alignment can be performed by `.skip` assembly directives to line-up instructions on a specific boundary.

Now by multiplying the value of x by 64, the value of a relative displacement can be obtained, then added to the instruction pointer and stored in a branch register. A single branch using that computed address will jump directly to the correct leaf.

```
switch(X) {
  case 0:
  | code0; break;
  case 1:
  | code1; break;
  case 2:
  | code2; break;
}
```

```
X*64: compute displacement
Computation of the target address
 ... delay slots
 ... (7+ cycles)
Branch to the computed address
a:    code0;
a+64: code1;
a+128: code2;
```

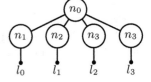

Fig. 6. Target code structures   **Fig. 7.** Indirect linear method

6.2   General One-Level Switch Structures: The Indirect Linear Method

To extend the previous method, it is sufficient to compute the maximum code size over all leaves and to round it to the next power of two. The corresponding code generation strategy is named *indirect linear*. The key advantage of such method is that there is a single branch instruction (always taken) instead of running down a chain of branches. The main drawback is that code layout may be fairly sparse when leaves are disproportionate or when the dispersion of selection constants is too wide.

This problem can often be worked around by using intermediate nodes consisting of a single unconditional branch. This layer of intermediate nodes will reduce the impact on memory. There is a high risk of target address misprediction for these branches when the decision tree is large, because the address prediction tables are far smaller than the outcome prediction ones. Fortunately, the address computation only takes one cycle on the Itanium2 (cf. Section 3). Figure 7 presents an example with a one-level `switch` and intermediate node layer. An alternative followed by ICC consists in storing target addresses in a table, indexed by the value of the `switch` argument. This increases the L1 cache pressure and may lose the benefit from instruction prefetching streams of the previous implementation.

Cost evaluation of the indirect linear method. We implemented a generic version of the indirect linear method in assembly (not shown for lack of space). From this implementation, and assuming a perfect instruction cache locality, the cost of the indirect linear selection of an arbitrary leaf is: $c_{indirect,linear} = 11$.

As explained in Section 3, instruction prefetching is initiated by the assignment to a branch register, therefore, in practice it could be beneficial to extend the delay beyond the minimal time required to update the branch register (7 cycles). Conversely, this code can be further optimized through code motion and hoisting. In the best case, this 7 delay cycles can be concealed, but it means that a large number of instructions must be displaced and possibly speculated (7 cycles x 6 instructions per cycle = 42 instructions).

Inserting an intermediate layer of unconditional branches adds only one or two cycles: the branch and, possibly the address calculation, likely to be mispredicted: $c_{indirect,linear+intermediate} = 13$.

6.3 General One-Level Else If Structures: The Indirect Compare Method

The difficulty in extending the previous technique to `else if` structures is the evaluation of the condition. This is not as simple as with `switch` structures.

First of all, comparisons corresponding to all `else if` conditions have to be performed. From these comparisons, the fastest way to derive a target address is to set a predicate register guarding an `add` instruction to compute the target address. If the comparison is true, the correct target address will be computed, otherwise no operation is performed. Eventually, after all comparisons have been made, an indirect branch always taken will jump to the correct address.

This approach is called the *indirect compare* strategy. In this case, we do not need to make any assumption about the size or layout of the leaves of the tree.

Cost evaluation of the indirect compare method. The cost of the compare indirect can be split in three parts: the cost of all comparisons is $L/3$ (2 comparisons per node, 6 per cycle); the cost of target address updates is $L/6$ (6 additions per cycle); the cost of the branch register assignment, the delay for the indirect branch and its intrinsic latency is $1 + 6 + 2 = 9$. Therefore the cost for the Itanium2 is: $c_{indirect,compare} = \lceil \frac{L}{2} \rceil + 11$.

This formula counts the number of slots used, but the remaining free slots might be filled through (speculative) code motion and hoisting.

Clearly, this strategy is less effective than the indirect linear method in general, because its cost is linear in the size of the decision tree. However, it may be useful for `switch` structures whose dispersion of selection values is too large.

7 Comparison of the Code Generation Strategies

We will now compare the various implementation strategies, taking the impact of hoisting into account. We will provide a worst case evaluation — called *no hoisting* — for which none of the free slots are filled, as well as a best case evaluation — called *hoisting* — assuming all empty slots are filled with useful instructions. For these cost models, we set *MpD* to 1 corresponding to the theoretical worst case when using the decision tree with random data.

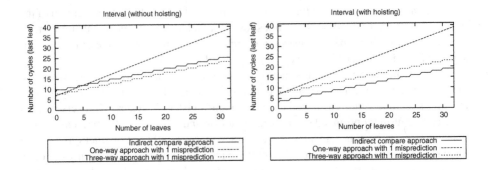

Fig. 8. Cost models comparison for `else if` structures, *last leaf*

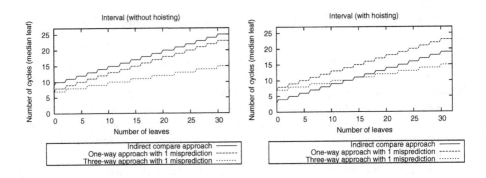

Fig. 9. Cost models comparison for `else if` structures, *median leaf*

7.1 Comparison for Else If Structures

We consider a size-L one-level `else if` structure. The *model-based* cost evaluation for the comb and indirect compare strategies are shown in Figures 8 and 9, respectively for the last and median leaf, and respectively with or without hoisting. The indirect compare method is interesting — especially on small decision trees — when code motion or hoisting can be applied very aggressively (30 to 40 instructions must be moved).

7.2 Comparison for Switch Structures

We consider a size-L one-level `switch` structure. The *model-based* cost evaluation for the comb and indirect linear strategies are shown in Figures 10 and 11, respectively for the last and median leaf, and with or without hoisting, respectively. Without hoisting, the indirect linear strategy leads asymptotically to the most effective implementation, but the merits of the different comb approaches are hard to distinguish on smaller decision trees. This complex interplay advocates for an iterative optimization approach to empirically select the best implementation, which is what the compiler does with Profile Guided Optimizations (PGO). The indirect linear approach benefits much more from code motion and hoisting, when performed aggressively the delay before the indirect branch can be completely concealed. This situation is optimistic but may occur in practice, e.g., when leaves have a many instructions in common, or when the code ahead of the decision tree can be moved into the delay slots.

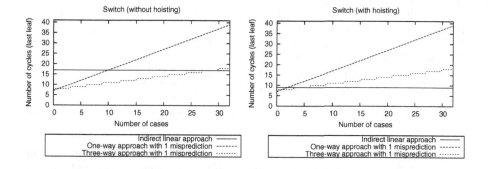

Fig. 10. Cost models comparison for `switch` structures, last leaf

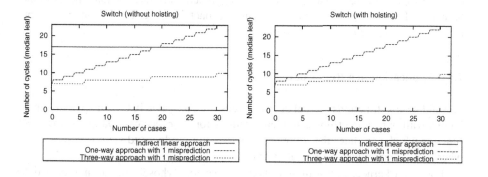

Fig. 11. Cost models comparison for `switch` structures, median leaf

7.3   First Experimental Analysis

We compare here some decision tree implementations. For such study, we considered `switch 16`, `switch 32`, `switch 64` and `else if 9` structures, where all leaves are reduced to a single arithmetic instruction limiting as much as possible the impact of hoisting. Looking at generated codes, rather than a constant degree comb, ICC favored a "mixed-way" approach trading multiway branches for speculative hoisting.

Table 4 compares the codes generated by ICC with different code variants : one-way, two-way, three-way comb and indirect linear variants. Empty cells correspond to irrelevant evaluations. These results clearly show that one-way and two-way combs are sub-optimal, the real confrontation being between ICC, three-way combs and indirect branches code variants. While ICC uses somehow complex heuristics involving combs

Table 4. Experimental Results: Misprediction per Decision and cycle count (random sequences) for a decision tree

		ICC	One-way	Two-way	Three-Way	Indirect compare	Indirect linear
Switch-16	MpD	0.91	1.10	1.05	0.98	n.a.	0
	Cycle count	10.5	16.5	12.3	10.3		11.2
Switch-32	MpD	0.94	1.08	1.06	0.98	n.a.	0
	Cycle count	12.3	24.3	16.5	13.3		11.1
Switch-64	MpD	0.94	1.08	1.05	0.98	n.a.	0
	Cycle count	12.3	40.4	24.4	18.4		11.2
Else-if-9	MpD	0.96	1.05	1.02	0.94	0	n.a.
(intervals)	Cycle count	12.4	13.3	12.3	11.3	16.2	n.a.

and even indirect branches — for a `switch` larger than 17, it can be outperformed by simpler approaches, and in general, the efficiency of hoisting is over-estimated by ICC. In addition, the implementation of indirect branches by ICC uses an intermediate look-up table; this only adds a one-cycle delay on small kernels, but may incur higher penalties on real benchmarks (compared to the linear approach with intermediate unconditional branches). Eventually, the indirect compare approach is less effective than combs, but its code motion potential is much higher.

7.4   Application to a Real Code

To validate cost functions on real decision trees, we compared ICC's Daxpy implementations with our indirect linear implementations for short vectors. Daxpy is a BLAS1 function which computes the following scalar-vector product and sum: $y = \alpha \times x + y$ where α is a scalar, and x and y are vectors.

For small kernels performing a Daxpy on vectors whose sizes do not exceed 16 elements, ICC generated a comb structure, mixing one-way and two-way branches. Empty slots are filled with hoisted instructions (mainly addresses computations). Over 16 elements, ICC generated an indirect branch version with hoisting where target leaf address is stored in a look-up table. But it failed use the delay cycles between the branch register update and the branch instruction for hoisting.

We implement three versions of indirect linear Daxpy with an increasing exploitation of delay slots to perform hoisting. `Hoist_adr` uses some of the delay slots to compute array addresses necessary for computations in each leaf. `Hoist_adr_load` derives from Hoist_adr, all the 16 loads on y and x are now hoisted. `Hoist_adr_load_fma` derives from `Hoist_adr_load`, some of the floating point multiply adds required to compute a vector element are now hoisted.

With such aggressive hoisting, leaves only contain floating point arithmetics and stores instructions. Note that in `Hoist_adr_load` and `Hoist_adr_load_fma` versions, special care was required to avoid potential load exception (which can be done using speculative load instructions of the Itanium2).

Table 5. Performance Gain (in %) of indirect versions over ICC with random vector size. For `switch 16`, ICC generates a comb shape decision tree while for `switch 17` it relies on indirect branch.

Indirect Linear	ICC `switch 16`		ICC `switch 17`	
	Cycles (vs ICC)	Gain	Cycles (vs ICC)	Gain
Hoist_adr	45.1 (53.5)	15.6 %	45.1 (53.9)	16.3 %
Hoist_adr_load	35.4 (53.5)	33.8 %	35.4 (53.9)	34.3 %
Hoist_adr_load_fma	31.8 (53.5)	40.6 %	31.8 (53.9)	41 %

Table 5 summarizes performance improvements of our indirect linear versions over ICC. All these indirect linear versions outperform the ICC version from 15.6% to 40%. The performance gain comes from two combined factors :

- Filling up the delay slots allows to execute up to 32 loads and to avoid a misprediction due to wrong branch target address.
- Instructions in leaves were scheduled in a better way than what the compiler did.

It is important to note that in Hoist_adr, performance improvement mainly comes from the instructions rescheduling within the leaves whereas for Hoist_adr_load and Hoist_adr_load_fma versions, performance gain really comes from their hoisting capabilities.

Additionally, our indirect linear versions also surpassed ICC indirect version (switch 17) which uses look-up table because the compiler failed to exploit delay slots for hoisting to compute the target address or to hoist other kind of instruction. We obtained similar results (with a slightly narrower gap with ICC) on a Copy kernel.

8   Conclusion

Studying the Itanium2 architecture, we show that the complexity of the branch mechanism does not hamper the design of accurate cost models, in the special case of decision trees. We build simple models that are both accurate and relatively independent of the input data. Based on these models, we compare the most significant code generation strategies for the Itanium processor family: tree of multiway conditional branches, indirect branch with predicated comparisons, and indirect branch with linear-computation of the target address. We show that no strategy dominates in all cases. Relying on this study we develop a simple kernel outperforming from 15% to 40% a state-of-the-art compiler such as the Intel ICC compiler.

Future works include the design of finer cost models, defining more precisely the impact of hoisting and code motion. Robustness toward either instruction cache locality or statistical distribution are also hot topic of interest. On the long run we also wish to extend our work to multiple levels of nested decision trees, and to integrate our cost models and implementation strategies in an adaptive automatic optimization tool.

Acknowledgments. This work is supported by research grants from CEA DAM, Bruyres-le-Chtel, Bull Les Clayes-sous-Bois and the French Ministry of Research.

References

1. A. Aho, R. Sethi, and J. Ullman. *Compilers: Principles, Techniques and Tools*. Addison-Wesley, 1986.
2. A. Ertl and D. Gregg. Optimizing indirect branch prediction accuracy in virtual machine interpreters. In *ACM Symp. on Programming Language Design and Implementation (PLDI'03)*, San Diego, California, June 2003.
3. P. Faraboschi, G. Brown, J. A. Fisher, G. Desoli, and F. Homewood. Lx: a technology platform for customizable VLIW embedded processing. In *ACM and IEEE Intl. Symp. on Computer Architecture (ISCA'00)*, Vancouver, BC, June 2000.
4. *Intel IA-64 Architecture Software Developer's Manual, Volume 3: Instruction Set Reference*, revision 2.1 edition.
   `http://developer.intel.com/design/itanium/family`.
5. X. Li, M.-J. Garzaran, and D. Padua. A dynamically tuned sorting library. In *ACM Conference on Code Generation and Optimization (CGO'04)*, Palo Alto, California, Mar. 2004.
6. C. McNairy and D. Soltis. Itanium 2 processor microarchitecture. *IEEE Micro*, pages 44–55, Mar./Apr. 2003.
7. Open research compiler. `http://ipf-orc.sourceforge.net`.
8. H. Packard. Inside the intel itanium 2 processor: an itanium processor family member for balanced performance over a wide range of applications. White paper, Hewlett Packard, July 2002.
9. Philips Semiconductors, Sunnyvale, CA. *TriMedia Compilation System, v.2.1 User and Reference Manual*, 1999.
10. T. Y. Yeh and Y. N. Patt. Alternative implementations of two-level adaptive branch prediction. In *19th International Symposium on Computer Architecture*, pages 124–134, Gold Coast, Australia, 1992. ACM and IEEE CS.

Extending the Applicability of Scalar Replacement to Multiple Induction Variables*

Nastaran Baradaran, Pedro C. Diniz, and Joonseok Park

University of Southern California/Information Sciences Institute,
4676 Admiralty Way, Suite 1001,
Marina del Rey, California 90292, USA
{nastaran, pedro, joonseok}@isi.edu

Abstract. Scalar replacement or register promotion uses scalar variables to save data that can be reused across loop iterations, leading to a reduction of the number of memory operations at the expense of a possibly large number of registers. In this paper we present a compiler data reuse analysis capable of uncovering and exploiting reuse opportunities for array references that exhibit Multiple-Induction-Variable (MIV) subscripts, beyond the reach of current data reuse analysis techniques. We present experimental results of the application of scalar replacement to a sample set of kernel codes targeting a programmable hardware computing device — a Field-Programmable-Gate-Array (FPGA). The results show that, for memory bound designs, scalar replacement alone leads to speedups that range between 2x to 6x at the expense of an increase in the FPGA design area in the range of 6x to 20x.

1 Introduction

Scalar replacement or *register promotion* is an important technique for computing systems with high memory latency and/or limited opportunities to mitigate it. This transformation replaces an array reference by a scalar to be mapped to a hardware register. Subsequent accesses to the data take advantage of the high availability of a register thereby eliminating cache memory or even external memory accesses.

Array variables with affine subscript functions in loop nests are ideal candidates for *scalar replacement*. Their data access patterns are very *regular* and can be summarized in well known abstractions developed in the context of data dependence analysis for high-performance compilation. For loops whose bounds are known at compile time, possibly by the application of loop tiling, the compiler can understand the reuse pattern of a given array reference and save the data in registers for reuse in subsequent iterations of the loop.

---

* This work is supported by the National Science Foundation (NSF) under Grants 0209228 and 0204040. Any opinions, findings, and conclusions or recommendations expressed in this material are those of the author(s) and do not necessarily reflect the views of the NSF.

R. Eigenmann et al. (Eds.): LCPC 2004, LNCS 3602, pp. 455–469, 2005.

The increasing high-cost of cache memories, both in area (for increased associativity) and power, makes it attractive to take advantage of high-capacity RAM blocks, as currently seen in emerging reconfigurable architectures. A compiler can exploit scalar replacement for array variables by explicitly managing and mapping the required scalars to a combination of registers and RAM blocks. In this context the compiler can also exploit internal memory bandwidth availability by distributing array data between multiple RAM blocks, while mitigating the complexity impact of using a large number of scalar variables in traditional register allocation algorithms.

In this paper we extend the previous work on *scalar replacement* for array variables by addressing the very challenging case of Multiple-Induction-Variables (MIVs) subscript functions. We developed a framework that examines data *self-reuse* using *reuse vectors*, as a refinement of the previous approaches that use *dependence distance* abstractions [1]. The refinement of the analysis framework is required to accurately capture the reuse in MIVs, which would otherwise be lost in the summarization used in current approaches.

This paper makes the following specific contributions:

- It presents a data reuse analysis framework based on *reuse vectors* to capture the *self-reuse* opportunities for array variables with affine MIV subscript functions in perfectly nested loops.
- Describes how to compute the number of registers required to capture the *self data* reuse of MIV array references across any level of the loop nest.
- Presents experimental results of the application of *scalar replacement* to a sample set of image/signal processing kernels that exhibit array references with MIVs targeting custom hardware implementation on Field-Programmable-Gate-Arrays (FPGAs).

The results presented here show that by exploiting self-reuse the hardware implementation eliminates a very large portion of the memory operations. This leads to a substantial performance improvement of up to 6x over an implementation that does not exploit the reuse. This improvement however comes at the cost of extra space for storing data. In some cases the extra space might be prohibitive leading to the need for compilers to develop good cost/benefit metrics that can allow them to gage the aggressiveness of the application of such transformation. The data reuse analysis presented in this paper enables the compiler to make time-space and cost-benefit trade-off analysis to evaluate which variables, and at which loop level, should be scalar replaced.

This paper is structured as follows. Section 2 illustrates a motivating example for the data reuse in the presence of MIVs. Section 3 describes the core of the reuse analysis using *reuse vectors* and explains the differences between the reuse in SIV (Single-Induction-Variable) and MIV subscripts. Section 4 represents the analytical formulas that indicate the number of registers required to capture the reuse at various levels of a loop nest along with a code generation scheme. In section 5 we present preliminary experimental results. We discuss related work in section 6 and then conclude in section 7.

2   Motivating Example

We now present an example of the application of scalar replacement to a computation that exhibits both SIV and MIVs, a Finite Impulse Response (FIR) computation. The computation is presented in figure 1(a) in C and is structured as a perfectly nested loop reading two array variables coeff and scan. For each iteration of the i loop, the computation reads N consecutive values of the coeff array and N consecutive values of the scan array.

To uncover the reuse opportunities in this example, a compiler examines the data access patterns of the references coeff[j] and scan[i+j]. For coeff[j], a compiler can understand that the same data element is accessed for the same loop iteration of j in every iteration of i. As such, the N values of coeff can be saved in registers during the execution of the first iteration of the i loop and reused in the subsequent iterations of that loop. The reference scan[i+j] reuses the same data element for every combination of the iterations $\{i,j\}$ such that i+j assumes the same value. Across iterations of the j loop the set of indices generated by the i+j indexing function are *shifted* by one element. As a result, from the N values read for scan in every iteration of i, $N-1$ values could be saved for the next iteration (as illustrated in figure 1(b)). As a result of saving data in registers, the code would require a total of $3N - 1$ read operations as opposed to $2N^2$ in the original computation, a substantial reduction. In fact, and for this specific example, this is the minimal number of memory read operations since each value required for the computation is only read once.

This example illustrates the kind of computation that the reuse analysis described in this paper is designed to handle. The compiler examines and uncovers

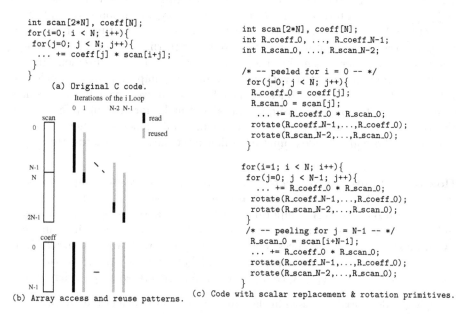

```
int scan[2*N], coeff[N];
for(i=0; i < N; i++){
  for(j=0; j < N; j++){
    ... += coeff[j] * scan[i+j];
  }
}
```
(a) Original C code.

(b) Array access and reuse patterns.

```
int scan[2*N], coeff[N];
int R_coeff_0, ..., R_coeff_N-1;
int R_scan_0, ..., R_scan_N-2;

/* -- peeled for i = 0 -- */
for(j=0; j < N; j++){
  R_coeff_0 = coeff[j];
  R_scan_0 = scan[j];
  ... += R_coeff_0 * R_scan_0;
  rotate(R_coeff_N-1,...,R_coeff_0);
  rotate(R_scan_N-2,...,R_scan_0);
}

for(i=1; i < N; i++){
  for(j=0; j < N-1; j++){
    ... += R_coeff_0 * R_scan_0;
    rotate(R_coeff_N-1,...,R_coeff_0);
    rotate(R_scan_N-2,...,R_scan_0);
  }
  /* -- peeling for j = N-1 -- */
  R_scan_0 = scan[i+N-1];
  ... += R_coeff_0 * R_scan_0;
  rotate(R_coeff_N-1,...,R_coeff_0);
  rotate(R_scan_N-2,...,R_scan_0);
}
```
(c) Code with scalar replacement & rotation primitives.

Fig. 1. Scalar replacement example in the presence of MIV variables

the reuse associated with each data reference and utilizes the scalar replacement to save values in registers across loop iterations. In the following sections we describe the analysis and code generation schemes that a compiler can use to perform the scalar replacement outlined in this example.

3   Reuse Analysis

We now describe the foundation of our reuse analysis, *reuse vectors*, that a compiler can use to understand which data elements are reused across which iterations of a loop nest. We describe how to determine these reuse vectors for the cases of SIV and MIV involving two or more induction variables.

3.1   Assumptions and Definitions

In this work we focus on data reuse analysis for array references whose subscripts are affine functions of the enclosed loop indices and constant loop bounds for perfectly or quasi-perfect nested loops. The iteration space of an `n-level` perfectly nested loops is represented by $I = (i_1, \ldots, i_n)$, where i_1 and i_n are respectively the outermost and innermost loops.

For affine references, the subscript indexing is represented as in a matrix form as $HI + C$, where H is the access matrix denoting the coefficient of the various index variables for each array reference dimension, I represents the iteration space vector, and C is a constant offset vector. The subscript function in each array dimension can define a Zero Induction Variable (ZIV) as in $A[0][1]$, a Single Induction Variable (SIV) as in $A[i+1][k]$, or a Multiple Induction Variable (MIV) as in $A[i + j][k]$. In terms of the H matrix, an array dimension subscript leads to a ZIV, SIV, or MIV, respectively if it has zero, one, or multiple nonzero coefficients in the corresponding dimensions row. We further impose a separability[1] requirement in order to simplify the code generation. This requirement greatly simplifies the implementation without substantially compromising its applicability. In the domain of kernel codes we have focused on, we have not seen a single example where the indices were not separable. Finally for multiple references to the same array we constrain our analysis to uniformly-generated references, *i.e.,* references whose array index functions differ in at most the constant terms.

How to Compute Reuse Vectors?. A *temporal data reuse*, or simply *temporal reuse*, occurs when the same array data item is accessed in two or more points in the iteration space. A temporal reuse is called a *self-reuse* if the reuse is induced by the same data reference and is called *group-reuse* if it is induced by two distinct array references. Given a reference A with access matrix H, its *self-reuse* occurs for distinct iterations I_1 and I_2 that satisfy the *reuse equation*: $I_2 - I_1 = \Delta I \in Null(H)$. Given two uniformly-generated array references, a

---

[1] A given index variable is used in the subscript of at most one of the dimensions of the array.

```
for(i=1; i < N; i++){
  for(j=1; j < N; j++){
    A[i][j] = A[i-1][j+1];
    C[i+j] = C[i+j+2];
    for(k=0; k < N; k++){
      D[2j+4k] = E[i+k] + B[i+j+k];
    }
  }
}
```

Fig. 2. Example code

group reuse occurs for iterations that satisfy the *reuse equation*: I_1 and I_2 if $I_2 - I_1 = \Delta I \in Null(H) + C$, where C is a vector satisfying $HC = C_2 - C_1$ (C_1 and C_2 are the constant offsets of the two references).

The solutions to the reuse equations above characterize the reuse space defined as the $Null(H)$ or $Null(H) + C$, and the basis that span these spaces are the *reuse vectors*. These vectors are selected to be always lexicographically positive as their linear combination will lead to feasible reuse distances. The number and structure of the reuse vectors depend on the structure of H itself. The dimension of $Null(H)$ is equal to $(n-r)$ where n and r are respectively the number of variables (columns) and independent rows (rank) of the matrix H. Each reuse vector, represented as $r = (r_1, \ldots, r_n)$, dictates the minimum iterations distance *along a set of loops* between reuses, as references can have more than a single reuse vector. For a reuse vector r we define $level(r)$ as the outermost non-zero element of r. For a given reference and loop level k, there exists at most one reuse vector r with $level(r) = k$ (proof omitted here). For vectors with more than one non-zero element, say at levels k_1 and k_2, the reuse is carried by the outermost k_1 loop and we say that level k_1 is *coupled* with k_2. For *group-reuse* the reuse space is characterized by the composition of two sets of reuse vectors. One set consists of the *self-reuse* vectors of each uniformly generated reference, whereas the other set (not necessarily orthogonal to the first set) consists of a set of *group-reuse* vectors derived by solving the *group-reuse* equations. In many cases the *group-reuse* space is simply defined by the composition of a constant vector with the space generated by the *self-reuse* vector. For example for array C in figure 2, this space is a composition of $(0, 2)$ with $(1, -1)$.

3.2   Reuse Vectors for SIV and MIV Subscripts

For an array reference with SIV indexing functions, we have n loop index variables and m free variables[2]. Matrix H has $(n - m)$ independent rows generating $n - (n - m) = m$ reuse vectors, each corresponding to one of the array's free variables. These vectors are in the form of elementary vectors e_k where k is the level of a free variable. In case of *group-reuse* between any two references with SIV indexing functions, the reuse vectors are defined by the linear combination of the *self-reuse* vectors of the uniformly-generated reference and the *group-reuse*

---

[2] A free variable for array A is a loop index that does not appear in any of the arrays' subscripts and therefore corresponds to a zero column in H matrix of A.

vectors. In the SIV case, the non-constant *group-reuse* vectors are a subset of the *self-reuse* vectors as the references are uniformly generated (proof omitted).

In case of *self-reuse* in an MIV array with n variables and m free variables, there are m reuse vectors corresponding to each free variable as well as $(s-1)$ vectors for each MIV subscript with s variables. Further, each reuse vector corresponding to an MIV subscript has exactly two nonzero elements. This structure of vectors is due to the assumption of separability. Since the subscripts are separable, all the rows in matrix H are independent and therefore each row with s variables results in $(s-1)$ vectors with two nonzero coefficients. Array D in the example code in figure 2 has reuse vectors of the form $(0, 2, -1)$ and $(1, 0, 0)$, corresponding to the MIV subscript $[2j + 4k]$ and the free variable i.

3.3   Reuse Vectors Versus Distance Vectors

A distance vector in an **n-level** loop nest is an **n-dimensional** vector that represents the difference between the iteration vectors of two dependent array references [7]. The elements of this vector are either a constant (constant difference), a '+' (all positive differences), or '*' (unknown difference). In case of SIV subscripts, the distance vector could give enough information as to where the reuse occurs. For example in figure 1(a), array `coeff` has a distance vector $(+, 0)$, which indicates a reuse at the same iteration of j for all iterations of i. However in case of MIVs, the distance vector does not provide exact information. In figure 1, array `scan` has distance vectors $(0, 0), (+, *)$. None of these vectors capture the relation between i and j when reuse occurs. Reuse vectors as defined in this paper on the other hand, not only indicate the relation between the variables in an MIV subscript, but also capture the exact iteration difference. In figure 1, the $(1, -1)$ reuse vector precisely captures the relation between iterations of i and j for reuses of the `scan` array.

4   Scalar Replacement

We now show how to use *self-reuse* vectors to determine the number of registers required to capture reuse for a given MIV array reference at a specific loop nest level. We also outline a code generation algorithm for scalar replacement.

4.1   Reuse Vectors and Scalar Replacement

For a given array reference, the reuse analysis determines the set of *reuse vectors* that span the *self-reuse* space for that reference. Each reuse vector defines the minimal distance between the iterations of a reference and its reuse. In general if a reuse is carried by level k (the outermost non-zero level), the data accessed by the inner loop levels needs to be saved for future reuse. An elementary reuse vector e_k means that the data accessed by the array reference is invariant with respect to the loop at level k, and therefore some reuse (not necessarily the outermost) is carried at this level. Array references with ZIV and SIV have exclusively elementary vectors as part of their *self-reuse* space (proof omitted).

The interpretation of a *self-reuse* vector with two non-zero elements (exclusive for MIV cases) is more complex. A reuse vector $(0, \ldots, \alpha, \ldots, -\beta, \ldots, 0)$, with α and β at levels k_1 and k_2, indicates that the data item accessed at the current iteration is first reused α iterations later at the loop at level k_1 and β iterations earlier at the loop at level k_2. This means that the loop at level k_1 carries the reuse, but the data is reused at an *offseted* iteration of the loop at level k_2. Overall, the set of reuse vectors define the various loop levels at which reuse occurs as well as which loop levels are *coupled*. Using this information, a compiler algorithm can understand the relationship between the data reuse and other loop transformations, as they might affect the iteration distance between reuses and hence the number of required registers to capture the full amount of reuse opportunities. Analyses that rely on aggregate dependence distance vectors cannot inherently represent the coupling between loop levels in MIV references.

4.2   Computing the Number of Required Registers

An important aspect of scalar replacement is to determine the number of registers required to capture the reuse of a given array reference. Compilers can use this metric along with the number of saved memory accesses to adjust the aggressiveness of scalar replacement in the presence of limited number of registers to a subset of the array references based on a cost-benefit measure.

In this description we make use of the auxiliary function γ_{k_i} for a given array reference ref and loop level k_i, as well as $Reg(l)$ the number of required registers for exploiting data reuse along all reuse vectors with $level(r) \geq l$ both defined below. Here $\mathcal{I}(k_i)$ denotes the number of iterations executed by the loop at index k_i. In the remainder of this section we present symbolic expressions for the function $R(l)$, denoting the number of registers required to exploit the reuse for all loops at level l or below under several scenarios.

$$Reg(l) = Max(R(k)) \text{ where } l \leq k \leq n, \text{ AND } \exists\, r \text{ st. } level(r) = k$$

$$\gamma_{k_i} = \begin{cases} \mathcal{I}(k_i) & \text{if } k_i \in \text{Subscript(ref)} \\ 1 & \text{otherwise} \end{cases} \tag{1}$$

MIV Subscripts with Two Variables. For an array reference of the form $[a * i_{k_1} + b * i_{k_2} + c]$, the reuse analysis uncovers a reuse vector (along with possibly many other vectors) with two non-zero entries at levels k_1 and k_2 that is of the form $r = (\underbrace{0, \ldots, 0}_{k_1 - 1}, b/\gcd(a,b), \underbrace{0, \ldots, 0}_{k_2 - k_1 - 1}, -a/\gcd(a,b), \underbrace{0, \ldots, 0}_{n - k_2})$. As an example, array D in figure 2 has a reuse vector of $(0, 2, -1)$ carrying reuse at the level j, in addition to the vector $(1, 0, 0)$ carrying reuse at the level i.

For a reuse vector r of this form, with non-zero values of $\alpha = b/\gcd(a,b)$ and $\beta = -a/\gcd(a,b)$ at levels k_1 and k_2, the number of required registers to exploit the reuse at level k_1 and all the loop level enclosed within k_1 is the number of distinct solutions to the reuse equations as described in section 3.1. While in general this problem can be solved using general frameworks such as Presburger formulas [4], for the special cases of loops with symbolically constant bounds, the number of such solutions is given by the equations below. In this equations we distinguish various levels of reuse relative to k_1, the reuse level of vector r.

$$R(k) = \begin{cases} \displaystyle\prod_{l=k+1}^{n} \gamma_l & \text{if } k > k_1 \\ \displaystyle\alpha \left[\prod_{l=k_1+1}^{k_2-1} \gamma_l \times (\mathcal{I}(k_2) - \mid \beta \mid) \times \prod_{l=k_2+1}^{n} \gamma_l \right] & \text{if } k = k_1 \\ \displaystyle\prod_{l=k+1, l \neq k_1, k_2}^{n} \gamma_l \times [\alpha \mathcal{I}(k_2) + (\mathcal{I}(k_1) - \alpha) \mid \beta \mid] & \text{if } k < k_1 \end{cases} \quad (2)$$

The first case occurs when the reuse is being exploited at a loop level inside the reuse level carried by r. As such the index variable at loop level k_1 remains constant and the total number of memory locations accessed is simply dictated by the index variables present in the subscript functions for the array reference. This is, essentially the SIV reuse case. The second case, for a reuse level k_1, dictates that we need a number that is given by the bound of the loop at level k_2 with the exception of the values accessed by the first β iterations. For the indices at the k_1 level, the number of distinct values are repeated after α iterations of the loop at level k_1, but need to be *offseted* by β for all loop levels nested below level k_2. Finally, for a level lower than k_1, *i.e.*, for a loop outside the loop at level k_1, one needs to accumulate all the values accessed by the combination of the indices at level k_1 and k_2. The number of such distinct combinations is $[\alpha \mathcal{I}(k_2) + (\mathcal{I}(k_1) - \alpha) \mid \beta \mid]$ as all but β values can be reused after the first α iterations of the k_1 loop. The other factors in the equations capture the presence of a given loop index variable in the subscript functions dictating the number of different elements. Notice that the number of registers for the scenario with $k = k_1$ does not reflect any possible reuse in a loop with index l between k_1 and k_2. If this is the case, the number of registers required for level k_1 is dictated by the number of required registers at l. This is the case for the array E in figure 2. Given that the $\mathcal{I}(k)$ distinct values are not immediately reused in the i loop, but rather in the j loop, all $\mathcal{I}(k)$ values need to be saved. As such the actual number of registers for a specific level, taking into account all reuse vectors, is calculated as the maximum value across all vectors as noted in (1).

We also note that for SIV subscripts the analysis presented above is greatly simplified. For SIV references the reuse analysis uncovers one elementary reuse vector e_{k_i} for each loop nest level, for which the corresponding loop index variable is not included in any of the array reference subscripts. This elementary reuse vector is a particular case of the MIV reuse vector with $k_1 = k_2 = k$ and $\alpha = 1/\gcd(0,1) = 1$ and $\beta = 0/\gcd(0,1) = 0$ yielding to $R(k) = \prod_{l=k+1}^{n} \gamma_l$.

MIV Subscripts with More Than Two Variables. For an array reference of the form $[a_1 i_{k_1} + a_2 i_{k_2} + \ldots + a_s i_{k_s}]$, the reuse analysis uncovers $(s-1)$ reuse vectors representing the $(s-1)$ levels of reuse, namely $k_1, k_2, \ldots, k_{s-1}$, for which there are s kernel representations. As an example, array B in figure 2 has three possible kernel representations, respectively $\{(1,-1,0),(0,1,-1)\}$, $\{(1,0,-1),$ $(0,1,-1)\}$ and $\{(1,-1,0),(1,0,-1)\}$. In order to preserve the coupling between variables in the loop, the analysis keeps a union of all the possible reuse vectors. There are a total of s individual vectors in the set of all possible reuse vectors, each having only two nonzero elements (due to separability), and each two vectors having a common nonzero level. In the above example the analysis keeps the 3 reuse vectors $\{(1,-1,0),(1,0,-1),(0,1,-1)\}$. The non-zero levels in this group of vectors specify the coupled levels. In this example level i is coupled with level j while level j is coupled with level k. We reduce this scenario to the case of a subscript with only two variables by choosing one of the s reuse vectors in the set. In effect, we ignore possible opportunities of reuse along other loops.

4.3   Limitations of Current Analysis

Equations (2) are used to derive the number of required registers for a specific loop level taking into account the reuse along one vector with two non-zero entries. For array references with more than one reuse vector with two non-zero elements, using these equations leads to an *upper bound* on the number of registers as its ignores reuse opportunities along other vectors. For *self-reuse*, either by input or output references, this approach simply means the compiler will miss some opportunities for eliminating memory accesses. For *group-reuse* (not addressed here), where one of the references is a *read* operation and the other is a *write* operation, ignoring opportunities of reuse means that the scalar replaced implementation can use the wrong data value. In addition to these limitations, we cannot handle more intricate references with non-separable subscripts such as $A[i+2j+3k][j+k]$ in a (i, j, k) loop nest. Using equations (2) and considering one of the MIVs independent of the others leads to incorrect results. Fortunately, these instances do not occur often, if hardly at all, in practice.

4.4   Code Generation

A complete description of the compiler code generation for exploiting the opportunities of *self-reuse* in the presence of MIVs is beyond the scope of this paper. Instead, we outline the basic principles for a code generation scheme that uses *loop peeling* to initialize and terminate the values of the various data references in registers when applying scalar replacement. We then illustrate the application of this scheme to the example in section 2.

Overall the idea of *loop peeling* is to structure a loop nest into three phases. A first phase where the computation loads data into registers; a second phase where the computation uses data previously loaded into registers, and a third phase where the results of the computation are written to memory. For a reference exhibiting *input self-reuse*, *i.e.*, a read operation, the last phase is absent. For this case, pre-peeling of the first iteration(s) of the loop that carries the reuse is used to load the data into registers. For a reference exhibiting *output self-reuse, i.e.,* a write operation, the transformed code uses back-peeling of the last iteration(s) to save data to memory. For a given loop and for a given array variable, these phases might be defined at different levels of the nest which makes the code generation scheme elaborate. The generated code also makes use of a *register rotation* primitive to position the data to be reused at the correct register while saving the data to be reused later, with the added benefit of eliminating any register addressing for the reused items. In a register-based architecture, rotating values across N registers requires N+1 instructions and N+1 registers, possibly a questionable implementation choice. Instead, a FIFO queue implementation with two pointer registers might be a much more suitable strategy. For FPGAs, and given the flexibility in the interconnection of registers, implementing a rotation across N registers can be accomplished in a single clock cycle. We use register *rotation* and *loop peeling* as a conceptual illustrative scheme. In practice the implementation can vary according to the specific target architecture.

For simplicity we focus on a single *input* reference with a single MIV reuse vector. The code generation scheme follows the three scenarios presented in section 4 for a MIV reuse vector with non-zero elements α and β at loop levels k_1 and k_2, respectively. To capture reuse at level $k > k_1$ the code peels the first iteration of the loop k. For the loop nest in this peeled section, the code reads data from memory, uses it in the computation and at the end of each iteration, rotates the data through registers so that in the next iteration of loop k the same data is ready to be reused at the same register locations. In the non-peeled iterations of k the code uses the data from the set of registers and rotates the values at each iteration. For a reuse level $k = k_1$ the generated code peels α iterations of the loop k_1. For each of these iterations the code will use a distinct set of $\mathcal{I}(k_2) - |\beta|$ registers. For each of the iterations of the inner loop, in this case for simplicity loop k_2, in the peeled section of the code the code rotates the values in each set. Since there are $\mathcal{I}(k_2)$ iterations in k_2 and only $\mathcal{I}(k_2) - |\beta|$ registers, this scheme effectively discards the first β values in the registers. For the non-peeled section of the k_1 loop, the code must now back-peel the last β iterations of the k_2 loop in order to fetch a set of β values. The code in figure 1(c) reflects these transformations for the example in figure 1(a). Finally, for the case where $k < k_1$ the code must accumulate all the values accessed in the iterations of the k_1 and k_2 loops. The loop nest is peeled for a single iteration of the k loop, followed by the peeling of the first α iterations of k_1. In this first peeled section the code reads the entire $\alpha \times \mathcal{I}(k_2)$ values into the α sets of registers while rotating. For the non-peeled section of loop k_1 the code in loop k_2 rotates values between the last $\mathcal{I}(k_2)$ elements of each set in the k_2 loop while adding β new elements in the last iteration(s) of the loop k_2. With these combined rotations the data can be reused in registers at the non-peeled iterations of the k loop.

5   Experimental Results

We validated the analysis presented in section 4 and observed the impact of using scalar replacement on hardware custom designs realized on an FPGA device.

Kernels Codes. For this evaluation we used a small set of kernel codes: a Decimation Filter (`Dec-FIR`), a pattern-matching computation (`PAT`) and a binary image correlation (`BIC`) computation. The `Dec-FIR` kernel computes the convolution of a 1024-long vector of 12-bit values against a 32-bit long sequence of coefficients structured as a 2-deep nested loop. The decimation factor for this FIR computation is 2, which means there is reuse between the *even* and *odd* iterations of the inner most loop in the nest. The `PAT` kernel searches for a specific 8-character pattern in a string. A set of 8 character string is compared one character at a time for a match. It is also structured as a 2-deep nested loop. The pattern string is loop invariant with respect to the outermost loop and because of a sliding window matching scheme there are opportunities for reusing most of the input data in a scheme similar to the one presented in the example code in section 2. Finally, the `BIC` computation implements a binary image correlation using a smaller template mask image. The computation scans the larger input image by sliding the mask image along two dimensions, and computing the aggregated sum for the input image values corresponding to locations in the mask that are non-zero. This computation is structured as a 4-deep loop nest and there are large opportunities for data reuse due to the sliding window scheme.

Methodology and Implementation. We have implemented the reuse analysis described in section 4 in SUIF taking advantage of the SUIFMath library. For each of the kernel codes, written in plain C, we used the results of our analysis and the code generation scheme outlined in section 4 to manually generate a scalar replaced version of each kernel in C. Next we used a `suif2vhdl` tool (developed as part of our research infrastructure) to automatically translate C/SUIF code to behavioral VHDL, which we then converted into a structural VHDL designs using Mentor Graphics' Monet™ high-level synthesis tool. We then used Synplify Pro 6.2 and Xilinx ISE 4.1i tool sets for logic synthesis and Place-and-Route (P&R) targeting a Xilinx Virtex™ XCV 1K BG560 device. After P&R we extracted the real area and clock rate for each design and used the number of cycles derived from simulation of the structural design with the memory latency information of our target FPGA board (read latency of 6 cycles and write latency of 1 cycle) to calculate wall-clock execution time.

Note that although the execution of the various loops in the hardware designs generated by VHDL exploits software pipelining techniques, the memory operations are not themselves pipelined. This leads to designs that are essentially memory-bound, an therefore ideal candidates to benefit from scalar replacement. For compute-bound designs it is expected that scalar replacement would have less performance impact except for a reduction in memory traffic.

All of our sample kernels have one array variable with an SIV subscript and a second array variable with an MIV subscript, both of which exhibit opportunities for *self-reuse* that can be captured by scalar replacement. In order to compare the effect of scalar replacement for different variables, we created 4 code versions. Version v1 is the original base code with no scalar replacement. Versions v2 and v3 denote the versions where scalar replacement is exclusively applied to SIV and

MIV variables respectively. Finally, in version v4 scalar replacement is applied to both SIV and MIV variables.

Results. Table 1 presents the results of the data reuse analysis for each of the kernel codes and its various versions. The third column depicts the reuse vectors exploited in each code version. The forth column includes the number of registers required to fully capture the data reuse, in all cases this reuse being exploited across the outermost loop level. Finally, the table presents the number of memory accesses along with a simple register efficiency metric defined as $\Delta(MemoryAccess)/\Delta(Registers)$ with respect to version v1.

Table 1. Reuse analysis and reduction on memory accesses results

Kernel	Code version	Reuse Vectors SIV	Reuse Vectors MIV	Registers	Memory Accesses	Reduction (%)	Register Efficiency
Dec-FIR	v1	—	—	2	32768	—	—
	v2	$(1,0)$	—	17	16400	49.5	1091
	v3	—	$(2,-1)$	31	17438	46.7	528
	v4	$(1,0)$	$(2,-1)$	46	1070	96.7	720
PAT	v1	—	—	2	4096	—	—
	v2	$(1,0)$	—	9	2064	49.6	290
	v3	—	$(1,-1)$	8	2320	43.3	296
	v4	$(1,0)$	$(1,-1)$	15	271	93.3	294
BIC	v1	—	—	2	8192	—	—
	v2	$\begin{cases}(0,1,0,0)\\(1,0,0,0)\end{cases}$	—	17	4112	49.8	272
	v3	—	$\begin{cases}(0,1,0,-1)\\(1,0,-1,0)\end{cases}$	13	5312	35.1	261
	v4	$\begin{cases}(0,1,0,0)\\(1,0,0,0)\end{cases}$	$\begin{cases}(0,1,0,-1)\\(1,0,-1,0)\end{cases}$	28	1232	84.9	267

As expected scalar replacement dramatically reduces the number of memory accesses (read operations in the case of these kernels). For the cases where a single array reference is scalar replaced (v2 and v3), the reduction values range between 40% and 50% whereas in the more aggressive cases of v4 it can reach values of more than 95%, in all cases with very modest number of registers. As a consequence, the register efficiency metric shows a high numeric value.

Figure 3 depicts the results that illustrate the practical impact of scalar replacement in the overall hardware design size, attained clock rate, and overall speedup relative to the base code version v1. The speedups are computed for two clock-rate scenarios. One scenario assumes a constant clock rate (the clock rate of v1) and uses the number of required clock cycles for the execution of the computation. A second scenario uses the real clock rate and reflects the impact of the larger design size, due to a large number of registers. We structure these results as two plots for each kernel. The first plot depicts the number of read and write memory operations along with the speedup results for the two clock-rate scenarios mentioned above. In the second plot we depict the number of registers used for scalar replacement and the number of FPGA slices used.

Reflecting designs that are memory-bound, the overall speedups track the reduction in the number of memory operations, with speedup values up to 6-fold.

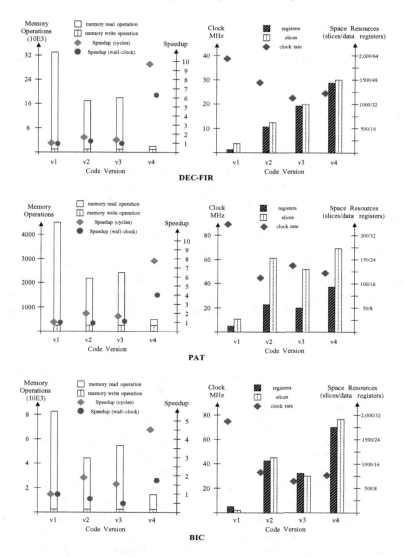

Fig. 3. Experimental results for DEC-FIR, PAT and BIC

This performance improvement comes at a steep price in terms of the required FPGA area as on average versions v4 are 15 times larger than versions v1. This is not as dramatic as it might seem as in all these kernels the base designs are really small. For computations with base versions using more hardware operators, the ratio between the resources used for operators and data is likely to be much higher than in these kernels leading to a smaller impact of scalar replacement on the overall design growth.

The results also show that the area (in slices) for each design tracks well the number of used registers for scalar replacement. This suggests that a compiler can effectively use the number of registers to project or estimate the impact of the scalar replacement for each individual variable in the overall design area. The data reuse analysis and number of required registers described in section 4 along with the number of memory accesses saved, provide an excellent mechanism for compilers to negotiate the area and time trade-off of hardware designs.

6   Related Work

Many other researchers have utilized the notion of reuse analysis as a way to guide compiler optimizations. The compiler detects and translates the reuse to locality, which can then be exploited by contemporary cache-based machines [5]. Previous work in this context has exclusively focused on high-end computing and ignores the issue of precision as to which iterations access which data items.

The work that has the most similarity to ours is done by So and Hall [1] who had extended the work by Carr and Kennedy [6] for scalar replacement while targeting FPGA devices. They use a single dependence distance vector to compute the number of registers required to capture an array's data reuse in a perfectly nested loop. This number is based on the minimal number of iterations between the source and the sink of a dependence. Their symbolic expressions are a particular case of the expressions presented in this paper, and generate accurate bounds on the number of required registers for the SIV cases. Their method also applies to particular cases of MIV where their approximation of the dependence distance vector matches the actual minimal reuse distance. Other than the fact that our approach can handle the case of MIV, another difference from [1] is the ability of our approach to determine the number of required registers at a particular loop level. This number can potentially guide the compiler to apply loop permutations to minimize the required registers at a given loop level.

Kandemir and Choudhray [2] describe a simple memory design algorithm that uses a condensed version of the reuse vectors to determine the required capacity of local memories for embedded systems. Due to the imprecision of their representation, their algorithm is not capable of determining tight upper bounds for the reuse cases that involve array references with MIVs. Even for the SIV cases their algorithm is not capable of determining tight bounds for the reuse cases that involve group-reuse. In previous work, Pande et. al. [3] developed an array-memory allocation algorithm by identifying the footprint associated with each array reference within a loop nest. They then use the array definitions and loop bounds and apply the Fourier-Motzkin elimination techniques to determine the required storage for each array variable.

The notions of data reuse and required registers presented in this paper can be viewed as particular cases of counting the solutions of Presburger formulas [4]. Although simple formulas would give the number of solutions corresponding to data reuse, they would not necessarily define the order in which the data elements are reused. To uncover such information it is necessary to specify more refined formulations where the minimal reuse distance, even if not known, would be determined by a search approach. The analytical closed form expressions presented here are applicable to common cases occurring in practice, covering a wide range of computations that programmers naturally express in high-level programming languages such as C or FORTRAN.

7 Conclusion

We presented a data reuse analysis for *self-reuse* of array references with MIV subscripts using *reuse vectors*. The increased precision of *reuse vectors* allows compilers to uncover and exploit scalar replacement for array variables with MIV subscripts, beyond the reach of previous techniques. We presented experimental results for the application of scalar replacement to a sample set of kernel codes targeting a configurable hardware computing device – a Field-Programmable-Gate-Array (FPGA). The results show that, for these memory bound designs, scalar replacement alone leads to speedups that range between 2x to 6x at the expense of an increase in the FPGA area in the range of 6x to 20x.

References

1. B. So, M. Hall. Increasing the Applicability of Scalar Replacement. In *Proc. of the Intl. Conf. on Compiler Construction (CC'04)*, In Lecture Notes in Computer Science (LNCS), Vol. 2985, Springer-Verlag Publishers, 2004.
2. M. Kandemir, A. Choudhary. Compiler-Directed Scratch Pad Memory Hierarchy Design and Management. In *Proc. of the 2002 ACM/IEEE Design Automation Conference (DAC'02)*, IEEE Computer Society Press, 2002.
3. D. Bairagi, S. Pande and D. Agrawal. Framework for Containing Code Size in Limited Register Set Embedded Processors. In *Proc. ACM Workshop on Languages, Compilers and Tools for Embedded Systems (LCTES 00)*, ACM Press, 2000.
4. W. Pugh. Counting Solutions to Presburger Formulas: How and Why. In *Proc. of the ACM Conf. on Prog. Language Design and Implementation (PLDI)*, 1994.
5. M. Wolf and M. Lam. A Data Locality Optimization Algorithm. In *Proc. of the ACM Conf. on Programming Language Design and Implementation (PLDI)* 1991.
6. S. Carr , K. Kennedy. Improving the Ratio of Memory Operations to Floating-point Operations in Loops. *ACM Trans. on Prog. Lang. and Syst.*, 16:1768-1810, 1994.
7. R. Allen , K. Kennedy. Optimizing Compilers for Modern Architectures. *Morgan Kaufmann Publishers.* , San Francisco, 2002.

Power-Aware Scheduling for Parallel Security Processors with Analytical Models

Yung-Chia Lin, Yi-Ping You, Chung-Wen Huang, Jenq-Kuen Lee, Wei-Kuan Shih, and Ting-Ting Hwang

National Tsing Hua University, Hsinchu 300 Taiwan
{yclin, ypyou, cwhuang, jklee, wshih, tingting}@cs.nthu.edu.tw

Abstract. Techniques to reduce power dissipation for embedded systems have recently come into sharp focus in the technology development. Among these techniques, dynamic voltage scaling (DVS), power gating (PG), and multiple-domain partitioning are regarded as effective schemes to reduce dynamic and static power. In this paper[1], we investigate the problem of power-aware scheduling tasks running on a scalable encryption processor, which is equipped with heterogeneous distributed SOC designs and needs the effective integration of the elements of DVS, PG, and the scheduling for correlations of multiple domain resources. We propose a novel heuristic that integrates the utilization of DVS and PG and increases the total energy-saving. Furthermore, we propose an analytic model approach to make an estimate about its performance and energy requirements between different components in systems. These proposed techniques are essential and needed to perform DVS and PG on multiple domain resources that are of correlations. Experiments are done in the prototypical environments for our security processors and the results show that significant energy reductions can be achieved by our algorithms.

1 Introduction

Techniques to reduce power dissipation for embedded systems have recently come into sharp focus in the technology development, as power consumption has become a crucial issue in the embedded SOC design. Among these techniques, dynamic voltage scaling (DVS), power gating (PG), and multiple-domain partitioning are regarded as effective schemes to reduce both dynamic and static power. Dynamic voltage scaling [1] is to reduce the dynamic power consumption P by dynamically scaling the supply voltage V_{dd} and corresponding frequency f of the PE if no demands for full throttle operating. The DVS uses the following equations for architecture-level power estimation:

$$P_{dynamic} = C \times \alpha \times f \times V_{dd}^2$$
$$f = k \times (V_{dd} - V_t)^2 / V_{dd}$$

---

[1] The work was supported in part by NSC-93-2213-E-007-025, NSC-93-2220-E-007-020, NSC-93-2220-E-007-019, MOE research excellent project under grant no. NSC93-2752-E-007-004-PAE, and MOEA research project under grant no. 92-EC-17-A-03-S1-0002 and no. 93-EC-17-A-03-S1-0002 of Taiwan.

R. Eigenmann et al. (Eds.): LCPC 2004, LNCS 3602, pp. 470–484, 2005.

where C is the switching capacitance, α is the switching activity, k is a circuit-dependent constant, and V_t denotes the threshold voltage. In the aspect of power gating [2, 3], the technique features in reducing leakage power dissipation; it uses the sleep circuit to disconnect the supply power from portions of the circuit when those portions are inactive. For leakage power estimation at architecture, we use the equation below:

$$P_{static} = V_{dd} \times N \times k_{design} \times I_{leakage}$$

where N is the number of transistors, k_{design} is a design-dependent constant, and $I_{leakage}$ denotes the normalized leakage current which depends on silicon technology, threshold voltage, and sub-threshold swing parameter. In the aspect of multiple domain partitioning, research issues remain for explorations when we try to integrate DVS, PG, and the scheduling for correlations of multiple domain resources. In this paper, we will have a scalable security processor as a case study to illustrate how to address this problem.

Variable Voltage Scheduling manages the tasks with execution deadlines and reduces power consumption without any task missing its deadline. We list the related research work as follows. The work in [4] gives a heuristic non-preemptive scheduling algorithm for independent tasks on a single processor. Works merely targeting on a single processor can be found in [5, 6, 7, 8, 9, 10, 11, 12, 13, 14, 15]. The works with distributed embedded systems can be found in [16, 17, 18, 19]. The main problem of using PG technology is to issue Gate-Off/On control at the proper time as to minimize performance degradation and maximize leakage power reduction. The works related to software-controlled power gating can be found in [20, 21, 22].

In this paper, we address the issue of variable voltage static scheduling in a heterogeneous distributed embedded system for independent periodic tasks with considering power gating to minimize both dynamic and static power dissipation. Our testbed is based on a scalable security processor (**SP**) which is developed in a collaborative research with the VLSI design group in our university [23, 24, 25, 26, 27, 28]. In the project, it aims to offer a configurable prototype of high-performance low-power security processors and incorporates the dynamic voltage scaling, power gating technology, and multiple domain partitioning in the designed processors. The interior of the security processors employs the architecture of heterogeneous distributed embedded system, in which processing elements (PEs) are various crypto-engine modules. Each crypto-engine module is designed to have DVS and PG capabilities. We propose a novel heuristic that integrates the utilization of DVS and PG, and increases the total energy-saving. Furthermore, we propose an analytic model approach to make an estimate about its performance and energy requirements between different components in systems. These proposed techniques are essential and needed to perform DVS and PG on multiple domain resources that are of correlation. Experiments are done in the prototypical environments for our security processors and the results show that significant energy reductions can be achieved by our proposed mechanisms.

The remainder of this paper is organized as follows. We first describe the architecture used in our target platform and power management design in Section 2. Next, we explain in detail our joint power-aware scheduling approach with both dynamic power reduction and leakage power reduction in Section 3. In Section 4, we present the experimental setup and the results. At last, we make an overall conclusion in Section 5.

2   Configurable SP Architecture with Power Management

In this section, we briefly describe a configurable architecture of **SP**s. The variations of this architecture have been used by many network device manufacturers, as Broadcom, Hifn [29], Motorola [30], and SafeNet. Key cryptographic functions in security processors may include:

- data encryption (DES, 3DES, RC4, and AES),
- user authentication only (DSS and DSA),
- hash function (SHA-1, MD5, and HMAC),
- public key encryption (RSA and ECC),
- public key exchange (Diffie-Hellman Key Exchange),
- and the compression (LZS and Deflate).

Fig.1 presents our architecture. It consists of a main controller, a DMA module, internal buses, and crypto modules [23, 24, 25, 26, 27, 28]. The main controller has a slave interface of external bus which accepts the control signals and returns the operation feedbacks via the interrupt port. In the main controller, there are resource allocation modules for managing resource such as external bus master interfaces, channels, transfer engines, internal buses, and crypto modules. Also, the process scheduler module and power management module are added into the main controller for task scheduling and low power control. The crypto operations are based on descriptors. The descriptor contains the type of en-/de-cryption functions, the length of raw data, the key information, and the destination memory address of the output data.

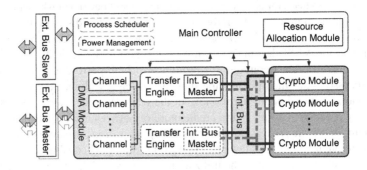

Fig. 1. Security processor architecture

The DMA module integrates master interfaces of external bus with the channels and the transfer engines. According to the data information in the channel, the transfer engine requests the external bus to transfer data from memory. The memory can be replaced by package processors which directly connect to the network by MAC modules. The transfer engine then passes the data to the dedicated crypto module via the internal bus. Furthermore, the internal buses are designed to support multiple layers for high-speed data transmission. Because the execution time of the crypto module may be varied, the crypto module will signal the main controller when the operations are done.

The power management module in the main controller presents a software-controllable voltage/speed adjustment of all components in the security processor. All components controlled by the power management module have four main power states: *Full*(1.8V), *Low*(1.5V), *Ultralow*(1.2V), and *Sleep*(0V). Cooperating with the process scheduler module, tasks can be assigned power states among *Full-Low-Ultralow*, and power gating as *Sleep* mode. For supplying multiple operating voltages, we have dynamic voltage generators which generate three level supply voltages for the security processor.

3   Power-Aware Scheduling Approach

In this section, we discuss the scheduling issues for low power in our security architectures and focus on the problem of independent periodic task scheduling. We assume a distributed embedded system containing major PEs (crypto modules) which are capable of k-level supply voltages and power gating mode. Moreover, we assume the other non-PE components (such as buses, channels) are capable of DVS. To simplify scheduling problems with all components in a complicated system, we propose a three-phases iterative scheme for power-aware scheduling in the following:

1. We employ the scheduling methods in Section 3.1 and assume the maximum performance of non-PEs (such as bus and channels) to determine running voltage/frequency of each task in major PEs and appropriate power gating occasions.
2. Apply analytic approximation techniques to rapidly determine running voltages/frequencies of the remaining components in the system. Analytic methods also give the proper estimation of computation latency in PEs caused by these components in the system.
3. Re-employ the scheduling methods with information generated in phase 2 and deliver final scheduled setting of each task. Iteratively proceed with phases 2–3 till the scheduling results are invariable. Other details would be described in Section 3.2.

3.1   Joint Variable-Voltage Scheduling with Power Gating for PEs

It is known that the scheduling problem of a set of nonpreemptable independent tasks with arbitrary execution time on fixed-voltage multiprocessors is NP-complete [31]. With reduction techniques, we find that the same scheduling problem on variable-voltage multiprocessors is NP-hard. To optimize the power or energy consumption in real-time systems, we propose a heuristic algorithm to schedule tasks under the condition of variable supply voltage.

The proposed scheduler maintains a list, called the *reservation list* [32], in which these tasks are sorted by deadlines. Since each periodic task arrives with a certain periodicity, we can get the information about the arrivals and deadlines of tasks in a given interval. At the beginning, all tasks are in the list and sorted by their deadlines, and the task with the earliest deadline is then picked for scheduling. The scheduler first checks if the task could be executed completely prior to the deadline at the lower voltage without influencing any unscheduled task in the reservation list. In this way the scheduler will decide how to schedule tasks at the lowest voltage as possible. For idle time of PEs, the scheduler will decide if it is deserved to gate off the idle PEs. The proposed heuristic would turn off unnecessary PEs completely as many as possible, so as to maximize static power reduction on top of dynamic power reduction.

Slack-Time Computation. We first give the definition for the slack time in the scheduling. Suppose we are going to schedule task T_i, and there are still $(n - i)$ unscheduled tasks (i.e., T_{i+1}, T_{i+2}, ..., T_n) in the reservation list. The slack time $\delta_i(V)$ is the maximum period allowed for T_i while the remaining $(n - 1)$ tasks are scheduled at supply voltage V in reverse order. To obtain the information for T_i, we first build a pseudo scheduler for the $(n - i)$ tasks with the following behaviors. The $(n - i)$ tasks are scheduled in a reversed way, which treats the deadlines as arrivals and the arrivals as deadlines and starts from the point of the latest deadline (i.e., d_n is the deadline of T_n) via the well-known earliest deadline first (EDF) algorithm [33]. We then record the time of the end point of the pseudo schedule as $\lambda_i(V)$.

The slack time of the pseudo schedule at a supply voltage V can be obtained from the following equation:

$$\delta_i(V) = \lambda_i(V) - Max(a_i, f_{i-1}),$$

where a_i is the arrival time of T_i, f_{i-1} is the finishing time of the last task T_{i-1}, and $Max(a,b)$ is a function that returns the maximum value of a and b. Figure 2 gives an example of the slack-time computation, in which there are four tasks in the reservation list. Here two reservation lists are maintained: one is created by a pseudo scheduler to schedule tasks at the lowest voltage, and the other is compiled by the highest-voltage scheduler. The slack time $\delta_i(V_H)$ and $\delta_i(V_L)$ is the time from the finishing time of the last task to the end point of the reservation list from the highest- and lowest-voltage schedulers, respectively. If we consider the overhead of DVS, the highest-voltage scheduler should add the maximum time-overhead of DVS to f_{i-1} to compute $\delta_i(V_H)$. It is noted that during the scheduling, we shall flag an exception if any deadline cannot be met when scheduling at the highest voltage.

Scheduling Algorithm. The proposed scheduling algorithm is based on the EDF algorithm [33]. Figure 3 lists the algorithm. Assume there are n periodic tasks to be scheduled. First, we sort tasks in ascending order by deadlines, namely $T_1, T_2, ..., T_n$, and put them in a list of unscheduled tasks, i.e., the reservation list. We then extract each task from the list on the basis of the schedule. Suppose the system provides m processing elements, and each processing element is capable of K-level supply voltages, where level 1 represents the lowest voltage and level K represents the highest voltage. Steps 1–3 in Figure 3 describe these procedures. For utilizing power gating capabilities, we shall try to make tasks run successively without intermissions and let idle time be together because PG mechanisms cost much more expense than DVS does in performance and power. Next, in step 4, we compute the slack time for task T_i with both the highest- and lowest-voltage pseudo schedulers, denoted as $\delta_i(V_H)$ and $\delta_i(V_L)$. The slack time $\delta_i(V)$ represents the maximum time interval allowed for task T_i to execute while all the remaining tasks in the reservation list are scheduled in reverse order with supply voltage V. In step 5, we compute the computation time of task T_i at both the highest-

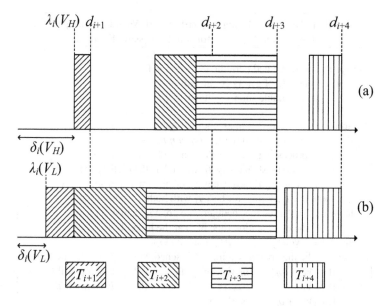

Fig. 2. Examples of slack-time computation while scheduling T_i: (a) tasks performed at the highest voltage; (b) tasks performed at the lowest voltage

and lowest-voltages, denoted as $c_i(V_H)$ and $c_i(V_L)$. In step 6, we compare $c_i(V_H)$ and $c_i(V_L)$ with $\delta_i(V_L)$ and $\delta_i(V_H)$ to decide which voltage should be applied to the task. This algorithm results in three possible scenarios as follows:

(a) $c_i(V_L)$ plus time-overhead of voltage-scaling is smaller than or equal to $\delta_i(V_L)$. If energy-overhead of voltage-scaling is less than energy-saving, we can schedule task T_i at the lowest voltage without affecting any task in the future because there are no overlaps between task T_i and the unscheduled tasks while those tasks are assumed to be executed at the lowest voltage.

(b) $c_i(V_L)$ plus time-overhead of voltage-scaling is larger than $\delta_i(V_L)$ and smaller than or equal to $\delta_i(V_H)$. If this happens, we call a decision algorithm described in Section 3.1 to decide at which voltage task should T_i be scheduled. It weights the alternatives to optimize the overall costs, using a criterion such as the power or energy consumption.

(c) $c_i(V_L)$ plus time-overhead of voltage-scaling is larger than $\delta_i(V_H)$. This means it is impossible for task T_i to complete its execution by its deadline at any voltage lower than the highest voltage, and hence we must schedule it at the highest voltage to let its deadline be met. If task T_i is un-schedulable for current PE, we put it in a new list called L_{un} that contains all un-schedulable tasks.

In step 7, we check the remained idle time between the scheduled tasks in the current PE and determine power gating commands to be inserted if it benefits energy-saving. In step 8 and step 9, if the list L_{un} generated in step 6 is not empty, we use the list as the reservation list for the next available PE and schedule it by the same procedures in steps 3–6. If no PE is available for scheduling, the scheduler should report the failure. At the

---

**Real-Time Scheduling Algorithm with Variable-Voltage
Reservation Lists in Multiple Processing Elements**

Input: n unscheduled periodic tasks and m PEs
Output: Schedule of gating commands and the n tasks
       with variable supply voltages at $PE_{1...m}$

1. Sort tasks by deadlines in ascending order; i.e., $T_1, T_2, ..., T_n$.
2. Put them in a list, called the *reservation list* of
   the target processing element PE_j. In the beginning, $j=1$.
3. Remove the first task, namely T_i, which has the earliest deadline, from
   the *reservation list*. Repeat steps 3–6 while the list is not empty.
4. Compute the slack time for task T_i with both the highest- and
   lowest-voltage pseudo schedulers, i.e., $\delta_i(V_H)$ and $\delta_i(V_L)$.
5. Compute the computation time of T_i at the highest-
   and lowest-voltages, i.e., $c_i(V_H)$ and $c_i(V_L)$.
6. Let $o_t(i)$ be the voltage scaling time, schedule T_i in the following rules:
   - If $c_i(V_L) + o_t(i) \leq \delta_i(V_L)$, schedule T_i for PE_j at V_L if possible[†].
   - If $\delta_i(V_L) < c_i(V_L) + o_t(i) \leq \delta_i(V_H)$, call the *decision algorithm*.
   - If $c_i(V_L) + o_t(i) > \delta_i(V_H)$ and
     - if $c_i(V_H) + o_t(i) \leq \delta_i(V_H)$, schedule T_i for PE_j at V_H.
     - if $c_i(V_H) + o_t(i) > \delta_i(V_H)$, put T_i in an unscheduled list L_{un}.
7. Check idle-time of PE_j and insert gating commands if possible[‡].
8. If PE_j is the last available PE and the list L_{un} is not empty,
   then report the possible failure of real-time scheduling.
9. If the list L_{un} is not empty, let $j = j + 1$ and use the list
   L_{un} as the *reservation list* of the target PE_j. Next, go to step 3.
10. If $j < m$, then gate off $PE_{j+1}...PE_m$ all the time.

[†]Schedule T_i at V_L if deadline is met and energy-overhead is acceptable.
[‡]Gate on/off if tasks are unaffected and energy-overhead is acceptable.

Fig. 3. Reservation-list scheduling algorithm for variable-voltage problems in multiple PEs

last step, we will turn off all unused PEs via power-gating to minimize both static and
dynamic power savings.

Decision Algorithm. Following the notations in the previous subsections, assume that
we are scheduling task T_i, and that $c_i(V_L) + o_t(i)$ is larger than $\delta_i(V_L)$ and smaller than or
equal to $\delta_i(V_H)$. To achieve the objective of power/energy reduction, we propose several
algorithms to decide at which voltage tasks should be scheduled when weighting trade-
offs between tasks. We use a probability density function,

$$f(x) = \frac{1}{\sqrt{2\pi}\sigma} e^{\frac{-(x-\mu)^2}{2\sigma^2}} \quad \text{where } -\infty < x < \infty,$$

which defines the probability density function for the value X of a random observation
from the population [34], to divide the population of a group into K equal parts in terms
of area under the distribution, and then schedule tasks at levels corresponding to the

parts that the tasks belong to. In other words, let W^1, W^2, ..., and W^{K-1} be demarcation that separates the population into K parts; a task will be scheduled at level t if its value falls between W^{t-1} and W^t. The detailed algorithms are described as follows:

(a) *Reservation list with first-come first-served scheduling*
    Tasks are always scheduled at the lowest voltage as possible without missing deadlines. This algorithm does not apply a cost model to the decision.
(b) *Reservation list with average power consumption*
    We use the switching activity α_i to select the voltage level for T_i. We schedule a task at level $(K - \tau + 1)$ if
    $$\int_{-\infty}^{W_\alpha^\tau} \frac{1}{\sqrt{2\pi}\sigma} e^{\frac{-(W_\alpha^\tau - \mu)^2}{2\sigma^2}} = \frac{\tau}{K} \text{ and } W_\alpha^\tau \text{ denotes the } \tau\text{-th watershed of the population of}$$
    switching activities of tasks.

3.2   Voltage/Speed Selection of Non-PEs

For non-PE components (such as buses and transfer engines) in the system, we apply analytic modeling techniques (to be described shortly) to compute the suitable voltage so that total performance of the system will fit the scheduling results of major PEs.

Suppose the system has multiple PEs that are labeled with an index in the range 1 to l. Several channels, which are labeled with an index in the range 1 to n, are built into the control unit for simultaneously accessing the PEs. The data transfer between channels and PEs are across a few of internal buses, which are labeled with an index in the range 1 to m. We can view each kth PE and j^{th} internal bus as a server with a constant service rate of M_{s_k} and M'_{s_j} bits per second, respectively. Let $P_{i,k}$ be the probability that channel i makes its next service request to the PE k. Define Φ_i to be the average fraction of the time that the ith channel is not waiting for a service request to be completed from any of PEs and internal buses. Also, let $\Omega_{k,i}$ and $\Omega'_{j,i}$ be the fraction of the time spent by the ith channel waiting for a service request to PE k and internal bus j, respectively. Define $\frac{1}{M_{r_{k,i}}}$ to be the ratio of the time that descriptors of the ith channel spend doing the overhead of PE service requests, not including the time of waiting in queues and having requests serviced by the kth PE to the total processing data size. Let

$$\eta_k = \sum_{i=1}^n P_{i,k} \frac{M_{r_{k,i}}}{M_{s_k}} \quad , \quad \lambda_k = \frac{(1+\varepsilon_k)M_{s_k}}{\sum_{j=1}^m M'_{s_j}},$$

where ε_k is the average scaling ratio of data size throughout the kth PE processing. The average time that each channel spends doing initiating, host memory communication, and descriptor processing Φ_i is related to the time spent waiting, $\Omega_{k,i}$ and $\Omega'_{j,i}$, as the following equations.

$$\Phi_i + \sum_{k=1}^l \Omega_{k,i} + \sum_{j=1}^m \Omega'_{j,i} = 1$$

$$\prod_{i=1}^n (1 - \Omega_{k,i}) + \eta_k \Phi_i = 1$$

$$\prod_{i=1}^{n}(1 - \Omega'_{j,i}) + \sum_{k=1}^{l} \eta_k \lambda_k \Phi_i = 1$$

We abbreviate the detailed model construction and proof which could be found in the appendix of this paper.

Suppose tasks for l PEs are scheduled by the scheduler as described in Section 3.1. We can derive Φ_i, $\Omega_{k,i}$, and $\Omega'_{j,i}$, which are the metrics of expected performance, from the scheduling results: the scheduling results offer the average service rate M_{s_k} of kth processing engines and $\eta_k \Phi_i$, which semantically equal to utilization of kth PE due to task assignments. Assume the security processor has n channels and m internal buses connecting PEs, so we can provide one proper selection among frequencies and corresponding voltages of internal buses and transfer engines through solving the equations previously: we use expecting values of M'_{s_j} to evaluate resulting Φ_i, $\Omega_{k,i}$, and $\Omega'_{j,i}$ and choose a minimal M'_{s_j} that causes the system to have the most load efficiency, for which Φ_i, $\Omega_{k,i}$, and $\Omega'_{j,i}$ are all positive and Φ_i should be the minimum as possible.

Apart from voltage/frequency selection, the proposed analytic modeling is used to revise the latency parameters in the schedulers during scheme phases 2–3. In the realistic environments of considered systems, the computation time of tasks in PEs should actually include the latency time caused by data transmission and bus contention. The data transmission latency could be calculated validly by data size, bus speed, and detailed transfer operations during scheduling. The bus contention latency, however, could not be correctly estimated if lacking any runtime information. Thus we shall use the worst-case estimation of the latency time to proceed with the calculation of task computation time and avoid deadline missing under any runtime condition. In the first phase of scheduling scheme, we use maximum performance settings of internal buses and transfer engines, which relax the slack time computation, to schedule tasks. We conservatively assume the worst case of each task is waiting for all tasks in PEs except the one in which it is scheduled to complete their data transmission with the maximum time spent by the possible largest data transmission. The proposed analytic approximation phase of voltage-selection estimates possible low power settings of internal buses and transfer engines which match the scheduling results, and is also able to estimate more accurate worst-case latency time in each PE than theoretical one by means of $\Omega'_{j,i}$ and $\eta_k \Phi_i$, which would reflect the possible worst-case latency in the scheduling results. We then perform the third phase of scheduling scheme that uses values derived by the second phase, and obtain final scheduling results. Due to the monotonic property of PE usage in our scheduling algorithms, iterative processing of phases 2–3 would converge on a stable scheduling result.

4   Simulator and Experiment

In the experiments, we have built a cycle-accurate simulator along with energy models for configurable security processors. The cycle-accurate simulator is written in SystemC in which each PE's simulation can be operated at assigned frequencies based on the voltage scaling. The energy consumption models, according to activity types and

Table 1. Benchmark settings and results

suite	1	2	3	4	5	6	7	8	9
arrival distribution	uniform			normal			exponential		
job number	300								
jobs/time (μs)	1500		375	1500		375	1500		375
AES:RSA	30:1								
max data size (bytes)	1280								
max AES deadline (μs)	3072	3430		3072	3430		3072	3430	
max RSA deadline (μs)	13312	15872		13312	15872		13312	15872	
dynamic energy reduction (%)	19.41	20.09	15.95	20.50	18.56	28.64	21.13	31.15	33.30
leakage energy reduction (%)	83.71	82.92	83.39	83.17	83.85	83.55	82.40	83.24	83.29
total energy reduction (%)	19.41	20.09	15.96	20.50	18.56	28.64	21.13	31.15	33.30

structure features of the hardware designs [35], are separated into functional units, control logics, memory, and clock distribution trees. Hence, the energy consumptions are weighted with various considerations. The simulation environment needs operated with a power library that contains synthesis values of PEs under UMC 0.18 CMOS library.

We implement a randomized security task generator to generate benchmark descriptor files for the simulator. The generator can generate the simulated OS-level jobs of de-/en-cryption and each job has randomized operation types, randomized data sizes, randomized keys and content, randomized arrival time, and randomized deadline on the basis of an adjustable configuration of job arrival distribution types, job numbers, job density, ratio of distinct operation types, job size variance, and job deadline variance. Each generated job is then converted by the generator to the corresponding descriptors which can be executed by the simulator. In our preliminary experiments, we assume the SP has the architecture configuration of 6 AES modules, 2 RSA modules, 5 internal buses, 8 channels and transfer engines. The generated benchmarks consist of 9 test suites with different task generator configurations listed in Table 1. They are mainly divided into three types of arrival distributions. Each distribution type has three suites with different task slackness, which are dependent on job density and job deadline range: the first suite features high density and short deadline; the second one features high density and long deadline; the third one features low density and long deadline.

We have generated 100 distinct descriptor files for each suite and computed their average energy consumptions of different components from the results of the simulator, as shown in Figure 4. The bars labeled by **N** are the scheduling results without power management and others labeled by **P** are the results with enabling our proposed power management. The energy-overhead of applying DVS and PG is too little to be exhibited

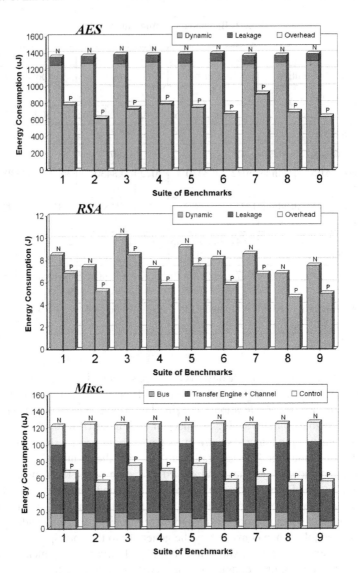

Fig. 4. Energy consumption estimated by the simulator

clearly on the charts, and so does the leakage of RSA modules. The top chart gives
the energy reduction for AES modules, the middle chart gives the energy reduction for
RSA modules, and the bottom chart shows the energy reduction for non-PE components
which are assigned by our analytic approximation phase, for all benchmark suites. The
final results with latency approximation are also confirmed by the simulator that no
deadline missing is reported in all benchmarks. Although the most energy consumptions
are dominated by RSA operations in our experimental architecture and workloads, the
charts show that our scheme performs well for all components in the system. Moreover,

the leakage reduction is great as shown in Table 1 and this portion is expected to be more important when CMOS process is going downward under $0.13\mu m$ [36]. Table 1 also gives the overall energy reduction for all test suites. The summary in the table presents that the total energy reduction up to 33% could be achieved by our power-aware scheduling scheme.

5   Conclusions

In this paper, we present a new approach of increasing power efficiency in complex distributed embedded systems with dynamic and static power reduction mechanisms. As the preliminary results show, our power management scheme gets significant power reduction for the experimental security processor. This work provides an exploration study on variable voltage scheduling resources of multiple domains with correlations.

References

1. Weiser, M., Welch, B., Demers, A., Shenker, S.: Scheduling for reduced cpu energy. In: Proceedings of USENIX Symposium on Operating Systems Design and Implementation (OSDI). (1994) 13–23
2. Butts, J.A., Sohi, G.S.: A static power model for architects. In: Proc. Int. Symp. on Microarchitecture. (2000) 191–201
3. Powell, M.D., Yang, S.H., Falsafi, B., Roy, K., Vijaykumar, T.N.: Gated-vdd:a circuit technique to reduce leakage in deep-submicron cache memories. In: Proc. ISLPED. (2000)
4. Hong, I., Kirovski, D., Qu, G., Potkonjak, M., Srivastava, M.B.: Power optimization of variable-voltage core-based systems. IEEE Trans. Computer-Aided Design **18** (1999) 1702–1714
5. Yao, F., Demers, A., Shenker, S.: A scheduling model for reduced cpu energy. In: Symp. Foundations of Computer Science. (1995) 374–382
6. Quan, G., Hu, X.: Energy efficient fixed-priority scheduling for real-time systems on variable voltage processors. In: Proc. DAC. (2001) 828–833
7. Pouwelse, J., Langendoen, K., Sips, H.: Energy priority scheduling for variable voltage processors. In: Proc. ISLPED. (2001)
8. Shin, Y., Choi, K.: Power conscious fixed priority scheduling for hard real-time systems. In: Proc. DAC. (1999) 134–139
9. Pering, T., Burd, T., Brodersen, R.: The simulation and evaluation of dynamic voltage scaling algorithms. In: Proc. ISLPED. (1998) 76–81
10. Krishna, C.M., Lee, L.H.: Voltage-clock-scaling adaptive scheduling techniques for low power in hard real-time systems. In: Proc. Real Time Technology and Applications Symp. (2000)
11. Ishihara, T., Yasuura, H.: Voltage scheduling problem for dynamically variable voltage processors. In: Proc. ISLPED. (1998) 197–202
12. Gruian, F., Kuchcinski, K.: Lenes: Task scheduling for low-energy systems using variable supply voltage processor. In: Proc. ASPDAC. (2001) 449–455
13. Manzak, A., Chakrabarti, C.: Variable voltage task scheduling for minimizing energy or minimizing power. In: Proc. ICASSP. (2000) 3239–3242
14. You, Y.P., Lee, C.R., Lee, J.K.: Real-time task scheduling for dynamically variable voltage processors. In: Proc. IEEE Workshop on Power Management for Real-Time and Embedded Systems. (2001)

15. Lee, C.R., Lee, J.K., Hwang, T.T., Tsai, S.C.: Compiler optimizations on vliw instruction scheduling for low power. ACM Transactions on Design Automation of Electronic Systems **8** (2003) 252–268
16. Luo, J., Jha, N.K.: Power-conscious joint scheduling of periodic task graphs and aperiodic tasks in distributed real-time embedded systems. In: Proc. ICCAD. (2000) 357–364
17. Luo, J., Jha, N.K.: Battery-aware static scheduling for distributed real-time embedded systems. In: Proc. DAC. (2001) 444–449
18. Schmitz, M.T., Al-Hashimi, B.M.: Considering power variations of dvs processing elements for energy minimisation in distributed systems. In: Proc. ISSS. (2001) 250–255
19. Luo, J., Jha, N.: Static and dynamic variable voltage scheduling algorithms for real-time heterogeneous distributed embedded systems. In: Proc. ASPDAC. (2002)
20. You, Y.P., Lee, C.R., Lee, J.K.: Compiler analysis and support for leakage power reduction on microprocessors. In: Proc. LCPC. (2002)
21. Duarte, D., Tsai, Y., Vijaykrishnan, N., Irwin, M.J.: Evaluating run-time techniques for leakage power reduction. In: Proc. ASPDAC. (2002)
22. Rele, S., Pande, S., Onder, S., Gupta, R.: Optimizing static power dissipation by functional units in superscalar processors. In: Proc. Int. Conf. on Compiler Construction. (2002) 261–275
23. Su, C.Y., Hwang, S.A., Chen, P.S., Wu, C.W.: An improved montgomery algorithm for high-speed rsa public-key cryptos ystem. IEEE Transactions on VLSI Systems **7** (1999) 280–284
24. Hong, J.H., Wu, C.W.: Cellular array modular multiplier for the rsa public-key cryptosystem based on modified booth's algorithm. IEEE Transactions on VLSI Systems **11** (2003) 474–484
25. Lin, T.F., Su, C.P., Huang, C.T., Wu, C.W.: A high-throughput low-cost aes cipher chip. In: 3rd IEEE Asia-Pacific Conf. ASIC. (2002)
26. Su, C.P., Lin, T.F., Huang, C.T., Wu, C.W.: A highly efficient aes cipher chip. In: ASP-DAC. (2003)
27. Wang, M.Y., Su, C.P., Huang, C.T., Wu, C.W.: An hmac processor with integrated sha-1 and md5 algorithms. In: ASP-DAC. (2004)
28. Lee, M.C., Huang, J.R., Su, C.P., Chang, T.Y., Huang, C.T., Wu, C.W.: A true random generator desing. In: 13th VLSI Design/CAD Symp. (2002)
29. Hifn: 7954 security processor Data Sheet. (2003)
30. Gammage, N., Waters, G.: Securing the Smart Network with Motorola Security Processors. (2003)
31. Stankovic, J.A., Spuri, M., Natale, M.D., Buttazzo, G.: Implications of Classical Scheduling Results For Real-Time Systems. Volume 28. (1995)
32. Shih, W.K., Liu, J.W.S.: On-line scheduling of imprecise computations to minimize error. SIAM Journal on Computing **25** (1996) 1105–1121
33. Liu, C.L., Layland, J.W.: Scheduling algorithms for multiprogramming in a hard read-time environment. Journal of the ACM **20** (1973) 46–61
34. Lapin, L.L.: Modern Engineering Statistics. Wadsworth Publishing Company, WBelmont, CA, (1997)
35. Chen, R.Y., Irwin, M.J.: Architecture-level power estimation and design experiments. ACM Transactions on Design Automation of Electronic Systems **6** (2001) 50–66
36. Doyle, B., Arghavani, R., Barlage, D., Datta, S., Doczy, M., Kavalieros, J., Murthy, A., Chau, R.: Transistor elements for 30nm physical gate lengths and beyond. Intel Technology Journal **6** (2002) 42–54
37. Hwang, K., Briggs, F.: Computer Architecture and Parallel Processing. Mc Graw-Hill (1984)
38. Bodin, F., Windheiser, D., Jalby, W., Atapattu, D., Lee, M., Gannon, D.: Performance evaluation and prediction for parallel algorithms on the bbn gp1000. In: Proc. of the 4th ACM International Conference on Supercomputing. (1990) 401–403

Appendix: Analytical Models

We describe the analytic model developed for the security architectures given earlier in Section 2 as follows. We consider a typical execution process of an operation in the system described in Section 2. The execution of each operation can be viewed as a procedure that a channel requests an internal bus twice to serve the data transmission and requests a PE to serve the data manipulation. Assume each channel execution can be treated as an exponentially distributed random process which produces sets of service request with three correlated operations in the fixed order: two for the internal bus, one for the PE. Following the notations in Section 3.2, let $system\_cycles_i$ be the total time spent by the ith channel on transmitting over system bus (including host memory accessing, descriptor processing, or idle). We now give the definition for $request\_cycles_i$. The $request\_cycles_i$ has two elements. It includes the total time spent by the ith channel on preparing PE request and internal bus request and processing time. Moreover, it includes the total time that the data are traversing among the channel, internal buses, and PEs. Now let $channel\_cycles_i = system\_cycles_i + request\_cycles_i$. Define $M_{r_{k,i}} = \frac{data\_amount_{k,i}}{channel\_cycles_i}$ which is the ratio of data request amount to the time that descriptors of the ith channel spend doing the overhead of PE service requests, not including the time of waiting in queues and having requests serviced by the kth PE.

If we neglect the interaction between channels and assume that all internal buses are utilizable by all channels and PEs, then we have the following analytic model developed on top of the previous parallelizing theorem [37, 38]:

Theorem 1. *Let*

$$\eta_k = \sum_{i=1}^{n} P_{i,k} \frac{M_{r_{k,i}}}{M_{s_k}} \quad , \quad \lambda_k = \frac{(1+\varepsilon_k)M_{s_k}}{\sum_{j=1}^{m} M'_{s_j}},$$

where ε_k is the average scaling ratio of data size throughout the kth PE processing. The average time that each channel spends doing initiating, host memory communication, and descriptor processing Φ_i is related to the time spent waiting, $\Omega_{k,i}$ and $\Omega'_{j,i}$, as the following equations.

$$\Phi_i + \sum_{k=1}^{l} \Omega_{k,i} + \sum_{j=1}^{m} \Omega'_{j,i} = 1, \quad \prod_{i=1}^{n}(1 - \Omega_{k,i}) + \eta_k \Phi_i = 1, \quad \prod_{i=1}^{n}(1 - \Omega'_{j,i}) + \sum_{k=1}^{l} \eta_k \lambda_k \Phi_i = 1$$

Proof. The first equation simply infers the time conservation. Let $C_{k,i}$ be the average channel-i-to-PE-k request cycle time for the system, $total\_cycle$ be the total operation time per request, and we get

$$\frac{1}{C_{k,i}} = \frac{data\_amount_{k,i}}{total\_cycles} \tag{1}$$

on average. By observing the workloads, we can compute $M_{r_{k,i}}$ which is the ratio of the request data amount to channel cycles. Based on the definition of $M_{r_{k,i}}$ and equation (1), we can derive

$$\frac{1}{M_{r_{k,i}} C_{k,i}} = \frac{channel\_cycles_i}{total\_cycles} = \Phi_i \tag{2}$$

Moreover, define

$$\delta_{k,i} = \begin{cases} 1 & \textit{if channel i is not waiting for module k} \\ 0 & \textit{otherwise} \end{cases}$$

$$\delta'_{j,i} = \begin{cases} 1 & \textit{if channel i is not waiting for bus j} \\ 0 & \textit{otherwise} \end{cases}$$

Let μ_k be the probability that PE k is busy and μ'_j be the probability that internal bus j is busy. We have

$$\mu_k = 1 - E(\delta_{k,1}\delta_{k,2}\cdots\delta_{k,n}) \tag{3}$$

$$\mu'_j = 1 - E(\delta'_{j,1}\delta'_{j,2}\cdots\delta'_{j,n}) \tag{4}$$

where $E(v)$ is the expected value of the random variable v. Therefore, $\mu_k M_{s_k}$ and $\mu'_j M'_{s_j}$ are the rate of completed requests to PE k and internal bus j, respectively. When the system is in equilibrium, $\mu_k M_{s_k}$ is equivalent to the rate of submitted requests to PE k and $\mu'_j M'_{s_j}$ is equivalent to the rate of submitted requests to internal bus j. Since $\sum_{i=1}^{n}\frac{P_{i,k}}{C_{k,i}}$ is the total rate of submitted requests to PE k from all channels, we have the equivalence,

$$\sum_{i=1}^{n}\frac{P_{i,k}}{C_{k,i}} = \mu_k M_{s_k} \tag{5}$$

Likewise, $\sum_{k=1}^{l}\sum_{i=1}^{n}\frac{P_{i,k}}{C_{k,i}}$ is the average rate of submitted requests to all internal buses from all channels. Due to the law of data indestructibility, we could have $\sum_{k=1}^{l}\sum_{i=1}^{n}\frac{P_{i,k}(1+\varepsilon_k)}{C_{k,i}}$ to be the average rate of submitted requests to all internal buses from all channels and all PEs. Accordingly, we have the equivalence as follows:

$$\sum_{k=1}^{l}\sum_{i=1}^{n}\frac{P_{i,k}(1+\varepsilon_k)}{C_{k,i}} = \sum_{j=1}^{m}\mu'_j M'_{s_j} \tag{6}$$

By combing equations (2), (3), (4), (5), and (6), we get

$$\begin{cases} \eta_k = \sum_{i=1}^{n} P_{i,k}\frac{M_{r_{k,i}}}{M_{s_k}} \\ E(\delta_{k,1}\delta_{k,2}\cdots\delta_{k,n}) + \eta_k\Phi_i = 1 \end{cases} \quad , \quad \begin{cases} \lambda_k = \frac{(1+\varepsilon_k)M_{s_k}}{\sum_{j=1}^{m}M'_{s_j}} \\ E(\delta'_{j,1}\delta'_{j,2}\cdots\delta'_{j,n}) + \sum_{k=1}^{l}\eta_k\lambda_k\Phi_i = 1 \end{cases}$$

Nevertheless, since both $\delta_{k,i}$ and $\delta'_{j,i}$ are binaries, we have by symmetry

$$E(\delta_{k,i}) = 1 - \Omega_{k,i} \quad , \quad E(\delta'_{j,i}) = 1 - \Omega'_{j,i}$$

for each channel i. We now make a critical approximation by assuming that all the channels have non-correlated activities and we get

$$E(\delta_{k,1}\delta_{k,2}\cdots\delta_{k,n}) = E(\delta_{k,1})E(\delta_{k,2})\cdots E(\delta_{k,n}) = \prod_{i=1}^{n}(1-\Omega_{k,i})$$

$$E(\delta'_{j,1}\delta'_{j,2}\cdots\delta'_{j,n}) = E(\delta'_{j,1})E(\delta'_{j,2})\cdots E(\delta'_{j,n}) = \prod_{i=1}^{n}(1-\Omega'_{j,i})$$

The result follows.

Author Index

Lecture Notes in Computer Science

For information about Vols. 1–3513

please contact your bookseller or Springer